Series Editors
Marc E. Fey, Ph.D
Alan G. Kamhi, Ph.D.

# Promoting Language and Literacy in Children Who Are Deaf or Hard of Hearing

Also in the *Communication and Language Intervention Series:*

*Late Talkers: Language
Development, Interventions, and Outcomes*
Edited by Leslie A. Rescorla, Ph.D.,
and Philip S. Dale, Ph.D.

*Treatment of Autism Spectrum Disorders:
Evidence-Based Intervention Strategies for
Communication and Social Interactions*
Edited by Patricia A. Prelock, Ph.D.,
and Rebecca J. McCauley, Ph.D.

*Dual Language Development and Disorders:
A Handbook on Bilingualism and Second
Language Learning, Second Edition*
By Johanne Paradis, Ph.D.,
Fred Genesee, Ph.D., and
Martha B. Crago, Ph.D.

*Interventions for Speech Sound
Disorders in Children*
Edited by A. Lynn Williams, Ph.D.,
Sharynne McLeod, Ph.D., and
Rebecca J. McCauley, Ph.D.

Communication
and Language
Intervention
Series

# Promoting Language and Literacy in Children Who Are Deaf or Hard of Hearing

edited by

**Mary Pat Moeller, Ph.D.**
Boys Town National Research Hospital
Omaha, Nebraska

**David J. Ertmer, Ph.D.**
Purdue University
West Lafayette, Indiana

and

**Carol Stoel- Gammon, Ph.D.**
University of Washington
Seattle

·P A U L·H·
BROOKES
PUBLISHING CO.®

Baltimore • London • Sydney

**Paul H. Brookes Publishing Co.**
Post Office Box 10624
Baltimore, Maryland 21285–0624

www.brookespublishing .com

Typeset by BMWW, Baltimore, Maryland.
Manufactured in the United States of America by
Sheridan Books, Chelsea, Michigan.

The individuals described in this book are composites or real people whose situations are masked
and are based on the authors' experiences. In all instances, names or identifying details have
been changed to protect confidentiality.

Photos are used by permission of the individuals pictured and/or their parents/guardians.

**Library of Congress Cataloging-in-Publication Data**

The Library of Congress has cataloged the print edition as follows:

    Names: Moeller, Mary Pat, editor. | Ertmer, David J., editor. | Stoel-Gammon,
      Carol, editor.
    Title: Promoting language and literacy in children who are deaf or hard of
      hearing / edited by Mary Pat Moeller, Ph.D., Boys Town National Research
      Hospital, David J. Ertmer, Ph.D., Purdue University and Carol
      Stoel-Gammon, Ph.D., University of Washington.
    Description: Baltimore, Maryland : Brookes Publishing, 2015. | Includes
      bibliographical references and index.
    Identifiers: LCCN 2015016100 (print) | LCCN 2015023951 (ebook) | ISBN
      9781598577334 | ISBN 9781681250304 (retail pdf) | ISBN 9781681250328
      (retail epub) | ISBN 9781681250304 (Retail PDF) | ISBN 9781681250328
      (Retail ePub) | ISBN 9781681250281 (Kindle/KF8)
    Subjects: LCSH: Deaf children--Education. | Hearing impaired
      children--Education. | BISAC: MEDICAL / Audiology & Speech Pathology. |
      EDUCATION / Special Education / Communicative Disorders. | LANGUAGE ARTS &
      DISCIPLINES / Speech.
    Classification: LCC HV2440 .P76 2015 (print) | LCC HV2440 (ebook) | DDC
      371.91/2--dc23

    LC record available at http://lccn.loc.gov/2015016100

British Library Cataloguing in Publication data are available from the British Library.

2020   2019   2018   2017   2016

10    9    8    7    6    5    4    3    2    1

# Contents

## III   Language and Literacy in the School Years

# Series Preface

The purpose of the Communication and Language Intervention Series is to provide meaningful foundations for the application of sound intervention designs to enhance the development of communication skills across the life span. We are endeavoring to achieve this purpose by providing readers with presentations of state-of-the-art theory, research, and practice.

In selecting topics, editors, and authors, we are not attempting to limit the contents of this series to viewpoints that we agree with or that we find most promising. We are assisted in our efforts to develop the series by an editorial advisory board consisting of prominent scholars representative of the range of issues and perspectives to be incorporated in the series.

Well-conceived theory and research on development and intervention are vitally important for researchers, educators, and clinicians committed to the development of optimal approaches to communication and language intervention. The content of each book in the series reflects our view of the symbiotic relationship between intervention and research: Demonstrations of what may work in intervention should lead to analysis of promising discoveries and to insights from developmental work that may, in turn, fuel further refinement by intervention researchers. We trust that the careful reader will find much that is of great value in this book.

An inherent goal of the series is to enhance the long-term development of the field by systematically furthering the dissemination of theoretically and empirically based scholarship and research. We promise the reader an opportunity to participate in the development of this field through debates and discussions that occur throughout the pages of the Communication and Language Intervention Series.

# Editorial Advisory Board

# About the Editors

**Mary Pat Moeller, Ph.D.,** Director, Center for Childhood Deafness, Boys Town National Research Hospital, 555 N. 30th Street, Omaha, Nebraska 68131

After many years of clinical work in rehabilitative audiology and early intervention, Dr. Mary Pat Moeller obtained a Ph.D. from the University of Nebraska at Lincoln. Her research interests include mother–child interaction, theory of mind development in children who are deaf or hard of hearing, and the study of factors influencing the outcomes of children who are hard of hearing. She directed a team at Boys Town National Research Hospital in the development of a web site for families whose infants are referred from newborn hearing screening (http://www.babyhearing.org; http://www.audiciondelbebe.org). She is co-principal investigator of a National Institutes of Health–funded multisite study of the longitudinal outcomes of children who are hard of hearing. Dr. Moeller has published widely and has lectured internationally on topics related to early development in children who are deaf or hard of hearing.

**David J. Ertmer, Ph.D.,** Professor, Department of Speech, Language, and Hearing Sciences, Purdue University, 715 Clinic Drive, West Lafayette, Indiana 47907

Dr. David J. Ertmer is a professor in speech, language, and hearing sciences at Purdue University in West Lafayette, Indiana. He received a B.S. from Marquette University, a M.S. from the University of Wisconsin–Milwaukee, and a Ph.D. from Purdue University. His clinical career includes experiences as a school speech pathologist in Wisconsin and Colorado and as a clinical supervisor at Purdue University. He has regularly taught courses in aural rehabilitation and clinical methods in communication disorders. His National Institutes of Health–funded research is focused on identifying the rate and completeness of prelinguistic vocal development, phonological development, and the attainment of intelligible speech in young children who receive cochlear implants and children who are typically developing. Dr. Ertmer has been an associate editor of *Language, Speech, and Hearing Services in Schools,* an editorial consultant for numerous professional journals, and a reviewer of National Institutes of Health and international research proposals. Along with numerous journal articles and book chapters, he is the author of *The Source for Children with Cochlear Implants* (PRO-ED, 2005). He and his wife, Peg, a professor in learning design and technology at Purdue University, have four adult children and three grandchildren.

**Carol Stoel-Gammon, Ph.D.,** Professor Emerita, Department of Speech and Hearing Sciences, University of Washington, 1417 Northeast 42nd Street, Seattle, Washington 98105

Dr. Carol Stoel-Gammon received her doctoral degree in linguistics from Stanford University and has taught, mentored, and carried out research in the area of phonological development and disorders for many years. Her book *Normal and Disordered Phonology in Children,* coauthored with Carla Dunn, was published in 1985 (PRO-ED). Her research interests focus on prelinguistic vocal development and early phonological development in children who are typically developing and speech development of children with autism, cleft palate, Down syndrome, fragile X syndrome, and childhood apraxia of speech and children who are deaf or hard of hearing and late talkers. Dr. Stoel-Gammon has served as associate editor of the *Journal of Speech and Hearing Disorders,* the *Journal of Speech and Hearing Research,* the *American Journal of Speech-Language Pathology,* and the *Journal of Child Language.*

# About the Contributors

**Stacy R. Abrams, M.S.,** Family Mentor Coordinator, Early Childhood and Family Education: Parent Outreach Program, Arizona Early Intervention Program (AZEIP), 2051 W Northern Avenue, Suite 200, Phoenix, Arizona 85021

During the writing of this book, Ms. Stacy R. Abrams was the Deaf Mentor Program coordinator at the New Mexico School for the Deaf. She has since then moved to Arizona and is the current Family Mentor Program coordinator, serving families with deaf children and giving them opportunities to learn from deaf adults. Stacy is also a proud Deaf mom of two bilingual deaf children.

**Cheryl L. Broekelmann, M.A., LSLS Cert. AVEd.,** Director, St. Joseph Institute for the Deaf, St. Louis, 1300 Strassner, Brentwood, Missouri 63144

Ms. Cheryl L. Broekelmann has more than 25 years of experience as an educator of children who are deaf or hard of hearing. She has served in a variety of roles at St. Joseph including teacher, supervisor of preschool and lower school, early childhood program director, and director of ihear Internet therapy and early intervention. She has a B.A. in deaf education and an M.A. in education, early childhood administration, from Fontbonne University and is certified as a teacher and deaf educator in Missouri and a listening and spoken language specialist–certified auditory-verbal educator through the A.G. Bell Listening and Spoken Language Academy. She has served as a lecturer at Fontbonne University and a presenter at numerous professional conferences as well as an author and coauthor of articles published in journals such as *Volta Voices, Volta Review,* and *ASHA Leader.* She is the coauthor of a chapter in *101 FAQs About Auditory-Verbal Practice.*

**Catherine Cronin Carotta, Ed.D.,** Associate Director, Center for Childhood Deafness, Boys Town National Research Hospital, 555 North 30th Street, Omaha, Nebraska 68131

Dr. Catherine Cronin Carotta is a licensed speech-language pathologist with many years of experience in the assessment and education of children who are deaf or hard of hearing using sign and spoken language modalities. Dr. Carotta has worked in public/private school settings, hospitals, and university-based clinical programs. She serves as a national consultant to school districts focused on providing optimal educational practices for students with hearing loss. With a doctorate in leadership education, she has actively worked to create learning organizations using current leadership models.

**Elizabeth B. Cole, Ed.D.,** Director, Soundbridge, Capitol Region Education Council, 123 Progress Drive, Wethersfield, Connecticut 06109

Dr. Elizabeth B. Cole is the director of Soundbridge, a statewide public school program in Connecticut, which provides a wide variety of audiological and instructional services to approximately 700 children (birth through secondary school) who are learning spoken language through listening. Prior to coming to Connecticut in 1996, Dr. Cole was a professor at McGill University in Montreal for 16 years, where she taught acoustic phonetics, language, speech, and aural habilitation courses to students in the Auditory-Oral ReHabilitation and Education of Hearing-Impaired Children (AORE) program, as well as to audiology and speech-language pathology students. Dr. Cole has coauthored a book with Carol Flexer titled *Children with Hearing Loss: Developing Listening and Talking* (Plural, 2010), which is a standard text for professional development of teachers who are seeking certification as Listening and Spoken Language Specialists.

**Leisha R. Eiten, Au.D., CCC-A,** Audiology Coordinator, Boys Town National Research Hospital, 555 North 30th Street, Omaha, Nebraska 68131

Dr. Leisha R. Eiten is a clinical coordinator at Boys Town National Research Hospital. She has served on task forces to develop pediatric amplification guidelines and remote microphone hearing assistance technology guidelines. She is a member of the KIPA (Knowledge Implementation in Pediatric Audiology) Work Group and American Speech-Language-Hearing Association's Health Care Economics Committee.

**Cheryl DeConde Johnson, Ed.D.,** Owner and Consultant, Audiology-Deaf Education vantage consulting (ADEvantage), Post Office Box 918, Leadville, Colorado 80461

Dr. Cheryl DeConde Johnson provides consultation and facilitation regarding initiatives in deaf education and systems improvement through her consulting practice, The ADEvantage—Audiology-Deaf Education vantage. In addition, she has adjunct faculty appointments at the University of Colorado, University of Northern Colorado, University of Arizona, and Salus University. Dr. Johnson is cofounder and former president of the board of directors for Hands & Voices.

**John L. Luckner, Ed.D.,** Professor, School of Special Education, University of Northern Colorado, 501 20th Street, Campus Box 141, Greeley, Colorado 80639

Dr. John L. Luckner is a professor and the coordinator of the Deaf Education teacher preparation program in the School of Special Education and the director of research for the Bresnahan/Halstead Center at the University of Northern Colorado. Dr. Luckner was a classroom teacher of students who are deaf or hard of hearing for 9 years. His current research interests include literacy, teacher preparation, social-emotional development, transition, and the provision of appropriate services for students who are deaf or hard of hearing and their families.

**Connie Mayer, Ed.D.,** Associate Professor, Faculty of Education, York University, 4700 Keele Street, Toronto, Ontario, Canada, M3J 1P3

Dr. Connie Mayer is an associate professor in the faculty of education at York University in Toronto, Canada, where she works in the graduate programs in education, linguistics and applied linguistics, and critical disability studies and is an academic coordinator of the teacher preparation program in the education of students who are deaf or hard of hearing (D/HH). Prior to coming to York, Dr. Mayer worked for more than 20 years as a consultant, administrator, and teacher of students who are D/HH from preschool through postsecondary. She is an associate editor for the *Journal of Deaf Studies and Deaf Education,* a former associate editor for the *Volta Review,* and a member of the editorial board of the *American Annals of the Deaf* and the *Reading Research Quarterly.* Her current research focuses on written language and literacy development in D/HH learners, early literacy and early intervention, cochlear implantation, bilingualism, and models of teacher education. She has presented widely on these topics both nationally and internationally as well as written numerous journal articles and book chapters and coauthored with Beverly Trezek the book *Early Literacy Development in Deaf Children* (Oxford University Press, 2015).

**Kristy Mixan, M.S.,** Early Childhood Coordinator, Center for Childhood Deafness, Boys Town National Research Hospital, 555 North 30th Street, Omaha, Nebraska 68131

Ms. Kristy Mixan has worked in the field of deafness for more than 30 years in the Omaha metro area. She has had varied experiences that include working at the Nebraska School for the Deaf, working with students in public school settings, and for the past 20 years, working at the Boys Town National Research Hospital. Her work at Boys Town National Research Hospital in the Center for Childhood Deafness has focused on providing parent–infant services, teaching and coordinating services for preschoolers, counseling services on the cochlear implant team, and counseling students in public school settings.

**Paula Pittman, Ph.D.,** Director, SKI-HI and Deaf Mentor Program Outreach, SKI-HI Institute, Utah State University, 6500 Old Main Hill, Logan, Utah 84322

Dr. Paula Pittman has been the director of SKI-HI Outreach at the SKI-HI Institute at Utah State University for 14 years and the director of the Deaf Mentor Outreach Project for 21 years. She has been a national trainer for the SKI-HI and Deaf Mentor Outreach Projects for more than 20 years. She was a creator of the Deaf Mentor Program and was involved in the development of the SKI-HI and Deaf Mentor Curriculum Manuals. She has provided direct services to infants, toddlers, and children who are deaf or hard of hearing, deaf-blind, or blind/visually impaired and their families for over 30 years.

**Amy McConkey Robbins, M.S., CCC-SLP, LSLS Cert. AVT,** Speech-Language Pathologist, Communication Consulting Services, Indianapolis, Indiana 46260

A speech-language pathologist in private practice, Ms. Amy McConkey Robbins is the author of several assessment tools widely used with children who are deaf or hard of hearing. She presents nationally and internationally on topics related to communication of children with cochlear implants and on vocational renewal for those in serving professions. Ms. Robbins's inclusive speech/music therapy curriculum, TuneUps, coauthored with Chris Barton, was named the "Most Valuable Product" by TherapyTimes.com readers.

**Jane Russell,** Doctoral Student, Social Research with Deaf People (SORD), School of Nursing, Midwifery and Social Work, University of Manchester, Oxford Road, M13 9PL, United Kingdom

Ms. Jane Russell is a part-time doctoral student, funded by the Economic Social Research Council (ESRC), at the University of Manchester, England. She is a trustee of a local deaf children's charity, Sign Hi Say Hi!, and is a mother to triplets, deaf and hearing.

**Marilyn Sass-Lehrer, Ph.D.,** Professor, Department of Education, Gallaudet University, 800 Florida Avenue Northeast, Washington, D.C. 20002

Dr. Marilyn Sass-Lehrer is a professor at Gallaudet University in Washington, D.C. She received a master's degree in deaf education from New York University and a Ph.D. from the University of Maryland in early childhood education and curriculum and instruction. She is the codirector of the Gallaudet University Graduate Interdisciplinary Certificate Program: Deaf and Hard of Hearing Infants, Toddlers and Their Families. She is editor of *Deaf and Hard of Hearing Infants, Toddlers and Their Families: Interdisciplinary Perspectives* (Oxford University Press, 2015), coauthor of *Parents and Their Deaf Children: The Early Years* (Gallaudet University Press, 2003), and coeditor of *The Young Deaf or Hard of Hearing Child: A Family-Centered Approach to Early Education* (Paul H. Brookes, 2003).

**Jeffrey Simmons, M.A.,** Clinical Coordinator, Hearing Services, Boys Town National Research Hospital, 555 North 30th Street, Omaha, Nebraska 68131

Mr. Jeffrey Simmons has been a practicing clinical audiologist since 1996. He currently serves as the cochlear implant clinical coordinator at Boys Town National Research Hospital in Omaha, Nebraska.

**Carol Westby, Ph.D., CCC-SLP,** Consultant, Bilingual Multicultural Services, 4821 Central Avenue Northeast, Albuquerque, New Mexico 87108

Dr. Carol Westby is a consultant for Bilingual Multicultural Services in Albuquerque, New Mexico, and holds an affiliate position with Brigham Young University in Provo, Utah. She has published and presented topics related to theory of mind; multicultural issues in assessment and intervention; and play, narrative, and language/literacy development. She has received honors from the American Speech-Language-Hearing Association.

**Deborah Wilson-Taber, M.Ed.,** Liaison, Santa Fe Public Schools, Bilingual Multicultural Services, Inc., 4821 Central Avenue Northeast, Albuquerque, New Mexico 87108

Ms. Deborah Wilson-Taber is the Santa Fe Public Schools liaison for students with hearing loss. For 9 years, she was the director of the preschool/kindergarten program of the New Mexico School for the Deaf. For many years, she has been developing programs and curricula and supporting access to learning for children who are deaf or hard of hearing in the state of New Mexico. She is currently affiliated with Bilingual Multicultural Services in Albuquerque.

**Alys Young, Ph.D.,** Professor of Social Work Education and Research, Social Research with Deaf People, School of Nursing, Midwifery and Social Work, University of Manchester, Oxford Road, M13 9PL, United Kingdom

Dr. Alys Young is a professor of social work and director of the SORD (Social Research with Deaf People) group at the University of Manchester, United Kingdom. She is also visiting professor at the Centre for Deaf Studies, University of the Witwatersrand, Johannesburg, South Africa. Her research work focuses on health and social care in relation to d/Deaf people across the life course, and she has a particular interest in social research methodologies associated with visual and spoken language contexts with d/Deaf children and adults.

# About the Video Clips

Purchasers of *Promoting Language and Literacy Development in Children Who are Deaf or Hard of Hearing* can access the illustrative video clips that accompany chapters 2, 4, 5, 6, 7, 8, 9, and 11 in two ways: on the DVD that is bound in the back of the print book or streaming it from brookespublishing.com/downloads with (case sensitive) keycode: 66eLLaD3g.

## List of Video Clips

### Video Clips for Chapter 2: Audiological Interventions for Infants and Preschoolers

Video clip 2.1: Demonstrating RECD Measurement Procedure

Video clip 2.2: Speech Perception Testing: ESP-Low Verbal Pattern Perception

Video clip 2.3: Speech Perception Testing: ESP Standard Version Pattern Perception

Video clip 2.4: Speech Perception Testing: Mr. Potato Head

Video clip 2.5: Prediction What a Child Can Hear From the Audiogram Results

Video clip 2.6: Equipment Check (CI): Sound Repetition

Video clip 2.7: Ling Sound Detection: CPA Task

Video clip 2.8: Sound Detection: Imitation of Sound Patterns

Video clip 2.9: Checking Device Function Recognition of Animal Sounds

### Video Clips for Chapter 4: Family-Centered Early Intervention: Principles, Practices, and Supporting Research

Video clip 4.1: Commenting on Imitation Routines

Video clip 4.2: Discussion about Meaningful Family Routines

Video clip 4.3: Coaching about Language Stimulation

Video clip 4.4: Reconnect and Review

Video clip 4.5: Join Problem Solving: Experimenting with What Works

Video clip 4.6: Summarizing Important Observations

Video clip 4.7: Observing Responses: Partners Share Expertise

Video clip 4.8: Father Shares Perspectives on Dual Language Use

Video clip 4.9: Father in Driver's Seat

**Video Clips for Chapter 5: Family-Centered Early Intervention: Supporting Spoken Language Development in Infants and Young Children**

Video clip 5.1: Temperament Questionnaire

Video clip 5.2: Discussing Consistency of Hearing Aid Use and Validating Parental Observations

Video clip 5.3: Encouraging Parents to Increase Auditory-First Opportunities in Play Routines

Video clip 5.4: Joint Experiment to Encourage Turn Taking During Familiar Routines (3 months post implant)

Video clip 5.5: Parent-Clinician Partnership Provides Opportunities for Speech and Grammatical Practice for a Child with Phonological Challenges

Video clip 5.6: News Commentator Role and Validation

Video clip 5.7: Coaching in Partnership During Book Sharing

Video clip 5.8: Acoustic Highlighting to Prompt Speech Production

**Video Clips for Chapter 6: Sign Language, Sign Systems, and Other Visual Modalities**

Video clip 6.1: Family Views of Raising a Child Bilingually

Video clip 6.2: Giving Wait Time and Securing Visual Attention When Learning Sigh Language is the Goal

Video clip 6.3: Learning Practical ASL Signs from a Deaf Mentor

Video clip 6.4: Deaf Mentor Guides Family in Use of ASL During Interaction with their Children (Blue bars in the section convey comments of non-primary communicators)

Video clip 6.5: Learning to Focus on Facial Expressions

Video clip 6.6: Learning to Express Emotions Using Signs and Facial Expression

Video clip 6.7: Family Goal of Meeting More Deaf People: Comfort is Increasing

Video clip 6.8: Encouraging Social Interaction, Turntaking, and Facial Expression

Video clip 6.9: Family Shares the Multiple Benefits of Working with a Deaf Mentor

Video clip 6.10: Learning ASL Signs to Support Turntaking

Video clip 6.11: Encouraging Gesture Use and Learning about ASL Classifiers

**Video Clips for Chapter 7: Auditory-Verbal Therapy:
A Conversational Competence Approach**

Video clip 7.1: Auditory-First Through Strategic Positioning

Video clip 7.2: Promoting Lexical Strategies During Conversation

Video clip 7.3: Promoting Narrative Development: Conversational Rules

Video clip 7.4: Auditory: Pitch Matching

Video clip 7.5: Ling 6-Sound Test: Mom Stands 10 Feet Away and Checks Left
Device

Video clip 7.6: Acoustic Highlighting During Phonological Awareness Training

Video clip 7.7: Boss Your Brain Strategies: Narrative and Listening to Text

Video clip 7.8: Making Predictions About a Poem and Using Auditory Closure

Video clip 7.9: Auditory First Through Positioning and Narrative Connectors

Video clip 7.10: Conversation: Information Seeking

Video clip 7.11: Incorporating Humor

Video clip 7.12: Holding Children Accountable for Clear Communication

Video clip 7.13: New, Nice, Noteworthy with Communication Temptation

Video clip 7.14: Narrative: Prompting Speech Self-Correction

Video clip 7.15: Mom Knows Why Nonsense Words Are Used to Promote
Phonological Awareness

Video clip 7.16: Parent Shares Home Language Examples

Video clip 7.17: What-Are-You-Wearing? Game: Listening, Conversation,
Taking Turns

Video clip 7.18: Eye Contact

Video clip 7.19: Teapot Game: Listening, Sequencing, Reauditorization, Music
Routine

Video clip 7.20: Tell-and-Show to Promote Listening, Perspective-Taking,
Conversation, Music Routine

Video clip 7.21: Rapid: Focused Practice: Phonological Awareness

**Video Clips for Chapter 8: Phonological Development and Intervention
Approaches for Children Who Are Deaf or Hard of Hearing**

Video clip 8.1: Open and Closed-Set Task

Video clip 8.2: Goldman-Fristoe Test of Articulation

Video clip 8.3: Beginner's Intelligibility Test

Video clip 8.4: Speech Intelligibility Sampling Monsen-IU Sentences: Cochlear Implant User

Video clip 8.5: Speech Intelligibility Sampling Monsen-IU Sentences: Hearing Aid User

Video clip 8.6: Speech Intelligibility Sampling Monsen-IU Sentences: Cochlear Implant User

Video clip 8.7: Speech Intelligibility Sampling Monsen-IU Sentences: Cochlear Implant User

Video clip 8.8: Speech Perception Testing: Compass Test of Auditory Discrimination

Video clip 8.9: Speech Perception Testing: Compass Test of Auditory Discrimination

Video clip 8.10: Speech Perception Testing: CAST

Video clip 8.11: Analytic Auditory Development Activities: CAST

Video clip 8.12: Analytic Auditory Development Activities

Video clip 8.13: Synthetic Auditory Development Activities: Story Presentation (Test of Narrative Language)

Video clip 8.14: Synthetic Auditory Development Activities: Story Comprehension (Test of Narrative Language)

**Video Clips for Chapter 9: Supportive Early Childhood Practices and Learning Environments**

Video clip 9.1: SCALES Discussion: Social Emotional

Video clip 9.2: Auditory-Visual Continuum Discussion

Video clip 9.3: Physical Learning Environment: Technology Checks and Listening Culture

Video clip 9.4: Physical Learning Environment: Speech Volume

Video clip 9.5: Emotional Climate and Social Relationship Practices: Peer Supported Problem Solving

Video clip 9.6: Instructional Learning Format Practices: Activity-Based Instruction with Embedded Goals

Video clip 9.7: Instructional Learning Format Practices: Reggio Amelia Project Approach with Peer Supported Conversation

Video clip 9.8: Communication Support Practices: Requesting with Picture-Supported Sign Language

Video clip 9.9: Communication Support Practices: Auditory Highlighting and Chunking

**Video Clips for Chapter 11: Reading the World: Supporting Theory of Mind Development in Deaf or Hard-of-Hearing Students**

# Acknowledgments

When we (the editors) began working with children who are deaf or hard of hearing, we could not have imagined the ways that technology would transform the intervention process. We are truly in a new era that allows interventions to begin early in life and to proceed in a developmental and proactive manner, helping children realize their potential. Our goal was to represent the ways in which interventions have evolved in this new era. This would not have been possible without the generosity and expertise of each of the chapter authors. We are grateful for their scholarly contributions, teamwork, and exceptional skill in providing contemporary views and practical considerations.

This book would not have been possible without the encouragement of Marc E. Fey. He recognized the need for this text and supported us with practical direction and advisement throughout the process. His previous intervention texts provided a model of excellence to follow. We appreciate his ongoing support and inspiring leadership.

We are also grateful for the many ways that the staff at Paul H. Brookes Publishing Co. actively supported us throughout each phase of the project. Astrid Zuckerman was our "rock"—there to provide calm guidance, reassurance, or cheerleading, depending on the issue. We owe her special thanks for her efforts, editorial skills, and constant encouragement throughout this journey. We also appreciate the responsiveness and expertise of Sarah Zerofsky. We could always count on Sarah to find answers to our questions and to assist us with whatever was needed to complete tasks. Finally, we are grateful for the careful copyediting and expertise provided by the editorial team at Scribe Inc.

Paul H. Brookes Publishing Co. has a history of providing video to accompany their intervention texts. This attracted us to the project, because we could see the value of bringing the words to life through multimedia. Our videos would not have been possible without the partnership of Catherine Cronin Carotta, who helped orchestrate and direct the process. We are grateful for her collaboration in this endeavor and her amazing leadership skills. We also express sincere appreciation to the production team at Boys Town National Research Hospital (Todd Sanford, Roger Harpster, and Diane Schmidt) for countless hours of travel, shooting, editing, captioning, design, and postproduction. The quality of the videos is to their credit, and we greatly appreciate their skills. We express sincere gratitude to the clinicians, teachers, parents, and children who generously shared their time and let us capture their intervention sessions on video. Their contributions to our learning are immeasurable and important.

Finally, this project would not have been possible without the steady and unconditional support of our families. They sacrificed, cheered, and supported without question. To our families, we express our gratitude and the recognition that we could not have done this without you.

*We dedicate this book in memory of
contemporary "giants" on whose shoulders we now stand.*

*Each was a visionary in developing the pioneering technologies
and innovative practices that have greatly enriched the lives of children
who are deaf or hard of hearing, their families, and society at large.*

*Orin Cornett
1913– 2002*

*Daniel Ling
1926– 2003*

*Julia Davis
1930– 2013*

*Doreen Pollack
1921– 2005*

*Marion Downs
1914– 2014*

*William Stokoe
1919– 2000*

*William House
1923– 2012*

# Promoting Language and Literacy Development in Children Who Are Deaf or Hard of Hearing

*An Introduction*

Mary Pat Moeller, David J. Ertmer, and Carol Stoel-Gammon

Children who are deaf or hard of hearing (D/HH) are adept learners with widely varied interests, talents, family backgrounds, hearing abilities, and specific needs. These diverse individual traits make the intervention process both challenging and engaging for service providers. One common and pressing need for children who are D/HH is that they have early and consistent access to rich language models in the environment. Access to linguistic input and communicative exchanges is known to be a critical factor that influences language development in children who hear (Hoff & Naigles, 2002; Hurtado, Marchman, & Fernald, 2008; Slobin, 1985) and is especially critical for children who are D/HH, who may experience reductions in quality and/or consistency of access to language exposure (Moeller & Tomblin, in press; Snow, 1994). Therefore, a central goal of interventions designed for children who are D/HH is the promotion of early and consistent communication access as a way of preventing or minimizing linguistic delays. Strategies for working toward these goals include the provision of 1) capacity-building supports for families, 2) linguistically rich environmental stimulation (either auditory, visual, or both), 3) well-fit and monitored hearing assistance technologies with focus on active promotion of auditory learning, and 4) effective early interventions that support families in implementing their chosen communication approach(es). The overall purpose of these strategies is to promote children's establishment of strong language foundations in the early years to support later literacy and social language competence.

## A NEW GENERATION OF CHILDREN
## WHO ARE DEAF OR HARD OF HEARING

Since the early 2000s, intervention needs of children who are D/HH could be described as a moving target— the landscape has changed dramatically and continues to change due to advancements in early identification, technology, and early service innovations. For service providers, this situation makes some previously familiar landmarks less recognizable and some tried and true intervention methods less applicable. As a result of early identification and changing technologies, providers are faced with the need to expand their knowledge and skill sets, including preparation for working across a wider range of ages (infants through young adults) and the management of complex technologies (e.g., cochlear implants, digital hearing aids, frequency-modulation [FM] systems). Children are served by intervention programs at much earlier ages than in the past, and **early intervention** services commonly begin in the first year of life, which requires a skill set for working within the context of the family system. In general, the service delivery process has shifted from emphasis on remedial approaches for late-identified children to preventative developmental approaches for those who are identified early. Prior to universal newborn hearing screening (UNHS), infants who were D/HH were often identified late, and this was especially true for infants who were hard of hearing (HH), typically identified at 2 years of age or later (Halpin, Smith, Widen, & Chertoff, 2010; Stein, Clark, & Kraus, 1983; Stein, Jabaley, Spitz, Stoakley, & McGee, 1990). Fortunately, studies confirm that early hearing screening has been effective in decreasing age of identification as well as the ages at which children receive follow-up care, such as confirmatory testing, enrollment in early intervention, and fitting of amplification devices (Dalzell et al., 2000; Durieux-Smith, Fitzpatrick, & Whittingham, 2008; Harrison, Roush, & Wallace, 2003; Holte et al., 2012; Spivak, Sokol, Auerbach, & Gershkovich, 2009; Vohr et al., 2008). Although some children are still identified late in the era of UNHS (Walker et al., 2014), this unfortunate situation occurs far less often than in the past, which alters the characteristics and experiences of families and children in ways that positively influence the nature of presenting intervention needs.

When early identification is linked efficiently with follow-up steps, families are placed in a proactive position, with opportunities to provide early linguistic stimulation (either auditory, visual, or both) that may minimize or prevent communicative delays. When early intervention services are effective with children and families, child outcomes are typically better than in the past (see Spencer & Marschark, 2006, for a review), and this positive shift has cascading effects, altering abilities and intervention needs at later stages in children's development. To stay abreast of these advancements, service providers are challenged to gain new skills, understand the impact of children's perceptual abilities on learning, rely less on past experiences, and remain current as children's technology offers advanced features and opportunities. This situation presents a compelling rationale for developing a book focused on language and literacy interventions for children who are D/HH— as Bob Dylan crooned in the 1960s, "The times, they are a-changin'."

Although the landscape is shifting, the need for an **individualized approach to intervention** endures. Children who are D/HH represent a heterogeneous group with highly varied outcomes, unique strengths, and individualized needs. Even when we see average outcomes improving for this group, studies consistently report wide ranges in individual outcomes; some children thrive and others struggle. What works for one child does not necessarily work for another. This makes it incumbent on the service provider to critically evaluate children's responses to intervention and to alter strategies as needed to address individual needs. Recent advances allow many children who are D/HH to develop spoken language. However, varied approaches are required and desirable to address the diverse array of child and family needs, family communication choices, cultural values, and learning styles. It is recommended practice that service providers have the professional qualifications and core knowledge and skills to optimize child development and family well-being, "regardless of the route or routes taken by the family (e.g., spoken language, American Sign Language, visually-supported spoken language)" (Joint Committee on Infant Hearing [JCIH], 2013, p. e1328). Thus, for some children and families, the intervention process requires service providers that have highly specialized skills. For example, some interventions require fluency in American Sign Language (ASL), and some require specialized skills in early auditory development and management of cochlear implants.

Furthermore, it is estimated that 35%–40% of children who are D/HH are reported to have other conditions/disabilities (Gallaudet Research Institute, 2010; Yoshinaga-Itano, Sedey, Coulter, & Mehl, 1998), sometimes referred to as "D/HH plus." The high incidence of special needs in this group of children adds to the need for expertise in developmental, medical, and communicative (e.g., augmentative) strategies on the part of service providers. Several authors in this book share challenging and interesting case studies in order to reinforce the concept that service providers must use diagnostically oriented interventions, keen observation, and careful tracking of responses to intervention to guide the adaptive intervention process and bring about successful outcomes with children who have complex developmental needs.

## PURPOSES OF THIS BOOK

A primary goal of this book is to describe and critically examine a broad range of intervention approaches that are specifically designed for and/or commonly used with children who are D/HH. Principles of **evidence-based practice** are incorporated into each chapter. The American Speech-Language-Hearing Association (2005) defines the term *evidence-based practice* (EBP) as "an approach in which current, *high-quality research evidence* is integrated with *practitioner expertise* and *client preferences and values* into the process of making clinical decisions." As part of these decision-making processes, service providers are expected to acquire and maintain knowledge and skills related to EBP to critically evaluate intervention approaches and the quality of evidence while incorporating new high-quality evidence into practice. Given these expectations, another key goal of this book is to support readers in gaining additional skills for critically examining intervention approaches and considering the evidence supporting them (or lack thereof). This is a tall order.

On a positive note, service innovations since the turn of the century have fueled opportunities for and interest in research on the outcomes of children who are D/HH. However, in some ways, technological progress has outpaced the garnering of evidence to support specific intervention approaches. We acknowledge at the outset that evidence supporting specific interventions for children who are D/HH is quite limited and, in some cases, only beginning to appear in literature. Comparative intervention studies are particularly rare. In spite of these constraints, efforts to purposefully integrate best available research evidence with practitioner expertise and client values and preferences are at the foundation of effective practice and are therefore endorsed and modeled throughout this text.

Children who are D/HH also benefit from many evidence-based interventions that were developed for children who hear. Thus, in the chapters that follow, authors describe widely implemented intervention approaches from the child language literature along with the evidence supporting them. When these approaches are implemented with children who are D/HH, they may require some specific adaptations that are based in service provider knowledge of the population and mastery of specialized skills. The authors have made every effort to describe their important insights regarding the process of adapting interventions and the unique skills that are required of the service provider.

Another purpose of this book is to provide comprehensive coverage of the diverse approaches that are typically implemented with children who are D/HH and their families. Some intervention practices for children who are D/HH are highly specialized and involve unique certifications or competencies (Listening and Spoken Language Specialist [LSLS]; bilingual-bicultural programs using American Sign Language). Other approaches adapt strategies that are designed for any child with speech- language challenges. Contributors to this book agree that a variety of strategies are often necessary, because it seems unlikely that a single approach will completely meet the wide array of auditory, visual, and communicative needs of the heterogeneous group of children who are D/HH. As editors, we have purposely recruited authors who present diverse intervention approaches that range on a continuum from primarily auditory focused to combined auditory-visual to primarily visually focused. We do so to promote understanding and evaluation of the specific interventions and to support the practice of individualization. The goal is not to polarize viewpoints but rather to present the varied strategies that are implemented singularly or in combination to support language development with this population. In reality, families may elect to use a variety of strategies and shift their emphasis based on the child's changing abilities. Many families of this new generation of children focus on the development of spoken language, yet others incorporate sign language within bilingual approaches. Some families elect to incorporate cued speech, manual codes of English, augmentative approaches, or a combination of strategies to serve as bridges to the development of spoken language. Selected authors share how the intervention process is adapted when auditory, visual, or combined approaches are implemented. Importantly, the chapter on family-centered practices (Chapter 4) discusses the concepts of informed choice and strategies for supporting families who are navigating the complexities of decision making around communication. Our overall goal is to promote a comprehensive understanding of the unique needs of children who are D/HH along with contemporary practices that are designed to promote optimal outcomes.

## ORGANIZATION OF THE BOOK

This book is organized into three main sections: Foundations of Intervention, Early Childhood Interventions, and Language and Literacy in the School Years. This organization reflects the developmental orientation of our work with children who are D/HH. These children may or may not present with persistent support needs throughout childhood, but regardless, their primary needs shift as linguistic skills develop and educational settings change. Intervention programs need to be developmentally appropriate, and there are distinct differences in the content focus of interventions for infants, preschoolers, and school-age children. Our overall organization respects how interventions change as children mature and service delivery settings shift (see Table 1.1).

### Principles Guiding Individual Chapters

Several guiding principles (premises) influenced the selection of topics that are presented in the forthcoming chapters. These main premises are highlighted here as we orient the reader to the content that is emphasized in the individual chapters and sections.

*Premise 1* Ongoing audiological management (Chapter 2) and provision of family supports (Chapter 3) are considered foundational to all service provision

**Table 1.1.** Developmental organization of topics covered in the book

| Section | Settings/developmental stages | Primary intervention focus | Chapters |
|---|---|---|---|
| Foundations | Family, community, and school systems (birth–young adult) | Managing amplification needs | 2 |
| | | Providing family support | 3 |
| Early childhood | Home based: on-site and distance via Internet (birth–3 years) Preschool and/or individual therapy (3–6 years) Home based, preschool, and individual settings (infant–school age) | Providing capacity-building interventions focused on early communicative development and family psychosocial support | 4, 5, 6, |
| | | Refining and strengthening auditory, visual, and linguistic foundations for learning | 10 |
| | | Promoting early literacy and social pragmatic skills | 7, 9 |
| | | Promoting ongoing development of phonology and conversational speech intelligibility | 8 |
| School age | School settings (6–18 years) | Promoting social cognitive skills that have an impact on literacy development | 11 |
| | | Supporting reading and writing development | 12, 13 |
| | | Promoting access to learning across the curriculum | 14 |

for children who are D/HH and their families. Although some families may not elect amplification for their children, all families interface with audiological services, and the majority receive ongoing services related to monitoring of auditory thresholds, fitting and verification of amplification, and/or mapping of cochlear implants. It is essential that service providers for children who are D/HH master and apply audiological principles and work in partnership with the audiologist to optimize the child's reliance on and consistent use of devices. Recent evidence supports the practices of early device fitting and optimizing the child's auditory access (audibility). Longitudinal studies demonstrate that age of fitting/implantation (Nicholas & Geers, 2007; Sininger, Grimes, & Christensen, 2010) and the amount of audibility provided by hearing aids (Stiles, McGregor, & Bentler, 2012; Tomblin, Oleson, Ambrose, Walker, & Moeller, 2014) contribute to child outcomes. Recent evidence also suggests that consistency of device use improves during the preschool years but is most variable in toddlers, less-educated families, and children with hearing thresholds in the mild range (Walker et al., 2013). We began this chapter with an emphasis on access to linguistic input. For the majority of children using amplification devices, verified high-quality fittings (McCreery, Bentler, & Roush, 2013), optimal audibility, and consistent device use are our first line of defense in supporting linguistic access for children learning spoken language.

Effective family support is known to be an influential aspect of intervention (Calderon & Greenberg, 1999) that is valued by families both early (Global Coalition of Parents of Children Who Are D/HH, 2010) and throughout the course of the child's development. In a recent qualitative study, families of newly identified children reported gaps in Early Hearing Detection and Intervention systems in the areas of social services and parent support (Fitzpatrick, Angus, Durieux-Smith, Graham, & Coyle, 2008). Chapter 3 introduces multidisciplinary perspectives from social work on the topic of family support. The authors consider four theoretical models for understanding parental and family experiences when a child in the family is D/HH: 1) the grief model, 2) the family systems model, 3) the stress and coping model, and 4) the social construction model. Importantly, this chapter reviews the evidential basis for specific components of family support practices and considers family-defined notions of support. This chapter also addresses unique considerations for supporting families when the parents are D/HH. The importance of supporting and respecting family decision-making authority is discussed.

**Premise 2**   Family involvement in promoting communication access and language development is a strong contributor to child success. Chapters 4–10 focus on developmental interventions for infants and young children (birth to 6 years), including interventions that support family roles (i.e., coaching models) as primary models of language and facilitators of communicative development. The section begins with an orientation to family-centered practice principles (Chapter 4) that are considered recommended practice in early childhood special education (ECSE). Many evidence-based practices from ECSE are required by federal legislation funding early intervention services and are endorsed by policy groups working with families who have infants who are D/HH (Moeller, Carr, Seaver, Stredler-Brown, & Holzinger, 2013). However, some components of intervention are unique to these families and require specialized areas of expertise. A model for building family capacity, including coaching them in the provision of an accessible, language-rich environment for the child, is described. The next two chapters explore the ways that coaching models are applied to promote auditory foundations for spoken language development in infancy (Chapter 5) and methods for coaching when sign language and/or other visual approaches are implemented (Chapter 6). These chapters include a discussion of specific interventions and strategies that are used to support families in the provision of a language-rich environment throughout daily routines to promote language development in infants and young children.

**Premise 3**  Children who are D/HH are educated in a variety of settings beginning at preschool, including child care and regular early childhood preschools. Interventions need to be tailored to these varied settings, and both individual and group interventions are designed to promote active learning, phonological development, social development, and literacy skills. Chapter 7 introduces the topic of auditory-based intervention approaches for preschoolers. This chapter describes the theoretical rationale and evidence supporting an auditory-first approach to the development of spoken language and literacy skills. This intervention approach focuses on the primacy of audition for the development of spoken language skills and is inclusive of auditory-oral and auditory-verbal methods. Through the provision of auditory access to rich and fluent conversational models, the emphasis is on natural language development with limited need for remedial interventions. Chapter 8 focuses on phonological development and interventions for children who are D/HH. This topic is particularly important given that recent studies suggest that phonological development, because of its dependence on the fidelity of the speech signal, may be vulnerable to delays in children who are D/HH (Moeller & Tomblin, in press; von Hapsburg & Davis, 2006). Thus, proactive developmental approaches are needed. Assessment strategies and evidence-based interventions that can be applied to meet habilitative and rehabilitative goals are described. This topic is addressed from a developmental viewpoint, beginning with vocal development in infancy and continuing through the stages to arrive at topics such as refinement of conversational speech intelligibility at the school-age level. Chapter 9 describes intervention delivered in the context of preschool settings and curricula. Following a discussion of the evidence promoting developmentally appropriate practices, this chapter demonstrates how auditory, language, and speech interventions are embedded in classroom routines. Methods for differentiating and accommodating individual child instructional needs are described.

**Premise 4**  Families also represent a "new generation," and they access information in new and technologically supported ways, which opens innovative avenues for service access/delivery. Chapter 10, the final chapter of the section on early childhood interventions, introduces a new frontier in intervention practices for children who are D/HH and their families—Internet therapy. Many families live far from qualified providers. Others may not have the means to access the specialized early intervention services they desire for their child. Modern telecommunication technology has the potential to overcome long-standing obstacles to service access, is readily accessible, and can be cost effective, reducing travel and time commitments for families and service providers (Stredler-Brown, 2013). Access to services should no longer be dictated by where the child lives, the language of the home, or the type of services or communication approaches chosen. Chapter 10 reviews the technological applications, types of interventions that can be delivered at a distance, and the competencies required of service providers. Internet therapy delivered at a distance is another area in which technological improvements have outpaced the collection of evidence, but practitioner experiences and existing evidence are valuable in guiding both research and practice.

*Premise 5*   The promotion of optimal literacy outcomes has been an elusive goal in the history of programs designed for children who are D/HH. However, outcomes and strategies are also improving in these areas, and a fresh consideration of reading and written language interventions is needed. The third and final section of the book, on language and literacy in the school years (Chapters 11–14), discusses the promotion of language, social cognition, and literacy in school-age students along with strategies for supporting students across the curriculum. Chapter 11 focuses on building strong foundations for reading comprehension and social interaction. This chapter includes strategies to develop theory of mind abilities as a way to promote the comprehension of academic discourse and socialization. It is known that theory of mind is a developmentally vulnerable domain for children who are D/HH, suggesting the need to consider current intervention strategies to prevent delays. Chapter 12 presents evidence-based contemporary reading interventions for students who benefit from audition and for those children who do not. Chapter 13 describes a model of process writing, which is a broad approach to written language development that is grounded in a view of writing as a recursive process, in which text is used as a tool for communication and learning. Chapter 14 wraps up the school age section by considering the topic of educational advocacy for students who are D/HH. This chapter explores ways to implement a tiered service delivery model and how to link interventions to Common Core State Standards in school programs. Tools for assessing communication access and classroom listening are discussed. Finally, the afterword brings the text to a conclusion in the form of five broad considerations that guide current and future practices.

## ORGANIZATION OF INDIVIDUAL CHAPTERS

The reader can expect to find parallel content areas across the chapters, although they may vary in specific organizational structure. Chapters include sections related to 1) reasons that selected intervention approaches are important for children who are D/HH (relevance); 2) the theoretical basis for the intervention approach(es); 3) the use of assessments to identify intervention priorities and to guide the intervention process; 4) discussion of intervention characteristics and strategies, evidence to support them, and adaptations to meet individual needs; 5) case studies illustrating the intervention process; and 6) future directions. Each chapter ends with suggested readings and learning activities to promote application of concepts.

## ADDITIONAL CONSIDERATIONS

This book is written with several audiences in mind. We expect that the content may be useful for students in university programs who are studying the process of aural habilitation/rehabilitation and/or child language interventions. This may include those studying the disciplines of speech-language pathology and audiology and those preparing to be teachers of D/HH students. We expect that service providers from each of these respective disciplines may find this book germane to their work. Finally, we envision that university professors may incorporate this book in their coursework related to interventions with children who are D/HH.

Current recommended practices for several chapters are modeled on the accompanying video clips (see DVD symbols and specific callouts in the chapters). Video demonstrations are intended to expand the readers' understanding of the specific intervention approaches described in the text. Furthermore, the demonstrations can assist readers in evaluating the applicability of specific techniques for the children and families in their practice settings. We have made an effort to show a range of child abilities and ages as well as adaptive intervention methods to increase generalizability. The DVD demonstrations are taken from actual intervention sessions (recorded either in educational settings at Boys Town National Research Hospital or by having videographers travel to the authors' communities).

Finally, the reader may notice that authors use terms that differ from some typically encountered in the literature. Rather than the more commonly used term *hearing age,* we use a term that captures the duration of a child's experience with cochlear implants or amplification. The selected term, **robust hearing** (Ertmer & Inniger, 2009, p. 1581), refers to the amount of time that children have had auditory access to speech at conversational-intensity levels. Use of this term highlights the need to consider children's exposure to spoken language models when making comparisons with age peers and younger children who are typically developing. For example, the phonological abilities of a 3-year-old child who was fitted with a cochlear implant (CI) at 12 months (i.e., has 2 years of robust hearing) are likely to be delayed compared with those of typically developing age peers who have experienced robust hearing since birth (Ertmer, Kloiber, Jung, Kirleis, & Bradford, 2012). Conversely, the time courses for making gains in prelinguistic speech development and expressive vocabulary have been shown to be more rapid for children implanted before 36 months than for younger, typically developing infants. This phenomenon appears to be due to the relatively advanced cognitive, social, and motor maturity levels of children who are D/HH when they first begin to hear via well-fit sensory aids (Ertmer & Inniger, 2009; Ertmer, Jung, & Kloiber, 2013). A similar concept could be extended to children in ASL programs, conceptualized as the duration of robust visual language exposure.

In addition, we adopt terms that are considered acceptable to the majority of stakeholders (i.e., family members, professionals, members of the Deaf community). Thus, we avoid terms that connote "impairment" and consistently use person-first terminology—in other words, *children who are deaf or hard of hearing.* Because this text may be used by multiple professional disciplines (speech-language pathologists, teachers of children who are D/HH, audiologists, early interventionists), we have elected to refer to the professionals as *service providers,* which we see as an inclusive term.

In summary, today's children who are D/HH have distinct advantages over those who were born before UNHS and improvements in hearing and visual technology. Indeed, their educational and vocational futures are bright. Yet early screening and technological advancements by themselves do not ensure the development of age-appropriate and adequate communication abil-i-ties. Readers of this text will find out how essential their efforts can be in help-ing children reach their communicative and academic potentials and become fully functioning citizens.

## REFERENCES

American Speech-Language-Hearing Association. (2005). *Evidence-based practice in communication disorders* [position statement]. Retrieved from http://www.asha.org/policy/PS2005-00221.htm#_ga=1.202345490.268001778.14310515

Calderon, R., & Greenberg, M.T. (1999). Stress and coping in hearing mothers of chil-dren with hearing loss: Factors affecting mother and child adjustment. *American Annals of the Deaf, 144*(1), 7–18.

Dalzell, L., Orlando, M., MacDonald, M., Berg, A., Bradley, M., Cacace, A., . . . Prieve, B. (2000). The New York State universal newborn hearing screening demonstration project: Ages of hearing loss identification, hearing aid fitting, and enrollment in early intervention. *Ear and Hearing, 21*(2), 118–130.

Durieux-Smith, A., Fitzpatrick, E., & Whittingham, J. (2008). Universal newborn hear-ing screening: A question of evidence. *International Journal of Audiology, 47*(1), 1– 10.

Ertmer, D.J., & Inniger, K.J. (2009). Characteristics of the transition to spoken words in two young cochlear implant recipients. *Journal of Speech, Language and Hearing Research, 52*(6), 1579–1594.

Ertmer, D.J., Jung, J., & Kloiber, D.T. (2013). Beginning to talk like an adult: Increases in speech-like utterances in young cochlear implant recipients and typically develop-ing children. *American Journal of Speech-Language Pathology, 22*(4), 591–603.

Ertmer, D.J., Kloiber, D., Jung, J., Kirleis, K., & Bradford, D. (2012). Consonant production accuracy in young children with cochlear implants: Developmental sound classes and word position effects. *American Journal of Speech-Language Pathology, 21,* 342–353.

Fitzpatrick, E., Angus, D., Durieux- Smith, A., Graham, I.D., & Coyle, D. (2008). Par-ents' needs following identification of childhood hearing loss. *American Journal of Audiology, 17*(1), 38–49.

Gallaudet Research Institute. (2010). *Regional and national summary report from the 2007–2008 annual survey of deaf and hard of hearing children and youth.* Retrieved from http://research.gallaudet.edu/Demographics/2008_National_Summary.pdf

Global Coalition of Parents of Children Who Are Deaf or Hard of Hearing (GPOD). (2010). *Position statement and recommendations for family support in the devel-opment of newborn hearing screening systems (NHS)/early hearing detection and intervention systems (EHDI) worldwide.* Retrieved from https://sites.google.com/site/gpodhh/Home/position_statement

Halpin, K.S., Smith, K.Y., Widen, J.E., & Chertoff, M.E. (2010). Effects of universal new-born hearing screening on an early intervention program for children with hearing loss, birth to 3 yr of age. *Journal of the American Academy of Audiology, 21*(3), 169–175.

Harrison, M., Roush, J., & Wallace, J. (2003). Trends in age of identification and inter-vention in infants with hearing loss. *Ear and Hearing, 24*(1), 89–95.

Hoff, E., & Naigles, L. (2002). How children use input to acquire a lexicon. *Child De-vel-opment, 73*(2), 418–433.

Holte, L., Walker, E., Oleson, J., Spratford, M., Moeller, M.P., Roush, P., . . . Tomblin, J.B. (2012). Factors influencing follow- up to newborn hearing screening for infants who are hard of hearing. *American Journal of Audiology, 21*(2), 163–174.

Hurtado, N., Marchman, V.A., & Fernald, A. (2008). Does input influence uptake? Links between maternal talk, processing speed and vocabulary size in Spanish-learning children. *Developmental Science, 11*(6), F31–F39.

Joint Committee on Infant Hearing (JCIH). (2013). Supplement to the JCIH 2007 position statement: Principles and guidelines for early intervention after confirmation that a child is deaf or hard of hearing. *Pediatrics, 131*(4), e1324–e1349.

McCreery, R.W., Bentler, R.A., & Roush, P.A. (2013). Characteristics of hearing aid fittings in infants and young children. *Ear and Hearing, 34*(6), 701–710.

Moeller, M.P., Carr, G., Seaver, L., Stredler- Brown, A., & Holzinger, D. (2013). Best practices in family-centered early intervention for children who are deaf or hard of hearing: An international consensus statement. *Journal of Deaf Studies and Deaf Education, 18*(4), 429–445.

Moeller, M.P., & Tomblin, J.B. (2015). Outcomes of children with hearing loss: An introduction to the inconsistent access hypothesis. Supplement to *Ear and Hearing*.

Nicholas, J.G., & Geers, A.E. (2007). Will they catch up? The role of age at cochlear implantation in the spoken language development of children with severe to profound hearing loss. *Journal of Speech, Language, and Hearing Research, 50*(4), 1048–1062.

Sininger, Y.S., Grimes, A., & Christensen, E. (2010). Auditory development in early amplified children: Factors influencing auditory-based communication outcomes in children with hearing loss. *Ear and Hearing, 31*(2), 166–185.

Slobin, D.I. (1985). Crosslinguistic evidence for the language-making capacity. *Crosslinguistic Study of Language Acquisition, 2*, 1157–1256.

Snow, C.E. (1994). *Beginning from baby talk: Twenty years of research on input and interaction.* New York, NY: Cambridge University Press.

Spencer, P.E., & Marschark, M. (2006). *Advances in the spoken language development of deaf and hard-of-hearing children.* New York, NY: Oxford University Press.

Spivak, L., Sokol, H., Auerbach, C., & Gershkovich, S. (2009). Newborn hearing screening follow-up: Factors affecting hearing aid fitting by 6 months of age. *American Journal of Audiology, 18*(1), 24–33.

Stein, L.K., Clark, S., & Kraus, N. (1983). The hearing- impaired infant: Patterns of identification and habilitation. *Ear and Hearing, 4*(5), 232–236.

Stein, L.K., Jabaley, T., Spitz, R., Stoakley, D., & McGee, T. (1990). The hearing-impaired infant: Patterns of identification and habilitation revisited. *Ear and Hearing, 11*(3), 201–205.

Stiles, D.J., McGregor, K.K., & Bentler, R.A. (2012). Vocabulary and working memory in children fit with hearing aids. *Journal of Speech, Language, and Hearing Research, 55*(1), 154–167.

Stredler-Brown, A. (2013). The future of telepractice for children who are deaf and hard of hearing. *Volta Review, 112*(3), 435–442.

Tomblin, J.B., Oleson, J.J., Ambrose, S.E., Walker, E., & Moeller, M.P. (2014). The influence of hearing aids on speech and language development of children with hearing loss. *JAMA Otolaryngology—Head & Neck Surgery, 140*(5), 403–409.

Vohr, B., Jodoin-Krauzyk, J., Tucker, R., Johnson, M.J., Topol, D., & Ahlgren, M. (2008). Early language outcomes of early-identified infants with permanent hearing loss at 12 to 16 months of age. *Pediatrics, 122*(3), 535–544.

von Hapsburg, D., & Davis, B.L. (2006). Auditory sensitivity and the prelinguistic vocalizations of early-amplified infants. *Journal of Speech, Language, and Hearing Research, 49*(4), 809–822.

Walker, E.A., Holte, L., Spratford, M., Oleson, J., Welhaven, A., & Harrison, M. (2014). Timeliness of service delivery for children with later-identified mild-to-severe hearing loss. *American Journal of Audiology, 23*, 116–128.

Walker, E.A., Spratford, M., Moeller, M.P., Oleson, J., Ou, H., Roush, P., & Jacobs, S. (2013). Predictors of hearing aid use time in children with mild-to-severe hearing loss. *Language, Speech, and Hearing Services in the Schools, 44*(1), 73–88.

Yoshinaga-Itano, C., Sedey, A.L., Coulter, D.K., & Mehl, A.L. (1998). Language of early- and later-identified children with hearing loss. *Pediatrics, 102*, 1161–1171.

# Foundations
of Intervention

# 2

# Audiological Interventions for Infants and Preschoolers

Leisha R. Eiten and Jeffrey Simmons

In March 1993, the National Institutes of Health (NIH) Consensus Development Conference recommended hearing screenings for all newborns before discharge from the hospital. Only two states had mandates for this practice at that time. At present, all 50 states and the territories of the United States have established their own Early Hearing Detection and Intervention (EHDI) programs. Typically, these EHDI programs follow the 2007 position statement of the Joint Committee on Infant Hearing (JCIH), which recommends that all infants have a hearing screening no later than 1 month of age with a diagnostic evaluation to be completed no later than 3 months of age for those children who are referred from the newborn hearing screening. For the most part, great success has been realized in meeting the screening goal. In 2011, 94.9% of infants were initially screened within the 1-month target frame, and 97.9% of all infants born that year received hearing screenings (Centers for Disease Control and Prevention [CDC], 2013). Unfortunately, current statistics also indicate that a significant percentage of children who do not pass newborn hearing screening do not complete the recommended follow-up testing. For 2011, this loss-to-follow-up rate was 34.9% (CDC, 2013). Despite ongoing concerns about the number of children lost to follow-up or lost to documentation (LTF/LTD), the average age of diagnosis appears to be dropping significantly, with 70% of infants diagnosed by age 3 months based on 2011 national statistics (CDC, 2013) and a mean age of hearing loss confirmation close to 7 months for a recent longitudinal study of children who are hard of hearing (Holte et al., 2012).

Despite improvements in the early diagnosis of hearing loss for many infants, challenges remain. Current screening technologies and protocols are most effective at identifying hearing loss of moderate degree or greater. Children with a degree of hearing loss in the milder range or for only isolated frequency regions may still pass a hearing screening (Johnson et al., 2005; Norton et al., 2000). Consequently, the total number of children born who are deaf or with some degree of either bilateral or unilateral hearing loss may be higher than the reported statistics suggest. Nevertheless, the number of children who are identified as deaf or hard of hearing (D/HH) in the first year of life (Holte et al., 2012) or even in the first 6 months of life (CDC, 2013) reflects a marked change from the years prior to the national adoption of EHDI programs, when the age of identification of permanent childhood hearing loss (PCHL) was often close to 2 to 3 years or greater (Harrison & Roush, 1996; Hoffman & Beauchaine, 2007; Mace, Wallace, Whan, & Stelmachowicz, 1991).

Every year, 1 to 3 of every 1,000 newborns are born D/HH (CDC, 2013). Without detection and intervention, hearing loss can have a negative impact on speech, language, academic, emotional, and psychosocial development (White & Munoz, 2008). With earlier identification of hearing loss, there is a greatly increased opportunity to stimulate auditory skills during the period most sensitive for their development. Accurate identification of hearing loss during the first few months of a child's life is not in itself sufficient for the development of listening and spoken language skills. Rather, identification is the launching pad in a process that must include appropriate fitting and consistent use of hearing technology such as hearing aids (HAs), cochlear implants (CIs), and other **hearing assistance technology (HAT)** in order to achieve optimal intervention outcomes (Tomblin et al., accepted). **Audibility** is essential to the development of spoken language skills (Tomblin et al., 2014; Tomblin et al., accepted) and to the development of a **soundscape**—that is, the sense and understanding of the full variety of sounds that surround each listener.

When spoken communication is the goal (either with or without visual communication supports), audiological intervention for infants and preschoolers forms a primary building block for promoting access to sound and speech awareness. Pediatric audiologists are among the first professionals to have contact with a family when hearing loss is identified, and they can be the first bridge between identification and intervention. The provision of well-fit HAs or CIs requires that an audiologist serving infants and children and their families be well-versed in the unique characteristics of children. This involves more than just the required technological expertise needed to program and adjust cochlear implants or advanced digital hearing aids. Pediatric audiologists must also form the bridge between sophisticated technology for an infant who cannot yet communicate and the parents and families who are still adjusting to their child's diagnosis of hearing loss.

## HEARING AID AND COCHLEAR IMPLANT CANDIDACY

National estimates indicate that from one-half to two-thirds of children with permanent hearing loss are considered hearing aid candidates. In 2011, the CDC reported that a total of 5,088 children born in the United States were

diagnosed with permanent hearing loss. Taking the CDC's data as an estimate, this would result in 2,500 to 3,400 infants with recommended hearing
aid fittings annually. Food and Drug Administration (FDA)– approved candidacy criteria for cochlear implants include children with profound hearing
loss in the 12- to 18-month age range as well those in the 2- to 17-year age
range with severe to profound deafness. Bradham and Jones (2008) utilized
a Gallaudet Research Institute analysis of the National Health Interview
Survey to estimate the number of children who met the candidacy criteria
for cochlear implantation and could benefit from the device. The researchers presented the number of 12,816 as a reasonable projection of the number
of children ages 12 months to 6 years who were potential cochlear implant
candidates. Dividing this into 1-year cohorts suggests that somewhere in the
range of 2,100 to 2,200 children are born each year who would be candidates
for cochlear implant technology.

## Hearing Aids

The recommended age for implementation of HA use is generally as soon
as the presence of permanent hearing loss has been confirmed. In addition to
the JCIH guidelines for the age of newborn hearing screening (1 month) and
hearing loss confirmation (3 months), the guidelines also call for intervention
to occur by age 6 months. This 1-3-6 model is being used internationally to
promote the earliest possible identification and intervention for infants with
hearing loss. Research supports the idea that there are increased benefits for
children who receive hearing instruments within the first few months of life
(Ambrose et al., 2014; Tomblin et al., accepted; Yoshinaga-Itano, Sedey, Coulter, & Mehl, 1998). Of course, if the presence of hearing loss is confirmed before 6 months of age, intervention with hearing aids can begin even earlier
than the JCIH guidelines recommend. A child's external ear and ear canal
need to be large enough to allow some type of earmold coupling so that sound
can be routed into the ear from an acoustic hearing aid. Binaural hearing
aid fitting is the standard approach for infants and children in order to promote the best possible development of the auditory neural pathways. Children
with external ear malformations such as microtia (malformed and/or under-
developed ear) or atresia (absence of external ear) may not be able to use
conventional air-conduction hearing aids and may require bone conduction
amplification that is worn attached to a band on the head to conduct sound
through the skull.

## Cochlear Implants

Children with severe and severe-profound degrees of hearing loss are considered to be possible cochlear implant candidates. However, cochlear implantation is not typically recommended until after the age of 12 months; it is
recommended at earlier ages only in specific cases such as following a menin-
gitis infection. If a child is identified with severe or profound hearing loss in
the first few months of life, pediatric audiologists will typically proceed with
hearing aid amplification to provide some experience with sound access rather
than waiting until cochlear implantation is approved.

The FDA has approved cochlear implantation in children as young as 12 months of age when bilateral profound hearing loss is present. There is a growing trend among professionals and researchers to pursue cochlear implantation for children prior to 1 year of age. The FDA's cochlear implant candidacy guidelines do not preclude the procedure in younger children or for those who are not profoundly deaf across the entire frequency range. Implant centers are able to exercise a practice known as "off-label" applications to provide implants for candidates who do not fall strictly within the FDA-approved criteria. The goal is to maximize early auditory development and speech-language outcomes by initiating robust stimulation of the hearing mechanism as early as possible. Those who support very early cochlear implantation (before age 12 months) make the argument that a critical time for development of listening and spoken language skills may be lost by waiting until age 12 months. A number of studies have demonstrated that age at implantation is an important variable that influences communication outcomes with a cochlear implant, and earlier implantation is better than later for development in areas such as language, speech perception, and reading (Dunn et al., 2013; Geers & Nicholas, 2013; Niparko et al., 2010). A determination of the optimal age at which cochlear implant surgery should occur or how early is early enough to maximize outcomes remains to be established. Research evidence with respect to CI in children younger than 12 months is somewhat mixed and variable, and the idea continues to generate debate.

Despite the debate about the optimal age to maximize cochlear implant benefit, earlier access to robust auditory input appears to result in better out-comes than later access. In their recent report on the benefits of extending cochlear implant candidacy, Nicholas and Geers (2013) expressed the opinion that "the earlier in his or her life that a child can achieve language skills commensurate with hearing peers, the better those later outcomes are likely to be" (p. 537). If a child for whom spoken communication is the ultimate goal has not shown significant progress toward that goal by 1 year of age, it is generally advisable to proceed with cochlear implantation as soon as possible.

## Bilateral Instruments for Cochlear Implant Users: Bimodal and Bilateral Cochlear Implant

As mentioned previously, binaural fitting has long been considered the standard of care for children who are D/HH bilaterally and use hearing aids. The auditory system uses input from both sides to perform binaural processes that are necessary for spatial hearing, sound localization, and optimal speech perception, especially in noisy environments (Ching, van Wanrooy, & Dillon, 2007). Stimulation of both ears is necessary to avoid neural degeneration that is associated with prolonged auditory deprivation (Olson & Shinn, 2008). Somewhat surprisingly, this same standard of binaural fitting has not always been applied to cochlear implants. In the recent past, monaural cochlear implantation was common practice, whereas bilateral cochlear implantation was not typical. Even when residual hearing was present in the nonimplanted ear, there was little emphasis placed on using a hearing aid in addition to the cochlear implant. There was even some suggestion that the electrical stimulation from the cochlear implant and the acoustic stimulation from the hearing aid might interfere with one another because they could not be assimilated in the central auditory system (Cullington & Zeng, 2010). In practice, the occurrence of clinically reported problems associated with simultaneous acoustic and electric input seems to be uncommon, and the recommendation to discontinue hearing aid use with initiation of the cochlear implant appears to have been based on historical practice rather than on compelling evidence in the literature (Olson & Shinn, 2008).

Many cochlear implant users now have auditory and speech perception abilities that exceed those exhibited by individuals who are severely hard of hearing and use hearing aids. Based on this newer evidence, candidacy for implants has expanded to include individuals with more residual hearing (Francart & McDermott, 2013; Novak, Black, & Koch, 2007; Sampaio, Araujo, & Oliveira, 2011). Many implant recipients have enough residual hearing sensitivity in the nonimplanted ear that some portion of the speech spectrum could be made audible with a hearing aid. Use of a hearing aid in the ear opposite to the implanted ear, commonly referred to as **bimodal** stimulation, takes advantage of an effect that Ching et al. (2007) refer to as "**complementarity.**" The cochlear implant is less successful at conveying low-frequency cues than is an acoustic hearing aid. The opposite is true for the hearing aid, which is less effective at providing audibility of high-frequency information for the listener who has little or no residual hearing for this spectral region. Bimodal stimulation utilizes the relative strengths of the two technologies to complement one another.

Evidence indicates that speech perception, sound quality, and music perception are all improved by bimodal stimulation more than by a cochlear implant alone (Francart & McDermott, 2013). Interestingly, a wide range of low-frequency audibility is not required in order to provide bimodal complementarity. A number of studies have indicated that even a limited amount of low-frequency audibility can be beneficial (Büchner, Schüssler, Battmer, Stöver, Lesinski-Schiedat, & Lenarz, 2009; Zhang, Dorman, & Spahr, 2010).

A number of arguments have been offered to provide a rationale for bilateral cochlear implantation. Binaural hearing is clearly better than monaural (Ching, van Wanrooy, & Dillon, 2007), and binaural hearing aids are the standard of care, so it is logical that the same practice should hold true for cochlear implants. Bilateral cochlear implantation ensures that the ear with the better performance for monaural implantation, if there is one, will be utilized. Even early monaural cochlear implantation does not suffice to adequately stimulate the auditory pathways for the nonimplanted ear, so bilateral implantation provides a means to avoid the effects of auditory deprivation in both ears (Ching, van Wanrooy, & Dillon, 2007; Sharma, Dorman, & Kral, 2005). There is a critical or sensitive period for developing and acquiring binaural integration skills (Sharma et al., 2005). Evidence is lacking to provide specific guidelines on whether bilateral cochlear implantation or bimodal stimulation is the best option for a given individual (Ching, van Wanrooy, & Dillon, 2007; Schafer et al., 2011). The evidence is clear that binaural stimulation is better than monaural, so implant recipients are more likely to be successful when using some type of hearing assistive device in both ears (Ching et al., 2007; Offeciers, Morera, Müller, Huarte, Shallop, & Cavallé, 2005).

## Special Candidacy Issues

Interventions for children with certain degrees and configurations of hearing loss have traditionally been more controversial and resulted in outcomes that were more variable across individuals. Hearing aid interventions for children with mild or minimal hearing losses, permanent conductive hearing losses, high-frequency hearing losses, and unilateral hearing losses are more often delayed than interventions for those with more severe bilateral hearing loss, partly because identification and confirmation of hearing loss may occur later (Gabbard, Schryer, & Ackley, 2008; Ross, Gaffney,Green, & Holstrum, 2008; White & Munoz, 2008). Parents may not see a need for hearing aid use when their infant or young child appears to consistently respond to voices and sounds in the home. Counseling and education is needed to help parents understand that mild, high- frequency, or unilateral hearing losses still present significant risk to speech and language development/learning (Yoshinaga-Itano, DeConde Johnson, Carpenter, & Stredler Brown, 2008).

***Minimal–Mild Hearing Loss*** Audiologists may vary in determining the exact decibel level at which a child with minimal or mild hearing loss becomes a hearing aid candidate. In order to provide more guidance for pediatric audiologists, the CDC EHDI program and the Marion Downs Hearing Center cosponsored a National Workshop on Mild and Unilateral Hearing Loss in 2005. The following working definitions of mild and unilateral hearing loss were adopted by the workshop participants:

> A permanent mild bilateral hearing loss was defined as a calculated or predicted average pure- tone air- conduction threshold at 500, 1000 and 2000 Hz between 20 and 40 dB hearing level (HL) or pure-tone air-conduction thresholds greater than 25 dB HL at two or more frequencies above 2000 Hz (i.e., 3000, 4000, 6000, 8000 Hz) in both ears. A permanent unilateral hearing loss was defined as a calculated or predicted average pure-tone air-conduction threshold at 500, 1000 and 2000 Hz of any level greater than or equal to 20 dB HL, or pure-tone air-conduction thresholds greater than 25 dB HL at two or more frequencies above 2000 Hz in the affected ear with an average pure-tone air-conduction threshold in the good ear less than or equal to 25 dB HL. (Ross et al., 2008, p. 142)

Recent evidence from a longitudinal outcomes study demonstrated benefits of the provision of hearing aids for children with mild hearing loss for both speech and language development (Tomblin et al., 2014).

Factors that should be considered in the candidacy process for children with milder degrees of hearing loss include the following:

- Evaluation of the individual ear corrections (real ear to coupler difference, or RECD) to determine the actual sound pressure arriving at the infant or child's eardrum

- The presence of risk factors for progression or fluctuation of the loss

- Any history of middle ear problems that may superimpose an additional conductive component or that could make use of an earmold problematic

***High-Frequency Hearing Loss***   Infants and young children with high-frequency hearing losses also present potential fitting problems. Audiologists need to minimize occlusion of the infant or child's small ear canal in order to provide natural, unamplified sound in regions of normal hearing. At the same time, high-frequency amplification needs to be provided. Being able to achieve both a significant opening or vent in the ear canal and high-frequency amplification in very small ears is a significant challenge.

***Unilateral Hearing Loss***   Unilateral hearing losses present another set of challenges to pediatric audiologists. The first challenge is whether to provide amplification based on the same time frames as children with bilateral hearing loss or to monitor for speech and language or learning delays before proceeding with amplification. The second challenge is to determine if the ear with hearing loss can or should be fit with conventional hearing aid technology or if other hearing assistance options would be preferable (McKay, 2002; Oyler & McKay, 2008; Updike, 1994). Other assistive options include the following:

- A frequency-modulated (FM) or digitally modulated (DM) remote microphone system with a receiver worn on the normal hearing ear in order to provide direct transmission from a primary talker via a microphone/transmitter

- A Contralateral Routing of Signal (CROS) system with a minimal gain acoustic hearing aid on the normal hearing ear and a wired or wireless microphone/transmitter on the ear with hearing loss to pick up and transmit sounds coming to the "off-side" or impaired hearing ear

- A bone conduction or Auditory **Osseointegrated** Implant (AOI) system that may be worn externally or implanted to act as a bone conduction CROS system

Cochlear implantation has recently been proposed as an additional option for unilateral hearing loss in cases when the affected ear is in the severe to profound range (Vlastarakos, Nazos, Tavoulari, & Nikolopoulos, 2013). In cases of single-sided deafness (SSD), the implant is the only means to provide useful stimulation to the deafened ear and is therefore the only option for potential provision of binaural/bilateral hearing. The initial published studies regarding this treatment involved only adults with SSD. Postoperative improvements in sound localization, speech perception in noise, auditory spatial perception, and tinnitus have all been reported (Sampaio, Araujo, & Oliveira, 2011; Vlasta-ra-kos et al., 2013). Although there have been some reports of this intervention in younger individuals (Cadieux, Firszt, & Reeder, 2013; Hassepass et al., 2013), at present, there is still limited available data regarding the application of cochlear implants in children with SSD.

***Additional Impairments***   Estimates of the number of children who are permanently D/HH who have additional medical complications and/or developmental disabilities run in the range of 30%–40% (Eze, Ofo, Jiang, & O'Connor, 2013; Gallaudet Research Institute [GRI], 2011; Palmieri et al., 2012). The general category of children with comorbid conditions beyond hearing loss is a heterogeneous group exhibiting significant variability in the impact of their disabilities on listening and learning language. Children with complex medical conditions may have limitations on their hearing device usage, especially if frequent hospitalizations or procedures have an impact on the ability to wear a device consistently. Children with cognitive impairments will have widely variable speech and language development even if hearing device use is established early and is consistent. Arguably, a significant portion of infants and children with additional impairments will experience outcomes that are more limited than what is seen in children who are D/HH with no additional conditions or concerns (Bagatto et al., 2011; Eze et al., 2013; Palmieri et al., 2012; Rafferty, Martin, Strachan, & Raine, 2013; Wiley, 2012). The presence of additional disabilities may make the early provision of hearing technology even more critical for maximizing speech and language outcomes. Children who do not experience significant improvements in auditory and oral communication skills as measured by standardized testing protocols may still be deriving notable benefit from hearing aids or cochlear implants in terms of a larger range of neuropsychological functions or skills that improve quality of life. Some children with additional impairments achieve outcomes in listening and spoken language that are comparable to typically developing children who are D/HH (Eze et al., 2013).

Cochlear implantation in this population has been more controversial. In the initial development of pediatric cochlear implant programs, children with comorbid conditions or complex needs tended to be excluded from implant candidacy due to concerns about being able to make acceptable progress (Edwards, Hill, & Mahon, 2012; Eze et al., 2013). This practice has changed within the last decade. A continuing issue, however, is the question of the usefulness of the CI or what can be expected in terms of benefit and whether that justifies implantation in this particular population of children with special needs. For the majority of individuals who receive a cochlear implant, the focus is on development of listening and spoken language skills (Palmieri et al., 2012). If this cannot be achieved, the overriding question is whether the cochlear implant would still be a worthwhile treatment. Parents and researchers have reported quality of life benefits from CI in children with additional developmental concerns, such as increased connectivity to and interest in the environment, better social interaction, and fewer problems with behavior management (Eze et al., 2013). Most parents of children who are D/HH with additional needs who are CI recipients are pleased with the benefits they perceive the device provides and would still select the implant for their children if given the choice again. Thus, the presence of additional disabilities does not automatically preclude the potential for benefit from cochlear implantation and should not be considered a contraindication to the procedure.

The decision about whether to proceed with cochlear implant or hearing aid fitting for a child with complex needs should be based on a thorough assessment by a multidisciplinary team. It is important that parents be counseled on how a given condition can have an impact on outcomes with either a hearing aid or cochlear implant and what realistically can be expected. In some cases, oral communication may not be an attainable goal for this particular population, and there may be cases where improvement or progress is minimal no matter how well-fit or programmed the HA or CI might be (Bagatto et al., 2011; Eze et al., 2013; Rafferty et al., 2013).

## HOW HEARING TECHNOLOGIES WORK

In a normally functioning auditory system, acoustic energy in the form of sound waves travels down the ear canal and causes vibration of the tympanic membrane. This causes the ossicles attached to the membrane to vibrate in the same pattern and transfer the energy to the fluid-filled cochlea, where the organ of hearing is located. The movement of the ossicles is translated into a series of wavelike motions in the cochlear fluid. This motion is referred to as a "traveling wave," and it results in displacement and stimulation of sensory cells distributed along the length of the cochlea. These receptor cells in turn release neurotransmitters that trigger a response in the fibers of the auditory nerve. When these nerve signals travel up the auditory brainstem to the auditory cortex, they are interpreted in the brain as sound. In children with permanent conductive losses, the middle ear does not transfer the sound efficiently to the sensory portion. In children with sensorineural hearing loss (SNHL), some portion of the cochlear sensory cells is not available to stimulate the auditory nerve. The fewer sensory cells that are available, the less sensitive the auditory system is to sound energy in the environment. The purpose of hearing technologies is to amplify the sound coming to the sensory system or to substitute for some portion of the auditory mechanism. (See an animation of ear anatomy and function at http://blausen.com/?Topic=9229.)

With severe-to-profound SNHL, the majority of the sensory cells may be damaged or absent, and the listener has limited detection of sound. Because the CI produces an electrical current that can directly stimulate the auditory nerve, this device can provide an alternative path for sound energy that bypasses the sensory cells that are not able to initiate a neural response.

### Hearing Aids

Acoustic hearing aids at their most basic, no matter what their style or size, use miniaturized microphones to take in sound, processors to filter and amplify sound, and miniaturized speakers (often called receivers) to send the amplified sound to the ear, all powered by small batteries (Figure 2.1). Almost all conventional hearing aids sold in the United States use digital circuits to process and amplify sounds. Hearing aids incorporate increasingly sophisticated digital sound processing, which may include amplification of more extended high frequencies, amplitude compression processing, noise reduction, and feedback cancellation. Digital circuitry now allows wireless communication between binaural hearing aids and between hearing aids and other devices such as cell phones and televisions.

### Advanced Hearing Aid Technology Features

***Extended Frequency Bandwidth***    Research shows that child and female voices carry important information up to 9,000 Hz, which is above the range of the typical audiogram frequencies (Stelmachowicz, Lewis, Choi, & Hoover, 2007). Older hearing aid circuits had limited amplification above 4,000 Hz. With advanced digital circuitry, hearing aids have been designed to provide amplification up to 8,000 or 10,000 Hz. The amount of amplified high-frequency

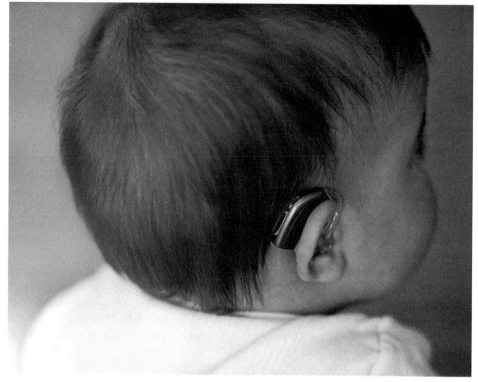

**Figure 2.1.**   Acoustic hearing aid on infant ear. (Image used with permission of Oticon Inc.).

audibility that can be achieved with extended bandwidth circuits will depend on the degree and configuration of an individual child's hearing loss. Other dig-ital circuitry uses frequency-lowering technology, which can transpose (move) or compress higher frequency speech sound information to a lower fre-quency range where the child may have better usable hearing.

*Amplitude Compression*   Amplitude compression allows the overall gain or amount of amplification to be actively and automatically changed in response to the loudness of the sound coming in to the hearing aid microphone. Amplitude compression processing provides the most amplification for soft sounds and automatically decreases amplification as incoming sounds get louder. Ampli-tude compression allows a wide range of sounds to be made audible within a more narrowed range of usable hearing.

*Noise Reduction*   Digital technology can use a variety of noise reduction techniques that may include the following:

- Directional microphone activation to reduce amplification coming from behind or from the side of the hearing aid user

- Impulse noise control to quickly detect and reduce amplification for sudden, very loud sounds

- Steady-state noise control that detects ongoing background noises and reduces the amplification in the frequency band/channel where the noise occurs

*Feedback Cancellation* Digital processors can provide feedback control, with reductions in peak gain in channels where feedback is detected. Active feedback cancellation is also available in many digital circuits. Feedback cancellation detects the sudden onset of feedback or whistling and provides a cancelling signal that is opposite in phase to the detected feedback, making the feedback inaudible.

## Bone Conduction and Osseointegrated Hearing Aids

Children who are born with small, malformed, or absent external ears and/or ear canals (congenital microtia, stenosis, or atresia) and children with severe and **chronic** ear infection and ear drainage may have permanent hearing loss and need amplification of sounds but not be able to wear conventional styles of hearing aids. The only available option to conduct sound to the ear in these situations is by bone conduction stimulation. Bone conduction stimulation substitutes for the conductive portion of the auditory mechanism by sending vibrations through the bones of the skull to stimulate the sensory organ more effectively. Bone conduction hearing aids may be external, with a vibrator (receiver) worn against the forehead or against the side of the head (see Figure 2.2, left panel). They can also be osseointegrated, with an implanted fixture in the mastoid bone. AOIs can be connected to an outside microphone and processor using a direct abutment to the implanted fixture or by using magnetic induction through the skin (see Figure 2.2, right panel). Implantation of an osseointegrated device is

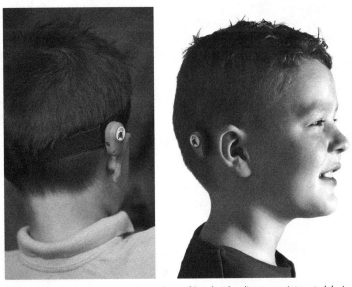

**Figure 2.2.** Bone conduction hearing aid on softband and auditory osseointegrated device. (Image used with permission of Oticon Inc.).

not currently approved by the FDA for infants and young children under 5 years of age, as the thickness of the skull in infants and young children may not be adequate to support an implanted fixture. A head-worn bone conduction processor is recommended before 5 years of age.

## Cochlear Implants

The CI system is composed of two sets of components. One set is internal, and the other is external. The surgically placed internal receiver/stimulator is composed of an electronics package, a radio-frequency receiving coil, and an electrode array. Extending from this implantable cochlear stimulator (ICS) is an electrode array that includes 12 to 22 electrodes, depending on the particular manufacturer. The ICS is placed under the skin behind the ear, and the electrode array is inserted into the cochlea. The external portion of the CI system is made up of a sound processor with one or more microphones, a power source, and a radio-frequency transmitting coil. The external components communicate with the internal components by means of a radio signal that passes through the skin rather than through a direct physical connection (see Figure 2.3).

Although different implant manufacturers vary in the details of both internal and external components, all cochlear implants follow the same general

**Figure 2.3.** Cochlear implant sound processor on a child.

process of providing acoustic stimulation to the auditory cortex. First, acous-tic sound energy is captured by the microphone(s) and passed to the external sound processor, where it is digitized and filtered into different channels or frequency bandwidths. The channels correspond to specific electrodes or com-binations of electrodes on the intracochlear array. Next, the electrical output from the processor is passed through a cable to the transmitting coil that is held in place on the skin over the internal receiving coil by means of magnets in the center of each coil. Radio-frequency (RF) pulses pass the signal through the skin to the ICS. In the next step, the ICS decodes the signal and sends it to the electrodes on the intracochlear array, which stimulates cells of the au-ditory nerve and can be perceived as sound. Information about the frequency or pitch is coded by the placement of the electrode array in the cochlea. The intensity or loudness of the stimulus is encoded in the amount of electrical current delivered from the electrodes.

## DEVICE VERIFICATION AND OUTCOME EVALUATION

Different intervention specialties are trained to obtain different types of **ver-ification** measures with children who use hearing aids or cochlear implants. Audiologists who specialize in hearing aid and cochlear implant fittings with children have specific objective and subjective verification measures to help determine if a device is working properly and if it is programmed or fit appro-priately to provide optimal audibility for a particular infant or child. Verifi-cation should be repeated over time to ensure that devices are functioning appropriately and is also repeated if a child's hearing thresholds change or as devices are updated.

The evaluation of outcomes moves beyond verification to determine if the hearing aid and/or cochlear implant is providing appropriate benefit or is resulting in appropriate progress in speech acquisition, sound discrimination/production, or listening performance in various environments. Outcome eval-uation is an ongoing process and may not always be measurable in a clinical or booth setting. It relies on a team approach with input and judgments from parents, early intervention specialists, speech-language pathologists, and class-room teachers in addition to the pediatric audiologist.

### Objective Verification Measures for Hearing Aids

*Electroacoustic Verification*  Audiologists use electroacoustic measures to verify the aided (amplified) audibility of actual speech signals or speech fre-quencies at a variety of loudness levels. A typical verification protocol includes evaluating the aided audibility of soft, average, and loud speech inputs and the verification of the maximum output or loudness of amplified sounds (maximum power output, or MPO) coming from the hearing aid(s). An example of electro-acoustic verification of a hearing aid is seen in Figure 2.4.

On this speechmap graph, frequency in Hz is shown on the horizontal axis and amplitude in dB is shown on the vertical axis. Amplification targets were generated by the Desired Sensation Level (DSL) prescriptive method and are indicated by the plus (+) symbol for speech and by the asterisk (*) for

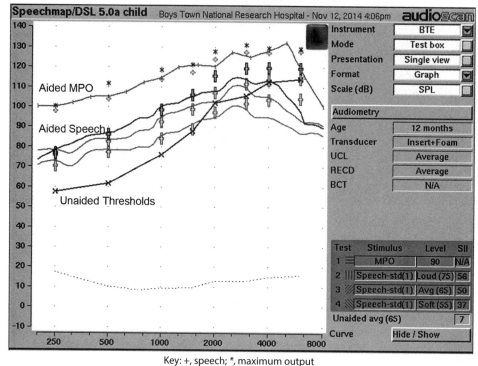

Key: +, speech; *, maximum output

**Figure 2.4.**  Electroacoustic hearing aid verification. The top curve represents maximum power output, the three middle curves represent the long- term average speech spectra for loud (75), average (65), and soft (55) amplified speech. The lowest curve with connected *Xs* represents unaided thresholds.

maximum output. The figure legend describes the different speech input levels used and the overall **Speech Intelligibility Index (SII)** audibility for each of the different input levels. Portions of the speech signals that are above the hearing threshold line will be audible. Portions that fall below the threshold line are inaudible. In this example, higher frequencies may not be audible with the hearing aid due to the severity of the high frequency hearing loss.

It is best if electroacoustic verification can be completed with the hearing aids on the child's ears. This takes into account the unique acoustic character- istics of the child's ear (size, shape, and middle ear status) and the coupling of the hearing aid to the ear (earmold fit and venting). On-ear electroacoustic verification requires that the child be able to sit quietly without moving for repeated measures. If this is not possible due to the child's age, developmen- tal level, or cooperation, another method that is used to estimate the on-ear response is the RECD measure. The RECD is a measure of the correction fac- tor between standardized test couplers and the child's individual ear. A brief on-ear measurement is completed with the child's earmold or a small foam eartip in place. This is compared with the response of the standardized test coupler. All other measures of the hearing aid response can be completed in the hearing aid test box, and the RECD corrections are added to estimate the audi- bility of speech through the hearing aid in the child's ear. Research indicates that although average age- specific RECD values are available, there is wide variability from child to child in the differences between average data and a specific child's RECD correction (Bagatto et al., 2005). Using only age-related average RECD data could result in significantly overfitting or underfitting HA gain and output characteristics for an individual child (see Video clip 2.1).

The use of prescriptive fitting formulas is recommended to ensure that amplified speech is audible and undistorted for the broadest possible range of speech input levels and for the broadest possible range of frequencies and that maximum output of the hearing aid in the child's ear is safe and does not cause discomfort or present a risk due to excessive loudness exposure. Pediatric-specific fitting prescriptions are available in hearing aid test systems and in hearing aid manufacturers' fitting software. In North America, the DSL prescriptive approach is commonly used by pediatric audiologists. The goal of DSL is to "define frequency/gain characteristics that would deliver to a child amplified speech that is audible, comfortable, and undistorted across the broadest relevant frequency range possible" (Seewald, Moodie, Scollie, & Bagatto, 2005, p. 146).

***Verification of Speech Audibility***   The SII is a value representing the proportion of speech that is audible to a listener and can be calculated both with and without hearing aids (American National Standards Institute [ANSI], 1997). It is an electroacoustic measure, not a behavioral prediction of speech recognition. SII values are provided in some hearing aid verification systems or as a stand- alone software application. The SII ranges from zero (no audibility of the speech spectrum) to one (full audibility of the speech spectrum) and can be expressed on a scale from 0 to 100 to indicate the percentage of accessible speech. The amount of SII that can be achieved with hearing aids will vary with the degree of hearing loss. Children with more severe hearing loss may not receive as much aided speech audibility as those with milder degrees of hearing loss, even with well-fit hearing aids. Beyond matching a prescriptive target, evaluating aided speech audibility is an informative verification function. Normative values and ranges for aided SII have been developed to assist audiologists in verifying pediatric hearing aid fittings (Bagatto et al., 2011). The SII provides a value that clinicians, caregivers, and teachers can use to estimate the proportion of speech that is available to the child and discuss the effects on word learning and speech. Stiles, Bentler, and McGregor (2012) found that for children fit bilaterally with hearing aids, a greater aided SII was associated with more accurate word recognition and nonword repetition and a larger receptive vocabulary. Tomblin et al. (2015) reported that greater relative aided audibility (controlling for unaided hearing) was associated with accelerating language growth curves in preschoolers who are hard of hearing. The aided SII provides the clinical audiologist with a useful reference tool that may reflect the long- term speech audibility with which a child will be acquiring spoken language (McCreery, Bentler, & Roush, 2013).

## Subjective Verification Measures

The choices for subjective or behavior verification measures include aided word recognition and/or aided speech detection and aided pure-tone thresholds.

Despite the fact that these measures have been used by audiologists for many years, subjective verification should typically be viewed as a supplement to electroacoustic verification rather than an alternative or substitute for careful electroacoustic measures.

**Aided Word Recognition**   Aided word recognition testing is an important and helpful supplement to electroacoustic verification. Speech testing is a more direct assessment of a child's functional hearing abilities both with and without hearing aids or cochlear implants in place. Speech materials must be tailored to the language age of the child. Due to limited vocabulary and test response options, it may not be possible to complete word recognition testing with children under the age of 3 years. If word recognition testing cannot be completed, aided speech detection may still be possible but will only provide an estimate of the softest speech levels detected through the HAs or CI. For preschool-age children, word recognition testing may be completed using an object-pointing or picture-pointing task with a restricted set of response choices. As children's expressive language and vocabulary develop, open-set testing using word or sentence repetition can be used. Some examples of word recognition test materials are listed in Table 2.1. Pediatric audiologists use aided word recognition tests in a variety of ways: Tests can be performed at multiple presentation levels to obtain a performance-intensity function; they can be administered in either quiet or background noise; and scoring can be done by words correct or by phonemes correct. Phonemic scoring is performed to look for specific error patterns  or to provide a more detailed picture of the child's functional ability (see Video clips 2.2, 2.3, and 2.4 for a variety of examples).

**Aided Pure-Tone and Aided Speech Detection Thresholds**   The current guidelines on pediatric amplification practices from the American Academy of Audiology (2013) state that behavior measures such as aided sound-field thresholds (ASFT) or functional gain should *not* be used as a primary method of verifying hearing aid function. What information *does* an ASFT provide? Essentially, it

**Table 2.1.**   Examples of aided word recognition tests

| Test | Task | Auditory skill hierarchy Language/cognitive age |
|---|---|---|
| Early Speech Perception (ESP) test (Moog & Geers, 1990) | Closed set, item and word identification | Identification 2–3 years |
| Open- and Closed-Set Task (Ertmer, 2015) | Open set, word repetition; closed set, picture identification | Identification 2–5 years |
| Northwestern University Children's Perception of Speech (NU-CHIPS; Elliot & Katz, 1980) | Closed set, picture identification | Identification 3–5 years |
| Multi-Syllable Lexical Neighborhood Test (MLNT; Kirk, Pisoni, & Osberger, 1995) | Open set, word repetition | Identification 3–5 years |
| Phonetically Balanced Kindergarten Vocabulary Test (PBK-50; Haskins, 1949) | Open set, word repetition | Identification 4–8 years |
| Hearing in Noise Test for Children (HINT-C; Nilsson, Soli, & Sullivan, 1994) | Open set, sentence repetition | Identification 4–8 years |

is an in situ (on-ear) estimate of the softest sounds detected through a hearing aid. However, current hearing aid processing can be highly compressed; the gain or amplification provided for soft sounds may be different from that for louder levels. Therefore, the hearing aid's performance at the lowest input levels where a detection response is obtained may or may not be related to how the device performs for conversational- level speech inputs. In short, with modern nonlinear hearing aid signal processing, the ASFT does not provide a predictable indication of the audibility of conversational or loud speech sounds (Stelmachowicz & Lewis, 1988).

Another important reason to avoid ASFT as a method of hearing aid verification involves test–retest reliability in the pediatric population, which can be significantly greater than the +/–5 dB variability commonly expected in the adult population (Hawkins et al., 1987; Stuart et al., 1990). Even if an increased variability in responses were not present, the use of aided behavioral thresholds provides limited amplitude resolution for the purposes of verifying hearing aid performance. Behavior measurements are typically performed in increments of no less than 5 dB steps. On the other hand, adjustments to hearing aid gain can occur in steps of 1 dB. In light of the behavioral test increment of 5 dB and higher test–retest variability in the pediatric population, it becomes exceedingly difficult to demonstrate the effects of small gain or output gain adjustments in the hearing instrument.

Compared with electroacoustic verification, ASFT methods are also lacking in terms of frequency resolution. With the limited span of attention/cooperation encountered in many infants and very young children, it is not uncommon for the audiologist to obtain reliable thresholds for only a few octave or half-octave frequencies in a given test session. Troughs and peaks that are readily visible in the hearing aid's electroacoustic frequency response can go unnoticed in behavioral thresholds obtained at widely spaced frequency intervals.

Although the American Academy of Audiology (2013) guidelines for pediatric amplification practices recommend that ASFTs not be used in verification of acoustic hearing aids, there are other types of hearing assistive technology for which these behavior measurements remain the best verification option. It is important to remember that the previously mentioned issues of test–retest reliability, amplitude resolution, and frequency resolution are still present for all the following devices.

- Performance of bone conduction amplification devices cannot be measured with real-ear probe microphone systems, and most clinics currently do not have access to the equipment necessary for electroacoustic testing of this category of device. Consequently, ASFT may be the only practical means of obtaining information about on-ear function of the bone conduction instrument.

- Another example of a device for which aided sound field responses may be useful is for hearing aids utilizing frequency lowering. This type of hearing instrument compresses or transposes high-frequency speech sounds to a lower frequency where audibility may be better achieved for the listener. Methods to electroacoustically assess frequency lowering processing are still being developed and are not readily available in all hearing aid testing systems. Using the ASFT to assess the functionality of the frequency compression and the audibility of high frequencies for the child is a valid verification option.

- There are no means to objectively measure the output of a cochlear implant, and audiologists must rely primarily on behavior measures to help assess and monitor the appropriateness of device parameters.

Historically, aided sound-field thresholds have been used to demonstrate to parents, teachers, and service providers that a child is obtaining benefit from amplification. Consequently, an audiogram showing aided thresholds may have utility as a counseling tool, as long as the audiologist is aware of its many limitations. Other than the exceptions with the devices mentioned, however, recommended practice dictates that ASFTs only be used as a supplement to objective **electroacoustic measurements** rather than the primary tool in the hearing instrument verification process.

## Outcomes Measurement

As previously discussed, outcome evaluation is an ongoing process. Early intervention specialists may perform a number of ongoing monitoring activities to measure the child's development of auditory and spoken language skills, but pediatric audiologists also contribute to the outcome evaluation process.

Appropriate outcome measurement instruments should be selected based on the child's emerging communication skills or abilities. The examples in Table 2.2 do not compose an exhaustive list, but rather they are a review of tools that can be used within the audiology clinic setting. They follow a hierarchy of

**Table 2.2.** Examples of outcome measures

| Test | Task | Auditory skills hierarchy |
|---|---|---|
| LittlEARS Auditory Questionnaire (Tsiakpini, Weichbold, Kuehn-Inacker, Coninx, D'Haese, & Almadin, 2004) | Parent questionnaire | Detection/discrimination/ identification |
| Parent's Evaluation of Aural/Oral Performance of Children (PEACH; Ching & Hill, 2007) | Parent questionnaire | Detection/discrimination/ identification |
| Infant-Toddler Meaningful Auditory Integration Scale (IT-MAIS; Zimmerman-Phillips, Osberger, & Robbins, 1997) | Parent questionnaire | Detection/discrimination/ identification |
| Auditory Skills Checklist (ASC; Anderson, 2004) | Parent questionnaire | Detection/discrimination/ identification |
| Ling Six-Sound Test (Ling, 2002) | Closed set, variable task; phonemic level | Detection or identification, nonverbal or verbal response |
| Early Speech Perception Test (ESP)/Low Verbal (Moog & Geers, 1990) | Closed set, pattern perception | Identification, nonverbal |
| Mr. Potato Head Task (Robbins, 1993) | Closed set, word/phrase level | Identification, nonverbal |
| Open- and Closed-Set (O&C) Task (Ertmer, 2015) | Closed set, word level Open set, word level | Identification, nonverbal and/or verbal |

auditory skills development from sound detection to auditory discrimination to identification to comprehension (Erber, 1982). Outcome assessment instruments may include parental questionnaires, tests of sound detection and pattern perception, or tests of closed-set or open-set word or sentence recognition. A variety of word and sentence recognition measures have already been listed in the behavior verification section in this chapter and may be used as both verification and outcomes assessment tools.

## HEARING ASSISTANCE TECHNOLOGY

The primary goal of any type of personal assistance technology is to promote or maintain independence and access to activities of daily living. The primary assistance technologies that infants who are D/HH will use are hearing aids and cochlear implants. However, additional technologies must also be considered as a child develops. The use of any assistive technology should be seen in the context of promoting daily activities that would be typical for the child's age and developmental level.

Technology applications can be used to do the following:

- Improve communication access in a variety of environments

- Provide access to electronic media

- Assist in fostering independence

- Promote awareness of environmental sounds

- Ensure safety

Formal tools to guide pediatric audiologists in discussing assistive technology applications with parents and caregivers are limited. Background knowledge about typical auditory development is helpful when considering the use of additional assistance technologies. The *Developmental Index of Audition and Listening* (DIAL; Palmer & Mormer, 1999) provides general milestones that may suggest when assistive technology use may be appropriate. For example, children typically begin attending to the television between 8 and 12 months and begin having interactive conversations on the telephone (without video support) around the age of 2 years. The use of assistive technology to provide direct inputs from the television or the telephone could be considered to foster these listening activities. The use of the *Auditory Skills Checklist* (Anderson, 2004) may also provide a means of giving caregivers and professionals a common reference for discussing early progress in development of functional auditory skills and whether additional technology options might be warranted.

### Alerting and Alarm Devices

Alerting and alarm devices must be considered for children and families who choose visual communication without auditory input or for situations when the child is not wearing his or her HA(s) or CI(s). Vibratory and visual signaling devices should be considered, particularly when environmental safety and increasing independence are the goal. For example, an older child, around 10 years of age, is allowed to be at home alone for certain hours of the day.

If the child is not wearing his or her HA(s) or CI(s) during this time, these assistive devices cannot contribute to safety. Visual or vibratory alerting is needed for smoke alarms in the house, especially if the child is not able to hear auditory alarms without amplification. In another instance, the goal is for the child to start waking up independently. Without HAs or CIs in place, the child cannot hear the alarm clock. An under- the- pillow vibrator can be attached to compatible alarm clocks to send vibration in addition to sound when the alarm goes off.

## Wireless Connection Options

Digital circuitry in HAs and CIs has improved the connection options between amplification devices and electronic media. Many different wireless connection options are available to connect amplification devices to cell phones, televisions, and computer tablets and laptops. Some connections use Bluetooth streaming, and others use the same transmission frequencies as cell phones. Audiologists and parents need to carefully consider the available connection options in terms of the age and independence of the child, as well as the type of wireless connection that is used. Some streaming devices that connect cell phones and electronic media inputs to hearing aids are worn around the user's neck. A necklace style can present safety concerns for infants and young children and would not be an appropriate option to consider until a child is older.

***Remote Microphone Technologies***   Remote microphones should always be considered a possible assistive listening technology for children who use hearing aids and/or cochlear implants. Remote microphone options provide improved listening and learning in environments with high levels of background noise and reverberation (echo) or where the primary talker moves farther than 1 to 2 meters from the listener. Examples of high noise or distance listening situations would be a noisy child care center or classroom, traveling in a car, playing in the park, or visiting a museum. In poor acoustic situations, the HA or CI user will experience increasing difficulty hearing and understanding speech clearly, even if their primary device is well fit and is functioning as intended. A remote microphone system can be used to wirelessly send signals from a small microphone/transmitter to a receiver directly connected to HAs or CIs. Remote microphone systems may use FM transmission, DM transmission, Bluetooth, cell phone, or other high-frequency transmissions (2.4 GHz or 900 MHz) to connect the microphone/transmitter to the receiver. Because the remote microphone is worn close to the talker's mouth (3 to 6 inches away), the signal that is sent to the user is as clear and undistorted as if the listener had their ear just as close to the talker, even if the talker and listener are much farther apart.

***Frequency-Modulated Transmission and Digitally Modulated Transmission Systems***   FM and DM systems are most often used in classroom/educational settings. FM and DM microphone/transmitter systems are able to transmit to multiple students at the same time. A variety of receivers and connections are available that can be used with most standard hearing aids, bone-anchored hearing devices, and cochlear implants (Eiten, 2010). Figure 2.5 shows typical DM remote microphone systems that can be used with hearing aids. Remote

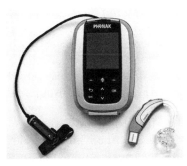 

**Figure 2.5.** Digitally modulated transmission system on acoustic hearing aid (left); checking frequency-modulated transmission receiver function with speaker (right).

microphone systems should also be considered for use in the home or in other situations outside of classroom listening. Additional decision making is needed to determine if an infant or young child is a possible candidate for home use of a remote microphone system. Considerations include determining if a parent/caregiver is able and willing to manage additional technology, determining if there is parental understanding about when the technology should be used, and determining if funding is available to purchase a system.

Pediatric audiologists must work closely with parents/caregivers and other members of the early intervention team when planning and implementing remote microphone technologies. Ownership and maintenance issues between home and school must be resolved in order to provide optimal access in all listening and learning environments.

***Verifying Remote Microphone Systems***   Any time a remote microphone device such as an FM/DM system is coupled or connected to a child's HA or CI, the pediatric audiologist should confirm the response of both the remote microphone and the primary device when the FM or DM system is connected and active. This is to ensure that a proper balance is maintained between the level of the primary talker using the remote microphone and other voices and sounds that are amplified from the HA or CI microphone. In addition, listening performance in noise should be evaluated in order to compare performance with the primary device alone versus performance with the remote microphone system active.

*Hearing Aids*   When evaluating a remote microphone connection to hearing aids, both electroacoustic and behavioral evaluation methods can be used. Electroacoustic verification of a remote microphone system is usually completed in a hearing aid test box. The response of the hearing aid can be compared with and without the remote microphone active. If the responses do not properly match, the hearing aid or remote microphone system may be adjusted.

*Cochlear Implants and Auditory Osseointegrated Implants*   As noted previously, cochlear implants and bone-anchored hearing aids (AOIs) cannot be evaluated using standard electroacoustic methods, and only behavioral verification has previously been available. The steps involved in behavioral verification include both informal and formal procedures. In the informal portion, an adult listener checks that the remote microphone receiver is receiving a signal through the use of a listening earphone. If such a listening check is not possible, as is the case with some CI processors, the receiver function can be verified by connecting it to a separate HA or a small speaker. Informal checks of the remote microphone system function can be accomplished by standing at a distance from the child and delivering simple commands or questions through the system's microphone/transmitter. Formal behavioral verification involves measuring speech recognition performance with standardized test materials. First, the child's word recognition performance is measured with the HA or CI alone in an "ideal," quiet environment. Next, testing is conducted with the primary device alone in a condition where background noise is present at the same loudness level as the test material or in a noise condition that closely approximates the child's classroom environment. Finally, speech understanding is tested in the noisy environment with both the primary device and the remote microphone system active. To demonstrate that the remote microphone device is set appropriately, the child's word or sentence understanding in the noise condition with both the primary device and the remote microphone active should be better than the performance in noise with the HA or CI alone, and it should be comparable to the results obtained for the primary device alone in the ideal quiet condition.

Extensive evidence-based guidelines are available to assist pediatric audiologists in verifying remote microphone hearing assistance technologies (American Academy of Audiology, 2011; Wolfe & Schafer, n.d.). Both the published guidelines and a companion DVD provide step-by-step verification instructions. More recently, Schafer and colleagues (2013) have developed an electroacoustic test approach to verify the response of an FM system connected to a cochlear implant. The proposed fitting procedure utilizes measurements of output from the sound processor's monitor earphones rather than measuring electrical output of the processor. As with hearing aids, the output of the CI processor alone is compared with the combination of the CI processor and FM/DM system. Various factors such as FM/DM gain settings, front-end sound processing in the CI equipment, and the type of coupling used with the CI must be taken into account when connecting a remote microphone system to a CI processor, but the measurements for the two conditions (CI processor alone and CI plus FM/DM) should be comparable to one another to indicate appropriate function of the FM/DM system.

## PROMOTING DEVICE USE

A great deal of a pediatric audiologist's clinical time is focused on technology. Evaluating hearing function, selecting devices, fitting ear molds and hearing devices, and determining assistive device needs can be time consuming. With so much technology to manage, it can be easy to lose sight of the fact that parents and caregivers may be in a grieving process because of their child's hearing diagnosis and may not be ready to participate in intervention activities. Parents and family members who are not familiar with the effects of hearing loss on language development may not understand the need for consistent hearing aid or cochlear implant use to promote language learning. Caregivers who do not speak English or who have limited reading literacy may not understand complicated device instructions. All of these issues present barriers to consistent hearing device use and successful intervention. Audiologists and early interventionists need to be aware of a family's **health literacy** level as they seek to introduce technology and establish hearing device use. The term *health literacy* can be defined as the degree to which individuals have the capacity to obtain, process, and understand basic health information and services needed to make appropriate health decisions (NIH, 2015). Health literacy and the idea of practicing health literacy universal precautions with all individuals are relatively new concepts that are being discussed and promoted in the field of health care. The goal is to promote a person's understanding and participation in the health care process. This can, in turn, improve compliance with important health recommendations and overall wellness.

## Health Literacy

The Agency for Healthcare Research and Quality (AHRQ) has published a helpful toolkit to promote health literacy in the medical field (AHRQ, 2010). The toolkit reviews key communication strategies that promote patient understanding and participation. These include the following:

- *Greet warmly:* Greet individuals with a smile and a welcoming attitude.

- *Make eye contact:* Make appropriate eye contact throughout the interaction. Don't just look down at the computer or equipment when speaking with individuals.

- *Use plain, nonmedical language:* Use common words when speaking to individuals. Take note of what words they use to describe their situation and use them in your conversation.

- *Slow down:* Speak clearly and at a moderate pace.

- *Limit content:* Prioritize what needs to be discussed and limit information to 3 to 5 key points.

- *Repeat key points:* Be specific and concrete in your conversation and repeat key points.

- *Use graphics:* Draw pictures, use illustrations, or demonstrate with 3-D models. Medical information provided to individuals often exceeds the 10th-grade reading level despite the fact that the average reading level of adults in the United States is below high school level.

- *Teach back:* Confirm that individuals understand what they need to do by asking them to restate the directions that are provided in their own words.

- *Promote individual participation:* Encourage individuals to ask questions and be involved in the conversation during visits and to be proactive in their health care. This goes beyond using yes/no questions or inquiring if individuals or parents have questions. Establish a plan of action together, with small goals and established check-in times (for more examples of a family-centered approach, see Chapter 4).

Some of the strategies may seem obvious to practitioners who work with children and families. This list of strategies is an important reminder that clinicians should not assume that parents and family members are able to remember all the instructions that are provided. The clinician should remember that parents may not understand the need to do everything that is recommended.

A variety of tools are available to educate parents and others on the implications of hearing loss and the benefits of consistent device use. Keeping the principles of health literacy in mind, the emphasis should be on clear pictures  and graphs that do not have jargon or technical vocabulary. An example of a simplified audiogram graph is shown in the video clips (see Video clip 2.5).

## Hearing Loss Simulations

Simulations can have a forceful impact on parents who question whether hearing aids are necessary for their child. These simulations are sound recordings that are altered to provide an example of how speech might sound for a given hearing loss. Infants and children with milder degrees of hearing loss or those with regions of better hearing often respond to environmental sounds and voices when they are not wearing hearing aids. Parents may question whether full-time hearing aid use is important because their child responds even when hearing aids are not worn. An opportunity to hear what the child hears can have a lasting impact on caregivers who struggle with establishing device use.

Several hearing aid test systems have hearing loss simulation options. The audiologist can enter the child's hearing test results into the system, and a simulation of the effect of that loss on a passage of speech is sent through the system's loudspeakers. Some simulations are available through the Internet but may not be able to incorporate the child's specific hearing threshold information into the simulation; many have been designed for adult hearing losses but can be used to illustrate the general effects of different degrees of hearing loss. Although not as individualized, online simulations give parents tools to share information with others (grandparents, family/friends) who may also be questioning hearing aid recommendations.

## Graphical Information

Graphics can provide an excellent starting point when discussing what speech information is audible both with and without hearing technology. Parents and caregivers frequently ask questions related to what kinds of sounds a child who is D/HH is able to perceive. A simple tool that can be used to support discussion about this is an audiogram of familiar sounds. An online search reveals that there are several versions available, but all follow the same theme. Various common environmental sounds as well as the phonemes or sounds that make up conversational speech are plotted on the audiogram based on their primary pitch (in Hertz) and loudness level (in decibels). A child's hearing sensitivity can be plotted on this audiogram to show the relationship to environmental or speech sounds. Sounds that are louder than the child's hearing thresholds will likely be audible. Conversely, sounds that are quieter than the child's thresholds will not be detected (see Video clip 2.5).

Another type of graph that pediatric audiologists use is an **SPLogram graph**. It gives an illustration of the typical speech spectrum (the range of pitches and loudness levels that make up speech) for conversational speech as it relates to the child's individual hearing loss. All available information, including hearing thresholds, RECD measures, and hearing aid gain levels can be referenced to the level of sound at the child's eardrum to give all measures a common reference point. The amount of speech that is loud enough to hear both with and without hearing aids can be compared. Individual speech sounds and their audibility can be explained. Many hearing aid test systems provide speechmapping to display hearing aid results. A downloadable program called SHARP (Situational Hearing Aid Response Profile, http://audres.org/rc/sharp/) is also available to illustrate audibility of a variety of different speech inputs, including typical infant listening positions and classroom speech levels, which may not be available in hearing aid test systems (Brennan, McCreery, Lewis, Kopun, & Stelmachowicz, 2013). The three SPLogram graphs that can be seen in Figure 2.6 provide a clear contrast of unaided and aided speech audibility for a child with a mild to moderate degree of hearing loss. Frequency (in Hz) is represented on the horizontal axis, and amplitude (in dB) is represented on the vertical axis. The child's thresholds are represented by the *O* symbols connected by a solid line. The top section of the graph shows the speech spectrum of an unaided female voice. The entire range of conversational speech is quieter than the child's thresholds. Note the SII value of *0* that is also seen beside the graph. The middle and bottom sections of the graphs illustrate the amount of aided audibility that is provided for speech from 1 meter and speech from 4 meters. For average conversation at 1 meter, audibility increases dramatically with the use of a hearing aid, with a majority of the speech spectrum now louder than the child's thresholds (SII=87). For speech coming from a distance of 4 meters, audibility is limited to the louder portions of the speech spectrum (SII=59). This contrast among different listening distances is helpful in illustrating how a child may respond differently in varying listening situations. The accompanying video clips provide further illustrations of how to use the SPLogram graphical information as a counseling tool when instructing parents (see also Figure 2.6).

### Percentages and Number Indexes

Percentages and indexes may be important supplemental information for some parents and caregivers when explaining the effects of hearing loss on speech understanding. Any comparison of unaided versus aided speech audibility indexes or percentages should be used in the context of health literacy awareness, which includes consideration for a person's literacy with numbers (defined as numeracy). The SII is one such number that estimates the amount of speech information that can be heard. As previously described, it represents the proportion of speech that is audible and can be calculated both with and without hearing aids.

### Listening Checks

Using hearing technology to facilitate auditory skills development requires not only that children wear the technology consistently but that devices function

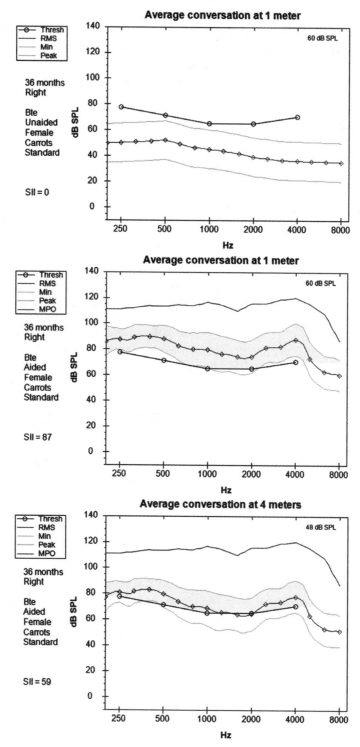

**Figure 2.6.** Situational hearing aid response profiles; top panel = unaided SPLogram graph (unaided speech is quieter than hearing thresholds); middle panel = aided speech at 1 meter (shaded area above threshold is audible); bottom panel = aided speech at 4 meters (shaded area above threshold is audible).

consistently. Parents, caregivers, and service providers can obtain information about how a hearing aid or cochlear implant is working by performing some type of listening check regularly. Listening stethoscopes or listening tubes can be connected to hearing aids to monitor sound quality and the amplification being provided. It is not possible to listen to the electrical output of a cochlear implant device, but many current implant processor models are compatible with monitor earphones that allow a listening check of the processor's microphone. As mentioned in the section on remote microphone sys-tems, this type of biologic listening check can also be used to monitor FM/DM equipment function when it is coupled to a hearing aid or implant processor. When children are developmentally able, it is also advisable to do regular listening checks with their participation (see Figure 2.7). The Ling Six-Sound Test (Ling, 2002) is a tool that can easily be adapted and modified for use as a listening check activity. The test involves oral presentation of six speech sounds (/m/, /u/, /i/, /a/, /ʃ/, and /s/). For children with less developed auditory or speech skills, detection of the sounds can be indicated with a conditioned response such as hand raising, putting a ring on a peg, or putting a block in a bucket. For other children, detection and recognition can be checked by having them imitate the target sounds or point to pictures that represent the sounds (see Video clips 2.6, 2.7, 2.8, and 2.9). Once a baseline has been established when the device is functioning, the child's responses can be monitored. If performance decreases from one listening check to the next, it could be an indication that the hearing technology is not functioning properly or that an adjustment of settings is warranted.

**Figure 2.7.**    Informal frequency-modulated (FM) system listening check.

### Device Maintenance

Both pediatric audiologists and early interventionists play an important role in educating and training parents to care for their child's hearing devices. A variety of maintenance and device-retention tools are available and should be introduced in the early phases of the device-fitting process. Introduction of the tools and hands-on training with their use should be done in steps as the parents show readiness and understanding:

- Device maintenance tools may include a battery tester, a blower for cleaning earmold tubing, a listening stethoscope or listening tube for hearing aids or monitor earphones for cochlear implant processors, a drying system/dehumidifier, and cleaning tools such as brushes and wax removal loops.

- Device retention and loss prevention tools may include a proper fitting of hearing aid ear mold tubing, the use of pediatric-size ear hooks to fit over the ear, double-stick wig tape or water-soluble adhesives to enhance HA or CI processor retention against the skin, thin fabric caps to cover the device(s), manufacturer-specific CI processor retention devices such as Snuggie and Snug-Fit, and loss-prevention tools such as Otoclips and EarGear. Extended manufacturer loss and damage warranty policies should be recommended and obtained when possible.

### Telepractice

In recent years, a number of specialized areas in the field of medicine have taken advantage of technological advances to provide telemedicine or telehealth services. The terms *telemedicine* and *telehealth* refer to the provision of health care at a distance (the American Speech-Language-Hearing-Association, n.d.; Swanepoel et al., 2010; see Chapter 10, this volume). These services can be synchronous, with the individual and the service provider interacting in real time; asynchronous, with data collected and later sent to the service provider; or a combination of synchronous, asynchronous, and/or face-to-face services. With respect to audiology and speech-language services, the American Speech-Language-Hearing Association (n.d.) recommends the use of the term *telepractice* to avoid conveying the idea that services would only be provided in health care settings. Telepractice overall will be addressed in greater detail in Chapter 10. For the current chapter, we will primarily focus on its use for audiological intervention.

Because a single audiologist can serve a large population base, many audiologists tend to be concentrated in larger communities and metropolitan areas. Consequently, children in rural, remote, or sparsely populated areas may have limited or no access to audiology services without traveling several hours to reach a clinic that specializes in pediatric audiology. Both the American Academy of Audiology (2008) and the American Speech-Language-Hearing Association (n.d.) have developed guidelines in support of this practice.

A critical issue when validating the efficacy of teleaudiology practice is to demonstrate that the services provided from a distance are equivalent or nearly equivalent to those provided in face- to- face situations (American Academy of Audiology, 2008; Hughes et al., 2012; Swanepoel et al., 2010). At present, there are reports of telepractice being used in virtually all facets of audiology practice (see Swanepoel & Hall, 2010, for review). This includes administering essentially the entire battery of commonly used clinical tests with either synchronous or asynchronous practices. Acoustic immittance testing, otoacoustic emissions (OAE) measurements, auditory brainstem response (ABR) testing, vestibular testing, and behavioral audiometry have been performed through Internet-based methods.

It has been suggested that fitting amplification may also be compatible with telepractice. For instance, the programming or adjusting of aids is routinely accomplished by using computers and software that can be controlled with remote access technology. Pediatric audiologists could potentially use interactive video to supervise trained personnel in the taking of ear impressions at a remote site (Swanepoel et al., 2010). Fitting and verification of hearing aids using probe microphone measures has reportedly been successfully conducted with an adult population (Ferrari & Bernardez-Braga, 2009). There is a need for additional data, however, and studies with young children remain to be reported.

There are only a few published studies that have examined the use of telepractice for setting program parameters for cochlear implants. In one of the first reports in the literature, researchers generated sound processor programs in both face-to-face and remotely controlled situations for five adults (Ramos et al., 2009). Comparisons of the program maps generated and the resulting speech perception scores with the different maps showed no significant differences. Similarly, a study by Wesarg and colleagues (2010) reported that maps generated in a remote session were comparable to those from a face-to-face fitting for a group of 70 implant recipients. Speech perception was not tested, but the authors noted that no difference in scores would be expected because the map parameters did not differ between the two conditions. Recently, Hughes and colleagues (2012) compared five different measurements (ECAP thresholds, psychophysical thresholds, programming levels, electrode impedances, and speech perception) that were performed both remotely and in face-to-face clinic sessions. In general, there were no significant differences among the first four of these measures obtained remotely versus those from face-to-face situations. However, the speech perception performance in quiet measured remotely was significantly poorer than performance measured in the face-to-face setting. This was attributed to the lack of a sound booth at the remote site, a situation that would not be uncommon in telepractice (Goehring et al., 2012). The researchers reported no adverse events, and they noted that they were able to complete all measures at the remote site without requiring an assistant with specialized knowledge of audiology or cochlear implants.

In addition to calls for further validation studies involving telepractice, a number of challenges to widespread implementation are frequently described as warranting consideration or resolution. These include reimbursement, licensure issues, and privacy/confidentiality (Hughes et al., 2012; Swanepoel et al., 2010). For individuals who depend on speechreading, communication may be more challenging in the remote condition than what the individual typically experiences in a clinic visit. This is especially true when audio and/or video signals are not optimal or are suffering from delay or interruption. It may be necessary to rely on sign language or written text in some telepractice circumstances. None of the challenges are necessarily insurmountable. If these issues can be successfully addressed, there appears to be a great deal of potential for the use of telepractice to provide audiology services to those who experience difficulty accessing clinic-based services.

## FUTURE DIRECTIONS

With rapid changes in all digital technologies, pediatric audiologists must continuously evaluate the value of new processing strategies and technology applications. When new HA technologies become available, they are most often directed to adult populations first. This is expected, as a majority of HA users are adults. However, not all technologies or processing strategies are appropriate for infants and young children. Safety and benefits for the young child should be clearly established before implementing the newest and most popu -lar technology interventions. Improved verification and outcome measurement  tools will continue to be needed to assess advanced speech processing and to  support early intervention service delivery.

Ongoing improvements are expected to continue in remote-microphone applications. Beginning in 2012, there has been a trend to replace traditional FM systems with DM systems, which is resulting in less signal interference between the transmitter and receiver as well as smaller receiver and transmitter sizes. This trend of decreasing size may result in pediatric-specific HA and CI products that have DM receivers completely incorporated into the processor with no additional pieces or parts to maintain. Wireless connections between HAs or CIs and other media such as phones, televisions, and music devices continue to progress, particularly with ongoing developments in smartphone applications. New smartphone apps are entering the market that allow direct wireless connections (pairing) between the phone and hearing aids with no intermediate streaming device. This allows the smartphone to function as a remote control and even as a remote microphone. With each new technology innovation, the pediatric audiologist must determine the value of its application to the infants, young children, and families that they serve.

Another area experiencing changes is candidacy for CI, which is rapidly evolving. Prompted by evidence of good outcomes in speech and language development and improved auditory access to a broader range of the speech spectrum, cochlear implants are now being considered for children with more residual hearing. Other changes include a trend toward younger age of implantation (under 12 months) and use of hybrid technology that provides the combination of HA and CI in the same ear for listeners with residual low-frequency hearing. Ongoing changes to signal processing strategies and implant hardware continue to improve outcomes, which in turn expands candidacy.

## SUMMARY

This chapter has provided basic information to highlight the important audiological components that help build the bridge between identification of hearing loss and high-quality speech and language intervention. If the desired outcome for a child who is D/HH is the optimal development of spoken language and listening skills, there must be a foundation of appropriate hearing technology that is individualized for the child. Without audibility and consistent access to sound, the journey from identification of hearing loss to spoken communication is a difficult and challenging one.

As members of the early intervention team, pediatric audiologists ensure that each child's hearing aids and/or cochlear implants are selected, fit, and verified using evidence-based recommended practices. They also participate in the process of assessing auditory and communication skill development with other service providers. Providing these critical services enables children who are D/HH to have enhanced access to the auditory speech signal and the opportunity to benefit from the therapeutic activities provided by other members of the team.

## SUGGESTED READINGS

A.G. Bell Listening and Spoken Language Knowledge Center. Retrieved from http://listeningandspokenlanguage.org/Tertiary.aspx?id=1213

Faulkner, K.F., and Pisoni, D.B. (2013). Some observations about cochlear implants: Challenges and future directions. *Neuroscience Discovery, 1*(9). Retrieved from http://www.hoajonline.com/neuroscience/2052-6946/1/9

Hearing Journal. (2012). *Building blocks.* Retrieved from http://journals.lww.com/the hearingjournal/Pages/collectiondetails.aspx?TopicalCollectionId=12

Hughes, M.L. (2012). Processes in receiving and maintaining a cochlear implant: What life care planners need to know. *Journal of Nurse Life Care Planning, 12*(2), 618–630. Retrieved from http://c.ymcdn.com/sites/www.aanlcp.org/resource/collection/8E724A1B-C4F2-4B8B-84B4-5D2411EBCE0D/Summer_2012_journal.pdf

## LEARNING ACTIVITIES

1. Explain the SPLogram from Figure 2.4, compare an unaided and aided graph, and find the SII value.

2. Complete a listening self-check with a hearing aid using the sounds from the Ling Six-Sound Test or check a child's detection of Ling sounds with cochlear implant use.

3. Visit the Success for Kids with Hearing Loss site and review at least three examples of hearing loss simulations (http://www.successforkidswithhearingloss.com/demonstrations).

4. Visit the Ear Channel on the Blausen Medical website (http://blausen.com/ ?Topic=9229) and review the animation of ear structure and function.

## REFERENCES

Agency for Healthcare Research and Quality. (2010). *Health literacy universal precautions toolkit.* AHRQ Publication No. 10-0046_EF.

Ambrose, S.E., Unflat-Berry, L., Walker, E.A., Harrison, M., Oleson, J., & Moeller, M.P. (2014). Speech sound production in two-year-olds who are hard of hearing. *American Journal of Speech- Language Pathology, 23,* 91–104.

American Academy of Audiology. (2008). *The use of telehealth/telemedicine to provide audiology services.* Retrieved August 17, 2014, from http://www.audiology.org/advocacy/publicpolicyresolutions/Documents/TelehealthResolution200806

American Academy of Audiology. (2011). *American Academy of Audiology clinical practice guidelines: Remote microphone hearing assistance technologies for children and youth from birth to 21 years.* Retrieved from http://www.audiology.org/publications-resources/document-library/hearing-assistance-technologies.pdf

American Academy of Audiology. (2013). *American Academy of Audiology clinical practice guidelines on pediatric amplification.* Retrieved from http://www.audiology.org/resources/documentlibrary/Documents/PediatricAmplificationGuidelines.pdf

American National Standards Institute (ANSI). (1997). ANSI S3.5–1997. *American national standard methods for calculation of the speech intelligibility index.* New York, NY: ANSI.

American Speech-Language-Hearing Association. (n.d.). *Telepractice: Overview.* Retrieved February 10, 2014, from http://www.asha.org/Practice-Portal/Professional-Issues/Telepractice

Anderson, K. (2004). *Auditory skills checklist.* Success for Kids with Hearing Loss. Retrieved from https://successforkidswithhearingloss.com/resources-for-professionals/early-intervention-for-children-with-hearing-loss

Bagatto, M.P., Moodie, S.T., Malandrino, A.C., Richert, F., Clench, D., & Scollie, S. (2011). The University of Western Ontario pediatric audiological monitoring protocol (UWO PedAMP). *Trends in Amplification, 15*(1–2), 57–76.

Bagatto, M., Moodie, S., Scollie, S., Seewald, R., Moodie, S., Pumford, J., & Liu, K.P. (2005). Clinical protocols for hearing instrument fitting in the desired sensation level method. *Trends in Amplification, 9*(4), 199–226.

Bradham, T and Jones, J. (2008). Cochlear implant candidacy in the United States: prevalence in children 12 months to 6 years of age. *International Journal of Pediatric Otolaryngology, 72*(7), 1023–1028.

Brennan, M., McCreery, R., Lewis, D., Kopun, J., & Stelmachowicz, P. (2013). *Incorporating measures of nonlinear frequency compression into the situational hearing aid response profile (SHARP).* Poster presented at A Sound Foundation Through Early Amplification, December 8–11, 2013, Chicago, IL.

Büchner, A., Schüssler, M., Battmer, R.D., Stöver, T., Lesinski-Schiedat, A., & Lenarz, T. (2009). Impact of low-frequency hearing. *Audiology and Neurotology, 14*(suppl. 1), 8–13.

Cadieux, J.H., Firszt, J.B., & Reeder, R. (2013). Cochlear implantation in nontraditional candidates: Preliminary results in adolescents with asymmetric hearing loss. *Otology & Neurotology, 34,* 408–415.

Centers for Disease Control and Prevention (CDC). (2013). *Summary of 2011 national CDC EHDI data.* Retrieved February 22, 2014, from http://www.cdc.gov/ncbddd/hearingloss/2011-data/2011_ehdi_hsfs_summary_a.pdf

Ching, T.Y.C., & Hill, M. (2007). The Parents' Evaluation of Aural/Oral Performance of Children (PEACH) scale: Normative data. *Journal of American Academy of Audiology, 18*(3), 220–235.

Ching, T.Y.C., Incerti, P., & Hill, M. (2004). Binaural benefits for adults who use hearing aids and cochlear implants in opposite ears. *Ear and Hearing, 25,* 9–21.

Ching, T.Y.C., Psarros, C., Hill, M., Dillon, H., & Incerti, P. (2001). Should children who use cochlear implants wear hearing aids in the opposite ear? *Ear and Hearing, 22,* 365–380.

Ching, T.Y.C., van Wanrooy, E., & Dillon, H. (2007). Binaural-bimodal fitting or bilateral implantation for managing severe to profound deafness: A review. *Trends in Amplification, 11,* 161–192.

Colletti, L., Mandala, M., & Colletti, V. (2012). Cochlear implants in children younger than 6 months. *Otolaryngology Head and Neck Surgery, 147,* 139–146.

Colletti, L., Mandala, M., Zoccante, L., Shannon, R.V., & Colletti, V. (2011). Infants versus older children fitted with cochlear implants: Performance over 10 years. *International Journal of Pediatric Otorhinolaryngology, 75,* 504–509.

Cosetti, M., & Roland, J.T. (2010). Cochlear implantation in the very young child: Issues unique to the under-1 population. *Trends in Amplification, 14,* 46–57.

Cullington, H.E., & Zeng, F.-G. (2010). Comparison of bimodal and bilateral cochlear implant users on speech recognition with competing talker, music perception, affective prosody discrimination, and talker identification. *Ear and Hearing, 32,* 16–30.

Dettman, S.J., Pinder, D., Briggs, R.J.S., Dowell, R., & Leigh, J.R. (2007). Communication development in children who receive the cochlear implant younger than 12 months. *Ear and Hearing, 28,* 11S–18S.

DeWalt, D.A., Callahan, L.F., Hawk, V.H., Broucksou, K.A., Hink, A., Rudd, R., & Brach, C. (2010). *Health Literacy Universal Precautions Toolkit.* Prepared by North Carolina Network Consortium, the Cecil G. Sheps Center for Health Services Research, the University of North Carolina at Chapel Hill, under Contract No. HHSA290200710014. AHRQ Publication No. 10-0046-EF. Rockville, MD: Agency for Healthcare Research and Quality.

Dunn, C.C., Tyler, R.S., & Witt, S.A. (2005). Benefits of wearing a hearing aid on the unimplanted ear in adult users of a cochlear implant. *Journal of Speech, Language, and Hearing Research, 48,* 668–680.

Dunn, C.C., Walker, E.A., Oleson, J., Kenworthy, M., Van Voorst, T., Tomblin, J.B., . . . Gantz, B.J. (2013). Longitudinal speech perception and language performance in pediatric cochlear implant users: The effect of age at implantation. *Ear and Hearing, 35,* 148–160.

Edwards, L., Hill, T., & Mahon, M. (2012). Quality of life in children and adolescents with cochlear implants and additional needs. *International Journal of Pediatric Oto-rhinolaryngology, 76,* 851–857.

Eiten, L. (2010). *New developments in FM systems for infants and children in R.C. Seewald and J.M. Bamford (Ed.),* A Sound Foundation Through Early Amplification, 2010 (167–177). Chicago, IL: Phonak AG.

Elliott, L.L., & Katz, D. (1980). *Development of a new children's test of speech discrimination* (technical manual). St. Louis, MO: Auditec.

Erber, N.P. (1982). *Auditory Training.* Washington DC: Alexander Graham Bell Association.

Ertmer, D.J. (2015). *The open- and closed-set task.* Durham, NC: MED-EL Corporation.

Eze, N., Ofo, E., Jiang, D., & O'Connor, A.F. (2013). Systematic review of cochlear implantation in children with developmental disability. *Otology & Neurotology, 34,* 1385–1393.

Ferrari, D.V., & Bernardez-Brag, G.R. (2009). Remote probe microphone measurement to verify hearing aid performance. *Journal of Telemedicine and Telecare, 15,* 122–124.

Francart, T., & McDermott, H.J. (2013). Psychophysics, fitting and signal processing for combined hearing aid and cochlear implant stimulation. *Ear and Hearing, 34,* 685–700.

Gabbard, S.A., Schryer, J., & Ackley, R.S. (2008). Diagnosis: Mild and unilateral hearing loss in children. *Seminars in Hearing, 29*(2), 159–168.

Gallaudet Research Institute (GRI). (2011). *Regional and national summary report of data from the 2009–10 annual survey of deaf and hard of hearing children and youth.* Washington, DC: Gallaudet University.

Geers, A., & Nicholas, J. (2013). Enduring advantages of early cochlear implantation for spoken language development. *Journal of Speech, Language, and Hearing Research, 56,* 643–655.

Goehring, J.L., Hughes, M.L., Baudhuin, J.L., Valente, D.L., McCreery, R.W., Diaz, G.R., . . . Harpster, R. (2012). The effect of technology and testing environment on speech perception using telehealth with cochlear implant recipients. *Journal of Speech, Language, and Hearing Research,* 55, 1373–1386.

Harrison, M., & Roush, J. (1996). Age of suspicion, identification, and intervention in infants with hearing loss: A national study. *Ear and Hearing, 10,* 254–258.

Haskins, H. (1949). *A phonetically balanced test of speech discrimination for children.* (Unpublished master's thesis). Northwestern University, Evanston, IL.

Hassepass, F., Aschendorff, A., Wesarg, T., Kröger, S., Laszig, R., Beck, R.L., . . . Arndt, S. (2013). Unilateral deafness in children: Audiologic and subjective assessment of hearing ability after cochlear implantation. *Otology & Neurotology, 34,* 53–60.

Hawkins, D., Montgomery, A., Prosek, R., & Walden, B. (1987). Examination of two issues concerning functional gain measurements. *Journal of Speech and Hearing Disorders, 52,* 56–63.

Hoffman, J., & Beauchaine, K. (2007). Babies with hearing loss: Steps for effective intervention. *The ASHA Leader, 12*(2), 8–9, 22–23.

Holman, M.A., Carlson, M.L., Driscoll, C.L.W., Grim, K.J., Petersson, R.S., Sladen, D.P., et al. (2013). Cochlear implantation in children 12 months of age and younger. *Otology & Neurotology, 34,* 251–258.

Holt, R.F., & Svirsky, M.A. (2008). An exploratory look at pediatric cochlear implantation: Is earliest always best? *Ear and Hearing, 29,* 492–511.

Holte, L., Walker, E., Oleson, J., Spratford, M., Moeller, M.P., Roush, P., . . . Tomblin, J.B. (2012). Factors influencing follow-up to newborn hearing screening for infants who are hard of hearing. *American Journal of Audiology, 21*(2), 163–174.

Houston, D.M., & Miyamoto, R.T. (2010). Effects of early auditory experience on word learning and speech perception in deaf children with cochlear implants: Implications for sensitive periods of language development. *Otology & Neurotology, 31,* 1248–1253.

Houston, K.T., & Caraway, T. (2010). For children with hearing loss: The times they are a-changin'. *SIG 9 Perspectives on Hearing and Hearing Disorders in Childhood, 20,* 48–55.

Hughes, M.L., Goehring, J.L., Baudhuin, J.L., Diaz, G.R., Sanford, T., Harpster, R., & Valente, D. (2012). Use of telehealth for research and clinical measures in cochlear implant recipients: A validation study. *Journal of Speech, Language, and Hearing Research, 55,* 1112–1127.

Jerger, J., Silman, S., Lew, H.L., & Chmiel, R. (1993). Case studies in binaural interference: Converging evidence from behavioral and electrophysiological measures. *Journal of the American Academy of Audiology, 4,* 122–131.

Johnson, J.L., White, K.R., Widen, J.E., Gravel, J.S., James, M., Kennalley, T., . . . Holstrum, J. (2005). A multicenter evaluation of how many infants with permanent hearing loss pass a two-stage otoacoustic emissions/automated auditory brainstem response newborn hearing screening protocol. *Pediatrics, 116,* 663–672.

Jöhr, M., Ho, A., Wagner, C.S., & Linder, T. (2008). Ear surgery in infants under one year of age: Its risks and implications for cochlear implant surgery. *Otology & Neurotology, 29,* 310–313.

Joint Committee on Infant Hearing (JCIH). (2007). *Principles and guidelines for early hearing detection and intervention* [position statement]. Retrieved from http://www.jcih.org/posstatements.htm

Kirk, K.I., Pisoni, D.B., & Osberger, M.J. (1995). Lexical effects on spoken word recognition by pediatric cochlear implant users. *Ear and Hearing, 16,* 470–481.

Knudsen, E.I. (2004). Sensitive periods in the development of the brain and behavior. *Journal of Cognitive Neuroscience, 16,* 1412–1425.

Ling, D. (2002). *Speech and the hearing-impaired child* (2nd ed.). Washington, DC: Alexander Graham Bell Association for the Deaf and Hard of Hearing.

Mace, A., Wallace, K., Whan, M., & Stelmachowicz, P. (1991). Relevant factors in the identification of hearing loss. *Ear and Hearing, 12,* 287–293.

McCreery, R., Alexander, J., Brennan, M., Hoover, B., Kopun, J., & Stelmachowicz, P. (2014). The influence of audibility on speech recognition with nonlinear frequency compression for children and adults with hearing loss. *Ear and Hearing, 35,* 440–447.

McCreery, R., Bentler, R., & Roush, P. (2013). Characteristics of hearing aid fittings in infants and young children. *Ear and Hearing, 34*(6), 701–710.

McKay, S. (2002). *To aid or not to aid: Children with unilateral hearing loss.* Retrieved from http://www.audiologyonline.com

Moog, J.S., & Geers, A.E. (1990). *The Early Speech Perception Test (ESP).* St. Louis, MO: Central Institute for the Deaf.

National Institutes of Health (NIH). (2015). *Health literacy: Clear communication.* Retrieved May 18, 2015, from http://www.nih.gov/clearcommunication/healthliteracy.htm

Nicholas, J.G., & Geers, A.E. (2013). Spoken language benefits of extending cochlear implant candidacy below 12 months of age. *Otology & Neurotology, 34,* 532–538.

Nilsson, M., Soli, S.D., & Sullivan, J.A. (1994). Development of the hearing in noise test for the measurement of speech reception thresholds in quiet and in noise. *Journal of the Acoustic Society of America, 95,* 1085–1099.

Niparko, J.K., Tobey, E.A., Thal, D.J., Eisenberg, L.S., Wang, N.-Y., Quittner, A.L., & Fink, N.E. (2010). Spoken language development in children following cochlear implantation. *JAMA, 303*(15), 1498–1506.

Nittrouer, S., & Chapman, C. (2009). The effects of bilateral electric and bimodal electric-acoustic stimulation on language development. *Trends in Amplification, 13,* 190–205.

Norton, S.J., Gorga, M.P., Widen, J.E., Folsom, R.C., Sininger, Y., Cone-Wesson, B., . . . Fletcher, K. (2000). Identification of neonatal hearing impairment: Evaluation of transient evoked otoacoustic emission, distortion product otoacoustic emission, and auditory brainstem response test performance. *Ear and Hearing, 21,* 508–528.

Novak, M.A., Black, J.M., & Koch, D.B. (2007). Standard cochlear implantation of adults with residual low-frequency hearing: Implications for combined electro-acoustic stimulation. *Otology & Neurotology, 28,* 609–614.

Offeciers, E., Morera, C., Müller, J., Huarte, A., Shallop, J., & Cavallé, L. (2005). International consensus on bilateral cochlear implants and bimodal stimulation. *Acta Otolaryngologica, 125,* 918–919.

Olson, A.D., & Shinn, J.B. (2008). A systematic review to determine the effectiveness of using amplification in conjunction with cochlear implantation. *Journal of the American Academy of Audiology, 19,* 657–671.

Oyler, R., & McKay, S. (2008, January). Unilateral hearing loss in children: Challenges and opportunities. *The ASHA Leader, 13,* 12–15.

Palmer, C.V., & Mormer, E. (1999). Goals and expectations of the hearing aid fitting. *Trends in Amplification, 4*(2), 61–71.

Palmieri, M., Berrettini, S., Forli, F., Trevisi, P., Genovese, E., Chilosi, A.M., . . . Martini, A. (2012). Evaluating benefits of cochlear implantation in deaf children with additional disabilities. *Ear and Hearing, 33,* 721–730.

Rafferty, A., Martin, J., Strachan, D., & Raine, C. (2013). Cochlear implantation in children with complex needs—outcomes. *Cochlear Implants International, 14,* 61–66.

Ramos, A., Rodriguez, C., Martinez-Beneyto, P., Perez, D., Gault, A., Falcon, J.C., & Boyle, P. (2009). Use of telemedicine in the remote programming of cochlear implants. *Acta Oto-Laryngologica, 129,* 533–540.

Robbins, A.M. (1993). *Mr. Potato Head task.* Indianapolis: Indiana University School of Medicine.

Ross, D.S., Gaffney, M., Green, D., & Holstrum, W.J. (2008). Prevalence and effects: Mild and unilateral hearing loss in children. *Seminars in Hearing, 29*(2), 141–148.

Sampaio, A.L.L., Araujo, M.F.S., & Oliveira, C.A.C.P. (2011). New criteria of indication and selection of patients to cochlear implant. *International Journal of Otolaryngology,* Article ID 573698.

Schafer, E.C., Amlani, A.M., Paiva, D., Nozari, L., Verret, S. (2011). A meta-analysis to compare speech recognition in noise with bilateral cochlear implants and bimodal stimulation. *International Journal of Audiology 50*(12), 871-880.

Schafer, E.C., Musgrave, E., Momin, S., Sandrock, C.and Romine, D. (2013) A proposed electroacoustic test protocol for personal FM receivers coupled to cochlear implant sound processors. *Journal of the American Academy of Audiology, 24*(10), 941-954.

Seewald, R., Moodie, S., Scollie, S., & Bagatto, M. (2005). The DSL method for pediatric hearing instrument fitting: Historical perspective and current issues. *Trends in Amplification, 9*(4), 145–157.

Sharma. A., Dorman, M.F. and Kral, A. (2005). The influence of a sensitive period on central auditory development in children with unilateral and bilateral cochlear implants. *Hearing Research 203,* 134–143.

Stelmachowicz, P.G., & Lewis, D.L. (1988). Some theoretical considerations regarding the relation between functional gain and insertion gain. *Journal of Speech and Hearing Research, 31,* 491–496.

Stelmachowicz, P., Lewis, D., Choi, S., & Hoover, B. (2007). Effect of stimulus band-width on auditory skills in normal- hearing and hearing- impaired children. *Ear and Hearing, 28,* 483–494.

Stiles, D., Bentler, R., & McGregor, K. (2012). The Speech Intelligibility Index and the pure-tone average as predictors of lexical ability in children fit with hearing aids. *Journal of Speech, Language and Hearing Research, 55,* 764–778.

Stuart, A., Durieux-Smith, A., & Stenstrom, R. (1990). Critical differences in aided sound field thresholds in children. *Journal of Speech and Hearing Research, 33,* 612–615.

Swanepoel, D.W., Clark, J.L., Koekemoer, D., Hall, J.W., III, Krumm, M., Ferrari, D.V., et al. (2010). Telehealth in audiology: The need and potential to reach underserved communities. *International Journal of Audiology, 49,* 195–202.

Swanepoel, D.W., & Hall, J.W., III. (2010). A systematic review of telehealth applica-tions in audiology. *Telemedicine and e-Health, 16,* 181–200.

Tomblin, J.B., Oleson, J.J., Ambrose, S.E., Walker, E., & Moeller, M.P. (2014). The influence of hearing aids on the speech and language development of children with hearing loss. *JAMA Otolaryngology—Head & Neck Surgery, 140*(5), 403–409.

Tomblin, J.B., Oleson, J.J., Harrison, M.E., Ambrose, S.E., Walker, E.A., & Moeller, M.P. (2015). Language outcomes in young children with mild to severe hearing loss. *Ear and Hearing.*

Torres, J., & Zeitler, D.M. (2013). Cochlear implantation for single-sided deafness in a child. *Audiology Today, 25*(5), 28–35.

Tsiakpini, L., Weichbold, V., Kuehn-Inacker, H., Coninx, F., D'Haese, P., & Almadin, S. (2004). *LittlEARS Auditory Questionnaire.* Innsbruck, Austria: MED-EL.

Updike, C.D. (1994). Comparison of FM auditory trainers, CROS aids and personal amplification in unilaterally hearing impaired children. *Journal of the American Academy of Audiology, 5,* 204–209.

Vlastarakos, P.V., Nazos, K., Tavoulari, E.-F., & Nikolopoulos, T. (2013). Cochlear implantation for single-sided deafness: The outcomes. An evidence based approach. *European Archives of Otorhinolaryngology.*

Vlastarakos, P.V., Proikas, K., Papacharalampous, G., Exadaktylou, I., Mochloulis, G., & Nikolopoulos, T. (2010). Cochlear implantation under the first year of age—The outcomes. A critical systematic review and meta-analysis. *International Journal of Pediatric Otorhinolaryngology, 74,* 119–126.

Wesarg, T., Wasowski, A., Skarzynski, H., Ramos, A., Gonzalez, J.C.F., Kyrianfinis, G., et al. (2010). Remote fitting in Nucleus cochlear implant recipients. *Acta Oto-Laryn-gologica, 130,* 1379–1388.

White, K.R. (2006). Early intervention for children with permanent hearing loss: Fin-ishing the EHDI revolution. *Volta Review, 106,* 237– 258.

White, K.R., & Munoz, K. (2008). Screening: Mild and unilateral hearing loss in chil-dren. *Seminars in Hearing, 29*(2), 149–158.

Wiley, S. (2012). Children who are deaf or hard of hearing with additional learning needs. *SIG 9 Perspectives on Hearing and Hearing Disorders in Children, 22,* 57–67.

Wolfe, J., & Schaefer, E. (n.d.). *Contemporary audiologic management to optimize cochlear implant benefit.* Retrieved August 12, 2014, from http://www.asha.org/aud/articles/Contemporary-Audiologic-Management-to-Optimize-Cochlear-Implant Benefit

Yoshinaga- tano, C., DeConde Johnson, C., Carpenter, K., & Stredler Brown, A. (2008). Outcomes of children with mild bilateral hearing loss and unilateral hearing loss: Mild and unilateral hearing loss in children. *Seminars in Hearing, 29*(2), 196–211.

Yoshinaga-Itano, C., Sedey, A.L., Coulter, D.K., & Mehl, A.L. (1998). Language of early- and later-identified children with hearing loss. *Pediatrics, 102,* 1161–1171.

Zhang, T., Dorman, M.F., & Spahr, A.J. (2010). Information from the voice fundamental frequency (F0) region accounts for the majority of the benefit when acoustic stimula-tion is added to electric stimulation. *Ear and Hearing, 31,* 63–69.

Zimmerman-Phillips, S., Osberger, M.J., & Robbins, A.M. (1997, May). *Assessment of auditory skills in children two years of age or younger.* Paper presented at the 5th International Cochlear Implant Conference in New York, NY.

# 3

# Supporting Families (Birth to 3)

Alys Young and Jane Russell

Families are our first developmental environment. They are the linguistic, relational, and social spaces in which we start to develop our human capacities and personal characteristics. They possess the resources and opportunities we require in childhood to unlock our potential and set us on the road to mature development. Children who are deaf or hard of hearing (D/HH) disrupt this developmental environment because of their differing needs and strengths in comparison with children who have "regular hearing."[1] The issue is not one of deficit because the child is not a hearing child or because the child's parents are not deaf parents. Rather, the issue is one of *fit*. To what extent can the familial environment meet the developmental requirements of the individual child who is D/HH and who is part of that particular family? To what extent will parents be able to enact their values, culture, and priorities in rearing their child in their family?

Too often these questions are discussed primarily in terms of language and communication choices with intervention provided to parents to support a child's spoken and/or signed language development. This is clearly

---

1. We borrow the term *regular hearing* from a father of a deaf child who took part in one of our research studies. He said he had thought for some time about how to describe his hearing daughter in comparison with his daughter who was deaf. He did not like the idea of *typical* or *average* hearing because that seemed to imply his deaf daughter was atypical or not normal. Then one day he was ordering in a fast food restaurant and was struck by the answer to his dilemma when an assistant asked him if he wanted a large or a "regular" soft drink. Regular for him was a neutral word implying what one might expect unless an exception was made. It seemed to him nonjudgmental and apt.

important as addressed by many chapters in this volume. However, the questions we are asking in this chapter are broader and concern understanding the family developmental context as a whole, in which any specific intervention or support has to be made real and has to make sense to the family in order to prove effective.

Specifically, in this chapter we address family support in the early years for a child who is D/HH (from birth to 3 years). We do not begin from the position of defining what a family may need or the different domains of support that may be required. Rather, we begin from the proposition that *how* the impact of a child who is D/HH on family life is conceptualized will fundamentally affect the approach taken to support its components. We propose four models for conceptualizing the impact of a child who is D/HH on (hearing) family life: 1) the grief model, 2) the family **systems** model, 3) the **stress** and coping model, and 4) the social construction model. In each case, we consider their theoretical underpinnings, their consequences for the provision of support, and potential criticisms of their application as a basis for working together with families with children who are D/HH. See Table 3.1 for a summary of the key emphases and implications for practice of each of the four models.

We use the term **model** to imply a way of understanding family support needs that has a theoretical basis and that privileges some courses of action

**Table 3.1.**  Summary of models related to provision of family supports

|  | Focus | Mechanism | Implications for family support |
|---|---|---|---|
| Grief model | Individual, personal, emotional, and psychological processes of adjustment | Resolution of psychological/emotional state over time | Counseling; psychological "holding"; purposeful working toward grief resolution, acceptance, and greater emotional availability |
| Family systems model | All members of the family and the system as a whole of which they are constituent | Admitting and/or resisting change to the system; return to steady state | Address all parts of the system and their interrelatedness and effects in any assessment, intervention, and evaluation of impact |
| Stress and coping model | The individual, their environment(s), others to whom they relate | Utilize preexisting coping mechanisms; enhance resources and repertoire of coping strategies; change appraisals of stressors; reduce environmental stressors | Introduce new cognitive and behavioral resources; address practical and economic issues; increase social support; maximize networks of opportunity |
| Social construction model | Society as a whole and its various subgroups, subcultures, divisions, and diversities | Institutionalized and structural prioritization of discourse; meaning generation through communication and interaction; unequal power dynamics in the privileging of meanings | Open up multiple versions of what it might be to be deaf in experiential and gently challenging ways that assume an unconditional positive regard for all possibilities and support informed choice |

and some explanations and interpretations over others. However, it would be wrong to consider the four models as mutually exclusive or that any one on its own might provide a universal explication of the essentials of family support. Rather, each exposes concepts, theories, and assumptions that will challenge readers to be **reflexive** and consider the implications of each approach for supporting families with children who are D/HH. In this sense, a model is neither prescriptive nor proscriptive but rather is best understood as a lens through which we might see families and our work alongside them. All lenses have the potential to reveal, magnify, and obscure, and with this in mind, we will also draw attention to relevant research studies that are associated with these ways of seeing and the strength of evidence they provide.

Finally, toward the end of the chapter, we consider the relevance of D/HH people, whether parents or not, to the issues we have explored. Fewer than 5% of parents with D/HH children are D/HH themselves (in the developed world) (Mitchell & Karchmer, 2004). However, parents, professionals, and ordinary citizens who are D/HH are an important resource on which to draw in considering the means by which families may be supported.

## THE GRIEF MODEL

> No one ever told me that grief felt so like fear. I am not afraid, but the sensation is like being afraid. The same fluttering in the stomach, the same restlessness, the yawning. I keep on swallowing . . . It gives life a permanently provisional feeling.
>
> — Lewis (1961), p. 15

The grief and loss model is the theoretical model most commonly used to explain the early experiences of hearing parents who learn that their child is D/HH (Kampfe, 1989; Kurtzer-White & Luterman, 2003; Luterman, 1999a, 1999b; Moses, 1985; Paget, 1983). Loss is written about by parents and professionals alike as the loss of expectations or loss of dreams. In some instances, this is expressed in terms of expectations of a "perfect" child not being met, where perfect usually implies "hearing" and refers to a child not having a "problem," "disability," or "impairment." Loss of expectations is also more generally considered in terms of expectations of a usual developmental trajectory and the likely satisfactions associated with parenting and raising a family:

> Most parents find disability to be the great spoiler of their dreams and fantasies about who or what their child was to be. Most dreams require an unimpaired child; therefore the initial diagnosis of disability often marks the point when a cherished and significant dream has been shattered. It is that dream that must be grieved for. (Moses, 1985, p. 86)

The accompanying emotional and psychological processes that parents go through in response to loss are predominantly thought of in terms of a grief response. Consequently, being sensitive to this psychological effect and responding to it become key bases of family support, particularly in the period immediately following diagnosis.

Founded on research into the personal consequences of experiencing a disaster (Lindemann, 1944), the grief process following a death (Kubler-Ross,

1969), and crisis theory (Caplan, 1964), grief is understood as a series of affective states. Despite the fact that terminology may differ among reports, the emotions generally ascribed to these states are connected with periods of shock, denial, anger, depression, and acceptance.

Although initially conceived of as a linear and deterministic process, with each stage being necessary to progress to the next, it is now more commonly understood as sequential or cyclical, depending on the individual. Some stages may be experienced more than once or in a different order. For some parents, grief may be revisited at different developmental stages in a child's life, which may prompt additional experiences of loss. For example, a child's first day at school may reveal the ways in which a son or daughter is not like his or her classmates; the beginning of adolescence may prompt new concerns about what may or may not be possible in young adulthood in comparison with normative expectations (Gregory, Bishop, & Sheldon, 1995). These may be understood as new experiences of loss. Kurtzer-White and Luterman (2003) explain that for parents of children who are D/HH, grief is not time bounded in the way in which grief resulting from death might be. It is open ended and thus presents a different kind of challenge for parents coping with loss.

## Supporting Families

In terms of supporting families, grief and mourning is considered to be not just a healthy and natural process that should be facilitated but an essential one. Resolution of the psychological and emotional processes of grief is regarded as a prerequisite to constructive action (Boison, 1987) and to personal mental well-being (Kampfe, 1989). Without such resolution, a parent may remain emotionally unavailable to his or her deaf child and unable to engage with professional services (Kurtzer- White & Luterman, 2003). Indeed, one of the early presumptions about the impact of universal newborn hearing screening (UNHS) and early identification of deafness was that it would facilitate a faster resolution of the grieving process (CWGCH, 2005; Siegel, 2000). It was argued that parents would not experience a protracted period of diagnostic uncertainty and would avoid the retrospective guilt of not having known and therefore not having adapted to their child's needs. In reality these presumptions have not quite proven correct, as we discuss later, but the emphasis on a quicker resolution of grief as one of the arguments supporting the introduction of UNHS demonstrates the influence of this model in understanding parental experience.

That said, one of the key criticisms and concerns about the consequences of newborn hearing screening and confirmation of deafness in the first weeks of life is that it allows no room to grieve and diverts attention from the necessity of grieving (Kurtzer-White & Luterman, 2003; Yoshinaga- Itano & de Uzcategui, 2001). The sequence of events from birth through confirmation of deafness to the start of early intervention is highly compressed (Joint Committee on Infant Hearing [JCIH], 2007). Consequently, the prompts to action and decision making that come with professional interventions may overtake the time to feel and grieve, which are viewed as necessary psychological processes in coming to terms with having a child who is D/HH.

The actual research evidence is limited, but studies have shown that from the perspective of hearing parents, early identification does not take away nor necessarily lessen a grief response (Fitzpatrick, Graham, Durieux-Smith, Angus, & Coyle, 2007; Young & Tattersall, 2007). However, it does add another dimension to it because for the majority, the experience of grief and loss occurs simultaneously with an appreciation for knowing early and positive expectations about the advantages of early detection (Young, 2010). Holding these two responses of grief and positivity simultaneously is neither psychologically nor emotionally easy. It characterizes a new consideration within a grief model approach as we seek to respond to parents' needs in the age of early identification (Young & Tattersall, 2007).

Understanding parents' responses to their child's deafness and the basis of family support in terms of grief and its resolution is not without criticism. There are three concerns related to this approach: First is the assumptions about being D/HH that a response of loss might imply, second is the extent to which the model is applied prescriptively, and third is that a grief model focuses on the individualized experience from a psychological perspective.

For the vast majority of parents who will have no experience of deafness or of D/HH people, it is entirely natural to consider deafness as an impairment, a deviation from the "normal," a disability, or a handicap. The aberration from normative expectations and the loss of the "perfect child" in this context makes sense. All of us begin from what we know already in responding to a new experience. However, just as "disability is not measles" (Rioux & Bach, 1994), deafness is not an illness (Young, 2011). The conceptualization of being D/HH in terms of an impairment to be rectified or a problem to be cured is not the only way to look at things (Young & Temple, 2014). Therefore, some writers have questioned whether the trajectories of loss and grief experienced by parents are not to some extent socially constructed (a point we return to in greater depth later) through the attitudes and assumptions of the professionals who hearing parents first encounter (Beazley & Moore, 1995). Common phrases such as "I'm sorry, your child is deaf" or "Don't worry, we can do something about it" reinforce from the start an understanding of deafness as loss and something to be fixed.

From this point of view, approaches to supporting families founded on acceptance of a grief process as natural and to be expected have the potential to create rather than respond to various stages of the grief process perceived in parents. In this respect, the grief model is challenged on the grounds that it is a main effects model. That is to say, all parental responses become explicable in terms of a stage of grief. Disagreement with advice is evidence of denial, failure to engage is explicable as depression, agreement with a course of action is evidence of acceptance, and so forth. One would hope the insights and contribution of a grief model in understanding parents' experiences and responding to them would be applied in a manner that is sensitive to the individual and the specific circumstances of complex personal and family realities. However, there are plenty of examples to the contrary that have used it as a blunt instrument in guiding professional behavior. For example, Moses (1985) cautions, "A professional's over-zealousness to save the child will frustrate the parents' ability to resolve the anxiety phase of grieving"

(p. 98). Is the model driving the response to parent and child over and above the specifics of person and context?

Evidence from parents looking back on their earliest experiences has also begun to push the boundaries of the grief model as applied to the earliest experiences of families with a deaf child. For example, whereas some parents portray their experiences of coming to terms with having a child who is D/HH as healing and moving on from grief and loss, others discuss their experiences as transformation, not resolution. Young and Greally (2003) identified two kinds of parental narratives: 1) "time as a healer" and 2) "time as a revealer." The former was characterized by parental reflections such as "things get better" or "it hurts less with time," and these types of responses very much confirm the significance of the psychological processes of grief resolution experienced by parents. The latter is characterized by parental reflections on having had experiences that they would never have previously dreamt of or meeting new people and developing skills that were unknown. Although seeming to point outward to new experiences and to the social world, the transformative narrative is nonetheless anchored in the internal and psychological, as parents discover new facets of themselves as individuals through the experiences of bringing up a child who is D/HH (an issue we return to in the family systems model later). DesGeorges (2003), writing as a parent about her experiences of grief and resolution, sug -gests the final stage is not acceptance but rather advocacy for your child who is D/HH. Importantly, her statement pushes the boundaries of what is often conceived of only as a psychological process to one that is recognized as a social process, too.

## Summary

The grief model conceptualizes parents' responses to learning that their child is D/HH in terms of a powerful emotional and psychological reaction that must be addressed. Interventions focused on the resolution of the state of grief and loss over time will enable parents and their families to move on, make decisions, consider appropriate courses of action, and come to terms with what has happened to them. Effort is directed to the individual as grief processes are highly personal, even between couples and within more extended family groups. Professionals supporting families require skills in counseling, empathy, and the psychological containment of emotion, regardless of whether person-centered, psychotherapeutic, or behavioral approaches are used. From the parents' perspective, acknowledgement of the powerful emotions they may experience when learning their child is D/HH is vital, as well as sensitivity to the individual and personal nature of that experience for them. From a professional's point of view, grief and loss may follow well-recognized stages, but from a parent's point of view, the experience is likely to be unique. The grief model is an important basis from which to understand and respond to parents' emotional reactions and responses to their child who is D/HH, at least in the earliest stages of that experience. However, it is not predictive necessarily of what "should" happen or the entirety of how families' responses and support needs might be considered, as we illustrate in addressing alternative models below.

## FAMILY SYSTEMS MODEL

> If the family were a fruit, it would be an orange, a circle of sections, held together but separable—each segment distinct. If the family were a boat, it would be a canoe that makes no progress unless everyone paddles.
>
> —Pogrebin (1983), chap. 2

Without wishing to deny or diminish the powerful psychological disorganization and affective reactions that may be termed *grief responses,* there is a problem in using that model as *the* basis for understanding the support needs of parents, whether in the early years or later in the child's life. The problem is that, on its own, it fails to account for the interrelatedness of the family as a whole; the impact of an individual's response, strengths, and needs on those of others; and the character of how a family might function as a unit. Understanding the impact of a child who is D/HH on family life requires a family systems approach. Its insights provide a very different basis for considering the assessment and provision of support with families.

Family systems theory emerged out of general systems theory (Laszlo & Krippner, 1998), whose principles were applied to understanding how a family functions and changes. Although later developed into a therapeutic model of "family systems therapy" with foundations in the psychotherapeutic tradition (Bowen, 1978), we are using family systems theory in a more general sense to understand the impact of change and family development in association with a child who is D/HH. Family systems theory encompasses five basic assumptions.

1. *The whole is more than the sum of its parts:* Although a family is made up of a number of individuals, what makes a family work, its resources and character, are not simply described by the sum of all of its components; it is how those components work together.

2. *Interdependence characterizes family life:* Families are relational structures in which roles, actions, and potential are interconnected in order to function (Skynner, 1982). One member's ability to carry out a task might be dependent on another fulfilling his or her role (whether practically or emotionally). For example, the confidence one parent experiences in carrying out his or her job at work may be codependent on the emotional security and support he or she receives at home from his or her partner.

3. *Systems vary in their capacity to admit change and adapt to new experiences* (Bernier, 1990): For example, faced with an unexpected life event or change in material circumstances, some families find it easier to cope than others.

4. *Systems tend toward seeking a steady state, or homeostasis* (Barker & Chang, 2013): A sense of chaos or shifting sands cannot be maintained for long, and systems will strive toward balance.

5. *The new state that results from the system making changes in response to events may not necessarily be **functional** (a positive transformation):* It

might be dysfunctional because new modes of interaction and inter-depen-dence may not be fit for purpose. This is because families and individuals within them vary in their capacity to welcome changes in usual ways of doing things and responding to new challenges with new approaches. Some will stick with the tried and tested responses to new situations even if these do not work. This is sometimes conceptualized in terms of different states of balance between flexibility and cohesion within the family system (Olsen, 2000).

In different ways, these five principles that drive a family systems approach provide alternative insights to the potential support needs of families with a child who is D/HH. They have been applied in a range of research studies and are also evident in some parental accounts of experience.

### The Family as a Unit that Is Greater than the Sum of Its Parts

There is a problem in much of the literature on family support, because what is often referred to is parent support (or in reality maternal support), with the implication that by supporting parents we are supporting families. Although that might be true (unless we support parents, we cannot support a child who is D/HH), it narrows the focus of what we might mean by family support. Widening our focus to begin from "family" rather than individuals within that family fundamentally forces the question, who or what is family? The culturally diverse nature of society today, the increasing tendency toward blended families, and the growth of lesbian and gay parenthood are just three examples of social trends that should cause us to reflect on whether we understand well enough what might be encompassed by "family."

Understanding the family as a unit, however, is also about understanding the character of a family. By character, we mean the values, traditions, priorities, preferences, and culture of a family. These aspects are highly significant influences on decision making, preferences for type of intervention, and engagement with the support that is offered (Young, 2002). This is because "input" (support offered by professionals, family, and other parents) does not equate to "uptake," the extent to which the support is utilized and becomes effective (Gascon-Ramos, Campbell, Bamford, & Young, 2010; Young, Gascon-Ramos, Campbell, & Bamford, 2009). A host of mediating factors intervene, one being the extent to which support is seen to tune into, cohere with, and make sense in families' terms (not professionals' terms). For example, Fletcher (1987), writing as a parent of a deaf child as well as a teacher, reflects on the advice she is given about how to support her son's spoken language development:

> What Jan has just demonstrated *is simply not our way of doing things* . . . The [ideas] that most appeal to us are those which have as their basis a firm respect for the right of children as originators and decision makers in their own learning; our own experience with Sarah, and with the children in our classes, gives ample support to this view, and over the years it has become our own. *It fits in with us as people,* with our way of thinking. (p. 53, emphasis ours)

The parent-driven organization Hands and Voices in the United States, in response to the diversity of families' approaches to bringing up a child who is D/HH, reiterates, "What makes the choice work for your child and family is what makes the choice right" (Seaver, 2004). Studies concerning the effectiveness of early intervention programs, in relation to both children who are D/HH and their families and children with disabilities, identify that coherence with family values and priorities (the family's way of doing things) is a significant influence on the effectiveness of intervention (Aytch, Cryer, Bailey, & Selz, 1999; Fitzpatrick et al., 2007; Gascon-Ramos et al., 2010; King, Rosenbaum, & King, 1996; Young et al., 2009). This order of influence can only be appreciated by focusing on the significance of the *family as a unit* and the family character rather than only its individual constituent members.

**Interdependence**

The experience of having a child who is D/HH in the family ushers in a whole new set of experiences, expectations, and knowledge demands. These can take the form of new people who in the usual course of events a family might never have had occasion to meet, whether professionals—such as teachers of the deaf, speech-language pathologists, or social workers—or other parents who happen to share the same experience of having a child who is D/HH. The demands of clinic appointments, making time for deliberate routines, exercises to support language development, and the drive to acquire and process vast amounts of new information are just a few of the influences on routines that will affect all members of the family (Jackson & Turnbull, 2004). For example, older siblings report changes in patterns of care and attention over and above what might be expected from a new addition to a family. Parents report changes in roles within the family. For example, a mother might take on more of the interactions with professionals, leaving her less time for other roles and tasks she would have routinely done within the family. In some cases, parents make difficult individual choices to set aside career ambitions or reduce working hours in order to prioritize the additional needs a child who is D/HH may have. Decisions made for the support of their child who is D/HH might bring changes in material and economic circumstances for the whole family. In other words, changes experienced by any family member in response to the new people, experiences, routines, tasks, and decisions made to support the development of the child who is D/HH are felt by the whole family system because previous *patterns of daily life* are disrupted. Also, on an emotional and psychological level, patterns of family life change as parents discover capacities and talents they had previously not realized. In contrast, capacities and talents may be expected of them, but they may feel they cannot fulfill these expectations. As one parent remarked of herself, "Having deaf children has emphasized my own difficulties with life: I am not good at asking questions, accessing information or demanding things and my children need me to be" (Young & Greally, 2003).

These psychosocial voyages of discovery initiated through the secondary effects of having a child who is D/HH in the family also challenge previous patterns of interrelationships within the family and established patterns of interdependence. Instruments such as the Family Needs Survey (Dalzell, Nelson, Haigh, Williams, & Monti, 2007) or the My Views on Services (MVOS) questionnaire (Gascon-Ramos et al., 2010; Young et al., 2009) encompass important components of the knowledge, information, skills, and guidance that parents with a child who is D/HH might require. However, they do not directly consider the issues of interdependence and disruption to the patterns of family functioning. These issues also need to be addressed in the process of identifying family support needs.

## Change Capacity

As individuals and as members of family systems, we all vary in our capacity to cope with new and, in some cases, unexpected experiences; we vary in the extent to which we embrace change. This is an important factor in tailoring family support and in understanding the differential responses of families to any component of the support and intervention that might be offered. For example, in a study of confidence and competence in parenting a child who is D/HH, Hintermair (2000) demonstrated that there was a positive association between increased confidence/competence among hearing parents and degree of contact with D/HH adults. However, the association did not demonstrate causality, and the study concludes with the discussion that the effect might equally be explained by the fact that those parents who engaged more with D/HH adults were those who had a greater capacity to seek out new experiences, were less afraid of challenge and change, and were therefore more likely to make the best use of early intervention regardless.

Young and colleagues (2006) conducted a metasynthesis related to informed choice in families with children who are D/HH. A key principle identified was the importance of realizing that parents vary in their capacity to make decisions, whether as a result of lack of experience with choice and decision making or as a result of other aspects of the self that impede that process, such as low self-esteem. Addressing factors unrelated directly to parenting a child who is D/HH can be vital in enabling individuals and families as a whole to engage with change and overcome challenges to previously established ways of functioning. Understanding and supporting the capacity of families to admit and respond to change is a central component of effective family support from a family systems perspective.

## Steady State—Functional or Dysfunctional?

It is important to be cautious about any judgments about whether a family system, in making adjustments and reaching a steady state, might be functional or dysfunctional. Such terms are potentially value judgments imposed on the "other" with whom we might struggle to empathize. However, in terms of family life with a child who is D/HH, these are important considerations in the sense of whether the family is able optimally to meet the specific needs of the child within its *system,* whether in an emotional, psychological, or practical sense. There are numerous examples of D/HH adults who report that their parents or family as a whole never really accepted their deafness and never accommodated their needs, whether in terms of communication, socialization, or place within the family.

From a family systems perspective, the problem can be conceptualized in terms of whether the family evolves into a "family who has a child who is D/HH" or whether the whole family becomes a "deaf/hearing family" in a holistic and integrated sense. Henderson and Hendershott (1991), writing about American Sign Language (ASL; see Chapter 6) and the family system, argue that unless all family members as individuals and the family unit as a whole accept that they are in some way changed and transformed into a deaf/ hearing family because of the presence of a D/HH member, then a healthy, functional state has not been reached. West (2012), exploring the experiences of all family members in mixed deaf and hearing families, characterizes the experience as "deafhearing family life," which becomes itself an identity and through which families are "strong together." From a general family systems perspective, families may tend toward a steady state that is preservative (how things have always been) or transformative (significant change in patterns of functioning) with many gradations along the continuum. Assisting families to engage with aspects of those patterns of change and preservation in light of the new experiences associated with a family member who is a child who is D/HH is, from a family systems perspective, important if dysfunctional or destructive patterns of intrafamilial relationships are to be avoided.

## Summary

The family systems model conceptualizes families as units of interconnected and interrelated components with a collective identity and preferred ways of functioning. It forces attention on the dynamic nature of family support with intervention at an individual level having potential consequences for all. The character of families is a key mediator in the appropriateness and effectiveness of support and intervention with the emphasis on the need to tune in to and follow the preferences, resources, and strengths of families. The degree to which the child who is D/HH is integral to or detached from the family sys -tem is crucial.

## STRESS AND COPING MODEL

If you aren't in over your head, how do you know how tall you are?

—T.S. Eliot (1941)

The stress and coping model begins from the perspective that to have a child who is D/HH is a stress- producing experience, at least in the early years (Calderon & Greenberg, 1993, 1999; Feher-Prout, 1996; Hintermair, 2006; Lederberg & Goldbach, 2001; Pipp-Siegel, Sedey, & Yoshinaga-Itano, 2002; Quittner, Glueckauf, & Jackson, 1990). Although the birth of any child might be regarded as stressful because of the new experiences and adjustments parents and the family as whole might make, it is argued that the additional issues associated with a child being D/HH make it particularly stressful (Poon & Zaidman-Zait, 2014). These include additional caregiving demands, having to make more decisions, financial pressures, interactions with professionals, applying communication strategies, and getting to grips with new knowledge and experiences such as those arising from technology.

Stress in and of itself is not unusual, nor necessarily harmful. It is a natural process that everyone experiences in the face of difficult or challenging circumstances and serves an important motivational function in prompting action and making adjustments. The physiological changes we experience (e.g., sweaty palms, racing heart) and the psychological ones (e.g., brief anxiety, racing thoughts) can be actually helpful in engendering new insights, making decisions, enabling creativity, increasing energy, or preventing hesitation. However, if stress becomes too much or becomes a permanent rather than temporary state, then just the opposite might happen: the associated physiological and psychological responses (such as chronic anxiety and depression) become harmful and incapacitating. Therefore, to consider a child who is D/HH in a family as an inherently stress-producing experience is to ask not just why this might be the case but whether that stress is positive or negative and why its effects for one parent or one family may not be the same as for another.

In this respect, psychological theories of stress have been influential, particularly those arising from cognitive-behavioral traditions. Lazarus (1966, 1974) and Lazarus and Folkman (1984) developed an approach to understanding stress and therefore by implication how to manage and mediate it, based on three important insights: 1) that stress is relational, 2) that we do not all find the same events or experiences stressful in the same ways, and 3) that personal resources and social support can mediate the impact and effects of stress.

### Stress Is Relational

First, stress is a *relational* concept. The extent or degree of stress is not defined by or inherent within a given object, experience, or process that might be regarded as "the stressor." Rather, stress is a resultant and relational effect between the individual, his or her environment, and the potential stressor. For example, if a family is experiencing stress in their environment for a range of reasons unconnected with those arising from having a child who is D/HH (such as poor housing, abusive relationships, inadequate economic resources), then stress is a product of the impact and interaction of those multiple stress-producing experiences, how the individual might experience those, and the additional demands that raising a child who is D/HH might bring.

While there is good evidence that parents of children who are D/HH experience stress, it is not necessarily true to say that this is *because* the child is D/HH. Other factors determine whether and why stress might be experienced. Plotkin, Brice, and Reesman (2014), for example, investigated the relationship between parent personality characteristics, perceived stress, and child behavior problems in a sample of 114 parents with a child who was D/HH. They concluded that parental personality had a significant predictive power for their experience of stress and for the child's overall behavioral adjustment.

### Stress Depends on Appraisal

Second, the degree of stress individuals might experience is a result of their **appraisal** of something as stressful (or not). What is experienced by one person as negatively stressful (e.g., attending an audiology appointment to test a child's hearing or meeting signing adults who are deaf) is not experienced by another as stressful to the same degree:

Stress lies not in the environmental input but in the person's appraisal of the relationship between that input and its demands and the person's agendas (e.g. beliefs, commitments, goals) and capabilities to meet, mitigate, and alter those demands in the interest of well being. (Lazarus, De Longis, Folkman, & Greun, 1985, p. 770)

Appraisal, therefore, can be considered a mediating variable in whether and why something might be experienced as stressful. Appraisal is not just a synonym for perspective or point of view but is fundamentally connected with the range of features that constitute diversity: an individual's culture(s), values, faith(s), politics, priorities, context(s), and history/ies, which combine to render an experience meaningful, anxiety provoking, or motivational.

## Coping Resources and Strategies Influence Perceived Stress

Third, the *coping resources and strategies* used to deal with a situation/event/demand are also important in whether and how something is experienced as stressful and to what degree. For example, previous experiences of successfully managing an unexpected or similar demand provide approaches, whether cognitively or behaviorally, to rely on and utilize to reduce the extent of stress. However, everyone varies in his or her repertoire of coping strategies, and some of those may not be appropriate or work for specific purposes. Therefore the degree of fit between coping strategies and event/demand is also significant in rendering a situation or experience stressful.

For example, in a qualitative study of information preferences among parents of children who are D/HH, variations were identified between those who preferred to have all information in detail accessible from the start and to read everything at once and those who preferred a more sequential, bite-size approach extended over time (Young, Jones, Starmer, & Sutherland, 2005). In both cases, the reason was exactly the same: It was a preferred coping strategy. Parents were not in markedly different situations or facing very different challenges, but they did have different resources for coping based on their pre-vious experiences of what worked for them.

## Personal Resources and Social Support Moderate Stress

Whereas Lazarus and colleagues tended to view coping in terms of personal cognitive and behavioral strategies, others extended the notion of the relationship between potential stressors and coping to include a more resource-related and social notion of coping. From this point of view, coping also encompasses social resources such as size of social networks, uptake of available support, access to material resources (e.g., money, transport, employment), and personal resources such as optimism, self-advocacy, self-efficacy (Bandura, 1977), and sense of coherence (Antonovsky, 1979)—that is, a fundamental belief that the world is meaningful, benevolent, and to a large extent predictable and open to personal control and management.

Hintermair (2004) demonstrated that parents possessing a strong sense of coherence were more likely to be successful in coping with the demands that a child who is D/HH might bring than those with a weaker sense of coherence. Similarly, parents with access to greater resources (whether material or psychological) experienced less stress (Hintermair, 2006). Calderon and Greenberg (1999) conducted a survey, interview, and observational study of 36 hearing mothers of children who were D/HH and demonstrated that "mothers who reported high satisfaction with their social support were rated as better adjusted to their deaf or hard of hearing child despite degree of maternal neg-a-tive life stress or severity of the child's hearing loss" (p. 13). In other words, social support had an important buffering effect on stress and acted as a pos-i-tive predictor of maternal adjustment to a child who is D/HH. Quittner and colleagues (1990) further demonstrated that it was not levels of social support in an objective, measurable sense that made a difference in moderating the experience of stress but rather maternal perceptions of support. In a metare-view of studies of social support in relation to parents of children who are D/HH, Poon and Zaidman-Zait (2014) emphasize that for social support to be effective in reducing or modifying the impact of stress, that support must be contextually coherent for families with children who are D/HH. In other words, social support is meaningful and identified as useful in families' terms, not in relation to a general definition of what might be universally described as social support. Furthermore, that social support should be regarded as multidimen-sional, encompassing both professional and nonprofessional support, peer-to-peer support, and support that is specifically related to bringing up a child who is D/HH and that which is unrelated, too.

### Summary

The stress and coping model draws attention to the significance of stress not as something inherent in meeting the challenges and demands of raising a child who is D/HH but as something relational and resultant between those demands, the caregivers, and their environment. As such, it is open to modifi-cation and moderation through interventions that make the most of preexist-ing coping resources and strategies that supplement these with contextually coherent social support and that take actions to reduce environmental stress-ors that may have little to do with a child who is D/HH but that have a cumu-lative impact on coping.

## SOCIAL CONSTRUCTION MODEL

> We had the experience but missed the meaning,
> And approach to the meaning restores the experience
> In a different form.
>
> —T.S. Eliot (1941)

**Social constructionism,** or the social construction of reality, is a branch of sociology and philosophy that examines the notion that meanings, their rela-tive significances, and personal understanding develop through, and are main-tained by, social interactions (Berger & Luckman, 1966). Reality is neither singular nor fixed. It is open to interpretation, relative to individual, context, group, or society (Blumer, 1969; Spradley, 1979). For example, what *school* means to one person and what it means to another person are likely not the same; there is no single internally held meaning of *school*. Furthermore, language and more particularly how it is used should be thought of not as a means by which to merely reflect reality; there are words and phrases that refer to objects and experiences, and therefore they can be discussed and communicated. Rather, language creates reality(ies); that is, through choice of words, the contexts in which they arise, and how they become used through social interactions, words imbue specific meanings to that reality.

For example, what does *deaf* mean to you? What does your use of the term imply because of your personal/professional identities? What do others assume about you if you use the word *deaf*? Does that vary depending on the context in which you are having the conversation? Have you ever had a discussion in which everyone used the word *deaf* but there were several different meanings implied despite the same term being used?

Meanings and their significance are socially constructed, not fixed, and they are perpetuated or diminished through social interactions. Furthermore, some potential meanings can come to dominate over others, and the power of who controls the discourse(s) to which we are exposed is significant (Young & Temple, 2014, ch. 2). For instance, why use the term *deaf or hard of hearing* in this book? It implies that a differentiation is important and at the same time seeks to be inclusive. Yet other writers would suggest that to seek to divide a population of "deaf children" in this way is to seek to impose differentiations that are unhelpful and divisive (Ladd, 2003). Others would draw the line in a different place, recapturing "deaf" expressed by an uppercase *D* to emphasize a linguistic-cultural label (e.g., French) rather than as an adjective to describe the biophysiological state (Lane, 1995; Lane, Hoffmeister, & Bahan, 1996).

## Being Deaf

In thinking about parents and families with children who are D/HH, this social constructionist perspective is important because the vast majority will have no previous experience of deafness (Gregory, Bishop, & Sheldon, 1995). They will bring to the discovery that their child is D/HH their own meanings of what *deaf* or *hard of hearing* is. Their view of its significance, their expectations, and their fears associated with *being* D/HH will have been forged elsewhere and before the personal event of their own child. Their meanings are socially constructed.

In terms of family support, therefore, it is important to understand what the first meanings are that families bring to having a child who is D/HH and what it is that might influence these. In terms of family adjustment, what one thinks one is adjusting to will inevitably influence the decisions made, the expectations harbored, and the goals set (Young, 2002). For example, an interview study of 45 hearing parents whose children had been identified as D/HH following universal newborn hearing screening explored the assumptions about language and communication that parents brought initially to the new experience (Young & Tattersall, 2007). The average age of the children at the time of the parental interview was 25 weeks old. Parents' narratives framed the advantage of early identification in terms of the potential for their children to develop speech and follow what they regarded as a "normal" developmental trajectory. They strongly associated screening for deafness in similar terms to screening for an illness that could be treated. They were utilizing their preexisting understandings of what it meant to be deaf in comparison with being able to hear, and they turned to the nearest similar experience they could find to assist in making sense of the new experience.

Findings such as these should not be surprising, because for the vast majority of hearing parents, to be D/HH lies outside of their "sphere of relevance" (Schutz, 1962). The concept **sphere of relevance** implies that everyone has knowledge, experiences, interests, and skills that are particular to their everyday lives and reflect heritage, culture, and choices about how to lead those lives. It is not just that some interests, knowledge, and experiences are particular to individuals but rather that these are meaningful. It is the difference between just knowing about something and knowledge carrying with it a significance for individuality, character, and personality. Consequently, some experiences and knowledge are outside of an individual's sphere of relevance not simply because of a lack of knowledge or experience but because of a lack of relevance to who an individual *is*.

For the majority of hearing parents whose child is D/HH, it is not simply the case that understanding deafness and its implications is unknown territory, requiring acquisition of information, knowledge, and skills. It is that these and the experience of bringing up a child who is D/HH are outside parents' sphere of relevance (Young, 2002). It has never had to matter before; it has never been on their radar as anything that might be associated with who they are, who their family is, and the choices they make about how to lead their lives. Voysey (1975), writing in similar vein about parents of children with cerebral palsy, describes their experience of their children as constituting "an imposed set of relevancies." For parents of children who are D/HH, this imposed set of relevancies would encompass, for example, deliberately thinking about language acquisition (for most parents, that process is undeliberate, natural, and requires little effort on their part to ensure their child develops a full first language). Another example of an imposed set of relevancies would be having to interact with professionals that parents may have never previously had any reason to meet—for example, teachers of the deaf, speech-language pathologists, and/or social workers. This process also involves having to engage with the fundamental issue of identity.

The majority of parents will reasonably assume that the social, personal, and cultural identity of their children will be consistent with their own. For example, their children will use the one or more languages that the family uses; they will have an ethnicity that is derived and relates to that of their parents; and they will be brought up with the cultural values and practices that are of importance to their parents and wider family. Yet for children who are D/HH, parents will engage, be it in different ways, with the potentially problematic nature of their child's identity (Atkin, Ahmad, & Jones, 2002; Leigh, 2009; Young, 1999). Is this child disabled? Is this child just like his or her parents but needs to do something extra to confirm that likeness? Is this child going to use spoken language? Will this child be bilingual and use spoken and signed languages? Will this child grow up to be culturally Deaf? Such considerations are outside of most hearing parents' sphere of relevance, at least initially.

In considering such issues of identity and their relevance to family support, it is helpful to stop using the term *deaf or hard of hearing* and instead prefix it as *being* deaf or hard of hearing. By privileging the **ontological**, we force attention onto the social, interpersonal, communicative, and interactive experiences in the world that make up who we are and influence how we are known. What is it to be a woman? What is it to be African American? What is it to be deaf? The answer to questions framed in this way ("to be") will encompass, for example, a consideration of core values, how others react to us in specific contexts, assumptions that are made about us (ascribed identity; see Young & Ackerman, 2001), how we behave as social actors in everyday life, and the prejudices of the majority toward the "other" (Johnson et al., 2004). *Being* deaf or hard of hearing encompasses, from a social constructionist perspective, all such features.

## Meeting Deaf or Hard-of-Hearing People

The vast majority of parents begin from a very low base in understanding what it is to be deaf or hard of hearing. Their understanding of this grows with every social and interpersonal encounter with others, be they other parents, professionals, or children or adults who are D/HH. It grows through becoming aware of how society views D/HH people; how they are written about; and how D/HH people represent, show, and write about themselves (e.g., see McDonald, 2014). Understanding what it is to be D/HH does not grow from simply digesting information—from parents interacting with their own child or being advised by knowledgeable professionals. It is also fundamentally influenced by the social constructions of being D/HH they encounter.

In terms of family support, therefore, expanding the availability of encounters with multiple and varied experiences of being D/HH would seem vital. The JCIH position statement (2007) clearly states that it expects to see D/HH people serving at all levels on state advisory boards, in training of professionals, and as direct service providers, whether as professionals in their own right (teachers, social workers, psychologists) or as role models and mentors available to families:

> Role models who are deaf or hard of hearing can be significant assets to an intervention program. These individuals can serve on state EHDI (Early Hearing Detection and Intervention) advisory boards and can be trained as mentors for families and children with hearing loss who choose to seek their support. Almost all families choose at some time during their early childhood programs to seek out both adults and child peers with hearing loss. (JCIH, 2007, unpaginated)

This position was reinforced by the "2013 Supplement to the JCIH 2007 Position Statement: Principles and Guidelines for Early Intervention After Confirmation That a Child Is Deaf or Hard of Hearing" (JCIH, 2013), in which goals 10 and 11 (pp. e1337 and e1338) cement the centrality of D/HH people within EHDI systems and specifically promote their routine availability to families. Principle 8 of the international consensus statement "Best Practices in Family-Centered Early Intervention for Children Who Are Deaf or Hard of Hearing" also makes the same point within the framework of collaborative teams (Moeller, Carr, Seaver, Stredler-Brown, & Holzinger, 2013, pp. 440–441).

Yet around the world, it is still unusual for hearing parents to meet D/HH people routinely, whether in professional roles or socially. Deaf mentor and deaf role model services still largely remain written about as additions or extras to standard practice (but see Chapter 6 and DVD segments). The evidence for their benefit suggests that exposure to D/HH people assists hearing parents to envision a range of possibilities for their children, as they can see examples of the vast diversity of deaf or hard-of-hearing adults; most will never have encountered them before (Meadow-Orlans, Mertens, & Sass-Lehrer, 2003; Rogers & Young, 2011; Sutherland, Griggs, & Young, 2003; Watkins, Pittman, & Walden, 1998). It is possible to reinforce positive messages about D/HH adults leading normal lives by giving opportunities for parents to ask questions that have been on their mind that may be as simple as "Do you drive?" "Do you have children?" and "Was it hard to find a job?" Other questions may be more specifically related to growing up D/HH: "What do you think of cochlear implants?" "Were you bullied at school?" and "Do you enjoy music?" Meeting D/HH people also presents opportunities for direct teaching of sign language skills, exposure to deaf cultural norms, and reflections on how being hearing and/or being deaf might shape expectations and family life (Young, 1997, 1999). These mutual encounters can also be challenging in facing parents with multiple realities of strengths and difficulties that might be experienced by children who are D/HH as they grow up; it is not possible to pretend (Young, 1995).

**Diversity and Choices**

Exposure to the different constructions of what it is to be deaf or hard of hearing is not just about meeting D/HH people. It is also potentially integral to standard family support services and intervention practices in a structural sense. The British Columbia Early Hearing Program in Canada and the Colorado Home Intervention Program are two examples of early family support services that actively encourage parents to explore the multiplicity of what it might be to be D/HH before they come to any decisions about how to bring up their own child (see also Chapters 4, 6, and 9). Furthermore, choices parents might make—for example, with regard to language and communication—are regarded as provisional. Parents are free to change their minds about the matrix of support and its emphases as their understanding of their own child's strengths and their appreciation of the variety of possibilities grow. As parents' sphere of relevance expands, services in their structure and provision mirror that fluidity and change.

However, it would be wrong to suggest that in terms of family support options and the diversity of ways in which children might be deaf or hard of hearing, there are "open futures" (Feinberg, 1980) in an absolute sense. Some developmental achievements require specialization or an optimum time by which they should be mastered to make the most of possibilities. To use an analogy from a different context, if a gifted musician who could pick up and play any instrument as a child never specializes in one or another, he or she will not be a virtuoso on a given instrument but rather might be reasonably good at all of them. This might not be a problem; it depends on the goals of the child and family. Some approaches to early development emphasize critical time periods by which an intervention must have occurred—for example, optimum times for cochlear implantation to support maximal neuroplasticity (see Chapters 2 and 7). Others emphasize the significance of specialization of technique and approach largely to the exclusion of others that are cast as distractions—for example, the strict practice of auditory-verbal therapy (AVT) in its purest form.

However, beyond the debates over whether and to what extent claims for the necessity of critical periods of specialization are correct, each claim and each approach from a social constructionist perspective embodies *a particular version* of what it is to be D/HH and what might be desirable within that construction. Choices are not just being made for a language or a communication approach. They are being made for a potential trajectory of being D/HH because of the assumptions, values, and priorities that each approach tacitly or explicitly embodies. Of course, as children grow, they may make additional, alternative, augmentative, or different choices that might contradict or enhance the potential that their parents' choices have offered them. *Becoming D/HH* is a personalized narrative that has been explored through many different perspectives (e.g., see Ladd, 2003; McDonald, 2014; Wright, 1969). The point in terms of early family support is that the social constructionist model emphasizes that choices of approach are also choices about what it is to be/become D/HH. They imply and enact a preferred meaning and way of being that is highly influential for the identity formation of children who are D/HH. As many parents have remarked, the choices they make on behalf of their children are ones they will have to be able to justify and be comfortable with when their children are old enough to evaluate them for themselves.

## Summary

The social construction model emphasizes that what it is to be D/HH is a product of meanings that are created, perpetuated, or diminished as a result of social and communicative encounters and what the structures of society, including the nature of available services, infer and prioritize as normative. Parents are on journeys to discover what it means to be D/HH, because for the vast majority, this consideration has been outside of their sphere of relevance. The changing nature of that understanding is vital because its assumptions and emphases will shape the choices that parents and families will make and mold what it is they might prioritize in bringing up their child and in engaging with professional and parent-to-parent support. The diversity and multiplicity of being D/HH from the perspective of personal, social, and cultural identity(ies) is a key resource for families. The extent to which family support is able to facilitate access to and engage with this diversity is a vital component of family support.

## CONCLUSION

In this chapter, we have set out to examine critically what is meant by family support with respect to hearing families in the early years following the diagnosis (or "recognition," to use a different social construction) of a child as D/HH. We have set out the theoretical foundations of four potential models of understanding how parents and/or families respond, their needs and strengths, and the implications of these for how they are supported. We have not set out to be prescriptive nor are we suggesting that any of the models we have explored are mutually exclusive. Rather, they are different from, and to a greater or lesser extent complementary to, each other. Their importance lies in breaking away from an approach to family support that is rooted in any singular vision or explanatory framework that inevitably will be partial. Each, be it in different ways, draws attention to something central in families' experiences and highlights potential required resources and support and the manner in which their delivery would be most helpful.

## SUGGESTED READINGS

Gregory, S., Bishop, J., & Sheldon, L. (1995). *Deaf young people and their families.* Cambridge, England: Cambridge University Press.

Parents seek to make the best decisions they can at the time for their children. In the case of hearing parents of children who are D/HH, making choices can be very difficult because a lack of prior experience and many uncertainties makes envisioning their child's future very challenging. In this book, Gregory and colleagues revisit a large number of parents of D/HH young people who were first interviewed when their children were very young. Parents reflect back on their children's growing years and the influences of the choices they made, and the young people themselves participate in interviews, telling their own stories.

Leigh, I.W. (2009). *A lens on Deaf identities.* New York, NY: Oxford University Press.

Identity is not simply a feature of inherent characteristics or traits; it is also a product of how we present ourselves in different contexts, our backgrounds, and who we become through our relationships and social influences. This book addresses the many ways in which it is possible to be deaf or hard of hearing, including how identities arising from faith, culture, and sexuality might intersect with being D/HH. It is helpful in addressing the plurality of identity in everyday life and the full range of influences on the current and future identities of children who are D/HH.

Young, A., Gascon-Ramos, M., Campbell, M., & Bamford, J. (2009). The design and validation of a parent-report questionnaire for assessing the characteristics and quality of early intervention over time. *Journal of Deaf Studies and Deaf Education, 14*(4), 422–435.

In any early intervention and family support process, what is offered is no guarantee of uptake. Many factors intervene, including family values, timeliness of intervention, its content, and how the process of parent–professional interaction is undertaken. In this article, Young and colleagues explain how they sought to design an instrument that would enable parents to evaluate the quality, timeliness, content, and process of multiprofessional intervention. They include a discussion of some of the inherent challenges in delivering quality early intervention that is meaningful and effective to families of children who are D/HH.

## LEARNING ACTIVITIES

The summary Table 3.1 and content of the chapter as whole may be used in the following ways:

1. *As a framework for assisting in the identification and assessment of families' strengths and needs:* For example, in considering a family's situation through each of the model's perspectives in turn, do you identify

similar or different issues? Does each model help you to uncover a broader diversity of strengths and resources? How does each assist you to identify courses of action to resolve identified difficulties, tune in to family priorities, and increase individual and family capacities?

2.    *To support reflective practice and develop individual practitioner skills:* Practitioners can use the multiple models that contrast with each other to challenge the assumptions underpinning their practice with a particular family. They provide alternative ways of looking at a family's situation and the actions we take. Therefore, they can be used to reflect critically on the limits and strengths of our own vision as practitioners, the basis of the support we provide, the assessments we undertake, and the skills and  practices we employ.

3.    *To build new knowledge and skills:* Some of the models offered in this chapter are likely to be more familiar than others depending on our own backgrounds as parents and/or professionals. The references cited will assist to explore less familiar approaches that will increase the repertoire of knowledge and skills that we can bring to a family with a child  who is D/HH.

## REFERENCES

Antonovsky, A. (1979). *Health, stress, and coping.* San Francisco, CA: Jossey-Bass.

Atkin, K., Ahmad, W.I.U., & Jones, L. (2002). Young South Asian Deaf people and their families: Negotiating relationships and identities. *Sociology of Health and Illness, 24*(1), 21–45.

Aytch, L.S., Cryer, D., Bailey, D.B., & Selz, L. (1999). Defining and assessing quality in early intervention programs for infants and toddlers with disability and their families: Challenges and unresolved issues. *Early Education and Development, 10,* 8–23.

Bandura, A. (1977). Self-efficacy: Toward a unifying theory of behavioral change. *Psychological Review, 84,* 191–215.

Barker, P., & Chang, J. (2013). *Basic family therapy* (6th ed.). London, England: Wiley-Blackwell.

Beazley, S., & Moore, M. (1995). *Deaf children, their families and other professionals.* London, England: David Fulton.

Berger, P., & Luckman, T. (1966). *The social construction of reality: A treatise in the sociology of knowledge.* Garden City, NY: Anchor.

Bernier, J.O. (1990). Parental adjustment to a disabled child: A family systems perspective. *Journal of Contemporary Human Services,* December, 589–596.

Blumer, H. (1969). *Social interactionism: Perspective and method.* Upper Saddle River, NJ: Prentice Hall.

Boison, K.B. (1987). Diagnosis of deafness: A study of family responses and needs. *International Journal of Rehabilitation Research, 10*(2), 220–224.

Bowen, M. (1978). *Family therapy in clinical practice.* New York, NY: Jason Aronson.

Calderon, L., & Greenberg, M.T. (1993). Considerations in the adaptation of families with school-aged deaf children. In M. Marschark & M.D. Clark (Eds.), *Psychological perspectives on deafness* (pp. 27–48). Hillsdale, NJ: Laurence Erlbaum Associates.

Calderon, R., & Greenberg, M.T. (1999). Stress and coping in hearing mothers of children with hearing loss: Factors affecting mother and child adjustment. *American Annals of the Deaf, 144*(1), 7–18.

Canadian Working Group on Childhood Hearing (CWGCH). (2005). *Early hearing and communication development: Resource document.* Ottawa, ON: Minister of Public Works and Government Services Canada.

Caplan, G. (1964). Principles of preventative psychiatry. New York: Basic Books.

Dalzell, J., Nelson, H., Haigh, C., Williams, A., & Monti, P. (2007). Involving families who have deaf children using a family needs survey: A multi-agency perspective. *Child: Care, Health and Development, 33*(5), 576– 585.

DesGeorges, J. (2003). Family perceptions of early hearing detection and intervention systems: Listening to and learning from families. *Mental Retardation and Developmental Disabilities Research Review, 9*(2), 89–93.

Feher-Prout, T. (1996). Stress and coping in families with deaf children. *Journal of Deaf Studies and Deaf Education, 1,* 155–166.

Feinberg, J. (1980). The child's right to an open future. In W. Aiken & H. LaFollette (Eds.), *Whose child? Children's rights, parental authority, and state power* (pp. 124– 153). Totowa, NJ: Littlefield, Adams, & Co.

Fitzpatrick, E., Graham, I.D., Durieux-Smith, A., Angus, D., & Coyle, D. (2007). Parents' perspectives on the impact of early diagnosis of childhood hearing loss. *International Journal of Audiology, 46,* 97–106.

Fletcher, L. (1987). *Language for Ben.* London, England: Souvenir.

Gascon-Ramos, M., Campbell, M., Bamford, J., & Young, A. (2010). Influences on parental evaluation of the content of early intervention following early identification of deafness: A study about parents' preferences and satisfaction. *Child Care Health and Development, 36*(6), 868– 877.

Gregory, S., Bishop, J., & Sheldon, L. (1995). *Deaf young people and their families.* Cambridge, England: Cambridge University Press.

Henderson, D., & Hendershott, A. (1991). ASL and the family system. *American Annals of the Deaf, 136,*(4), 325–329.

Hintermair, M. (2000). Hearing impairment, social networks and coping: The need for families with hearing impaired children to relate to other parents and to hearing-impaired adults. *American Annals of the Deaf, 145*(1), 41–53.

Hintermair, M. (2004). The sense of coherence— A relevant resource in the coping process of mothers with hearing impaired children? *Journal of Deaf Studies and Deaf Education, 9,* 15–26.

Hintermair, M. (2006). Parental resources, parental stress, and socioemotional development of deaf and hard of hearing children. *Journal of Deaf Studies and Deaf Education, 11*(4), 493–513.

Jackson, C.W., & Turnbull, A.P. (2004). Impact of deafness on family life: A review of the literature. *Topics in Early Childhood Special Education, 24*(1), 15–29.

Joint Committee on Infant Hearing (JCIH). (2007). Year 2007 position statement: Principles and guidelines for early hearing detection and intervention programs. *Pediatrics, 120*(4), 898–921.

Johnson, J. L., J. L. Bottorff, Browne,A.J., Grewal, S., Hilton, B.A., & Clarke, H. (2004). Othering and being othered in the context of health care services. *Health Communication 16*(2), 255–271.

Joint Committee on Infant Hearing (JCIH). (2013). Supplement to the JCIH 2007 position statement: Principles and guidelines for early intervention after confirmation that a child is deaf or hard of hearing. *Pediatrics, 131,* e1324– e1349.

Kampfe, C.M. (1989). Parental reaction to a child's hearing impairment. *American Annals of the Deaf, 134,* 255–259.

King, A.M., Rosenbaum, P.L., & King, G. (1996). Parents' perceptions of caregiving: Development and validation of measure of processes. *Developmental Medicine and Child Neurology, 38,* 757–772.

Kubler-Ross, E. (1969). *On death and dying.* New York, NY: Macmillan.

Kurtzer-White, E., & Luterman, D. (2003). Families and children with hearing loss: Grief and coping. *Mental Retardation and Developmental Disabilities Research Review, 9,* 232–235.

Ladd, P. (2003). *Understanding Deaf culture: In search of Deafhood.* Clevedon, England: Multilingual Matters.

Lane, H. (1995). Constructions of Deafness. *Disability & Society, 10*(2), 171–189.

Lane, H., Hoffmeister, B., & Bahan, B. (1996). *A journey into the Deaf world.* San Diego, CA: Dawn Sign Press.

Laszlo, A., & Krippner, S. (1998). Systems theories: Their origins, foundations, and development. In J.S. Jordan (Ed.), *Systems theories and a priori aspects of perception* (pp. 47–74). Amsterdam: Elsevier Science.

Lazarus, R.S. (1966). *Psychological stress and the coping process.* New York, NY: McGraw-Hill.

Lazarus, R.S. (1974). Psychological stress and coping in adaptation and illness. *Journal of Psychiatry in Medicine, 5,* 321–333.

Lazarus, R.S., De Longis, A., Folkman, S., & Greun, R. (1985). Stress and adaptational outcomes: The problem of confounded measures. *American Psychologist, 40,* 770–779.

Lazarus, R.S., & Folkman, S. (1984). *Stress, appraisal, and coping.* New York, NY: Springer.

Lederberg, A., & Goldbach, T. (2001). Parenting stress and social support in hearing mothers of deaf and hearing children: A longitudinal study. *Journal of Deaf Studies and Deaf Education, 7,* 330–345.

Leigh, I.W. (2009). *A lens on Deaf identities.* New York, NY: Oxford University Press.

Lewis, C.S. (1961). *A grief observed.* London, England: Faber and Faber.

Lindemann, E. (1944). Symptomatology and management of acute grief. *American Journal of Psychiatry, 101,* 118–128.

Luterman, D. (1999a). Counselling families with a hearing impaired child. *Otolaryngologic Clinics of North America, 32,* 1037–1050.

Luterman, D. (1999b). *The young deaf child.* Timonium, MD: York Press.

McDonald, D.M. (2014). *The art of being Deaf: A memoir.* Washington, DC: Gallaudet University Press.

Meadow-Orlans, K.P., Mertens, D.M., & Sass- Lehrer, M. (2003). *Parents and their Deaf children: The early years.* Washington, DC: Gallaudet University Press.

Mitchell, R.E., & Karchmer, M.A. (2004). Chasing the mythical ten percent: Parental hearing status of deaf and hard of hearing students in the United States. *Sign Language Studies, 4*(2), 138–163.

Moeller, M.P., Carr, G., Seaver, L., Stredler-Brown, A., & Holzinger, D. (2013). Best practices in family-centered early intervention for children who are deaf or hard of hearing: An international consensus statement. *Journal of Deaf Studies and Deaf Education, 18*(4), 429–445.

Moses, K.L. (1985). Infant deafness and parental grief: Psychosocial intervention. In F. Powell (Ed.), *The education of the hearing impaired child* (pp. 86–102). San Diego: College Hill.

Olsen, D.H. (2000). Circumplex model of marital and family systems. *Journal of Family Therapy, 22,* 144–167.

Paget, S. (1983). Long term grieving of parents of hearing impaired children: A synthesis of parental experience. *Journal of the British Association of Teachers of the Deaf, 7*(3), 79–83.

Pipp-Siegel, S., Sedey, A.L., & Yoshinaga-Itano, C. (2002). Predictors of parental stress in mothers of young children with hearing loss. *Journal of Deaf Studies and Deaf Education, 7*(1), 1–17.

Plotkin, R.M., Brice, P.J., & Reesman, J.H. (2014). It is not just stress: Parent personality in raising a deaf child. *Journal of Deaf Studies and Deaf Education, 19*(3), 347–357.

Pogrebin, L.C. (1983). *Family politics.* New York, NY: McGraw-Hill.

Poon, B., & Zaidman-Zait, A. (2014). Social support for parents of deaf children: Moving toward contextualized understanding. *Journal of Deaf Studies and Deaf Education, 19*(2), 176–188.

Quittner, A.L., Glueckauf, R.L., & Jackson, D.N. (1990). Chronic parenting stress: Mod -erating versus mediating effects of social support. *Journal of Personality and Social Psychology, 59,* 1266–1278.

Rioux, M.H., & Bach, M. (1994). *Disability is not measles: New research paradigms in disability.* North York, ON: Roeher Institute.

Rogers, K.D., & Young, A.M. (2011). Being a deaf role model: Deaf people's experiences of working with families and deaf young people. *Deafness & Education International, 13*(1), 2–16.

Schutz, A. (1962). *Collected papers* (Vol. 2). The Hague, Netherlands: Martinus Nijhoff.

Seaver, L. (2004). *Hands and voices: Supporting families without bias.* Retrieved from http://www.handsandvoices.org

Siegel, S. (2000). *Resolution of grief of parents of young children with hearing loss* (Ph.D. dissertation). University of Colorado, Boulder, CO.

Skynner, A.C.R. (1982) Frameworks for viewing the family as a system. In A. Bentovim, G.G. Barnes & A. Cooklin (Eds.), *Family therapy, Complementary frameworks of theory and practice volume 1* (pp. 3–36). London, England: Academic Press.

Spradley, J. (1979). *The ethnographic interview.* Belmont, CA: Holt, Rinehart and Winston.

Sutherland, H., Griggs, M., & Young, A. (2003). Deaf adult role models in family intervention services. In C. Galloway & A. Young (Eds.), *Deafness and education in the UK: Research perspectives* (pp. 5–20). London, England: Whurr.

Voysey, M. (1975). *A constant burden.* London, England: RKP.

Watkins, S., Pittman, P., & Walden, B. (1998). The Deaf mentor experimental project for young children who are deaf. *American Annals of the Deaf, 143*(1), 29–34.

West, D. (2012). *Signs of hope: Deafhearing family life.* Cambridge, England: Cambridge Scholars Publishing.

Wright, D. (1969). *Deafness: A personal account.* London, England: Allen Lane.

Yoshinaga-Itano, C., & de Uzcategui, C.A. (2001). Early identification and social emotional factors of children with hearing loss and children screened for hearing loss. In E. Kurtzer-White & D. Luterman (Eds.), *Early childhood deafness* (pp. 13– 28). Baltimore, MD: York Press.

Young, A. (1995). *Family adjustment to a deaf child in a bilingual bicultural framework* (Ph.D. dissertation). University of Bristol, Bristol.

Young, A. (1997). Conceptualising parents' sign language use in bilingual early intervention. *Journal of Deaf Studies and Deaf Education, 2*(4), 264–276.

Young, A.M. (1999). Hearing parents' adjustment to a deaf child: The impact of a cultural-linguistic model of deafness. *Journal of Social Work Practice, 13*(2), 157–176.

Young, A. (2002). Parents of deaf children: Factors affecting communication choice in the first year of life. *Deafness & Education International, 4*(1), 1–12.

Young, A. (2010). The impact of early identification of deafness on hearing parents. In M. Marschark (Ed.), *The Oxford handbook of deaf studies, language, and education* (Vol. 2, pp. 241–250). New York, NY: Oxford University Press.

Young, A. (2011). Early intervention with deaf children and their families: "Why, sometimes I've believed as many as six impossible things before breakfast!" In D. Moores (Ed.), *Partners in education: Issues and trends from the 21st international congress on the education of the deaf* (pp. 75–88). Washington, DC: Gallaudet University Press.

Young, A., Gascon-Ramos, M., Campbell, M., & Bamford, J. (2009). The design and validation of a parent-report questionnaire for assessing the characteristics and quality of early intervention over time. *Journal of Deaf Studies and Deaf Education, 14*(4), 422–435.

Young, A., & Greally, A. (2003). *Parenting and deaf children: Report of the needs assessment study.* London, England: National Deaf Children's Society.

Young, A.M., & Ackerman, J., (2001). Reflections on validity and epistemology in a study of working relations between deaf and hearing professionals. *Qualitative Health Research 11*(2), 179-189.

Young, A.M., Jones, D., Starmer, C., & Sutherland, H. (2005). Issues and dilemmas in the production of standard information for parents of young deaf children: Parents' view. *Deafness & Education International, 7*(2), 63–76.

Young, A., & Tattersall, H. (2007). Universal newborn hearing screening and early identification of deafness: Parents' responses to knowing early and their expectations of child communication development. *Journal of Deaf Studies and Deaf Education, 12*(2), 209–220.

Young, A., & Temple, B. (2014). *Approaches to social research: The case of deaf studies* New York, NY: Oxford.

# Early
# Childhood Interventions

**4**

# Family-Centered Early Intervention

*Principles, Practices, and Supporting Research*

Mary Pat Moeller and Kristy Mixan

Family-centered approaches are those that recognize the primary role of the family in fostering children's development. They seek to establish parent–professional partnerships to build on family strengths, address family-identified needs, and promote children's development in the context of early intervention. There is a rich literature in the field of early childhood special education describing evidence-based models, principles, and practices that characterize **family-centered early intervention (FCEI)**. Borrowing from this extant literature and tradition, family-centered approaches have been widely endorsed as recommended practice for joining with families to promote the development of infants who are deaf or hard of hearing (Bodner-Johnson & Sass-Lehrer, 2003; Brown & Nott, 2006; Moeller, Carr, Seaver, Stredler-Brown, & Holzinger, 2013; Muse et al., 2013). Family-centered help-giving practices are particularly relevant in the era of universal newborn hearing screening. Typically, families in the United States are no longer seeking care for a late-identified toddler but rather are referred to the early intervention **system** with infants who are in the first few months of life. Our child-focused intervention models of the past are ill-adapted to this scenario. Service providers are now challenged to address family-identified needs and support the family in promoting development of their very young infants. This chapter has two primary goals. The first is to describe key components of FCEI and theories and evidence that support their application with families. The second goal is to discuss the implementation of FCEI with families who have an infant who is deaf or hard of hearing (D/HH), including some unique considerations.

Two key concepts pervade the approaches discussed in this chapter: *relationships* and *capacity building*. When service providers begin their work with families, at least four relationships are prominent. The first and primary one is the *family–infant relationship*. Fundamentally, we are in the home to support this relationship. It is established before we arrive, has a unique nature, and has inherent strengths that serve as the foundation for our work with families. A second relationship is that of the *service provider with the family*. The quality of this relationship may be a key contributor to intervention outcomes for the infant and family and thus requires investment and nurturing. Calderon and Greenberg (1997) observed that what may really make a difference in early intervention is the service provider's "ability to improve the parents' sense of efficacy in relating both with their deaf child and professionals, to influence the parents' sense of hope, and to foster realistic, positive expectancies" (p. 474). The collaborative nature of this relationship is a process that evolves and matures over time. Ultimately, the expectation is that a partnership will form and that the partnership will be based in mutual respect, trust, reciprocity, and honest communication (Dunst, Trivette, & Deal, 1988).

Relationships also serve to link the family with a variety of providers. This third relationship in early intervention ensures that the family and the service provider are connected with a *broader community of services and supports*. The service provider may act as a bridge—relying on skills in transdisciplinary collaboration to support families in gaining a full understanding of their child's strengths and needs. The service provider also plays a key role in helping the family identify sources of informal and formal community supports (Bailey, Nelson, Hebbeler, & Spiker, 2007). The final (fourth) relationship is the one *between the service provider and the infant.* In the past, this was the primary relationship in child-focused interventions, with family members being secondary observers. In contemporary practice, the service provider brings to the intervention the observational and developmental expertise to support the identification of strengths, developmental goal selection, and planning of next steps, but direct interaction/therapy with the infant is replaced by a role of **coaching** the family from the sidelines. This primary focus on the infant–family relationship recognizes that intervention will be effective to the degree that it has an impact on the family's ability to encourage the infant's development throughout natural interactions.

This primary focus is fundamentally about *capacity-building practices,* the second main concept pervading this chapter. Various models of FCEI implementation have evolved, but what they share is an emphasis on a paradigm of capacity building rather than correcting problems (Dunst & Trivette, 2009). In a **capacity-building** paradigm, children and families are seen as having unique strengths and assets, and the intervention focuses on supporting and promoting existing competence along with other positive aspects of family functioning (Trivette & Dunst, 2007). Capacity-building interventions seek to promote caregivers' competence and confidence in providing the child with learning opportunities that enhance development. Service providers help families adopt everyday practices that promote the child's learning by offering information, support, and **active learning** opportunities (Swanson, Raab, &

Dunst, 2011). In this chapter, we will consider how a capacity-building viewpoint shapes the process and content of early intervention.

## FAMILY-CENTERED PRACTICES:
## KEY PRINCIPLES, AND THEORETICAL AND EMPIRICAL SUPPORT

Four defining principles are foundational to family-centered philosophies and practices (Dempsey & Keen, 2008). These include recognition that 1) the family rather than the professional is the constant in the child's life, 2) the family is in the best position to determine the needs and well-being of the child, 3) by helping and supporting the family, the child is helped, and 4) families and professionals should work collaboratively by forming partnerships. The following definition by Dunst (2002) captures what is meant by family centeredness:

> Family-centeredness characterizes beliefs and practices that treat families with dignity and respect; individualized, flexible, and responsive practices; information sharing so that families can make informed decisions; family choice regarding any number of program practices and intervention options; parent-professional collaboration and partnerships as a context for family-program relations; and the provision and mobilization of supports necessary for families to care for and rear their children in ways that produce optimal child, parent, and family outcomes. (p. 139)

Family-centered practices can be grouped into two process categories: *relational* and *participatory* help-giving practices (Trivette & Dunst, 2007). **Relational practices** are those associated with compassion, active listening, empathy, and partnership-building skills, along with professional attitudes and sensitivity toward families and **cross-cultural competence**. **Participatory practices** respond to family-identified needs and engage the family in activities that strengthen existing competencies. They also promote collaboration and joint decision making (Dunst & Dempsey, 2007). The concurrent use of *both* sets of practices represents a hallmark of family-centered help giving.

An expanded model of help-giving practices adds a technical component to the relational and participatory practices (Trivette & Dunst, 2007). This technical quality component comprises the knowledge, skills, and experiences that the professional brings to the enterprise and how this competence is activated with families. These three components (relational, participatory, and technical quality) are an especially good fit for early interventions with families who have children who are D/HH. Relational practices address the affective concerns faced by families as they work to understand what it means for their child to be D/HH and are foundational to effective partnership formation. Similarly, participatory practices incorporate an adult learning model of hands-on, active learning to support family members in becoming strong language partners for their children who are D/HH. The need for early intervention service providers to have specialized knowledge and skills for working with children who are D/HH and their families has been emphasized in the Joint Committee on Infant Hearing (JCIH) 2007 supplement on early intervention (Muse et al., 2013). For example, providers need to be conversant with hearing technology, knowledgeable about communication approaches, and able to support the approach(es) implemented by the family. The reader is also referred to an international consensus statement that further supports the need for skilled providers and identifies 10 key principles that guide FCEI for families with children who are D/HH (Moeller et al., 2013).

Family-centered approaches have evolved in response to the recognition of the powerful influence of the ecological system of the family on child development. Family-centered philosophies have roots in family systems theory and models (Dunst et al., 1988), developmental theories in child language and child development, models of empowerment, and adult learning theories and consultative approaches (McWilliam, 2010b). According to McWilliam, families are like mobiles—when one part is moved, the other parts move in tandem. This focus on the family as a system acknowledges the bidirectional influences of child on family and family on child. Although family-centered approaches have gained wide acceptance as recommended practice in early intervention, it is important to consider the strength of the evidence supporting them. Because this is a vast literature, findings from a national study of early intervention outcomes and selected meta-analyses will be highlighted, followed by discussion of studies involving families of children who are D/HH.

The National Early Intervention Longitudinal Study (NEILS) team, led by Bailey and colleagues, has conducted numerous studies on early intervention outcomes, with a particular focus on the measurement of family outcomes. In one study from this team, 2,586 parents from 20 different states participated in a 40-minute interview regarding perceived outcomes near the end of early intervention (around the child's third birthday). In general, the find -ings suggested that parents felt competent in their roles as parents, able to work with professionals, and successful in advocating for services as a result of their experiences in early intervention. Most reported being hopeful about their child's future. At the same time, parents reported greater confidence in helping their children learn than in dealing with challenging behaviors (Bailey et al., 2005). This research team continues to advocate for research on family outcomes, and their work will be revisited later in this chapter.

Enhanced parental confidence is considered to be a key objective of early intervention and is often measured as an outcome. It is typically conceptualized as parental **self-efficacy**. This term comes from social learning theory and has to do with what parents *believe* about their own ability to perform specific tasks (Bandura, 1989). It has been broadly defined as the "expectations caregivers hold about their ability to parent successfully" (Jones & Prinz, 2005, p. 342). Caregivers with low levels of self-efficacy may find it difficult to persist or effectively parent when facing challenges with the child. High levels of maternal self-efficacy beliefs have been linked to parenting styles known to promote communicative development: responsiveness and provision of stimulating interactions (Coleman & Karraker, 2003).

Parental self-efficacy was among the measures examined in a meta-analysis of 47 studies that explored the relationship among family-centered practices and parent, family, and child outcomes (Dunst, Trivette, & Hamby, 2007). Six domains (satisfaction, self-efficacy, social support, child behavior, well-being, and parenting) were examined as outcomes, and all were significantly associated with family-centered help giving. The average **effect sizes** (a measure that shows the strength of a finding) ranged in stair-step fashion from large to small, respectively, for these six listed domains. The authors concluded that the more family-centered the practice, the more likely it was for parents to express satisfaction with providers and programs, to report higher levels of self-efficacy, and to judge supports and resources to be helpful. The meta-analysis also revealed that participatory practices were more strongly related to family outcomes than were relational practices. This finding was expected by the researchers, given evidence that active learner participation in acquiring new skills leads to a greater impact on capacity building. The authors also observed that family-centered practices may not be directly linked to child outcomes but rather are mediated through parental self-efficacy beliefs; parents who feel confident in their parenting capabilities are more likely to provide their children with learning opportunities, which, in turn, promotes development.

Additional meta-analyses provide further support for the impact of family-centered practices that promote family capacity (help-giving). One included 18 studies from the same early intervention program (Dunst, Trivette, & Hamby, 2006), and another included 52 studies (Dunst, Trivette, & Hamby, 2008). Collectively, these analyses revealed that family-centered help-giving practices had direct effects on family and child functioning, indirect effects mediated through self-efficacy, or both. A more recent meta-analysis using structural equation modeling showed that help-giving practices directly influenced parental self-efficacy and well-being and that there were indirect effects of help-giving practices on parent–child interaction and child development, mediated by self-efficacy (Trivette, Dunst, & Hamby, 2010).

Parental self-efficacy is a potential predictor of parenting competence that relates to child outcomes (Jones & Prinz, 2005). However, most previous studies have relied on cross-sectional and correlational designs that limit the conclusions that can be drawn about causal influences. Thus, there is a need for longitudinal, intervention, and experimental studies to confirm causal links. An intervention study employed a multiple baseline design with four caregivers to examine the extent to which capacity-building interventions influenced parental confidence and competence. Results revealed large effects on the measured outcomes and indicated that caregivers' interactions with the child and parental self-efficacy were influenced positively by the intervention (Swanson et al., 2011). The construct of parental self-efficacy may be especially important in the context of families of infants who are D/HH, as these beliefs could influence caregivers' willingness to get involved, persist, and implement the day-to-day parenting practices that promote communicative development (Ingber, Al-Yagon, & Dromi, 2010).

## EVIDENCE RELATED TO FAMILIES OF CHILDREN WHO ARE DEAF OR HARD OF HEARING

Studies examining the impact of FCEI on families and their children who are D/HH are relatively rare. However, a few studies have directly explored the contributions of parental self-efficacy and participation (involvement) on outcomes. Maternal ratings of self-efficacy and involvement were explored with 24 mothers of children who wore hearing aids (HAs) and 30 mothers of children with cochlear implants (CIs; DesJardin, 2005). The measures focused on the mothers' self-efficacy in managing the children's sensory devices and their involvement in developing their children's speech and language skills. Interestingly, mothers of children with CIs reported greater self-efficacy in managing sensory devices than parents of children with hearing aids. Mothers of children with CIs also felt more involved in their children's programs and in promoting listening and language activities at home than mothers of children with hearing aids. These contrasting outcomes suggest the need to further examine how interventions can promote self-efficacy in families, with additional attention to those with children who are HH. Notably, earlier ages of amplification and intervention were positively associated with maternal self-efficacy, suggesting that longer periods of time in early intervention may promote these important skills.

It is also pertinent to ascertain whether enhanced caregiver self-efficacy and involvement are associated with improved outcomes for children who are D/HH. This relationship was explored in a follow-up study involving 32 mothers of children with CIs (DesJardin & Eisenberg, 2007). Results showed that maternal self-efficacy and involvement were positively related to maternal use of facilitative language techniques and that maternal use of those techniques was directly related to children's language outcomes. Qualitative aspects of maternal talk, such as use of recasting strategies (see Chapter 5), were positively related to children's receptive language abilities, and parent's use of open-ended questioning promoted better expressive language in children. Quantitative aspects of maternal language (longer mean length of utterance, more diverse word use) were also associated with better language outcomes in children. These findings provide strong justification for the focus on parental self-efficacy and parental involvement in language-facilitating interactions. They also suggest that parental confidence and competence positively influence the children's communicative development.

Other studies have found that family involvement in intervention influences outcomes in children who are D/HH (Moeller, 2000; Sarant, Holt, Dowell, Rickards, & Blamey, 2009). However, previous studies have defined involvement in varying ways, and there is need for greater understanding of factors that influence involvement. Maternal personal and contextual factors that affect family involvement in intervention were examined in a large sample of mother–child dyads ($n$ = 114) in Israel (Ingber et al., 2010). Results showed that mothers reporting high levels of curiosity and motivation, greater perceived informal support, and lower levels of pessimism about the child's potential also reported higher levels of involvement in early intervention. These results support the practices of providing families with access to relational supports in early intervention and promoting families' reliance on their own sources of informal support. The focus on supporting parents in their roles as primary language models for children who are D/HH is also supported by child language theories and studies demonstrating the effectiveness of parent-implemented language interventions. Snow (1994) observed that children who are D/HH may receive inconsistent access to spoken language models provided in the environment, which places them at risk for language delays (Moeller & Tomblin, 2015). A number of factors are known to influence children's auditory access, including aided audibility (McCreery, Bentler, & Roush, 2013), amplification use history

(Tomblin, Oleson, Ambrose, Walker, & Moeller, 2014; Walker et al., 2013), and environmental effects on the signal (noise, distance, reverberation). To counteract these effects, early intervention programs seek to optimize linguistic input provided by the family by encouraging frequent conversational turns, quiet conditions in the home, and consistent use of HAs and CIs.

It has also been suggested that children who are D/HH may be more dependent than typical peers on the presence of optimal input for language learning due to these variations in access (Snow, 1994; Szagun & Stumper, 2012). Given that practitioners believe that families should be supported in their roles as primary and rich language facilitators, what does the evidence say about parent-implemented language facilitation? Is the approach effective overall?

Several qualitative features of caregiver–child interaction are known to promote child language development in young children, and these are commonly emphasized skills in early intervention with families of children who are D/HH (Brown & Nott, 2006). They include parental responsiveness to the child (Baumwell, Tamis-LeMonda, & Bornstein, 1997; Nittrouer, 2010; Tamis-LeMonda, Bornstein, & Baumwell, 2001) and use of specific language facilitation techniques, such as parallel talk, expansions, open-ended questions, and recasts (Fey, Krulik, Loeb, & Proctor-Williams, 1999; Proctor-Williams, Fey, & Loeb, 2001; Szagun & Stumper, 2012; see Chapter 5). Another meta-analysis focused on 18 studies to evaluate the effects of parent-implemented interventions for hearing toddlers and preschoolers with language impairments (Roberts & Kaiser, 2011). More than half the studies ($n = 11$) included home training or a home training component. The analysis showed that parent-implemented language interventions had a positive impact on children's language outcomes in comparison to a control group, and significant effects were observed for the majority of child language outcomes. Further, increasing parent–child turn taking in interactions and improving responsiveness to child communication were associated with positive outcomes in child language.

Finally, studies examining the relationships between caregiver input and outcomes suggest that children who are D/HH benefit from exposure to both quantity and quality features of input in the home environment (Ambrose, VanDam, & Moeller, 2014; Cruz, Quittner, Marker, & DesJardin, 2013; DesJardin & Eisenberg, 2007; Nittrouer, 2010; Szagun & Stumper, 2012). In particular, the frequency of engagement in conversational interactions has importance and is a strong influence on children's language abilities (Ambrose et al., 2014). Thus, a growing body of evidence clearly underscores the need for interventions that promote parental capacity as responsive communication partners and linguistic models for their children who are D/HH.

## FAMILY–PROFESSIONAL PARTNERSHIPS IN ASSESSMENT AND INTERVENTION

In the context of early intervention, assessment is an ongoing process that serves multiple purposes. The first purpose is to identify child and family strengths; these are the capabilities upon which we want to build. In addition, ongoing assessments can be effective in clarifying family-identified needs so that they can be addressed in intervention. **Authentic assessments** are defined as flexible processes of systematically recording observations of behaviors over time in natural contexts and are especially valued as ongoing assessment strategies (Bagnato, Neisworth, & Pretti-Frontczak, 2010). By observing the family and child during natural activities, service providers gain insights into the everyday functioning of both parties. The second purpose of assessment is for partners to engage in collaborative reflection during home visits as a way of figuring out what is working well (Shelden & Rush, 2010). By participating in this reflection process, families increase their skills in observing their child's behavior and noticing whether desired changes are occurring as a result of their efforts. This assists in planning intervention and guiding the promotion of developmental progress. The third purpose of an ongoing assessment is to document family and child outcomes. Because assessment of child outcomes is a topic covered in other chapters in this book (see Chapters 5–8), the discussion in this chapter will focus on selected assessments of family outcomes. Finally, assessments include quality indicators and benchmarks that can be used by service providers for self-reflection and to identify professional development goals and by programs to determine the degree to which they are adhering to recommended practices in family-centered early intervention (JCIH, 2007).

Discussion of these areas of assessment will be interwoven with the discussion on early intervention, because they are intrinsically related to and inseparable from the intervention process itself. It is hard to imagine how one would go about identifying family strengths and needs outside the context of collaboration with the family. Therefore, before implementing assessment processes, it is essential that providers work to establish a partnership relationship during early visits with the family. These early contacts, in the experience of the authors, set the tone and expectations for how families and professionals will work together over time. Forming partnerships is a process, and effective family–professional relationships are likely to mature as trust and reciprocity grow over time.

A number of factors may influence whether or not service providers are successful in kicking off and strengthening partnership relations on home visits. First of all, professionals and parents may have different values or expectations for their roles on intervention visits. A qualitative study revealed considerable diversity in parental expectations for the roles they would take in early intervention (Dromi & Ingber, 1999). Fifty Israeli mothers of 2- to 5-year-old children with mild to profound hearing loss reported role expectations that fell into four categories (*represented in italics*). Some mothers (14%) reported confidence in taking *independent responsibility* for addressing child needs. They viewed early intervention as a resource to support their goals, but they expected to take the lead. A second group (14%) viewed themselves as *full collaborators,* willing to engage in partnership with professionals. Another 26% of the mothers viewed themselves and the child as clients of the program, with *less well-developed* collaborative views. Interestingly, 46% of the mothers were classified as *relinquishing responsibility,* viewing the professionals as responsible for planning and implementing the child's educational program. Although this study was conducted some time ago, it highlights the importance of not assuming that the professional expectation about roles is necessarily shared by the family.

In early visits, it is essential that professionals seek to understand family expectations, provide information about the nature of a family-centered approach, and work toward joined perspectives about engagement on home visits. Service providers need to be clear with families during early visits that the job of professionals is to support caregivers emotionally, to provide information and resources, to help them encourage their child's development, and to respond to family needs (McWilliam, 2010b). Professionals should engage families in conversations during the earliest visits regarding the notion that intervention will actually happen *between* visits and that more help for the child will not come from more services—it will come from supporting the capabilities of the family (McWilliam, 2010b).

Following newborn hearing screening, families of referred infants become involved in a series of medical and audiological appointments that address diagnosis and next steps (see Chapter 2). It is understandable that a family might expect that the role of the early intervention professional is to provide therapy to "fix" any problems. This attitude can be seen in a parent who recently reported, "Well, the home visitor comes and just talks to me. She is not doing anything with my child!" This statement reveals that the intervention approach is not currently aligned with parental expectations. It suggests the need for further efforts to find common ground and increase understanding about what collaboration can accomplish and why this approach is helpful. Both parents and professionals share a desire to do what is in the best interest of the child. Thus, parental expectations can be shaped with clear explanations and experiences demonstrating that caregivers are essential to helping the child. Useful scripts for explaining a partnership and coaching approach are available online from the Family Infant and Preschool Program (FIPP Brief-CASE; Rush & Shelden, 2005; see http://fipp org/publications/briefcase).

It is important to recognize, however, that clear conversation about the focus of intervention is not the only approach to kicking off partnership. It is essential that providers "walk the walk" with families—in other words, their actions must demonstrate a sincere desire to work in partnership. This means starting first sessions with an attitude of learning from the family and observing what is going well before teaching and giving information. In a framework of empowerment, service providers work to avoid circumstances that can be "power robbing" for families. For hearing parents, the diagnosis of the child as D/HH itself can be power robbing (Luterman, Kurtzer-White, & Seewald, 1999). Families often begin intervention with very young D/HH infants while still in a period of intense adjustment to the birth of an infant. It is not uncommon for new parents to wonder if they have what it takes to parent this new little person who has entered their lives. When they discover that the infant is deaf or hard of hearing, it is natural for self-doubts to increase. A parent of a deaf child articulated the importance of this notion quite well. She said,

> I think it's normal for all first-time mothers to feel overwhelmed and lack the confidence that they will make the right decisions for their child. I had periods of insecurity before my son was identified, but my insecurity increased exponentially after I learned that he was deaf. My service provider was so encouraging; she was my own personal cheerleader at times. She gave me confidence that I was up to the task at hand.

This common stance is why service providers focus in early intervention on confidence building and on strengthening the parents' natural capacities (Dunst & Trivette, 2009). Professional skills, knowledge, and abilities are essential contributions to the early intervention collaborative process, and parents value this expertise (Ingber & Dromi, 2010). However, sensitive professionals recognize that their models and expertise can be overpowering, especially early in the interaction before a foundation of trust has been established. In early visits, there are opportunities to observe family members naturally interacting with the child, and this is a rich context for noticing what is already going well in the relationship and pointing it out. Families who have this experience soon figure out that the service provider is learning about the child by watching interactions with the family. They discover that the professional is not interested in judging their parenting skills. Experiencing a nonjudgmental and supportive approach sets the stage for future reciprocal coaching within the partnership.

Although professionals often remind families that "parents are the experts regarding the child," parents may not feel like experts, especially when the service provider has a great deal of knowledge and experience related to children who are D/HH. On the other hand, professionals may not be confident in methods for drawing out parental expertise, and this is a truly important step. When the service provider uses the tools of open-ended informal conversation, active listening, observing, and responding sensitively, it becomes obvious to family members that the service provider hears them and learns from their input. They see concrete evidence that they are contributing meaningful expertise. Here is an example with the father of an 11-month-old infant.

Service provider (SP):    So she likes to look at books with you?

Dad:  Yes, we try to read books every day.

SP:  Do you think she might like to look at one now?

Dad:  Sure—she loves this book. Come here, sweetie. *(Pulls daughter in his lap and begins to look at the book with her, pointing at simple pictures and naming them.)*

SP:  So you like to tell her the names of the pictures. It seems like she listens to you for a long time.

Dad:  Yeah, and if she is looking down and then I say a brand new word, she looks right up.

SP:  Do you think she is responding to your voice or is she noticing the change?

Dad:  I actually think she notices new words or unusual sounds. But sometimes I am not sure.

SP:  Oh, that's interesting. Please tell me more about that.

During this same conversation, a skilled service provider commented to the father, "Can you see that I am learning what we need to do next based on your input?" This objective comment reinforced both the purpose and process of their interaction. It also prompted a slightly reticent parent to continue sharing. The service provider is taking a stance of "learning from" *before* moving to advising and guiding.

Service providers also use *objective commenting* to point out something important and to encourage the parent to share more about what both parties are seeing. This is sometimes referred to as a "news commentator" strategy (Moeller & Condon, 1994). A news commentator keeps listeners informed of important events that are happening, sometimes in a blow-by-blow fashion. When working with families, the service provider may quietly make comments from the sidelines, pointing out child behaviors partners are learning about or noting caregiver–child interactions that are going well. Often, this approach is confidence building for caregivers as it points out capacities. In some cases, service providers comment on something parents just do automatically; parents may be unaware of the benefit of their actions for their child. This takes attunement, flexibility, and sensitivity on the part of the service provider—an ability to be a sideline observer who notices what matters in the interaction. Here is an example of the use of the *news commentator strategy:*

*Mother is playing with infant while service provider watches from the sidelines.*

> SP:  Every time she looks at you, you smile at her. Then she locks her gaze on you.

*Infant coos and the mother coos right back. Infant coos again.*

> SP:  And when you coo after her, she tries again. That keeps the conversation going.

An important point is that these are not pats on the back or "warm fuzzies." Rather, this is a process of objectively pointing out to caregivers something that is important. The service provider learns about strengths and capabilities, and caregivers recognize they are doing something that matters. The *news commentator role* is a coaching strategy that provides concrete feedback about  the interaction (see Video clip 4.1).

In FCEI, service providers strive to use family *routines* within their regular, natural environments as the context for providing support and building capacity. Based on longitudinal studies of families of children with disabilities, researchers concluded that "no intervention, no matter how well designed or implemented, will have an impact if it cannot find a slot in the daily routines of an organization, family, or individual" (Bernheimer & Weisner, 2007, p. 199). Families can and do make accommodations in their family routines, but interventions must fit existing practices and beliefs that are *in place.* Families with young children typically have busy daily schedules. Where will families fit in extra assigned therapy tasks? The principle of providing support and resources to assist families in enhancing their children's development through everyday routines is emphasized in a family-centered approach called routines-based intervention (McWilliam, 2010a). In this approach, routines are not considered to be the activities the professional implements. Rather, they are the families' naturally occurring events and activities that happen regularly.

In order to foster caregiver abilities within daily routines, it is essential to understand the activities and routines that are a part of their daily lives. A conversational approach can be used along with informal observations in the family context to gather this key information from families (Wilcox & Woods, 2011; see

Video clip 4.2). They encourage providers to include discussion of routines that the family finds challenging as well as those that bring enjoyment for both the child and the caregivers. Comprehensive guidelines, scripts, and tools for conducting a Routines-Based Interview (RBI) may be found in McWilliam's work (2010b). The RBI not only familiarizes the service provider with important family routines; it allows for identification of child interests, functional outcomes, and family strengths and priorities, all of which are relevant to the development of the individualized family service plan (IFSP; see Chapter 5) that will include goals and serve as a road map to guide services. The RBI is also intended to foster investment by caregivers other than the family (such as child care providers) in promoting outcomes. Recent evidence suggests that the RBI is a more efficacious process than traditional approaches to development of an IFSP; the effect sizes from this pilot study were large (McWilliam, Casey, & Sims, 2009).

The RBI is a dialogue-based assessment process that promotes family involvement in IFSP development. There is sometimes a misconception that being family centered means the families need to determine the goals single handedly. Family members have reported statements such as "I go to the meeting and they ask me what I want the goals to be. I don't know what the goals need to be. I end up feeling inadequate and losing confidence because I just don't know what to say." Looked at from this vantage point, a structured conversational process like the RBI has considerable merit, as it promotes the collaborative partnership process we have been discussing. *Both* sides of the partnership are contributing expertise.

### Partnering with Families on Home Visits: Support and Coaching Roles

Home visitation requires a host of skills of the provider, with effective, sensitive, and flexible communication being paramount. Relational help-giving practices are instrumental in providing support, and these are based on professional practices such as active listening, honesty, caring, empathy, and pos-itive attributions about the strengths and capabilities of caregivers (Dunst, Boyd, Trivette, & Hamby, 2002). Active listening is a process that incorporates several provider practices, such as responding with empathy to feelings expressed in a message, using questions to explore viewpoints and encourage elaboration, and paraphrasing and summarizing to verify that the caregiver's comments were heard and interpreted accurately. The intent of active listening is to develop a clear understanding of the concern expressed and to clearly convey that the service provider is interested in the caregiver's message (McNaughton, Hamlin, McCarthy, Head-Reeves, & Schreiner, 2008). It can be tempting to provide suggestions, tips, or advisement in response to parental expressions of concern. In active listening, the service provider is *listening past the words* to identify the feelings being expressed. The provider comments on the feelings in ways that convey empathy and a willingness to hear more. The following example illustrates the nonjudgmental and sensitive response of a service provider to a mother's expression of guilt.

A mother tearfully shared her gratitude for the responsiveness of her early intervention provider. This mother was a single parent who was parenting a child who was deaf with a variety of health issues and special needs (see Box 4.1).

> ### Box 4.1. Vignette recalled by a parent
>
> *Service provider (on arrival):* What's up? How did things go this week?
>
> *Mother (who confessed to being near panic):* It was an awful week. I feel terrible that I did not get his amplification on him very much. I did not have time to practice much of anything with him.
>
> *Service provider (seeking to help mom put the week in perspective):* Did you get meals on the table for your children? Did you give your little one his medications? Did you let your children know they are loved?
>
> *Mother (recalling this experience):* Suddenly, I was able to breathe again. This little bit of encouragement and empathy toward my struggle helped me find the strength to forgive myself, put things in perspective, and attend more to his needs the next week and the week after that. Her sensitivity was a lifeline that helped me find resilience . . . a precious and necessary skill.

How service providers respond to families is an essential ingredient in forming effective partnerships. It is beyond the scope of this chapter to provide comprehensive coverage of specific relational strategies. However, some general principles are provided as a guide (see Table 4.1).

The Vanderbilt Home Visit Script is a useful guide for providing relational supports (McWilliam, 2010a). The script incorporates a "4E" acronym to remind service providers of four primary relational tools needed in conversations: ears and eyes (meaning listen), elicit (ask questions), empathize, and encourage. Table 4.2 provides a practical illustration of the use of 4Es in response to a scenario where a child who is hard of hearing is with her grandmother during the day, and the grandmother is not promoting hearing aid use. Notice the various strategies the service provider uses to respond to the mother's feelings, engage her in planning and problem solving, empathize with her struggle, and provide encouragement to support the mother's process. Under the "Elicit" heading, four

**Table 4.1.** Characteristics of service providers found to be highly effective with families and questions to guide service provider self-refection

| Characteristics of effective service providers |
| --- |
| 1. Positivity about the family and child |
| 2. Responsiveness to needs (i.e., return calls and e-mails quickly, follow through) |
| 3. Orientation to the whole family |
| 4. Friendliness (building interpersonal connections) |
| 5. Sensitivity |

| Questions for service provider self-reflection |
| --- |
| 1. Does my service delivery embody these characteristics? |
| 2. Do I incorporate these practices with a range of families in varied circumstances? |
| 3. Are any of my attitudes or perceptions getting in the way? |

*Source:* McWilliam, Tocci, & Harbin (1998).

types of questions (Shelden & Rush, 2010) are illustrated in this same scenario. Suppose this mother is reticent to discuss this issue with her parent or mother-in-law who is providing helpful and essential support in the form of child care. If this is the case, it is important to seek understanding of the mother's perspectives and perceived barriers ("Can you tell me more?") and utilize varied question types (see Table 4.2) to help her form a concrete plan. In the "encourage" section, some concepts are included from Michael Brandwein (http:// www. michaelbrandwein.com/bionormal.html), a leadership consultant who promotes the use of positive communication with parents, especially by responding in ways that build confidence. Notice how the mother is reinforced for expressing her needs, for devising new solutions, and for her persistence and advocacy efforts. These messages focus on the parent's *process,* and they are likely to reinforce her efforts, whether or not they bring about the desired result.

The *participatory* goals of early intervention (Trivette & Dunst, 2007) are fostered through coaching practices in collaboration with families. Coaches are not seen as whistle-blowing dictators who call all the shots on the court. Rather, they are seen as helpful partners, there to support the growth process through reflection, sharing of information, and practicing of skills in real contexts (participatory practices; see Video clip 4.3). The coaching process provides opportunities to refine actions and strategies, develop new skills, and continuously self-assess and learn (Shelden & Rush, 2010). Based on a synthesis of research on coaching practices, the following definition of coaching was derived:

> An adult learning strategy in which the coach promotes the learner's ability to reflect on his or her actions as the means to determine the effectiveness of an action or practice and develop a plan for use of the action in immediate and future situations. (Rush & Shelden, 2005, p. 3)

Home visits tend to contain routine elements that are illustrated in Figure 4.1. Although we are presenting the elements in a cyclic fashion, they rarely unfold in an orderly sequence, and flexible partners may go in and out of different activities and conversations. For service providers who may be new to home visits, it can be helpful to see a structured framework, and as experience grows, flexible adaptation of the components will occur. Many service providers begin home visits with informal conversation (Block A in Figure 4.1 model), starting with open-ended questions (i.e., What's up?). This *reconnect and review* of what has happened since the last visit allows partners to share information and discuss what they would like to focus on in the current visit. Previous focus group research revealed that families value the *quantity* of communication (e.g., frequent, open communication) and see it as essential to positive partnerships (Blue-Banning, Summers, Frankland, Nelson, & Beegle, 2004). The "reconnect" time on home visits can foster opportunities for frequent informal conversations with families

(see Video clip 4.4). Consistent and regular contact with families may also foster this goal, and future research needs to explore the potential influence of regular contact on family and child outcomes. It is noteworthy that Blue-Banning and colleagues also found that parents desire communication that is open, honest, and free of hidden agendas or the candy coating of difficult news.

The next three components represented in B, C, and D in the model (Figure 4.1) may work as an iterative process. In B, the partners engage in discussion, observing and reflecting on observations and identifying priorities for

**Table 4.2.** Relational family-centered practice examples

| Four Es guiding relational help giving | Description | Application: Scenario—Grandparents are watching the child during the day. They are not consistent with hearing aid (HA) use. |
|---|---|---|
| Ears and eyes (listen) | Take the time to really listen and avoid quick judgments or advice giving; respond to the feeling expressed, not just content; avoid efforts to minimize or fix the pain. | Parent: My mom just won't keep the hearing aids in. She insists that Shelby can hear. Service provider (SP): That sounds quite concerning to you. Can you tell me more? |
| Elicit (ask) | Question types (Shelden & Rush, 2010) *Awareness:* What have you tried? What do you typically do when she . . . ? | SP: What have you tried with your mother? You said it was tricky . . . what makes it tricky for you? |
| | *Analysis:* How does this compare with what you would like to have happen? | SP: How does this compare with what you want your mother to do? |
| | *Alternatives:* What are the possible options to consider? It is important to allow parents to explore their ideas before jumping in with suggestions or trying to "fix" things. | SP: Do you have ideas about how to change this situation? |
| | *Action:* Who will do what? Some families may need support to come up with a concrete action plan: who, how, and when it will happen. | Parent: I was thinking it might help her to talk with another grandmother of an infant with hearing aids. SP: From what you told me, it sounds like you want to suggest that to her first. How will you approach her? What might you say? When do you want to try that? |
| Empathize | Acknowledge and respond sensitively to caregivers' feelings. | Parent: I am being consistent with her hearing aid, and I can't seem to get everybody on board. SP: It must be hard to feel so responsible and not get the support you need. |
| Encourage | Confidence-building responses (Brandwein, 2010) Use responses that comment on the family's process of the following: • Communication | Parent: Sometimes I need help from others in talking to her. That's why I thought of another grandmother. SP: By finding support, you are looking out for yourself. That is important. |
| | • Problem solving | Parent: Maybe I'll have Shelby wear the bonnet at mom's. If she doesn't bother her HAs, maybe mom won't take them out. SP: You are willing to try another way—that is flexible problem solving. |
| | • Gaining confidence in own abilities | SP: When I last saw you, you were going to talk to your mom about visiting with another grandmother. How did that conversation go? Parent: Well, she seemed reluctant, but I reminded her that she was only agreeing to share a cup of coffee with another grandmother . . . and that the conversation might benefit Shelby. So she said okay in the end. SP: Your persistence paid off. Sounds like you found common ground in that you both want what is best for Shelby. Parent: Yeah, I guess that did work to bring that in. SP: The practice you are getting now advocating for Shelby will help in the future, too. |

*Source:* McWilliam (2010a).

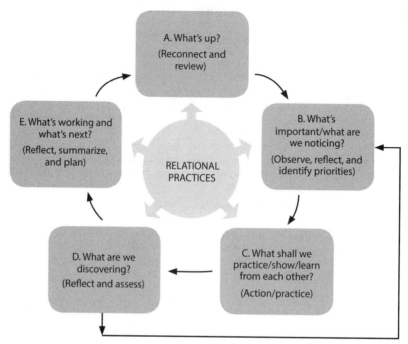

**Figure 4.1.**  A framework for home visits representing both relational and participatory practices. (*Sources:* Carotta, 2011; Shelden & Rush, 2010; Stredler-Brown et al., 2004.)

what to do next. In C, partners engage in joint problem solving and discovery. It is action and practice but with a strong reflection component. Perhaps the partners are capitalizing on the child's interest in playing peekaboo with famil- iar family members. They wonder out loud if the little one might recognize familiar voices if three family members hold up blankets and only one calls the child's name. As they try it out, they move to D by assessing how the child responds and reflecting on what just happened. It may be that the toddler turned consistently to the correct voice, and the parents are able to "own" the success and understand what it means. This might send the partners back to the B-C-D cycle, with perhaps an increase in the auditory challenge. Maybe the toddler loves Hide and Seek, and family members can call him or her from dif- ferent doorways down the hall. This turns into a joyful family game of listening at greater distance, localizing, and finding those favored voices. Perhaps the service provider models from the sideline pragmatically appropriate comments such as "Hi, Daddy. I found you!" The parent picks up on the strategy and later observes the child responding positively to their efforts (e.g., caregivers owning the success).

The outer arrows linked with the B-C-D cycle are intended to show that this process might be repeated several times during a session as partners pose priorities or questions, try something out (typically with the parents in the driver's seat and the provider on the sidelines), observe and reflect on the responses, and perhaps pose something else to try (see Video clip 4.5). Ser- vice providers will sometimes model a strategy directly but quickly create opportunities for the parent to try it on for size. Throughout the process, the service provider makes summarizing statements so that partners keep track of important observations (see Video clip 4.6). Importantly, the B-C-D process helps caregivers learn to observe the child and take cues from the child's responses. This is a valuable way of getting to know the child's strengths and needs, and it can aid decision making.

Summarizing is also a key component of E, particularly as the session is wrapping up. That is a good time for a big picture summary that allows partners to reflect on what was accomplished today and what should be the focus of efforts in the weeks to come. All of these steps should be reciprocal—both caregivers and service providers are contributing expertise (see Video clip 4.7), sharing tasks, negotiating meanings, and reflecting. Notice that relational practices (discussed earlier) are situated in the "heart" of this model. It is impossible to separate relational and participatory help-giving practices; service providers are integrating both when working with families. Service provider sensitivity to families is truly at the heart of FCEI.

It has been suggested that early intervention providers should strive to provide three types of support to families on home visits: emotional, material, and informational (McWilliam, 2010a). Consider this overall approach in relation to the family described earlier, who is struggling to establish consistent hearing aid use, especially in the child care setting with grandparents. Suppose the family identifies this as a priority area of need and they are expressing guilt over their difficulties establishing consistent device use as a family. Figure 4.2 provides examples of supports that might be useful in addressing this family-identified need from McWilliam's support framework.

In an era of evidence-based practices, accountability for early intervention outcomes is emphasized. There is a pressing need to measure *family outcomes* (beyond satisfaction with services) as part of our determination of whether FCEI is achieving its desired results (Bailey, Raspa, & Fox, 2012). What outcomes do we expect for families as a result of their early intervention experiences? This question was addressed by a research team called the Early Childhood Out-comes (ECO) Center (Bailey et al., 2006). This team of investigators gathered stakeholder input and applied an evidence-based process to identify five primary outcomes that are useful in determining if early intervention programs are providing benefits for families. Table 4.3 lists these five primary family outcomes but expands the information with specific examples that are relevant to parents who have a child who is D/HH. These examples can guide our thinking about what we are trying to accomplish with these families in the early intervention process. The ECO team also developed an evidence-based and well-validated tool called the Family Outcomes Survey (Bailey, Hebbeler, Olmsted, Raspa, & Bruder, 2008; Bailey et al., 2011) to support the measurement of family outcomes. This tool is available from the Early Childhood Technical Assistance Center (http://ectacenter.org/eco/pages/tools.asp#SurveyVersions). In the first section of this tool, families rate their abilities in the five primary outcome areas listed in Table 4.3. In the second section, families are asked to rate the helpfulness of early intervention in promoting families' knowledge of their rights, ability to advocate for the child's needs, and ability to help their child develop and learn.

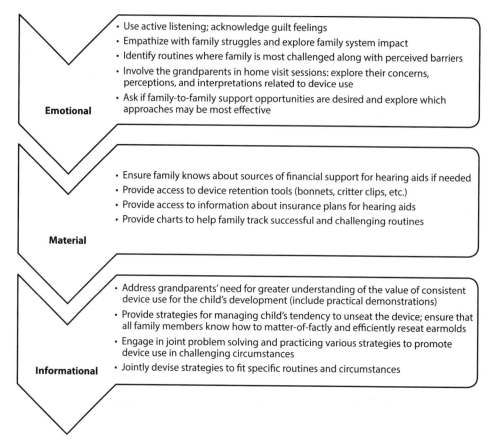

**Emotional**
- Use active listening; acknowledge guilt feelings
- Empathize with family struggles and explore family system impact
- Identify routines where family is most challenged along with perceived barriers
- Involve the grandparents in home visit sessions: explore their concerns, perceptions, and interpretations related to device use
- Ask if family-to-family support opportunities are desired and explore which approaches may be most effective

**Material**
- Ensure family knows about sources of financial support for hearing aids if needed
- Provide access to device retention tools (bonnets, critter clips, etc.)
- Provide access to information about insurance plans for hearing aids
- Provide charts to help family track successful and challenging routines

**Informational**
- Address grandparents' need for greater understanding of the value of consistent device use for the child's development (include practical demonstrations)
- Provide strategies for managing child's tendency to unseat the device; ensure that all family members know how to matter-of-factly and efficiently reseat earmolds
- Engage in joint problem solving and practicing various strategies to promote device use in challenging circumstances
- Jointly devise strategies to fit specific routines and circumstances

**Figure 4.2.**    Three areas of support recommended by McWilliam and applied to a family-identified need around consistent hearing aid use. (*Source:* McWilliam, 2010a,b.)

Earlier in this chapter, the contributions of parental self-efficacy and involvement to child outcomes were described. Although more research is needed, the concept is that by strengthening parental self-perceptions of competence, actual parenting abilities may be enhanced, which in turn promotes child outcomes. Service provision with families of children who are D/HH is predicated on these notions, which justifies the incorporation of measures of parental self-efficacy and involvement as part of the outcomes assessment. Two tools were developed to support service providers in monitoring parental self-efficacy and/or involvement. The Early Intervention Parenting Self-Efficacy Scale (EIPSES) tool was developed to assess family competence beliefs that relate to early intervention (Guimond, Wilcox, & Lamorey, 2008). Factor analysis revealed that this scale measures two aspects of parental self-efficacy: 1) parental outcomes expectations and 2) parental competence. This scale may be useful in identifying strengths and areas of need related to parental perceived competence in supporting their children's development.

Another tool, called the Scale of Parental Involvement and Self-Efficacy, was developed by DesJardin (2003) and is specific to families who have young children who are D/HH. The scale (available in English and Spanish) provides

**Table 4.3.**   Family outcomes from early intervention and their application to families who have a child who is deaf or hard of hearing

| Family outcomes | Examples specific to families of children who are deaf or hard of hearing (D/HH) |
|---|---|
| 1. Families understand their child's strengths, abilities, and special needs. | • Know expectations for typical development; understand barriers to language access and consequences for language development in children who are D/HH<br>• Know expectations for auditory development and how to promote reliance on hearing and vision for language learning<br>• Know how child is developing and what might be the next developmental abilities to encourage<br>• Observe their child's behavior and notice whether changes are resulting from efforts<br>• Learn about what it means to be D/HH, understand audiogram and the need for well-fit and functioning devices<br>• Understand etiology and any related health risks/needs<br>• Maintain hopefulness about the child's ability to achieve now and in the future<br>• Understand varied perspectives about the communicative needs of children who are D/HH<br>• Detect bias and evaluate varied opinions in light of family goals and their child's unique abilities and needs |
| 2. Families know their rights and advocate effectively for their children. | • Know their rights and responsibilities related to service provision<br>• Identify experiences that will support their family in becoming informed decision makers<br>• Know different service options and the types of services offered by different providers; understand benefits and risks of various approaches and programs<br>• Feel comfortable talking with professionals and asking questions<br>• Know how to use the Internet or other sources to find out about rights and services<br>• Participate effectively in team meetings to plan goals and services; know who they want to involve in the discussions<br>• Know what to do if they feel that needed services are not provided<br>• Ensure that family system understands and is responsive to child's needs |
| 3. Families help their children develop and learn. | • Know and use positive and responsive styles of parenting<br>• Know how to promote language access for their child who is D/HH<br>• Know how to engage the child in conversational turns by recognizing and responding to the child's various communicative attempts<br>• Know how to engage the child's auditory and visual attention and involve the child in joint engagement routines<br>• Provide a nurturing and stimulating environment for their child; know how to create language rich, responsive interactions<br>• Manage auditory and visual distractions in the environment to optimize input<br>• Use effective techniques to enhance learning and manage behavioral challenges<br>• Manage devices effectively; seat earmolds easily; conduct daily integrity checks of devices; promote consistent use; consistently take child to audiologist and/or cochlear implant team to ensure optimal audibility with devices<br>• Aggressively manage ear infections by medical team<br>• Know how to assess and evaluate the appropriateness of recommendations offered in relation to child's needs<br>• If electing to implement a bilingual-bicultural approach, become as fluent and proficient as possible in American Sign Language (ASL)<br>• If electing a bilingual-bicultural ASL approach, recognize the value of exposing the child to fluent language models<br>• If electing a total communication approach, gain fluency in manual signs and ability to promote both visual and auditory learning |
| 4. Families have support. | • See Chapter 3 for comprehensive discussion |

*(continued)*

**Table 4.3.**   *(continued)*

| Family outcomes | Examples specific to families of children who are D/HH |
|---|---|
| 5. Families access desired services, programs, and activities in their community. | • Have quality child care services and child care providers that are knowledgeable about managing the child's devices and communicative needs<br>• Have sufficient knowledge and skills to make informed decisions with confidence<br>• Have medical providers who are informed about the child's hearing loss, potential medical and educational needs, and the need for community collaborations<br>• Participate in family-to-family support groups, activities, and/or social networks that are relevant to the family's style and priorities<br>• Access D/HH role models to support learning about the meaning of being D/HH and to foster hopefulness about the child's future |

*Source:* Bailey et al. (2006).

insight on parents' perceived roles in early intervention and their perceived self-efficacy on specific knowledge and skill areas necessary to promote communicative development in children who are D/HH (e.g., managing amplification, promoting speech and language, participating in intervention). This scale appears to have high utility for measuring family needs and outcomes in relation to help-giving practices.

## Supporting the Process of Informed Decision Making

As a result of participation in FCEI, it is expected that families will have the knowledge and skills to make informed decisions (Moeller et al., 2013; Muse et al., 2013). Families with newly identified children who are D/HH encounter a number of complex decisions early in their child's life. These include decisions regarding how they will support the child's communicative development, which specific technologies will be used, and whether or not surgical interventions (e.g., cochlear implants, bone-anchored hearing aids) will be pursued, among many others. Families are also striving to navigate educational programs and determine what community services will best meet child and family needs. Often families are in a position of making decisions when evidence may be unclear or limited and when professional and community opinions are contradictory or varied.

Professionals are in agreement that families should have information about all service options for their child but may not agree that various approaches are equally necessary or appropriate (Young et al., 2006). One mother reported that her service provider gave her several pamphlets describing various communicative approaches (e.g., auditory-verbal therapy, cued speech, bilingual-bicultural). The mother added, "She told me to read all this by Monday so I could tell her what I wanted to do with my child." Although written materials may be helpful for some families, they do not make up the entire process of gaining knowledge, insights, and skills that leads to making informed decisions. Further, the pamphlet approach may suggest that approaches are dichotomous and there is one "right" choice. This can make the process especially daunting for families.

Decision making can be conceptualized as a collaborative process that is addressed *over time* within the family–professional partnership in early intervention. Families will need the ability to make informed decisions and advocate for the child over the course of their child's life; it is critical that these abilities be fostered in early intervention. Early intervention provides a context for ongoing conversations, getting to know the infant and his or her needs, and figuring out and reflecting on what works for this family and child. Young and colleagues (2006) emphasize that informed choice is not synonymous with providing information that is neutral or functionally descriptive. Rather, it is important to provide evaluative information that supports families in understanding inherent benefits, risks, uncertainties, and expectations associated with particular choices.

As an example, the family of a child with auditory neuropathy had a strong desire to use cued speech with their preschooler. They devoted themselves to learning cued speech, but struggled to master the system and incorporate it as they communicated with their child. They subsequently decided to pursue cochlear implantation, and their child was successful in developing spoken language without the aid of visual methods. As illustrated by the example, it is not possible to say one decision or approach was right and the other was wrong. The point is that families benefit from actively pursuing their goals and learning to reflect and evaluate how the decision is working for them. Knowing that decisions can be altered in response to the child's needs and successes may make decisions less weighty and daunting.

FCEI principles reinforce the view that decision-making authority rests squarely with the family (Dunst et al., 1988). Families desire that professionals respect and support the decisions that they make (DesGeorges, 2003). This requires flexible professionals who can reflect on their own value judgments in their work with families. Families will vary in what experiences and information will best support their ongoing efforts to make informed decisions. The challenge to the service provider is to flexibly support the families' process of gaining knowledge, skills, and experiences that lead to strengthened abilities in decision making, reflection, problem solving, and advocacy.

### Are Early Intervention Programs Truly Family Centered?

The need for family-centered approaches in early intervention is widely accepted as recommended practice, yet evidence suggests that there are major gaps in implementation. Several investigators have studied home visit practices in early childhood special education and have reported that many providers are not implementing participatory, **relationship-focused** interventions (Campbell & Sawyer, 2007; McBride & Peterson, 1997). Direct examination of videotapes from home visits revealed that most providers (70%) were working directly with the child while caregivers observed (Campbell & Sawyer, 2007). This finding is concerning, given the challenges of fostering caregiver competence when learners are engaged only as spectators. When parents are observing rather than participating, they miss opportunities to discover how strategies work in their own natural interactions with the child, and service providers miss the chance to learn from and support those efforts. Given that the goal is to promote what happens between visits, it is critical to engage caregivers in participatory learning.

Another study of early intervention practices explored providers' understanding of participation-based services and beliefs about factors that hindered or promoted the provision of recommended practice with families (Fleming, Sawyer, & Campbell, 2011). Results suggested that providers had an incomplete understanding of participation-based services. For example, only a few providers discussed the importance of embedding interventions into families' routines, and only half of the 31 providers interviewed talked about their roles in teaching caregivers rather than the child. A majority of the providers reported working directly with the child on home visits, and some discussed this as a way to teach families. Interestingly, providers were asked to estimate the percentage of visits in which they were able to implement ideal services. The average response was 55.4% ($SD = 28.47$, range = 0–100). Notably, most providers identified factors related to the families (rather than to their own capabilities or attributes) as barriers to provision of optimal services. They discussed issues such as caregiver characteristics (e.g., level of education, motivation), home environment (e.g., disruption from siblings, phone calls, physical environment issues), and other major family stressors (e.g., poverty, illness). Parents' limited understanding of their roles in early intervention was also seen as a barrier. Given the diverse and challenging circumstances providers encounter in contemporary times, a high level of knowledge, skills, and personhood is required. Fleming and colleagues concluded from their results that there is need for service provider training that would result in better understanding of participation-based methods, their use on home visits, and participation in reflection to hone professional skills.

Programs may benefit from systematically evaluating the extent to which their services reflect the principles of family-centered early intervention. There are a number of helpful resources in this regard, and some are specific to families whose children are D/HH. The reader is referred to recent policy statements (Moeller et al., 2013; Muse et al., 2013) and recently developed early intervention outcome measures (Young, Gascon-Ramos, Campbell, & Bamford, 2009) that are specific to families of children who are D/HH. In addition, the reader can find many practical online resources from the Family, Infant and Preschool Program (FIPP; http://fipp.org/publications). This site includes many evidence-based checklists and tools for monitoring coaching practices and implementation of family-centered help-giving models.

### Addressing Unique Needs in Early Intervention: Working with Families from Culturally and Linguistically Diverse Backgrounds

Service providers must also have the knowledge and skills to work with families from diverse backgrounds, whose cultural practices, linguistic histories, and families of origin may differ considerably from that of the service provider (Brotherson et al., 2010). The term *cross-cultural competence* refers to the knowledge and skills needed by providers to appropriately partner with families from culturally and linguistically diverse (CLD) backgrounds. Specifically, cross-cultural competence is defined as "the ability to think, feel, and act in ways that acknowledge, respect, and build upon ethnic, sociocultural, and linguistic diversity" (Lynch & Hanson, 2004, p. 50).

The literature suggests that there are major gaps in implementation of recommended practices related to cross-cultural competence (Harry, 2008). Barriers to implementation include cultural misunderstandings and mistrust, tendencies by professionals to maintain deficiency views of CLD families, and conflicts in beliefs about appropriate goals for individuals with disabilities. The topic of cross-cultural competence is critically important in contemporary society. Unfortunately, it is beyond the scope of this chapter to explore the topic in any depth, so instead, two key points are emphasized. First, research suggests that there is an ongoing need to strengthen and prioritize preprofessional and in-service training related to cross-cultural competence (Harry, 2008). Second, early intervention service providers may want to strive for **cultural reciprocity** in their interactions with families. *Cultural reciprocity* is defined as a process of dialogue in which professionals "engage in explicit discussions with families regarding differences in cultural values and practices, bringing to the interactions an openness of mind, the ability to be reflective in their practice, and the ability to listen to the other perspective" (Kalyanpur & Harry, 2012, p. 19). They emphasized the need for professionals to learn from the discussions and make allowances for differences in perspectives as they seek to respond to family needs. Within this process, professionals cultivate the skills of introspection, reflection, and questioning—are there assumptions about the ways things should be in early intervention that are based in values of the majority culture and may not be a fit for this family? For example, the professional may have been raised to value achievement and self-reliance, whereas an Asian family may value the group more than the individual (Cook & Sparks, 2008). Another family may have culturally determined views about their role in teaching academic concepts early in development, which may differ from the views of the professional. Families and professionals may differ in how they define being D/HH, as in the case of culturally Deaf parents. A reflective process should support partners in navigating and accommodating to such differences in cultural practices, beliefs, and values.

## Case Study: Application to a Family

Rose is a charming, happy 2-year-old who has a bilateral, mild to moderately severe hearing loss, first detected through newborn hearing screening. She was fit with binaural hearing aids at 6 months of age, and shortly thereafter, the family relocated to a midwestern state due to the father's military service. Rose is the first and only child of this young couple. The mother's first language is Mandarin Chinese, although she is bilingual in English and Chinese. The father's first language is English, and he also speaks some Mandarin Chinese. During early home visits, the parents shared with their service provider their interest in using a bilingual approach with Rose, with plans for the mother to expose Rose primarily to Mandarin while the father would expose her primarily to English. The service provider began working in partnership with the family in support of their goal.

The mother was at home with Rose during the day while the father worked. When the father was deployed, he was typically gone for 2 to 3 months at a time, which limited family communication to weekly Skype calls. The mother sometimes took Rose on trips to visit her family in Taiwan for periods of 1–3 months. These changes in the family member's locations had an impact on service delivery and the balance of roles in the family system, including roles related to Rose's care, education, and language exposure. The mother became the primary communicative partner, and Rose's Mandarin Chinese began to flourish. The father had a strong desire for his daughter to master English, yet his opportunities to provide English exposure were limited by his work circumstances. When he returned to the United States, he would find that his daughter was progressing at a slower rate in English than in Mandarin, and at times he struggled to understand her Mandarin expressions. Although it was not possible for him to be more involved, he may have felt "left out" regarding Rose's language development and perhaps uneasy about how to achieve the family's bilingualism goals. It was essential to directly address possible concerns within the family–professional partnership.

With time and the establishment of trust in the relationship, the father began to participate more during home visits and share his concerns with the provider and his wife (see Video clip 4.8). The provider worked to respect and involve both parents in problem solving around this issue. During one visit, she asked the father what he and Rose enjoyed doing with each other. He invited Rose to climb in his lap so he could demonstrate their favorite book-reading activity. Rose pointed at pictures and named some in Mandarin. After labeling "apple" in Mandarin, the father said, "Yes, apple." Rose immediately smiled, looked at him, and imitated, "Apple!" The father was so proud that Rose was able to copy his model. This small example bolstered his confidence that his models were also contributing to her development. Importantly, owning the success allowed the father to be more hopeful about his daughter's potential to learn English, even if his models could not be as consistent as he desired (see Video clip 4.9). Maternal and paternal roles as language models remain an ongoing topic for discussion, and they continue to work to intentionally integrate both languages into activities at their home visits.

The service provider also found the need to accommodate to some of the cultural values of the mother. The mother's cultural orientation led her to strongly value education and to see a primary role for herself in teaching academic concepts to her daughter from an early age. The service provider commented that the family home was rich with instructional supplies and that a section of the living room "looked like a wonderful preschool." The service provider's orientation included values for developmentally appropriate practices—for example, following the child's lead and engaging in playful interactions around the child's interests. The service provider reflected on their different approaches with Rose and found ways to accommodate and appreciate the mother's values. She was able to promote the extension of some of these routines for the benefit of the child. For example, the mother took pride in her daughter's ability to name flashcards. The service provider shared the mother's and child's delight in this accomplishment. Then from the sidelines, she encouraged the mother to see what would happen if she presented four of the pictures and named them for Rose. Would she be able to identify them through auditory cues alone? The mother was successful in using this familiar routine to challenge Rose in new ways. As the partnership relationship grew, both parties began to expand familiar and new routines. For example, the mother enjoyed reading with her daughter, but her typical strategy was to ask Rose to name each picture in the book. With coaching, the mother became comfortable with allowing Rose to explore the pages while she commented and described.

Interestingly, the audiologist later reported data-logging values showing that Rose was not wearing her hearing aids during her full waking hours. The service provider opened a dialogue about this with the mother, who explained that after dinnertime, she and Rose were both ready for a break from the hearing aids. The service provider helped the mother put the hearing aid use in the context of her value for a high level of education for her daughter. She helped her see that nighttime book reading was a prime time for language stimulation. This discussion supported the mother in reframing her goals for hearing aid use in relation to her ultimate educational goals for her daughter. This case illustrates the importance of the reflective practices that are inherent in honoring families' cultures, values, and goals for their children.

## SUMMARY AND FUTURE DIRECTIONS

Today's families of infants who are D/HH typically enter the early intervention process at very early stages in their infants' lives. A primary goal of early intervention is to optimize infants' linguistic development by taking advantage of sensitive developmental periods. Fundamentally, this goal is best addressed in the context of the family system by supporting family members' confidence and competence in parenting the child and promoting developmental outcomes through natural, daily interactions. Service providers need the sensitivity and skills to build trusting, balanced partnerships with families and to incorporate both adult learning models and knowledge of the linguistic needs of young infants who are D/HH. Rather than providing direct therapy services for the infant, the service provider seeks to support and empower family members. In many respects, this is a tall order, and the implementation of family-centered models appears to be inconsistent in actual practice. Yet a large body of research documents the value of these practice principles for families. This leads to several implications for research and practice:

1.  There is a shortage of service providers with the specialty knowledge and skills needed to work with young infants and their families using both relational and participatory approaches. Family-centered early intervention requires that providers have expertise in infancy, deafness, and family-centered coaching models. Innovative in-service models should be considered to enhance provider expertise, including provision of mentoring experiences, opportunities to watch experienced providers, and experiences learning from families themselves.

2.  There are pressing research needs related to early intervention with families of children who are D/HH. Research is needed to determine the degree to which recommended practices are actually implemented with families and how effective they are in bringing about expected child and family outcomes. Typically, early intervention models and methods need to be adapted to the unique needs of the individual child and family. How effective are practitioners in making accommodations to family needs while fostering optimal outcomes?

3.  Measurement tools need to be developed to support programs in monitoring 1) the fidelity of early intervention implementation; 2) the degree to

which services are responsive to family-identified needs; 3) the degree to which family and child outcomes are affected; and 4) the degree to which family members feel supported, empowered, and confident for their journey with the child.

Effective parent–professional partnerships often lead to increased confidence and competence on the part of caregivers. These ingredients are fundamental to optimizing early development in infants who are D/HH.

## SUGGESTED READINGS

Brown, P.M., & Nott, P. (2006). Family-centered practice in early intervention for oral language development: Philosophy, methods, and results. In P.E. Spencer & M. Marschark (Eds.), *Advances in the spoken language development of deaf and hard-of-hearing children* (pp. 136–165). New York, NY: Oxford University Press.

This chapter describes the SOLAR model of early intervention for children who are D/HH. SOLAR stands for setting the scene (S), observing (O), listening (L), assessing (A), and responding (R). The model is based in family-centered practice principles.

Carr, G., Young, A., Hunt, R., McCracken, W., Skipp, A., Tatersall, H. (2006). *Informed choice, families and deaf children: Professional handbook*. Retrieved from http://media. education.gov.uk/assets/files/pdf/i/informed%20choice%20families%20and%20deaf %20children%20-%20professional%20handbook.pdf

This handbook offers practical tools and guidance on the principles of informed choice and ways to help families be informed decision makers.

Kalyanpur, M., & Harry, B. (2012). *Cultural reciprocity in special education: Building family-professional relationships*. Baltimore, MD: Paul H. Brookes Publishing Co.

This is an excellent resource that helps practitioners and families learn to examine their own values, appreciate and respect one another's differences, and collaborate on behalf of children.

## LEARNING ACTIVITIES

1.  Go to the resources provided at the Family, Infant and Preschool Program web site (http://fipp.org/publications/casetools). Review the Coaching Practices Scale provided by Rush and Shelden (2005). Consider how you might implement such practices on a home visit. What might be challenging?

2.  Interview a professional who is experienced in working with families on home visits. What is his or her approach if a family elects not to participate in sessions? What strategies have been successful in addressing this issue?

3.  Visit the Promoting Cultural & Linguistic Competency page (http://nccc .georgetown.edu/documents/ChecklistEIEC.pdf) and review the checklist on cultural competency. Assess yourself on this scale and consider goals you want to set for yourself on this topic.

4.  Visit the Hands & Voices web site (http://www.handsandvoices.org). Read about the Guide by Your Side program. Write a summary of the program and any advantages you see for families of a child who is D/HH.

## REFERENCES

Ambrose, S.E., VanDam, M., & Moeller, M.P. (2014). Linguistic input, electronic media, and communication outcomes of toddlers with hearing loss. *Ear and Hearing, 35*(2), 139–147.

Bagnato, S.J., Neisworth, J.T., & Pretti-Frontczak, K. (2010). *LINKing authentic assessment and early childhood intervention: Best measures for best practices* (2nd ed.). Baltimore, MD: Paul H. Brookes Publishing Co.

Bailey, D.B., Bruder, M.B., Hebbeler, K., Carta, J., Defosset, M., Greenwood, C. . . . Spiker, D. (2006). Recommended outcomes for families of young children with disabilities. *Journal of Early Intervention, 28*(4), 227–251.

Bailey, D.B., Hebbeler, K., Olmsted, M.G., Raspa, M., & Bruder, M.B. (2008). Measuring family outcomes: Considerations for large-scale data collection in early intervention. *Infants & Young Children, 21*(3), 194–206.

Bailey, D.B., Hebbeler, K., Spiker, D., Scarborough, A., Mallik, S., & Nelson, L. (2005). Thirty-six-month outcomes for families of children who have disabilities and participated in early intervention. *Pediatrics, 116*(6), 1346–1352.

Bailey, D.B., Nelson, L., Hebbeler, K., & Spiker, D. (2007). Modeling the impact of formal and informal supports for young children with disabilities and their families. *Pediatrics, 120*(4), e992–e1001.

Bailey, D.B., Raspa, M., & Fox, L.C. (2012). What is the future of family outcomes and family-centered services? *Topics in Early Childhood Special Education, 31*(4), 216–223.

Bailey, D.B., Raspa, M., Olmsted, M.G., Novak, S.P., Sam, A.M., Humphreys, B.P., . . . Guillen, C. (2011). Development and psychometric validation of the family out-comes survey—revised. *Journal of Early Intervention, 33*(1), 6–23.

Bandura, A. (1989). Regulation of cognitive processes through perceived self-efficacy. *Developmental Psychology, 25*(5), 729.

Baumwell, L., Tamis-LeMonda, C.S., & Bornstein, M.H. (1997). Maternal verbal sensitivity and child language comprehension. *Infant Behavior and Development, 20*(2), 247–258.

Bernheimer, L.P., & Weisner, T.S. (2007). "Let me just tell you what I do all day . . .": The family story at the center of intervention research and practice. *Infants & Young Children, 20*(3), 192–201.

Blue-Banning, M., Summers, J.A., Frankland, H.C., Nelson, L.L., & Beegle, G. (2004). Dimensions of family and professional partnerships: Constructive guidelines for collaboration. *Exceptional Children, 70*(2), 167–184.

Bodner-Johnson, B., & Sass-Lehrer, M. (2003). *The young deaf or hard of hearing child: A family-centered approach to early education.* Baltimore, MD: Paul H. Brookes Publishing Co.

Brandwein, M. "Motivating communication." Workshop presentation at Boys Town National Research Hospital, Omaha, NE, September 24, 2010.

Brotherson, M.J., Summers, J.A., Naig, L.A., Kyzar, K., Friend, A., Epley, P., . . . Turn-bull, A.P. (2010). Partnership patterns: Addressing emotional needs in early intervention. *Topics in Early Childhood Special Education, 30*(1), 32–45.

Brown, P.M., & Nott, P. (2006). Family-centered practice in early intervention for oral language development: Philosophy, methods, and results. In P.E. Spencer & M. Marschark (Eds.), *Advances in the spoken language development of deaf and hard-of-hearing children* (pp. 136–165). New York, NY: Oxford University Press.

Calderon, R., & Greenberg, M.T. (1997). The effectiveness of early intervention for deaf children and children with hearing loss. In M.J. Guralnick (Ed.), *The effectiveness of early intervention* (pp. 455–482.). Baltimore, MD: Paul H. Brookes Publishing Co.

Campbell, P.H., & Sawyer, L.B. (2007). Supporting learning opportunities in natural settings through participation-based services. *Journal of Early Intervention, 29*(4), 287–305.

Carotta, C. (2011). Auditory consulting resource network. Unpublished resource materials. BTNRH: Omaha, NE.

Carotta, C. Cline, K. M., & Brennan, K. (2014). *Auditory consultant resource network handbook.* Omaha, NE: Boys Town National Research Hospital.

Coleman, P.K., & Karraker, K.H. (2003). Maternal self-efficacy beliefs, competence in parenting, and toddlers' behavior and developmental status. *Infant Mental Health Journal, 24*(2), 126–148.

Cook, R.E., & Sparks, S.N. (2008). *The art and practice of home visiting: Early intervention for children with special needs and their families:* Baltimore, MD: Paul H. Brookes Publishing Co.

Cruz, I., Quittner, A.L., Marker, C., & DesJardin, J.L. (2013). Identification of effective strategies to promote language in deaf children with cochlear implants. *Child Development, 84*(2), 543–559.

Dempsey, I., & Keen, D. (2008). A review of processes and outcomes in family-centered services for children with a disability. *Topics in Early Childhood Special Education, 28*(1), 42–52.

DesGeorges, J. (2003). Family perceptions of early hearing, detection, and intervention systems: Listening to and learning from families. *Mental Retardation and Developmental Disabilities Research Reviews, 9*(2), 89–93.

DesJardin, J.L. (2003). Assessing parental perceptions of self-efficacy and involvement in families of young children with hearing loss. *Volta Review, 103*(4), 391–409.

DesJardin, J.L. (2005). Maternal perceptions of self-efficacy and involvement in the auditory development of young children with prelingual deafness. *Journal of Early Intervention, 27*(3), 193–209.

DesJardin, J.L., & Eisenberg, L.S. (2007). Maternal contributions: Supporting language development in young children with cochlear implants. *Ear and Hearing, 28*(4), 456–469.

Dromi, E., & Ingber, S. (1999). Israeli mothers' expectations from early intervention with their preschool deaf children. *Journal of Deaf Studies and Deaf Education, 4*(1), 50–68.

Dunst, C.J. (2002). Family-centered practices: Birth through high school. *Journal of Special Education, 36*(3), 139–147.

Dunst, C.J., Boyd, K., Trivette, C.M., & Hamby, D.W. (2002). Family-oriented program models and professional helpgiving practices. *Family Relations, 51*(3), 221–229.

Dunst, C.J., & Dempsey, I. (2007). Family–professional partnerships and parenting competence, confidence, and enjoyment. *International Journal of Disability, Development and Education, 54*(3), 305–318.

Dunst, C.J., & Trivette, C.M. (2009). Capacity-building family-systems intervention practices. *Journal of Family Social Work, 12*(2), 119–143.

Dunst, C.J., Trivette, C.M., & Deal, A.G. (Eds.). (1988). *Enabling and empowering families: Principles and guidelines for practice.* Cambridge, MA: Brookline Books.

Dunst, C.J., Trivette, C.M., & Hamby, D.W. (2006). *Family support program quality and parent, family and child benefits. Winterberry Press Monograph Series:* ERIC. Retrieved from http:// www .wbpress .com

Dunst, C.J., Trivette, C.M., & Hamby, D.W. (2007). Meta-analysis of family-centered helpgiving practices research. *Mental Retardation and Developmental Disabilities Research Reviews, 13*(4), 370–378.

Dunst, C.J., Trivette, C.M., & Hamby, D.W. (2008). *Research synthesis and meta-analysis of studies of family-centered practices. Winterberry Press Monograph Series:* ERIC. Retrieved from http://www.wbpress.com

Fey, M.E., Krulik, T.E., Loeb, D.F., & Proctor-Williams, K. (1999). Sentence recast use by parents of children with typical language and children with specific language impairment. *American Journal of Speech-Language Pathology, 8*(3), 273.

Fleming, J.L., Sawyer, L.B., & Campbell, P.H. (2011). Early intervention providers' perspectives about implementing participation-based practices. *Topics in Early Childhood Special Education, 30*(4), 233–244.

Guimond, A.B., Wilcox, M.J., & Lamorey, S.G. (2008). The Early Intervention Parenting Self-Efficacy Scale (EIPSES): Scale construction and initial psychometric evidence. *Journal of Early Intervention, 30*(4), 295–320.

Harry, B. (2008). Collaboration with culturally and linguistically diverse families: Ideal versus reality. *Exceptional Children, 74*(3), 372–388.

Ingber, S., Al-Yagon, M., & Dromi, E. (2010). Mothers' involvement in early intervention for children with hearing loss: The role of maternal characteristics and context-based perceptions. *Journal of Early Intervention, 32*(5), 351–369.

Ingber, S., & Dromi, E. (2010). Actual versus desired family-centered practice in early intervention for children with hearing loss. *Journal of Deaf Studies and Deaf Education, 15*(1), 59–71.

Joint Committee on Infant Hearing (JCIH). (2007). Year 2007 position statement: Principles and guidelines for early hearing detection and intervention programs. *Pediatrics, 120*(4), 898–921.

Jones, T.L., & Prinz, R.J. (2005). Potential roles of parental self-efficacy in parent and child adjustment: A review. *Clinical psychology review, 25*(3), 341–363.

Kalyanpur, M., & Harry, B. (2012). *Cultural reciprocity in special education: Building family-professional relationships.* Baltimore, MD: Paul H. Brookes Publishing Co.

Luterman, D., Kurtzer-White, E., & Seewald, R.C. (1999). *The young deaf child.* Hollister, CA: York Press.

Lynch, E.W., & Hanson, M. (2004). *Developing cross-cultural competence: A guide for working with children and their families* (3rd ed.). Baltimore, MD: Paul H: Brookes Publishing Co.

McBride, S.L., & Peterson, C. (1997). Home-based early intervention with families of children with disabilities: Who is doing what? *Topics in Early Childhood Special Education, 17*(2), 209–233.

McCreery, R.W., Bentler, R.A., & Roush, P.A. (2013). Characteristics of hearing aid fittings in infants and young children. *Ear and Hearing, 34*(6), 701–710.

McNaughton, D., Hamlin, D., McCarthy, J., Head-Reeves, D., & Schreiner, M. (2008). Learning to listen: Teaching an active listening strategy to preservice education professionals. *Topics in Early Childhood Special Education, 27*(4), 223–231.

McWilliam, R.A. (2010a). *Routines-based early intervention: Supporting young children and their families.* Baltimore, MD: Paul H. Brookes Publishing Co.

McWilliam, R.A. (2010b). *Working with families of young children with special needs.* New York, NY: Guilford Press.

McWilliam, R.A., Casey, A.M., & Sims, J. (2009). The routines-based interview: A method for gathering information and assessing needs. *Infants & Young Children, 22*(3), 224–233.

McWilliam, R.A., Tocci, L., & Harbin, G.L. (1998). Family-centered service providers' discourse and behavior. *Topics in Early Childhood Special Education, 18*(4), 206–221.

Moeller, M.P. (2000). Early intervention and language development in children who are deaf and hard of hearing. *Pediatrics, 106*(3), E43.

Moeller, M.P., Carr, G., Seaver, L., Stredler-Brown, A., & Holzinger, D. (2013). Best practices in family-centered early intervention for children who are deaf or hard of hearing: An international consensus statement. *Journal of Deaf Studies and Deaf Education, 18*(4), 429–445. doi:10.1093/deafed/ent034

Moeller, M.P., & Condon, M. (1994). A collaborative, problem-solving approach to early intervention. In J. Roush and N.D. Matkin (Eds.), *Infants and toddlers with hearing loss: Identification, assessment and family-centered intervention* (pp. 163–192). Parkton, MD: York Press, Inc.

Moeller, M.P., & Tomblin, J.B. (2015). An introduction to the outcomes of children with hearing loss study. *Ear and Hearing.*

Muse, C., Harrison, J., Yoshinaga-Itano, C., Grimes, A., Brookhouser, P.E., Epstein, S., . . . Martin, B. (2013). Supplement to the JCIH 2007 position statement: Principles and guidelines for early intervention after confirmation that a child is deaf or hard of hearing. *Pediatrics, 131*(4), e1324–e1349.

Nittrouer, S. (2010). *Early development of children with hearing loss.* San Diego, CA: Plural.

Proctor-Williams, K., Fey, M.E., & Loeb, D.F. (2001). Parental recasts and production of copulas and articles by children with specific language impairment and typical language. *American Journal of Speech-Language Pathology, 10*(2), 155–168.

Roberts, M.Y., & Kaiser, A.P. (2011). The effectiveness of parent-implemented language interventions: A meta-analysis. *American Journal of Speech-Language Pathology, 20*(3), 180–199.

Rush, D., & Shelden, M. (2005). Evidence-based definition of coaching practices. *CASEinPoint, 1*(6), 1–6.

Sarant, J.Z., Holt, C.M., Dowell, R.C., Rickards, F.W., & Blamey, P.J. (2009). Spoken language development in oral preschool children with permanent childhood deafness. *Journal of Deaf Studies and Deaf Education, 14*(2), 205–217.

Shelden, M.L., & Rush, D.D. (2010). A primary-coach approach to teaming and supporting families in early childhood intervention. In R. McWilliam (Ed.), *Working with families of young children with special needs* (pp. 175–202). New York, NY: Guilford Press.

Snow, C.E. (1994). *Beginning from baby talk: Twenty years of research on input and interaction.* New York, NY: Cambridge University Press.

Stredler-Brown, A., Moeller, M. P., Gallegos, R., & Corwin, J., & Pittman, P. (2004). *The art and science of a home visit* (DVD). Boys Town, NE: Boys Town Press.

Swanson, J., Raab, M., & Dunst, C.J. (2011). Strengthening family capacity to provide young children everyday natural learning opportunities. *Journal of Early Childhood Research, 9*(1), 66–80.

Szagun, G., & Stumper, B. (2012). Age or experience? The influence of age at implantation, social and linguistic environment on language development in children with cochlear implants. *Journal of Speech, Language, and Hearing Research, 55*(6), 1640–1654.

Tamis-LeMonda, C.S., Bornstein, M.H., & Baumwell, L. (2001). Maternal responsiveness and children's achievement of language milestones. *Child Development, 72*(3), 748–767.

Tomblin, J.B., Oleson, J.J., Ambrose, S.E., Walker, E., & Moeller, M.P. (2014). The influence of hearing aids on the speech and language development of children with hearing loss. *JAMA Otolaryngology—Head & Neck Surgery, 140*(5), 403–409.

Trivette, C.M., & Dunst, C.J. (2007). Capacity-building family-centered help-giving practices. *Winterberry Research Reports, 1*(1), 1–10.

Trivette, C.M., Dunst, C.J., & Hamby, D.W. (2010). Influences of family-systems intervention practices on parent-child interactions and child development. *Topics in Early Childhood Special Education, 30*(1), 3–19.

Walker, E.A., Spratford, M., Moeller, M.P., Oleson, J., Ou, H., Roush, P., & Jacobs, S. (2013). Predictors of hearing aid use time in children with mild-to-severe hearing loss. *Language, Speech, and Hearing Services in the Schools, 44*(1), 73–88.

Wilcox, M.J., & Woods, J. (2011). Participation as a basis for developing early intervention outcomes. *Language, Speech, and Hearing Services in Schools, 42*(3), 365–378.

Young, A., Carr, G., Hunt, R., McCracken, W., Skipp, A., & Tattersall, H. (2006). Informed choice and deaf children: Underpinning concepts and enduring challenges. *Journal of Deaf Studies and Deaf Education, 11*(3), 322–336.

Young, A., Gascon-Ramos, M., Campbell, M., & Bamford, J. (2009). The design and validation of a parent-report questionnaire for assessing the characteristics and quality of early intervention over time. *Journal of Deaf Studies and Deaf Education, 14*(4), 422–435.

# 5

# Family-Centered Early Intervention

*Supporting Spoken Language Development in Infants and Young Children*

Mary Pat Moeller and Elizabeth B. Cole

Early identification that is linked with effective interventions places families in a proactive position to promote spoken language development in their infants who are deaf or hard of hearing (D/HH). Consider the typical experience of a family around the year 1995. The youngest child in the Jones family turned 2 years of age. For several months, the family has expressed concerns about her limited speech and language development. They were reassured by professionals that she was probably just a "late talker." Now they discover that she has hearing levels in the moderate range and that they need to fit her with bilateral hearing aids (HAs), at a time when she is in the throes of the "terrible twos." The parents feel guilty about the time they lost and about the occasions when they reprimanded her for not paying attention. This was an all-too-familiar scenario for families in the era before the widespread implementation of newborn hearing screening (NHS). Children were typically identified around 2 years of age (Halpin, Smith, Widen, & Chertoff, 2010; Stein, Jabaley, Spitz, Stoakley, & McGee, 1990), which in today's terms is quite late, and families were placed in the awkward position of needing to make up for lost time.

Fast forward to the era following NHS—families routinely get an early start with support to naturally promote their infants' communicative development. National statistics indicate that 97% of infants are screened *at birth,* and 69.2% of those referred for diagnosis are identified by 3 months of age as either hearing or D/HH (Centers for Disease Control and Prevention [CDC], 2013). The viability and success of spoken language approaches have been bolstered by these service advancements that include access to technologies and early interventions.

This chapter explores the implementation of family-centered early intervention principles when the family's goal is to promote spoken language development through primarily an auditory route with their child who is D/HH. As emphasized throughout this text, no one intervention approach can be expected to meet the individual needs of all children. Families require support in the informed decision-making process (see Chapter 4). However, many families elect spoken language intervention approaches given the access to effective early interventions. This is not surprising, given that 95% of children who are deaf are born to hearing parents (Mitchell & Karchmer, 2004), who often choose for their children to communicate in the spoken language used in the home. Chapter 4 provides a comprehensive discussion of the principles of family-centered early intervention (FCEI). This chapter discusses some unique components of family-centered practice that are considered to be essential for the success of spoken language approaches.

Interventions focused on spoken language development through maximal use of residual hearing were historically known as aural or oral approaches (Beattie, 2006). In the United States, both auditory-verbal and auditory-oral interventions have been widely implemented. Auditory-verbal methods had their roots in unisensory (acoupedic) approaches that emphasized maximal development of listening skills as the route to spoken language. Auditory-oral methods also focused on listening development but incorporated some level of visual support (speechreading). Beattie (2006) suggests that these differences may be disappearing in contemporary practice; given the improvements in hearing instruments, many practitioners focus on developing spoken language through listening. As described in Chapter 7, the evolution of Listening and Spoken Language Specialist (LSLS) Certification through the Alexander Graham Bell Association provides a rigorous specialty certification process to support quality in implementation of early auditory-verbal intervention.

## THEORETICAL BASIS SUPPORTING EARLY INTERVENTION PRACTICES: WHAT MATTERS?

### Access to Input Matters

Auditory access to linguistic input is considered to be essential to the successful development of spoken language in young children. There are two issues related to access that serve as theoretical underpinnings of spoken language interventions for children who are D/HH. The first recognizes the primary role that auditory perception and processing plays in accessing relevant features of spoken linguistic input to promote learning. This recognition of the primacy of audition (see Chapter 7) in the service of spoken language learning leads to a major focus on developing and honing aided listening skills as a primary route to spoken language development for young children who are D/HH. The second issue is that children who are D/HH are at risk to experience reductions in overall language exposure due to distorted, incomplete, or **inconsistent access** to the input (Moeller & Tomblin, in press). Because reduced exposure could lead to language delays, the intervention process focuses on optimizing **audibility** with assistive technologies to reduce or remove barriers to listening to spoken language. Caregiver–child interaction styles that are known to support linguistic development are encouraged in order to counteract the reductions in overall language exposure imposed by the child's hearing levels.

Infants who are typically developing make remarkable advances in auditory-perceptual skills in the first year of life. Consider just a few of these achievements. In the first year of life, infants' auditory perceptual biases "increasingly conform to native language patterns" (Werker & Yeung, 2005, p. 525). For example, infants who are only 9 to 10 months of age prefer to listen to words that follow the permissible patterns of sound combinations in their native language (phonotactics) and not to those of nonnative languages. Infants also prefer words that follow their native language stress patterns (Werker & Yeung, 2005). Kuhl (2000) stressed that simply by listening to language, infants become pattern detectors. They attend to statistical patterns in the input, including distributional and phonological cues, in order to identify word boundaries in running speech and to learn words and grammar (Monaghan, Charter, & Chistiansen, 2005; St. Clair, Monaghan, & Christiansen, 2010). Language development also requires that infants learn essential phonetic contrasts that distinguish one word from another (Farmer, Monaghan, Misyak, & Christiansen, 2011). These accomplishments require tuning into the acoustic-phonetic information in the speech signal. Social interaction plays a key role in these developments (Kuhl, 2010) along with regular language exposure that is meaningful and varied (Tomblin et al., in press) Thus, the value of auditory-linguistic exposure for spoken language learning is evident from very early stages of development. This supports the emphasis in spoken language interventions with infants on fine-tuning listening skills to enable typical perceptual processes to unfold. *Early* access to optimized audibility and intervention is also considered important for taking the greatest advantage of sensitive periods of brain development.

The desired situation is that the child is identified as D/HH at birth and appropriate hearing aids are fit and worn all waking hours from a very young age, with educational support provided for the family throughout at least the first three years of the child's life. However, for a number of reasons, children who are D/HH may experience reductions or inconsistency in language exposure that can place them at risk for language delays. Unfortunately, even when children have their hearing screened at birth and hearing status diagnosed soon after, months can elapse before device fitting is accomplished, resulting in diminished or incomplete exposure to sounds and speech. Several studies from the post-NHS era report average ages of first hearing aid fitting of 6 to 11 months (Harrison, Roush, & Wallace, 2003; Holte et al., 2012; Spivak, Sokol, Auerbach, & Gershkovich, 2009). Thus, even though a child may be identified as D/HH at an early age, there may be a period of auditory deprivation during a portion of the first year of life. Assistive technologies that are not fit optimally, are not worn consistently, present distortion, or limit perception of certain consonants may also lead to reduced or inconsistent access to input. The degree and configuration of the child's hearing levels can impose limits on the potential for providing audibility with amplification (Bagatto et al., 2011). Furthermore, excessive noise and nonideal reverberation times in the environment can create additional barriers to linguistic access for children who are

D/HH. Child care settings, for example, are often far from ideal acoustically, which means that the child is listening to speech for major parts of the day under adverse conditions (Crandell & Smaldino, 2000). Distance from the speaker also affects signal level in a way that creates challenges for language access, including learning through overhearing the speech of others. Given the numerous and varied elements that can compromise access to linguistic input, the key emphasis on promoting auditory access is well justified.

## Caregiver–Child Interactions with High Quality Input Matters

Considerable research in the typical development context has documented features of caregiver–child interaction that promote language learning. Spoken language interventions seek to promote these identified language-facilitating features of maternal input and caregiver–child interaction. Specifically, there is extensive evidence that children's early language development is shaped by the linguistic input to which they are exposed. For example, children who are exposed to larger quantities of talk tend to demonstrate stronger vocabulary growth and faster lexical processing than children exposed to less talk (Hoff & Naigles, 2002; Hurtado, Marchman, & Fernald, 2008; Huttenlocher et al., 1991). In addition, higher levels of maternal education and richer language models are associated with better language outcomes in children who hear (Hoff, 2003).

Due to limitations in access and overall exposure, some have suggested that children who are D/HH may be more dependent than typical peers on the presence of optimal input for language learning (Cole & Flexer, 2016; Snow, 1994; Szagun & Stumper, 2012), and naturalistic early intervention strategies are predicated on this notion. Nittrouer (2010) found that language development was more sensitive to parental responsiveness in children who are D/HH compared with typical peers, providing further support for naturalistic approaches that foster responsive interactions.

Novel evidence is emerging about features of mother–child interaction that promote spoken language development in children with cochlear implants (CIs). DesJardin and Eisenberg (2007) reported that mothers' use of two facilitative language techniques (recasts and open-ended questions) positively influenced children's language outcomes. The complexity of mothers' utterances also appeared to influence children's language development. Cruz, Quittner, Marker, and DesJardin (2013) also found that parents' use of higher level language facilitation strategies, such as parallel talk, recasts, and open-ended questions, was related to children's expressive language outcomes. They also found that the number of different words mothers used benefited children's receptive language. Children with the strongest language outcomes had mothers who were highly sensitive responders and used many high-quality features in their talk (Quittner, Cruz, Barker, Tobey, Eisenberg, Niparko, & Childhood Development After Cochlear Implantation Investigative Team, 2013). Similarly, Szagun and Stumper (2012) found that the richness of maternal language input, including higher mean length of maternal utterances and more frequent **expansions**, was related to better linguistic progress in children with CIs. Collectively, this body of work supports promoting families' responsiveness to their children's growing communicative skills in early intervention.

Families of children who are D/HH also benefit from strategies that encourage responsive interactions and high-quality features in talk. Ambrose, Walker, Unflat-Berry, Oleson, and Moeller (in press) found that children who were D/HH were exposed to language input that was more limited in quality and quantity than the talk directed to a matched group of 3-year-old hearing peers. In addition, directive styles were associated with poorer language out -comes for children who are D/HH. The results suggested that some caregivers need support in order to provide optimal conditions for language learning, including encouragement to adopt a style that elicits conversation.

Another large-scale study examined longitudinal samples of caregiver–child interactions in children with moderate to profound hearing levels (Nittrouer, 2010). Several important findings came from this study that should guide early intervention practices. Parents of children who were D/HH responded less often to their children's communicative attempts than did parents of hearing children. This was considered to be especially concerning because the study results showed that language development is *more sensitive* to parental responsiveness in children who are D/HH than in hearing children. The key factor found to influence language development was parental responsiveness to children's communicative attempts, especially when those attempts included at least one spoken word. It was concluded that service providers should promote interaction styles that 1) encourage children to generate language, 2) respond sensitively to children's communicative attempts (especially those with words), and 3) expand upon the language that the child is explicitly trying to produce (Nittrouer, 2010, p. 277). Taken together, these studies provide support and direction for what should be emphasized in early intervention.

### Adult Learning Methods Matter

Because family-centered early intervention focuses on empowering parents as the child's primary teachers, there is simultaneous focus on infant and adult learning. This dictates the need for service providers to be conversant with principles and theories of adult learning and be able to identify the preferred learning approaches within individual families. Malcolm Knowles (1970) described five characteristics of adult learners, which are listed here along with implications for early intervention:

1.  *Self-directed learning is preferred:* This suggests that adults prefer to have a sense of agency or a sense of control over their learning. As adults, we want to have some sense of direction about where we want to go with our learning. In the early intervention context, this means that we want to position the adult to help direct both the learning and how the partnership will form and evolve. Through shared direction, adults gain ownership of the process and the learning.

2.  *Life experiences support new learning:* Caregivers come to the intervention process with a wealth of life experiences that are foundational to their learning. Connection to caregivers' experiences promotes

self-efficacy and efficiency in new learning. This suggests that the service provider should draw on concepts and experiences that are already familiar to the learner when practicing new strategies (e.g., find ways to secure the child's joint attention and utilize this knowledge when learning to secure attention through audition). Caregivers should practice and problem-solve while drawing on their personal experiences.

3.  *Learning needs are dictated by changing roles:* Caregivers of children who are D/HH engage in multiple roles each day. They may shift in a single day through roles as a worker, a parent, a partner in early intervention, a consumer of child care services, and a volunteer. A mother may be confident in parenting her child but uncertain how to guide the child care providers in providing what her child needs. Service providers should be prepared to support caregivers in addressing the skills needed for new roles.

4.  *Interest is in immediate application of knowledge:* Knowledge is most meaningful when it can be applied and adapted to authentic life situations. Use of natural routines is a means for applying relevant intervention strategies in a meaningful context. This supports active adult participation in intervention during natural routines. When practice is embedded in daily routines, the application to daily life is supported.

5.  *Internal rather than external factors provide motivation for learning:* As adults, we tend to pursue learning about topics that align with what we value or are passionate about. A father who loved fishing made sure that his son knew the names and functions of every tool in the tackle box. A mother who valued connecting with others was innovative in pursuing social experiences for her deaf preschooler. Service providers can support families in both recognizing these inherent values and capitalize on them as they parent their children.

Notably, adults vary in their learning styles and preferred methods for accessing information. Service providers need to be sensitive to this issue and provide resources that support individual adults' styles and preferences.

## EMPIRICAL BASIS

Researchers have recently examined the effectiveness of auditory-verbal therapy (AVT), and international findings have been summarized by Fitzpatrick, Rhoades, Dornan, Thomas, & Goldberg (2012). Although the limitations of existing studies are acknowledged, results suggest that many children enrolled in AVT programs develop spoken language skills commensurate with typical peers. Another systematic review of the research on auditory-verbal therapy pointed to the lack of well-controlled studies and suggested that the overall evidence was inconclusive (Brennan-Jones, White, Rush, & Law, 2014). Previously, Rhoades (2006) reviewed research outcomes on AVT from an evidence-based perspective. In her review of the extant literature, she identified several class II studies (quasi-experimental) that she concluded yielded *emergent justification* for auditory-verbal methods (Fratalli, 1998). Importantly, Rhoades used her analysis to promote the need for multisite studies of children's outcomes in AVT programs using norm-referenced procedures. She posed a number of future directions for research, including the need to ascertain if auditory-verbal methods are as effective for low-income families as they are for middle-or high-income families. She also cited the need to examine fidelity of interventions and how strategies may need to be adapted for children with multiple disabilities or those from multilingual families. Clearly, Rhoade's suggestions would go a long way toward determining the efficacy and efficiency of AVT and other approaches to intervention.

As explained in the introductory chapter to this text, contemporary interventions are targeted at a new generation of families and children, who have much earlier access to improved technology and early education programs. These major advancements are a somewhat recent phenomenon (over the past 10 to 15 years). In many ways, it is not surprising that research documentation has failed to keep pace with service innovations. For the first time in history, a majority of the youngest children are identified early enough that researchers can examine the impact of technology and interventions on foundational language stages. Several multisite collaborations have worked to study large population-based samples of children with CIs (Ching et al., 2009; Geers, Strube, Tobey, & Moog, 2011; Niparko et al., 2010), hearing aids (Tomblin, Oleson, Ambrose, Walker, & Moeller, 2014), or combined groups (Ching et al., 2013; Nittrouer, 2010), and additional monitoring of early intervention efforts on a large scale are ongoing (e.g., Colorado Home Intervention Program). Two conclusions that can be drawn from these studies are that 1) the average spoken language outcomes are improving for young children who are D/HH in contrast to the historical literature but 2) there is considerable between-subject variability in outcomes. This common variability underscores the need for further research directed at understanding the mechanisms and factors that leave some children who are D/HH at risk for delayed language while others perform like typically developing age-mates in spoken language.

Service providers need to recognize the limitations in current evidence, monitor the efforts to expand the evidence base, follow recommended practice guidelines (JCIH; Moeller, Carr, Seaver, Stredler-Brown, & Holzinger, 2013; Muse et al., 2013), and incorporate the values and preferences of the family in individualizing the intervention process.

## Use of Assessment Tools and Processes to Monitor Growth and Guide Next Steps

Assessment in birth-to-3 programs is typically envisioned as a collaborative decision-making process. Parents and professionals systematically observe the infant's/young child's responses, revise their appraisals, and reach consensus about the developmental growth and changing needs of the child and family. This flexible, ongoing process has a different purpose than administration of a battery of norm-referenced, standardized tests. Norm-referenced measures are particularly useful for identifying individual differences in development and determining if the child is performing like typically developing peers. However, they may be less helpful in identifying targets for intervention. It is beyond the scope of this chapter to provide comprehensive coverage of standardized tests, criterion-referenced tools, and parent report measures and checklists available for infants and young children (see Bradham & Houston, 2015, for an annotated list of assessments commonly used with children who are D/HH). Rather, this chapter will focus on selected **criterion-referenced measures**, checklists, and other observational procedures that are useful in guiding the intervention process (e.g., measuring progress, forecasting next steps). It is important to recognize that there remains a great need for further research and development of sensitive assessment tools for use in **early intervention**. Service providers need to recognize the limitations of assessment tools designed for the youngest groups of children and interpret them with caution, given the wide ranges in ages at which specific linguistic developmental landmarks are achieved by individual children, especially in the second year of life. In the sections that follow, assessment resources are described in relation to several foundational areas of early intervention progress monitoring:

1. Family–child interactions

2. **Temperament**

3. Characteristics of the language environment

4. Listening development

5. Vocal development

6. Early communicative development

7. Early stages of sentence development

**Family–Child Interactions**   Given that the goal of family-centered intervention is to support families in nurturing the infant through responsive interactions, joint engagement, and promotion of communication through daily routines, it is helpful to routinely observe family–child interactions over time. For some families, rich, positive interactions seem to proceed intuitively with minimal support. Yet these parents may not feel confident in their skills, and observation with feedback can promote both confidence and enjoyment. Other families may experience barriers as they seek to interact in warm and nurturing ways. It is natural and common for parents to be overwhelmed by the information that the infant is D/HH, the multiple appointments, and the flood of new technical terms. One parent of an infant who was premature and HH remarked, "She came home from the hospital with all this equipment, and then we added hearing aids. To be honest, I just wanted a baby without equipment." Even earmolds can be a daily reminder of an initially painful circumstance the parents would rather forget. An empathic and responsive service provider can support the family in addressing these natural reactions.

The process of joint observation of family–child interactions in the context of a trusting parent–professional partnership is a *confidence-building* process. To guide this process, the service provider needs to focus on behaviors that are known to promote early social, cognitive, auditory, and spoken language development. Figure 5.1 is an adaptation of a framework proposed by Cole & Flexer (2016) to maximize caregiver effectiveness in promoting auditory-linguistic

| Facilitative caregiver behavior | Comments/observations |
|---|---|
| ***Sensitivity to child*** | |
| 1. Handles and interacts with the child in a positive manner (e.g., parenting style) | |
| 2. Recognizes the infant's/child's cues, interprets them correctly, and responds | |
| 3. Understands and accommodates to the child's temperament | |
| 4. Paces play and talk in synchrony with child's tempo | |
| 5. Follows the child's interests much of the time; is flexible as child's interests and attention shifts | |
| 6. Provides stimulation and play opportunities that are appropriate for age and stage | |
| 7. Encourages and facilitates child's play with objects and materials | |
| 8. Shows enthusiasm and is attentive to the interaction | |
| ***Conversational behaviors:*** ***Responsiveness and quality dimensions*** | |
| 1. Interprets the intent of infant presymbolic communication and comments (e.g., infant points; caregiver r esponds, "You want the ball.") | |
| 2. Recognizes the child's communicative attempts regardless of form (e.g., gesture, eye gaze, vocalization, body language) | |
| 3. Responds to the child's communicative attempts | |
| 4. Imitates the child's productions if developmentally appropriate | |
| 5. Provides labels for objects child is attending to or gesturing toward | |
| 6. Describes object, event, or activity on which the child is focused (i.e., parallel talk: "You are building with blocks") | |
| 7. Provides the child with words appropriate to what he or she is trying to express (including thoughts, desires, and feelings) | |
| 8. Uses techniques that offer the child a chance to take conversational turns (e.g., wait time, pausing expectantly) | |
| 9. Expands the child's utterances grammatically | |
| 10. Expands the child's utterances by adding new meanings | |
| 11. Prompts play and exploration ("Should we feed your baby? What else can we try?") | |
| 12. Asks open-ended questions that promote talking and/or thinking outside the immediate context (e.g., "Have you ever been fishing?") | |
| 13. Gives reasons for events and actions of others | |

*(continued)*

**Figure 5.1.**    An observational tool for supporting caregiver effectiveness in promoting child development. (*Sources:* Cole & Flexer, 2016, with additions from Baumwell, Tamis-LeMonda, & Bornstein, 1997; Cruz, Quittner, Marker, & DesJardin, 2013; Hoff & Naigles, 2002; Tamis-LeMonda, Bornstein, & Baumwell, 2001.)

**Figure 5.1.** *(continued)*

| Facilitative caregiver behavior | Comments/observations |
|---|---|
| ***Maintaining shared attention*** | |
| 1. Follows child's lead and attempts to engage the child | |
| 2. Talks about what interests the child | |
| 3. Uses voice (first) to attract child's attention to objects, events, or self | |
| 4. Uses body movement, facial expression, gestures, and touch appropriately in attracting child's attention to objects, events, or self | |
| 5. Uses phrases and sentences of appropriate length and complexity | |
| ***Caregiver speech characteristics*** | |
| 1. Uses interesting, animated voice that conveys warmth | |
| 2. Facial expressions match what is expressed | |
| 3. Speaks to the child with appropriate rate, intensity, and pitch | |
| 4. Uses typical, unexaggerated mouth movements | |
| 5. Uses audition-maximizing techniques | |
| 6. Anticipates auditory access barriers and addresses them | |
| 7. Uses gestures as appropriate | |

development in little ones who are D/HH. This framework provides a guide to major aspects of interaction and caregiver behaviors that are known to facilitate child development: sensitivity to the child, conversational behaviors (including responsiveness and quality dimensions), maintaining shared attention, and use of child-directed speech features. These essential characteristics of interaction will be covered in more detail in the intervention section of this chapter in terms of promoting their use with families.

Cole and Flexer (2016) recommend that the service provider video-record about 15 minutes of caregiver–child interaction in a natural routine. The evidence-based content in Figure 5.1 can then be used as a general guide regarding adult behaviors that matter for the child's development and nurturing. Parents are engaged in a reflective process of reviewing video segments with the service provider. In the trusting context of family-centered early intervention, this becomes an objective, nonjudgmental process of joint discovery. This type of checklist may require adaptation when applied across cultures (Brown & Nott, 2006).

As Cole and Flexer (2016) point out, the skills of the service provider are paramount so that the time spent reviewing the video is a helpful learning process for both partners. In many cases, the service provider will work in partnership with the caregivers to identify what is already going well. In other cases, a challenge in the interaction might be observed, and the joint discovery process can be helpful in overcoming the barrier. For example, a father of a deaf tod-dler was experiencing difficulty securing his daughter's attention during a play interaction, and he openly expressed his frustration to the service provider. Rather than focus on the negative, the service provider found a segment of the video where joint attention and turn taking were well-established, and the partners watched that interaction. She then said, "It seems that she is pay-ing attention to you quite well here, and you two took several turns back and forth. How did you make that happen?" He thought about it and said, "Oh, I see—I was talking about what she was interested in!" He appeared a bit more confident right away with this discovery, and the discussion led him to identify goals for himself. Reflection with guided questioning was an essential tool in this process.

Partnership is further supported when questioning seeks to confirm what parties are thinking and/or to join perspectives. Perhaps the parent is observed in the video using gestures when giving the child simple instructions (e.g., "Oh we need a new diaper. Can you get mommy the diaper [parent points at diaper]?"). There are also multiple examples of the toddler looking right at objects when the object names are used conversationally. The service provider could use open-ended questions to guide the parental observation: "It looks to me that in some situations, you find it helpful to gesture [looks at example with parents], but in others, she responds right away to your words. Is that how it usually happens? What prompts you to use gesture sometimes and not others?" In this circumstance, the parent reported that she finds the need to use visual support when the child is farther away from her. This explanation was quite reasonable and helped the service provider understand the paren-tal perspective. The discussion then led to a parent-identified goal to create opportunities for the child to listen at a distance. The mother decided to try a strategy of using auditory-first input at a distance and then adding a gesture if she was not understood. This reflective process was more effective than hav-ing the service provider simply "remind" the mother to provide auditory-first opportunities.

A standardized tool for assessing positive aspects of caregiver–child inter-action was developed by Roggman and colleagues and is called the Parenting Interactions with Children Checklist of Observations Linked to Outcomes™ (PICCOLO™; Paul H. Brookes Publishing Co., 2013). This checklist includes 29 developmentally supportive parenting behaviors for children ages 10 to 47 months, with sections on affection, responsiveness, encouragement, and teaching. It is also intended for rating a video-recorded parent–child inter-action. Although not specifically designed for observing families of children who are D/HH, it covers many of the broad parenting behaviors that influence children's early development. A training DVD is provided along with extensive scoring guidelines. This procedure has been demonstrated to be reliable and valid, and it is available in multiple languages.

***Temperament***    A primary goal of family-centered early intervention is to support responsiveness and synchrony in caregiver–child interactions. Part of being responsive is accommodating to the child's pace and temperament. Many parents do this naturally, but in some cases, it can be helpful to enhance parents' understanding of their children's unique temperaments in comparison to their own as a way to foster synchrony and responsiveness in interactions. Temperament is often described as a constellation of inborn traits that influence the ways in which the child is likely to experience and react to the world (Kristal, 2005). Frameworks for assessing infant temperaments often use rating scales (low to high or almost never to almost always) to explore a child's typical responses to situations. Many conceptualizations of temperament categories are based on seminal work from the New York Longitudinal Study (Thomas, Birch, Chess, Hertzig, & Korn, 1963), which described individual differences in children's behaviors in categories including activity level, rhythmicity, approach-withdrawal, adaptability, intensity, mood, persistence, distractibility, and sensory threshold. Kristal (2005) provides descriptions of behaviors associated with various temperament traits and informal rating scales that can be used with families to gain a better understanding of the child's unique temperament. A discussion guided by the Quick Survey of a Child's Temperament (Kristal, 2005) may increase caregiver understanding of and appreciation for the child's unique temperament, which could support responsiveness.  The video clips include an example (see Video clip 5.1) of the use of temperament scales to discuss parent and child temperaments and ways that parents accommodate to temperament differences within their family system. Helping caregivers address children's unique behaviors and behavioral challenges is foundational for improvements in spoken language and communication.

**Language Environment** Early interventionists often work to support families in engaging their infants and young children in frequent conversational turns. The **Language Environment Analysis (LENA)** system is a technological tool for monitoring conversational turns and amount of talk in the home context. LENA collects and analyzes full-day recordings of the child's language and auditory environments (http://www.lenafoundation.org). Two studies have demonstrated the feasibility of using LENA to monitor quantitative and qualitative aspects of caregiver input using automated methods. In one study, LENA was used to measure the frequency of conversational turns in a study of 28 HH toddlers. Results indicated that toddlers who were engaged in more conversational turns demonstrated stronger receptive language outcomes than those who were exposed to fewer turns (Ambrose, VanDam, & Moeller, 2014). Another study included children who are D/HH from Spanish-speaking and English-speaking homes and found that the rates of adult words and conversational turns matched that of families of children with normal hearing (NH). These results suggested the possible benefits of early intervention (EI) on home language use in families of children who are D/HH with diverse linguistic backgrounds (Aragon & Yoshinaga-Itano, 2012). Some early intervention programs have used LENA to provide objective and ongoing feedback to families on their communication with their children as an intervention tool. Although not all EI programs will have access to LENA, it is valuable for service providers to be aware of this resource and the ongoing intervention work incorporating this device (Sacks et al., 2013; Suskind et al., 2013). This tool holds promise as an objective way to monitor selected intervention effects such as increasing the frequency of conversational turns on the communicative outcomes of children and families.

*Listening Development*   When spoken language development is the goal, it is imperative that the family expect the child to respond through listening, be aware of cues that the infant is listening, and monitor these cues to ensure that the child has consistent access to linguistic input. Clearly, most parents have little experience in helping their child "learn to listen." Specific information is needed to facilitate parental understanding in this area.

A useful approach for thinking about global stages in auditory-linguistic learning was provided by Cole and Flexer (2016) and is adapted in shorter form for the current chapter. Figure 5.2 includes targets for auditory-linguistic learning that Cole and Flexer organized into four key categories: 1) being aware of sound, 2) connecting sound with meaning, 3) understanding simple language through listening, and 4) understanding complex language through listening. This framework can serve as a checklist for monitoring accomplished skills, emerging behaviors, and next steps. It can also serve as an overall guide to a hierarchical set of skills that are fostered in early intervention. Another auditory learning guide developed by Simser is provided in Chapter 7. Along with monitoring the infant's listening development, the service provider works closely with the family to ensure that they have the knowledge and skills to promote listening throughout the child's waking hours and that they regularly monitor both the child's devices and the child's responses to sound and speech so that any device issues can be identified and addressed quickly.

*Vocal Development*   Landmarks in **prelinguistic vocal development** are discussed in Chapter 8, and those guidelines are particularly useful as a basis for monitoring auditory-based changes in infants' spoken productions. Some investigators have used typical vocal and speech development benchmarks to create parent report measures to monitor production changes that signal auditory development. Previous research has documented that caregiver reports are useful in examining infant behaviors, such as the onset of canonical babbling (Oller, Eilers, & Basinger, 2001), characteristics of vocal categories (Ramsdell, Oller, Buder, Ethington, & Chorna, 2012), and early lexical development (Dale & Fenson, 1996). The parent report scales have been developed to measure early vocal development in children who are D/HH, including Infant Monitor of Production (IMP; Cantle Moore, 2004), Production Infant Scale Evaluation (PRISE; Kishon-Rabin, Taitelbaum-Swead, Ezrati-Vinacour, & Hildesheimer, 2005), and Vocal Development Landmarks Interview (VDLI; Moeller, Bass-Ringdahl, Ambrose, VanDam, & Tomblin, 2011).

The IMP (Cantle Moore, 2004) was developed in response to the need for a tool that would guide very early intervention (birth to 12 months) in the promotion of timely prelinguistic stages of development. This criterion-referenced tool uses an authentic assessment process to collect information and guide parental understanding regarding infants' progress in vocal development. The instrument involves a series of guided conversations and a visual scale that support the parents in systematically observing their infant's vocal development. The questionnaire supports the documentation of incremental changes in the infant's vocal development from neonatal, reflexive stages to first word imitation. As of 2015, this tool continues to be developed and validated, and

**Auditory skills profile**

| | | R | S | A |
|---|---|:---:|:---:|:---:|
| **I.** | **Being aware of sounds** | | | |
| 1. | Responds reflexively to sounds (blinks, widens eyes, becomes startled, changes breathing or sucking motion) | | | |
| 2. | Searches for sound / attempts to lateralize or localize (early auditory attention) | | | |
| 3. | Sustains auditory attention to sound (moves, smiles, or coos to music; dances, claps, stops at end) | | | |
| 4. | Demonstrates learned responses to sound without seeing source (points to ear, looks, responds to sound in a conditioned play task) | | | |
| 5. | Indicates nonworking device (auditory attention—takes off and hands to adult; tells adult) | | | |
| 6. | Detects sounds from the Ling Six-Sound Test (orients to sound, puts ring on stacker, puts object in bucket) | | | |
| **II.** | **Connecting sound with meaning** | **R** | **S** | **A** |
| 1. | Responds to speech (auditory association—smiles or coos in response; turns to talker) | | | |
| 2. | Responds to novel sounds (auditory association— quiets, becomes excited, searches, asks about sound) | | | |
| 3. | Responds to loud, unexpected noises (auditory association— cries, fusses, widens eyes, becomes startled) | | | |
| 4. | Responds to devices being turned on (auditory association— quiets, changes vocalization, smiles) | | | |
| 5. | Produces speechlike vocalizations (early auditory feedback— uses syllables, varied intonation) | | | |
| 6. | Responds to calling (speaker not in sight—child searches for sound, turns, stops activity; does so in quiet, in noise, at some distance) | | | |
| 7. | Anticipates what comes next in simple nursery rhymes, songs, stories (auditory closure) | | | |
| 8. | Engages in brief vocal turn taking (one or two exchanges) | | | |
| 9. | Engages in three or more vocal turn taking exchanges | | | |
| **III.** | **Understanding simple language through listening** | **R** | **S** | **A** |
| 1. | Responds to Ling sounds by imitating | | | |
| 2. | Responds appropriately to simple questions or requests without seeing talker's face | | | |
| | a.  In a closed set of up to seven objects | | | |
| | b.  In a typical, everyday situation ("Go get your shoes"; "Where's Daddy?") | | | |
| 3. | Engages in pragmatically correct conversation regarding everyday topic for one to two turns (auditory only) | | | |

**Figure 5.2.**  Targets for auditory-linguistic learning that children who are learning spoken language through listening should demonstrate. (*Sources:* Cole & Flexer, 2016; Carotta, Cline, & Brennan, 2014.)

| IV. *Understanding increasingly complex language through listening* | R | S | A |
|---|---|---|---|
| 1. Responds to familiar, everyday expressions and questions without watching talker's face | | | |
|    a. In quiet | | | |
|    b. In noise (auditory figure ground) | | | |
|    c. At a distance when engaged in play or task (auditory scanning/overhearing) | | | |
| 2. Spontaneously imitates phrases spoken by others (may or may not understand: auditory memory) | | | |
| 3. Recognizes recordings of familiar songs or rhymes (sings along, fills in missing parts) | | | |
| 4. Imitates an increasing sequence of digits in random order (auditory memory) | | | |
| 5. Understands and repeats utterances of increasing length (auditory tracking and memory) | | | |
| 6. Begins using words and colloquial expressions not directly taught ("no way"; "oh man!") | | | |
| 7. Responds through listening to increasing grammatical and semantic complexity (live, phone) | | | |
| 8. Responds through listening to commands with increasing steps (two-step, three-step) | | | |
| 9. Identifies object, person, or activity through listening based on clues (simple, then complex) | | | |
| 10. Answers personal questions about given topic through listening (simple, then complex) | | | |
| 11. Answers questions (open set)—no topic given through listening (simple, then complex) | | | |
| 12. Retells stories presented auditory only that include two, three, or four events/concepts in order | | | |
| 13. Understands and supplies whole word or message to fill in the blank (auditory closure) | | | |
| 14. Listens to a story or paragraph and answers questions about main idea and supporting details | | | |
| 15. Communicates on the telephone for a specific purpose (chats with grandparent) | | | |
| 16. Engages in longer, pragmatically appropriate conversations without the need for visual cues | | | |
| 17. Tunes in to conversations in vicinity while multitasking (overhearing, distance listening) | | | |

*Key:* R, rarely observed; S, sometimes observed; A, acquired.

*Note:* Not all behaviors are expected at each age level. Please use "BNE" to indicate "behavior not expected."

training materials for administration can be accessed by registering at the IMP web site (http:// ridbcrenwickcentre .com/ imp).

The second tool, the PRISE, was developed as a structured interview technique designed to explore the nature and frequency of 11 early speech behaviors using parent report (Kishon-Rabin et al., 2005). The first six questions on the scale focus on initial vocal stages (phonation, cooing, and expansion), whereas questions 7 to 11 focus on auditory-based developments such as canonical and variegated babbling and early word production. PRISE data have been collected on more than 260 typically developing infants and more than 200 children who are D/HH (Kishon-Rabin, Taitelbaum-Swead, & Segal, 2009), providing a reference base against which to compare individual infants.

A third research team followed the **model** of both the IMP and PRISE to create an alternative approach to the use of parent report to measure infant vocal stages. The experimental version of the VDLI (Moeller et al., 2011) was designed to promote parental understanding of target behaviors and enhance their reporting accuracy by reducing the need to rely on verbal descriptions of vocal stages. Instead, parents participate in an interactive interview that includes audio examples of infant vocal behaviors, often presented in a paired comparison format (e.g., vowels and glides versus true babble). The parent judges whether his or her child is producing sounds similar to the model and judges the frequency with which the child is producing them. As of 2015, tool refinement and validation studies (involving typically developing infants, ages 5–21 months) are in progress, with the ultimate goal of making this resource available to service providers for use in the home visit context. Readers are referred to Chapter 8 for more comprehensive coverage of prelinguistic and phonological assessments.

***Early Communicative Development***   In the early intervention context, service providers need to determine if the child is appropriately advancing from prelinguistic to early and subsequent linguistic development stages. Tools that examine prelinguistic predictors of later linguistic development are helpful in gathering evidence that the infant is progressing in expected ways or supporting the early identification of any concerns.

A valuable evaluation model for assessment of infants and toddlers is the Communication and Symbolic Behavior Scales Developmental Profile™ (CSBS DP™; Prizant & Wetherby, 2002). This well-validated scale (Wetherby, Allen, Cleary, Kublin, & Goldstein, 2002; Wetherby, Goldstein, Cleary, Allen, & Kublin, 2003) includes a caregiver questionnaire and an infant-toddler behavioral sample video that is rated across multiple dimensions. The caregiver questionnaire will be the focus of the current chapter, but the reader is encouraged to explore the behavioral sample online (http://firstwords.fsu.edu). The CSBS DP caregiver questionnaire is a parent report scale with 41 multiple choice items. Parents can complete the questionnaire independently every 3 months between the infant-toddler ages of 6 and 24 months. The scale provides a norm reference that was based on 790 caregiver reports. Importantly, the comprehensive model of the CSBS DP sections guide service providers in the scope of behaviors that are relevant to track, including prelinguistic skills that have been demonstrated to predict later linguistic stages (Watt, Wetherby, & Shumway, 2006). The questionnaire includes items related to emotion and eye gaze, communication, gesture, sounds, words, understanding, and object use. Measures such as the CSBS DP that reflect a comprehensive view of behaviors contributing to early communicative development can be an important addition to the service provider's toolbox.

Several methods have been developed for tracking early lexical development. For example, parent report is one efficient way to monitor children's early lexical development. A study by Nott, Cowan, Brown, and Wigglesworth (2009) used diaries of lexical development to track the time hearing children and those with cochlear implants took to achieve some specific lexical milestones (age at 50 words, age at 100 words, and age at true word combinations). Another method for tracking lexical growth, using a systematic recognition format, was developed in the MacArthur-Bates Communicative Development Inventories (CDI; Fenson et al., 2007). This instrument, which includes forms for words and gestures (8–18 months) and for words and sentences (15–30 months), has become widely used to monitor early words, gestures, and sentences and has been adapted for multiple languages. Normative data support the comparison of the child's rate of vocabulary development to that of typically developing peers. Lexical milestones are appropriate to track in early intervention, as they are foundational to later linguistic stages.

***Early Stages of Sentence Development***    A helpful framework for monitoring steps in early sentence development and emergence of morphology was proposed by Hadley (2014). Although this work was developed to monitor linguistic development in hearing children with language impairments, it has applicability for children who are D/HH who may experience delays in morphosyntax development (Koehlinger, Owen Van Horne, & Moeller, 2013; McGuckian & Henry, 2007). Hadley conceptualizes the process as a series of building blocks or steps: Infants and toddlers first develop a core set of vocabulary words (step 1). However, in order to advance to sentence production, the child needs to know a core set of verbs (step 2) that support production of subject-verb (SV) and subject-verb-object (SVO) sentence frames (see Hadley, 2014, for more detail). Lexical verbs are those that carry meaning (*put, want*) rather than solely a grammatical function (such as the auxiliary verb *is*). Hadley points out that assessing how the child uses lexical verbs with a variety of subjects (first, second, third person, singular and plural) reveals a great deal about progress in sentence development (step 3). Tense marking (e.g., *I want, he wants, they wanted;* step 4) builds on top of the three foundational steps (words, lexical verbs, and sentence frames). Children figure out tense marking through the use of varied SV and SVO combinations. By three years of age, typically developing children have a diverse verb lexicon, are able to frequently produce an array of simple sentences, and then begin to show tense marking (Hadley, 2014).

To monitor these steps in sentence development and the emergence of tense marking, Hadley and colleagues created a measure of the child's unique subject-verb (USV) combinations. Table 5.1 shows an example of a USV anal-y-sis completed for a female child with cochlear implants who was 27 months of age. A check of her vocabulary records (CDI) showed that she was credited with 87 lexical verbs, which is considered age appropriate. Table 5.1 shows a subgroup of utterances from her spontaneous language sample (for illustration purposes). Notably, she used a variety of subjects (singular and plural; first, second, and third person) with a variety of lexical verbs. In this case, the analysis reveals that the foundational behaviors (lexical verbs, varied SV and SVO combinations) are present. Although tense markers were infrequent in her sample at this age, they appeared to be emerging (e.g., *open/s, come/ing*), and the service provider can expect that the conditions are ripe for those to emerge next. Rapid progress in tense marking was observed on the next language sample that was collected at 30 months. Readers are referred to Hadley's work (2014) for a more thorough discussion. This section and Table 5.1 were intended to illustrate the value of paying attention to the child's verb lexicon and how verbs are used with a variety of subjects to document that the child is progressing in ways that will support the emergence of tense marking.

This section has emphasized the importance of measuring both caregiver and child behaviors that are relevant to early communicative development. The assessment process provides a road map, giving insights into various aspects of the child's communication development journey.

### Supporting Families in Fostering Spoken Language Through Listening

Cole and Flexer (2016) identified three key ingredients of spoken language intervention as 1) beginning with technology and instruction as early in life as possible, 2) following a typical developmental sequence, and 3) promoting parental roles as the child's primary teachers.

### Case Study: Beginning the Balancing Act

Early one morning, the first author of this chapter overheard a mother interacting with her 3-year-old son who had bilateral cochlear implants. He commented on some flowers sitting on a shelf, and she automatically responded, "Yes, that is a beautiful flower arrangement. Do you know why it is also called a centerpiece?" He answered, "Nope, I don't." Mom explained, "People call it a centerpiece because it usually is placed in the center of the table as a decoration. Remember how we decorated for your birthday? I think your cake was the centerpiece!" On this day, generating such rich language exposure came so naturally and automatically to her, but this was not always the case. She had previously shared that in the months following cochlear implantation, she felt pressure to elicit language and speech from her child, which led to some overly directive interactions. In her urgency to teach language and coax it from her son, she sensed a loss of joy and increasing struggle in their interactions. Over time and with support, she gained confidence in using natural ways to promote conversational interaction and began to trust that this process was bringing about positive engagement and learning.

Families and service providers often start the communication journey very early in an infant's life (e.g., 1–2 months of age). From the earliest visits with

**Table 5.1.**   Examples of a unique subject-verb combination analysis to support assessment of children's sentence development

Examples from a subset of unique subject-verb (USV; Hadley, 2014) combinations for a child with bilateral cochlear implants who was assessed at 27 months of age. Number of verbs = 90; lexical verbs = 87.

| First person singular (I) | Second person singular (you) | First person plural (we) | Third person singular | Third person plural |
|---|---|---|---|---|
| I take bus out. | You open. | We play bus. | It come/ing. | They run. |
| I said get out. | You want some. | | Mommy drive in front seat. | |
| Me put in microwave. | | | And Goofy fall out too. | |
| I wash my hands. | | | It open/s. | |
| I knock over my chair. | | | And Pluto want seat belt on. | |

From Dr. Pam Hadley.

the family, the process can be characterized as both a holding environment and a balancing act. The concept of a "holding environment" is used in therapeutic settings to mean a relationship that is dependable, consistent, responsive, and empathic toward the individual's needs. The holding environment that is created in family-centered early intervention permits the family to sort through natural feelings of loss and/or uncertainty, to wade through confusing information with an understanding guide, and to get to know and appreciate the child's unique temperament and strengths.

The holding environment respects that parenting, itself, is a developmental process. First-time parents of a child who is D/HH may be finding their way on two levels: as a parent and as a parent of a child who is D/HH. A holding environment can reinforce the secure attachment that is present with the infant while promoting mutual enjoyment and discovery of the child's responsiveness to the family's efforts. In relation to the infant, it is a period of "getting to know you." Most parents anxiously await their infant's first words; for families with an infant who is D/HH, first words might be concrete evidence of a step toward their desired goal of spoken language. But when intervention begins in early infancy, 10 to 11 months is a long time to wait for this evidence. Service providers help families learn to recognize prelinguistic changes and growth in auditory abilities that serve as critical foundations to spoken language. The efforts of the service provider in these early months is not directed at the infant but rather at creating a safe holding environment in which parents can express and resolve fears, grow in appreciation for the infant's emerging skills, and develop knowledge and skills needed to support development.

Service providers also work to achieve balance in the implementation and focus of home visits. A primary goal is for parents to be empowered with beliefs that they are principal and effective agents of change. This requires a balance in the distribution of power in the parent–professional relationship (Moeller & Condon, 1994). In the experience of the authors, imbalance can result from an overpowering of professional skills, an attitude of teaching rather than facilitating, and inattention to recruiting existing strengths in the family. Parental feelings of powerlessness are also associated with imbalance and with poorer long-term child outcomes (Schlesinger, 1987). A focus on caregiver empowerment requires that service providers develop self-awareness as they interact with families. Effective service providers work on self-management to maintain a balance between the desire to help the family and the goal to promote independence. This is a particularly challenging aspect of being a skilled provider, because there are a number of ways to respond to any question, comment, or child behavior. Yet foremost is the need for the service provider to calibrate responses and actions, figuring out when to lead and when to follow, when to suggest and when to inquire, when to model and when to watch and learn, and when to share information and when to invite perspectives. These delicate balances maintain the sharing of power in the relationship, which is foundational to the process of joint problem solving. At the foundation is a service provider mind-set and commitment to adherence to family-centered principles. Table 5.2 provides a set of **self-reflection** questions that support service providers in determining whether their practices are aligned with these tenets.

**Table 5.2.**  Self-reflection questions to guide service providers

| Self-reflection questions | Child-centered examples | Family-centered examples |
|---|---|---|
| Use the following four questions to judge the degree to which a service provider is implementing principles of family-centered early intervention. | | |
| What is the physical arrangement? | Service provider sits close to child, interacting directly. Family members observe from couch or observation room. | Caregiver interacts with infant; service provider sits on the sidelines providing support and guidance. |
| What is my role? | Service provider provides direct therapy to child, informs parents about goals, and suggests ideas for carry-over. | Service provider identifies family strengths and builds on strengths to promote family confidence in interacting in natural routines in ways that foster the child's development. |
| What language do I use to promote partnership? | Service provider selects goals and activities and directs the efforts of the family, telling them how to work with the child: "Remember to try calling his name to get his attention every day this week." | Service provider actively recruits parental expertise and learns from it: "What have you noticed about her responses when you call her name? When has it worked best for you? Can you show me?" |
| How do my services build on the strengths of the family? | Service provider models new listening and language stimulation techniques for parents to see. (Note: It is unclear if this builds on strengths.) | Service provider frequently observes natural interactions and makes observations about what's working ("Each time she vocalizes, you copy her. See how she is starting to copy you back? Seems like turn taking is starting to happen . . . what do you think?") |

## Promoting Essential Family Outcomes from Early Intervention When Spoken Language Is the Goal

Although a major goal of early intervention is to maximize the child's potential for language and communicative development, the route to that goal is through the family. This prompts one to consider the *family outcomes* that are necessary to support a child in developing spoken language skills through listening. The following sections outline expected family outcomes along with strategies to promote parental self-efficacy and skill in integrating these components in everyday interactions with the child. Fundamentally, early interventions aimed at developing spoken language also focus on rigorous and appropriate audiological and technology management in partnership with the family (Cole & Flexer, 2016).

*Outcome 1: Families Provide Their Infants with Consistent Access to Well-Fit and Well-Maintained Hearing Devices*   Much has been written in the literature on spoken language interventions about the critical importance of consistent use of well-managed listening technology (see Estabrooks, 2012). Cole and Flexer (2016) emphasize the key role of the child's technology in providing access to spoken language input that is vital for cognitive-linguistic development.

Given the vital role of technology, a foundational parent-related outcome is that the child will use hearing technology (hearing aids and/or cochlear implants) during all waking hours (Cole & Flexer, 2016), and parents of infants need to understand why consistent device use is fundamental to achieving their goals with the child. In a study of more than 200 HH children, consistency of hearing aid use was significantly associated with child language outcomes, and this finding applied to a wide range of hearing levels (Tomblin et al., in press). This work demonstrated the positive impact of consistent hearing aid use on linguistic development for children with mild-to-severe hearing levels. Unfortunately, infants and toddlers, who are in a particularly sensitive period for language development, were found to be at greatest risk for inconsistent device use (Moeller, Hoover, Peterson, & Stelmachowicz, 2009; Walker et al., 2013). Studies showed that families vary in their ability to accomplish consistent hearing aid use, particularly when children were young (e.g., toddlers) and/or when families had more limited resources (Walker et al., 2013). Attaining consistent device use is equally vital for children with cochlear implants. Challenges in device use may arise from issues related to the infant (e.g., health status, behaviors, temperament), the family (e.g., adjustment to diagnosis, parenting style, beliefs about the reduced importance of learning in infants and toddlers, a lack of support from extended family), or situational context (e.g., child care, riding in the car; see Moeller et al., 2009). The fundamental importance of the child wearing the hearing technology cannot be overemphasized. Service providers need to identify and understand unique barriers individual families are facing and to provide specific supports in response to the identified needs. Generally speaking, an infant or toddler will adjust to what a calm, determined, and consistent parent wants him or her to adjust to. If a trusting partnership has been established, parents are likely to be comfortable openly discussing any practical and/or affective barriers and developing their own approaches to overcoming the barriers. Without parent "buy-in," progress in spoken language will be limited. Ultimately, there is little that the service provider can do until the barriers to equipment wearing are addressed. If the parent is not willing to have the child wear equipment, then pursuing spoken language through audition is not an appropriate communication modality.

Families should have access to tools that support device retention (see http://www.babyhearing.org/HearingAmplification/AidChoices/practical.asp) along with tools (stethoscope, battery tester, etc.) and techniques for device checking (see http://evdcweb.org/level100/lesson104/lesson104.html). Over time, some families have been observed to become complacent about devices, cupping their hand around the hearing aid to see if it produces feedback as a way of checking devices. Parents need to understand that this approach will not allow them to detect device malfunction. It can be helpful to provide audio simulations that demonstrate what it sounds like to listen through malfunctioning technology (see http://www.utdallas.edu/~thib/ EARRINGFINAL/ EARRINGWEB_files/frame.htm). Parents can easily appreciate the impact of listening all day with a malfunctioning device. One mother with a high level of expertise noted, "Why bother putting hearing aids on my child if I have not checked each day to ensure they are functioning properly?" As a result of early intervention, parents should come to appreciate this central point. Parents also need to become keen observers of their children's subtle and not so sub-tle auditory responses and changes in vocalizations that signal benefits from am-plification. Recognition of growth in auditory skills may further reinforce their commitment to the child's consistent use of technology (see Video clip 5.2).

For devices to benefit children, they must also be properly fit and well maintained. Well-fit technology optimizes an individual child's access to sound (audibility). As explained in Chapter 2, audiologists verify hearing aid fittings and seek to optimize the child's audibility by fitting the device to individually prescribed targets. Hearing aid fitting data were examined in 195 children with mild to severe hearing loss. Results showed that not all devices are fit optimally; 55% of the hearing aids deviated from prescriptive targets, which had conse-quences for aided audibility (McCreery, Bentler, & Roush, 2013). This finding is important because the same research team documented that children with better aided audibility from hearing aids demonstrated faster rates of language growth during the infant–preschool period (Tomblin et al., in press). The key point is that both parents and service providers need to be informed consumers of audiological services. Parents should understand the importance of hearing aid verification procedures (see Chapter 2) and request that the audiologist pro-vide ongoing information about the child's aided audibility levels. Families are best served by working in close partnership with the audiologist in maintaining optimized audibility through well-fit and well-maintained technology.

Family members also need to be conversant with procedures for con-ducting daily listening checks and observing children's functional responses to sound with the equipment. For example, parents should become skilled in using the Ling sounds (presented in Chapters 2 and 7) daily as part of checking the child's function with amplification. Often this can be incorporated during the morning dressing routine. For young infants, this will involve learning early signs of auditory detection, such as quieting, eye widening, or orienting toward the sound source. Figure 5.3 provides a form that may be useful with families who appreciate some structure as they are learning to conduct daily device and functional listening checks. With appropriate support, family members and other caregivers can develop high levels of self-efficacy related to these top-ics (see DesJardin, 2005; DesJardin & Eisenberg, 2007). However, it is inter-esting to reflect on the study (discussed in Chapter 4) showing that mothers of children with cochlear implants reported greater self-efficacy in managing the technology than mothers of children with hearing aids (DesJardin, 2005). This finding warrants further consideration in early intervention programs. Par-ents of infants with hearing aids may experience unique challenges, including the fact that some children may respond to sound without devices. It is essen-tial to provide supports that clearly link consistent device use to the parental goals of optimal spoken language development for the child.

*Outcome 2: Families Optimize Auditory-Linguistic Access and Learning by Manag-ing the Environment in Specific Ways*  Children who are D/HH require consistent access to linguistic input, but several factors can lead to reductions in the qual-ity and quantity of access and auditory experience, which over time will have

**Daily device checking chart**

Child: _____

Parents/service provider: _____

| Key | |
|-----|--|
| ✓ | Device function okay |
| ? | Possible problem |
| – | Device not working |

| Date | Device | | Performance checks | | | | | | | Comments and plan |
|------|--------|------|-------|---|----|----|----|----|----|-------------------|
| | Right | Left | Child detects<br>Child repeats what I say | | | | | | | |
| | | | Lings | m | oo | ah | ee | sh | ss | |
| | | | Right | | | | | | | |
| | | | Left | | | | | | | |
| | | | Both | | | | | | | |
| | | | Right | | | | | | | |
| | | | Left | | | | | | | |
| | | | Both | | | | | | | |
| | | | Right | | | | | | | |
| | | | Left | | | | | | | |
| | | | Both | | | | | | | |
| | | | Right | | | | | | | |
| | | | Left | | | | | | | |
| | | | Both | | | | | | | |
| | | | Right | | | | | | | |
| | | | Left | | | | | | | |
| | | | Both | | | | | | | |
| | | | Right | | | | | | | |
| | | | Left | | | | | | | |
| | | | Both | | | | | | | |

**Figure 5.3.**  A form that can be used to support parents who appreciate structure to log daily device and performance monitoring in their child. (Adapted with permission from Johnson, Benson, & Seaton, [1997]. *Educational Audiology Handbook.* Cengage Learning; Carotta et al. [2014]. *Auditory Consultant Resource Network Handbook.* Boys Town National Research Hospital.)

an impact on spoken language development. Caregivers (including child care providers) need to be aware of common barriers to access so that they manage them in everyday life with the child. This aspect of knowledge and skills involves family members becoming cognizant of the listening conditions and whether or not they support optimal communication with the child (Cole & Flexer, 2016). Families should gain skills in monitoring background noise and reverberation as well as their distance from the child. As a result of coaching in early intervention, parents should become astute about the need to reduce

barriers to access by removing or reducing noise sources, getting in close prox-
imity to the child (behind or to the side), and/or using frequency modulated
(FM) or digitally modulated (DM) technology.

Part of structuring an optimal language environment entails being
mindful of noise sources and their potential deleterious effects on language
access. Ambrose and colleagues (2014) explored the impact of noise on conversational turns and child language outcomes in a study using full-day
LENA recordings of the home environments of young children who were HH.
Results showed that more frequent television (or other electronic media) use
was associated with reductions in parent–child conversational turn taking
and lower child language scores. This study supports the need for families
to understand how noise acts as a barrier to turn-taking opportunities and
conversational access. Furthermore, children's speech recognition suffers
in conditions of excess noise and reverberation (Finitzo-Hieber & Tillman,
1978). Armed with an understanding of the deleterious effects of these environmental factors on children's language access, families can make effective
choices (e.g., FM/DM technology; see Chapter 2) and/or accommodations,
such as minimizing background noise whenever possible. Accommodations
and awareness may be especially important as parents advocate for their
children's access to language in child care settings.

Parents also manage the auditory environment when they use speech and
vocal characteristics that are expected to facilitate young children's language
development and engagement/attention. The observational tool in Figure 5.1
(the section on caregiver speech characteristics) includes some of these key features. For example, expression of warmth and interest in the tone of the voice is
likely to create interest and support affective engagement. Audition-maximizing
techniques include strategic positioning (close and to the side), use of audition
(voice) to attract attention, and pausing to give children time to process what
they hear. Parental use of natural rate, appropriate intensity, and varied intonation are encouraged in interaction with young children who are D/HH. Parents may incorporate these characteristics naturally, but monitoring using the
checklist in Figure 5.1 can ensure that this is the case. Appendix 5.1 includes
a handout that can be used with parents to reinforce key concepts involved in
maximizing children's auditory access.

*Outcome 3: Families Establish a Language-and Auditory-Rich Environment, Provid-
ing an Abundance of Developmentally Appropriate, High-Quality Interactions*   Another
major goal of early intervention is to support family members and other caregivers in providing auditory-and language-rich exposure and conversational
opportunities throughout daily routines. As discussed earlier in this chapter, children who are D/HH may experience inconsistent access to linguistic
input due to a number of factors. One way to counteract the effects of inconsistent access is to provide frequent, high-quality input (Snow, 1994; Szagun
& Stumper, 2012) within abundant conversational turns. Fundamentally,
effective early interventions support parents' skills as robust language models who maintain high expectations that children will learn through audition
following typical developmental sequences. Many of the strategies used in this
approach are similar to those of enhanced milieu teaching (EMT), a naturalistic

approach that seeks to combine responsive interactions (semantically **contin-gent responses**, modeling, expansions, balance in turn taking) with use of language prompts (wait time, models that elicit language, incidental teaching; Hancock & Kaiser, 2006). Spoken language early intervention for infants who are D/HH differs from EMT in its focus on promoting language development through conscious efforts to develop reliance on listening skills.

Incidental learning through natural interactions are promoted (e.g., parenting as you would any child), but parents also learn to *embellish* the interactions in ways that promote auditory-linguistic growth (Cole & Flexer, 2016). **Embellishments** include those strategic efforts throughout the day to max-imize communication and auditory opportunities and make them accessible. In spoken language early intervention, caregivers are encouraged to inter-act in typical ways but to do so frequently with deliberate focus on auditory/linguistic targets (see Video clip 5.3).

Early intervention typically begins by supporting parental *responsive-ness* to the infant and his or her emerging communicative signals. At least in Western cultures, parents regard their tiny infants as conversational part-ners, building on smiles, burps, kicks, or other behaviors ("Oh, you are such a big kicker! You gonna kick some more? Yes, there it is!"; Hoff, 2006). Some suggest that these exchanges establish a foundation for later intentional com-munication by the child (Locke, 1995). It is known that quality of caregiver–child engagement, including sensitivity and responsiveness of the caregiver to the child, and the provision of cognitively stimulating ideas support language learning (Tamis-LeMonda & Rodriquez, 2009). The service provider's role is to know what developmental steps are next for the child in order to guide goal selection. In addition, the service provider maintains a focus on the family's typical routines while supporting the parents' use of language scaffolding tech-niques and responsive, nurturing interactions (Brown & Nott, 2006).

The observational tool provided in Figure 5.1 provides a framework for the effectiveness of family members in promoting auditory-linguistic devel-opment through embellished incidental interactions (Cole & Flexer, 2016). Parents are encouraged to create an engaging and interesting communicative environment and to interact in ways that promote the child's motivation and increasing skill in understanding and expression through verbal means. It is beyond the scope of this chapter to fully illustrate the details in each section of Figure 5.1, but the reader can find detailed guidance in Cole and Flexer (2016). The framework can guide the service provider in recognizing the scope and ingredients of facilitative parenting behaviors. The eventual goal of con-versational interaction begins with sensitivity to the child, being responsive to the infants' cues, pacing interactions in tune with the child, and following the child's interest to promote joint attention and engagement. Parents are supported in providing stimulation and play opportunities that are develop-mentally appropriate and engaging.

Responsiveness to the infant's communicative attempts is an essential step toward building conversation. It begins with caregivers recognizing the child's communicative attempts in their various forms. Caregivers are typi-cally eager for the child's first words and may find it encouraging to recog-nize the various means by which the infant is attempting to communicate—for example, using gestures, eye gaze, changes in body movement, vocalizations, facial expressions, and so forth (Prizant & Wetherby, 2002). Caregivers can be supported in their awareness of the importance of responding to communicative attempts such as gestures. Parents who respond contingently to their children's gestures are likely to have children who demonstrate stronger language skills than children of less responsive parents (Goldin-Meadow, Goodrich, Sauer, & Iverson, 2007; Masur, 1982). Thus, early home visits include emphasis on tuning in to *what* and *how* infants are trying to communicate to support adults in replying consistently by responding with interest (smile, move closer) and/or putting the child's intended message into words (see Video clip 5.4).

Cole and Flexer (2016) promote responding in ways that encourage the child to take a turn. For example, during a feeding routine, the little one might bang his or her spoon on the high chair tray. The parent interprets this as communication and responds, "Oh, do you want more?" (Parent looks expectantly and waits.) The infant then leans in to take another bite. A toddler in the same scenario might gesture and vocalize while looking at the apple slices. The caregiver responds with a "turnabout" such as "You see apples. You want some?" The child then gets excited and attempts to say, "Apple," taking his or her next conversational turn. These types of caregiver responses (turnabouts or conversational reflectives) are encouraged because they are known to facilitate children's language learning (Proctor-Williams, Fey, & Loeb, 2001). These strategies also seek to achieve balance in turn-taking interactions between caregiver and child.

Another parent-focused intervention approach designed to empower parents' language facilitation strategies in naturalistic contexts is It Takes Two to Talk: The Hanen Program for Parents (Girolametto & Weitzman, 2006). This program was developed as an intervention for toddlers and preschoolers with language disorders. Some programs serving families of children who are D/HH have had service providers trained in the Hanen program and have found that selected resources are especially useful in training parents. Many of the support materials are parent friendly in design and reinforce key concepts through the use of easy-to-remember acronyms. For example, three *A*s are used to emphasize the importance of **a**llowing the child to lead, **a**dapting to share the moment, and **a**dding new experiences and words. Skills that are emphasized under "allowing the child to lead" include observing the child (for communicative attempts or nonverbal expression of intentions), imitating the child (if developmentally appropriate), and interpreting what the child is trying to say or asking questions to offer another turn. The "adapting to share the moment" material focuses on playful interactions and adjusting to the child's interest and language levels. "Adding new experiences and words" helps parents see the value of rich and varied input that can be embedded in any daily routine. One caveat is important, however: Some of the Hanen recommended strategies are intended for children with disabilities who benefit from reductions in the cognitive load (i.e., providing single-word models—"Apple. Want."). This is not a useful practice with a child who is D/HH because the child needs to hear the entire normal acoustic envelope of an utterance one would typically use ("I have an apple. Do you want some, too?"). Another helpful resource for encouraging facilitative caregiver behaviors is *Learn to Talk Around the Clock*

(Rossi, 2003). These types of materials can be adapted to promote caregiver–child interaction in natural routines.

Caregivers of infants and toddlers are also encouraged to *imitate and encourage* their children's vocalizations. This practice, especially with children under 12 months of age, draws the caregiver into the interaction. When caregivers give contingent social feedback, including models of vocal production timed to typically developing infant's babbling, vocal development is facilitated; infants learn new vocal forms by discovering phonological patterns in the caregiver's model (Goldstein & Schwade, 2008). As children's language matures, imitation may be replaced by expansions of the child's utterances. Expansions include responses that repeat part or all the child's previous utterance and add to it with semantic content, grammatical cues, or both. Recall that Nittrouer (2010) found that caregiver-contingent responses to the child's utterances that included spoken words were powerful in promoting language development in children who are D/HH. She recommended that service providers promote caregiver effectiveness in expanding upon the language that the child is explicitly trying to produce.

Early language development is bidirectional in nature, with the child influencing the parent and the parent influencing the child. As service providers promote facilitative caregiver behaviors, it is also important to monitor these adaptive adjustments over time (see Figure 5.1). As children's language and auditory skills advance, caregivers should be observed to increase the complexity of their input, including using more complex utterances and a variety of different words (Szagun & Stumper, 2102). As noted earlier, researchers have begun to identify higher level facilitative techniques that are associated with better language outcomes for children who are D/HH. These provide direction about more advanced caregiver behaviors that can be encouraged. These include the use of recasts (e.g., restating the child's verbalization into a grammatically correct form—"want more milk" is recasted as "Oh, you want some more milk?"), parallel talk (commenting on the child's action or focus of attention), and open-ended questions (e.g., "What else can we try?"; (Ambrose et al., in press; Cruz et al., 2013; DesJardin & Eisenberg, 2007; Quittner et al., 2013).

Incidental learning and embellishment strategies are also emphasized in the development of listening skills. Cole and Flexer (2016) discuss ways that everyday activities can be embellished in a purposeful way to give infants regular opportunities to attend selectively through audition; to discriminate and identify; to make associations; and eventually to integrate, interpret, and comprehend what is heard. The skills listed in Figure 5.2 can serve as a guide for the service provider and the parents regarding auditory behaviors that are expected to develop in response to systematic stimulation. Cole and Flexer also advise that parents and service providers internalize selected auditory strategies and incorporate them in all interactions with the child. For example, adults are expected to place themselves near and behind or beside the microphones of the child's technology to provide auditory stimulation. If they need to cue the child to tune in, they are apt to say "listen" rather than "watch" or "look at me." Other strategies include talking to the child and expecting understanding, including when the child is not watching. When the child accesses visual cues, the information may be presented again to provide auditory exposure.

Messages are presented auditory only the first time (see Chapter 7) and whenever possible. Children are observed to gain confidence in the ability to respond through listening alone when given regular practice. Several key resources provide direction for naturalistic incorporation of auditory learning opportunities into daily routines (see Cole, Carroll, Coyne, Gill, & Paterson, 2005; Cole & Flexer, 2016; Estabrooks, 2006; Rossi, 2003).

## Tools of the Trade: Provider Behaviors that Matter in Bringing About Family Outcomes

There are certain provider behaviors and/or roles that are foundational to promoting balanced partnership and promotion of knowledge and skills within a family-centered approach. Up to this point, much of the focus has been on the content of early intervention. In this section, we return to the process: how the service provider interacts to support the family. These service provider roles will be illustrated in this section in regard to spoken language approaches, but these behaviors are broadly applicable to a range of intervention approaches. This set of behaviors and their definitions can be characterized as "tools of the trade." They have evolved from the literature on family-centered early intervention practices and through collaborations of the authors with colleagues involved in early intervention (Cole & Flexer, 2016; Moeller & Condon, 1994; Moeller, Schow, & Whitaker, 2013; Stredler-Brown, Moeller, Gallegos, & Corwin, 2006).

 **Partner**   At the core of family-centered early intervention is the value for working in balanced partnership with families (see Video clip 5.5; see also Chapter 4). Balanced partnerships evolve over time and are partly dependent on the dispositions of the service provider. The National Council for Accreditation of Teacher Education (NCATE, 2013) defines dispositions as professional attitudes, values, and beliefs that are conveyed both verbally and nonverbally in interactions with families. The service provider seeks to convey an attitude of collaboration ("Let's solve this together") and unconditional support ("You can do this!"; Klein & Gilkerson, 2000). Service providers maintain confidentiality and are trustworthy (do what they say they will), which allows families to put their trust in the relationship. Sometimes, the service provider's own values and cultural influences may differ from the families in their caseload. To form collaborative partnerships, service providers may need to recognize and put aside some of their own values and presuppositions (Sass-Lehrer, Moeller, & Stredler-Brown, 2015). As Chapter 4 notes, the ability to listen beneath the words and respond with compassion is essential to building a partnership. The partnership approach is a mind-set that focuses away from expert-driven ideas to learner-focused techniques (Hanft, Rush, & Shelden, 2004). Table 5.3 illustrates this notion by comparing partner-oriented problem solving to expert-driven approaches.

**Validator**   Another role of the service provider is to validate parental observations and concerns. Validation differs from praise; validation is an effort to demonstrate or support that a statement or concept has truth value (see Video clip 5.2). In the early intervention context, this can mean empathic responses to parental expression of feelings as natural and important human

**Table 5.3.**   A partnership approach contrasted with an expert-driven approach

| Service-provider-directed example | Partnership example | Advantages of partnership |
|---|---|---|
| Example A<br>Service Provider (SP): "You noticed he is not hearing as well, yet his cochlear implants (CIs) are working fine. Let me contact the CI team to see if they can get you in to check the map." | SP: "You are noticing a change in his responses with his CIs. I suspect that is concerning to you. Is that accurate? What steps do you want to take next and how can I support you?"<br>Parent: "Maybe I should contact the CI team."<br>SP: "Yes, checking the map makes sense as a first step." | In example B, the SP seeks to explore the level of family concern and responds with empathy. The SP respects the family's authority by inquiring about their plan to address the present need and by offering to help in finding a solution. The SP promotes family independence and acknowledges the benefit of their suggested solution. |
| Example C<br>Parent: "I am an introvert, so it is not natural for me to talk to her all the time even though I know it is best for her."<br>SP: "Well, please keep up the talking because research shows that it will benefit her in the long run."<br>Example B | Example D<br>Parent: "I am an introvert, so it is not natural for me to talk to her all the time even though I know it is best for her."<br>SP: "So constant talking is challenging for you. Yes, it can feel really odd at first and in some situations. Sometimes parents say they don't know what words to use or what to talk about. You need to be kind to yourself about it. Don't feel like you have to talk with her every single minute—just try to talk a bit more; ease yourself into this talking-a-lot thing!" | In example D, the SP responds to the parental concern rather than the content of the message. This conveys that the session is a safe place to share concerns and they will be listened to and honored. |

responses to a challenging situation. Validation also involves acknowledging and accepting parental interpretations. The following vignette illustrates the validator tool of the trade:

Situation:   *Parent and SP discuss latest audiogram suggesting possible progression of thresholds.*

Parent:   The audiologist said there may be a drop in hearing, but I don't believe it.

Service Provider (SP): So you are skeptical . . . tell me about that. (Validates)

Parent:   Well, he was tired and I don't think he was giving his best effort.

SP:   So you are wondering if the results are accurate? (Validate and check understanding)

Parent:   Yeah, but what if it is true? I'm so scared.

SP:   If it is true there is a drop in hearing, that feels scary (nodding) (Validates)

Parent:   Yeah (tearing up), but the audiologist is going to try to work us in again later this week.

SP:   So the waiting and not knowing is hard. (Validates)

Parent:   Really hard.

The validation tool allows parents to know that their concerns and observations are heard and understood. Feelings are not judged, and there are no attempts to find a simple fix. Validation is an essential tool for building trust and creating an atmosphere that welcomes the expression of feelings, interpretations, and perspectives.

***News Commentator***    The role of the provider as "news commentator" was first described by Moeller and Condon (1994) as a technique where the service provider gives objective, on-the-spot commentary about what is happening, much like a news commentator reporting through a blow-by-blow narrative of an event (see Video clip 5.6). In early intervention, this tool is used quietly by the service provider from the sidelines and is designed to highlight something important in the interaction—something notable that partners take as signals of progress, strengths to recognize, or needs to address. The following vignettes provide examples of use of the news commentator role:

Situation 1:    *SP watches young dad seat the infant's earmold.*

SP:    That earmold went in easily that time. (News commentator)

Dad:    I am starting to get the hang of this. (Self-affirms)

SP:    How does that feel? (Recruits parental interpretation)

Dad:    Pretty darn good. I am not so worried that I am going to hurt her anymore.

Situation 2:    *A mother is engaging her infant in rounds of peekaboo.*

SP:    Each time you cover your face, she seems to wait expectantly for your voice. Then she smiles and reaches. (News commentator)

Mother:    We have started to notice that, too. I think she is starting to be aware of the sounds of our voices! (Parent contributes expertise)

SP:    Yes. There it is again. She waited, you vocalized, she tugged the blanket. (News commentator)

Situation 3:    *SP observes as parent changes a diaper.*

SP:    Your voice is soothing as you rub the lotion. Your voice is dramatic when you say "phew!" (News commentator)

Mom:    Oh, I didn't realize I was doing that. Maybe that gives her nice contrast? (Self-affirms)

SP:    It sure seems so. Let's think about how we might expect her to respond—what should we watch for? (Invitation to partner)

***Joint Problem Solver Through Experiments***    Joint problem solving is a tool of the trade that helps maintain balance in any problem-solving endeavor in early intervention (Moeller & Condon, 1994). This tool involves addressing questions or curiosities that arise as "miniexperiments." Here is a scenario illustrating this approach:

Situation: *Toddler sits on mother's lap during book sharing.*

Mom: She is so quiet when I read to her. I know she has things to say about the book.

SP: I wonder what would happen if you give more pause time before telling her about the next page. (Offers experiment)

Mom: Hmm, I'm not sure. Let's try it and see. (Pauses and waits expectantly)

Child: (Looks at mom and points at the page) Boat!

Mom: You love riding in boats . . . especially with Daddy! (Responsive expansion)

SP: Pausing invited her to join the conversation. (News commentator summary)

Mom: I want to try it again to see if she will take more turns! (Suggests another experiment)

In this example, the professional may have already had a sense that wait time could help, but in offering the idea as an experiment, there is an opportunity for shared discovery. This maintains partnership, as both parties contribute expertise, observations, and opportunities to try things out. Importantly, the use of experiments to discover what works supports family members in the use of observation as a guide for planning and decision making. Obviously, the service provider's developmental knowledge is a valuable ingredient here, as is parental knowledge. Within joint experiments, parents often develop areas of competence, such as the ability to recognize and support early communicative signals and the ability to recognize important but subtle auditory responses by the infant. Experimentation and joint problem solving allow partners to make unique discoveries about what works or what strategies might need to be altered.

***Sounding Board*** The service provider often serves in a role as a neutral sounding board. Imagine a trusted colleague who is willing to listen to your concerns without giving unwelcome advice. This confidant is patient yet willing to question to help you see alternative ways to think about the problem. The confidant does not insist on his or her way but offers support for you to arrive at your own solution. Service providers are called to serve in this very capacity—to be as neutral and supportive as possible in responding to a family's plan or concern. The following vignette illustrates the sounding board role:

Situation: *Parent is exploring options for child care.*

Parent: I really like the teachers and the atmosphere of this one, but it is so noisy.

SP: So it sounds attractive to you on most levels but not in terms of her access. (Sounding board restates and validates)

Parent: Right, but her audiologist said we could maybe try an FM system.

SP: And what do you think? (Recruits parental interpretation)

Parent:  I don't know if the child care can handle all that equipment, and I am worried about the cost.

  SP:    Would more information support your decision? (Identifies support needs)

Parent:  Yes, and I think I'd like to talk to a parent who got an FM system. (Clarifies support needs)

  SP:    Should we explore together how we might get more information and identify a parent you could visit with? (Joint problem solving)

**Information Resource**   As in the previous example, families often rely on service providers to point them to helpful resources and opportunities that may address a concern, expand their horizons, and/or support decision making. Obviously, families consume information and resources in a variety of ways. Families may access information on the Internet and/or through social media, finding resources that may vary in accuracy. Service providers need to determine families' preferred routes for accessing information, guide them to reliable sources, and support them in detecting when information may be biased. When serving as an information resource, service providers should consider how to share the responsibility for information gathering and synthesis (as in the previous sounding board example). Furthermore, the service provider can support families in coming to their own conclusions about the applicability of the information for their personal situation.

**Supporter**   A final role worthy of mention is that of supporter. Although all the tools of the trade covered in this chapter could be considered "supportive," this role comprises identifying family support needs and linking them with responsive supports. The vast majority of families emphasize the importance of family-to-family support (see http://www.gpodh .org), and it is considered recommended practice to provide such opportunities (JCIH; Muse et al., 2013; Moeller et al., 2013). Skilled service providers are sensitive to the individual needs of families in regard to support from others. They help families identify and access informal supports as well as more formal community services and programs that will meet family-identified needs. This is a process of getting to know together what resources are an appropriate fit for an individual family.

## Case Study: Application to a Child

Lukas was the first-born child of a young couple in a Midwestern city. The parents were informed shortly after Lukas's birth that he did not pass the newborn hearing screening and was in need of follow-up pediatric audiological testing. The family followed through quickly, and Lukas was soon identified as deaf—with auditory brainstem response (ABR) results showing profound bilateral hearing levels. Follow-up services were initiated promptly, including enrollment in family-centered early intervention and fitting of binaural hearing aids. The family observed that Lukas rarely responded to sound even though he was wearing his hearing aids in full waking hours, and they began working in partnership with their audiologist and service provider to explore intervention options. As they became informed decision makers, they elected to meet with a cochlear implant team and determine if Lukas was a candidate for surgical intervention.

The early intervention service provider who was conducting home visits also linked them with family-to-family support programs, including the opportunity to attend a weekend-long program called Roots and Wings. This cross-agency collaborative program was designed for families of newly identified infants who are deaf or hard of hearing (D/HH). This family-support program was held in a retreat atmosphere with child care provided to promote full family participation. The program included multiple informal social opportunities with veteran and new parents, content learning sessions, "hands-on practice" (e.g., troubleshooting technology, interpreting an audiogram, "stretching" one's language exposure), and opportunities to meet and ask questions of older children and adults who were D/HH and veteran parents. The program content supplemented or complemented what families were learning on home visits, and, critically, the Roots and Wings experience provided invaluable opportunities for mutual support and making family-to-family connections. After exploring their options, the family elected to pursue cochlear implantation to support their goals for Lukas to learn spoken language.

Lukas received bilateral cochlear implants at 12 months of age. Following activation, his early intervention program expanded to individual family–infant sessions focused on listening development to promote spoken language. His service provider recalled that Lukas adjusted quickly to his cochlear implants, and the parents were successful in implementing full-time use very early in the process. It helped that Lukas was lateralizing and searching for sounds around him, turning in response to his parents' voices, and beginning to connect meaning to sound (microwave means food!). He would vocalize responsively each time his devices were turned on in the morning, and his vocalizations appeared to be getting more complex. His changing auditory behaviors reinforced the parents' goals. Their new habits of daily device checking and monitoring became "a given" as part of the early morning dressing routine. Device use was promoted during full waking hours by all family members. Many aspects of this case seemed ideal—the parents formed a partnership readily with their providers, became informed decision makers, and were able to clearly articulate needs and goals to their early intervention team. The service provider observed that they seemed to be able to put deafness in perspective and get on with parenting their curious little boy. So one might ask what else they needed from the early intervention process. Several of the answers make this a more interesting story to share.

The service provider who began working with the family following cochlear implantation recalled what she valued most about forming a partnership with this family. She stated that working closely with the family gave her important insights about what they especially valued in their daily routines with their son. For example, they took pride in their well-established routine of daily book reading with Lukas. By 1 year of age, he was already in love with books, and books were constantly in his diaper bag as the family went about the community. The service provider recognized the value of linking auditory-linguistic routines to the books they were already enjoying. Early on, they experimented together with strategies that would connect sound with meaning by offering auditory contrasts (e.g., finding the vehicle that goes "ahhhhh" [airplane] versus the one that goes "vrmmm vrmmm beep-beep" [car]—see *Learning to Listen Sounds* from Dave Sindrey at http://www.hearingjourney.com/userfiles/File/1_05instr.pdf). Lukas quickly associated these highly contrastive sounds with the objects and then began to recognize their labels, pointing to the pictures as they were named during story sharing.

The service provider noted that these gregarious and friendly parents quickly picked up on language stimulation strategies, providing very rich input. They also figured out how to embellish by engineering opportunities for Lukas to listen. They consistently used an auditory-first approach (see Chapter 7) and often used the strategy of "tell then show," providing labels and descriptions in joint attention routines followed by showing Lukas what they meant and then telling him again. Lukas's receptive abilities grew quickly, but supports were needed to encourage his expressive language, which appeared to be lagging well behind what he was able to comprehend as he approached his second birthday. The service provider coached the family to use his comprehension as a gauge for increasing expectations for his expressive participation in their conversations. In addition, she supported them in strengthening his listening skills as a route to promoting his speech production. One of the more effective strategies was to ascertain what would happen (experiment) if they increased expectations for his conversational turns and their clarity.

Interestingly, a temperament discussion was useful in discovering ways to increase Lukas's participation as a conversational partner. The mother explained that her son is fairly withdrawn, especially in new situations and/or with new people (see Video clip 5.1). In contrast, his parents are highly social and enjoy engaging with others. The mother went on to describe how she accommodated to Lukas's style in these situations by toning down her natural desire to approach and allowing him to gradually warm up. This discussion revealed some parent–child differences in temperament and also demonstrated the mother's ability to attune and adapt to her son's style. This flexibility could be built on as the parents sought to draw Lukas more actively into conversations. The parents were so accustomed to providing rich input. It helped to raise the expectation for Lukas's conversational turns, which required a focus on conversation, not just high-quality input. The parents discovered that it helped pace their input, provide more pause time, and use expectant waiting to encourage Lukas to contribute. As his expressive language grew, they regularly responded contingently, following his conversational lead and expanding his comments. During book reading, they gave him opportunities for auditory closure ("And then baby bear said, '_____'") and encouragement to sequence by predicting the next event in a familiar book. They purposely left out parts or used an inaccurate statement, which he quickly refuted and corrected. As his language grew, the focus shifted to asking more complex questions, talking about thoughts and feelings, and conversing more than they questioned. They also worked together with the service provider on natural and supportive ways to

increase the expectations for the clarity of speech (see Video clips 5.7 and 5.8).

The family became strong advocates for Lukas. Both parents worked outside the home in busy careers. They worked closely with the child care setting to ensure Lukas's auditory access. The staff became conversant with managing his technology and ensuring its function and use. Lukas's spoken language skills were formally assessed when he was 2 years, 10 months of age as the family was preparing to make the transition out of the birth-to-3 program. He achieved age-appropriate scores in spoken language on norm-referenced measures (total standard score of 110 on the Preschool Language Scale, Fifth Edition; standard score of 99 on the Goldman-Fristoe Test of Articulation). The family continues to receive support services to ensure that Lukas will maintain and exceed these promising performance levels.[2]

---

2. Case study contributed by Katie Brennan, M.S., CCC-SLP.

## SUMMARY AND FUTURE DIRECTIONS

Early interventions that focus on promoting spoken language in infants and young children who are D/HH share many of the features of any family-centered approach. For example, primary emphasis is placed on empowering family members as the child's most influential teachers and supporting them in gaining the confidence and competence for this role. Service providers seek to build on strengths in the family–infant relationship and support the family in natural language facilitation throughout daily routines. Particularly unique components of spoken language interventions include the promotion of 1) rigorous and appropriate management of hearing technology, 2) caregiver self-efficacy in managing the child's technology and monitoring functional auditory skills, 3) caregiver skill in encouraging the child's reliance on listening as a route to spoken language learning, 4) embellished opportunities for the child to listen and communicate, and 5) parental contingent responses to the child's verbalizations and use of strategies that promote turn taking in conversation with the child. This chapter has focused on expected family out-comes and supportive service provider behaviors that are integral to spoken language interventions. The viability of spoken language approaches has been bolstered by early identification and early provision of improved hearing technologies. Emerging evidence suggests that average spoken language outcomes are improving for children who are D/HH; but the field cannot be complacent, given the wide individual differences in outcomes observed in most studies. The following future directions deserve our attention so that more children may reach their potential:

1.  We concur with Rhoades (2006) that there is an ongoing need for research collaborations and prospective, longitudinal study of the spoken language outcomes of children and families who receive listening-based approaches to intervention. Do these approaches meet the needs of underresourced families (e.g., lower socioeconomic status)? If not, what can we do to help the approach better meet those needs? How do approaches need to be adapted when the child has multiple disabilities?

2.  In principle, interventions that promote spoken language through listening require close collaboration among the service provider, the family, and the pediatric audiologist. Future research should document the degree to which such collaborations are operationalized along with any barriers to implementation. Because harnessing the technology to optimize audibility is so central to the intervention approach, it would be worthwhile to determine how this collaborative factor may be contributing to positive outcomes.

3.  Service providers should engage in an ongoing process of self-reflection to determine how to optimize their interventions for individual families.

4.  Efforts to develop ecologically valid and sensitive measures to guide the work on home visits should continue.

## SUGGESTED READINGS

Cole, E.B., & Flexer, C. (2016). *Children with hearing loss: Developing listening and talking, birth to six* (3rd ed.). San Diego, CA: Plural.

This comprehensive resource describes the foundations of listening and spoken language approaches applied to young children who are D/HH. The authors describe methods for developing high levels of family involvement in the promotion of language and listening skills. This is a valuable resource for students and practitioners as well as parents of young children who are deaf or hard of hearing.

Estabrooks, W. (2012). *101 FAQs about auditory-verbal practice.* Washington, DC: Alexander Graham Bell Association for the Deaf or Hard of Hearing.

This text contains contributions from numerous Listening and Spoken Language Specialists (LSLS) certified practitioners and is edited by Warren Estabrooks. It describes the history of auditory-verbal and LSLS practices, collaborations, educational elements, and outcomes research. This is a valuable resource for practitioners interested in listening and spoken language intervention.

Rhoades, E.A., & Duncan, J. (Eds.). (2010). *Auditory-verbal practice: Toward a family-centered approach.* Springfield, IL: Charles C. Thomas.

This innovative, edited text explores the implementation of auditory-verbal practices in the context of family-centered practices. It offers multidisciplinary perspectives, including family systems theory, and a goal is to support practitioners in understanding the multitude of concepts underlying family-centered practices.

## LEARNING ACTIVITIES

1.  Examine the information in Table 5.2. If you have conducted home visits with families, ask yourself the self-reflective questions. Did you encounter any barriers to implementing family-centered practices? If you have not yet conducted home visits, interview a professional who has, getting that service provider's views on the self-reflective questions. In practice, does that professional encounter barriers to the implementation of family-centered practices? If so, what are they and how are they addressed?

2.  Visit the Listening Room web site (http://thelisteningroom.com) and sign up for a free account. Navigate to infant-toddler lessons provided by Dave Sindrey. Review one of the lessons provided and determine how the idea could be incorporated in a natural routine on a home visit.

## REFERENCES

Ambrose, S.E., VanDam, M., & Moeller, M.P. (2014). Linguistic input, electronic media, and communication outcomes of toddlers with hearing loss. *Ear and Hearing, 35*(2), 139–147.

Ambrose, S.E., Walker, E.A., Unflat-Berry, L.M., Oleson, J.J., & Moeller, M.P. (in press). Quantity and quality of caregivers' linguistic input to 18-month and 3-year-old children who are hard of hearing. *Ear and Hearing.*

Aragon, M., & Yoshinaga-Itano, C. (2012). Using Language ENvironment Analysis to improve outcomes for children who are deaf or hard of hearing. *Seminars in Speech and Language, 33*(4), 340–353.

Bagatto, M.P., Moodie, S.T., Malandrino, A.C., Richert, F., Clench, D., & Scollie, S. (2011). The University of Western Ontario pediatric audiological monitoring protocol (UWO PedAMP). *Trends in Amplification, 15*(1–2), 57–76.

Baumwell, L., Tamis-LeMonda, C.S., & Bornstein, M.H. (1997). Maternal verbal sensitivity and child language comprehension. *Infant Behavior and Development, 20*(2), 247–258.

Beattie, R. (2006). The oral methods and spoken language acquisition. In P.E. Spencer & M. Marschark (Eds.), *Advances in the spoken language development of deaf and hard of hearing children* (pp. 103–135). New York, NY: Oxford University Press.

Bradham, T.S., & Houston, K.T. (2015). *Assessing listening and spoken language in children with hearing loss.* San Diego, CA: Plural.

Brennan-Jones, C.G., White, J., Rush, R.W., & Law, J. (2014). *Auditory-verbal therapy for promoting spoken language development in children with permanent hearing impairments.* The Cochrane Library. Retrieved from http://onlinelibrary.wiley.com/doi/10.1002/14651858.CD010100.pub2/full

Brown, P., & Nott, P. (2006). Family-centered practice in early intervention for oral language development: Philosophy, methods and results. In P.E. Spencer & M. Marschark (Eds.), *Advances in the spoken language development of deaf and hard of hearing children* (pp. 136–165). New York, NY: Oxford University Press.

Cantle Moore, R. (2004). *The infant monitor of vocal production (IMP).* North Rocks, New South Wales, Australia: Royal Institute for Deaf and Blind Children. Retrieved from http://ridbcrenwickcentre.com/imp

Carotta, C., Cline, K.M., & Brennan, K. (2014). *Auditory consultant resource network handbook.* Omaha, NE: Boys Town National Research Hospital.

Centers for Disease Control and Prevention. (2013). *Hearing loss in children: Data and statistics.* Retrieved May 19, 2015, from http://www.cdc.gov/ncbddd/hearingloss/data.html.

Ching, T.Y., Dillon, H., Day, J., Crowe, K., Close, L., Chisholm, K., & Hopkins, T. (2009). Early language outcomes of children with cochlear implants: Interim findings of the NAL study on longitudinal outcomes of children with hearing impairment. *Cochlear Implants International, 10*(Suppl. 1), 28–32.

Ching, T.Y., Dillon, H., Marnane, V., Hou, S., Day, J., Seeto, M., . . . Yeh, A. (2013). Outcomes of early-and late-identified children at 3 years of age: Findings from a prospective population-based study. *Ear and Hearing, 34*(5), 535–552.

Cole, E.B., Carroll, E., Coyne, J., Gill, E., & Paterson, M. (2005). Early spoken language through audition. In *The SKI-HI Curriculum* (Vol. 2, pp. 1279–1394). Logan, UT: Hope.

Cole, E.B., & Flexer, C. (2016). *Children with hearing loss: Developing listening and talking, birth to six* (3rd ed.). San Diego, CA: Plural.

Crandell, C.C., & Smaldino, J.J. (2000). Classroom acoustics for children with normal hearing and with hearing impairment. *Language, Speech, and Hearing Services in Schools, 31,* 362–370.

Cruz, I., Quittner, A.L., Marker, C., & DesJardin, J.L. (2013). Identification of effective strategies to promote language in deaf children with cochlear implants. *Child Development, 84*(2), 543–559.

Dale, P.S., & Fenson, L. (1996). Lexical development norms for young children. *Behavior Research Methods Instruments and Computers, 28*(1), 125–127.

DesJardin, J.L. (2005). Maternal perceptions of self-efficacy and involvement in the auditory development of young children with prelingual deafness. *Journal of Early Intervention, 27*(3), 193–209.

DesJardin, J.L., & Eisenberg, L.S. (2007). Maternal contributions: Supporting language development in young children with cochlear implants. *Ear and Hearing, 28*(4), 456–469.

Estabrooks, W. (Ed.). (2006). *Auditory-verbal therapy and practice.* Washington, DC: Alexander Graham Bell Association for the Deaf and Hard of Hearing.

Estabrooks, W. (Ed.). (2012). *101 FAQs about auditory-verbal practice.* Washington, DC: Alexander Graham Bell Association for the Deaf and Hard of Hearing.

Farmer, T.A., Monaghan, P., Misyak, J.B., & Christiansen, M.H. (2011). Phonological typicality influences sentence processing in predictive contexts: Reply to Staub,

Grant, Clifton, and Rayner (2009). *Journal of Experimental Psychology-Learning Memory and Cognition, 37*(5), 1318–1325.

Fenson, L., Marchman, V.A., Thal, D., Dale, P.S., Reznick, J.S., & Bates, E. (2007). *MacArthur-Bates Communicative Development Inventories: User's guide and technical manual* (2nd ed.). Baltimore, MD: Paul H. Brookes Publishing Co.

Finitzo-Hieber, T., & Tillman, T.W. (1978). Room acoustics effects on monosyllabic word discrimination ability for normal and hearing-impaired children. *Journal of Speech, Language, and Hearing Research, 21*(3), 440–458.

Fitzpatrick, E., Rhoades, E.A., Dornan, D., Thomas, E., & Goldberg, D. (2012). What are some of the evidence-based outcomes of auditory-verbal practice? In W. Estabrooks (Ed.), *101 FAQs about auditory-verbal practice* (pp. 419–436). Washington, DC: Alexander Graham Bell Association for the Deaf and Hard of Hearing.

Frattali, C.M. (1998). *Measuring outcomes in speech-language pathology.* New York, NY: Thieme.

Geers, A.E., Strube, M.J., Tobey, E.A., & Moog, J.S. (2011). Epilogue: Factors contributing to long-term outcomes of cochlear implantation in early childhood. *Ear and Hearing, 32*(Suppl. 1), 84S.

Girolametto, L., & Weitzman, E. (2006). It takes two to talk: The Hanen program for parents: Early language intervention through caregiver training. In R. McCauley & M. Fey (Eds.), *Treatment of language disorders in children* (pp. 77–103). Baltimore, MD: Paul H. Brookes Publishing Co.

Goldin-Meadow, S., Goodrich, W., Sauer, E., & Iverson, J.M. (2007). Young children use their hands to tell their mothers what to say. *Developmental Science, 10*(6), 778–785.

Goldstein, M.H., & Schwade, J.A. (2008). Social feedback to infants' babbling facilitates rapid phonological learning. *Psychological Science, 19*(5), 515–523.

Hadley, P.A. (2014). Approaching early grammatical intervention from a sentence-focused framework. *Language, Speech, and Hearing Services in Schools, 45*(2), 110–116.

Halpin, K.S., Smith, K.Y., Widen, J.E., & Chertoff, M.E. (2010). Effects of universal newborn hearing screening on an early intervention program for children with hearing loss, birth to 3 yr of age. *Journal of the American Academy of Audiology, 21*(3), 169–175.

Hancock, T.B., & Kaiser, A.P. (2006). Enhanced milieu teaching. In R. McCauley & M. Fey (Eds.), *Treatment of language disorders in children* (pp. 203–236). Baltimore, MD: Paul H. Brookes Publishing Co.

Hanft, B.E., Rush, D.D., & Shelden, M.L.L. (2004). *Coaching families and colleagues in early childhood.* Baltimore, MD: Paul H. Brookes Publishing Co.

Harrison, M., Roush, J., & Wallace, J. (2003). Trends in age of identification and intervention in infants with hearing loss. *Ear and Hearing, 24*(1), 89–95.

Hoff, E. (2003). The specificity of environmental influence: Socioeconomic status affects early vocabulary development via maternal speech. *Child Development, 74*(5), 1368–1378.

Hoff, E. (2006). *Language development* (4th ed.). Belmont, CA: Cengage Learning.

Hoff, E., & Naigles, L. (2002). How children use input to acquire a lexicon. *Child Development, 73*(2), 418–433.

Holte, L., Walker, E., Oleson, J., Spratford, M., Moeller, M.P., Roush, P., . . . Tomblin, J.B. (2012). Factors influencing follow-up to newborn hearing screening for infants who are hard of hearing. *American Journal of Audiology, 21*(2), 163–174.

Hurtado, N., Marchman, V.A., & Fernald, A. (2008). Does input influence uptake? Links between maternal talk, processing speed and vocabulary size in Spanish-learning children. *Developmental Science, 11*(6), F31–F39.

Huttenlocher, J., Haight, W., Bryk, A., Seltzer, M., & Lyons, T. (1991). Early vocabulary growth: Relation to language input and gender. *Developmental Psychology, 27*(2), 236–248.

Johnson, C.D., Benson, P.V., & Seaton, J.B. (1997). *Educational audiology handbook.* Independence, KY: Cengage Learning.

Kishon-Rabin, L., Taitelbaum-Swead, R., Ezrati-Vinacour, R., & Hildesheimer, M. (2005). Prelexical vocalization in normal hearing and hearing-impaired infants before and after cochlear implantation and its relation to early auditory skills. *Ear and Hearing, 26*(Suppl. 4), 17S–29S.

Kishon-Rabin, L., Taitelbaum-Swead, R., & Segal, O. (2009). Prelexical infant scale evaluation: From vocalization to audition in hearing and hearing impaired infants. In L. Eisenberg (Ed.), *Clinical management of children with cochlear implants* (pp. 325–68). San Diego, CA: Plural.

Klein, R., & Gilkerson, L. (2000). Personnel preparation for early childhood intervention programmes. In J.P. Shonkoff & S.J. Meisels (Eds.), *Handbook of early childhood intervention* (pp. 454–483). New York, NY: Cambridge University Press.

Knowles, M.S. (1970). *The modern practice of adult education.* New York, NY: Association Press.

Koehlinger, K.M., Owen Van Horne, A.J., & Moeller, M.P. (2013). Grammatical outcomes of 3 & 6 year old children who are hard of hearing. *Journal of Speech, Language, and Hearing Research, 56*(5), 1701–1714.

Kristal, J. (2005). *The temperament perspective: Working with children's behavioral styles.* Baltimore, MD: Paul H. Brookes Publishing Co.

Kuhl, P.K. (2000). A new view of language acquisition. *Proceedings of the National Academy of Sciences, 97*(22), 11850–11857.

Kuhl, P.K. (2010). Brain mechanisms in early language acquisition. *Neuron, 67*(5), 713–727.

Locke, J.L. (1995). *The child's path to spoken language.* Boston, MA: Harvard University Press.

Masur, E.F. (1982). Mothers' responses to infants' object-related gestures: Influences on lexical development. *Journal of Child Language, 9*(1), 23–30.

McCreery, R.W., Bentler, R.A., & Roush, P.A. (2013). Characteristics of hearing aid fittings in infants and young children. *Ear and Hearing, 34*(6), 701–710.

McGuckian, M., & Henry, A. (2007). The grammatical morpheme deficit in moderate hearing impairment. *International Journal of Language & Communication Disorders, 42*(Suppl. 1), 17–36.

Mitchell, R.E., & Karchmer, M.A. (2004). Chasing the mythical ten percent: Parental hearing status of deaf and hard of hearing students in the United States. *Sign Language Studies, 4*(2), 138–163.

Moeller, M.P., Bass-Ringdahl, S., Ambrose, S.E., VanDam, M., & Tomblin, J.B. (2011). Understanding communication outcomes: New tools and insights. In R.C. Seewald & J.M. Bamford (Eds.), *A sound foundation through early amplification: Proceedings of the 2010 international conference* (pp. 245–260). Stafa, Switzerland: Phonak AG Immediate Proceedings.

Moeller, M.P., Carr, G., Seaver, L., Stredler-Brown, A., & Holzinger, D. (2013). Best practices in family-centered early intervention for children who are deaf or hard of hearing: An international consensus statement. *Journal of Deaf Studies and Deaf Education, 18*(4), 429–445.

Moeller, M.P., & Condon, M. (1994). A collaborative, problem-solving approach to early intervention. In J. Roush and N.D. Matkin (Eds.), *Infants and toddlers with hearing loss: Identification, assessment and family-centered intervention* (pp. 163–192). Parkton, MD: York Press.

Moeller, M.P., Hoover, B., Peterson, B., & Stelmachowicz, P.G. (2009). Consistency of hearing aid use in infants with early-identified hearing loss. *American Journal of Audiology, 18*(1), 14–22.

Moeller, M.P., Schow, R.L., & Whitaker, M.M. (2013). Audiologic rehabilitation for children: Assessment and management. In R.L. Schow & M.A. Nerbonne (Eds.), *Introduction to audiologic rehabilitation* (pp. 305–375). Boston, MA: Pearson.

Moeller, M.P., & Tomblin, J.B. (in press). An introduction to the outcomes of children with hearing loss study. *Ear and Hearing.*

Monaghan, P., Chater, N., & Christiansen, M.H. (2005). The differential role of phonological and distributional cues in grammatical categorisation. *Cognition, 96*, 143–182.

Muse, C., Harrison, J., Yoshinaga-Itano, C., Grimes, A., Brookhouser, P.E., Epstein, S., . . . Martin, B. (2013). Supplement to the JCIH 2007 position statement: Principles and guidelines for early intervention after confirmation that a child is deaf or hard of hearing. *Pediatrics, 131*(4), e1324–e1349.

National Council for Accreditation of Teacher Education. (2013). *NCATE glossary.* Retrieved from http:// www .ncate .org/ Standards/ NCATEUnitStandards/ NCATE Glossary/ tabid/ 477/ Default .aspx

Niparko, J.K., Tobey, E.A., Thal, D.J., Eisenberg, L.S., Wang, N.Y., Quittner, A.L., & Fink, N.E. (2010). Spoken language development in children following cochlear implantation. *JAMA, 303*(15), 1498–1506.

Nittrouer, S. (2010). *Early development of children with hearing loss.* San Diego, CA: Plural.

Nott, P., Cowan, R., Brown, P.M., & Wigglesworth, G. (2009). Early language development in children with profound hearing loss fitted with a device at a young age: Part I—the time period taken to acquire first words and first word combinations. *Ear and Hearing, 30*(5), 526–540.

Oller, D.K., Eilers, R.E., & Basinger, D. (2001). Intuitive identification of infant vocal sounds by parents. *Developmental Science, 4*(1), 49–60.

Prizant, B.M., & Wetherby, A.M. (2002). *Communication and Behavior Scales Developmental Profile* (First Normed Edition). Baltimore, MD: Paul H. Brookes Publishing Co.

Proctor-Williams, K., Fey, M.E., & Loeb, D.F. (2001). Parental recasts and production of copulas and articles by children with specific language impairment and typical language. *American Journal of Speech-Language Pathology, 10*(2), 155–168.

Quittner, A.L., Cruz, I., Barker, D.H., Tobey, E., Eisenberg, L.S., Niparko, J.K., & Childhood Development After Cochlear Implantation Investigative Team. (2013). Effects of maternal sensitivity and cognitive and linguistic stimulation on cochlear implant users' language development over four years. *Journal of Pediatrics, 162*(2), 343–348.

Ramsdell, H.L., Oller, D.K., Buder, E.H., Ethington, C.A., & Chorna, L. (2012). Identification of prelinguistic phonological categories. *Journal of Speech, Language, and Hearing Research, 55*(6), 1626–1639.

Rhoades, E.A. (2006). Research outcomes of auditory-verbal intervention: Is the approach justified? *Deafness & Education International, 8*(3), 125–143.

Roggman, L.A., Cook, G.A., Innocenti, M.S., Norman, V.J., & Christiansen, K., & Anderson, S. (2013). *Parenting interactions with children: Checklist of observations linked to outcomes.* Baltimore, MD: Paul H. Brookes Publishing Co.

Rossi, K. (2003). *Learn to talk around the clock.* Washington, DC: Alexander Graham Bell Association of the Deaf and Hard of Hearing.

Sacks, C., Shay, S., Repplinger, L., Leffel, K.R., Sapolich, S.G., Suskind, E., . . . Suskind, D. (2013). Pilot testing of a parent-directed intervention (Project ASPIRE) for underserved children who are deaf or hard of hearing. *Child Language Teaching and Therapy, 30*(1), 91–102.

Sass-Lehrer, M., Moeller, M.P., & Stredler-Brown, A. (2015). What every early intervention provider should know. In M. Sass-Lehrer (ed.). *Early Intervention for Deaf and Hard-of-Hearing Infants, Toddlers, and Their Families: Interdisciplinary perspectives,* New York: Oxford University Press.

Schlesinger, H.S. (1987). Effects of powerlessness on dialogue and development: Disability, poverty, and the human condition. In B.W. Heller, L.M. Floor, & L.S. Zegans (Eds.), *Psychosocial interventions with sensorially disabled persons* (pp. 1–27). Mind and medicine series. New York, NY: Grune & Stratton.

Snow, C.E. (1994). Beginning from baby talk: Twenty years of research on input and interaction. In C. Gallaway & B.J. Richards (Eds.), *Input and interaction in language acquisition* (pp. 3–12). London, England: Cambridge University Press.

Spivak, L., Sokol, H., Auerbach, C., & Gershkovich, S. (2009). Newborn hearing screening follow-up: Factors affecting hearing aid fitting by 6 months of age. *American Journal of Audiology, 18*(1), 24–33.

St. Clair, M.C., Monaghan, P., & Christiansen, M.H. (2010). Learning grammatical categories from distributional cues: Flexible frames for language acquisition. *Cognition, 116,* 341–360.

Stein, L.K., Jabaley, T., Spitz, R., Stoakley, D., & McGee, T. (1990). The hearing-impaired infant: Patterns of identification and habilitation revisited. *Ear and Hearing, 11*(3), 201–205.

Stredler-Brown, A., Moeller, M.P., Gallegos, R., & Cordwin, J. (2006). *Early intervention illustrated: Language partners: Building a strong foundation* (DVD). Boys Town, NE: Boys Town Press.

Suskind, D., Leffel, K.R., Hernandez, M.W., Sapolich, S.G., Suskind, E., Kirkham, E., & Meehan, P. (2013). An exploratory study of "quantitative linguistic feedback": Effect of LENA feedback on adult language production. *Communication Disorders Quarterly, 34*(4), 199–209.

Szagun, G., & Stumper, B. (2012). Age or experience? The influence of age at implantation, social and linguistic environment on language development in children with cochlear implants. *Journal of Speech, Language, and Hearing Research, 55*(6), 1640–1654.

Tamis-LeMonda, C.S., Bornstein, M.H., & Baumwell, L. (2001). Maternal responsiveness and children's achievement of language milestones. *Child Development, 72*(3), 748–767.

Tamis-LeMonda, C.S., & Rodriguez, E.T. (2008). Parents' role in fostering young children's learning and language development. *Encyclopedia on Early Childhood Development*. Retrieved from http://www.child-encyclopedia.com/Pages/PDF/Tamis-Lemonda-RodriguezANGxp-Language.pdf

Thomas, A., Birch, H.G., Chess, S., Hertzig, M.E., & Korn, S. (1963). *Behavioral individuality in early childhood*. New York, NY: New York University Press.

Tomblin, J.B., Harrison, M., Ambrose, S.E., Walker, E.A., Oleson, J.J., & Moeller, M.P. (in press). Language outcomes in young children with mild to severe hearing loss. *Ear and Hearing*.

Tomblin, J.B., Oleson, J., Ambrose, S.E., Walker, E.A., & Moeller, M.P. (2014). The influence of hearing aids on speech and language development in children with hearing loss. *JAMA Otolaryngology—Head & Neck Surgery, 140*(5), 403–409.

Walker, E.A., Spratford, M., Moeller, M.P., Oleson, J., Ou, H., Roush, P., & Jacobs, S. (2013). Predictors of hearing aid use time in children with mild-to-severe hearing loss. *Language, Speech, and Hearing Services in the Schools, 44*(1), 73–88.

Watt, N., Wetherby, A., & Shumway, S. (2006). Prelinguistic predictors of language outcome at 3 years of age. *Journal of Speech, Language, and Hearing Research, 49*(6), 1224–1237.

Werker, J.F., & Yeung, H.H. (2005). Infant speech perception bootstraps word learning. *Trends in Cognitive Sciences, 9*(11), 519–527.

Wetherby, A., Allen, L., Cleary, J., Kublin, K., & Goldstein, H. (2002). Validity and reliability of the Communication and Symbolic Behavior Scales™ Developmental Profile with very young children. *Journal of Speech, Language, & Hearing Research, 45*, 1202–1219.

Wetherby, A., Goldstein, H., Cleary, J., Allen, L., & Kublin, K. (2003). Early identification of children with communication delays: Concurrent and predictive validity of the CSBS Developmental Profile. *Infants and Young Children, 16*, 161–174.

**APPENDIX 5.1**

# Optimizing Auditory Access

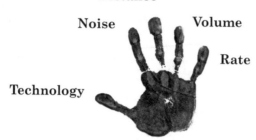

## TECHNOLOGY

❑ How is my child doing with wearing hearing technology each day? Could we use help?

❑ Did we check the devices today? Did he or she respond as expected on the Ling Six-Sound Test?

❑ Do I need to touch base with the audiologist on questions or issues?

## NOISE

❑ What noises in the background can I reduce (television, computer, appliances)?

❑ What are the noisiest places we go and what can we do about it?

❑ How can conversation be most accessible at the dinner table?

## DISTANCE

❑ How does my child usually respond close by and at a distance?

❑ Do I move close to my child to share activities and important ideas?

❑ Do I check to make sure my child understood communication at a distance?

## VOLUME

❑ Am I speaking at a natural volume that is appropriate for my child?

❑ Do I use stress to emphasize new words or important ideas?

❑ Do I sometimes whisper to draw attention to something interesting?

## RATE OF SPEECH

❑ Am I speaking naturally and not too fast?

❑ Am I pausing to give my child time to understand and respond?

❑ Am I expecting my child to take turns? Do I use expectant waiting to encourage turns?

*Source:* Carotta, Cline, and Brennan (2014).

**6**

# Sign Language, Sign Systems, and Other Visual Modalities

Paula Pittman, Marilyn Sass-Lehrer, and Stacy R. Abrams

Joyful and carefree communicative interactions between infants and their families are a thing of beauty. Loving communication partners are in tune with one another, each watching the other for cues that indicate when to initiate or respond to a communicative event. These free-flowing interactions can be thought of as "a dance" (Raikes & Edwards, 2009) because each partner interprets the other's behaviors to determine the next steps and then responds accordingly (Pressman, Pipp-Seigel, Yoshinaga-Itano, & Deas, 1999). Whereas parents and other caregivers often lead the dance, infants have an innate desire to participate and quickly learn how to respond to their communication partner's facial expressions, touch, voice, or signs. Through these interactions, a bond of trust and enjoyment develops—a bond that provides a foundation for the development of social-emotional well-being and linguistic competence.

When a parent and child share the same **hearing status** and **communication approach** (e.g., listening and speaking, watching and signing, using cued speech), this dance tends to go smoothly, with parent and young child in rhythm with one another. But being deaf from an early age has the potential to strain the communicative dance—especially when the primary caregivers have typical hearing (Lederberg & Mobley, 1990; Lederberg & Prezbindowski, 2000; Meadow-Orlans, 1994; Spencer, 2003). Regardless of the hearing status and the senses (vision, auditory, touch, or a combination of the three) used to communicate with a child who is deaf or hard of hearing (D/HH), the ultimate goal for the family and child is to achieve synchrony in their communicative dance.

We receive information about the world around us through our senses. We rely primarily on our senses of vision, hearing, and touch to communicate. Infants who are typically developing (TD) use all three of these senses to communicate with and understand others. Typically, most children rely increasingly on vision and audition as they develop communication skills and acquire language. For children who have hearing thresholds in the average range, spoken language is acquired primarily through the auditory channel; however, information gained visually is also vitally important. For a child who is D/HH and does not have sufficient access to audition, visual support may be needed to develop the skills required to communicate clearly (Spencer & Koester, in press), and for some children, **American Sign Language (ASL)** may be essential for language acquisition.

A variety of communication approaches may be used to enhance visual learning in children. These approaches include 1) **bilingual** approaches that combine ASL with English in some form—written, spoken, signed; 2) **cued speech**, which relies on hand shapes and spatial positioning of these shapes around the face along with speechreading cues to convey meaning; and 3) **simultaneous communication**, which uses both a system of signs (e.g., **Manually Coded English [MCE]**) and spoken language. Whereas ASL is a true language (Stokoe, 1960/2005) represented in the visual-gestural **modality**, the other approaches are systems that have been created to help children who are D/HH have access to English through a visual modality (Moores, 2001). Other ways in which signs are used as bridges between ASL and English include Pidgin Signed English (PSE) and sign-supported speech.

Some communication approaches emphasize an auditory modality and may or may not include a visual component. For example, an auditory-verbal (AV) approach focuses on listening as the primary avenue to understand and acquire spoken language during intervention activities (see Chapter 7). In con-trast, multisensory approaches incorporate listening as well as speechread-ing, gestures, and facial expression to comprehend spoken language. Many children who are D/HH use a combination of visual and auditory modalities and communication approaches to understand others and express themselves. Children who have limited vision and are D/HH may benefit from tactile modalities in addition to auditory and visual modalities for communication and language development. However, tactile communication systems will not be covered in this chapter. A brief description of the commonly used communication approaches with children who are D/HH can be found in Table 6.1.

Various terms are used to describe how deaf people communicate. These include *options, methodologies, approaches, modalities, choices,* and since 2011, *communication opportunities*. In this chapter, we will be using the term *modality* to represent a sensory modality (e.g., visual, auditory, or tactile) and *communication approaches* to describe the systems used to communicate (e.g., cued speech, MCE, simultaneous communication, listening, spoken language). We will focus on spoken English and ASL to represent the two most common languages used in the education of children who are D/HH in the United States. The day-to-day communication patterns of families may not fit solely into any of the previous descriptions. For example, a child whose language preference is

**Table 6.1.**   Communication approaches

| Approach | Description | Languages incorporated | Modalities incorporated |
|---|---|---|---|
| Bilingual-bimodal | Incorporates the use of two languages, one visual and one spoken. American Sign Language (ASL) is a full and complete visual language with complex grammatical structures that incorporate signs and nonmanual markers expressed on the face and body. ASL has no spoken or written form. ASL is used separately but in the same environments as a true, full, and complete spoken language. The two languages are given equal value and equal representation. | ASL or a native sign language and English or another spoken language | Listening/speaking<br>Print<br>Visual system of signs or cues that represent a spoken language visually<br>Facial/body expression/ gestures<br>Speechreading |
| Simultaneous communication | A true spoken language is used simultaneously with a system of signs (not a true visual language) that borrow from ASL but are put in English order and then said and signed simultaneously. | Spoken English or another spoken language | Visual system of signs or cues that represent a spoken language visually<br>Facial/body expression/ gestures<br>Listening/speaking<br>Speechreading |
| Sign-supported speech | Signs are used to clarify and support the use of spoken language. Primarily used when children rely on mostly audition and spoken language to communicate but may need visual support to understand spoken language in loud settings or for new information. | Spoken English or another spoken language | Listening/speaking<br>Visual system of signs that represent a spoken language visually<br>Facial/body expression/ gestures<br>Speechreading |
| Pidgin Signed English | Used when native English speakers are learning ASL and use ASL signs without using appropriate ASL grammar and sign in an incomplete way. Used as a bridge to link spoken and signed language and is not seen as a true representation of either language. | Parts of spoken language and parts of ASL or a signed English system | Listening/speaking<br>Signs (may be ASL signs or signs from an English-based sign system)<br>Facial/body expressions/ gestures<br>Speechreading |
| Cued speech | A system of eight arbitrary hand shapes placed in one of four positions near the face that visually presents a phonetic representation of syllables used in spoken English. Cued speech systems have been created to represent the sounds in 48 different languages to make visual the phonemes that are spoken that cannot be visually distinguished through lipreading. | Spoken English or another spoken language | Listening/speaking Spee-chreading<br>System of cues that phonetically represents a spoken language<br>Facial/body expression/ gestures |

*(continued)*

**Table 6.1.**    *(continued)*

| Approach | Description | Languages incorporated | Modalities incorporated |
|---|---|---|---|
| Auditory-oral | Using listening to understand speech along with speechreading, facial expression, and gestures and using spoken language to interact with others. | Spoken English or another spoken language | Listening/speaking Speechreading Facial/body expression/ gestures |
| Listening and spoken language (previously known as auditory-verbal) | Using primarily listening and audition to understand spoken language and using spoken language to interact and communicate with others. | Spoken English or another spoken language | Listening Speaking |

ASL may need to rely on speechreading cues when playing with hearing cous-ins who don't sign well. Similarly, a child who uses predominately listening for information reception may have to rely on speechreading, gestures, and facial expressions at a noisy family reunion.

Children who are D/HH often require visual access to information they cannot gain through hearing alone. As Marschark and Hauser (2011) state, "Regardless of whether or not they have hearing aids or cochlear implants and whether they primarily use sign language or spoken language, it is through vision and touch that deaf infants will gain access to the world of experience" (p. 56). For children who are D/HH, there may be an innate need to experience the world through their sense of vision very early on. For parents who are not aware of this need, the development of communicative synchrony with their infant can be challenging. Most hearing parents have a lifetime of experience communicating through listening and speaking but very limited experience communicating their ideas visually. As a result, the transition from a fully auditory way of communicating to one that emphasizes visual information is not easy for many parents. This chapter will provide an overview of visual approaches to language development, including sign language (ASL) and sign systems.

## THEORETICAL FRAMEWORK

There is a large body of evidence that supports the presence of a sensitive time period for language development early in life (Bailey, Bruer, Symons, Lichtman, & National Center for Early Development & Learning, 2001; Grimshaw, Adelstein, Bryden, & MacKinnon, 1998; Johnson & Newport, 1989; Lederberg & Spencer, 2005; Mayberry & Eichen, 1991; Newport, 2002; Uylings, 2006). Therefore, it is essential that infants, toddlers, and young children who are D/HH gain optimal access to communication and language early on (Baker, 2011). For some children, visual language, such as ASL, or visual communication systems (e.g., MCE, PSE, cued speech) can help in acquiring language and facilitating communication.

### Communication and Language Continuum

There are a variety of communication approaches available for children who are D/HH (see Table 6.1), all of which have shown to be successful when matched with the needs and abilities of individual children (Stredler-Brown, 2011). The two continua depicted in Figures 6.1 and 6.2 provide a visual representation of the many possible ways that children who are D/HH and their family members may receive information and express themselves. When families freely use the communication strategies that best fit their needs in any given situation, it allows them the opportunity to strive to achieve comfort and ease in their communication interactions.

When families understand there is a range of communication modalities and language approaches (as illustrated in Table 6.1 and Figures 6.1 and 6.2), they are better able to explore different options and make an informed decision about what is best for themselves and their child. The **communication continuum** helps families understand the value of both visual and auditory modalities in receptive and expressive communication and can encourage them to consider all the communication tools available. Families can then respond to their children's communication needs in a manner that places more emphasis on effective communication interaction than on a specific communication approach (see Chapter 9 for more information).

### Receptive Communication Continuum

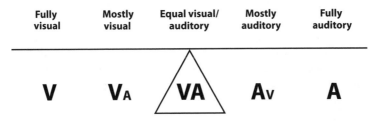

**Figure 6.1.** Possible ways along a continuum that children who are deaf or hard of hearing understand and take in information, communication, and language from receiving information visually to receiving information auditorily. (From McConkey-Robbins, *Loud and Clear,* Advanced Bionics, 2001.)

### Expressive Communication Continuum

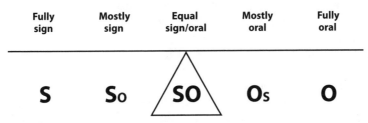

**Figure 6.2.** Possible ways along a continuum that children who are deaf or hard of hearing express themselves, from using sign language only to using spoken language only. (From McConkey-Robbins, *Loud and Clear,* Advanced Bionics, 2001.)

## Bilingualism and Children Who Are Deaf: American Sign Language and English

All children use vision to learn about the world around them, but children who are D/HH with limited auditory access rely heavily on what they see to understand and process information. Yet parents may be advised to avoid using visual input of language and to limit visual communication in order to enhance the development of listening skills. And so researchers ask, does the use of visual language (ASL) or a visual communication or visual sign system impede the development of language overall or hinder the development of spoken language? This question has been debated since before the establishment of formal education for children who are D/HH in the United States.

Research has provided support for the value of early access to sound through hearing aids or cochlear implants to provide stimulation to the auditory nerve (Sharma, Dorman, & Spahr, 2002). Even for children with hearing levels in the severe to profound range, the use of hearing aids stimulates the auditory nerve and can, in some cases, help them comprehend meaningful speech. Likewise, children with profound hearing levels may benefit from auditory stimulation via cochlear implants. Thus, for many children who use hearing aids or cochlear implants, the question becomes, will exposure to two languages—ASL and spoken English—early on enable children to learn both languages fully? Or will exposure to a spoken and a visual language prevent and/or limit the development of one or both languages? Fortunately, research is beginning to provide new insights into these important questions.

For several years, it has been hypothesized that spoken language input received through auditory channels is essential to the overall development of language. One hypothesis was that children who are D/HH and do not receive language input auditorily would lose volume in the auditory cortex. This loss would result in a restructuring of the brain, preventing children from developing and processing language typically. This possibility was investigated by Penhune, Cismaru, Dorsaint-Pierre, Pettito, and Zatorre in 2003. In their study, adults who were born deaf and were visual language users and who had no auditory input from birth were examined using magnetic resonance imaging (MRI) technology. Two areas of the auditory cortex, Heschl's gyrus and the planum temporale, were measured to determine if cortical volume in these centers was reduced when compared with hearing participants. The results indicated that there was no volume difference between deaf and hearing participants and that the location and degree of volume in both areas of the auditory cortex were identical. The only difference noted between the brains of deaf participants in comparison to hearing participants was increased gray matter density in the motor cortex of the brain for the left hand, which was attributed to sign language use by the deaf adults, but there was no difference between the groups in any auditory cortical region. Most importantly, the researchers reported that expected asymmetries in Heschl's gyrus and the planum temporale thought to be related to auditory language processing were preserved in the deaf participants. This suggests that the development, preservation, and maintenance of the auditory cortex do not depend solely on auditory language experience.

More recently, researchers have had the benefit of observing and measuring activity within the brain using functional Near-Infrared Spectroscopy (fNIRS) as both spoken language and visual language (ASL) are being processed. The researchers found that language is processed in the same centers of the brain, regardless of whether that language is presented through a visual or spoken mode (Kovelman et al., 2009). Speculation in years past has been that spoken language is processed in the auditory centers of the brain and visual language processed in the visual cortex. These studies have provided scientific evidence that, in fact, the brain does not discriminate between visual and spoken language; it processes language as language.

Prior to this research, Pettito and Kovelman (2003) studied five children who were early bilinguals. Two of the children were exposed to two spoken languages, and the other three were exposed to a visual language and a spoken language. The study revealed that the children, who were exposed to two languages from birth, displayed no language confusion and met linguistic milestones for both languages at the appropriate ages, regardless of whether the languages used were spoken or visual.

The notion that exposure to a visual language might impede the development of spoken language was also refuted in a study conducted by Hassanzadeh (2012). In this study, the spoken language outcomes of seven deaf children who had cochlear implants and also had deaf parents who used Persian Sign Language as the primary language of the home were compared with the same number of deaf children with cochlear implants who had hearing parents who used spoken language. The children who were native Persian Sign Language users and had deaf parents had spoken language outcomes that were the same or better than the children whose parents were hearing on tests of auditory perception, speech intelligibility, and sentence imitation.

Similar results were found in an earlier study where young children who were deaf and their hearing families had the benefit of home-based early intervention services provided by a trained deaf adult through the experimental Deaf Mentor Program (Watkins, Pittman, & Walden, 1998). Thirty-six children and their families were involved in the study. Eighteen children and their families received weekly home visits from trained **Deaf mentors** who acted as ASL language models for children and families, taught formal ASL skills to family members that helped the family communicate fully with their children during everyday routines and events, and acted as guides for families into the local **Deaf community**, teaching them about **Deaf culture**. Families in the experimental group used ASL with their children and also exposed them to English through print as well as signed English (MCE) and spoken English using simultaneous communication. These families received support from early intervention specialists weekly who taught them skills and strategies for using signed and spoken English. The 18 children and families in the control group used either spoken language only or simultaneous communication using signed and spoken English. They also received weekly visits from early intervention providers who taught them strategies for using English in their daily routines. At the end of the study, children who were in the experimental group that were exposed to both ASL and English had higher scores on tests of English competency than the children in the control group who had been exposed only to English that was either spoken or spoken and signed (Watkins et al., 1998).

These studies suggest that visual language, when used fluently and frequently in meaningful ways throughout the day, does not limit the development of spoken language or vice versa. These studies are in contrast to several demonstrating that children in oral environments outperformed children in educational environments that use both spoken and signed communication (Boons et al., 2012; Dettman, Wall, Constantinescu, & Dowell, 2013; Geers, Nicholas, & Sedey, 2003). Additional research is needed to clarify variables that lead to successful outcomes in different communication environments. Children who are D/HH who gain access to spoken language through listening devices and also have access to visual language in a bilingual environment appear to achieve communication and language milestones in each language in similar time lines to children who have exposure to only visual or only spoken language. In addition to the linguistic and cognitive benefits, bilingual children who are D/HH rate themselves as socially content with a positive sense of themselves (Pittman, 2003) (see Video clip 6.1). Being bilingual allows the child who is D/HH access to individuals who are hearing and to hearing culture as well as the Deaf community and individuals who are D/HH, enriching their lives.

In summary, when children who are D/HH have limited access to spoken language, they can benefit from visual support to acquire language visually. Infants who are D/HH use their most intact systems—vision and touch—to learn about their world, and for some children, the limited auditory information they receive may be insufficient to acquire a strong language foundation. Visual language, such as ASL, and visual communication systems, such as MCE, have a positive impact on the development of children's overall language skills and abilities, including the development of social cognition and literacy skills. Visual systems such as cued speech and fingerspelling (i.e., hand shapes used to represent syllable sequences) can also provide support in the development and recognition of particular linguistic details that a child may miss when in a spoken language environment. Fingerspelling is an essential component of ASL and also manually coded English sign systems (Padden, 2006). Both have demonstrated benefits to the development of literacy. Communicative success—this precious exchange of emotion and language—between the parent or caregiver and the child is the ultimate goal. Communication approaches used with each child who is deaf or hard of hearing should enhance rather than hinder this dance. When parents understand that this communication interaction is the goal and that communication and language success can be found in all communication approaches available to them, they can more easily and confidently find the communication match that best meets the needs of their unique relationship with their child.

### Intersubjective Developmental Theory

In 2003, Loots and Deviś e proposed an intersubjective developmental theory that was based on earlier work by Stern (1985) and Trevarthen (1979). This theory proposes four stages that occur in the development of intersubjectivity (shared understanding) in the interactions between a mother and her child. Each developmental stage is identified by unique mother–child interaction. The four stages are 1) emerging (birth–2 months of age), 2) physical (2–8 months), 3) existential (8–12 months of age), and 4) symbolic (13 months of age and older).

***Emerging and Physical Intersubjectivity***   In the first two phases of development, emerging and physical, the communicative dance between a parent and child is created. In these stages of development, a parent responds to the needs, movements, actions, sounds, and expressions of his or her infant, creating a synchronized cycle of communication and interactivity. It is during this phase that an infant watches his or her parent and responds, stimulating social behavior and creating reciprocity of interactions between parent and child. Parents use aspects of "motherese" or "parentese," which are characterized by exaggerated words and facial expressions, repetition of words and phrases, variations in pitch that create a sing-song quality to the voice, and shorter and clearer enunciation of words (Cooper & Aslin, 1990; Jung, Cumming, & Rodda, 1992; Messer, 1994). Parents and other family members will engage their child with questions, often providing a response for the child, calling the child's name, as if the child is participating in a conversational dialogue with them. This interchange occurs even when the child is only a few days or a few weeks old and unable to carry on a conversation (Koester, 1988; Papoušek, Papoušek, & Bornstein, 1985).

Interactions that employ features of parentese seem almost intuitive for hearing parents as they engage their hearing infant in a manner that captures and maintains their attention, knowing exactly what their infant needs to visually and auditorily connect with them as they learn how to communicate with one another. Signing parents who are deaf use a variation of "parentese" that looks a bit different from that used by hearing parents. Just as hearing parents may intuitively know what a hearing infant needs to attend to spoken language, deaf parents may also have an intuitive understanding of the visual and tactile input needed by their child who is deaf in order for the child to attend to and begin to capture the nuances of communication and language (Koester, Papoušek, & Smith-Gray, 2000). The parentese used by signing deaf parents has distinctive features that differ significantly from the way that deaf adults communicate with one another. Deaf mothers tend to use signs that are made larger and are more exaggerated, produce signs slowly and purposefully, use sign phrases that are short and simple, repeat words and phrases frequently, hold signs longer than usual, exaggerate facial and body expressions; tap the infant's body to gain his or her attention before signing; orient the infant so he or she can visually attend to what is being communicated, and often sign directly on the child's face and/or body (Chen, 1996; Reilly & Bellugi, 1996; Swisher, 2000).

When parents encourage and respond to their child's communication attempts, they send a message to their child that he or she is a valued communication partner. Children, in turn, sense acceptance and find enjoyment and security in the predictable pattern of communicative interactions. This communicative partnership between the parent and child allows the child to move into the next phase of development, existential intersubjectivity, which requires the child not only to interact with a parent but to respond to a parent's social input while also being able to attend to an external object or event.

*Existential Intersubjectivity* The third phase of development within this theory is a phase of development that results in infants displaying the ability to use social referencing, gain and maintain joint attention through the imitation of others, and make decisions based on the reactions of others. In this phase, infants and their parents and caregivers share emotions and interactive and communicative intent and engage in shared interests. Social referencing is typically developed in an infant between 10 and 13 months of age (Walden & Ogan, 1988). Children who have developed social referencing are able to perceive a situation solely through the facial expressions on a trusted caregiver's face or the intonation in his or her voice. In a study conducted by Scorce, Emde, Campos, and Klinnert (1985), researchers created a false visual cliff by placing glass safely over a space below that had a drop off or cliff that appeared unsafe to cross. Infants were divided into two groups, with mothers in the first group encouraging their infants to cross over to the deep side of the cliff to reach a toy solely by using smiles and a positive and relaxed look on their faces. The second group of mothers was told to show a fearful face as the infant approached the false cliff edge. The infants all looked to their mother's faces for information about what they should do upon approaching the cliff's edge. Not one of the 17 infants whose mothers expressed fear in their faces attempted to cross the false cliff to obtain the toy, whereas 14 of the 19 infants whose mothers smiled and did not act concerned about the false cliff crawled across the "cliff" to the toy. This ability to read the emotions and facial expressions of the mother and trust the information being provided to the child is one end result of an effective early communication dance between infant and parent.

The ability of the communication partners to attend to the same object or event is critical to the development of language and social interaction. In this phase of development, children are able to gain joint attention on an object, such as the false cliff, and they gain information about that object through the facial expressions of the parent. During the existential intersubjectivity phase of development, children begin to learn more individual words—mostly words that label objects, emotions, or actions. The interactions and communication between parent and child are frequently concrete in nature, referring to emotions that are expressed visually and tonally referring to objects and actions that are present. From these interactions, children develop an early set of vocabulary and comprehension of language-based words, facial and body expressions, and vocal intonation.

*Symbolic Intersubjectivity* In this final phase of development, the child moves from the use of single words to learning new words at a more rapid pace than previously and develops comprehension of new phrases. This phase is facilitated by the child's and parent's ability to jointly attend to an object or event and the child's ability to attach symbolic meaning by hearing a series of words or seeing a series of connected signs. The child begins to develop new words and then phrases frequently and quickly. Language is initially limited to objects and events that are visible to the child and gradually extends to conversations overheard by the child without needing to draw the child's attention directly to the conversation. In the latter portion of this phase of development, the child becomes involved in conversations; parents respond to the child and expand his or her expressions to encourage linguistic development. In this stage of development, rapid language acquisition occurs, and the child becomes a true language partner.

## Implications of Being Deaf for Language Acquisition

Being D/HH can have an impact on the natural process of language acquisition, be it spoken or signed. Hearing individuals learn language by hearing language used throughout the day in ways that are meaningful and interesting. When a child who is D/HH is a member of a hearing family, he or she does not have full access to the spoken language of the family. With limited language accessibility, the process of acquiring language is challenging at best. In some cases, listening devices (e.g., hearing aids, cochlear implants) may not provide adequate auditory access to spoken language to allow a child to acquire the foundational aspects of language.

Even the simple process of obtaining joint attention, essential for the purpose of language acquisition, may be greatly affected when a hearing parent has a child who is deaf (Gale & Schick, 2009). For example, hearing parents typically attempt to gain their child's attention by using auditory prompts such as saying, "Look!" as they point to an object and describe what they see. When children don't hear the "Look!" prompt, they may also miss the pointing gesture until the parent's hand is on the way down, thus missing the parent's communicative intention. Parents who are deaf, on the other hand, use visual communication strategies to ensure shared visual attention (Spencer, Bodner-Johnson, & Gutfreund, 1992). When attempting to gain their child's attention, a parent who is deaf may first tap their child on the shoulder or wave their hand in their child's line of vision before saying or signing, "Look!" The parent will then wait for the child to visually inspect the object and then look back to the parent before the parent begins to describe the object. In this way, shared attention, shared emotion, and shared intent all take place.

With spoken language, important information is shared through prosodic features of the language such as intonation, stress, rhythm, and loudness. These features often convey emotional aspects of communication as well as meaning. For example, warmth is expressed through soft, quiet, or slow expression of words, whereas danger or warning comes with use of loud, fast, and repetitive use of words such as "No! No!" Children who cannot hear these intonational markers in their parents' or caregivers' voices often miss out on the very meaning and intention of a communicative exchange. These same emotional aspects of communication may be salient to children who are deaf when facial expressions and body language are used to enhance understanding.

Children who are D/HH who have limited access to the auditory signal from their listening devices may have difficulty developing symbolic intersubjectivity through spoken language alone. Learning object names and information is challenging if the child's communication partner is pointing at an object and talking about it before the child has shifted focus from the object to his or her partner to see what he or she is saying or signing. The child who has limited auditory access must choose to either look at the object or look at his or her partner for information about the object, but he or she is unable to do both simultaneously.

It is important to remember that in the introduction of visual information, regardless of whether parents and other caregivers use spoken language, sign language, cued speech, or a visual sign system (see Table 6.1), children who are D/HH need to be given time to look at the object, person, or event that is the subject of the communicative interaction and then look to the parent for  additional information (see Video clip 6.2). Parents who are D/HH appear to use these strategies intuitively (Koester et al., 2000), whereas hearing parents tend to need intentional teaching and guidance.

Deaf parents use a variety of visual strategies to make certain their children are getting the visual information they need to acquire language. As noted earlier, deaf parents will wait until the child turns his or her gaze back to the parent for information about the object before describing or commenting. Parents who are deaf often describe or comment about an object, person, or event while the child is engaged by signing within the child's line of vision. In other words, the parent will move the sign away from his or her own body where it is typically made and sign in the child's visual field. Deaf parents might also sign on the child's body, using the parent's hand and putting it in the appropriate location on the child's body. For example, the mother may point at the father and then take her hand and place it on the child's temple, signing "daddy" on the child (see Figure 6.3).

For a child who is D/HH to acquire language in a typical developmental sequence through vision, audition, or both, it is essential that parents and caregivers understand that the key to communication and language development is not about a specific communication approach or modality but about the effectiveness of parent–child interactions. Communication requires filling in of gaps for the child when there is insufficient visual or auditory input to understand what is being conveyed. Families need support to develop skills along the auditory-visual continuum that will help them engage in the reciprocity of communication and language interaction using whatever is appropriate for the child at that particular moment in time. This will allow the child to move through the developmental stages of intersubjectivity successfully, providing the child with a strong foundation for language acquisition, social-emotional well-being, and the potential to develop age-appropriate literacy and critical thinking skills.

The communication continua described in Figures 6.1 and 6.2 illustrate the concept of a continuum of different communication modalities. These are intended to be used and/or tailored according to the individual, his or her communication partners, or his or her environment/setting. Children who are D/HH may move along these continua fluidly, depending in part on their

**Figure 6.3.** Mother signing "Daddy" on the child.

communication skills and the opportunities they have had throughout their lives to use these modalities and approaches.

Children who are D/HH, like hearing children, need access to language input from birth. A hearing child born into a hearing family acquires language naturally in response to language exposure from the moment of birth forward. The same is true of a deaf child who is born to parents who are deaf and use a full visual language, such as ASL. A deaf child of deaf parents will have full access to a complete language that is totally accessible to the child through his or her eyes from birth. These children, assuming they have no disabilities that have an impact on the acquisition of language (e.g., severe cognitive delays), will acquire language in a natural, spontaneous manner (Marschark & Hauser, 2011). Children who have a different hearing status than their families may struggle with the development of language, literacy, and critical thinking skills to the degree that they do not have full access to language from birth. These families will need support from highly trained early intervention specialists to maximize the children's access to language in the first months and years of life (see Video clips 6.3 and 6.4).

### Visual Communication Approaches

Descriptions of the most commonly used visual communication approaches are provided in Table 6.1 and will not be described again here, but a brief summary of some of the benefits and limitations of each approach are discussed.

***Simultaneous Communication***    The visual communication approaches that have been designed, created, or developed with the intent of making grammatical aspects of English visible on the hands were all designed to be used simultaneously with spoken English. By combining a visual approach with spoken English, the expectation was that children would be able to use visual input to fill in any gaps they might experience due to missing auditory input. Historically, simultaneous communication, or SimCom, has been used to describe spoken English in combination with signs used in English order and coded to represent grammatical morphemes present in spoken English (Moores, 2001). The term *sign-supported speech* may also be used to describe the use of spoken language and signed English used simultaneously. In reality, each of the created visual communication systems was intended to be used simultaneously with spoken language.

**Manually Coded English**   Many signed English systems have been developed since the 1960s to visually support children who were D/HH develop both spoken and sign language skills, with an ultimate end result of helping children who are D/HH to visually capture the morphology of English so they could not only communicate effectively with hearing individuals but also learn to read and write in English (Nielsen, Luetke, & Stryker, 2011). The first recorded signed English system developed in the United States was developed in 1966, called Seeing Essential English (SEE-1; Anthony, 1971), followed by Signing Exact English (SEE-2; Gustason, Pfetzing, & Zawolkow, 1975), Signed English (Bornstein, 1990), and since the late 1990s, Conceptually Accurate Signed English (CASE), which uses ASL signs in English order but also embeds the use of ASL concepts.

All of these systems have drawn strong criticism as well as support. The primary limitations of these systems presented simultaneously with speech include 1) stilted spoken language due to the limited speed by which the hands can move to present words at the speed of spoken language; 2) frequent omission of words or components of English, such as morphological markers (Schick & Moeller, 1992); and 3) the fact that these systems are not true languages like ASL or English but contrived systems that are designed to make a spoken language visually accessible (Meadow-Orlans, Spencer, & Koester, 2004; Supalla, 1991). However, the benefits of MCE systems have also been reported in literature. Whereas MCE systems have not resulted in children expressing 100% accuracy of morphological structure of English, they do appear to have improved communicative interaction between parents and their child, provided a strong foundation for English acquisition, and showed no evidence of limiting or negatively affecting the development of spoken language skills (Hyde & Power, 1992; Marschark, Sapere, Convertino, & Pelz, 2008; Maxwell & Bernstein, 1985; Mayer & Akamatsu, 1999; Power, Hyde, & Leigh, 2008; Schick & Moeller, 1992). It appears that the key to successful use of MCE in terms of production of signed or written English in children is consistent and complete presentation of English in the hands of skilled parents and teachers alike.

**Cued Speech**   Cued speech was designed by Orin Cornett in 1967 in an attempt to create a visual system to be used in conjunction with speechreading and listening to help children who are D/HH access the phonological structure of spoken language (Cornett, 1967). The system was designed to eliminate the ambiguity of speechreading and ultimately improve the reading skills of children who are D/HH. Cued speech is described by many as an oral approach because it incorporates the use of listening and speechreading, but it is included in this chapter because it is also a visual communication approach, adding visual cues to a spoken language to make the language more accessible to children who are D/HH (Movallali & Rafi, 2012).

Several studies report positive outcomes for children using cued speech. Children who were D/HH exposed to cued speech from early childhood performed better than matched children who did not have access to cued speech and performed as well as their hearing peers on rhyming tasks (LaSasso, Crain, & Leybaert, 2003; MacLean, Bryant, & Bradley, 1987). There is a positive correlation between a child's phonological awareness, such as rhyming, and his or her reading skills (Bryant, MacLean, & Bradley, 1990; Ellis & Large, 1987; Leybaert, 1993; Mirus, 2014). The phonologic accessibility that cued speech provides has, in fact, resulted in improved reading skills in children who are D/HH (Bouton, Bertoncini, Serniclaes, & Cole, 2011; LaSasso & Crain, 2010; Torres, Rodriguez, Garcia-Orza, & Calleja, 2008). Cued speech also has proven to increase speechreading abilities, even when cues are not present (Aparicio, Peigneux, Charlier, Neyrat, & Leybaert, 2012; Bouton, Serniclaes, Bertoncini, & Cole, 2012; Leybaert, J., 2000).

***Bilingualism*** The benefits of bilingualism or multilingualism for children who are hearing are strongly supported in literature (Bialystok, Craik, & Luk, 2012; Lieberman, 2012; Marian & Shook, 2012; Marian, Shook, & Schroeder, 2013). Children who are exposed to two or more languages in the early years of life naturally acquire those languages and achieve fluency in both languages by an early age. There is strong evidence that suggests that exposure to two or more languages results in scaffolding from one language to support the development and understanding of the other language or languages (Cummins, 1991). Hearing children who are bilingual develop cognitive skills more rapidly than children who are monolingual, understand concepts more rapidly than monolinguals, and show an ability to "play with language" at an earlier age (Kovács & Mehler, 2009). The spoken language skills of children who are bilingual may lag behind their monolingual peers in the first 2 years of life because they are learning to process and acquire the grammar, structure, and sounds of different languages, but their receptive language abilities in both languages keep pace with their monolingual peers (Fish & Morford, 2012). These children do "catch up" in their expressive skills in both languages by approximately 5 years of age and tend to develop cognitive advantages that include mental flexibility that enables them to be more malleable learners, solve problems more easily, and have higher levels of executive function (Bialystok, 2011; Kovács & Mehler, 2009). These benefits of bilingualism appear to continue through the child's academic career and into adulthood (McConnell, 1982).

Evidence suggests that children who are hearing and born to parents who are deaf who use ASL as their primary language acquire both ASL and spoken language similarly to other hearing children exposed to two spoken languages (Petitto, Katerelos, Levy, Gauna, Tétreault, & Ferraro, 2001). Children who are deaf with deaf parents who use ASL also acquire ASL, written English, and often spoken English, depending on whether the child has auditory access to spoken language and opportunities to learn spoken language skills. In fact, deaf children of deaf parents who are ASL users typically perform at the same levels linguistically as hearing children of hearing parents on tests of English ability (Newport & Meier, 1985). These children who have the benefit of a full visual language from birth have little difficulty learning a second language, such as English, and many have access to both from birth depending on the child's hearing level and access to spoken and written English. If hearing children can be successfully bilingual when exposed to two spoken languages or a spoken and a visual language and if children who are D/HH who have parents who are D/HH can be successful bilinguals using both ASL and English, then it would stand to reason that children who are D/HH who are born to hearing parents could also acquire and use two languages—ASL and English—successfully if given access to both languages. Since the bilingual education approach took hold in the early 1990s (at the time called the Bi-Bi, or Bilingual-Bicultural Approach), there has been a great deal of controversy whether children who are D/HH could or should be exposed to both sign language and spoken language due to a fear that developing one language would limit the development of the other. This discussion permeates the field and warrants exploration.

## THE USE OF ASSESSMENTS TO IDENTIFY INTERVENTION PRIORITIES

Assessment data serve many purposes, including providing a baseline of a child's overall linguistic, social, cognitive, and motor development; information to select appropriate programming; and evidence of developmental progress. Through this process, we can also gather information that indicates the effectiveness of the sensory modalities used to promote language development (e.g., visual, auditory, tactile) and the effectiveness of the services provided. The focus of this section will be on the latter area. Readers are referred to Carotta, Cline, and Brennan (2014) for a detailed discussion of assessment for children who are D/HH.

### Assessment Team Members

The first step in the assessment process would be to determine the members of the interdisciplinary team that will be conducting the assessment. For a child who is using ASL, it is essential for professionals on the team to be familiar with ASL milestones (Simms, Baker, & Clark, 2013). If the child is using a visual approach such as cued speech or MCE, team members should be proficient users of the approach(es) that the child and family use. In order to gain an accurate picture of a child's language ability in ASL, the specialist or specialists conducting the assessments must include a native or native-like fluent user of ASL. The assessment team should include a deaf professional who is a native ASL user skilled at recognizing a young child's visual, and often subtle, communicative intentions that may be missed by hearing professionals. Parents are also essential members of the team. Additional members of the team may include a speech-language pathologist, school audiologist, and additional specialists as needed, including an occupational or physical therapist, psychologist, or social worker. Regardless of the communication modalities or language of the child, it is critical that team members are able to communicate clearly to the child and understand the child's expressive communication.

## Assessment Tools

Once a team is established, they should then determine which assessment tools are most appropriate. There are a multitude of assessment tools that are accessible to early intervention providers and early childhood educators. Yet different educational programs often require different types of assessments that may be specified by the state or the program's participation in data-tracking systems. Some programs will require standardized tests such as the Battelle Developmental Inventory (Newborg, 2005), whereas others will permit checklists, interviews, and criterion-referenced assessments. Effective tools should provide the following information:

- The amount and quality of visual and auditory information available to the child in all of the child's everyday environments

- The functioning of listening devices (e.g., hearing aids, cochlear implants, frequency-modulated [FM] units, visual technologies such as glasses) as well as augmentative communication devices

- Description of the child's status and growth in all five developmental domains (communication/language, fine and gross motor, adaptive behavior, social-emotional, and cognition)

- Estimates of the child's vocabulary, pragmatic skills, grammar, and phonological ability in each language (if bilingual)

- Descriptions of parent–child interaction patterns

- The child's ability to use language(s) with peers, adults, and other communication partners

- A description of the quality and consistency of language input from primary caregivers

## Assessment Environment

The environment where the assessments are administered is of special concern for a child who is D/HH. If the administrator is using spoken language to provide instructions and to elicit responses from the child, the environment must be quiet and background noise should be minimized or eliminated to the greatest extent possible. Reverberation can be reduced by introducing soft surfaces on floors and walls that will absorb random environmental sounds (e.g., heating/cooling units and outside noises) and ensure that the child will be able to use his or her hearing optimally.

Equal care should be given to creating an assessment environment that is free from visual clutter. This includes removing items that are visually distracting, such as colorful toys and electronic equipment, and putting loose toys in organized boxes or bins. The assessor should sit in a location where natural light is not impeding the visual clarity of the hands or face (e.g., no windows behind the test administrator or the child) and should wear a solid-colored shirt or smock that is not visually distracting (e.g., large or bright flowers, distracting stripes). Windows in the assessment environment should be covered if there are visual distractions outside. The room should be well lit so that assessment objects and the hands and face of the specialists and others involved can be fully and easily seen.

As in any assessment environment, it is important that the child and the parents and caregivers are comfortable and feel at ease. Spoken language and/or sign language interpreters may be necessary to ensure that families are comfortable enough to participate in the assessment tasks. Young children will not perform optimally if they are in a strange environment or surrounded by unfamiliar adults. In many situations, the best environments to assess a child's receptive and expressive language skills will be in the home with a limited number of people present. The team might consider using video recordings of the child's behaviors and parent–child interactions to ensure accurate documentation that can be reviewed at a later time by specialists who are not physically present. People can be the greatest visual distraction for a child who is being assessed, so individuals who may be observing the child rather than administering the assessment should sit behind the child throughout the assessment. All assessment items needed for the evaluation should be kept in a container out of visual range of the child but easily accessible to the assessor.

## Analyzing Assessment Results

It takes a skilled assessment team to use the assessment results to 1) describe the child's current skills, 2) monitor progress, and 3) design or modify services for the child and family in a manner that will help the child attain or maintain language levels that are individually and developmentally appropriate for that child.

The assessment results will drive the goals that are established for the child, and those goals will drive program services. For example, if a child who is bilingual and bimodal (e.g., incorporates two languages and uses both auditory and visual modalities) is struggling with listening skills, then the early intervention provider knows that the audiologist should be contacted to make certain that the child's listening devices are functioning properly and are set appropriately. Speech and language services might also be needed to improve listening and spoken language skills. Children who are acquiring ASL can ben-efit from ASL facilitation from a native signing deaf adult. For example, if a child is struggling with a particular language skill, such as expressing plurals in ASL or describing language tenses appropriately in ASL, services from a trained deaf adult who can demonstrate and describe to parents and other family members how these elements are expressed in ASL may be especially beneficial. ASL language modeling and increased opportunities for the whole family to use ASL will support the child's development of fluent ASL skills.

One primary purpose of an assessment is to identify children's developmental and communication strengths and needs so that an individualized family service plan (IFSP) or an individualized educational plan (IEP) can be written. Effective language and communication assessments can help families understand the value of both visual and spoken languages and honor the range of modalities their children need to comprehend and express language. By capitalizing on their children's strengths and matching appropriate services to their children's needs, families and early intervention specialists can enhance their children's linguistic development. The ultimate goal is the establishment of a strong language foundation that not only accelerates language and literacy in the early years but also strengthens the communication partnership between children and their families.

## INTERVENTIONS TO PROMOTE VISUAL COMMUNICATION

When parents, with guidance from their interdisciplinary team, decide that a visual communication approach will support their child's development, they often need guidance to learn how to use the visual system or visual language that matches the child's and family's needs (see Video clips 6.5 and 6.6). For most hearing people, visual language or visual communication systems are unfamiliar and initially feel awkward to use. Families need assistance to learn how to use visual language comfortably and fluently. The most effective way for hearing parents to learn to use a visual language, such as ASL, or to use visual communication systems, such as cued speech, is through interacting with native or native-like users of ASL and experienced users of a visual communication system (see Video clip 6.7). This support can happen in informal ways, but there are also formal programs for families that focus on teaching families the skills they need, such as the Deaf Mentor Program, which is described below, or local sign language classes like the family sign language program coordinated by Gallaudet University Regional Center at Northern Essex Community College.

### Deaf Mentor Program

In 1991, the Deaf Mentor Program was designed by the SKI-HI Institute at Utah State University and funded by a grant as a combined program development and research grant. This program trained adults who were deaf to provide home-based early intervention services to families, acting as a language model for children who were deaf and teaching families ASL formally through topics from the Deaf Mentor Curriculum (Pittman, 2001) and informally through conversations with family members. Deaf mentors also teach families about the Deaf community and encourage them to get to know their local Deaf community. After 2 years of participation, parents in the Deaf Mentor Program reported that their children understood what they were communicating to them in sign language 84% of the time. This compared favorably to the 50% of the time reported by families who did not have Deaf mentors. In addition, mothers in the program reported knowing and using six times more signs than parents in a control group that did not have Deaf mentors. Fathers reported similar benefits from having a Deaf mentor (Watkins et al., 1998). The Deaf Mentor Program has been established in several states, in one province in Canada, and in three provinces in South Africa. Opportunities to observe interactions among a child, the child's family, and his or her deaf mentor are available to the reader in the DVD that accompanies this text.

### Deaf and Hard of Hearing Role Model Program

The power of having D/HH adults involved in early intervention programming was experienced in Colorado a few years after the Deaf Mentor Program began.

The Deaf and Hard of Hearing Role Model Program was organized by the Colorado Home Intervention Program in 1995. This program included deaf adults who were ASL users, deaf adults who were signed English users, and deaf adults who were spoken language users. Families in this program reported many advantages from their interactions with their D/HH role model.

These benefits go beyond learning sign language or other visual modalities from the deaf adult who visits their home. Participating families also value the opportunity to watch how deaf adults interact and communicate with their children who are deaf, taking advantage of the child's visual senses to soak up communication and language (Pittman, 2003). It is one thing to know that individuals who are deaf take advantage of the visual modality to teach children who are deaf about their world, but it is a totally different experience to see those skills in practice. By watching adults who are D/HH working directly with children, parents can see how readily and easily the child acquire language and communication skills visually; this in turn encourages them to use more visual strategies with their child, enhancing that early communication dance so critical for the child's early development (see Video clip 6.8).

## Shared Reading Project

A third program that has been in existence since 1995 that introduces adults who are D/HH to children and families and assists families in learning and using ASL skills with their children and emphasizes reading skills that bring literacy alive for children who are D/HH is the Shared Reading Project (SRP; Schleper, 1995). SRP has been a very beneficial program for families who are learning ASL and is described in detail in Chapter 13.

All the programs discussed in this section provide families with opportunities to acquire ASL and visual modalities from adults who are D/HH. Families who participate in these programs benefit on multiple levels from the experience. Research has provided evidence that parents, caregivers, siblings, and extended family members who engage with individuals who are D/HH learn more about the experiences, skills, challenges, and culture of individuals who are D/HH than families who do not have this experience (Hintermair, 2000, 2006; Rogers & Young, 2011; Watkins et al., 1998). This relationship can be very rich and rewarding for both the family and the adult who is D/HH who is providing services (Rogers & Young, 2011) (see Video clip 6.9). Interaction with adults who are D/HH may also result in better parenting skills. Hintermair (2000) found that parents of children who were D/HH who had multiple interactions with adults who were D/HH had a stronger level of confidence raising their child than parents who did not have that opportunity.

## Principles of a Bilingual Approach

Many hearing families decide that they want to learn to use ASL with their children and also want their children to have exposure to spoken English. For such families, several principles are essential for the development of a bilingual-bimodal approach in their home.

1. Ensure that the languages being used are not "mixed." In other words, when using ASL and English, for example, read a story or say a full

sentence in English (with or without visual cues or signed English) and then go back and sign it in ASL (no voice) using ASL grammar. Children who are exposed to a full and complete form of a language will acquire that language. When they are exposed to incomplete or partial aspects of a language mixed with other incomplete forms of another language with limited clarity of rules or structure, children tend to struggle learning either language.

2.  Set up specific times to use ASL and specific times to use spoken English or spoken English with or without other visual modalities. For example, a family may decide to establish ASL times of the day where everyone is using ASL (no voice) such as mealtime, bath time, storytime, and playtime outside. Spoken English times might be during dressing, preparing meals, or laundry time. Some families opt for mothers to use spoken English all the time and dads to use just ASL. *How* it is done is not nearly as important as ensuring that *it is* done and that each language is used as fully and completely as possible.

3.  Take every opportunity to learn to use ASL and/or the visual modality or modalities that the child needs (see Video clips 6.10 and 6.11). When parents, caregivers, and family members have the skills and the desire to provide as full and complete a language model as possible to their child, their child has a much greater chance of developing a complete language or languages.

## Family-Centered Early Intervention Principles

Family-centered early intervention (FCEI) principles are at the core of any effective early intervention program. Ten FCEI principles that should guide early intervention service (Moeller, Carr, Seaver, Stredler-Brown & Holzinger, 2013) are described in detail in Chapter 4 of this text. It is within the parameters of effective family-centered early intervention that families learn how to appropriately respond to their children's communication needs, using visual language or visual modalities necessary for their child to have full access to language and communication. This, in turn, enables families to develop the confidence and competence to engage in the communicative dance essential to the development of the children's communication and language.

## Addressing Unique Needs in Early Intervention Services

Many children who are D/HH have developmental or learning challenges that demand unique strategies to acquire language and communicative competence. Early intervention specialists must also be responsive to families whose life situations require specialized approaches to deliver effective services, support, and guidance. The use of ASL or a communication approach that incorporates visual and auditory approaches may open a door to communication between the child and his or her family. For example, children who cannot access spoken language through audition and whose home language (e.g., Spanish) is different from the language used in the school or community may benefit from the use of ASL or a visual communication system to support overall communication and allow access to the family's home or native language if it is inaccessible to the child through audition alone. Visual strategies may help families communicate more easily with their children while simultaneously honoring and supporting the language of the home.

**Nonmajority Language Speakers**   Many families whose native language is different from that of the greater community in which they live choose to use a bimodal approach, using both spoken and sign language. These families support their children's early access to their native spoken language through listening devices to provide their children with the opportunity to acquire the native language of the home through listening. At the same time, they learn ASL so their children can use a visual language. Children are also provided with formal strategies to learn and use English upon entering preschool.

**Children with Additional/Multiple Special Needs**   Children who have additional special needs present unique challenges acquiring language that can be facilitated by the use of visual language or visual modalities. For example, a 2-year-old boy with cerebral palsy who has hearing levels within the moderate range and can access spoken language with the help of hearing aids may struggle with the motor demands required to produce intelligible spoken language. As a result, he may be frustrated because, although he can hear and understand others communicating with him, he is unable to express his thoughts, wants, and desires in a way that can be understood by others. If he has some control of his arms, legs, eyes, or head, he might benefit from the use of a visual augmentative communication system. This child might also benefit from listening and spoken language with the simultaneous support of signs presented in English word order. In this way, he might hear some aspects of spoken English and see the signs to help clarify what he may be missing through listening alone. If he has some control of his arms, hands, and fingers, he may be able to use signs to convey his own thoughts, needs, emotions, and feelings to others. In other words, the child should be encouraged to take advantage of as many visual supports as he possibly can to be able to express himself fully.

**Progressive Hearing Loss**   Children who become D/HH after they have begun to acquire spoken language may also benefit from visual support. These children may use hearing aids or cochlear implants to augment their residual hearing and ASL or visual approaches to express their ideas. Children who benefit from their listening devices may reduce the amount of signing they use or limit signing to situations when they do not have optimal listening conditions. Thus, such children have the option of communicating through listening or through vision according to the situation at hand (Nussbaum, Waddy-Smith, & Doyle, 2012).

Children who progressively lose their hearing may be able to use their listening devices effectively initially but over time lose clarity of the speech signal and listening ability due to changes in their hearing sensitivity. Such children might benefit from the use of simultaneous communication or cued speech to provide continual access to language input as their hearing deteriorates. They might also benefit from ASL for full visual language access as their hearing levels no longer permit access to the conversational speech around them. Speechreading practice and cued speech might also be considered. Children in this situation may choose or their families may elect to receive a cochlear implant when their hearing deteriorates to a level where they are not able to access spoken language easily through the auditory channel. Visual systems may continue to be of benefit to these children as they learn to listen with their new device and also use vision to access language as the need arises.

***Children with Cochlear Implants*** There has been some controversy over the years regarding the benefits of ASL and visual communication approaches with children who have cochlear implants. However, individuals who have cochlear implants and who have access to sound and spoken language with the assistance of their cochlear implant(s) have reported that access to ASL or visual communication systems such as MCE or cued speech often are of assistance—in particular, when there is background noise that cannot be controlled or reduced, when there is new or unfamiliar information being shared (e.g., classroom lectures, workshops, conferences), or when the speaker is using an amplification device that provides a somewhat distorted signal (Paludneviciene & Leigh, 2011; Spencer & Marschark, 2006).

These examples in no way exhaust the potential for the benefit of visual communication systems or visual language use with children who are D/HH who have unique or additional challenges. **Visual language and visual communication** systems simply provide access to language and communication for a child who is D/HH who has an intact visual system. Taking advantage of that intact system as the primary modality for language input or in combination with auditory access can create opportunities for the child and family to continually be connected to one another so communication and language can grow and develop naturally and comfortably, giving that child the foundation to reach his or her full linguistic potential.

## Case Study: Braden

Braden is a bright-eyed, visually attentive, and communicative 14-month-old who has hearing levels that are severe to profound bilaterally. He received bilateral hearing aids at 3 months of age, and he wears his hearing aids consistently, using them all his waking hours. He also has some physical challenges due to mild cerebral palsy. He can sit independently and has just mastered a "commando crawl" but is not yet pulling to stand or cruising. He can reach and pull items to him, uses four signs expressively, and responds appropriately to some spoken phrases and several signed phrases.

Braden's family's early interventionist is a teacher of the deaf with a specialty in early intervention. The family also has a Deaf mentor who is teaching them American Sign Language (ASL) and about Deaf culture. Braden's family uses both ASL and English with him. They use ASL exclusively when he will not or cannot wear his hearing aids (e.g., bath time, bedtime, when he is not feeling well), when they want to introduce new concepts, and when they are in noisy environments, as well as when they are engaged in play or storytelling, or when they are communicating with him when there are no other hearing people in the room. They also use simultaneous communication consistently with one another when Braden and either or both of his two hearing siblings are together or when there are people in the home who are hearing and speak English but do not know signs. Braden receives deaf-specific services from his early intervention provider (e.g., strategies to encourage language development, communication skills, listening skills practice, family sign classes, audiological monitoring), and he also receives physical therapy to address gross motor needs and occupational therapy for feeding issues and fine motor skills.

Recently, Braden's parents told their early intervention provider and their Deaf mentor that Braden was really struggling with his physical therapy visits. At the next early intervention team meeting, the team recommended that the Deaf mentor, David, and the physical therapist, Allison, attend the next visit together. During the visit, David watched as Allison explained to the family the skill she would be working on and the purpose of the movements she was going to take Braden through. He also noticed that Allison approached Braden (playing on the floor) from the side and a bit behind him. Then she put her hand on his back and began to move him into a new position. Braden's first response was a startle and then he began to move in opposition to her. As Allison started moving his upper arms and shoulders from behind, Braden continually attempted to turn around to see what Allison was doing. Allison then told him what she was doing and tried to comfort him, but because Braden relies on both visual information and auditory information, he didn't seem to understand her. As a result, Braden's frustration levels escalated, he became agitated and uncooperative, and Allison became exasperated. Within a few minutes, Braden was in tears and was inconsolable.

It did not take long for David to realize the causes of Braden's behavior. He explained that Braden, who relies on visual information to understand his world, probably had no idea that Allison was even sitting behind him. He was engaged in play, did not have on his hearing aids due to an ear infection and draining ear, and received no signs or visual cues to let him know Allison was going to be working with him. David explained that if Allison would face Braden; obtain eye contact; sign something simple like, "Ready to work?"; and *then* touch his back, Braden wouldn't startle at her touch. David went on to explain that clear visual communication means more than simply signing. It also requires being in tune with a person's behaviors, watching his or her facial and body expressions and movement, reading cues, and moving in response to one another. David asked the parents if they might have a large mirror they could use and explained that the mirror might help Braden see what Allison was doing and allow him to "read" her communication attempts. This, in turn, might help him be less frustrated and more compliant. David explained that even if Alison didn't know all the "right" signs, she could still use visual strategies to express her intentions so Braden would be aware of what was happening.

They set the mirror up against the wall, making sure it was at eye level for both Braden and Allison. David showed Alison how she could sit behind Braden with both of them facing the mirror. David also taught Allison and Braden's parents some visual communication strategies they could use with Braden. They practiced using gestures, facial expressions, eye contact, and wait time to ensure that Braden was watching and understood what was happening next. David explained that touch is a powerful communication tool, showing Allison how to tap Braden's back to let him know she was going to move to another position on his back or was going to begin working on his arm, leg, or neck. The combination of the mirror and the new visual strategies did the trick! Braden was immediately more cooperative, and Alison commented that this was the best visit she ever remembered having with Braden. Braden's parents also felt they learned a lot and realized that there were other situations when Braden's frustrations and negative behaviors might be the result of a communication breakdown.

At the end of the visit, Allison, David, and Braden's parents agreed that it might be worthwhile for them to do joint visits periodically so they could continue to learn from one another. David suggested that in future visits, he could sit in front of Braden and describe in signs what Allison was doing or was going to do to him, and then Allison could show the parents what they c ould do in their everyday routines to encourage Braden's physical development.

The visual adaptation that David suggested in this scenario was simple but impactful because it opened visual opportunities for Braden to be able to understand what was happening to him. The experience also had a positive impact on Alison and on Braden's parents, who were able to see the impact of using good visual communication with Braden. They learned that taking the time to ensure that Braden was engaged and aware of his environment through visual language and visual communication strategies could result in pleasant and meaningful interactions with Braden. Everyone learned the value of working together as a team to learn from Braden and from one another.

## FUTURE DIRECTIONS

There are many things we do not yet understand about the use of visual language (ASL), visual communication systems, and the development of language or the best ways to help families develop these skills. As we move forward as a profession, we must continue to investigate and report on the effectiveness of visual communication systems and ASL for children who are D/HH. These studies are needed to determine the most successful interventions for children and families.

Whereas research supports the involvement of adults who are D/HH in early intervention, additional research on the use of Deaf mentors and role models is still needed. These investigations should focus on 1) the impact of these services on families (including siblings and extended family members) and interactions with their children; 2) families' and children's development of ASL over time; and 3) the use of innovative strategies including visual technology to provide Deaf mentor services to families living in rural areas or other locations where it is challenging to find adults who are D/HH (see Chapter 10).

The following areas related to the use of visual approaches and visual language should also be considered for future research:

1. How well do children with cochlear implants or hearing aids develop both ASL and spoken English skills?

2. How well does spoken language develop when supported by the use of cued speech, MCE, or other visual approaches?

3. How does the use of ASL and/or the use of other visual approaches have an impact on children's social cognition and pragmatics?

4.  How do we effectively assess the development of communication, visual skills, and language in young children who use ASL and/or visual communication approaches?

5.  How do specific visual communication approaches and visual languages have an impact on neurological development in children?

6.  Can we develop standardized assessments to measure typical ASL development and effectively evaluate visual interaction or communication?

7.  What strategies are most successful in helping hearing parents learn ASL and other visual communication approaches?

## CONCLUSION

The early years of a child's life are a precious time. Infants are learning about this new world they are in, and parents are learning about their new infant. These very early interactions between a parent and a child are symbiotic, with every action and reaction from either party feeding into the next action. It is in these early months of life that a pattern of communication emerges between the parent and child that is unique, is understood by both, and creates a foundation for language and social emotional development that will influence that child for a lifetime. This communication "dance" can be greatly affected when a hearing parent has a child who is D/HH. The parent, being hearing, will have expectations for the child to respond to voice and sound in order to develop a connection. When that does not happen, a breakdown in the dance can occur. However, as parents learn to convey information through vision and touch, they can successfully help their child develop their unique interaction patterns and create a communication dance that is rewarding to all and beautiful to observe.

## SUGGESTED READINGS

Erting, C., Prezioso, C., & O'Grady-Hynes, M. (1990). The interactional context of deaf mother-infant communication. In V. Volterra & C. Erting (Eds.), *From gesture to language in hearing and deaf children* (pp. 97–106). Berlin: Springer-Verlag.

Meadow-Orlans, K., Spencer, P.E., & Koester, L.S. (2004). *The world of deaf infants: A longitudinal study.* New York, NY: Oxford University Press.

Schick, B., Marschark, M., & Spencer, P.E. (2006). *Advances in the sign language development of deaf children.* New York, NY: Oxford University Press.

*Visual Language and Visual Learning Science of Learning Center: Research briefs.* Retrieved from http://www.issuu.com/vl2newsletter

## SUGGESTED LEARNING ACTIVITIES

There are a multitude of activities that will make learning ASL or visual communication approaches a fun experience:

1.  Watch the music videos created by D-PAN (Deaf Professional Arts Network) including "Waiting for the World to Change," "Beautiful," "Watch These Hands," and "We're Going to Be Friends" as well as community videos and other D-PAN productions (http://www.d-pan.org).

2. Take an ASL class online with Bill Vicars at ASLU (American Sign Language University) at the university's web site (http://www.lifeprint.com). There are a wide variety of video classes available that will allow you to learn ASL online. Follow up with live classes and visits into your local Deaf community.

3. Explore the information on visual communication at the VL2 web site (http://vl2parentspackage.org). If you follow the VL2 Parent Tool Kit link, you will have the opportunity to watch a video titled "Through Your Child's Eyes," which describes the importance of visual language for children who are deaf or hard of hearing. You can also access this video on YouTube (https://www.youtube.com/watch?v=FV69iJuXwP4).

4. Watch videos about cued speech at the National Cued Speech Association's web site (http://www.cuedspeech.org) to see children and families using cued speech and to learn more about cued speech.

5. Learn more about the Deaf community and the lives of D/HH people by watching the television series *Deaf Mosaic*, available on YouTube (https://www.youtube.com/watch?v=OtsYVeRuBuw). This television series provided an in-depth look at the Deaf community in the 1980s, but the topics are still pertinent today.

## REFERENCES

Anthony, D. (1971). *Signing essential English (S.E.E.) manual.* Anaheim, CA: Anaheim Union School District, Educational Services Division.

Aparicio, M., Peigneux, P., Charlier, B., Neyrat, C., & Leybaert, J. (2012). Early experience of cued speech enhances speechreading performance in deaf. *Scandinavian Journal of Psychology, 53*(1), 41–46.

Bailey, D.B., Bruer, J.T., Symons, F.J., Lichtman, J.W., & National Center for Early Development & Learning. (2001). *Critical thinking about critical periods: A series from the National Center for Early Development and Learning.* Baltimore, MD: Paul H. Brookes Publishing Co.

Baker, S. (2011). Visual language and visual learning research brief: Advantages of early visual language. In *Science of Learning Center on Visual Language and Visual Learning* (pp. 1–2). Washington, DC: Gallaudet University.

Bialystok, E. (2011). Coordination of executive functions in monolingual and bilingual children. *Journal of Experimental Child Psychology, 110*(3), 461–468.

Bialystok, E., Craik, F.I., & Luk, G. (2012). Bilingualism: Consequences for mind and brain. *Trends in Cognitive Sciences, 16*(4), 240–250.

Boons, T., Brokx, J.P., Dhooge, I., Frijns, J.H., Peeraer, L., Vermeulen, A., . . . Van Wieringen, A. (2012). Predictors of spoken language development following pediatric cochlear implantation. *Ear and Hearing, 33*(5), 617–639.

Bornstein, H. (Ed.). (1990). *Manual communication: Implications for education.* Washington, DC: Gallaudet University Press.

Bouton, S., Bertoncini, J., Serniclaes, W., & Cole, P. (2011). Reading and reading-related skills in children using cochlear implants: Prospects for the influence of cued speech. *Journal of Deaf Studies and Deaf Education, 16*(4), 458–473.

Bouton, S., Serniclaes, W., Bertoncini, J., & Cole, P. (2012). Perception of speech features by French-speaking children with cochlear implants. *Journal of Speech, Language, and Hearing Research, 55*(1), 139–153.

Bryant, P., MacLean, M., & Bradley, L. (1990). Rhyme, language, and children's reading. *Applied Linguistics, 11,* 237–252.

Carotta, C., Cline, K.M., & Brennan, K. (2014). *Auditory consultant resource network handbook.* Omaha, NE: Boys Town National Research Hospital.

Chen, D. (1996). Parent-infant communication: Early intervention for very young children with visual impairment or hearing loss. *Infants and Young Children, 9*(2), 1–12.

Cooper, R., & Aslin, R. (1990). Preference for infant-directed speech in the first month after birth. *Child Development, 61,* 1584–1595.

Cornett, O. (1967). Cued speech. *American Annals of the Deaf, 112,* 3–13.

Cummins, J. (1991). Interdependence of first- and second-language proficiency in bilingual children. In E. Bialystok (Ed.), *Language processing in bilingual children* (pp. 70–89). New York, NY: Cambridge University Press.

Dettman, S., Wall, E., Constantinescu, G., & Dowell, R. (2013). Communication out-comes for groups of children using cochlear implants enrolled in auditory-verbal, aural-oral, and bilingual-bicultural early intervention programs. *Otology & Neurotology, 34,* 451–459.

Ellis, N., & Large, B. (1987). The development of reading: As you seek so shall you find. *British Journal of Psychology, 78,* 1–28.

Fish, S., & Morford, J. (2012, June). *Visual language and visual learning science of learning center: The benefits of bilingualism* (Research Brief No. 7). Washington, DC: Gallaudet University.

Gale, E., & Schick, B. (2009). Symbol-infused joint attention and language use in mothers with deaf and hearing toddlers. *American Annals of the Deaf, 153*(5), 484–503.

Geers, A.E., Nicholas, J.G., & Sedey, A.L. (2003). Language skills of children with early cochlear implantation. *Ear and Hearing, 24*(1), 46S–58S.

Grimshaw, G.M., Adelstein, A., Bryden, M., & MacKinnon, G.E. (1998). First-language acquisition in adolescence: Evidence for a critical period for verbal language development. *Brain and Language, 63*(2), 237–255.

Gustason, G., Pfetzing, D., & Zawolkow, E. (1975). *Signing exact English.* Silver Spring, MD: Modern Signs Press.

Hassanzadeh, S. (2012). Outcomes of cochlear implantation in deaf children of deaf parents: Comparative study. *Journal of Laryngology and Otology, 126*(10), 989–994.

Hintermair, M. (2000). Hearing impairment, social networks, and coping: The need for families with hearing-impaired children to relate to other parents and to hearing-impaired adults. *American Annals of the Deaf, 145*(1), 41–53.

Hintermair, M. (2006). Parental resources, parental stress, and socioemotional development of deaf and hard of hearing children. *Journal of Deaf Studies and Deaf Education, 11*(4), 493–513.

Hyde, M.B., & Power, D.J. (1992). The receptive communication abilities of deaf students under oral, manual, and combined methods. *American Annals of the Deaf, 137*(5), 389–398.

Johnson, J.S., & Newport, E.L. (1989). Critical period effects in second language learning: The influence of maturational state on the acquisition of English as a second language. *Cognitive Psychology, 21,* 60–99.

Jung, V., Cumming, C., & Rodda, M. (1992). Paralinguistic and cross-modal behaviours during early infant-caregiver interactions: Implications for social-emotional development in deaf children. *Journal of the British Association of Teachers of the Deaf, 16,* 110–117.

Koester, L.S. (1988). Rhythmicity in parental stimulation of infants. In P.G. Fedor-Freyburgh & M.V. Vogel (Eds.), *Prenatal and perinatal psychology and medicine* (pp. 143–152). Nashville, TN: Parthenon Publishing Group.

Koester, L.S., Papoušek, H., & Smith-Gray, S. (2000). Intuitive parenting, communication, and interaction with deaf infants. In P.E. Spencer, C.J. Erting, & M. Marschark (Eds.), *The deaf child in the family and at school: Essays in honor of Kathryn P. Meadow-Orlans* (pp. 55–71). Mahwah, NJ: Lawrence Erlbaum Associates.

Kovács, Á.M., & Mehler, J. (2009). Cognitive gains in 7-month-old bilingual infants. *Proceedings of the National Academy of Sciences, 106*(16), 6556–6560.

Kovelman, I., Shalinsky, M.H., White, K.S., Schmitt, S.N., Berens, M.S., Paymer, N., & Petitto, L.A. (2009). Dual language use in sign-speech bimodal bilinguals: fNIRS brain-imaging evidence. *Brain & Language, 109,* 112–123.

LaSasso, C., & Crain, K. (2010). Cued language for the development of deaf students' reading comprehension and measured reading comprehension. In C. LaSasso, K. Crain,

& L. Leybaert (Eds.), *Cued speech and cued language for deaf and hard of hearing children* (pp. 217–241). San Diego, CA: Plural.

LaSasso, C., Crain, K., & Leybaert, J. (2003). Rhyme generation in deaf students: The effect of exposure to cued speech. *Journal of Deaf Studies and Deaf Education, 8*(3), 250–270.

Lederberg, A.R., & Mobley, C.E. (1990). The effect of hearing impairment on the quality of attachment and mother–toddler interaction. *Child Development, 61,* 1596–1604.

Lederberg, A., & Prezbindowski, A. (2000). Impact of child deafness on mother-toddler interaction: Strengths and weaknesses. In P. Spencer, C. Erting, & M. Marschark (Eds.), *The deaf child in the family and at school: Essays in honor of Kathryn P. Meadow-Orlans* (pp. 73–92). Mahwah, NJ: Lawrence Erlbaum Associates.

Lederberg, A.R., & Spencer, P.E. (2005). Critical periods in the acquisition of lexical skills: Evidence from deaf individuals. In P. Fletcher & J.F. Miller (Eds.). *Language disorders and developmental theory* (pp. 121–145). Philadelphia, PA: John Benjamins.

Leybaert, J. (1993). Reading in the deaf: The roles of phonological codes. In M. Marschark & D. Clark (Eds.), *Psychological perspectives on deafness* (pp. 269–311). Hillsdale, NJ: Lawrence Erlbaum Associates.

Leybaert, J. (2000). Phonology acquired through the eyes and spelling in deaf children. *Journal of Experimental Child Psychology, 75,* 291–318.

Lieberman, A.M. (2012). Visual language and visual learning research brief: Eye gaze and joint attention. In *Science of learning center on visual language and visual learning.* Washington, DC: Gallaudet University.

Loots, G., & Devisé, I. (2003). An intersubjective developmental perspective on interactions between deaf and hearing mothers and their deaf infants. *American Annals of the Deaf, 148,* 295–307.

MacLean, M., Bryant, P., & Bradley, L. (1987). Rhymes, nursery rhymes, and reading in early childhood. *Merrill-Palmer Quarterly, 33,* 25–282.

Marian, V., & Shook, A. (2012, September). *The cognitive benefits of being bilingual.* Cerebrum: The Dana Forum on Brain Science. Dana Foundation. Retrieved from http://www.ncbi.nlm.nih.gov/pmc/articles/PMC3583091

Marian, V., Shook, A., & Schroeder, S.R. (2013). Bilingual two-way immersion programs benefit academic achievement. *Bilingual Research Journal, 36*(2), 167–186.

Marschark, M., & Hauser, P. (2011). *How deaf children learn: What parents and teachers need to know.* New York, NY: Oxford University Press.

Marschark, M., Sapere, P., Convertino, C., & Pelz, J. (2008). Learning via direct and mediated instruction by deaf students. *Journal of Deaf Studies and Deaf Education, 13*(4), 546–561.

Maxwell, M., & Bernstein, M. (1985). Synergy of sign and speech in simultaneous communication. *Applied Psycholinguistics, 6,* 63–81.

Mayberry, R.I., & Eichen, E. (1991). The long-lasting advantage of learning sign language in childhood: Another look at the critical period for language acquisition. *Journal of Memory and Language, 30,* 486–512.

Mayer, C., & Akamatsu, C. (1999). Bilingual-bicultural models of literacy education for deaf students: Considering the claims. *Journal of Deaf Studies and Deaf Education, 4*(1), 1–8.

McConkey-Robbins, A. (2001). A sign of the times: Cochlear implants and total communication. *Advanced Bionics Loud and Clear, 42*(2), 1-7.

McConnell, B.B., & California State University. (1982). *Bilingual education: Will the benefits last?* Bilingual Education Paper Series (Vol. 5, No. 8). Evaluation, Dissemination, and Assessment Center, California State University, Los Angeles.

Meadow-Orlans, K.P. (1994). Stress, support and deafness: Perceptions of infants' mothers and fathers. *Journal of Early Intervention, 18,* 91–102.

Meadow-Orlans, K., Spencer, P.E., & Koester, L.S. (2004). *The world of deaf infants: A longitudinal study.* New York, NY: Oxford University Press.

Messer, D. (1994). *The development of communication: From social interaction to language.* West Sussex, England: Wiley.

Mirus, G. (2014). Articulatory play among American cuers. *Sign Language Studies, 14*(3), 382–401.

Moeller, M., Carr, G., Seaver, L., Stredler-Brown, A., & Holzinger, D. (2013). Best practices in family-centered early intervention for children who are deaf or hard of hearing: An international consensus statement. *Journal of Deaf Studies and Deaf Education, 18*(4), 429–445.

Moores, D.F. (2001). *Educating the Deaf: Psychology, principles, and practices* (5th ed.). Boston, MA: Houghton Mifflin.

Movallali, G., & Rafi, M. (2012). Cued speech: Full access to spoken language for the hearing impaired. *Audiology, 21*(2), 1–18.

Newborg, J. (2005). *Battelle developmental inventory* (2nd ed.). Itasca, IL: Riverside Publishing.

Newport, E.L. (2002). Critical periods in language development. In L. Nadel (Ed.), *Encyclopedia of Cognitive Science* (pp. 737–740). London, England: Macmillan/Nature Publishing Group.

Newport, E.L., & Meier, R.P. (1985). *The acquisition of American Sign Language*. Mahwah, NJ: Lawrence Erlbaum Associates.

Nielsen, D.C., Luetke, B., & Stryker, D.S. (2011). The importance of morphemic awareness to reading achievement and the potential of signing morphemes to supporting reading development. *Journal of Deaf Studies and Deaf Education, 16*(3), 275–288.

Nussbaum, D., Scott, S., Waddy-Smith, B., & Koch, M. (2004, June). *Spoken language and sign: Optimizing learning for children with cochlear implants*. Paper presented at Laurent Clerc National Deaf Education Center, Washington, DC. Adapted from McConkey-Robbins, Loud and Clear. Advanced Bionics, 2001.

Nussbaum, D., Waddy-Smith, B., & Doyle, J. (2012). Students who are deaf and hard of hearing and use sign language: Considerations and strategies for developing spoken language and literacy skills. *Seminars in Speech and Language, 33*(4), 310–321.

Padden, C. (2006). Learning to fingerspell twice: Young signing children's acquisition of fingerspelling. In M. Marschark & P.E. Spencer (Eds.), *Advances in the sign language development of children* (pp. 189–201). New York, NY: Oxford University Press.

Paludneviciene, R., & Leigh, I. (2011). *Cochlear implants: Evolving perspectives*. Washington, DC: Gallaudet University Press.

Papoušek, H., Papoušek, M., & Bornstein, 1985). The naturalistic vocal environment of young infants: On the significance of homogeneity and variability in parental speech. In T. Field & N. Fox (Eds.), *Social perception in infants* (pp. 269–297). Norwood, NJ: Ablex.

Penhune, V., Cismaru, R., Dorsaint-Pierre, R., Petitto, L.A., & Zatorre, R. (2003). The morphometry of auditory cortex in the congenitally deaf measured using MRI. *NeuroImage, 20,* 1215–1225.

Petitto, L.A., Katerelos, M., Levy, B.G., Gauna, K., Tétreault, K., & Ferraro, V. (2001). Bilingual signed and spoken language acquisition from birth: Implications for the mechanisms underlying early bilingual language acquisition. *Journal of Child Language, 28*(2), 453–496.

Petitto, L.A., & Kovelman, I. (2003). The bilingual paradox: How signing-speaking bilingual children help us to resolve bilingual issues and teach us about the brain's mechanisms underlying all language acquisition. *Learning Languages, 8*(3), 5–18.

Pittman, P. (2001). *Deaf Mentor Curriculum*. SKI-HI Institute. Logan: Utah State University.

Pittman, P. (2003). *Starting small: A qualitative study of families of deaf children who have experienced early intervention services*. Retrieved from *Dissertation Abstracts International, 64*(5), 1600A. (UMI No. 3091770).

Power, D., Hyde, M., & Leigh, G. (2008). Learning English from signed English: An impossible task? *American Annals of the Deaf, 153*(1), 37–47.

Pressman, L., Pipp-Siegel, S., Yoshinaga-Itano, C., & Deas, A. (1999). Maternal sensitivity predicts language gain in preschool children who are deaf and hard of hearing. *Journal of Deaf Studies and Deaf Education, 4*(4), 294–304.

Raikes, H.H., & Edwards, C.P. (2009). *Extending the dance in infant and toddler caregiving: Enhancing attachment and relationships*. Baltimore, MD: Paul H. Brookes Publishing Co.

Reilly, J., & Bellugi, U. (1996). Competition on the face: Affect and language in ASL motherese. *Journal of Child Language, 23,* 219–239.

Rogers, K., & Young, A. (2011). Being a deaf role model: Deaf people's experiences of working with families and deaf young people. *Deafness & Education International, 13*(1), 2–16.

Schick, B., & Moeller, M.P. (1992). What is learnable in manually coded English sign systems? *Applied Psycholinguistics, 13*(3), 313–340.

Schleper, D.R. (1995). Reading to deaf children: Learning from deaf adults. *Perspectives in Education and Deafness, 13*(4), 4–8.

Scorce, J.F., Emde, R.N., Campos, J., & Klinnert, M. (1985). Maternal emotional signaling: Its effect on the visual cliff behaviour of 1-year-olds. *Developmental Psychology, 21*(1), 195–200.

Sharma, A., Dorman, M., & Spahr, A. (2002). A sensitive period for the development of the central auditory system in children with cochlear implants: Implications for age of implantation. *Ear and Hearing, 23*(6), 532–539.

Simms, L., Baker, S., & Clark, M. (2013). The standardized visual communication and sign language checklist for signing children. *Sign Language Studies, 14*(1), 101–124.

Spencer, P.E. (2003). Straight talk about cochlear implants for children. *Journal of Deaf Studies and Deaf Education, 8*(4), 498.

Spencer, P.E., Bodner-Johnson, B., & Gutfreund, M. (1992). Interacting with infants with hearing loss: What can we learn from mothers who are deaf? *Journal of Early Intervention, 16,* 64–78.

Spencer, P., & Koester, L. (in press). *Development of deaf and hard-of-hearing infants and toddlers.* New York, NY: Oxford University Press.

Spencer, P., & Marschark, M. (2006). *Advances in the spoken language development of deaf and hard-of-hearing children.* New York, NY: Oxford University Press.

Stern, D. (1985). *The interpersonal world of the infant: A view from psychoanalysis and developmental psychology.* New York, NY: Basic Books.

Stokoe, W.C. (1960/2005). Sign language structure: An outline of the visual communication system of the American Deaf. Studies in Linguistics, Occasional Papers 8. Buffalo, NY: Department of Anthropology and Linguistics, University of Buffalo. Reprinted in *Journal of Deaf Studies and Deaf Education, 10,* 3–37.

Stredler-Brown, A. (2011). *Early intervention: Serving infants and toddlers.* In C. DeConde-Johnson & J. Seaton (Eds.), *Educational audiology handbook* (pp. 445–466). New York: Thompson Delmar Learning.

Supalla, S. (1991). Manually coded English: The modality question in signed development. *Theoretical Issues in Sign Language Research, 2,* 85–109.

Swisher, M.V. (2000). Learning to converse: How deaf mothers support the development of attention and conversational skills in their young deaf children. In P.E. Spencer, C.J. Erting, & M. Marschark (Eds.), *The deaf child in the family and at school: Essays in honor of Kathryn P. Meadow-Orlans* (pp. 21–39). Mahwah, NJ: Erlbaum.

Torres, S., Rodriguez, J., Garcia-Orza, J., & Calleja, M. (2008). Reading comprehension of an inferential text by deaf students with cochlear implants using cued speech. *Volta Review, 108*(1), 37–59.

Trevarthen, C.B. (1979). Communication and cooperation in early infancy: A description of primary intersubjectivity. In M. Bullowa (Ed.), *Before speech* (pp. 321–348). Cambridge, England: Cambridge University Press.

Uylings, H.M. (2006). Development of the human cortex and the concept of "critical" or "sensitive" periods. *Language Learning, 56*(1), 59–90.

Walden, T., & Ogan, T. (1988). The development of social referencing. *Child Development, 59,* 1230–1240.

Watkins, S., Pittman, P., & Walden, B. (1998). The Deaf mentor experimental project for young children who are deaf. *American Annals of the Deaf, 143*(1), 29–34.

# 7

# Auditory-Verbal Therapy

*A Conversational Competence Approach*

Amy McConkey Robbins

This chapter focuses on auditory-verbal (AV) therapy, an intervention approach for young children who are deaf or hard of hearing (D/HH) that places emphasis on audition as the foundation for competence in spoken language, conversation, and literacy. The notion that children who are D/HH can learn to listen and speak is not a new one. As far back as the 17th century, there have been proponents of techniques to develop spoken language in children who are D/HH. Advocates of this approach used methods that emphasized lipreading and tactile cues. More recently, AV therapy evolved from the conviction that through maximum use of residual hearing, children could learn spoken language by relying on audition. (The reader is referred to Goldberg & Flexer, 2012, for historical background on the AV method and its pioneers.) The viability of the AV approach has increased dramatically over the last 25 to 30 years, owing to a confluence of remarkable advances in hearing instruments, changes in health care policies, and mandates for special education services, topics mentioned in Chapter 1. Because many of the innovations that make the AV approach broadly applicable have occurred since the 1990s, there is a need within the profession for heightened awareness of the approach and the positive outcomes associated with it.

One of the crucial factors supporting success with the AV approach has been the provision of advanced hearing technology to infants and toddlers. Whereas early fittings of hearing instruments have the potential to greatly enhance listening and spoken language outcomes, these benefits may not be realized if children's potentials are under-or overestimated. An example of an underestimate is the misconception that age-appropriate spoken language skills are not realistic in children who are born profoundly deaf. An example of an overestimate is the mistaken notion that simply placing hearing instruments on children's ears will lead to spoken language mastery—although today's hearing technology gives access to sound, access alone does not guarantee comprehension of spoken language. Meaning is acquired only with purposeful, repeated listening experiences and motivating interactions that allow the child to make sense of what is heard. Tyszkiewicz and Stokes (2006) suggest that, without purposeful emphasis on meaning, hearing technology merely increases the quantity and volume of sound the child hears, resulting in auditory learning that is likely to be random and unfocused. In this chapter, I describe factors that must align and work in concert in a successful AV approach. These include early, state-of-the-art hearing technology that is worn, monitored, and upgraded with vigilance; focused habilitation by clinicians who are highly skilled in developing spoken language through listening; strong family engagement; and a daily environment rich in meaningful sound that provides *motivation* to listen and learn.

The growth in the number of children using the AV approach is not the result of a single factor but rather may be characterized as a virtuous circle. *Virtuous circle* is a term borrowed from economics that refers to a complex chain of beneficial events, each having a positive effect on the next. Each iteration of the circle reinforces the previous one, producing mutually reinforcing effects and creating sustainable momentum. Figure 7.1 shows the growth of the AV approach over the last 25 to 30 years, illustrated as a virtuous circle. As cochlear implants (CIs) underwent major technological advances and were routinely provided to infants and toddlers, published studies reported on the increasingly successful outcomes of children using auditory approaches (Geers, Nicholas, Tye-Murray, Uchanski, Brenner et al., 2000; Osberger, Robbins, Todd, & Riley, 1994). This success led to growth in funding for and availability of auditory-based programs, both public and private. The expansion of available programs meant, in turn, that more families who selected the AV approach could be served. With the growth in AV programs, clinicians had opportunities to see the method in action by doing observations or internships, often as part of grants from private foundations. A certification process for clinicians using listening and spoken language was made widely available in 2007, increasing the number of practitioners certified through a voluntary, rigorous mentoring, education, and examination process. This program has resulted in Listening and Spoken Language Specialists (LSLS) certifications, including both certified AV therapists (LSLS Cert. AVT) and certified AV educators (LSLS-AVEd). Thus, this process is considered one certification with two designations (Goldberg & Flexer, 2012). It is encouraging that, in the first 4 years of LSLS certification, the number of Cert. AVT and AVEd specialists increased by more than 100% (Goldberg & Estes, 2012), and the number of enrollees continues to grow. As a result, families of newly identified infants have increased access to credentialed service providers who specialize in the AV approach. The virtuous circle pattern continues. Statistics from some state agencies indicate that between 75% and 95% of families have selected listening and spoken language competence as the desired goal for their infant (Alberg, 2014).

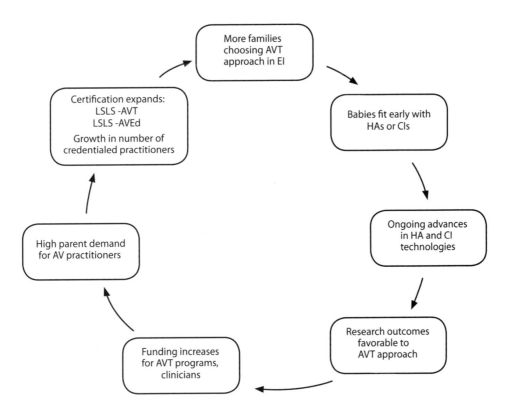

**Figure 7.1.** Virtuous circle representing factors that resulted in increased growth of the auditory-verbal therapy approach. Key: *AV*, auditory-verbal; *AVT*, auditory-verbal therapy; *CIs*, cochlear implants; *EI*, early intervention; *HAs*, hearing aids; *LSLS-AVEd*, listening and spoken language specialist, auditory-verbal education; *LSLS-AVT*, listening and spoken language specialist, auditory-verbal therapy

## THEORETICAL BASES

### Rationale for Auditory-Verbal Therapy and the Primacy of Audition

The foundation of the AV approach is listening development. The approach seeks to replicate—as closely as possible—the stages of auditory development through which typical children pass. Infants who can hear at birth receive auditory input all day every day, eventually benefitting from thousands of hours of hearing experience before they ever say a meaningful word. Auditory input to the brain is the foundation upon which spoken language is built. Thus, the AV approach emphasizes the primacy of auditory development by employing the term *auditory first*. The term also applies to the sequence of presentation of information in therapy. Rather than always presenting information with visual and auditory information simultaneously, the AV approach advocates creating opportunities to present stimuli through the auditory channel first. In this way, it is possible to determine whether children have understood via listening alone or whether visual information (i.e., speechreading cues) is needed to ensure comprehension. The practice of strategically presenting information in this sequence is referred to as the auditory-first technique. A practitioner can achieve an auditory-only context through natural means, such as sharing joint visual attention on an object or activity with the child, strategically speaking when the child is looking away, or sitting next to (rather than across from) the child when playing or reading. These techniques are seen in the accompanying video clips (see Video clip 7.1). Other auditory-only techniques are contrived events wherein adults use an acoustic hoop or their hand to cover their mouth when speaking, a technique known as the *hand cue* (see Estabrooks, 2012, for perspectives on the changing use of the hand cue). Though considered unnatural by some, these techniques are useful in certain teaching situations, a point revisited later in the chapter.

LSLS practitioners acknowledge that real-world communication is a multisensory event and support the balance between periods of auditory-only practice and everyday experiences that are multimodal. This is important because typically developing (TD) children integrate auditory and visual information—a process needed for word learning—as neural pathways mature and form connections between the auditory cortex and other cortices. This integration process is impaired when early auditory deprivation occurs (Kral, Hartmann, Tillein, Held, & Klinke, 2000) but appears to be restorable in children who receive cochlear implants at very young ages (Houston, Ying, Pisoni, & Kirk, 2003). In addition, watching the face of the speaker gives cues about the corresponding emotional content that are critical for interpersonal communication. Eye contact is a strong signal that a person is attending to the message conveyed by a communication partner. For these reasons, children need to experience much of their daily communication looking at and receiving eye contact and facial/body language.

There is a reciprocal and dependent relationship among hearing, speech, and language. Listening to language encourages speech development, and using speech provides reinforcement through the auditory-oral feedback loop. Segal and Kishon-Rabin (2011) note that *auditory* exposure to linguistic input is essential for developing an interest in spoken language. Their findings from children with typical hearing show that the preference for listening to *child-directed speech* is developmental. As the authors note,

> Infants may first prefer speech because they are drawn to the dynamicity of the acoustic signal, and this attraction might intensify later when this signal becomes a source of communication and linguistic information. The latter bias toward speech may occur toward the end of the first and beginning of the second years of life when infants can recognize familiar words, associate words with objects, and acquire initial receptive and expressive vocabularies. (p. 364)

### The Primacy of Audition for Cognitive Development

The AV approach also is grounded in the fact that sound is inherently a temporal and sequential signal. With tasks that require learning or remembering temporally ordered events, people do best when they can rely on hearing (Collier & Logan, 2000; Glenberg & Jona, 1991). Growing evidence indicates that experience with sound may provide a sort of scaffolding for the development of general cognitive skills that depend on the representation of temporal or sequential patterns, as suggested by Conway, Pisoni, and Kronenberger (2009). These authors posit that sound, compared with vision, may specifically carry higher level patterns of information related to timing and sequencing, suggesting that hearing is the primary gateway for perceiving *sequential* patterns of input that change over time (rather than over space, as in vision). They assert that "the development of fundamental sequence-learning mechanisms would be delayed when this type of [sequential-pattern] input is unavailable, as is the case in deafness" (p. 4). Considered in this light, hearing is not simply a matter of sound perception but potentially of fortified cognition. At its crux, the AV approach is not just about listening and spoken language acquisition but about *cognitive enrichment.*

## Underlying Assumptions

Three assumptions that undergird the AV approach are discussed next. These are based on published studies of TD children and those who are D/HH.

*Sensitive Periods and Early Cortical Input*    Early auditory stimulation of the brain leads to maturation of primary auditory cortex and auditory association areas that are critical for listening and spoken language proficiency (Froemke et al., 2014). Sensitive periods have been established for these cortical regions, with evidence that, minus adequate stimulation, regions designated for auditory development undergo crossmodal plasticity and take on functions of other sensory modalities, particularly vision (Buckley & Tobey, 2011). Thus, early, consistent auditory input to promote maturity of the auditory cortex is essential for children whose parents have chosen a listening and spoken language approach. Though a degree of **neuroplasticity** remains throughout the lifespan, Gordon et al. (2011) verify that hearing research supports a "use it or lose it" hypothesis related to higher level cortical regions. The AV approach is consistent with findings that early cochlear implant stimulation in children who are D/HH results in auditory cortical maturation that approaches or matches that of typical hearing children (Sharma & Campbell, 2011). Specifically, researchers have documented latencies in P1 cortical auditory evoked potential—a biomarker that provides a measure of auditory cortical maturity—in large groups of children with congenital deafness who received cochlear implants at varying ages. Sharma and Dorman (2006) reported that children who received a cochlear implant before age 3 1/2 years had typical P1 latencies after 6 months of consistent CI use. In contrast, children who received a CI after age 7 years had atypical cortical response latencies that did not reach typical limits, even after several years of implant experience. The middle group, who received a CI between ages 3 years 6 months and 7 years, showed highly variable response latencies. These researchers concluded that the optimal time for central auditory development is during the first 3.5 years of life and that in all likelihood, the sensitive period for such development ends at age 7 (Sharma & Nash, 2009). Our approach promotes the potential of CIs and hearing aids (HAs) by pairing early hearing technology fittings with aggressive AV input.

*What We Do in Intervention Matters*    A second underlying assumption driven by research is that environment and sensory experience alter cortical development and plasticity (Ryugo & Limb, 2009). The way the brain organizes and reorganizes as a result of rehabilitation is highly influenced by the characteristics of the input and by a multitude of factors that make up rehabilitation (Moucha & Kilgard, 2006). Although children acquire spoken language in biologically determined stages, the nature of that acquisition varies widely in children who are D/HH because the auditory input they receive is degraded and limited when compared with that available to TD children. In intervention, we seek to influence the amount, quality, and characteristics of auditory-linguistic input from the environment so as to maximize the potential for the biological system to do what it was intended to do. To quote Margaret Tait (personal communication, 1993), intervention seeks to "help the natural happen."

***Early Input, Developmental Synchrony, and Cumulative Practice***  A third assumption is the importance of an early age of auditory input to replicate typical development as closely as possible. This is one of the driving principles behind cochlear implantation at early ages. There is mounting evidence (Nicholas & Geers, 2006; Niparko, Tobey, Thal, Eisenberg, Wang, Quittner et al., 2010) that implantation at a young age produces an auditory learning advantage, even in children younger than 24 months. Robbins, Koch, Osberger, Phillips, and Kishon-Rabin (2004) found that, in three groups of children implanted by 36 months, those implanted by 18 months of age reached auditory benchmarks earlier and had a higher likelihood of falling within typical auditory norms than did those implanted between 19 and 36 months. Their findings were in concordance with the "earlier is better" conclusion. These authors discussed the notion of developmental synchrony, where, for TD children, skills in various developmental domains, such as physical, cognitive, motor, linguistic, emotional, and social, emerge together—that is, *in synchrony*. Children are biologically programmed to develop certain subskills in each of these domains during specific periods of time. Sensory deprivation, if not ameliorated, will inevitably result in developmental asynchrony, a concept that Boothroyd (1982) applied years ago to children wearing hearing aids. When **developmental dyssynchrony** occurs, a child's auditory skills (and subsequent spoken language abilities) are out of synch with skills in other domains, such as gross motor, fine motor, and visual processing. Providing access to sound at a very young age helps prevent or minimize the negative consequences of developmental dyssynchrony, a view supported by the findings of Tomblin, Barker, and Hubbs (2007). Early fitting of hearing instruments is also supported by the fact that mastery of any developmental skill depends on **cumulative practice**. The more delayed the acquisition of an expected skill, the further behind children are in the amount of cumulative practice they have had to perfect that skill (Robbins et al., 2004).

A major focus of any intervention is to help a child acquire developmental milestones as closely as possible to the time that he or she is biologically intended to do so. In the case of the AV approach, we seek to replicate the time course and sequence of skill acquisition across a broad range of developmental domains, taking into account the whole child and the goal of synchrony across developmental domains. Special attention is given to auditory development, taking into consideration that this is a primary modality for spoken language acquisition.

## Auditory Milestones in Typically Developing Children

Children with typical development follow a predictable sequence of auditory milestones from the time they are newborns. Knowledge of this sequence and the ages when milestones are usually attained is essential for clinicians who use the AV approach. Such knowledge allows practitioners to informally assess children's listening development while working with them in a diagnostic-teaching paradigm. In addition, the ability to identify intervention priorities is dependent on a clear understanding of the sequence and time course of other developmental behaviors, as will be reviewed later in the chapter. Readers may access a chart of auditory and speech milestones for children with typical hearing at the American Speech-Language-Hearing Association web site (http://www.asha.org/public/speech/development/chart). When children hear from birth, they demonstrate the milestones shown on this chart without any conscious effort or formal instruction and without adults setting goals or planning for the next step. These milestones emerge as a result of biological readiness; environmental influence; access to sound all day, every day; and participation in meaningful social interactions.

The milestones shown on the chart reflect auditory and speech behaviors observed in TD children at different chronological ages. Figure 7.2 shows a useful clinical tool, the Auditory Learning Guide (Walker, 2009). This tool helps practitioners set goals and monitor ongoing progress for children who are D/HH. Notice how many units there are. Many small steps are identified, with each of the milestones for TD children broken down into separate steps. Years ago, it was necessary for clinicians and parents to formally work on each of these steps because auditory progress in children with profound hearing losses was dependent on formal, didactic instruction. With early identification, early fitting of technology, and access to spoken language at conversational levels, today's children who are D/HH have the potential to acquire many—although not necessarily all—of these skills through **incidental learning**, just as TD children do. It is exciting for practitioners to observe that, for increasing numbers of children who use the AV approach, some milestones emerge *without direct therapy to address them,* often as a result of generalization from other skills they have acquired. These children's mastery results from biological readiness; environmental influence; access to sound all day, every day; and participation in meaningful social interactions, just as it does in TD children. When we "help the natural happen" by teaching parents how to utilize all waking moments as enriching communication opportunities with their children, our approach becomes one of habilitation (facilitating progress) rather than rehabilitation (remediating deficits). It is important to query parents directly about the communication skills they observe at home that may have emerged without direct teaching, presumably via overhearing. Such discussions help parents identify and celebrate instances of spontaneous learning and generalization in their child. Robbins (2009) has noted, "The purpose of mastering

**AUDITORY LEARNING GUIDE**

| Sound awareness (speech and environmental sounds) | Phoneme level** (speech babble) | Discourse level (auditory processing of connected speech) | Sentence level | Word level |
|---|---|---|---|---|
| Step 1—Detect* the presence of any speech syllable. | Step 2—Imitate physical actions (before speech imitations). | Step 1a—Imitate motions of nursery rhymes/songs with accompanying vocalizations. | Step 1—Identify familiar stereotypic phrases or sentences. | Step 1a—Identify and imitate approximations of Learning to Listen sounds varying in suprasegmentals and vowel content (e.g., [a-a-a]/airplane, [u]-[u]/train, [oil] [oil] pig in isolation) at the end and then in the middle of a sentence. |
| Step 2—Detect* vowel variety ([u] [a] [i]) and raspberries ([b-r-r]). | Step 2—Imitate any phoneme that child produces spontaneously when given hand cue (or other cue). | Step 1b—Identify nursery rhymes or songs. | Step 2—Recall two critical elements in a message. | Step 1b—Identify one-, two-, and three-syllable words in isolation (e.g., cat versus chicken versus kangaroo). |
| Step 3—Detect* consonant variety (e.g., [mm-m], [bʌ], [bʌ] [bʌ], and [wa] [wa]). | Step 3—Imitate varying suprasegmental qualities in phonemes (vary intensity, duration, and pitch); [aeeee] (long) versus [ae ae] (pulsed); [ae-ae] loud/quiet/ whispered; [ae] high/mid/ low pitch, whispered; [ae] high/mid/low pitch. | Step 2—Answer common questions with abundant contextual support (e.g., "Where's that?" "What's that?" "Where's Mama?" "What is ___ doing?"). | Step 3—Recall three critical elements in a message. | Step 2—Identify words having the same number of syllables but different vowels/ diphthongs and consonants (e.g., horse versus cow versus sheep). |
| Step 4—Detect* the presence of environmental sounds at loud, medium, and soft levels at close range, at a distance of 6–12 ft, and at a distance of greater than 12 ft. | Step 4—Imitate vowel and diphthong variety (e.g., /u/, / ae/, /au/, /i/). | Step 3—Identify a picture that corresponds to a story phrase in a three- or four-scene story. | Step 4—Complete known linguistic messages from a closed set (e.g., nursery rhymes songs, familiar stories). | Step 3a—Identify words in which the initial consonants are the same but the vowels and final consonants are different (e.g., ball versus bike). |
| Step 5—Detect* whispered [hae] [hae] and [p] [p] [p]. | Step 5—Imitate alternated vowels and diphthongs (e.g., /a-u/ /e-I/ /a-I/). | Step 4—Identify an object from several related descriptors (closed set). | Step 5—Answer common questions about a disclosed and familiar topic 1) without pictorial cues, 2) over the telephone, or 3) on audio/ video. | Step 3b—Identify words in which the final consonants are the same but the vowels and initial consonants are different (e.g., food versus card). |

**Figure 7.2.** Auditory learning guide demonstrating stages in auditory development. The information on the chart was compiled by Beth Walker and adapted from the following sources: Los Angeles County Schools (1976). Auditory skills curriculum. North Hollywood, CA: Foreworks; Romanik, S. (2008). Auditory skills program. Sydney, Australia: New South Wales Dept. of Education; Simser, J.I. (1993). Auditory verbal intervention: Infants and toddlers. *Volta Review 95*(3): 217–229.

| | | | | |
|---|---|---|---|---|
| Step 6—Detect* the sounds of the Ling Six-Sound Test. | Step 6—Imitate consonants varying in manner (fricatives, nasals, and plosives). Use phonemes previously produced (e.g., /h/ versus /m-m-m/ versus /p/). | Step 5—Follow a conversation with the topic disclosed. | Step 6—Recall four or more critical elements in a message to follow multiple element directions. | Step 4—Identify words in which the initial and final consonants are identical but the vowels/diphthongs are different (e.g., *book* versus *back*). |
| Step 7—Detect* the sounds of the Ling Six-Sound Test at various distances. | Step 7—Imitate consonants differing in voiced versus unvoiced cues (e.g., /bʌ/ /bʌ/ versus /pʌ/ /pʌ/ and then with vowel variety, /bobo/ /paepae/). | Step 6a—Answer questions about a story with the topic disclosed. | Step 7—Complete known linguistic messages (open set). | Step 5a—Identify words in which the vowels and final consonants are identical but the *initial* consonants differ by three features—manner, place of articulation, and voicing (e.g., *mouse* versus *house*). |
| Step 8—Locate the direction of sound if amplified binaurally. | Step 8—Alternate consonants varying in place cues, first with varying vowels (e.g., /ma-ma/ /no-no/; /go-go/ /bi-bi/). | Step 6b—Answer questions about a story with the topic disclosed; story is teacher recorded. | Step 8—Follow open set directions and instructions (disclosed). | Step 5b—Identify words in which vowels and initial consonants are identical but the *final* consonants differ by three features—manner, place of articulation, and voicing (e.g., *comb* versus *coat*). |
| | Step 9—Alternate syllables with varying consonants and same vowel (e.g., [bi] [di], [ho] [go]). | Step 7—Recall details of a story (topic disclosed). | Step 9—Recall specific elements in a sentence by answering questions about an undisclosed but familiar topic. | Step 6—Identify words in which the vowels and the final or initial consonants (Cs) are identical but one C (initial/final) differs by two features: 1) manner and place (voicing in common: *moat* versus *goat*; 2) manner and voicing (place in common), *man* versus *mat*; 3) place and voicing (manner in common), *boat* versus *coat*. |
| | | Step 8—Sequence the events of a story (topic disclosed). | Step 10—Repeat each word in a sentence exactly: 1) predictable sentences (e.g., "I'm going to the grocery store to buy cereal and milk."); 2) less predictable sentences (e.g., "A woman hit me so I told her to calm down.") | Step 7a—Identify words in which the initial and final consonants are identical but the *initial* consonants differ by only one feature – manner of articulation (e.g., *ball* versus *mall*). |

*(continued)*

# AUDITORY LEARNING GUIDE

| Sound Awareness (speech and environmental sounds) | Phoneme level** (speech babble) | | |
|---|---|---|---|

| | | Step 11—Recall specific elements in a sentence by answering questions on an undisclosed topic. | Step 7b—Identify words in which the vowels and initial consonants are identical but the **final** consonants differ by only one feature—manner of articulation (e.g., *cloud* versus *clown*). |
| | | | Step 8a—Identify words in which the vowels and final consonants are identical but the **initial** consonants differ by only one feature—voicing (e.g., *coat* versus *goat*). |
| | | | Step 8b—Identify words in which the vowels and initial consonants are identical but the **final** consonants differ by only one feature—voicing (e.g., *bag* versus *back*). |
| | | | Step 9a—Identify words in which the vowels and final consonants are identical but the **initial** consonants differ by only one feature—place of articulation (e.g., *bun* versus *gun*). |
| | | | Step 9b—Identify words in which the vowels and initial consonants are identical but the **final** consonants differ by only one feature—place of articulation (e.g., *sheep* versus *sheet*). |

| Step 9—Retell a story with the topic disclosed, recalling all the details in sequence. |
| Step 10—Make identification based on several related descriptors (open set). |
| Step 11—Follow a conversation on an undisclosed topic. |
| Step 12—Retell a story about an undisclosed topic, recalling as many details as possible. |
| Step 13—Process information in noise and at various distances. |
| Step 14—Process group conversations. |

The shading codes in the chart designate auditory behaviors to be mastered by the end of the specified year, given optimally fitted hearing devices.

KEY
YEAR 1
YEAR 2
YEAR 3
YEAR 4

This guide is intended to aid professionals in the *beginning* stages of learning an auditory-based approach. As professionals acquire more experience in auditory teaching, children should progress more rapidly.

The information on the table was compiled by Beth Walker (2009) and adapted from Judy Simser's article in the Volta Review (1993; ** items); the Auditory Skills Program, New South Wales Department of School Education; the Foreworks Auditory Skills Curriculum (1976, North Hollywood, CA); and teacher input.

**Note \***
A detection response could include turning head, pointing to ear, clapping, dropping a toy in a container, and so forth.

**References**
Simser, J.I. (1993). Auditory-verbal intervention: Infants and toddlers. Volta Review, 95(3), 217–229.
Walker, B. (2009). Auditory Learning guide. Retrieved May 13, 2015, from http://www.firstyears.org/c4/alg/alg.pdf

**Figure 7.2.** *(continued)*

skills [in therapy] is not so that the child can perform there but so that he or she can utilize those skills outside of it" (p. 271).

## Target Areas within the Auditory-Verbal Approach

The first "target" in this approach is family guidance. AV practice seeks first to guide and coach parents, who then become the main force in advancing their child's communication. Chapter 4 discusses parent coaching practices. The overarching target for children is to learn to listen and talk with full communicative competence and to excel in the academic setting. Estabrooks (2012) notes that in the AV approach, listening and spoken language become major forces in nurturing the development of a child's personal, social, and academic life. With this whole-child approach, skills are emphasized in such domains as listening, receptive and expressive language, speech intelligibility and phonology, social and pragmatic skills, music, literacy, and neurocognition including working memory (i.e., the ability to hold a thought until the brain has a chance to think something through) and executive functions (i.e., self-control).

These targets are addressed within the context of a habilitation approach in which the parent and clinician are partners in nurturing the child's communicative competence. Parent engagement is a key component of the AV approach, consistent with the finding that family involvement is a primary factor in predicting outcomes in children who are D/HH enrolled in early intervention (Moeller, 2000). In this approach, parents (the term *parent* is used to refer to those individuals who care about and nurture the child) are present in every session, partnering with the clinician. This partnership involves both observation, where the clinician takes the lead, and active participation, where the clinician "passes the baton" to the parent, who takes leadership of an activity. Experienced clinicians agree that creating this partnership is a formidable but worthwhile task. Talbot and Estabrooks (2012) wrote, "It is rare that a parent comes to the initial session prepared to truly partner with the practitioner. In addition, it takes significant awareness and practice for the AV practitioner to share control of the session with a parent" (p. 23). Clinicians may justify seeing a child alone in therapy by stating that the child's behavior is poor when parents are present and therefore the value of the sessions is reduced. This observation should compel *more*, not *less*, parent involvement in the session, because the parents need assistance to get compliance from their child and to learn behavior management techniques. If a child cooperates during 1 hour of therapy each week but is noncompliant during the remaining hundreds of hours spent in the home, the impact of therapy upon real-life communication will be limited.

Estabrooks (2012, p. 4) lists nearly a dozen key tasks of parents in AV sessions:

- Model techniques for stimulating speech, language, and communication activities at home

- Plan strategies to integrate listening, speech, language, and communication into daily routines and experiences

- Communicate as partners in the therapeutic and educational processes

- Inform the professional of the child's interests and abilities
- Interpret the meaning of the child's early communication
- Discuss and practice appropriate behavior management techniques
- Record and discuss progress
- Interpret short-and long-term goals
- Build confidence in parent–child interaction
- Make informed decisions
- Advocate on behalf of their child

Additional important tasks include the following:

- Interpret the purpose of a game or activity while observing/ participating
- Summarize a session to solidify what has been learned
- Problem-solve with the practitioner on issues of concern
- Review how insights from the session will be communicated to other family members

Clearly, parents are essential partners, not just observers, in the AV approach. Examples of active parental involvement can be seen in the accompanying video clips.

## USE OF ASSESSMENTS TO IDENTIFY INTERVENTION PRIORITIES

There are a variety of reasons for assessing the communication skills of a child who is D/HH. This chapter specifically addresses assessments whose purpose is *to identify intervention goals* (see Robbins, 2006, for general principles of communication assessment with children who are D/HH and a suggested battery of measures). A battery containing both formal and informal measures is recommended because this combination yields the most helpful information from different sources under varying conditions.

In order to set intervention goals, the clinician needs knowledge about the child's abilities that falls within four different sectors, and obtaining that knowledge is what dictates the measures that will make up the assessment (see Figure 7.3). These four sectors are 1) the child's current level (CL); 2) the concepts and skills the child would be expected to acquire at the next level (NL; for this, a clinician must be familiar with the developmental trajectories for these specific concepts and skills); 3) the factors or techniques that make learning easier (FTE) for this child; and 4) the factors or techniques that make learning harder (FTH) for this child.

Knowledge within these four sectors guides the assessment. The four sectors also provide support for the notion that different kinds of measurement tools, including those that are both formal and informal, are needed in order to gain rich understanding from an assessment. Knowledge about the child's current level is mostly (not exclusively) found in formal, standardized measures,

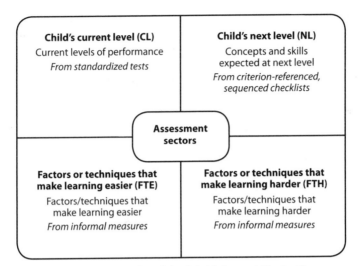

**Figure 7.3.**    The four sectors of knowledge (in bold) about a child, gained from assessment, that enable the clinician to set intervention goals. The primary though not exclusive source of information used in each sector is noted in italics.

which yield norm-referenced scores, comparing a child to peers. Knowledge of NL is primarily but not exclusively revealed in criterion-referenced measures or sequenced checklists where the clinician is able to view what developmental skills are expected to follow the child's current ones. Knowledge about FTE and FTH is primarily but not exclusively revealed in informal measures, which allow the clinician to manipulate a host of different variables and to document how such manipulations affect learning. The following are examples of the latter: If I reduce the set size, what percentage of the time will the child be successful? What percentage of the time will the child remain successful at answering complex questions if I remove vision and provide language through audition alone? Informal measures are not standardized or normed but should be systematic. Note the suggested use of percentages, which the examiner would compute by tallying both the opportunities in which the target occurs and the child's response to each opportunity. In this way, informal measures yield a percentage and can, therefore, be tracked and repeated over time and used to support data on goal attainment in the child's individualized education program (IEP). The IEP is a legal document used in special education that spells out a child's learning goals, the services the school will provide, and how progress toward goals will be measured.

***Intervention Priorities and the Zone of Proximal Development***    The following framework for assessments is based on Vygotsky's concept of the **zone of proximal development** (ZPD; Vygotsky, 1978). In the 1930s, Vygotsky asserted that children have a level of *independent performance* (what they are able to do without help) and a level of *assisted performance* (what they can do if given support). In Vygotskian theory, ZPD is the area between the child's *independent* and *assisted* performance levels. Skills found inside the child's ZPD are those that have not yet emerged but could emerge if the child had meaningful interactions with "knowledgeable others" (both peers and adults) or was placed in supportive environments such as group pretend play scenarios for young children. It was Vygotsky's conviction that the most powerful teaching is directed not at a child's independent performance but rather within the ZPD. Such teaching is thought to do more than simply work on adding new skills; rather, it actually enhances gains in child development. How do we focus teaching so that it is just above the child's current level? We must know the child's current level and what factors help or hinder learning to answer that question.

***Strengths, Weaknesses, Recommendations Approach***  When a battery of tests is administered, it is useful to report individual scores but more useful to consolidate the information obtained into *strengths, weaknesses,* and *recommendations* and represent these in written form. Parents often understand test results if they are presented in this format. Moeller (1989) advises that, following an assessment, service providers should be able to list four or five observed child strengths. For a child who is not at expected age level in any area, the clinician still may lift up relative strengths (a skill in the profile that is stronger than others) or mention positive traits such as the child's willingness to persevere at a task or the child's desire to relate to others using communication. Expression of the following strength may reinforce family efforts: "This child comes from a warm and supportive home." Focusing only on weaknesses or what the child cannot do is discouraging for parents, as it would be for any of us who face a task that will require years of effort.

In order to identify intervention priorities, we review evaluation results with the following questions in mind: What are the relative strengths and weaknesses in this child's profile when comparing across all measures, both formal and informal? How does the child's learning increase or decrease when I vary factors such as rate of presentation, complexity of information, presence of distractions, or background noise? What skills, if successfully targeted in intervention, would have the strongest impact on the child's communication? Where are the skills that are already emerging and could be mastered quickly if targeted? Is there a skill that has been resistant to mastery on which other skills depend? Parent input about family priorities for communication is integral to this approach. When gathering data to present to a family, it is done with the purpose of working together with them to review the findings and to receive their input about goals that are important at home among family members and in other real-world situations.

## INTERVENTION TO PROMOTE AUDITORY LEARNING IN YOUNG CHILDREN

### Empirical Evidence from the Literature on Children Who Are Deaf or Hard of Hearing

Published studies have documented the performance of children served in programs with a strong auditory emphasis. Rhoades (2001) found that prior to beginning AV therapy at chronological ages between 4 months and 8 years, a group of 40 children wearing either hearing aids or cochlear implants had average spoken language scores that were significantly delayed relative to their ages. The children were enrolled in AV therapy for various time periods throughout the 4-year study, and growth rates in receptive and expressive language exceeded a month-for-month gain (i.e., they had a faster rate of acquisition than that observed in children with typical hearing). This meant that they showed a pattern of closing the gap between their language age and chronological age. At the end of 4 years of AV therapy, a subgroup of 14 of the children "graduated" from therapy and achieved language scores equivalent to their chronological ages and were successfully enrolled in inclusive educational classrooms. Notably, the parent education levels for the children in this study were higher than average. Three fourths of the parents were college educated, which was a positive prognostic factor for their children's communication outcome. On the other hand, the children had not benefitted from newborn hearing screening and had an average age of identification of 17 months, which could be considered a relative disadvantage for communication development.

In another study, researchers investigated speech and language outcomes for 19 children wearing hearing aids or cochlear implants who were enrolled in AV intervention (Dornan, Hickson, Murdoch, Houston, & Constantinescu, 2010). Each participant was matched with a TD child and evaluated over a 4-year period. Measures of receptive vocabulary, receptive and expressive connected language, articulation, reading, and mathematics were administered. The participants' self-esteem was also studied. Results showed that the children enrolled in AV therapy had communication outcomes that closely approximated the matched TD controls. There were periods of time when the children who were D/HH had faster rates of language learning than those expected of children with typical hearing. Reading and math scores were also comparable between the children who were D/HH and their matched peers, although too few for statistical analysis. The authors concluded that AV therapy was highly effective in fostering age-appropriate speech and language skills. Limitations of the study were that the AV families had mostly moderate to high socioeconomic status and very few children with complex needs were included in the study cohort. On the other hand, the participants did not have a particularly early age at implantation (mean = 27 months) yet were able to demonstrate excellent communication progress when their families engaged in AV practice.

Dettman, Wall, Constantinescu, and Dowell (2013) compared spoken receptive vocabulary and speech perception skills of 39 children with cochlear implants who used different intervention approaches. Participants were matched for characteristics such as gender, age at implantation, and cognitive status. The results showed that children who had spoken language emphasis, either AV therapy (n = 8) or AV education (n = 23), outperformed children from bilingual-bicultural programs (n = 8) on all outcome measures. When participants were individually matched on demographic variables, early age at implantation was the most significant factor for spoken language performance. The authors interpreted their results as providing support for consistent emphasis on oral-aural input to achieve optimum spoken communication outcomes for children with cochlear implants. The study did not match participants for parent education level or socioeconomic status, factors the authors acknowledge may have affected outcomes.

Finally, another 4-year study tracked communication progress of 181 children in North America who received a cochlear implant by age 5 (Geers & Brenner, 2003). A host of variables was evaluated, including the degree to which auditory and speech skills were emphasized in each child's classroom. A rating scale reflected how much speech emphasis existed in the "signing" classrooms and how much auditory emphasis existed in "oral" classrooms of the children with CIs. Better speech and spoken language scores were associated with children in signing programs whose classrooms were rated as *strong speech emphasis*. Among oral children, higher levels of speech and language were associated with programs rated as *strongly auditory*. There was variability in the data, as is seen in virtually all studies of children who are D/HH. Even after all other factors had been accounted for, the analysis revealed strong associations between classroom communication mode and speech perception, speech production, and expressive language (Moog & Geers, 2003). Overall, the more auditory emphasis in the child's classroom, the higher the child's ability to understand and use age-appropriate, intelligible spoken language. This study demonstrated that the information-rich signal provided by the CI was best used to understand and produce speech when children were educated in a classroom with an emphasis on listening and talking.

Some limitations of the studies should be recognized. The first three involved small sample sizes and quasi-experimental designs, relying on pretest and posttest assessment to document progress. The families in all studies had either higher-than-average or undocumented levels of parent education, which remains a possible confounding factor. It has been observed that the nature of longitudinal studies may result in a selection bias regarding families who are able to participate (Sininger, Grimes, & Christensen, 2010). The "burdens" of study participation are considerable and are related to employment, absenteeism from work, finances, and child care for other children in the family, to name a few. Such burdens likely discourage parents with lower-than-average socio-economic status from participating, regardless of the communication approach their child uses. Indeed, data-based findings on communication methodology are limited, and more research is needed. However, when taken together, these studies provide some evidence that a strong emphasis on auditory development, in the context of therapy, home, and classroom, allows many children who are D/HH to achieve high levels of spoken language competence. AV therapy is designed to provide this strong emphasis.

### Commitment to Hearing Technology Is a Principle of Auditory-Verbal Practice

Hearing technology walks hand-in-hand with the other therapy elements of the AV approach. In fact, this approach cannot be carried out unless there is a commitment to vigilant audiological management using state-of-the-art hearing technology (see Chapter 2). Table 7.1 shows the 10 Principles of AV Therapy, the first two principles being focused on technology for auditory access. This aspect of AV therapy finds concordance in current research findings: "Early development of the auditory system is dependent on stimulation from a rich acoustic environment of relevant sound" (Sininger et al., 2010, p. 166). The key words in this statement affirm the importance of multiple aspects of the AV approach, including *early* development, an acoustic environment that is *rich*,

**Table 7.1.** The principles of Listening and Spoken Language Specialists auditory-verbal therapy

The following are the Principles of Auditory-Verbal Therapy (from the 2012 LSLS Certification Handbook, Alexander Graham Bell Academy for Listening and Spoken Language):

1. Promote early diagnosis of hearing loss in newborns, infants, toddlers, and young children, followed by immediate audiologic management and auditory-verbal therapy.
2. Recommend immediate assessment and use of appropriate, state-of-the-art hearing technology to obtain maximum benefits of auditory stimulation.
3. Guide and coach parents[1] to help their child use hearing as the primary sensory modality in developing listening and spoken language.
4. Guide and coach parents to become the primary facilitators of their child's listening and spoken language development through active and consistent participation in individualized auditory-verbal therapy.
5. Guide and coach parents to create environments that support listening for the acquisition of spoken language throughout the child's daily activities.
6. Guide and coach parents to help their child integrate listening and spoken language into all aspects of the child's life.
7. Guide and coach parents to use natural developmental patterns of audition, speech, language, cognition, and communication.
8. Guide and coach parents to help their child self-monitor spoken language through listening.
9. Administer ongoing formal and informal diagnostic assessments to develop individualized auditory-verbal treatment plans, to monitor progress, and to evaluate the effectiveness of the plans for the child and family.
10. Promote education in regular schools with peers who have typical hearing and with appropriate services from early childhood onward.

Adapted from the principles originally developed by Doreen Pollack in 1970. Adopted by the Alexander Graham Bell Academy for Listening and Spoken Language on November 6, 2009.

[1]The term *parents* also includes grandparents, relatives, guardians, and any caregivers who interact with the child.

and the purposeful presentation of sounds that are *relevant,* not random, to young children during their waking hours. Sininger et al. (2010) based their conclusions on a longitudinal study of auditory-based outcomes (i.e., speech perception, speech production, and spoken language) in 44 children whose degree of hearing losses ranged from mild to profound. For every outcome measure, earlier fitting of amplification predicted improved performance. Other factors associated with outcomes were degree of hearing loss and cochlear implant use. The results clearly demonstrated the importance of early amplification on communication outcomes. The authors summarized that "children with the earliest access to the speech signal through amplification, overall, will have the best outcomes on auditory-based communication measures" (Sininger et al., 2010, p. 178). The AV approach has a key component: the vigilant fitting, monitoring, and upgrading of technology. When considering the AV model, then, it is not just a partnership between parent and therapist. Rather, there is a triad of adults who must be actively engaged when parents' stated outcomes focus on spoken language through listening (Robbins & Caraway, 2010). This triad is made up of family members, an AV practitioner, and a pediatric audiologist (Joint Committee on Infant Hearing [JCIH], 2007), whose involvement is irreplaceable. By way of analogy, a milking stool supports weight elegantly when there is balance among the three legs. However, it is rendered almost useless when there are only two legs or when the three legs are imbalanced. Similarly, the AV approach depends on the balancing of input and energy from each of the three parts of the therapy triad. This is just one of the ways in which intervention for children who are D/HH varies significantly from interventions for children who have developmental diagnoses other than D/HH, and it is a distinguishing feature of AV practice.

***Use of Ongoing Assessments to Guide Intervention***    Children's progress can be effectively monitored via evidence-based or criterion-referenced tools that show both where a child is functioning and what skills are expected next. Progress monitoring tools include the Cottage Acquisition Scales for Listening, Language, and Speech (CASLLS; Wilkes, 2009), the Auditory Learning Guide (Walker, 2009), the Early Listening Function (ELF; Anderson, 2000), the Infant-Toddler Meaningful Auditory Integration Scale (IT-MAIS; Zimmerman-Phillips, Osberger, & Robbins, 1997), the Red Flags Matrix (Robbins, 2005b), and the Children's Home Inventory of Listening Difficulties (CHILD; Anderson & Smaldino, 2000). Collection of data during intervention sessions is often completed using spontaneous language samples and regular charting of response data related to prioritized goals. The clinical concepts of listening age (see Flexer & Madell, 2009) or months of robust hearing (Ertmer & Inniger, 2009) may be useful when measuring the progress a child has made since receiving full-time access to audition via HA or CI use. A second aspect of monitoring progress focuses on the spontaneous use of learned behaviors in real-world situations. With guidance, parents may become excellent observers/ reporters of children's auditory and spoken language behaviors such as repeating something overhead from another room, understanding conversation not directed at the child, using a new word or phrase without being directly taught, or reauditorizing (i.e., talking to oneself as a way of processing or remembering linguistic information). One could argue that these types of behaviors are actually the most important evidence about progress because they represent the spontaneous, unrehearsed use of a skill, not in the confines of an intervention session, but in a meaningful real-world environment.

## Addressing Special Needs in Intervention

***Children from Bilingual Homes***    An increasing number of children who are D/HH come from families with diverse linguistic and cultural backgrounds. Use of more than one language in the home or parents who are *new learners of English* should never be considered contraindications for the use of the AV approach. Several studies suggest impressive outcomes in achieving bilingualism by children who use listening and spoken language (Bunta & Douglas, 2013; Robbins, Green, & Waltzman, 2004). When counseling bilingual families about the use of the AV approach, it is important to review the principles of AV therapy so that parents understand how intervention will be structured. There are differences across cultures in how individuals with disabilities are viewed. For some families, wearing hearing technology in public would be inconsistent with their cultural experiences and expectations. However, in the context of the AV approach, families need to commit to their child's use of technology during all waking hours every day. Parents from certain cultures may also feel uncomfortable participating in every therapy session. Experience suggests that when families fully understand the rationale for techniques that may at first seem unusual, they often commit to using them. Different therapy models for bilingual families have been described, including the tag-team model (Robbins, 2007, 2009), where the clinician and parent speak a different language to the child during therapy using bilingual simultaneous (immersion in two languages at the same time) or sequential (immersion in one language to begin, then adding a second language) models (Bunta & Douglas, 2013).

***Children with Complex Developmental Needs***    It is estimated that approximately 40% of children who are D/HH have one or more additional special needs. Selection of a communication approach for these children is an ongoing and important process. Recent studies suggest that many children with complex needs show benefits from a cochlear implant, although relatively slower rates of progress are consistent with the severity of the disability (Donaldson, Heavner, & Zwolan, 2004; Holt & Kirk, 2005). Aligning intervention goals with family priorities is highly valued in every case, but especially so for children with severe complex needs. When these families choose a listening and spoken language approach, it is essential to monitor progress in a variety of ways. If using formal tests, we may compare the child to his or her past performance on the test rather than use the test norms. Ongoing assessment for this population should include the parents' perception of their child's communication progress and benefit from hearing instruments. Tools to utilize for this purpose include the Sound Access Parent Outcomes Instrument (Hayward, Ritter, Grueber, & Howarth, 2013) and the Champions Evaluation Profiles for Paediatric Cochlear Implant Users with Additional Disabilities (Herrmannova, Phillips, O'Donoghue & Ramsden, n.d.). Intervention suggestions from experienced AV practitioners can be found in Estabrooks (2012).

## Listening and Spoken Language Sessions: Why Conversation?

The context of my[3] approach to AV sessions is conversation. Identified goals and strategies are embedded into exchanges that are as close as possible to the rich, natural language that surrounds children with typical hearing. I use a conversational approach even at the earliest stages of language development with very young children. Understanding the rationale for this is important. By its very nature, therapy is contrived, and the language of therapy is often stilted and didactic. By employing conversation, we retain many of the benefits of real-life language learning. For example, children observe conversational  (see Video clips 7.2 and 7.3) turn taking and topic maintenance and hear new words used in discourse where there are redundant cues that aid in deciphering meaning. During sessions, the parent and I comment as much as we question, a guideline wisely suggested years ago by Blank and Marquis (1987). We try not to ask many disingenuous questions whose answers we already know; rather, whenever possible, we pose questions whose answers we genuinely seek. Conversation supports our frequent use of mental state words (e.g., think, know, wonder, remember, agree, decide), which are important for the

---

3. *Editors' note:* Amy Robbins has a wealth of clinical experience working with children who are deaf or hard of hearing. She is internationally recognized for her work with children who have cochlear implants. She has elected to use first person in the following sections to share her intervention experiences and perspectives.

development of theory of mind (see Chapter 11). Words and their corresponding emotions (i.e., what we say and how we feel about it) may be separated in a stilted therapy task. Conversation reunites them.

Parents need to witness their child's participation in conversation so that they 1) know to use natural language at home and 2) gain trust in hearing as an effective modality for spoken language acquisition. If the language of intervention is unnatural and "therapized," how will parents know to use natural, rich discourse at home? Early fitting of state-of-the-art technology gives most children access to rich ambient language, and so it is ill-advised for adults to limit or stifle their input. Children learn what they hear, so our input to them must be high in its quality and interest level. Traditional therapy tasks are sometimes not meaningful and therefore not intrinsically motivating (e.g., note how often clinicians reinforce with stickers or other external rewards just to keep children on task). Appropriate conversation aimed at a child's developmental and interest levels supplies its own reward: authentic connection with other human beings.

## Session Format

A conversational approach starts as soon as the family and I greet each other at the door. As we make our way to the therapy studio, we may engage in meaningful conversation or use an established music routine. A musical pitch-matching technique combines such goals as orienting to a schedule by singing the day of the week and the date and sharing recent news or anticipating upcoming events, which encourages use of past or future tense and prediction. The child matches a descending musical pitch, all accomplished via audition  alone (see Video clip 7.4). As with most activities, sometimes I am the leader and the child imitates; at other times our roles are switched.

Once settled, I ask the parent to give an update since our last session. I use the routine, "What's new, what's nice, what's noteworthy?" (based on Caraway, personal communication, 2011). Parents provide updates when children are young, but the children themselves, as they get older, also will share news. I set the stage for the rest of the session by describing what plans I have in mind and encourage families to tell me if there is something they'd like to add. We preview the session using appropriate temporal and sequence words by reviewing, "*First,* we're going to do the Ling Six-Sound Test. *Then* let's read a poem and talk about it. The *next* thing will be Tell and Show." These session-opening routines provide a natural context for working on listening and promoting narrative and thinking skills.

Checking the functioning of the child's technology has top priority in this approach because of the importance of optimal hearing at all times. The Ling Six-Sound Test (Ling, 2002) is administered by the parent or clinician, who produces the six sounds /m/, /ah/, /oo/, /ee/, /s/, and /sh/ one at a time, in random order, while the other adult records the child's response. Each ear is tested separately by disabling the technology in the opposite ear. There are  a variety of ways to elicit reliable responses from the child. On the DVD (see Video clip 7.5), we see Annabelle repeating the sounds she hears. These sounds represent frequencies across the speech spectrum from low to high pitch and confirm that a child's technology is working as usual and that all sounds are accessible to the child on that day. I encourage parents to include a repeated voiceless consonant (p-p-p, t-t-t, or k-k-k) to see if their child has access to place-of-articulation cues and to say one or more real words after administering the Ling sounds. For children who do not yet demonstrate a conditioned response (if practiced regularly, we often see this emerge as early as 18 to 24 months), a parent and I may do a listening check of each HA separately, listening to each of the sounds from varying distances.

Within sessions and across time, we observe the child's listening effort. Listening effort is the perceived amount of internal resources that must be expended in order to listen and understand. These resources include vigilance to task, ignoring distractions, and filling in missing pieces of the auditory message. Older CI users, including those without the benefit of bilateral hearing, often self-report fatigue as a result of listening in demanding environments, especially noisy ones (Hicks & Tharpe, 2002). Other clinical reports of high listening effort include headaches, irritability, and emotional lability. Tracking listening effort is vital because chronic, high degrees of listening effort reduce the cognitive resources available to learn in the classroom (Hughes & Galvin, 2013). Decisions about technology upgrades, cochlear implantation, and classroom placement, among other academic considerations, can be informed by having cumulative notes regarding a child's listening effort.

As we work, I include the family in activities throughout the session in various ways by asking for their input and bringing them in as conversational partners and modelers of language targets. If a child is struggling with a task, the parent and I often discuss the best way to modify the task so the child is successful. Because parents know their children so well, they offer input that is informative to the clinician. Techniques for **acoustic highlighting** (emphasizing certain elements of spoken language to make them more audible) are  used throughout the session when appropriate (see Video clip 7.6), including use of a whispered voice to increase the salience of voiceless consonants, singing, and emphasizing target syntactic or suprasegmental features (aspects of speech such as pitch, juncture patterns, and stress that occur simultaneously with vowels and consonants). Pausing to give children time to process is a skill that develops with practice, given that it is natural to add more information if a child looks puzzled. Often, we inadvertently clutter the acoustic environment with language when we would be wise to wait. In these situations, we are sometimes surprised to find that the child is successful when given a period of time to process the information. *Auditory hooks* are employed to secure the child's auditory attention through listening. An auditory hook is a conversationally natural way to express interest or surprise, which is intended to provoke curiosity and draw the child into the dialogue. Such hooks include "Neat!" "Oh, no!" "My goodness!" and others mentioned by Estabrooks (2012).

I incorporate **Boss Your Brain (BYB)** strategies (Robbins, 2005a) to help children learn ways of organizing, remembering, and retrieving what has been heard and understood (see Video clips 7.7 and 7.8). For example, the **reaudi-**  **torization** or "say it aloud to yourself" strategy aids memory by hearing one's own voice repeat information. The *finger cue* strategy is useful for information that is a list or series of steps because each finger marks a single item in the list or series as it is spoken, aiding both memory of the items and their sequence. I sometimes tell children this is the world's best memory aid because you'll never forget your fingers at home or leave them in your backpack. They are always with you. A *visualization strategy* is used frequently because it is known that adept listeners and readers form visual images in their mind (Bell, 1991). The parent and I make this process explicit by describing our images and using vocabulary such as *picture, image,* and *visualize.* I might say, "Mom, I'm visualizing a girl with Little Orphan Annie hair." The parent replies, "I saw her hair differently in my mind." I add, "The words made me picture a girl with short, red, curly hair," and so forth. These strategies set the stage for important executive function and theory of mind behaviors. Sometimes, I use BYB techniques with children as young as age 2 to model selected strategies and teach them to the parents. Children this young are generally not required to use the strategies themselves.

As mentioned earlier, *auditory first* is now achieved primarily through positioning—joint visual attention to a toy or natural opportunities when the child looks away (see Video clip 7.9). AV practitioners historically used their hand to obscure lipreading cues during listening practice, a technique known as the hand cue. Because children were diagnosed as late as age 3 or older, discouraging use of visual cues was seen as a necessary part of helping them rely on listening. Critics of this technique expressed concerns about the unnaturalness of the hand cue and about distortion or attenuation of the auditory signal that resulted from using the technique. In recent years, the prevailing thought is that the hand cue is almost never needed. Estabooks (2012) interviewed a number of AV therapists and found that many rarely use the hand cue anymore.

Competencies in pragmatics and social language are part of our long-term goals as well. For some early implanted children, these areas take on more of the focus in our sessions because other speech and language skills are developing rapidly and at a rate commensurate with peers with typical hearing. I use *authentic provocation* of the parent—for example, "Mom, is that how you remembered it?" The parent and I consistently model interactions that teach pragmatics, including conversational repair and clarification. If I pose a question (e.g., "Thomas, how do you know Bill and Kathy?") and the child doesn't know the answer, parents learn not to rescue the child by automatically answering. Rather (see Video clip 7.10), after pausing to see if the child employs an information-seeking strategy on his or her own, I offer the comment, "Hmmm—somebody at this table knows" (Caraway, personal communication, 2011). This prompts the child toward an appropriate strategy but avoids whenever possible the awkward practice of my requiring direct imitation: "Ask Mom, 'Mom, how do we know Bill and Kathy?'" Our sessions incorporate humor and laughter as we comment on what is funny, absurd, or witty (see Video clip 7.11). This provides a lightheartedness that is appealing to all participants and reinforces the idea that parenting a child who is D/HH is not all serious, grim business. I hold the child accountable (see Video clip 7.12) for  clear communication, often by repeating a child's tangled sentence (e.g., "Mom and Dad are going to Hawaii *to see if your dog likes child care?*") so he or she can use my auditory model to repair his or her syntax. I offer **communication**

**temptation** comments (see Video clip 7.13) that have considerable emotional value, using the corresponding vocal tone. I want to see how a child reacts to a statement such as "Something happened to my cat last night." If the child fails to respond with empathy or appropriate language, I use eye contact with the parent, who then models, "Oh, no, what happened last night?" using a concerned tone (Robbins, 2009). This kind of social-language discourse occurs throughout sessions, maintaining cohesion between the words used and their corresponding emotions.

I also *hold children accountable* for articulation and voice production. For example, I tuck in a simple auditory challenge when Danny produces a distorted /s/ (see Video clip 7.14) and give Kenady feedback about vocal intensity at an appropriate level. I say to her, "Your voice is too loud; tell your mom in a softer voice," rather than demonstrating a loud voice, because Kenady doesn't need a model to correct her loudness, only a verbal reminder. I am adjusting my expectations and correction techniques based on the most sophisticated level of feedback the child is able to handle. For a list of other therapy tips I employ, see Table 7.2.

We end sessions by reviewing (see Video clip 7.15) in a way that doesn't make parents feel they are being graded. For example, asking Mom, "How will you explain these concepts to those at home?" creates a pragmatically appropriate environment for the mother to describe what she learned that day.

### The Therapeutic Alliance

Family-centered therapy (see Chapters 3, 4, and 10) is most constructive when clinicians and parents have established a foundation of mutual trust, respect, and authentic communication in what is termed the **therapeutic alliance** (Bordin, 1979), a concept widely used in psychotherapy. A therapeutic alliance is based on collaborative problem solving, accountability, and alignment of purpose. In other words, the parent and clinician know that they are both fully committed to doing everything they can to help a child fulfill his or her potential. Establishing such an alliance with families over time is the platform that makes even difficult conversations civil and productive. Bordin (1979) identified three main elements of a successful therapeutic alliance: 1) agreement on the goals of treatment, 2) agreement on the tasks to achieve those goals, and 3) a personal bond made up of reciprocal positive feelings. The optimal therapeutic alliance is forged when the parent and therapist share beliefs with regard to the goals of treatment and view the methods used to achieve these as efficacious and relevant. I consider the establishment of a therapeutic alliance as essential to successful intervention using any approach (Robbins, 2013). Though this concept evolved from psychotherapy, I have found its contribution to the AV therapy model to be invaluable.

Part of the connection I forge with the family includes discussing how much energy the parents put into making communication exchanges successful with their child. This concept of *adult effort* operates in tandem with the listening effort that we monitor in children. Ling (2002) advises clinicians to evaluate how much responsibility the child and the adult take on to repair broken lines of communication. Conversation assumes that all parties expend

**Table 7.2.**   Therapy tips from the author's experience

| Therapy tip | Example/purpose |
|---|---|
| Start sessions asking parent, "What's new, nice, and noteworthy?" (see Video clips 7.1 and 7.2) | Affirms the value of home carryover and parent as partner |
| Use mental state words; make your thought process transparent. | "Oh, I can see that in my mind" or "My image for that was different." (see Video clip 7.8) |
| Use supportive routines to clarify roles in conversation. | "What are you wearing?" game (see Video clip 7.17) |
| Scaffold child's use of more mature conversational repair strategies over time. | "Where does your aunt live?" [Child shrugs.] "Someone at this table knows." (see Video clip 7.10) |
| Comment as much as you question (see Video clip 7.20; Blank & Marquis, 1987). | Mimics real conversation: "What a cute animal!" not "What animal is this?" Models for parent; invites rather than demands participation |
| Establish signals for important language routines. | "Instruction!" "Synonym!" (see Video clip 7.2) "Connection" "Text to self"; spotlights critical language; prepares child for classroom routines |
| Utilize communication sabotage (Arwood, 1991; Robbins & Kirk, 1996; review Video clip 7.17). | Is a window on child's auditory comprehension and confidence in hearing |
| Incorporate Boss Your Brain techniques (Robbins, 2005a) to support working memory, retrieval, strategy selection, and executive function. | Finger cues (the "world's best memory aids"; see Video clip 7.7); reauditorization (talk to self); act it out (motor rehearsal); visualization; invisible blackboard |
| Switch roles so child is the talker and clinician the listener (see Video clip 7.12). | Mimics conversation; different skills required in each role |
| If appropriate, act on/repeat what child said, not what he or she meant. | Clinician: "Your best friend is *gravy?*" [Child corrects production.] Clinician: "Oh, *Gracie.*" |
| Use drills such as speech babble or phonics rules with the motto *Quick, fun, get it done.* | Efficient use of time; affords rapid, focused practice (see Video clip 7.21) |
| Be creative using music to enhance listening and language. | Use piggyback technique (see Video clip 7.20) or narrate your actions with song, like an opera |
| Incorporate poetry (see Video clips 7.7 and 7.8), even with preschoolers. | May facilitate humor, double meanings, phonological awareness, point of view, cultural references; has rhythm and melody so is a "cousin" to music |
| Ensure language has a genuine purpose. | Barrier games (see Video clip 7.12) and Tell and Show (see Video clip 7.20) require rich description and authentic questions because the receiver can't see what the sender sees |
| Respect silence as another person in the room. (What is it telling us?) | Provides more processing time (see Video clip 7.13); encourages reflection over impulsivity |
| Teach story conventions (e.g., "Once upon a time…") and narrative connectors (e.g., then, so, because of that, finally). | Play "Story in a Suitcase" game (see Video clip 7.9) with increasing number of cards/elements |
| Employ humor naturally and liberally. Remind parents that like the U.S. Peace Corps, this is the toughest job they'll ever love. | Lightheartedness (see Video clip 7.11) and fun break tension and seriousness child and parent may feel |

reasonable effort toward successful interaction (Grice, 1975). I discuss progress toward this goal openly with families, and the parent and I address it via our therapy conversational language and techniques.

I previously wrote about using silence to contrast with sound, particularly in the early stages of listening and technology use. As children mature, *silent periods* are just as important, although for a host of different reasons. Silence encourages a reflective rather than an impulsive approach to learning. In silence, the words just spoken hang in the air and are available for listeners to analyze, ponder, agree with, or challenge. Developing a comfort level with silent periods is an important clinical skill for service providers. Parents feel welcomed to ask questions or otherwise participate in discussions when periods of silence are available, whereas they might feel rushed or have a sense of interrupting if the clinician never leaves open spaces that invite participation. The notion that silence should be respected, almost as if it is another person in the room, was suggested in a workshop taught by Parker J. Palmer (personal communication, 2007).

## Case Study: Auditory-Verbal Intervention with a Young Child

Kenady was developing normally until 15 months of age. She had a vocabulary of about 40 words and was reported to understand much of what was said around her. She experienced a sudden loss of hearing and balance and long waiting times for audiological and medical appointments that delayed a diagnosis. A severe-to-profound bilateral loss was confirmed around 24 months, and she was fit with two hearing aids at 28 months. Some benefit was observed from the left hearing aid but no benefit from the right. She was enrolled at age 2 years 4 months in early intervention with this clinician utilizing an auditory-verbal (AV) approach, and she and received a cochlear implant (CI) in her right ear at 2 years 8 months. At age 3 years, Kenady began full-time placement in an AV education preschool. She and her mother continued to attend individual AV therapy sessions for 1 hour each week.

A number of characteristics of the AV approach within a conversational context are seen on the accompanying DVD. Note the confidence with which Kenady's mother participates in the session. Having been a part of therapy since its beginning, she picks up quickly on the goals of activities and provides good language models. The previous week, I had asked her to write down some of the questions Kenady used at home because question forms are one target in therapy. Her mother had written these down exactly as Kenady said them, capturing the utterances very accurately (see Video clip 7.16). As we reviewed them, her mother was able to identify what Kenady does to form questions. She correctly reported that Kenady "just puts a question mark" on statements, using rising intonation to turn a statement into a question. Her mother and I also have *review time* near the end of the session where we discuss conversational turns and the ways in which we signal that it is Kenady's turn. Her mother notes that this is accomplished at various times by telling Kenady directly that it's her turn or by using a visual prompt in a routine that signals whose turn it is (e.g., the triangle on the floor in the "What Are We Wearing?" game; see Video clip 7.17). I remind her that eye contact is another powerful signal (see Video clip 7.18). Garcia Winner (2007) suggests a prompt for eye contact by saying, "Show that you're thinking about me," where the eyes are not simply movable body parts but actually tell others about one's internal focus and mental state. We used many mental state words during our session, including *know, think,* and *visualize,* and observed that Kenady used some of these spontaneously, including *remember.*

We administer the Ling Six-Sound Test at the beginning of each session to verify the functioning of Kenady's CI and hearing aid individually. Our routine for board games provides a

**template in therapy** for organizing what we say to others in conversation (see Video clip 7.19) so that the most important information is expressed first, such as a skeletal outline, and then details are given that fill in the outline. This is early practice with the important academic skill of knowing the main idea and the supporting facts. Kenady is learning that the three most important rules of a board game are *how you win, how you play or move,* and *something else. Something else* is the twist most games have, such as losing a turn if you land on a certain space or the option of sharing an earned card if you already have one. Her mother has practiced carryover of this template at home when Kenady returns from school and excitedly shares many details about an unknown event in a disordered sequence. Her mother reminds her, "Tell me three important things that happened, in order. First..." Having these key prompts allows parents to show genuine interest and affirms the child's desire to feel connected to and share his or her experiences with family members.

The tell and show game (see Video clip 7.20) addresses many goals of an AV approach because Kenady talks about the item she brought before I am allowed to see it. At some sessions, we reverse roles, and I bring the item and describe it without showing it, and Kenady creates a picture of it in her mind. We are forming the building blocks of visualization by making mental images from the words we hear, an important learning skill for reading comprehension and auditory memory. When Kenady is the sender, as she was in this session, the game gives her practice using specific, descriptive language with many details so that the image the listener forms is accurate. I narrated my visualization process, as suggested by Bell (1991), in ways that included mental states, such as "I can see that in my mind."

Conversational conventions were used naturally during the session. When Kenady offered, "My favorite colors are yellow and red," I responded with communication temptation in the form of a comment: "Oh, my favorite colors are different." Kenady maintained the topic and responded to the temptation by asking what my favorite colors were. This is an example of a *conversational volley* in which each speaker adds something but volleys the conversation back, rather than ending it. If I had replied to her comment by saying, "That's nice," that branch of the conversation would have ended. Improvisation comedians utilize an analogous rule known as the "Yes, and..." rule to keep a sketch alive. This rule requires speakers to accept the topic (the "Yes") chosen by their improv partner and to build upon it (the "and") in the response they offer. If one comedian suggests entering a triathlon, the second comedian is obliged to pick up on this topic and propose an additional, supportive idea such as competing in the triathlon in the nude. If the second person says, "No, I hate triathlons," the sketch comes to a screeching halt and isn't funny. Even an art form that seems as spontaneous as improv comedy has strict rules that all participants agree upon. Without them, the purpose of it—to make people laugh—is thwarted. And so it is with spoken communication, its rules, and its purpose.

We discuss many things in a natural, matter-of-fact way, such as giving Kenady feedback about her vocal intensity—"Your voice is too loud. Tell us with a softer voice."—and reminding her that it's rude to point her finger at people. We also discuss deafness head-on (see Video clip 7.17)  when she offers the comment, "I can't hear [without] my ears!" meaning her hearing aid and cochlear implant. Mom states that she needs her glasses to see, and later I ask Kenady if she wears glasses, to which she responds, "No, I can see with my eyes." Music, an essential part of AV practice, is used liberally, often to mark transitions or as a clue to a new activity. We created the "Tell and Show" song using the **piggyback technique**—in other words, adding new words to an existing melody—with the tune to "Frère Jacques" so that it explains the sequence of the game: "Tell and show / tell and show / we can't see / we can't see / we will talk about it / we will talk about it / then we'll see / then we'll see." For the teapot game, we sing "I'm a Little Teapot," acoustically highlighting a new word, *stout*, and providing synonyms for it.

When reviewing the session at the end, we expect developmentally appropriate behavior from children. Requiring a 5-year-old to sit patiently for 2 or 3 minutes as the parent and I go over our notes is not just about behavioral compliance. All children, including those who are D/HH, need practice with self-regulation, an important component of executive function. While waiting without disturbing their parent, they are learning to entertain themselves, a key skill of resourcefulness. They also demonstrate instances of overhearing conversation that is not focused directly on them. Children may chime in briefly (e.g., "I just heard you say we're going to the zoo tomorrow, Mommy!"), indicating that they use their listening skills to monitor the discourse of others, to make sense of it, and to comment on it. It's a gratifying way to end the session.

## FUTURE DIRECTIONS

AV therapy is a dynamic, family-centered approach for parents who choose listening and spoken language for their child. Published findings suggest encouraging outcomes for many children enrolled in AV therapy, though there is a need for more treatment efficacy research. Additional research is required about ways to individualize AV therapy, particularly for children who are not making expected progress. Guidelines are needed for using AV therapy with children who have complex needs such as those from bilingual homes and the many children who have additional diagnoses along with deafness. More research is required to better understand the critical periods of auditory learning, including the sensitive period for making use of bilateral sound input.

## SUGGESTED READINGS

Cole, E.B., & Flexer, C. (2011). *Children with hearing loss: Developing listening and talking birth to six* (2nd ed.). San Diego, CA: Plural.

Estabrooks, W. (Ed.). (2012). *101 FAQs about auditory-verbal practice*. Washington, DC: A.G. Bell Publications.

Nicholas, J.G., & Geers, A.E. (2006). Effects of early auditory experience on the spoken language of deaf children at 3 years of age. *Ear and Hearing, 27*(3), 286–298.

The first recommended reading gives comprehensive coverage to such topics as auditory technology, auditory development, spoken language development, and intervention for young children with hearing loss whose parents have chosen listening and spoken language as their goal. In the second reading, experts in auditory-verbal therapy provide up-to-date information about the history, theory, and practice of the approach. The last reading provides support for the notion that younger age at cochlear implantation serves as a strong determinant of spoken language competence.

## LEARNING ACTIVITIES

1.  Consider a child currently or previously in your practice or university clinic. What modifications would be required if you were to utilize techniques consistent with the AV approach, keeping in mind the 10 principles of AV practice (Table 7.1)?

2. You have reviewed a model of assessment whose purpose is to establish intervention priorities (Figure 7.3). Plan and/or conduct an evaluation with this model in mind. What have you added or deleted from a typical evaluation? Describe the components that are least familiar to you (e.g., informal assessment procedures) and how you could become more proficient with them.

3. Review Video clips 7.2, 7.3, 7.10, 7.13, 7.17, and 7.20 with the goal of noting conversational exchanges. Observe the intersection of dialogue among clinician, parent, and child. What opportunities did the clinician seize and when did she miss them? Document the points at which the child was held accountable for communication clarification by an adult.

4. Identify instances in Video clips 7.1, 7.4, 7.5, 7.6, 7.7, 7.12, 7.19, and 7.21 where listening skills are emphasized (e.g., commitment to high-functioning technology, rhyming task, music routines, use of positioning and joint attention, acoustic highlighting). Give examples of ways in which a clinician would modify these techniques as a child's auditory and spoken language skills mature.

## REFERENCES

Alberg, J. (2014). *BEGINNINGS for parents of children who are deaf or hard of hearing annual report*. Raleigh, NC: GuideStar.

Alexander Graham Bell Academy for Listening and Spoken Language. (2012). *Certification handbook*. Retrieved May 13, 2015, from http://listeningandspokenlanguage.org/uploadedFiles/Get_Certified/Getting_Certified/Final%202012%20Handbook.pdf

Anderson, K. (2000). *Early learning function (ELF)*. Retrieved August 26, 2014, from http://successforkidswithhearingloss.com/uploads/ELF

Anderson, K., & Smaldino, J. (2000). *Children's Home Inventory of Listening Difficulties (CHILD)*. Retrieved August 26, 2014, from http://successforkidswithhearingloss.com/life-r

Arwood, E.L. (1991). *Semantic and pragmatic language disorders* (2nd ed.). Gaithersburg, MD: Aspen.

Bell, N. (1991). *Visualizing and verbalizing for language comprehension and thinking*. San Luis Obispo, CA: Gander Publications.

Blank, M., & Marquis, M.A. (1987). *Directing discourse*. Tucson, AZ: Communication Skill Builders.

Boothroyd, A. (1982). *Hearing impairments in young children*. Upper Saddle River, NJ: Prentice Hall.

Bordin, E.S. (1979). The generalizability of the psychoanalytic concept of the working alliance. *Psychotherapy, 16*, 252–260.

Buckley, K.A., & Tobey, E.A. (2011). Cross-modal plasticity and speech perception in pre-and postlingually deaf cochlear implant users. *Ear and Hearing, 32*(1), 2–15.

Bunta, F., & Douglas, W.M. (2013). The effects of dual-language support on the language skills of bilingual children with hearing loss who use listening devices relative to their monolingual peers. *Language, Speech, and Hearing Services in Schools, 44*, 281–290.

Cole, E.B., & Flexer, C. (2011). *Children with hearing loss: Developing listening and talking birth to six* (2nd ed.). San Diego, CA: Plural.

Collier, G., & Logan, G. (2000). Modality differences in short-term memory for rhythm. *Memory & Cognition, 28*(4), 529–538.

Conway, C., Pisoni, D., & Kronenberger, W. (2009). The importance of sound for cognitive sequencing abilities: The auditory scaffolding hypothesis. *Current Directions in Psychological Science, 18*(5), 275–279.

Dettman, S., Wall, E., Constantinescu, G., & Dowell, R. (2013). Communication outcomes for groups of children using cochlear implants enrolled in auditory-verbal, aural-oral, and bilingual-bicultural early intervention programs. *Otology & Neurotology, 34,* 451–459.

Donaldson, A., Heavner, K., & Zwolan, T. (2004). Measuring progress in children with autism spectrum disorder who have cochlear implants. *Archives of Otolaryngology Head & Neck Surgery, 130*(5), 666–671.

Dornan, D., Hickson, L., Murdoch, B., Houston, T., & Constantinescu, G. (2010). Is AVT effective for children with hearing loss? *Volta Review, 110*(3), 361–387.

Ertmer, D.J., & Inninger, K.J. (2009). Transition to spoken words in two young cochlear implant recipients. *Journal of Speech, Language, and Hearing Research, 52,* 1579–1594.

Estabrooks, W. (2012). *101 FAQs about auditory-verbal practice.* Washington, DC: A.G. Bell Association.

Flexer, C., & Madell, J. (2009). The concept of listening age for audiologic management of pediatric hearing loss. *Audiology Today, 21,* 31–35.

Froemke, R., Heman-Ackah, S., & Waltzman, S.B. (2014). Auditory neuroplasticity. In S.B. Waltzman & J.T. Roland (Eds.), *Cochlear implants* (3rd ed., pp. 38–46). New York, NY: Thieme.

Garcia Winner, M. (2007). *Thinking about you, thinking about me* (2nd ed.). San Jose, CA: Think Social Publishing.

Geers, A., & Brenner, C. (2003). Background and educational characteristics of prelingually deaf children implanted by five years of age. *Ear and Hearing, 24*(1), 2S–14S.

Geers, A.E., & Hayes, H. (2010). Reading, writing, and phonological processing skills of adolescents with 10 or more years of cochlear implant experience. *Ear and Hearing, 32*(Suppl.), 48S–59S.

Geers, A., Nicholas, J., Tye-Murray, N., Uchanski, R., Brenner, C., Davidson, L.S., Toretta, G., & Tobey, E.A. (2000). Effects of communication mode on skills of long-term cochlear implant users. *Annals of Otology, Rhinology, and Laryngology, 109*(12, Suppl. 185), part 2.

Glenberg, M.A., & Jona, A. (1991). Temporal coding in rhythm tasks revealed by modality effects. *Memory & Cognition, 19,* 514–522.

Goldberg, D.M., & Estes, E.L. (2012). How do practitioners in AV therapy and education work together? In W. Estabrooks (Ed.), (pp. 31–34). *101 FAQs about auditory-verbal practice.* Washington, DC: Alexander Graham Bell Association for the Deaf or Hard of Hearing.

Goldberg, D.M., & Flexer, C. (2012). What is the history of AV practice? In W. Estabrooks (Ed.), (pp. 6–9). *101 FAQs about auditory-verbal practice.* Washington, DC: Alexander Graham Bell Association for the Deaf or Hard of Hearing.

Gordon, K., Wong, D., Valero, J., Jewell, S., Yoo, P., & Papsin, B. (2011). Use it or lose it? Lessons learned from the developing brains of children who are deaf and use cochlear implants to hear. *Brain Topography, 24*(3–4), 204–219.

Grice, H.P. (1975). Logic and conversation. In A.P. Martinich (Ed.), *Philosophy of language* (pp. 165–175). New York, NY: Oxford University Press.

Hayward, D., Ritter, K., Grueber, J., & Howarth, T. (2013). Outcomes that matter for children with multiple disabilities who use cochlear implants. *Canadian Journal of Speech-Language Pathology and Audiology, 37*(1), 58–69.

Herrmannova, S.D., Phillips, R., O'Donoghue, G., & Ramsden, R. (n.d.). *Champions evaluation profiles for paediatric CI users with additional disabilities.* Nottingham, England: Ear Foundation.

Hicks, C.B., & Tharpe, A.M. (2002). Listening effort and fatigue in school-aged children with and without hearing loss. *Journal of Speech, Language and Hearing Research, 45,* 573–584.

Holt, R.F., & Kirk, K.I. (2005). Speech and language development in cognitively delayed children with cochlear implants. *Ear and Hearing, 26,* 132–148.

Houston, D.M., Ying, E.A., Pisoni, D.B., & Kirk, K.I. (2003). Development of preword-learning skills in infants with cochlear implants. *Volta Review, 103*(4), 303–326.

Hughes, K., & Galvin, K. (2013). Measuring listening effort expended by adolescents and young adults with unilateral or bilateral cochlear implants or normal hearing. *CI International, 14*(3), 121–129.

Joint Committee on Infant Hearing (JCIH). (2007). Year 2007 position statement: Principles and guidelines for early hearing detection and intervention programs. *Pediatrics, 120*(4), 898–921.

Kral, A., Hartmann, R., Tillein, J., Held, S., & Klinke, R. (2000). Congenital auditory deprivation reduces synaptic activity within the auditory cortex in a layer-specific manner. *Cerebral Cortex, 10,* 710–726.

Ling, D. (2002). *Speech and the hearing-impaired child* (2nd ed.). Washington, DC: Alexander Graham Bell Association for the Deaf and Hard of Hearing.

Los Angeles County Schools (1976). Auditory skills curriculum. North Hollywood, CA: Foreworks.

Madell, J.R., & Flexer, C. (2008). *Pediatric audiology: Diagnosis, technology and management.* New York, NY: Thieme.

Moeller, M.P. (1989). Combining formal and informal strategies for language assessment of hearing-impaired children. In L. Krestchmer (Ed.), *Evaluation of the communicative skills of hearing-impaired students* (Monograph of the *Journal of the Academy of Rehabilitative Audiology*, pp. 73–99).

Moeller, M.P. (2000). Early intervention and language development in children who are deaf and hard of hearing. *Pediatrics, 106*(3), E43.

Moog, J.S., & Geers, A. (2003). Epilogue: Major findings, conclusions and implications for deaf education. *Ear and Hearing, 24*(1),121S–125S.

Moucha, R., & Kilgard, M.P. (2006). Cortical plasticity and rehabilitation. *Progress in Brain Research, 157,* 111–122.

Nicholas, J., & Geers, A. (2006). Effects of early auditory experience on the spoken language of deaf children at 3 years of age. *Ear and Hearing, 27*(3), 286–298.

Niparko, J.K., Tobey, E.A., Thal, D.J., Eisenberg, L.S., Wang, N.-Y., Quittner, A.L., & Fink, N.E. (2010). Spoken language development in children following cochlear implantation. *JAMA, 303*(15), 1498–1506.

Osberger, M.J., Robbins, A.M., Todd, S., & Riley, A. (1994). Speech intelligibility of children with cochlear implants. *Volta Review, 96,* 169–180.

Rhoades, E. (2001). Language progress with an A-V approach for young children with hearing loss. *International Pediatrics, 16*(1), 1–7.

Romanik, S. (2008). Auditory skills program. Sydney, Australia: New South Wales Dept. of Education.

Robbins, A.M. (2005a, July/August). Bossing your brain: A history lesson with a middle school student who is hard of hearing. *Volta Voices,* pp. 38–40.

Robbins, A.M. (2005b). Clinical red flags for slow progress in children with cochlear implants. *Loud and Clear, 1,* 1–8.

Robbins, A.M. (2006). Language development in children with cochlear implants. In S. Waltzman & J.T. Roland (Eds.), *Cochlear implants* (2nd ed.) (pp. 153–166). New York, NY: Thieme Medical.

Robbins, A.M. (2007). Clinical management of bilingual families and children with cochlear implants. *Loud and Clear, 1,* 1–12.

Robbins, A.M. (2009). Rehabilitation after cochlear implantation. In J. Niparko (Ed.), *Cochlear implants principles & practices* (2nd ed.) (pp. 269–312). Philadelphia, PA: Lippincott Williams & Wilkins.

Robbins, A.M. (2013, January). Difficult conversations. *British Association of Teachers of the Deaf Magazine,* pp. 4–6.

Robbins, A.M., & Caraway, T.H. (2010). Missing the mark in early intervention for babies who are hard of hearing or deaf learning spoken language. *Perspectives on Hearing and Hearing Disorders in Childhood, 20*(2), 41–47.

Robbins, A.M., Green, J., & Waltzman, S. (2004). Bilingual oral language proficiency in children with cochlear implants. *Archives of Otolaryngology Head & Neck Surgery, 130,* 644–647.

Robbins, A.M. & Kirk, K.I. (1996). Speech perception assessment and performance in pediatric cochlear implant users. *Seminars in Hearing 17*, 353–369.

Robbins, A.M., Koch, D.B., Osberger, M.J., Phillips, S., & Kishon-Rabin, L. (2004). Effect of age at cochlear implantation on auditory skill development in infants and toddlers. *Archives of Otolaryngology Head & Neck Surgery, 130*, 570–574.

Ryugo, D.K., & Limb, C.J. (2009). Brain plasticity: The impact of the environment on the brain as it relates to hearing and deafness. In J. Niparko (Ed.), *Cochlear implants: Principles and practices* (pp. 19–37). Philadelphia, PA: Lippincott, Williams & Wilkins.

Segal, O., & Kishon-Rabin, L. (2011). Listening preference for child directed speech versus nonspeech stimuli in normal-hearing and hearing-impaired infants after cochlear implantation. *Ear and Hearing, 32*(3), 358–372.

Sharma, A., & Campbell, J. (2011). A sensitive period for cochlear implantation in deaf children. *Journal of Maternal, Fetal, Neonatal Medicine, 24*(Suppl. 1), 151–153.

Sharma, A., & Dorman, M.F. (2006). Central auditory development in children with cochlear implants: Clinical implications. *Advances in Otoryinolaryngology, 64*, 66–88.

Sharma, A., & Nash, A. (2009, April 14). *Brain maturation in children with CI.* ASHA Leader. Retrieved May 13, 2015, from http://www.asha.org/Publications/leader/2009/090414/f090414b.htm

Simser, J.I. (1993). Auditory verbal intervention: Infants and toddlers. *Volta Review 95*(3): 217–229.

Sininger, Y.S., Grimes, A., & Christensen, E. (2010). Auditory development of early amplified children: Factors influencing auditory-based communication outcomes in children with hearing loss. *Ear and Hearing, 31*(2), 166–185.

Talbot, P., & Estabrooks, W. (2012). What are the characteristics of an effective parent-practitioner relationship in AV therapy? In W. Estabrooks (Ed.), (pp. 23–26). *101 FAQs about auditory-verbal practice.* Washington, DC: Alexander Graham Bell Association for the Deaf or Hard of Hearing.

Tomblin, J.B., Barker, B.A., & Hubbs, S. (2007). Developmental constraints on language development in children with cochlear implants. *International Journal of Audiology, 46*, 512–523.

Tyszkiewicz, E., & Stokes, J.S. (2006). Pediatric habilitation. In H. Cooper & L. Craddock (Eds.), *Cochlear implants: A practical guide* (pp. 322–337). London, England: Whurr Publishers.

Vygotsky, L.S. (1978). *Mind in society: The development of higher psychological processes* (M. Cole, V. John-Steiner, S. Scribner, & E. Souberman., Eds.; A.R. Luria, M. Lopez-Morillas, & M. Cole [with J.V. Wertsch], Trans.). Cambridge, MA: Harvard University Press. (Original manuscript ca. 1930–1934)

Walker, B. (2009). *Auditory learning guide (ALG).* Retrieved May 13, 2015, from http://www.firstyears.org/c4/alg/alg.pdf

Wilkes, E. (2009). *Cottage Acquisition Scales for Listening, Language & Speech (CASLLS).* San Antonio, TX: Sunshine Cottage School.

Zimmerman-Phillips, S., Osberger, M.J., & Robbins, A.M. (1997). *Infant-Toddler Meaningful Auditory Integration Scale (IT MAIS).* Washington, DC: A.G. Bell Association.

# 8

# Phonological Development and Intervention Approaches for Children Who Are Deaf or Hard of Hearing

David J. Ertmer and Carol Stoel-Gammon

This chapter is about ways to help children who are deaf or hard of hearing (D/HH) develop phonology—the speech sound system of a language. Early identification of hearing loss and the provision of well-fit hearing aids (HAs) and cochlear implants (CIs) are the foundations of contemporary spoken language interventions for children who are D/HH. Although receiving well-fit hearing instruments at a young age often leads to substantial progress in phonological development, children who are D/HH tend to lag behind their hearing peers in this area. Phonological intervention seeks to facilitate listening and speech skill development so that children can become effective oral communicators as soon as possible.

The "style" of phonological intervention is often determined by the age and abilities of the child. During the first 3 years of life, service providers help caregivers learn ways to use language facilitation strategies (e.g., modeling words, expanding child utterances; see Chapter 5) in their everyday interactions with the child. By using these strategies, family members help children to associate spoken words with their meanings in the context of their daily activities—just as typically developing (TD) infants and toddlers do. For such young children, evidence of auditory-guided speech development is first heard as their **prelinguistic vocalizations** become progressively more speechlike and recognizable words and word combinations begin to emerge. As children reach preschool age, they continue to receive spoken language stimulation at home while also participating in child-centered intervention sessions. Using child-centered intervention, service providers continue to apply language stimulation techniques during intervention sessions while also providing abundant opportunities to expand vocabulary, syntax and grammar, and phonological skills during play-based activities. Many early identified children are subsequently mainstreamed for preschool or kindergarten (Wilkins & Ertmer, 2002). At these ages, direct instruction can be used to provide auditory training and phonological interven-tion aimed at helping children perceive and produce a full array of phonemes and acquire speech that is natural sounding and readily intelligible.

The interventions described here are not "one size fits all." They are most effective when adapted for the specific needs of individual children. For example, children who have normal hearing until 3 years of age and then experience hearing loss are more likely to make relatively rapid progress after receiving hearing instruments because they have previous knowledge of characteristics of mature speech. In contrast, some children who are born D/HH and those who have secondary disabilities such as autism, cerebral palsy, or speech-motor difficulties—even though identified early in life—may require specialized intervention strategies such as visual and tactile cues to make phonological gains (Ertmer, Leonard, & Pachuilo, 2002; Holt & Kirk, 2005; Ling, 1988). Similarly, those who are born deaf but not identified until after the brain has undergone a period of neural organization (e.g., after 3.5 years) may require more intensive intervention because spoken language development is out of synchrony with other developmental processes (Cole & Flexer, 2007; Higgins, McCleary, Carney, & Schulty, 2003). It is also important to point out that children who are hard of hearing (i.e., those with mild or moderate hearing losses) often respond well to the combination of HA use and intervention and become readily intelligible talkers early in life.

Two broad approaches to intervention have recently arisen in response to different patterns of spoken language development in children who are D/HH. **Habilitative intervention** is provided for children who make efficient—or even rapid—progress in developing early listening, language, and speech abilities. These children can acquire many aspects of spoken language through listening in context—just as children who are TD do. **Rehabilitative intervention** is used for children who make relatively slower progress and do not easily acquire spoken-language knowledge and skills through everyday interactions with others. Whereas many of the same objectives and activities are used in both approaches, children's proficiency in auditory-guided speech learning often dictates the rate at which objectives are introduced and progress is made. Examples of these two approaches can be found in the case studies at the end of this chapter.

In addition to children's hearing levels, age at identification, and the presence/absence of secondary disabilities, service providers can optimize learning by tailoring interventions to the personal needs, interests, and familial strengths of each child and by encouraging parents and teachers to expect children to use newly acquired skills in everyday communication.

## RELATIONSHIPS BETWEEN HEARING AND PHONOLOGICAL DEVELOPMENT

We begin discussion of the relationship between hearing and speech with the well-accepted premise that hearing is critical for the development of a

**phonological system.** If hearing were not critical, then children who are D/HH would produce readily intelligible conversational speech without intervention. However, numerous research studies from the 1970s to 1990s showed that the speech of children who are deaf contained many misarticulations (Smith, 1975) and was, on average, only 20% intelligible to listeners with normal hearing—even after years of HA use and speech intervention (see Osberger, 1992, for review). Developing a phonological system and readily intelligible speech requires that children perceive mature speech models, modify their own speech toward these models through auditory feedback, and produce a full range of phonemes and suprasegmental features (e.g., stress and intonation patterns, acceptable rate of speaking). Thus hearing is critical for phonological development. Fortunately, today's children who are D/HH are much more likely to become successful oral communicators than was possible in the recent past. The relatively recent adoption of newborn hearing screening has made it possible to identify hearing loss in infants and to provide HAs and CIs within an age range when many fundamental prelinguistic and phonological skills are typically acquired. For the benefits of these advancements to be realized, however, service providers must have a solid understanding of the nature of phonological development in children who have normal hearing. Studies of children who are TD provide many useful insights for serving children who are D/HH. The following is a synopsis of the main findings of this area of research.

### Acquiring a Phonological System

Phonological development in children—whether TD or D/HH—involves two components: a biological component associated with the development of auditory and speech-motor skills and a cognitive-linguistic component associated with the phonological patterns of the language being acquired. Our understanding of the biological component is based on experimental and observational data gathered in laboratories and naturalistic settings. These studies show that the auditory system is well developed at birth and allows infants to perceive the segmental (consonants and vowels) and suprasegmental (stress, intonation, rhythm) features of a language. In contrast, infants' first vocalizations are limited by the anatomical configuration of the vocal tract, which becomes more adult-like by 6 months, and by a lack of control over speech-motor movements. The ability to match adult-like articulation patterns increases with age, albeit very slowly. For many American children, accurate production of English phonology is not fully achieved until the age of 8 years or later.

While we know a good deal about the biological component of phonological acquisition, our knowledge of the cognitive-linguistic component is more limited, as it is difficult to observe and/or measure the processes associated with this type of learning. In this domain, we must try to determine how infants recognize recurring phonological patterns of their language, how they segment words from a stream of speech and store these words in the mental dictionary, how they access the stored forms in order to recognize and produce words, and how they recognize the link between the sounds of the language (what they hear) and the articulatory movements they must make in order to produce those sounds. By 12 to 13 months, a good deal of cognitive-linguistic learning has occurred, as most children have a receptive vocabulary of about 50 words, indicating they have stored these forms; in contrast, the expressive vocabulary at this age is typically very small, and many children have yet to say their first word.

## Chapter Overview

The following sections present information on various aspects of phonological development in children who are D/HH. We begin with an overview of vocal development in the prelinguistic period, followed by a brief comparison of phonological acquisition in children who are TD and those who are D/HH. Sections on assessment and treatment of the latter population are presented along with case studies that illustrate the developmental patterns and interventions for two young children. The research cited focuses primarily on studies published since 2000, as phonological development in children who are D/HH has changed dramatically following the widespread adoption of newborn hearing screening.

## THE PRELINGUISTIC PERIOD

The prelinguistic period plays an important role in speech and language development. Babies learn to articulate a variety of sounds and to "tune in" to their own vocal output and adult input. As they listen to their parents and caregivers, they begin to create a "mental dictionary" of word forms—stored representations (also called "underlying representations") that allow them to understand and produce words. As they hear their own babbles, they begin to associate their articulatory movements with the resulting acoustic signal—an association that plays an important role in learning to produce the articulatory movements associated with word production. Thus the baby who repeatedly produces the nonmeaningful syllable [ba] at 7 months becomes aware of the tactual and kinesthetic (movement) sensations associated with this syllable and hears the acoustic output associated with the production, creating an auditory-articulatory loop that is fundamental to speech production throughout life (Fry, 1966; Stoel-Gammon, 1992, 2011).

### Infants with Typical Development

Babies produce cries at birth and make a series of "vegetative" sounds such as burps, wheezes, and coughs in early infancy. By around 3 months of age, they begin to smile in social settings and produce "coos" and "goos." The baby's vocalizations are often imitated by the parent or caregiver, after which the baby, in turn, may respond with another coo. In this way, parent–baby vocal turn-taking can become primitive conversations. From 4 to 6 months, infant vocalizations become more diverse, with yells, whispers, sustained vowels, and raspberries (bilabial trills), among other types of production. By 6 to 7 months, most infants produce vocalizations that include consonant-vowel (CV) syllables. Although these vocalizations are nonmeaningful, they resemble adult words, and adults often respond as though they are indeed words. Thus if her baby produces [ma], a mother may repeat it and add, "Yes, Mama."

The range of infant vocal types changes and increases dramatically in the first year. Vegetative noises, coos, and elongated vowels tend to predominate in the early months; most consonantal sounds are produced in the back of the mouth—hence the name "cooing" or "gooing." With the onset of CV babbling (also referred to as **canonical babbling**), bilabial (e.g., [b, m]) and alveolar (e.g., [d, n]) consonants are frequent, and babies produce many one- and two-syllable utterances like [di] or [baba]. Between 6 and 12 months, vocalizations include a variety of consonants, but a small set of sound classes tends to be most frequent: stops (e.g., [b, d, g]), nasals (e.g., [m, n]), and glides (e.g., [w, j]). Around the time they begin to produce words, many babies produce "jargon speech"—long utterances with sentence-like intonation patterns but lacking identifiable words. An online resource for learning about prelinguistic vocalizations can be found in the Learning Activities section at the end of the chapter.

In order to determine if a baby's vocalizations are developing in accordance with the typical pattern, we need measures that allow us to compare children to expected developmental norms. A useful measure is based on age of onset of canonical babble: normally, most babies begin to produce canonical babble (i.e., CV syllables) between 6 and 9 months of age. If 20% or more of an infant's spontaneous utterances fail to contain CV syllables by 10 months, a hearing test is recommended (Oller & Eilers, 1988). Other measures are based on comparisons of vocalization *types* (coos, vowels, CV syllables) and *quantity* of vocalizations.

### Implications for Children Who Are Deaf or Hard of Hearing

The crucial role of hearing is highlighted in several aspects of early vocal development. As noted, the conversational exchanges that occur in the "cooing" period are based, in part, on the infant's ability to hear adult vocalizations. If a baby engages in cooing and cannot hear his mother imitate his productions, he is less likely to imitate her coo response, and thus the likelihood of conversational turn-taking is greatly decreased. Hearing also plays a fundamental role in the development of the auditory-articulatory loop (described previously), which allows a baby to link the articulatory movements associated with the production of [bu] or [ma] with the resulting sounds that occur. Finally, hearing allows babies to notice similarities between the sound of their own vocalizations and adult input (Stoel-Gammon, 1998).

Prior to the advent of newborn hearing screening, children who had profound hearing loss were not identified until 21 months, on average (Harrison & Roush, 1996; Sininger, Martinez, Eisenberg, Christensen, Grimes, & Hu, 2009). Those who were hard of hearing were sometimes not identified until 3 or even 5 years of age. This delayed identification meant that children missed out on spoken language input during a time when many basic auditory perceptual and phonological skills are acquired. Infants who were D/HH had very limited access to adult speech models during the first 2 years of life and, as a result, made relatively slow and incomplete progress in vocal development. Compared to children with normal hearing, their difficulties included late onset and a limited variety of vowels, CV syllables, and babbling (Oller & Eilers, 1988) and small consonant and syllable shape inventories (Moeller et al., 2007a; see Ertmer & Iyer, 2010, for review). Children with moderate to severe hearing loss are also at risk for delays in the onset of canonical babbling (Moeller et al., 2007a). However, some children who are hard of hearing begin to babble within the normal age range (Nathani, Oller, & Neil, 2007; Oller & Eilers, 1988). Delays in vocal development appear to contribute to later phonological difficulties in children who are D/HH (e.g., Osberger, 1992; Smith, 1975).

The convergence of newborn hearing screening and modern hearing technologies (CIs, digital HAs, and wireless hearing assistance technologies [HATs]; see Chapter 2) have created new opportunities to introduce environmental sounds and speech input to infants. These efforts initially aim to help children become aware of sounds in their environments and then quickly shift to the detection, discrimination, and recognition of speech and the meanings associated with spoken words. Well-fit HAs and CIs greatly increase auditory access to conversational speech models. Improved access to spoken communication via a CI has enabled many but not all deaf infants and toddlers to make noticeable advancements in vocal development (Ertmer, Jung, & Kloiber, 2013; Ertmer, Young, & Nathani, 2007; McCaffrey, Davis, MacNeilage, & von Hapsburg, 1999; Moore & Bass-Ringdahl, 2002).

### Assessments to Identify Progress in Prelinguistic Vocal Development

Progress in vocal development after HA or CI fitting has been analyzed by recording speech samples and classifying child utterances into developmental levels (Ertmer et al., 2013; Nathani, Ertmer, & Stark, 2006; see Oller, 2000; Vihman, 2014, for comprehensive reviews). However, speech sample analysis is very time-consuming and might not be practical in most intervention settings. The Conditioned Assessment of Speech Production (CASP) was developed as a time-efficient alternative to speech sample analysis (Ertmer & Stoel-Gammon, 2008). Research has shown that CASP scores have a high correlation with the results of speech sample analysis (Ertmer & Jung, 2012). Thus the CASP can be a time-efficient way to determine whether children are using hearing to guide speech development.

The CASP is a criterion-based assessment tool that is useful for monitoring changes in vocal development after infants and toddlers have received hearing instruments. Using the CASP, children are asked to imitate 10 short utterances that increase in developmental complexity from isolated vowels to basic canonical syllables, to diphthongs and more complex syllable shapes. A video demonstration can be found at http://www.listeningandspokenlanguage .org/uploadedFiles/Connect/Publications/The_Volta_Review/CASPDemo.mpg.

A recently developed behavioral checklist can also provide information about progress in vocal development. Ertmer and Iyer (2010) have identified four kinds of vocalizations that indicate auditory-guided speech development. Tracking the emergence of these behaviors can also be an informal method of assessing prelinguistic speech development (Table 8.1).

In summary, advances in prelinguistic vocalizations reveal that children are using hearing to guide speech development. Service providers who use the CASP and monitor the four indicators described in Table 8.1 can document advancements even before children begin to say words regularly. Young children who demonstrate slow or limited progress in vocal development may be in need of rehabilitative intervention.

**Table 8.1.**   Indicators and examples of auditory-guided vocal development in infants and toddlers

1. *Vowels and diphthongs become more diverse:* Children's spontaneous vocalizations begin to include not only [ʌ] but vowels produced at the front and back of the mouth, such as [i, u]. Children begin to imitate a variety of vowels and diphthongs.

2. *Consonant-vowel (CV) syllables become more frequent and a variety of consonants and vowels are produced:* CV syllables with adult-like (rapid) timing (e.g., [ma], [ba], [ki], [go], [no]) and strings of CV syllables (babbling) become common; consonants with less-visible places of articulation (e.g., [t, d, k, g, s, l]) and manners of production (i.e., fricatives and affricates) are observed.

3. *Consonant-vowel-consonant (CVC) and vowel-consonant (VC) syllables and "jargon" emerge:* Children produce consonants at the end of a syllable (closed syllables): [ʌp], [op], [bum], [dɑf]. Syllable strings with different consonants and vowels are produced with adult-like stress and/or intonation patterns.

4. *First words begin to appear:* Productions contain at least one consonant or vowel that matches the adult word, have the proper number of syllables, and are produced in appropriate contexts (e.g., [dɑi] for *doggie*, [dus] for *juice*).

*Source:* Ertmer & Inniger (2009); Ertmer & Iyer (2010).

## A Rehabilitative Intervention Approach for Stimulating Prelinguistic Vocal Development

Short Periods of Prelinguistic Input (SPPI; Ertmer et al., 2002; Ertmer, 2005) is an intervention approach that employs *focused stimulation* to facilitate advancements in prelinguistic vocal development (see Chapter 5). When used with toddlers and preschoolers who have language delays, focused stimulation involves repeated modeling of words or grammatical structures so that children are exposed to linguistic targets multiple times. Focused stimulation has been shown to be effective in increasing vocabulary, grammar, and phonological skills in children with language disabilities (see Ellis-Weismer & Robertson, 2006, for a review).

SPPI applies focused stimulation to prelinguistic vocalizations by having parents model vocalizations (e.g., vowels, basic canonical syllables, advanced forms) that are likely to be within the child's zone of proximal development (Allal & Ducrey, 2000; Vygotsky, 1978). For example, children who produce mainly isolated vowels or strings of vowels would be exposed to repeated productions of new vowels and simple CV syllables such as [ba], [ma], or [wa]. Similarly, children who produce basic canonical syllables but not advanced forms (see http://www.vocaldevelopment.com; Ertmer & Galster, 2002) would be exposed to new CV syllables (e.g., [fɑ], [ʃo], [gi]) and a variety of advanced forms (e.g., [ʌt], [bon], [obot]). In this way, children hear repeated models that are at or slightly above their current developmental level.

Using SPPI, parents produce target vocalizations once every 5 seconds for a period of 1 minute, five times per day. Pausing between models provides opportunities for imitation. SPPI is likely to be most engaging when used with toys or actions. Parents are encouraged to continue to use other language facilitation techniques (see Chapter 5) throughout the day so that both prelinguistic and early linguistic skills are stimulated. Although the efficacy of SPPI has not been assessed directly, focused stimulation has been shown to be effective for children with specific language impairment (SLI; see Ellis-Weismer & Robertson, 2006, for review), and a study by Kuhl and Meltzoff (1996) targeting vowels showed an influence on the vocal output of 20-week-old children.

## PHONOLOGICAL DEVELOPMENT IN
## CHILDREN WHO ARE TYPICALLY DEVELOPING

Words have two essential elements, sound and meaning, and to be considered a word, a child's production must have a consistent link between these two elements. For example, the vocalization [mama] produced at 7 months is a word only if there is a consistent sound–meaning link between [mama] and the mother (or a female caregiver). This sound–meaning link underlies comprehension and production of early words and is encoded in the child's mental dictionary, where each entry contains information about the phonological and semantic properties of a word.

Most TD babies produce their first words around 12 months, although the onset can vary substantially, with words appearing at 9 months in some cases and at 15 months in others. This variation is within the expected range for children who can hear. Regardless of the age of onset of meaningful speech, most children who are TD have an expressive vocabulary of ~50 words at 18 months and 250 to 300 words by their second birthday.

### The Phonology of First Words

Canonical babble and words co-occur for several months after the onset of meaningful speech and share many phonetic properties; consonants in both babble and speech are predominantly stops, nasals, and glides, and early words, like babble, are formed of CV syllables, yielding CV and CVCV word shapes (e.g., the CV [du] for *shoe*; the CVCV [gaga] for *cracker*). As the number of words in a child's vocabulary increases, the variety of consonants expands to include some fricatives (e.g., /f/, /s/) and a greater variety of word shapes, including words with final consonants (CVC) and a few with consonant clusters (CCV; VCC).

In the first-word period, accuracy of production varies extensively and depends, to some extent, on the phonological characteristics of the target word. Thus young children may produce *mommy* and *daddy* quite accurately, but the pronunciation of *elephant* (a three-syllable form with a liquid, a fricative, and a consonant cluster) or of *cheese* (with an initial affricate and a final fricative) may bear little resemblance to the adult form.

### Expanding the System

Between 2 and 6 years of age, children with normal hearing make great advances in phonological development. By age 2, children's word productions contain many of the basic elements of the adult system, although some sound classes and syllable types are missing. The segmental inventory at this age includes voiced and voiceless stops, labial and alveolar nasals, and a few fricatives (Stoel-Gammon, 1985, 1987). In terms of syllable structures, 2-year-olds produce CV and CVC syllables that can combine to form disyllabic words (CVCV; CVCVC) and a few forms with consonant clusters (i.e., two adjacent consonants), as in **tw**in or **h**ats. Their vowel repertoire is more complete than the consonantal repertoire (Ingram, 1976). By age 3, the typical phonetic inventory has expanded to include consonants from nearly all places and manner classes and a range of syllable and word types.

## Phonological Analyses

For the analysis of early words, two complementary approaches are commonly used: *independent* analyses that focus on the child's productions without reference to the adult model and *relational* analyses that compare the child's production relative to the adult model. Each type of analysis provides important information.

Independent analyses are based on an inventory (i.e., a list) of segments (consonants and vowels), sound classes, and syllable and word structures in a child's speech and can be used to analyze both intelligible and unintelligible utterances (Stoel-Gammon & Dunn, 1985). One advantage of independent analyses is that they can be used with children who have relatively small vocabularies (50–100 words) and are useful in analyzing both intelligible and unintelligible utterances. A summary of information from independent analyses of 2-year-old hearing children is provided in the upper rows of Table 8.2. As shown in the table, TD children have larger inventories in the word-initial than word-final position, and word shapes are limited to relatively simple forms.

Relational analyses are based on a comparison of the child's pronunciation of a word and the adult form and provide information on accuracy and on the nature of errors. This type of analysis reveals that accuracy of consonantal production improves markedly between 2 and 3 years, as a majority of children can accurately produce all stops, nasals, and glides as well as some fricatives during this period (see lower rows of Table 8.2). Relational analyses are also used to describe differences between the adult form and the child's productions; the differences are not random but adhere to "rule-based" error patterns (or "phonological processes"). Two types of error patterns, deletions and substitutions, occur commonly between 24 and 36 months (Stampe, 1969). In terms of deletions, young children may omit the final consonant, producing a CV rather than a CVC syllable (e.g., producing [ka] for *car*) or producing a single consonant rather than a sequence of consonants (e.g., [bu] for *blue*).

Substitution errors are often described in terms of sound classes rather than individual segments. Common substitution errors include "stopping," whereby fricatives (e.g., /f/, /v/, /s/, /z/) and affricates (/tʃ / and /dʒ/) are produced as stops, and "gliding," in which the liquids /l/ and /r/ are produced as

**Table 8.2.** Expectations for phonological development in children who are typically developing

| Aspect of development | Expectations |
|---|---|
| *Independent analysis:* Consonantal inventory and word shapes at 24 months (Stoel-Gammon, 1985, 1987) | Word-initial consonants: [b t d k g m n h w f s]<br>Word-final consonants: [p t k n r s]<br>Word shapes: consonant-vowel, consonant-vowel-consonant, consonant-vowel-consonant-vowel, consonant-vowel-consonant-vowel-consonant |
| *Relational analysis:* Order of acquisition of consonants, grouped by early, middle-, and late-mastered phonemes (Shriberg, 1993) | Early eight: / m b j n w d p h / (stops, nasals, glides)<br>Middle eight: / t ŋ k g f v tʃ dʒ / (stops, fricatives, affricates)<br>Late eight: / ʃ θ ð s z l r ʒ / (fricatives, liquids) |
| *Accuracy:* Percent consonants correct (PCC) in conversational speech (Campbell et al., 2007)<br>*Intelligibility:* The proportion of speech that can be understood by a stranger (Coplan & Gleason, 1988) | Age 2 years: Accuracy = 70%; Intelligibility = 50%<br>Age 3 years: Accuracy = 87%; Intelligibility = 75%<br>Age 4 years: Accuracy = 92%; Intelligibility = 100%<br>Age 5 years: Accuracy = 94% |

glides. (See Ingram, 1976; Grunwell, 1981; and Stoel-Gammon & Dunn, 1985, among others, for more complete descriptions of common error patterns in children's speech.)

Findings from relational analyses are presented in the second row of Table 8.2, showing the *order of acquisition* of groups of consonantal phonemes. There is great variation in the precise age at which individual phonemes are acquired, but we can obtain a general picture of acquisition by considering groups of phonemes. The table shows early-, middle-, and late-acquired consonantal phonemes (the early eight, middle eight, and late eight), with no attempt to delineate order of acquisition among the consonants in this set (Shriberg, 1993). Order of acquisition is of interest to researchers and clinicians as a means of identifying children whose acquisition patterns differ markedly from the established norms.

The lowest row in Table 8.2 presents expectations for two aspects of development in TD children: overall accuracy of productions in conversational speech (measured as percent consonants correct) and level of **speech intelligibility** (the proportion of speech that can be understood by a stranger). As shown, typical accuracy levels are quite high at age 3 (87%), rising to 94% by age 5. This is due in part to the samples on which the measure is based—conversational speech. In this medium, children's words tend to have a high proportion of early acquired consonants and syllable/word shapes.

Segmental accuracy is a major factor in the intelligibility of speech, although intelligibility is also affected by rate of speech (faster speech is linked to lower intelligibility) and syntactic complexity (longer, more complex sentences are harder to understand). The intelligibility of a 2-year-old is expected to be 50%, and by age 4, intelligibility doubles to 100% (Coplan & Gleason, 1988). This does not mean that all productions are accurate but rather that the errors have little effect on intelligibility (e.g., "wabbit" for "rabbit").

## COMPARING PHONOLOGICAL DEVELOPMENT IN TYPICALLY DEVELOPING AND DEAF OR HARD-OF-HEARING CHILDREN

The transition from prelinguistic (nonmeaningful) to linguistic (meaningful) productions among children who are D/HH is affected by a number of factors, including age at identification, degree/severity of hearing loss, and age at which the child receives a HA or CI. Yet several trends have been documented: When compared to their age-matched hearing peers, children who are D/HH 1) produce their first words at a later age and 2) have a longer period of overlap of nonmeaningful and meaningful productions. At 24 months, data from Moeller and colleagues show that children who are D/HH, on average, had a productive vocabulary of 108 words (*SD* 84), compared with an average of 316 words (*SD* 157) for TD peers (Moeller et al., 2007b; Nott, Cowan, Brown, & Wigglesworth, 2009). Although delays in vocabulary development are common, children who receive intervention from a young age often make impressive gains.

It is difficult to summarize studies of phonological development among children who are D/HH, due to important differences in the characteristics of the participants and selected research methods. For instance, research participants can differ in their ages at time of data collection, the severity of their hearing losses, and the amount of **robust hearing experience** (i.e., "auditory access to speech at conversational intensity levels"; Ertmer & Inniger, 2009, p. 1581), among other within-child differences. Similarly, research methods can differ from study to study in terms of the way speech data are collected and analyzed (e.g., imitated words versus spontaneous speech samples), the focus of the research (e.g., assessing speech production accuracy versus speech intelligibility), and the presence or absence of TD controls.

Mindful of these differences, the following sections are restricted to a few studies that address three main questions about early identified children: How closely do children who are D/HH approximate the phonological skills of children who are TD? Do children who are D/HH and children who are TD acquire consonants in the same developmental order? What do studies tell us about the special intervention needs of children who are D/HH?

### Question 1: General Phonological Skills

Ambrose and colleagues (2014) made direct comparisons of the phonological abilities of a group of children who are hard of hearing (mild to severe hearing losses) and a group of 2-year-olds who are TD. In the study, 70 early identified children who used HAs and their TD counterparts were asked to imitate 10 early emerging words; all word productions were transcribed and analyzed for consonant and vowel accuracy. Whereas 63% of the hard-of-hearing group achieved scores similar to that of the NH group, scores of more than one third of the hard-of-hearing group were found to be more than one standard deviation below the mean of the TD group. In addition, 10 children from the hard-of-hearing group were unable to perform the imitation task satisfactorily and were not included in the study. Another recent study of 3-year-old children who are hard of hearing noted that their development appeared to be strongly influenced by the severity of their hearing losses (Tomblin et al., 2014). Children with unaided pure-tone averages (PTA) greater than 45 dB hearing loss had greater phonological delays than those with lower PTAs. Taken together, these studies illustrate the wide differences in early phonological abilities that are seen in young children with mild to severe hearing losses.

Comparisons between young CI recipients with severe-profound hearing loss and TD children are also available. Ertmer and colleagues (2012) asked 11 CI users, ages 33–61 months, and 11 age-and gender-matched TD controls to imitate 50 short sentences containing key words that were transcribed and analyzed. Members of the CI group were implanted at 17.6 months on average and were tested upon completing their second year of device experience. Consonant production scores were examined for overall accuracy (across all words), accuracy in the initial position in words, accuracy in the final position, and accuracy of consonants from early, middle, and late developmental sound classes (see Table 8.2).

The results showed that children in the TD group had greater overall accuracy scores than those in the CI group ($M = 83\%$ versus 53%, respectively). Both groups produced initial consonants with greater accuracy than final consonants ($M = 73\%$ versus 63%, respectively), and the CI group had lower accuracy for consonants in each word position. Although the scores of the CI group were significantly lower than those of the TD group, it should be remembered that they indicate substantial improvements during the first 2 years of robust hearing. In fact, the scores of these young CI recipients were within 10 percentage points of the mean score of children implanted at older ages who had more than 5 years of CI experience (Tobey, Geers, Brenner, Altuna, & Gabbert, 2003). In sum, the CI group did not match the phonological skills of their TD same-age peers, but continued improvement is expected as they gain further experience in auditory-guided speech development.

## Question 2: Order of Acquisition of Consonants

It is important to consider whether children who are D/HH follow typical patterns of phonological development once they receive their HAs or CIs. Knowledge in this area can be useful in selecting the order in which vowels and consonants are introduced during intervention. Several comparisons of consonant acquisition order have recently been completed. Ambrose and colleagues (2014) concluded that children who are hard of hearing follow a typical developmental pattern during the first 2 years of life. Similar conclusions have also been reached for children with severe-profound hearing losses. In general, these studies have noted a typical developmental order but a comparatively slower pace of consonant acquisition (Flipsen, 2011; Moeller et al., 2007b; Serry & Blamey, 1999).

Recent data show that this conclusion appears to be reliable for initial consonants (Ertmer et al., 2012). As can be seen Figure 8.1, both groups of children produced initial consonants from the early, middle, and late developmental classes with progressively decreasing accuracy. Thus both groups

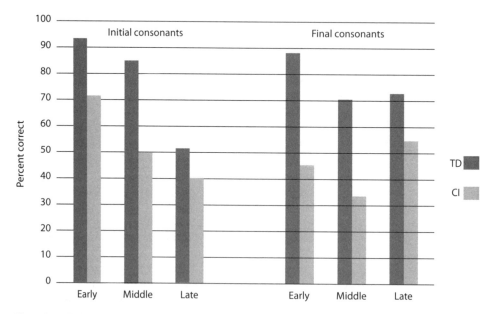

**Figure 8.1.** Mean percent correct for initial and final consonants produced by 11 children with cochlear implants (CIs) and their typically developing (TD) same-age peers. (Adapted with permission of American Speech-Language-Hearing Association, from Ertmer, D.J., Kloiber, D., Jung, J., Kirleis, K., & Bradford, D. [2012]. Consonant production accuracy in young cochlear implant recipients: Developmental sound classes and word position effects. *American Journal of Speech-Language Pathology, 21*, 348; permission conveyed through Copyright Clearance Center, Inc. Copyright © 2002, American Speech-Language-Hearing Association.)

acquired *word-initial* consonants in a typical developmental order. However, the order of acquisition for consonants in *word-final* position was not as predictable.

In Figure 8.1, the TD group shows a decrease in consonant-final mean scores from the early to the middle class, but the middle and late classes are comparable. The lack of progressively lower accuracy across the latter classes might be due to factors such as the small number of TD participants and narrow age range in the Ertmer et al. study, compared to the much larger norming study by Smit and colleagues (1990). A close look at the data for the CI group reveals a surprising profile: Consonants from the late class were actually produced with greater accuracy than those from the early or middle classes. Figure 8.2 provides a look at individual consonants in each developmental class for final consonants. As this figure reveals, there is much overlap in the accuracy scores across the developmental classes—as if all final consonants are emerging at the same time. In sum, initial consonants seem to be acquired in a typical order, but final consonants were not. Possible reasons for this discrepancy will be discussed as question 3 is considered below.

Finally, early identified children who receive HAs and CIs often make substantial improvements in speech intelligibility with intervention, although improvements may take considerable time. Peng, Spencer, and Tomblin (2004) found that 24 CI users who communicated through speech and sign and who were implanted between 2 years and 6 months and 11 years of age ($M$ = 5 years and 1 month) produced sentences that were 70% intelligible after 7 years of device experience. Ertmer (2010) examined HA and CI users (ages 2 years and 10 months to 15 years and 5 months at time of testing) who used oral

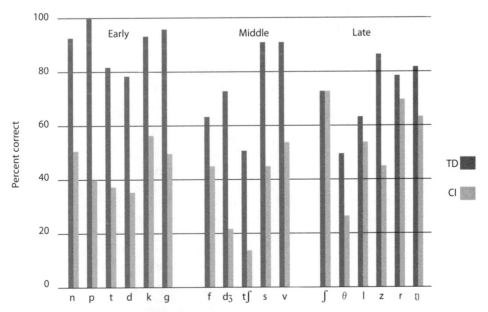

**Figure 8.2.** Mean percent correct for final consonants produced by 11 children with cochlear implants (CIs) and their typically developing (TD) same-age peers. (Adapted with permission of American Speech-Language-Hearing Association, from Ertmer, D.J., Kloiber, D., Jung, J., Kirleis, K., & Bradford, D. [2012]. Consonant production accuracy in young cochlear implant recipients: Developmental sound classes and word position effects. *American Journal of Speech-Language Pathology, 21,* 349; permission conveyed through Copyright Clearance Center, Inc. Copyright © 2002, American Speech-Language-Hearing Association.)

communication to determine whether their scores on word articulation tests could predict their level of intelligibility for sentences. One finding of the study was that children's speech was nearly 55% intelligible. Both of the mean scores in these studies were well above the well-supported average intelligibility level noted prior to the introduction of newborn hearing screening (Osberger, 1992). However, they also indicate that there is quite a bit of room for improvement. As Monsen (1981, p. 350) concluded, listeners are "confronted by overwhelming difficulty in understanding" when children's speech is less than 59% intelligible. This "cutoff" level can serve as an indicator of children's functional oral communication ability.

## Question 3: Special Intervention Needs

Several segmental error patterns are common in the speech of children who are D/HH. The sources of these difficulties may be related to the severity and configuration of the hearing loss, intervention effectiveness, and/or the signals that hearing instruments provide—among other possibilities. As Tomblin and colleagues (2014) pointed out, as the severity of hearing loss increases, HA users experience more limited access to conversational speech models and auditory feedback for phonological development. In addition, those with sensorineural hearing loss and sloping audiometric configurations may have little or no access to high-frequency consonants—a situation that can lead to the protracted development of fricative and affricate consonants (Ambrose et al., 2014; Moeller et al., 2007a; Stelmachowicz, Pittman, Hoover, Lewis, & Moeller, 2004). Children with CIs, on the other hand, usually have relatively flat auditory threshold configurations across the range of speech frequencies. As a result, their access to high frequency information can be quite good—as evidenced by the high-level accuracy for /ʃ/ in Figure 8.2. Thus, in this area, CI users may actually outperform children who are hard of hearing and use HAs.

Another error pattern is evident in comparatively poorer production of final versus initial consonants by CI users (Figures 8.1 and 8.2) and children who use HAs (Ambrose et al., 2014; Moeller et al., 2007b). Final consonants have been shown to be more difficult to perceive than initial consonants in adults with normal hearing (Redford & Deihl, 1999). This difficulty has been attributed to the reduced amplitude and duration of some final consonants in connected speech. It seems reasonable to infer that children who use HAs and CIs would also experience this difficulty (see Ertmer et al., 2012, for more discussion). Yet it is puzzling that some final consonants (/ʃ/ and /r/; see Figure 8.2) were produced with relatively high accuracy by young CI recipients. In comparison to the least accurate final consonants (/tʃ/ and /dʒ/), /ʃ/ and /r/ can be prolonged and emphasized during child-directed speech. Increasing auditory saliency might be a useful intervention technique for stimulating the perception and production of other final consonants (e.g., /m/, /n/, / ŋ /) as well. Improvements in final (and likely medial) consonant accuracy will require special emphasis during intervention.

Finally, it is important to remember that hearing instruments do not restore normal hearing. CIs present children with an electrical rather than an acoustic signal, and so children with CIs have internal representations of speech sounds that may differ from those of children who are TD. Likewise, HA users may experience distortion that could interfere with recognizing and representing phonemes. Users of both devices also "battle" the interference of background noise, reverberation, and decreased speech signal strength as their distance from the speaker increases. All these perceptual constraints can have negative consequences for phonological development. The upcoming sections will consider ways to evaluate children's phonological abilities and provide interventions that address child-specific needs.

## PHONOLOGICAL ASSESSMENTS OF CHILDREN WHO ARE DEAF OR HARD OF HEARING

Phonological assessments have a variety of purposes. These include 1) examining children's ability to produce a variety of phonemes and word shapes, 2) identifying intervention targets (i.e., phonemic errors) for intervention, 3) assessing the suprasegmental characteristics of children's connected speech (e.g., rate and intonation), 4) assessing the level of children's speech intelligibility, and 5) analyzing speech patterns for systematic errors (phonological processes). Children's phonological awareness (i.e., awareness of aspects of the sound structure of language, including syllables, phonemes, and rhymes) can also be examined but will be discussed in relation to literacy in Chapter 12. A detailed discussion of all aspects of a phonological evaluation, including oral mechanism exams, **stimulability** testing, and target selection options, can be found in Bauman-Waengler (2016); Bernthal, Bankson, and Flipsen (2013); and Williams (2003). We will focus on assessments that are especially useful for children who are D/HH.

The main purposes of a phonological assessment are met through a variety of procedures for children who are D/HH. Spontaneous speech samples can be elicited by having children tell stories or talk about their day as service providers listen and note the kinds of misarticulations that are produced during the sample. Although sampling provides an opportunity to observe children's natural, conversational speech, a full range of speech sounds might not be produced by the child. As a result, sampling is considered an informal speech screening tool. The remainder of this section examines commercially available assessment tools.

### Assessments for Children with Limited Expressive Vocabularies

A unique assessment tool has been developed especially for young children who are D/HH. The Identifying Early Phonological Needs tool (Paden & Brown, 1992) examines children's spontaneous productions of 25 early emerging vocabulary words. The results are then analyzed to determine how consistently consonant features (voicing, manner, and place), vowels and diphthongs, and syllable shapes are produced. Repeated administration is useful for monitoring progress during the early stages of phonological development.

The Open-and Closed-Set Task (Ertmer, 2015) is aimed at examining young children's early gains in phonology and auditory comprehension. It consists of 3 lists of 10 words that are common in the vocabularies of 2-year-old children who are TD. Children who are D/HH are asked to imitate a spoken word and then select a photograph of that word from three choices. Children's responses are scored for the number of phonemes produced correctly, the acceptability of the production as a match for the target word, and the number of stimulus words that are correctly identified. The Open-and Closed-Set Task can be administered to children as young as 18 months and, when given at regular intervals, provides objective estimates of phonological development and receptive vocabulary during the first 2 years of hearing instrument use (see Video clip 8.1).

### Assessments for Children with Larger Vocabularies

Commercially available articulation tests are designed so that a full range of consonants and some consonant clusters are examined. The target consonants appear in various positions in familiar words (i.e., word initial, word medial, and word final). Although developed for preschool and school-age children who have speech sound disorders, these tests can also be used with children who are D/HH. To administer these tests, service providers transcribe children's productions and calculate an overall score based on the number of phonemes that were produced correctly. Standardized tests allow children's speech scores to be compared to norms for children within the same age range. The Goldman-Fristoe Test of Articulation 2 (Goldman & Fristoe, 2000; see Video clip 8.2) and the Arizona Articulation Proficiency Scale (3rd edition; Fudala & Reynolds, 2000) are especially useful because they examine phonemes in connected speech as well as single words. However, vowel production accuracy is not explicitly assessed on most articulation tests. Because vowels can be problematic for children who are D/HH, it is important to pay close attention to vowel accuracy during both word articulation testing and spontaneous speech samples. Children's rate of speech, habitual pitch, use of intonation and stress, and loudness levels should also be observed so that inappropriate characteristics can be identified as intervention targets.

The productions of children with normal hearing but moderate to severe speech sound disorders (SSDs) are often examined using analysis of error patterns (also called phonological processes). This type of analysis examines the system, structure, and stability of children's utterances for error patterns (Grunwell, 1997). For example, children who often omit the final consonant in words show the process of "final consonant deletion"; those who produce final voiced consonants without voicing ([dak] for *dog*) show the process of "final consonant devoicing." Identifying phonological processes enables service providers to target multiple phonemes at the same time (e.g., final /d/, /g/, and /z/ when targeting the process of final devoicing or deletion) to more efficiently improve speech production. Children who are D/HH might also benefit from this analysis when systematic deviations from adult standards are noted (Bernthal et al., 2013).

### Specialized Assessments for Children Who Are Deaf or Hard of Hearing

Whereas the aforementioned procedures are applied to both children with normal hearing and those who are D/HH, two other kinds of assessments are usually reserved for the latter group. Recognizing that children who have very limited robust hearing require specialized speech assessments, Daniel Ling developed two complementary tools. The Phonetic Level Speech Evaluation (Ling, 1980) is an elicited imitation task in which children imitate 1) nonsegmental aspects of speech (e.g., long versus short vocalizations, loud versus soft sounds, and vowels at low, mid, and high pitches), 2) vowels and diphthongs, and 3) consonants in CV syllables. Children are asked to produce each stimu-lus item individually, three times per second, and while alternating targets in syllables (e.g., [tikitikitiki]). Service providers judge each production as either consistently acceptable, inconsistent, or absent. Because the stimuli of the Phonetic Level Speech Evaluation are thought to represent a continuum of speech skills, the evaluation can be discontinued whenever children reach a level at which they are unable to imitate stimuli consistently. This level then provides a starting point for intervention.

The Phonologic Level Speech Evaluation (Ling, 1980, 1988) examines how well children actually use their phonological skills in everyday situations. To administer the Phonological Level Speech Evaluation, service providers listen to children in a variety of settings to determine whether they transfer their newly acquired speech sounds to everyday conversational speech. Careful records are kept to indicate when phonological skills become consistent, and progress is tracked from year to year.

## Assessment of Intelligibility

As mentioned earlier, the intelligibility of children's speech is another important area for assessment. Speech intelligibility can be examined via subjective listener ratings called "scalings" (e.g., poor, fair, good; 1-to 5-point rating scales) and through listener write-down tasks. Many research studies have used the latter, more objective approach of having children say sentences and having listener-judges write down the words that they understood in recordings of those sentences. This form of assessment has the advantage of quantifying the number of words produced in connected speech rather than words produced in isolation. The primary finding of Ertmer's (2010) study was that word articulation test scores did not predict speech intelligibility levels in children who are D/HH. Thus it was recommended that speech intelligibility be assessed directly through write-down assessments. Thanks to handheld digital recorders (and smartphones) and readily available sentence lists, sentence write-down assessments can be completed in a relatively short  amount of time (see Video clips 8.3–8.7). For more information about how to assess intelligibility and sentence lists, see Ertmer (2011) and Kloiber and Ertmer (2015).

## Assessments to Identify Speech Perception Abilities

Children's aided hearing levels and the configuration of their hearing losses can influence how well they detect vowels and consonants. It is important to remember that children differ greatly in their frequency-specific thresholds and the phonemes that they perceive. In addition, some phonemes may be detectable via a sensory aid but not perceived clearly. Children who have little or no auditory access to conversational speech models are likely to need visual and tactile cues to supplement auditory-based phonological intervention.

Familiarity with the audibility of speech features based on the audiogram is foundational for phonological intervention so that appropriate auditory training and phonological goals can be developed.

An assortment of tools is available to assess auditory speech perception ability for a wide age range of children. These tools fall into two main kinds of procedures: closed-set and open-set tests. Closed-set tests provide several choices from which a response is selected. For example, this could include asking a child to listen to a stimulus word before pointing to the corresponding picture in a set of four pictures or circling a word in a list of words. Scores on closed-set tests are interpreted according to the probability of guessing the correct answer. For instance, if there are three picture choices for each stimulus word, children who correctly identify ~33% of all the words would demonstrate only chance-level speech perception ability. Open-set tests, in contrast, provide no choices for the listener and therefore have a chance performance level of 0% correct. The latter kind of test is likely to provide a closer estimate of listening ability in everyday conditions. Both closed-and open-set procedures can be administered with auditory and visual (speechreading) cues or through audition only, usually with the aid of an acoustic screen (e.g., cloth-covered embroidery hoop; see Video clips 8.8–8.10). Children's audiological records typically include the results of speech perception testing.

During formal audiometric evaluations in sound booths, speech perception stimuli are presented at controlled loudness levels to determine the percentage of words or sentences that children can recognize (see Chapter 2). However, some less formal assessment tools can be administered in face-to-face settings in order to determine the kinds of speech features that children can identify. Using this method, care must be taken to produce stimuli at a conversational intensity level while using an acoustic screen to block speechreading cues. Informal speech perception tools assess a variety of perceptual skills, ranging from the detection and discrimination of suprasegmental information such as speech intensity (e.g., loud versus soft), intonation (e.g., rising versus falling), and timing characteristics (e.g., continuous versus interrupted vowel sounds; see Glendonald Auditory Screen Procedure [Erber, 1982], Early Speech Perception Test [Moog & Geers, 1990]), to closed-set word identification (e.g., New Children's Test of Speech Discrimination [Elliott & Katz, 1980], Contrasts for Auditory and Speech Training [Ertmer, 2005]) and open-set words (e.g., Lexical Neighborhood Test [Kirk, Pisoni, & Osberger, 1995]). The results of these assessments enable service providers to select target speech features and monitor progress toward auditory development goals. Before using these tools, children's speech perception abilities should also be screened using the Ling Six-Sound Test to ensure that hearing instruments are working properly (see Video clips 8.8–8.10 and Chapter 7).

In summary, many tools are available for assessing children's speech production and perception abilities. The results of these assessments help identify areas of strength and need. It should not be surprising—given their relatively late introduction to hearing and reliance on technology—that many children who are D/HH require intensive intervention to reach age-level functioning in these areas. The next section describes intervention approaches that are intended to facilitate progress toward these important goals.

## INTERVENTIONS TO PROMOTE PHONOLOGICAL AND AUDITORY SKILLS

There are many similarities between preschool and school-age children with normal hearing who have speech sound disorders (SSDs) and similar-age children who are D/HH. For instance, both groups are delayed in phonological development compared to their same-age peers, both have difficulty producing a full range of consonants accurately, and their speech errors can interfere with oral communication. However, two basic differences call for specialized intervention strategies for children who are D/HH. First, children who are D/HH do not detect or recognize speech sounds as well as children with normal hearing. Their peripheral hearing losses affect both phonetic (i.e., the ability to perceive and produce speech patterns acceptably) and phonological (i.e., the meaningful use and understanding of speech in communication) aspects of spoken language (Ling, 1980). These difficulties arise from comparatively poorer auditory access to mature speech models and auditory feedback about their own speech. In addition, children who are D/HH often experience auditory perceptual difficulties even with well-fit hearing instruments. The second difference is that children who are D/HH do not necessarily have a speech production disorder—that is, upon attaining robust hearing via hearing instruments, many begin to acquire phonetic and phonologic skills without explicit instruction and, in contrast to many children who have SSDs, make steady progress in developing intelligible speech. Yet despite expectations for spontaneous improvement following HA or CI fitting, special strategies are often needed to increase phonetic and phonological skills in children who are D/HH. Much has been written about intervention approaches that can be effective in remediating SSDs in children who have normal hearing (e.g., Bleile, 2013; Williams, McLeod, & McCauley, 2010). A detailed description of the many intervention models available for this population is beyond the scope of this chapter. However, many of these approaches might also be effective for children who gain robust hearing through their hearing instruments. Interested readers are referred to Bauman-Waengler (2016) and Williams et al. (2010) for discussions of traditional therapy, minimal pairs therapy, and the cycles approach for phonological process errors and other approaches that are potentially useful for children who are D/HH.

Unfortunately, there is a paucity of research that explores the efficacy of phonological interventions for children identified through newborn hearing screening—the majority of children who are D/HH today. Several factors have contributed to this situation. First, since the early 1990s, much more research has focused on determining the effects of CIs on speech development than the efficacy of phonological intervention models. Second, newborn hearing screening has changed the research landscape by shifting intervention to much younger children. Although treatment studies are beginning to appear in the literature (e.g., Bow, Blamey, Paatsch, & Sarant, 2004), the efficacy of phonological intervention for today's preschool and school-age children who are D/HH has not yet been sufficiently explored in the research.

In lieu of well-grounded models of intervention, several strategies to optimize auditory-guided speech development are offered. The next sections discuss *habilitative* approaches for children who are making steady or even rapid progress in acquiring spoken language skills and *rehabilitative* approaches for children who make slow or insufficient progress. In most cases, strategies for the former group can also be applied to the latter group. Three ways to stimulate auditory development will also be described. These approaches are intended to improve children's ability to distinguish between speech segments and comprehend meaningful speech. Integrating auditory and phonological activities can help children expand and integrate their listening and oral communication abilities.

## Habilitative Intervention Approaches

Early identified toddlers and preschoolers with well-fit hearing instruments often benefit from child-centered intervention to stimulate speech and language development (see Chapter 7). In this approach, parents and service providers follow the child's lead during play activities while also implementing language facilitation techniques such as modeling words and phrases to match the child's desires and recasting children's utterances to more adult forms. Adult speech models can also be highlighted by making the target word or a phoneme in the word slightly louder and/or longer, by repeating the target several times (focused stimulation), and by contrasting the child's and the adult production aloud (e.g., "Shees? . . . Oh, you want cheese."). In this way, speech sounds are emphasized in social situations when the child is likely to be paying attention (i.e., teachable moments). Developmentally appropriate speech targets that are missing from the child's phonetic inventory can be introduced through play with toys whose names contain the new targets or by emphasizing their occurrence during teachable moments. Continuing these language facilitation strategies after children are old enough for more direct intervention helps to ensure the generalization of new skills to everyday speaking situations. The first case study provided later in the chapter illustrates this approach for a child making steady progress in spoken language abilities.

## Rehabilitative Intervention Approaches

Figure 8.2 shows that, on average, preschool-age children who are D/HH (in this case CI users) have poorer consonant production accuracy than their TD same-age peers. This is not surprising, given that the former group experienced less exposure to speech models and auditory feedback and has poorer hearing acuity than their same-age peers (see Chapter 2). Most children who are D/HH will need phonological intervention to "catch up" to their same-age peers. As children mature, they become better able to attend to clinician-directed instruction and can benefit from some of the intervention approaches designed for children with SSD. However, special strategies to optimize auditory learning hold the potential to stimulate progress.

The A.G. Bell Academy for Listening and Spoken Language (http://www.listeningandspokenlanguage.org/AGBellAcademy/) recommends three main principles for phonological intervention with children who are D/HH. These are 1) create and maintain acoustically controlled environments that support listening and talking (i.e., reasonably quiet therapy rooms and classrooms), 2) coach parents to become effective facilitators of their child's listening and spoken language development, and 3) promote each child's ability to self-monitor spoken language through listening. Self-monitoring is crucial for making gains in speech intelligibility. Children who show poor carryover to conversational speech may need explicit practice in evaluating their own speech through review of audio and video recordings (see Ertmer & Ertmer, 1998).

Suggestions to increase auditory-guided speech development include 1) maximizing children's reliance on audition by introducing and practicing new targets in an auditory-only condition using an acoustic screen or a side-by-side seating arrangement that facilitates auditory-only presentation (see Chapter 7), 2) letting children be the "teacher" by judging the correctness of the service provider's models (both correct and false assertions) and giving instructions on how to "fix" errors, 3) conveying high expectations for carry-over of new skills to spontaneous speech, and 4) keeping parents and teachers informed of the child's targets and progress so that generalization to all environments is expected (Ertmer, 2005). Applying the A.G. Bell principles with these suggestions can help children become more reliant on listening to guide speech productions throughout the day.

Finally, children who have little robust hearing are likely to require a highly structured rehabilitation program that emphasizes visual and tactile cues as well as listening (i.e., multisensory stimulation). In the Ling (1980) approach, phonetic targets are selected and ordered after completing the previously discussed Phonetic Level Speech Evaluation. Skills that are foundational for speech production such as voicing and breath control are taught whenever necessary. Vowels and diphthongs are practiced through contrast of vowel height and place characteristics targeting jaw position, tongue shape and placement, and lip shapes. Similarly, groups of consonants are taught simultaneously through contrasts of manner, place, and voicing features. For example, [du], [tu], and [ʃu] provide opportunities to highlight the voicing difference between the first two targets and the manner differences between the first two and the third target. Single syllable productions ([ko]) are emphasized at first, then rapid, multiple productions of the same syllable ([kokoko]), followed by rapidly alternating syllable strings ([kogokogokogo]). Once targets can be produced rapidly, they are practiced in words and sentences. The use of new skills is monitored by parents and teachers to ensure generalization to meaningful speech.

### Auditory Development in Preschool and School-Age Children

Children who are D/HH and who use HAs or CIs typically experience substantial increases in the audibility of speech via their hearing instruments. That is, they are able to *detect* sounds and speech at lower intensity levels with amplification or CI input. Learning to *understand* what they hear, however, often requires special intervention combined with consistent sensory aid use. *Auditory training* has been defined as "instruction designed to maximize an individual's use of residual hearing or electrical hearing by means of both formal and informal listening practice" (Tye-Murray, 2015, p. 699). Auditory training has been found to be effective with adults who have hearing losses in a systematic review of research by Sweetow and Palmer (2005) and to produce positive changes in related neurological processing abilities (e.g., Russo, Nicol, Zecker, Hayes, & Kraus, 2005). However, studies of its efficacy for children, especially those identified since 2000, are scarce. Currently, the broader term "auditory development" is often used to encompass the activities previously known as "auditory training." This more contemporary terminology will be used in the following discussion.

Auditory development programs typically focus on improving the ability to detect, discriminate, recognize, and comprehend environmental sounds and speech (Erber, 1982). It is important to keep in mind that children will differ in their rate of progress in auditory training and that training goals must be individualized. As Chapter 7 provides a discussion of auditory development in young children, the focus of the following sections will be on listening activities for relatively older children. Three complementary types of auditory development—analytic, synthetic, and pragmatic—and a way to combine them in an eclectic approach will be discussed next. As each addresses different and important aspects of speech perception and spoken language development, it is recommended that all three be implemented together in an eclectic approach.

***Analytic Auditory Development***    **Analytic auditory development** is considered a "bottom-up" approach in which the "parts" of speech (i.e., suprasegmental, vowel, and consonant features) are highlighted and contrasted (Blamey & Alcantara, 1994). At first, grossly different sounds (e.g., silence versus [a]; [ba] versus [bababa]; [i:] versus [o:]) are introduced and contrasted. Later, increasingly finer acoustic distinctions (e.g., [fæt] versus [kæt] or [teɪk] versus [teɪp]) are introduced and practiced. Research has shown that vowels are easier to identify than consonant manner, voicing, and place cues (Fryhauf-Bertschy, Tyler, Kelsay, Gantz, & Woodworth, 1997; Miyamoto, Osberger, Robbins, Myers, & Kessler, 1993). These findings provide the basis for auditory training programs such as the Contrasts for Auditory and Speech Training (CAST; Ertmer, 2005), the Speech Perception Instructional Curriculum Evaluation (SPICE; Moog & Geers, 1990), and the Bridge to Better Communication program from the MED-EL corporation.

In analytic auditory development, minimal pair words (i.e., those differing by a single phoneme only) are used to present targeted contrasts. For example, the words "hat" and "hoot" can be used to contrast low-front and high-back vowels, and the words "fan" versus "tan" to contrast manner of production (i.e., a voiceless fricative with a voiceless stop). Minimal pair words are spoken through an acoustic screen so that the child uses only auditory cues to identify the correct word. The child's performance is documented by tallying the number of correct and incorrect responses. A criterion is selected (e.g., greater than 80% accuracy for two consecutive sessions) so that the effects of training can be documented and training progresses efficiently. Speech *production* practice is also incorporated by having children repeat each stimulus word out loud and by changing roles so that the child acts as the "talker" while the clinician acts as the "listener" (see Video clips 8.11–8.12).

It is important to remember that some children may quickly learn to identify speech features. Habilitative intervention for such children may require only short-term practice with a relatively small set of contrasts. Other children may require rehabilitative intervention with extensive practice of a full range of speech feature contrasts (see Ertmer et al., 2002, for descriptions of individualized programs).

*Synthetic Auditory Development*   Children who are D/HH participate in conversations with family, friends, and teachers daily. Their success in these interactions can strongly influence their attitudes toward oral communication and their progress in developing listening skills. **Synthetic auditory development** is a "top-down" approach that places emphasis on the *comprehension of meaningful speech*, rather than the identification and discrimination of the "parts" of the speech signal, as seen in analytic development (Blamey & Alcantara, 1994). Using a synthetic approach, phrases and sentences are presented, and children are asked to repeat, answer questions, demonstrate comprehension (e.g., by pointing to pictures or words), or participate in conversations. In this way, all contextual, syntactic, and semantic cues are available for understanding messages (see Video clips 8.13 and 8.14).

Synthetic auditory development is likely to be more engaging when the topic of discussion is of genuine interest to the child. Synthetic listening activities are also designed to integrate practice with language targets. For example, pivot sentences with simple syntax may be presented for children who are beginning to combine words (e.g., "want . . . [color] [vehicle]"). Stimuli are then adjusted to include longer, more complex, and varied sentences as the child's language skills improve. For example, a **barrier game** format can be used to develop comprehension of longer sentences (e.g., "I want the small, red car"). Allowing the child to take turns as the "talker" ensures that both auditory comprehension and phonology are emphasized. Practice can be conducted with both auditory-only and auditory-plus-speechreading cues, depending on the child's abilities and the clinician's instructional philosophy.

*Pragmatic Auditory Development*   Background noise, reverberation, and excessive distance from the source of a sound or a speaker can make auditory comprehension difficult for children who are D/HH. Children who deal with these troublesome situations assertively increase their chances of communication success. **Pragmatic auditory development** introduces facilitative and communication repair strategies to overcome difficult listening situations (Tye-Murray, 2015). Facilitative strategies include statements and actions that influence talkers to speak more slowly, provide better visual cues (e.g., "Please let me see your face when you talk"), or move to a quieter environment. Repair strategies are used to fix communication breakdowns after they occur. These might include asking for repetition or rephrasing what was understood before asking about missed information. Although these strategies may seem to be common sense, children typically need explicit instruction before applying them in a variety of situations. Teachers and parents play key roles in encouraging the use of these strategies throughout the day.

*An Eclectic Approach to Auditory Development*   Meeting the many listening needs of children who are D/HH calls for an approach in which analytic, synthetic, and pragmatic skills are emphasized concurrently. At first glance, such an approach might seem unwieldy, but it can be implemented efficiently when short periods of analytic practice (approximately 5 minutes) are followed by activities that integrate language, speech, and listening practice (synthetic auditory development). Although introducing and practicing pragmatic strategies will take some time at first, the use of the strategies can be easily reinforced within the context of other intervention activities once children understand them. In sum, eclectic auditory training can help children develop a base of speech perception skills while promoting the linguistic and social skills needed to communicate in everyday situations. Additional suggestions for implementing auditory development activities with children can be found in Robbins (1990), Koch (1999), Ertmer et al. (2002), Ertmer (2005), and Tye-Murray (2015). Finally, computerized auditory training for children who are D/HH is becoming increasingly available. A variety of programs and Internet resources now address analytic, synthetic, and pragmatic goals. Tye-Murray (2015) cites numerous advantages to computer applications, including training that is self-paced, adjustment of task difficulty to the listener's performance, use of different talkers to present stimuli, and costs that may be less than those associated with clinician-provided intervention.

## Case Studies[4]

The following case studies illustrate many of the intervention principles and practices that have been previously discussed. The first case describes a *habilitative* intervention program; the second case describes a *rehabilitative* intervention approach.

### Case 1: Habilitative Intervention for a Toddler Who Has Cochlear Implants

Nathan has severe to profound bilateral hearing loss secondary to mutations in the Connexin 26 gene. His hearing loss was identified at 6 months of age, and he was fit with hearing aids (HAs) shortly afterward. He began receiving early intervention services at 9 months of age. After a 3-month trial with HAs, it was determined that Nathan did not have enough access to sound to acquire spoken language. Nathan's parents decided to pursue bilateral cochlear implants (CIs), and he was sequentially implanted in his right ear at 12 months and his left ear at 15 months of age. The following are some of the activities used to facilitate his speech perception, speech production, and language development after his CIs were activated. Nathan's intervention is considered "habilitative" because he made relatively rapid progress in listening and speech development once his CIs were activated.

Nathan received in-home, family-centered intervention services twice a week for 1 hour with his mother (see Chapters 3, 4, 5, and 6). Parent coaching began with activities to facilitate auditory detection skills. During these activities, attempts were made to minimize background noises, and Nathan was observed for reactions to sounds and his mother's voice as they were presented to him. He would usually stop vocalizing and quit what he was doing in reaction to sounds and speech. These behaviors provided the first evidence of auditory detection. His parents were encouraged to stage listening activities throughout the day with Nathan.

---

4. Contributed by Susan Sehgal, CCC-SLP, LSLS-AVEd.

Structured activities were also used to draw attention to sounds. First, Nathan's mother was taught to make a surprised look while pointing to her ear to alert him to both elicited and spontaneous sounds that occurred during sessions (i.e., a hearing response; see Chapter 7). Next, the interventionist and Nathan's mother worked together to condition him to respond to sound. This involved having Nathan's mother put a block in a bucket whenever a sound occurred and then waiting while looking expectantly for Nathan to do the same. Wait time was provided to give Nathan an opportunity to respond without a model. Nathan quickly began to associate sounds and voices with events and people in his environment. For example, Nathan would look for his father to enter the house after he heard the garage door or turn to his mother when he heard her voice.

Becoming aware of speech was a high priority during early sessions; for example, the vowels /a/, /i/, and /u/ were selected as targets because they carry substantial acoustic power, making them easier to detect. The early interventionist sat slightly behind Nathan's side in order to produce vowels without speechreading cues. His mother then sat in front of him and put a block in the bucket as each vowel was modeled. The early interventionist produced the vowel sounds with varied suprasegmental features (e.g., interrupted, like [ah-ah-ah] versus long and continuous, like [aaaaaaaah]). Nathan made relatively rapid progress in detecting environmental sounds and responding to speech.

The next stage of auditory skill development was aimed at helping Nathan learn that speech sounds and spoken words have meaning. At 15 months of age, Learning to Listen sounds (Sindrey, 2002) were introduced with objects to help Nathan connect sounds with meaning and produce a variety of vowels and consonant-vowel (CV) syllables. The Learning to Listen sounds are mostly onomatopoeia syllables that are associated with toys (e.g., *sheep* = "baaaa baaaa," *train* = "choo chooooo") but can be supplemented with words and phrases (e.g., "weeee" for objects going down, "round and round" for items that spin). The main advantages of these stimuli are that they span the spectrum of speech frequencies and have gross acoustic differences in duration, intensity, and pitch. The early interventionist first encouraged Nathan to pay attention to sounds by hiding the corresponding toy in a bag. She would then make the sound that went with the object and wait to see if Nathan imitated her production before taking it out of the bag. In this way, the relationship between speech sounds and meaning was introduced and reinforced. When Nathan's productions mirrored the model, it was clear that he perceived the stimuli. His progress was steady, although it was interesting to note that he was able to reproduce the Learning to Listen sounds well before he was able to match syllables and words to their corresponding toys.

Music was another medium that provided suprasegmental features, including rhythm, pitch, and duration. Nathan was eventually able to identify songs through listening alone. Some of the songs, like the "Wheels on the Bus," included the Learning to Listen sounds that the early interventionist had been working previously (e.g., bus = "buh buh buh," wheels = "round and round"). With continued exposure to instrumental music and song, Nathan's voice quality and prosody began to match his typically developing (TD) peers. These improvements highlight the value of including music when working with young children.

During the first year of intervention, therapy sessions also emphasized perception and production of "power" words such as *open, more, push, up*. By 30 months, Nathan's language skills approximated those of TD children ages 20 to 24 months: He had acquired approximately 150 words, was combining words (e.g., "Mommy walk," "sit chair"), and was comprehending familiar one-step commands (e.g., "Throw it in the trash") and simple questions (e.g., "Where is the kitty?"). It was clear that he was learning new words vicariously by "overhearing" words that had not purposefully been taught to him. The intelligibility and quality of his speech also showed steady improvement and became comparable to that of other 2-year-olds. The role of Nathan's parents in facilitating his growth cannot be overstated. They provided abundant spoken language models and opportunities for oral communication in everyday situations. Active parental involvement, combined with auditory-verbal intervention, enabled Nathan to optimize his auditory and spoken language development early in life.

### Case 2: Rehabilitative Intervention for a Child with Cochlear Implants and a Secondary Disability

Rebecca was born with a bilateral, profound sensorineural hearing loss and complications arising from her birth mother's addiction to cocaine. Rebecca's first intervention program focused on learning American Sign Language (see Chapter 6). However, her adoptive parents decided to pursue cochlear implantation and oral communication following limited success during a HA trial. Rebecca received a CI in her right ear at 2 years old and in her left ear at 3 years old. Soon after her first surgery, Rebecca began attending a full-day preschool where intensive auditory-oral rehabilitation was provided by a teacher of the deaf or hard of hearing (D/HH) and a speech-language pathologist (SLP) who were both certified as listening and spoken language specialists (LSLS).

Rebecca was an inconsistent user of her CI when she first began attending preschool. To overcome this situation, the importance of exposure to sounds and speech throughout the day and the value of audiological appointments were emphasized to her parents. Subsequent hearing tests revealed that, when using both CIs, Rebecca could detect sounds across the spectrum of speech frequencies (e.g., 250–8000 Hz) at 25 to 30 dB hearing loss. Thus her CIs provided substantial auditory access to speech at conversational intensity levels.

Early therapy sessions also sought to help Rebecca acquire a foundation for listening and deriving meaning from what she was hearing. Similar to Nathan's program, perception and production of the Ling six sounds, the Learning to Listen sounds, and early developing vocabulary words were mainstays of her early sessions. Because Rebecca had a tendency to talk at the same time as she was receiving a model, turn-taking was an early listening goal: It was important that she learn to actively listen to the target *prior* to repeating a model so that her auditory feedback loop and speech production accuracy could be developed.

Various auditory-verbal strategies were used to improve Rebecca's speech production skills. *Acoustic highlighting* was applied to targets during speech practice by increasing the duration, intensity, or pitch of various speech sounds (e.g., "Oh, that's an *apple. Aaaaaaple.* You have a red *apple.*"). A three-step teaching technique known as an *auditory sandwich* was also used frequently. Using this technique, speech targets were initially presented in an auditory-only condition. If Rebecca did not produce an acceptable approximation of the target, additional information (acoustic emphasis, visual support, or visual/motor cues) was provided before giving her a second try. The third model of the target was then represented in an auditory-only condition using normal intonation and prosody. These rehabilitative strategies were used across all of Rebecca's speech targets.

Using her auditory skills alone, Rebecca began to imitate vowels accurately and count the number of syllables in modeled words. Vowels such as /a/, /i/, and /u/ showed much improvement at first. Rebecca's consonant repertoire also began to emerge. Her early acquired sounds were /m/, /n/, /p/, /b/, /t/, and /d/ in word-initial position and /s/ and /ʃ/ in word-final position.

Rebecca's speech production skills were observed to improve in single words and short commonly used phrases (2–3 words) during practice. Her spontaneous speech, however, contained very few intelligible words interspersed with jargon during the first 2 years of preschool. This pattern persisted longer than expected. It was also noted that Rebecca often became "stuck" in her productions of new sentences. Articulatory groping and difficulty sequencing words in sentences were also observed. Taken together, these behaviors suggested the possibility of childhood apraxia of speech (CAS; Strand, 1995).

Several special strategies, including visual cues, were implemented in Rebecca's therapy sessions. These strategies would not typically be used for oral children who are D/HH but were added because of her CAS diagnosis. The auditory sandwich technique continued to be used along with finger-tapping cues and/or printed words to identify the number of syllables in multisyllabic words and the number of words in a sentence. Another useful technique was to chunk sentences into short phrases before presenting the entire target (e.g., "The girl is sleeping. The girl [pause] is sleeping. The girl is sleeping."). The backward chaining of syllables was also used to facilitate multisyllabic word production (e.g., "tornado, do-nay-tor, tornado"). Additional helpful strategies for children with CAS can be found in Strand (1995). Extensive practice was required before progress in speech production skills was observed.

Rebecca eventually made significant progress in her development of spoken language. She returned to her local school at age 7 and was placed in a mainstreamed classroom with support from a teacher of the D/HH and an SLP. Consultation from a LSLS specialist was provided to public school personnel to assist in this transition. At that time, she demonstrated excellent articulation skills with appropriate voice quality and prosody. Rebecca's remaining phonological and syntactical concerns appeared to be due more to her CAS than hearing, and she continued to receive speech-language services in her school.

## FUTURE DIRECTIONS

Although the widespread adoption of newborn hearing screening and early fitting of hearing instruments have created significant opportunities for auditory-guided phonological development in children who are D/HH, room for further improvement remains. In the interest of conciseness, we will highlight three areas where innovation is needed: technology, assessment, and intervention.

Advances in hearing instruments themselves are often aimed at improving children's speech perception. Improvements in perception are likely to, in turn, result in better phonological and prosodic abilities for children. For example, CI electrode arrays that represent a wider range of speech frequencies—especially low frequencies—could lead to improved pitch perception and result in prosodic patterns that more closely resemble those of TD children. At present, developments in this area are well underway. We anticipate other exciting advancements in digital HAs, CIs, and hearing assistance devices that will provide rich auditory experiences and lead to more natural patterns of phonological acquisition.

Additional norms for assessment tools are urgently needed so that children who do not make expected progress in prelinguistic and phonological development can be identified as soon as possible. Many children who are D/HH show relatively limited improvement in these areas due to secondary conditions such as autism spectrum disorders, intellectual disabilities, speech-motor disorders, and cerebral palsy (Gallaudet Research Institute, 2010). New normative studies with widely used speech perception and speech production assessment tools would help determine the degrees to which children are delayed. Ideally, these norms could be applied within the first and second year of CI or HA fitting. Early identification of secondary conditions can also assist in designing and implementing appropriate interventions as soon as possible.

Finally, innovative interventions are needed to help children fully realize natural sounding and readily intelligible speech. In particular, elements of music therapy appear to hold promise for expanding the perceptual and phonological abilities of very young children. Kanata and colleagues (Nakata, Trehub, Mitani, & Kanda, 2006) found that CI users ages 5 to 10 years had smaller pitch ranges and poorer control of pitch directionality during the singing of familiar songs. Efforts to overcome these difficulties might be more successful when musical concepts are introduced at a young age. For example, including musical instruments (e.g., xylophones, tambourines, bells) and childhood songs during family-centered intervention and preschool activities have face validity for expanding pitch range and improved control of pitch and intonation. Further, musical activities such as songs and nursery rhymes also provide motivating language stimulation and opportunities to develop and reinforce speech production skills. Of course, many treatment studies are needed to determine the efficacy of current and new intervention approaches. The fundamental quest of this research is to determine whether early identification and specialized interventions can enable children who are D/HH to achieve the phonological proficiency of their peers who have normal hearing.

## SUGGESTED READINGS

The 2014 e-book *A Resource Guide for Early Hearing Detection and Intervention* is now available and posted on the National Center for Hearing Assessment and Management web site. This guide contains up-to-date information from a wide variety of authors on every aspect of early hearing detection and intervention. Each of the 30 chapters is posted as a separate PDF, allowing the user to read online, download, or print any or all the chapters at will. The link to the most recent edition is http://www.infanthearing.org/ehdi-ebook/index.html.

Eisenberg, L.S. (2009). *Clinical management of children with cochlear implants.* San Diego, CA: Plural.

## LEARNING ACTIVITIES

1.  Visit http://www.vocaldevelopment.com to listen to the kinds of prelinguistic vocalizations that children produce prior to saying words regularly.

2. Visit http://abclocal.go.com/wls/story?section=news%2Fdisability_issues
   &id=8949135 to contrast the speech of a deaf reporter with that of a student who is D/HH and received a CI before 3 years of age. How intelligible are the two talkers? What differences do you notice in their speech?

3. Visit the resources pages of the Cochlear Implant Education Center at
   Gallaudet University for more information on spoken language assessment tools: http://www.gallaudet.edu/clerc_center/information_and
   _resources/cochlear_implant_education_center/resources/suggested
   _scales_of_development_and_assessment_tools.html.

## REFERENCES

Allal, L., & Ducrey, G. (2000). Assessment of—or in—the zone of proximal development. *Learning and Instruction 10*(2), 137–152.

Ambrose, S.E., Unflat-Berry, L., Walker, E.A., Harrison, M., Oleson, J., & Moeller, M.P. (2014). Speech sound production in two-year-olds who are hard of hearing. *American Journal of Speech-Language Pathology, 23,* 91–104.

Bauman-Waengler, J. (2016). *Articulatory and phonological impairments: A clinical focus* (5th ed.). Boston, MA: Allyn & Bacon.

Bernthal, J.E., Bankson, N.W., & Flipsen, P.P., Jr. (2013). *Articulation and phonological disorders* (7th ed.). Boston, MA: Allyn & Bacon.

Blamey, P.J., & Alcantara, J.I. (1994). Research in auditory training. *Journal of the Academy of Rehabilitative Audiology, 27*(suppl.), 161–192.

Bleile, K.M. (2013). *The late eight* (2nd ed.). Independence, KY: Cengage Learning.

Bow, C.P., Blamey, P.J., Paatsch, L.E., & Sarant, J.Z. (2004). The effects of phonological and morphological training on speech perception scores and grammatical judgments in deaf and hard-of-hearing children. *Journal of Deaf Studies and Deaf Education, 9,* 305–314.

Campbell, T., Dollaghan, C., Janosky, J., & Adelson, P.D. (2007). A performance curve for assessing change in Percentage of Consonants Correct–Revised (PCC-R). *Journal of Speech, Language, and Hearing Research, 50*(4), 1110–1119.

Cole, E.B., & Flexer, C. (2007). *Children with hearing loss: Developing listening and talking, birth to six.* San Diego, CA: Plural.

Coplan, J., & Gleason, J. (1988). Unclear speech: Recognition and significance of unin-telligible speech in preschool children. *Pediatrics, 82,* 447–452.

Elliott, L., & Katz, D. (1980). *Development of a new children's test of speech discrimina-tion.* St. Louis, MO: Auditech.

Ellis-Weismer, S., & Robertson, S. (2006). Focused stimulation approach to language intervention. In R. McCauley & M. Fey (Eds.), *Treatment of language disorders in children* (pp. 175–202). Baltimore, MD: Paul H. Brookes Publishing Co.

Erber, N.P. (1982). *Auditory training.* Washington, DC: A.G. Bell Association.

Ertmer, D.J. (2005). *The source for children with cochlear implants.* East Moline, IL: LinguiSystems.

Ertmer, D.J. (2010). Relationships between speech intelligibility and word articulation test scores in children with hearing loss. *Journal of Speech, Language, and Hearing Research, 53,* 1075–1086.

Ertmer, D.J. (2011). Assessing speech intelligibility in children with hearing loss: Toward revitalizing a valuable clinical tool. *Language Speech and Hearing Services in Schools, 42,* 52–58.

Ertmer, D.J. (2015). *The open-and closed-set task.* Durham, NC: MED-EL Corporation.

Ertmer, D.J., & Ertmer, P.A. (1998). Constructivist strategies in phonological inter-vention: Facilitating self-regulation for carryover. *Language, Speech, and Hearing Services in Schools, 29,* 67–75.

Ertmer, D.J., & Galster, J. (2002). An interactive web site for instruction in prelin-guis-tic vocal development. *Educational Technology, 42*(5), 21–23.

Ertmer, D.J., & Inniger, K. (2009). Characteristics of the transition to spoken words in two young cochlear implant recipients. *Journal of Speech, Language, and Hearing Research, 52*(6), 1579–1594.

Ertmer, D.J., & Iyer, S. (2010). Prelinguistic vocalizations in infants and toddlers with hearing loss: Identifying and stimulating auditory-guided speech development. In M. Marschark & P. Spencer (Eds.), *The Oxford University handbook of deaf studies, language, and education* (Vol. 2, pp. 360–375). New York, NY: Oxford University Press.

Ertmer, D.J., & Jung, J. (2012). Prelinguistic vocal development in young cochlear implant recipients and typically developing infants: Year 1 of robust hearing experi-ence. *Journal of Deaf Studies and Deaf Education, 17*, 116–132.

Ertmer, D.J., Jung, J., & Kloiber, D. (2013). Beginning to talk like an adult: Increases in speech-like utterances in young cochlear implant recipients and toddlers with nor-mal hearing. *American Journal of Speech-Language Pathology, 27*, 591–603.

Ertmer, D.J., Kloiber, D., Jung, J., Kirleis, K., & Bradford, D. (2012). Consonant produc-tion accuracy in young cochlear implant recipients: Developmental sound classes and word position effects. *American Journal of Speech-Language Pathology, 21*, 342–353.

Ertmer, D.J., Leonard, J.S., & Pachuilo, M.P. (2002). Communication intervention for children with cochlear implants: Two case studies. *Language, Speech, and Hearing Services in Schools, 33*, 205–217.

Ertmer, D.J., & Stoel-Gammon, C. (2008). The Conditioned Assessment of Speech Pro-duction (CASP): A tool for evaluating auditory-guided speech development in young children with hearing loss. *The Volta Review, 108*, 59–80.

Ertmer, D.J., Young, N., Grohne, K., Mellon, J., Johnson, C., Corbett, K., & Saindon, K. (2002). Vocal development in young children with cochlear implants: Assessment and implications for intervention. *Language, Speech, and Hearing Services in the Schools, 33*, 185–196.

Ertmer, D.J., Young, N.M., & Nathani, S. (2007). Profiles in vocal development in young cochlear implant recipients. *Journal of Speech, Language, and Hearing Research, 50*, 393–407.

Flipsen, P. (2011). Examining speech sound acquisition for children with cochlear implants using the GFTA-2. *The Volta Review, 111*(1), 25–37.

Fry, D. (1966). The development of the phonological system in the normal and deaf child. In F. Smith & G.A. Miller (Eds.), *The genesis of language* (pp. 187–206). Cam-bridge, MA: MIT Press.

Fryhauf-Bertschy, H., Tyler, R.S., Kelsay, D.M.R., Gantz, B.J., & Woodworth, G.G. (1997). Cochlear implant use by prelingually deafened children: The influences of age at implant and length of device use. *Journal of Speech, Language, and Hearing Research, 40*, 183–199.

Fudala, J., & Reynolds, W. (2000). *Arizona Articulation Proficiency Scale* (2nd ed.). Los Angeles, CA: Western Psychological Services.

Gallaudet Research Institute. (2010). *Regional and national summary report from the 2007–2008 annual survey of deaf and hard of hearing children and youth.* Retrieved from http:// research .gallaudet .edu/ Demographics/2008_National_Summary.pdf

Goldman, R., & Fristoe, M. (2000). *Goldman-Fristoe Test of Articulation 2.* Minneapolis, MN: Pearson Assessments.

Grunwell, P. (1981). The development of phonology: A descriptive profile. *First Lan-guage, 2*, 161–191.

Grunwell, P. (1997). Developmental phonological disability: Order in disorder. In B.W. Hodson & M.L. Edwards (Eds.) *Perspectives in applied phonology* (pp. 61–103). Gaith-ersburg, MD: Aspen.

Harrison, M., & Roush, J. (1996). Age of suspicion, identification, and intervention for infants and young children with hearing loss: A national study. *Ear and Hearing, 17*(1), 55–62.

Higgins, M.B., McCleary, E.A., Carney, A.E., & Schulte, L. (2003). Longitudinal changes in children's speech and voice physiology after cochlear implantation. *Ear and Hear-ing, 24*, 48–70.

Holt, R.F., & Kirk, K.I. (2005). Speech and language development in cognitively delayed children with cochlear implants. *Ear and Hearing, 26,* 132–148.

Ingram, D. (1976). *Phonological disability in children.* London, England: Edward Arnold.

Kirk, K.I., Pisoni, D.B., & Osberger, M.J. (1995). Lexical effects on spoken word recognition by pediatric cochlear implant users. *Ear and Hearing, 16,* 470–481.

Kloiber, D.J., & Ertmer, D.J. (2015). Can children substitute for adult listener-judges in assessments of speech intelligibility? Implications for children who are deaf or hard of hearing. *Language, Speech, and Hearing Services in the Schools, 46,* 56–63.

Koch, M. (1999). *Bringing sound to life.* Baltimore, MD: York.

Kuhl, P.K., & Meltzoff, A.N. (1996). Infant vocalizations in response to speech: Vocal imitation and developmental change. *Journal of the Acoustic Society of America, 100,* 2425–2438.

Ling, D. (1980). *Speech and the hearing-impaired child: Theory and practice.* Washington, DC: A.G. Bell Association.

Ling, D. (1988). *Foundations of spoken language for hearing-impaired children.* Washington, DC: A.G. Bell Association.

McCaffery, H.A., Davis, B.L., MacNeilage, P.F., & von Hapsburg, D. (1999). Multichannel cochlear implantation and the organization of early speech. *The Volta Review, 101,* 5–28.

Miyamoto, R., Osberger, M.J., Robbins, A., Myres, W., & Kessler, K. (1993). Prelingually deafened children's performance with the Nucleus multichannel cochlear implant. *American Journal of Otology, 14,* 437–445.

Moeller, M.P., Hoover, B., Putman, C., Arbataitis, K., Bohnenkamp, G., Wood, S., & Peterson, B. (2007a). Vocalizations of infants with hearing loss compared with infants with normal hearing: Part I—Phonetic development. *Ear and Hearing, 28*(5), 605–627.

Moeller, M.P., Hoover, B., Putman, C., Arbataitis, K., Bohnenkamp, G., Wood, S., & Peterson, B. (2007b). Vocalizations of infants with hearing loss compared with infants with normal hearing: Part II—Transition to words. *Ear and Hearing, 28*(5), 628–642.

Monsen, R.B. (1981). A usable test for the speech intelligibility of deaf talkers. *American Annals of the Deaf, 126,* 845–852.

Moog, J.S., & Geers, A.E. (1990). *Early Speech Perception Test.* Washington, DC: A.G. Bell Association.

Moore, J.A., & Bass-Ringdahl, S. (2002). Role of infant vocal development in candidacy for and efficacy of cochlear implantation. *Annals of Otology, Rhinology, and Laryngology, 111,* 52–55.

Nakata, T., Trehub, S.E., Mitani, C., & Kanda, Y. (2006). Pitch and timing in the songs of deaf children with cochlear implants. *Music Perception: An Interdisciplinary Journal, 24,* 147–154.

Nathani, S., Ertmer, D.J., & Stark, R.E. (2006). Assessing vocal development in infants and toddlers. *Clinical Linguistics and Phonetics, 20,* 351–369.

Nathani, S., Oller, D.K., & Neal, A.R. (2007). On the robustness of vocal development: An examination of infants with moderate-to-severe hearing loss and additional risk factors. *Journal of Speech, Language, and Hearing Research, 50,* 1425–44.

Nott, P., Cowan, R., Brown, P.M., & Wigglesworth, G. (2009). Early language development in children with profound hearing loss fitted with a device at a young age: Part I—the time period taken to acquire first words and first word combinations. *Ear and Hearing, 30*(5), 526–540.

Oller, D.K. (2000). *The emergence of the speech capacity.* Mahwah, NJ: Lawrence Erl-baum Associates.

Oller, D.K., & Eiler, R. (1988). The role of audition in infant babbling. *Child Development, 59,* 441–449.

Osberger, M.J. (1992). Speech intelligibility in the hearing impaired: Research and clin-ical implications. In R.D. Kent (Ed.), *Intelligibility in speech disorders* (pp. 233–265). Philadelphia, PA: John Benjamins.

Paden, E., & Brown, C.J. (1992). *Identifying early phonological needs in children with hearing impairment.* Washington, DC: A.G. Bell Association.

Peng, S., Spencer, L.J., & Tomblin, J.B. (2004). Speech intelligibility of pediatric cochlear implant recipients with seven years of device experience. *Journal of Speech, Language, and Hearing Research, 47,* 1227–1236.

Redford, M.A., & Diehl, R.L. (1999). The relative perceptual distinctiveness of initial and final consonants in CVC syllables. *Journal of the Acoustic Society of America, 106,* 1555–1565.

Robbins, A.M. (1990). Developing meaningful auditory integration in children with cochlear implants. *The Volta Review, 96,* 361–370.

Russo, N.M., Nicol, T.G., Zecker, S.G., Hayes, A.E., & Kraus, N. (2005). Auditory training improves neural timing in the human brainstem. *Behavioural Brain Research, 156,* 95–103.

Serry, T.A., & Blamey, P.J. (1999). A 4-year investigation into phonetic inventory development in young cochlear implant users. *Journal of Speech, Language, and Hearing Research, 42,* 141–154.

Shriberg, L. (1993). Four new speech and prosody-voice measures for genetics research and other studies in developmental phonological disorders. *Journal of Speech and Hearing Research, 36,* 105–140.

Shriberg, L.D., Austin, D., Lewis, B.A., McSweeney, J.L., & Wilson, D.L. (1997). The Percentage of Consonants Correct (PCC) metric: Extensions and reliability data. *Journal of Speech Language and Hearing Research, 40,* 708–722.

Sindrey, D. (2002). *Listening games for littles* (2nd ed.). London, Canada: WordPlay.

Sininger, Y.S., Martinez, A., Eisenberg, L., Christensen, E., Grimes, A., & Hu, J. (2009). Newborn hearing screening speeds diagnosis and access to intervention by 20–25 months. *Journal of the American Academy of Audiology, 20*(1), 49–57.

Smit, A.B., Hand, L., Freilinger, J.J., Bernthal, J.E., & Bird, A. (1990). The Iowa articulation norms project and its Nebraska replication. *Journal of Speech and Hearing Disorders, 55,* 779–798.

Smith, C. (1975). Residual hearing and speech production in deaf children. *Journal of Speech and Hearing Research, 18,* 795–811.

Stampe, D. (1969). *A dissertation on natural phonology.* New York, NY: Garland.

Stelmachowicz, G., Pittman, A.L., Hoover, B.M., Lewis, D.E., & Moeller, M.P. (2004). The importance of high frequency audibility in the speech and language development of children with hearing loss. *Archives of Otolaryngology Head & Neck Surgery, 130,* 556–562.

Stoel-Gammon, C. (1985). Phonetic inventories, 15–24 months: A longitudinal study. *Journal of Speech and Hearing Research, 28,* 505–512.

Stoel-Gammon, C. (1987). The phonological skills of two-year-old children. *Language, Speech, and Hearing Services in Schools, 18,* 323–329.

Stoel-Gammon, C. (1992). Prelinguistic vocal development: Measurement and predictions. In C.A. Ferguson, L. Menn, & C. Stoel-Gammon (Eds.), *Phonological development: Models, research, implications* (pp. 439–456). Timonium, MD: York Press.

Stoel-Gammon, C. (1998). The role of babbling and phonology in early linguistic development. In A.M. Wetherby, S.F. Warren, & J. Reichle (Eds.), *Communication and language intervention series, Vol. 7: Transitions in prelinguistic communication* (pp. 87–110). Baltimore, MD: Paul H. Brookes Publishing Co.

Stoel-Gammon, C. (2011). Relationships between lexical and phonological development in young children. *Journal of Child Language, 38,* 1–34.

Stoel-Gammon, C., & Dunn, C. (1985). *Normal and disordered phonology in children.* Austin, TX: Pro-Ed.

Strand, E. (1995). Treatment of motor speech disorders in children. *Seminars in Speech and Language, 16,* 126–138.

Sweetow, R., & Palmer, C.V. (2005). Efficacy of auditory training in adults: A systematic review of the evidence. *Journal of the American Academy of Audiology, 16,* 494–501.

Tobey, E.A., Geers, A.E., Brenner, C.B., Altuna, D., & Gabbert, G. (2003). Factors associated with development of speech production skills in children implanted by age five. *Ear and Hearing, 24,* 36S–45S.

Tomblin, J.B., Oleson, J.J., Ambrose, S., Walker, E., & Moeller, M.P. (2014). The influence of hearing aids on the speech and language development of children with hearing loss. *JAMA Otolaryngology—Head & Neck Surgery, 140*(5), 403–409.

Tye-Murray, N. (2015). *Foundations of aural rehabilitation* (4th ed.). Stamford, CT: Cengage Learning.

Vihman, M.M. (2014). *Phonological development: The first two years.* Chichester, UK: Wiley-Blackwell.

Vygotsky, L.S. (1978). *Mind in society: The development of higher psychological processes.* Cambridge, MA: Harvard University Press.

Wilkins, M., & Ertmer, D.J. (2002). Introducing young children who are deaf or hard of hearing to spoken language: Child's Voice, an oral school. *Language, Speech, and Hearing Services in the Schools, 33,* 197–205.

Williams, A.L. (2003). *Speech disorders: Resource guide for preschool children.* Clifton Park, NY: Singular.

Williams, A.L., McLeod, S., & McCauley, R. (2010). *Interventions for speech sound disorders in children.* Baltimore, MD: Paul H. Brookes Publishing Co.

# 9

# Supportive Early Childhood Practices and Learning Environments

Catherine Cronin Carotta

Children who are deaf or hard of hearing (D/HH), like all children, have innate potential and extraordinary promise. They can be supported in discovering their talents and actualizing their dreams if we promise to attend to their potential. What are the promises we, as educators, service providers, and families, need to make to the children we serve?

Children rely on our promise to provide them with combined recommended practices from many fields: early childhood education, early childhood special education, deaf education, and the wide variety of hearing and medical specialty fields. We support optimal outcomes when we cultivate reciprocal relationships among children, their families, and the specialists who work together to reach educational goals. We dedicate ourselves to understanding the individuality of children and their families when we listen to families' expectations and recognize children's natural inheritances. It is our intention, then, to ensure that early childhood learning environments support children's potential. We believe that it is each child's right to have these innate characteristics recognized, cultivated, and supported.

This chapter identifies the influence of early and contemporary learning theorists on today's early childhood education practices. Current approaches in early childhood education and special education will be reviewed. A **blended framework** for creating supportive early childhood environments for children who are D/HH will be presented. This blended framework is founded on **developmentally appropriate practices** (DAPs) from the National Association for the Education of Young Children (NAEYC), the National Association of

Early Childhood Specialists in State Departments of Education (NAEYCS/ SDE), the Council for Exceptional Children's Division for Early Childhood (DEC), and the speech-language-hearing specialty fields.

## THEORETICAL BASIS OF EARLY CHILDHOOD EDUCATION

There is a dearth of evidenced-based research available to advise the early childhood deaf educator, speech-language pathologist, or audiologist on the best pedagogy to be used with preschool-age children who are D/HH. However, there is a wealth of early childhood literature available that can be applied to the education of children who are D/HH.

For more than 300 years, theorists have observed, contemplated, and engaged in lively dialogue about the nature of childhood. Today's early child-hood educators continue the conversation in an effort to promote positive out -comes for young children. In fact, the early learning theorists' ideas can be seen clearly in educational settings that support all children and especially those who are D/HH. Interestingly, early intervention and early childhood special education practices have evolved from what would appear to be incompatible theoretical perspectives ranging from traditional behaviorist theories, to constructivist theories, to ecological theories (Odom & Wolery, 2003). Let's take a closer look at the blend of diverse theories evident in today's classrooms.

Educators activate the value of Maria Montessori's notions when learning is orchestrated in prepared and accessible environments (Montessori, 1967). Montessori's theories also can be seen in speech therapy and classrooms where children work using self-correcting materials (e.g., those that include feedback that guides the child to independently complete the task with minimal adult direction). Locke's individual differences theory is present as teachers differentiate instruction by modifying their teaching based on children's auditory and visual needs (Gordon & Browne, 2004). Piaget's notion that children need to learn about the world by active manipulation is evident in activities such as reaching into a partially carved pumpkins to experience "slimy seeds" (Piaget, 1970). Rousseau's ideas about children using their senses to learn is obvious when we witness what children do in sand boxes and in mud left behind after a spring shower (Rousseau, 1961). Itard's early attempts to educate a child found in a jungle using games and meaningful activities are evident in the principles of **activity-based intervention** (Pretti-Frontczak & Bricker, 2004). The Skinnerian approach is woven throughout clinical and educational settings. It is clearly visible in the audiologist's booth when the child puts a block in a bucket upon hearing a sound and is rewarded by a light shining on a dancing monkey (Skinner, 1953).

The value that Dewey placed on the daily activities of life as active and engaging ways for children to learn in meaningful educational and social contexts can be witnessed firsthand when children work together to make a xylophone (Dewey, 1976). Sharing ideas about how to build a town, recounting how a toy was broken, and cocreating classroom rules for listening are all examples of Vygotsky's theory focused on constructing and modifying our knowledge through social interactions. Educators' mindful attention to adding visual strategies or additional auditory support to promote a child's ability to understand new content is an example of Vygotsky's well-known scaffolding strategies and zone of proximal development theory (Bodrova & Leong, 2007; Vygotsky, 1987). Bronfenbrenner's ecological approach is activated when the teacher goes to the home and child care center to help the family and child care workers learn how to put on the child's hearing aids (Bronfenbrenner, 1979). When an educator stops instruction to feed the child who came to school hungry, Maslow's hierarchy of needs is being addressed (Maslow, 1970). And finally, when teachers and specialists choose not to implement a deficit-driven model of education but instead choose to focus on what the child can do and the diverse ways the child can learn and grow, the teacher is actively promoting Reggio Emilia educators', Malaguzzi's, and Rinaldi's belief that children should be viewed "as active, competent, strong, and capable of exploring and finding meaning, not as predetermined, fragile, needy, and incapable" (Rinaldi, 2012).

## CHILD DEVELOPMENT AND LEARNING PRINCIPLES

These early developmental theories permeate our current early childhood practices. The National Association for the Education of Young Children has identified 12 principles that support national standards of DAPs for young children. The principles are based on the work of theorists and researchers to guide early childhood educators with recommended practices. It should be noted that no one set of principles can fully describe the complex nature of child development and learning, and the principles presented are frequently interrelated. Knowledge of these principles is not only necessary for implementing a quality early childhood educational framework but essential, as it serves as a touchstone for guiding our understanding of children's development. Table 9.1 provides the NAEYC's child development and learning principles (Copple & Bredekamp, 2009, pp. 9–16).

## CURRICULUM FRAMEWORK

How can we construct an environment where these principles of development and learning are evident not only in one classroom but throughout all early childhood educational settings? Most early childhood specialists would agree that it is a well-designed and articulated curriculum that leads the way. While there seems to be no clear definition for the term *curriculum*, experts in the field of early childhood education would agree that the curriculum is a guide to instruction that is composed of several active functions requiring 1) a caring and rich learning environment, 2) a scope and sequence of learning content, 3) interesting and meaningful activities to explore the content, 4) specific strategies to support access to the learning interaction, and 5) engagement in ongoing assessment to determine the effectiveness of instruction (DEC, 2007).

Given the complex nature of all of the elements described, the term **curriculum framework** is proposed here to "represent the idea that a curriculum is not a single resource or feature but rather a set of concepts or a structure of classifying and organizing the many elements and processes involved when creating learning ecologies for young children" (Grisham-Brown, Hemmeter, & Pretti-Frontczak, 2005, p. 20). The term *learning ecologies* refers to environments in which children and adults coexist with relative stability and

**Table 9.1.**   National Association for the Education of Young Children principles of child development and learning

1. All the domains of development and learning—physical, social and emotional, and cognitive—are important, and they are closely interrelated. Children's development and learning in one domain influence and are influenced by what takes place in other domains.
2. Many aspects of children's learning and development follow well-documented sequences, with later abilities, skills, and knowledge building on those already acquired.
3. Development and learning proceed at varying rates from child to child, as well as at uneven rates across different areas of a child's functioning.
4. Development and learning result from a dynamic and continuous interaction of biological maturation and experience.
5. Early experiences have profound effects, both cumulative and delayed, on a child's development and learning, and optimal periods exist for certain types of development and learning to occur.
6. Development proceeds toward greater complexity, self-regulation, and symbolic or representational capacities.
7. Children develop best when they have secure, consistent relationships with responsive adults and opportunities for positive relationships with peers.
8. Development and learning occur in and are influenced by multiple social and cultural contexts.
9. Always mentally active in seeking to understand the world around them, children learn in a variety of ways; a wide range of teaching strategies and interactions are effective in supporting all these kinds of learning.
10. Play is an important vehicle for developing self-regulation as well as for promoting language, cognition, and social competence.
11. Development and learning advance when children are challenged to achieve at a level just beyond their current mastery and also when they have many opportunities to practice newly acquired skills.
12. Children's experiences shape their motivation and approaches to learning, such as persistence, initiative, and flexibility; in turn, these dispositions and behaviors affect their learning and development.

*Source:* Copple and Bredekamp (2009).

interdependence. The environments are activated, assessed, and aligned with the children's development when teachers engage in obtaining information about children's developmental level, discovering children's content strengths and gaps, seeking attunement of the teaching approach with how children learn, and watching for the children's questions, curiosities, confusions, and emerging theories.

Single resources often do not contain all the elements needed to establish a curriculum framework. For example, the NAEYC's and the DEC's guidelines for DAPs remind us of what is important and how we should work with children, but these practices should not to be seen as the entire curriculum. Further, a child's individualized education program (IEP) addresses the specific skills needed in order for the child to access the curriculum, but the IEP's goals should not be seen as the only content to be taught (Grisham-Brown et al., 2005). The Division for Early Childhood's position statement, *Promoting Positive Outcomes for Children with Disabilities: Recommendations for Curriculum, Assessment, and Program Evaluation,* emphasizes that a key component of the curriculum framework is ensuring that all children have *access to and full participation in* all learning opportunities. According to the Individuals with Disabilities Education Improvement Act (IDEA) of 2004 (PL 108-446), the principles of universal design are necessary to ensure access, participation, and progress of all learners, including those with special learning needs. The three essential principles of universal design for access to learning include providing *multiple means* of 1) *representation* to increase understanding, to address different ability levels, and to attend to auditory, visual, and kines-thetic learning styles; 2) *engagement* to arouse children's attention and moti-vation by attending to their interests and to support their learning using a variety of scaffolding strategies; and 3) *expression* to ensure children can use a variety of formats to express themselves, to demonstrate what they know, or to inform us of their preferences (DEC, 2007).

It is important that early childhood educators be well versed in these foun-dational concepts of development and learning as they partner with children and families. A variety of approaches has been developed to integrate this wide array of principles into cohesive classroom curricula well suited to support the learning strategies for exceptional child education. The activity-based inter-vention approach and the Reggio Emilia approach will be highlighted, as they have specific features that support children who are D/HH. Following a review of the activity-based intervention and Reggio Emilia approaches, additional examples of commercially available curriculum frameworks and supplemen-tary resources for children who are D/HH will be provided.

### Activity-Based Intervention

This approach capitalizes on functional skill development within natural everyday routines, transitions, and activities in classroom or home environ-ments with familiar adults and peers. "Activity-based intervention is a child-directed, transactional approach in which multiple learning opportunities are embedded into authentic activities and logically occurring antecedents and timely feedback are provided to ensure functional and generative skills are acquired and used by children" (Pretti-Frontczak & Bricker, 2004, p. 11). For a child who has a language goal of using three-word phrases, the educator may target this goal through natural activities, such as opening circle role call (e.g., "I am here"), snack time (e.g., "We need milk"), playtime (e.g., "You play house"), or transition time (e.g., "Time to swing").

Pretti-Frontczak and Bricker (2004) reviewed their first-generation stud-ies examining the effects of activity-based intervention and concluded that long-term effects of activity-based intervention have not been determined due to a number of factors, including limited resources and difficulties with design-ing studies that have sufficient scientific control while accommodating the re-ality of conducting research within educational settings. Their early stud-ies revealed improvements in children's test scores following activity-based in-tervention. Subsequent studies comparing the activity-based approach with a direct teaching approach revealed more vocabulary learning in the direct teaching approach, but generalization of vocabulary items was greater in the activity-based approach. While it is acknowledged that a second set of research is needed to determine the effects of specific features of the approach, Pretti-Frontczak and Bricker conclude that the "implementation of the elements of activity-based intervention by well-prepared interventionists produces consis-tent positive change in children" (Pretti-Frontczak & Bricker, 2004, p. 218).

The activity-based intervention approach is widely used and is particu-larly useful when working with children who are developing listening, speech, and language skills, as this approach is activated within natural learning contexts rather than adult-directed therapy or teaching models that lack nat-ural contexts. The skills children learn are relevant to their lives, and there are numerous opportunities for practicing and generalizing. There is limited need for specific training on the generalization of skills, as the training occurs within the environment in which it is to be used. Further, the assessment of a child's acquisition of a skill can be conducted within the natural context in which the skill is used. Because this approach does not contain learning con-tent or suggested instructional strategies specific to D/HH education, educa-tors must have a strong understanding of child development and knowledge of DAPs. The intervention section of this chapter provides multiple examples of embedded learning using this approach.

### Reggio Emilia Approach

The Reggio Emilia approach subscribes to social constructivism theory and fosters partnerships between children and the educator, who engage in "nego-tiated learning" (Edwards, Gandini, & Forman, 2012). The approach often uses projects to explore areas of in-depth study based on children's interests, focus-ing attention on the discourse of learning, and documentation of the learning process using photographs, audio recordings, notes, and the children's work samples. As educators document and engage in discourse with the children about their work, they shift from their role of teaching children to studying children and hence learning alongside them. Included in the Reggio Emilia ap-proach is a public display of the children's work, which extends the dis-course to children communicating with other children, children engaging with teach-ers, teachers reflecting with other teachers, and families communicating with children and teachers about their children's work. "The curriculum is not child-centered or teacher-directed. The curriculum is child-originated and teacher-framed" (Forman & Fyfe, 2012, p. 248).

This approach is particularly supportive of children who are D/HH with developing language skills, as it promotes the use of a variety of means to communicate using the **hundred languages**, a term coined by Reggio Emilia founder, Loris Malaguzzi, which refers to children using a variety of mediums (e.g., cloth, textiles, paint, wire, clay, wood, music, dance, photography) to rep-resent their ideas about their world. In essence, the approach explores the ways these media become a visual, aesthetic, and kinesthetic sketchpad or canvas representing children's feelings, thinking, and creating. When this approach is used with children who are D/HH, it provides multiple opportunities for educators to honor children's internal conceptualizations while promoting the emergence of spoken or sign language. The type of learning path explored is a negotiated process between the child and teacher. "In negotiated learning, it is essential for teachers to listen with the third ear, to hear the implied meanings of children's words," or representations (Forman & Fyfe, 2012, p. 249). This is particularly important for young developing communicators. When we truly listen to what children are trying to tell us, we are positioned to better under-stand what they already know and we are situated to negotiate and scaffold their future language learning. Further details on the use of this approach with children who are D/HH can be found in Edwards and Carotta (2015).

## Commercial Curriculum Frameworks

Commercially available curriculum frameworks, in varying degrees, provide educators with a scope and sequence of developmental behaviors, suggestions for creating the educational environment, instructional strategies, parent education materials, and curriculum-embedded assessment. It is important to remember that children who are D/HH may require a blend of approaches, including child initiated and teacher led, in order to acquire necessary skills. In other words, relying completely on embedded learning opportunities without intensive teacher-directed training on specific listening skills or relying on intensive teacher-directed listening skills without attending to purposefully embedding skills into the natural environment may not produce the outcomes desired. Table 9.2 includes examples of curricular frameworks providing components recommended by NAEYC and DEC (left column) and curricular resources that include a scope and sequence of discrete auditory, speech, and language skills that may be necessary for children who are D/HH (right column).

In summary, learning theorists, early child educators, early childhood special education educators, and speech and hearing specialists offer numerous ways of designing rich learning environments. Educators may wish to select from the following specific components in order to create a balanced and blended curriculum framework for children who are D/HH:

1.  Provide children with educational materials that support independence in solving problems, rather than solely using approaches requiring children to be reliant on adult feedback.

2.  Encourage children to follow High/Scope Curriculum's Plan-Do-Recall process (Hohmann & Weikart, 1995), including discussing their work or play intentions, following through with what they have planned, and recalling their activities to promote initiative, organization, persistence, recall, and oral narrative abilities.

3.  Use an activity-based intervention approach to learning, as it embeds development and assessment of functional skills into daily routines, transitions, and activities across a range of natural settings and individuals to support generalization.

**Table 9.2.**   Commercial curricular frameworks for use with preschoolers

| Selected early childhood curricular frameworks | Supplemental resources about the deaf or hard of hearing |
|---|---|
| 1. *Assessment, Evaluation, and Programming System for Infants and Children,* 2nd edition (Bricker & Waddel, 2002) | 1. *Children with Hearing Loss: Developing Listening and Talking, Birth to Six* (Cole & Flexer, 2007) |
| 2. *Carolina Curriculum for Preschoolers with Special Needs,* 2nd edition (Johnson-Martin, Attermeier, & Hacker, 2004) | 2. *Cottage Acquisition Scales for Listening, Language, and Speech* (Wilkes, 1999) |
| 3. *Hawaii Early Learning Profile* (Holt, Gilles, Holt, & Davids, 2004) | 3. *Learn to Talk Around the Clock* (Rossi, 2003) |
| 4. *HighScope Curriculum* (Hohmann & Weikart, 1995) | 4. *101 FAQs About Auditory-Verbal Practice* (Esterbrooks, 2012) |
| 5. *The Creative Curriculum for Preschool,* 5th edition (Dodge, Colker, Heroman, & Bickart, 2010) | 5. *SKI-HI Curriculum* (Watkins, Taylor, & Pittman, 2004) |
| | 6. *The Speech Instructional Curriculum and Evaluation* (Moog, Bildenstein, & Davidson, 1995) |

4    Incorporate the Reggio project-based approach, as it engages children in areas of extended study about their areas of interest, encourages mean-ingful discourse, promotes active listening, and activates negotiated learning, an approach that is particularly well suited for children who are D/HH because it provides **multiple means of representation**, engagement, and **expression**.

5.   Expand early childhood curriculum frameworks with specialized resources designed to develop discrete auditory, speech, and language skills in children who are D/HH.

## ASSESSMENT

Assessment is key to ensuring that learning expectations for children are met. Comprehensive discussion regarding assessment for children who are D/HH is beyond the scope of this chapter. Suffice it to say, there are numerous factors to consider when assessing young children. A comprehensive framework for assessing children who are D/HH can be found in the *Auditory Consultant Resource Network Handbook* (Carotta, Cline, & Brennan, 2014). This section will review developmentally appropriate assessment principles and practices. In addition, two components of a student assessment framework from Carotta and colleagues (2014) will be introduced: the SCALES model for obtaining a holistic view of children and the Communication Performance Summary,  a guide to assist families and professionals in determining how children who are D/HH best understand information and expressively communicate.

Let's consider the essential components of appropriate assessments for young children. According to Bagnato and Neisworth, early childhood assess-ment should be a "flexible, collaborative decision-making process in which teams of parents and professionals repeatedly revise their judgments and reach consensus about the changing developmental, educational, medical, and mental health service needs of young children and their families" (Bag-nato & Neisworth, 1991, p. xi).

Early childhood assessment experts have proposed the following principles and practices to guide the process (Bagnato, Neisworth, & Pretti-Frontczak, 2010; DEC, 2007; Grisham-Brown et al., 2011; Losardo & Notari Syverson, 2011; NAEYC & NAECS/SDE, 2003; Sandall, Hemmeter, Smith, & McLean, 2005):

1.   Focus on identifying strengths and needs using a child- and family-cen-tered approach.

2.   Include families at multiple levels as equal and contributing partners.

3.   Individualize assessments to the child and family.

4.   Select tools and procedures that take into account children's develop-mental status across all domains.

5.   Consider how specific sensory, motor, and temperament factors may affect performance.

6.   Determine visual, auditory, tactile, processing, and expression charac-teristics that may affect ability to access or demonstrate knowledge.

7. Identify the child's and family's primary language or communication method.

8. Use a multimodal model including formal and informal tools to provide a holistic view of children.

9. Blend a variety of assessment approaches including norm-referenced, criterion-referenced, routine- and activity-based, curriculum-based, portfolio, documentation, dynamic, and classroom-based processes.

Now let's consider two specific tools that can be used to design assessments and ensure appropriate access for children who are D/HH.

### SCALES Model: Social-Emotional, Cognition-Curriculum, Auditory, Language, Extra, Speech

The SCALES model is a tool that is designed to obtain a holistic picture of the child by engaging the family or professional team in a conversation about how they view the child's development across broad developmental domains or areas (Carotta et al., 2014; Tyler Krings & Robinson, 2011). The model serves as a guide to assist families, educators, and assessment specialists with defining and prioritizing assessment and intervention needs. It can be used as part of the intake interview with a family to obtain a profile of the child's notable strengths, areas of typical development, and concerns about learning. The child's SCALES profile can support assessment specialists in determining the specific domains that need to be explored further and can assist specialists in determining which particular assessment methods or measures should be used to examine the learning concerns. For an extensive list of tests that address each of the developmental domains, see Carotta et al. (2014). For an example of the SCALES model as a preassessment interview, see Video clip 9.1.

The SCALES model can also be used by the mainstream teacher or deaf educator who may have difficulty pinpointing the exact nature of a child's abilities. Exploration of the child's performance in the various domains includes inquiry into how the child performs in daily routines and activities occurring across multiple individuals and settings (i.e., home, school, child care, community). The developmental domains in the SCALES model include the following:

*S = Social-emotional:* Play skills, emotion expression, emotion regulation, social interaction, empathy, independence, positive self-image, cooperation, and temperament

*C = Cognition and/or curriculum:* Thinking, problem solving, representation, reasoning, and emerging writing, reading, and math skills

*A = Auditory:* Detection, discrimination, identification, and comprehension and listening skills

*L = Expressive and receptive language:* Vocabulary/basic concepts, sentence length and complexity of language, functional use of language, understanding language, conversation skills, and storytelling

*E = Extra areas:* Executive function (focus, attention, memory, organization, shift, regulation) and fine motor, gross motor, vision, and sensory functioning

*S = Speech:* Oral motor functioning, vocal production, articulation, and intelligibility

An example of the SCALES model for a preschool child who is deaf can be found in Figure 9.1.

## Communication Performance Summary

All children, regardless of their hearing capacity, have individual ways of understanding and expressing themselves. The manner in which children who are D/HH express and comprehend language depends on numerous factors, including but not limited to the following:

1. Their hearing, biological, and neurological characteristics

2. Their families' values for sign language or spoken language

3. The presence of other developmental delays

| S Social-emotional | C Cognitive | A Auditory | L Language | E Extra | S Speech |
|---|---|---|---|---|---|

| Skill area | Strength | Typical | Questions/concerns | Comments, questions, routines |
|---|---|---|---|---|
| Social-emotional | | | X | Play skills typical; frustration with communication/behavior |
| Cognitive/curriculum | | X | | Typical for non-language–related expectations |
| Auditory | | | X | Developing awareness of 1/2 syllables |
| Language | | | X | 1–2 sign/word language attempts |
| Extra | | | | |
| * Executive function | | | | |
| o Attention | X | | | |
| o Memory | | X | | |
| o Organization | | X | | |
| o Shift | | | X | Difficulty shifting attention to nonpreferred tasks |
| o Regulation | | X | | |
| * Fine motor | | X | | |
| * Gross motor | | X | | |
| * Vision | | X | | |
| * Sensory | | X | | |
| * Oral-motor: Feeding | | X | | |
| Speech | | | | |
| o Oral motor | | X | | |
| o Articulation | | | X | Developing production of vowels and consonants in words |
| o Intelligibility | | | X | |

**Figure 9.1.** Completed SCALES profile on a child with cochlear implant. (Adapted from Carotta, Koch-Cline, and Brennan, 2014, with additions from Tyler, Krings, and Robinson, 2011.)

4. Their level of auditory access

5. Their use of hearing technology

6. Their level of visual access

7. Their level of cognitive functioning

8. Their oral motor function for production of speech

9. Their motor skills for production of sign language

Children who are D/HH use a variety of means to communicate. Many of today's children who are D/HH use spoken language to communicate, whereas others use a combination of approaches. Some may be bilingual English and Spanish spoken language users. Others may be bilingual, using American Sign Language (ASL) with their friends who are D/HH and spoken language with their friends who can hear. Still others may be monolingual language users, using sign, spoken language, or picture symbols only. In addition, some children blend approaches, using spoken language with some sign support, or sign with some spoken language, or picture symbols with some sign language. It is important for the family to assist professionals in identifying how the child is currently communicating and how they hope their child will communicate in the future (see Chapters 5 and 6 for further discussion).

The Communication Performance Summary (see Figure 9.2) is a conversational interview tool used by families and educators to discuss children's current communication performance and families' goals for future performance. Children who are D/HH and their families may elect to use a variety of approaches to promote language development. The approaches range from primarily auditory and auditory plus visual to primarily visual (auditory to visual continuum, AV). The Communication Performance Summary integrates the view of representing current performance and change over time using a continuum approach. It is a tool that is intended to ensure the universal design principles for promoting use of multiple means of representation, engagement, and expression for children who are D/HH. The tool can be used to assist the families and educators in considering the best communication approach(es) for engaging and educating individual children. For example, if a child's family and educator view the child's performance to be on the auditory and spoken language end of the continuum (A), the child most likely will benefit from instruction presented using spoken language. Or, if the family and educator view the child's performance to be in the middle of the continuum (AV), the child most likely will benefit from instruction presented using spoken language and sign language or spoken language and the written word. And finally, if the family and educator view the child's performance to be on the visual end of the continuum (V), the child most likely will benefit from instruction presented using a visual language (e.g., ASL). It is important to note that visual information can be derived from print, speechreading, or sign language.

Multiple observations and assessments are used to determine where to place the child's current performance on a continuum in four areas: 1) receptive communication or language understanding (auditory to visual [e.g., print,

**Receptive communication: Understanding of language**

| Auditory | Av | AV | Va | Visual |
|---|---|---|---|---|
| Primarily uses auditory input | Mostly uses auditory input with some visual support | Equal use of auditory and visual input | Mostly uses visual input with some auditory awareness | Primarily uses visual input (print, speechreading, sign) |

Adapted from McConkey Robbins (2001); Nussbaum, Scott, Waddy-Smith, & Koch (2004).

**Expressive communication: Use of language**

| Oral | Ov | OV | Vo | Visual |
|---|---|---|---|---|
| Primarily uses oral communication | Mostly uses oral expression with some visual expression | Equal use of oral expression and visual expression | Mostly uses visual expression with some oral expression | Primarily uses visual expression (print, signs, gestures) |

Adapted from Waddy-Smith (2004).

**Expressive communication: Use of speech**

| Words | Wv | WV | Vw | Vocalizations |
|---|---|---|---|---|
| Primarily uses word productions | Mostly uses word productions with some vocalizations | Equal use of words/vocalizations | Mostly uses vocalizations with some word productions | Primarily uses vocalizations |

Adapted from Carotta, Koch Cline, & Brennan (2014).

**Supplemental continuum: Alternative expressive communication approaches**

| Pictures/Sign | P/S/g | P/S/G | G/p/s | Gestures |
|---|---|---|---|---|
| Primarily uses pictures or signs; more formal system | Mostly uses pictures/signs with some gestures | Equal use of pictures/signs and gestures | Mostly uses gestures with some pictures/signs | Primarily uses gestures; less formal system |

**Figure 9.2.**   Communication performance summary. (Adapted from Carotta, Koch, Cline, and Brennan, 2014.)

speechreading, sign language]), 2) expressive language use (oral to visual [e.g., print, sign language, gesture]), 3) expressive communication using speech and vocalizations (words to vocalizations), and 4) use of visual communication (picture/sign to gesture). This continuum is optional and reserved primarily for children who have additional developmental delays that may require the use of alternative or picture communication systems.

Integral to use of the continuum tool is the establishment of intervention goals that will either support the child's movement on the continuum or promote the stronger use of a particular approach. When a family identifies a priority for a child who does not have auditory access to establish a stronger visual language, the parents and educators work together to design multiple learning and social opportunities for the child to experience visual language. In this case, the goal is not for the child to move on the continuum but rather to strengthen the child's visual skills. If the family identifies a preference for the child to rely less on visual information by developing auditory skills, the family and educator work to create goals that will focus on movement on the continuum by providing intervention that will support the development of auditory and spoken language skills. While discussion of approaches to develop visual or spoken language are beyond the scope of this chapter, it is paramount that educators know that a high level of specialized expertise and training is needed to ensure optimal outcomes for children, regardless of the approach selected. See Video clip 9.2 for a discussion of the family auditory-visual continuum.

## INTERVENTION

The initial assessment results support the establishment of an intervention plan that is based on the child's strengths and needs and family priorities. The intervention plan for a given child or family may be implemented in a variety of settings. The range of options includes enrollment in individual listening and language sessions, enrollment in a mainstream preschool program, or enrollment in a specialized preschool program for children who are D/HH. A framework will be introduced here that can help guide professionals and families in designing the best program for the child, regardless of the placement.

The developmentally appropriate practices (DAP) framework for children who are D/HH is represented in Figure 9.3 (Carotta et al., 2014). The framework embraces developing strong family partnerships, maintaining a holistic view of children, attending to children's individual auditory-visual access needs, and conducting assessment and monitoring practices to ensure optimal outcomes for children. Children's developmental learning domains are addressed using the SCALES model. Children's preferences for accessing auditory and visual information are addressed using the Communication Performance Summary. The DAP framework is based on four fundamental principles:

1.  The learning environment affects the quality and nature of opportunities offered to children.

2.  Caring interactions create an emotional climate that promotes development and well-being.

3.  Multiple instructional formats provide an individualized approach to active learning.

4.  Communication is foundational to human development and learning interactions.

A discussion of the physical learning environment, emotional climate, communication support, and instructional learning formats recommended for children who are D/HH with specific suggestions for incorporating practices using the SCALES model during activity-based instruction follows.

### Physical Learning Environment

The provision of meaningful learning environments is a fundamental principle of early childhood educators and represents the manner in which they wish to partner with young children and their families. An environment prepared with the intention of respecting the unique nature of childhood sends messages to the community, the families, and most importantly, the children themselves about children's right to inhabit spaces that support their growth and development (Gandini, 2012). One of the more significant dialogues about

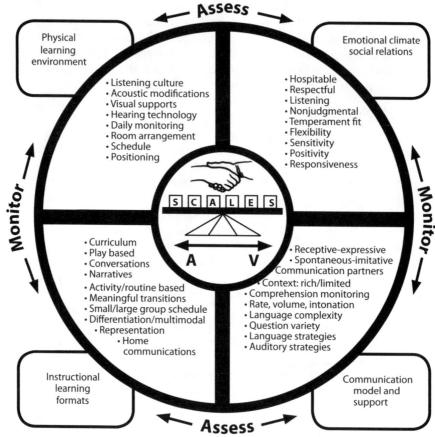

**Figure 9.3.** Developmentally appropriate practices framework.

the physical environment comes from the Reggio experience, specifically from Loris Malaguzzi, who referred to the environment as "the third teacher" (Gandini, 2012).

The notion that the environment is the third teacher is a powerful one. Educational spaces invite educators and students alike to discover what we value about each other and how we want to be with one another. Educational environments are places where children, with adults by their side, encounter experiences that provoke a sense of wonder and a need to explain life in meaningful ways, often in simple daily occurrences. Children's explorations take time and the willingness of adults to support children's need to *abide* by dawdling with what strikes their fancy and *venture* by getting carried away in leftover rain puddles. Environments for children cannot be too beautiful, too hospitable, or too accessible to young developing minds. And by their nature, these environments welcome questions, invite exploration, stimulate curiosity, and encourage discovery.

Designing learning environments for young children takes time, care, and thoughtfulness. Because all children bring unique dispositions, contributions, and special considerations into the educational spaces, they deserve a learning community that is committed to *fully* supporting who they are. That means creating opportunities to support not only their social-emotional, cognitive, adaptive, speech, language, and auditory dispositions but also their spiritual dispositions. Most recently, educators have proposed that spending time in natural outdoor environments promotes children's spiritual development—that is, a sense of belonging, a respect for self and others, and an awareness and appreciation of the unknown (Baumgartner & Buchanan, 2010; Schein, 2014). Providing quiet spaces for those who enjoy solitude, cozy spaces fit for two whisperers, open outdoor spaces for running with the wind, and window spaces for dancing with shadows supports individual dispositions and provides natural opportunities for children to explore the essence of life (Rinaldi, 2006).

Early childhood environments, designed to include both large group spaces for class discussions and smaller spaces supporting quiet interactions between a teacher and child, promote communication exchanges, relationship formation, and social constructivism. Educational spaces should be reassuring and predictable and yet flexible and modifiable in response to children's changing development. Provision of multiple sensorial experiences and materials that encourage exploration can lead children to make cognitive connections. Attention to the visual, tactile, olfactory, and auditory elements is essential in providing a stimulating environment for all children.

Special considerations are needed for children who are D/HH in order to provide them with the best listening, looking, learning, and loving environments. Even children with minimal/mild hearing loss experience greater difficulties understanding speech in unfavorable listening conditions than their peers with typical hearing (Bess, Dodd-Murphy, & Parker, 1998). Children who are D/HH may have difficulty following conversations, understanding speech from a distance, or overhearing casual comments. They may be distracted by noises within the room, in adjoining areas, or outside the classroom. According to the American National Standards Institute (ANSI, 2010), many classrooms fail to meet classroom standards for an auditory environment that is controlled for noise and reverberation (Knecht et al., 2002). As a result, many classrooms have a less-than-optimal environment for listening and learning. Specific acoustical modifications should be implemented to address distance, noise, and reverberation issues in classrooms (Crandell & Smaldino, 2005; see also Chapter 14). And most importantly, educators need to establish daily habits dedicated to ensuring that the highest quality auditory and visual learning environment is available for all children, but most specifically for children who are D/HH, so they have access to the auditory and visual information needed for their overall growth and development. The following auditory, visual, learning, and caring considerations may be helpful in preparing environments for children who are D/HH:

1. Establish a listening culture by maintaining classroom conversational guidelines for turn-taking and listening while another person communicates.

2. Attend to the acoustic environment by decreasing the distance between talkers and listeners during classroom activities. This will enhance the overall level of the talker's voice for the listener and reduce the effects

of noise and reverberation. Modify the acoustic environment by adding acoustic wall panels, ceiling tiles, or carpets to reduce the level of reverberation in the room.

3.  Provide the visual supports needed to supplement auditory information and minimize the effect of glare from lights or the sun. Establish a visual cue to signal when the class needs to listen, and ensure access to the speaker's face. Arrange the classroom with low barriers or transparent dividers so the children have visual access across the environment. (e.g., open bookshelves or see-through fabrics to divide the room).

4.  Utilize children's personal hearing devices (e.g., cochlear implants, hearing aids), hearing assistive technology (HAT), and classroom audio distribution systems (CAD).

5.  Institute daily monitoring practices for comprehensive device and listening checks (see Video clip 9.3).

6.  When arranging areas in the room, be mindful of how quiet activities may be situated next to other quiet areas (e.g., book reading situated next to fine motor or puzzle play).

7.  Create classroom schedules that take into account interfering noise in adjoining rooms (e.g., music activities scheduled when the classroom next door is outside playing).

8.  Position children away from interfering noises such as a fan or noisy hallway.

Children who are D/HH require specific learning opportunities focused on developing their listening skills and on understanding how the visual and auditory environment can support or interfere with their learning. Video clip 9.4 demonstrates how a teacher establishes a listening culture by addressing the use of appropriate speech volume. Table 9.3 provides intervention practices related to effective physical learning environments situated in the SCALES model.

### Emotional Climates and Social-Emotional Relationships

Designing a developmentally appropriate physical environment goes hand in hand with establishing an emotional climate for learning. An aesthetically beautiful and well-organized environment without a caring and engaging emotional climate will not support the child. Positive educational climates are established when there is a thoughtful and balanced approach to deciding *where* we will learn, *what* we will learn, and most importantly, *how* we will learn together.

The development of prosocial and social reasoning skills is foundational to young children's social-emotional competence and to their ability to establish relationships. Listening to others' perspectives, learning to share thoughts, persevering when problems arise, understanding emotions, and interpreting others' mental states are skills that affect all the developmental domains and are needed in order for children to fully benefit from learning.

**Table 9.3.** SCALES model: Physical learning environment practices

| | Skills: Auditory awareness, problem-solving, self-advocacy, self-regulation, and shift | | | | |
|---|---|---|---|---|---|
| S = Social-emotional | C = Cognitive | A = Auditory | L = Language | E = Extra | S = Speech |
| Encourage the child to identify when the environment is not supportive of their listening and thinking. For example, if block play becomes too loud, ask the children to listen, commenting on how hard it is to understand anything with all the noise. When it is very quiet, ask the children to listen, commenting on how easy it may be to think when things are quiet. | Incorporate listening comprehension and basic concepts into listening checks and routine classroom directions. For example, during listening checks with children working on auditory comprehension, give a direction such as "Tell Sally it's her turn for listening checks" or "Tell Joe to put the bell in the closet." | Engage children in discussing the types of classroom toys (e.g., quiet puzzles and books versus loud wind-up toys and blocks). Recruit the children's assistance in exploring ways to manage the use of toys that make noise (e.g., play with blocks on a carpet instead of on hard surfaces). | Establish routine language phrases or scripts that support children's ability to express their auditory needs (e.g., "I can't hear you," "It's too noisy," or "Please be quiet"). | To encourage self-regulation and shift to new activities, use timers or musical instruments as a way to notify children when an activity is finished. | Create self-advocacy scripts that have the children's targeted speech sounds. For example, for a child working on producing the /s/, /sh/, and /z/ sounds, practice the following scripts throughout the classroom day: "Say that again," "Please say it louder," "Please slow down," "Sh-sh, we should be listening," "Please let me see," or "Show me." |

How do we create positive emotional and social environments as we partner with young children? Early childhood, human development, and relationship-based practices provide educators with a variety of dispositions that will assist in creating supportive emotional climates. Caring and trusting relationships can be established and maintained when educators model these prosocial dispositions during experiences in the classroom by extending *hospitality* to multiple forms of expression and engagement, offering *appreciation* for varied perspectives and ideas, engaging in *respectful and nonjudgmental listening* to all members of the community, exercising *flexibility* and *sensitivity* to different temperaments and perspectives, practicing *positivity,* and demonstrating *responsiveness* (Barrera & Kramer, 2009; Ensher & Clark, 2011; Kristal, 2005). Research in the area of teacher–child relationships has indicated that positive relationships with adults support social development and academic success (Rudasill & Rimm-Kaufman, 2009). Furthermore, neuroscience research shows that relationships can affect the physical structure of the brain, as nurturing and positive interactions release chemicals that promote brain development (Eliot, 1999). Understanding the nature of teacher–child relationships requires knowledge and appreciation of attachment theory and how temperament affects interactions (Howes & Ritchie, 2002; Kristal, 2005). Howes (1999) found that children who have secure attachment with their caregivers form positive relationships with their teachers and peers. Close relationships between teachers and children promote prosocial development that facilitates children forming relationships with peers and being part of a group (Palermo, Hanish, Martin, Fabes, & Reiser, 2007). The modeling of prosocial dispositions is especially important for children who are D/HH who may have communication delays that can affect their social-emotional competency, social reasoning,  and their general sense of belonging. See Video clip 9.5 for a demonstration of practices supporting emotional climate and peer relationships. The list below describes components of a strong emotional climate.

1.  Nurturing responsiveness is demonstrated in all interactions.

2.  Hospitality is extended through multiple forms of expression and engagement.

3.  Appreciation is shown for new ideas and multiple perspectives.

4.  Respectful and nonjudgmental listening is practiced.

5.  Positivity is exhibited for each child and family's needs and interests.

6.  Sensitivity is demonstrated for children's temperaments and dispositions.

7.  Flexibility is present in shared decision making.

Table 9.4 provides intervention practices related to creating emotional climates and supporting social relationships situated in the SCALES model.

## Instructional Learning Formats

A variety of instructional learning formats should be used to maximize the children's interests, level of engagement, and functionality of skills (Pianta et

**Table 9.4.** SCALES model: Emotional climate and social relationship practices

| | Skills: Emotion awareness, emotion vocabulary, mental state, emotion sequences, initiation, and prosocial dispositions | | | | |
|---|---|---|---|---|---|
| S = Social-emotional | C = Cognitive | A = Auditory | L = Language | E = Extra | S = Speech |
| Increase individual and group awareness of feelings by assigning one child to be the "Feelings Namer." The "Feelings Namer" is then responsible for identifying the various feelings present throughout the day. | Incorporate problem solving and model mental state language as opportunities arise in daily routines. For example, after outdoor play, say, "I'm excited, I know I need to calm down," or, during arrival times, say, "You look sad, I think you may miss your mommy; Remember you will see your mom after school." | Incorporate a conversational approach into daily listening checks and demonstrate genuine care about how you or the children feel at the start of the day. For example, before or after the listening check, incorporate conversation about how you feel and then ask how the children feel. | Highlight one specific emotion during the week. Take pictures and put them in a classroom book. Create a language script that connects the reason to the emotion (e.g., "Casey is proud because he finished his puzzle," or "Miranda is worried because her friend is hurt."). | Document emotional sequences in pictures (e.g., "Here you are thinking about how to design your cake ... Now you are excited because you discovered that you could make the cake stand up better when you used tooth picks ... When the cake fell down, you became really frustrated."). | Model and set up situations where the child can use a range of intonation, loudness, and rate patterns associated with feelings and functional problems (e.g., "We're late; let's hurry!"; "I'm sooooo tired."; "WOW! That surprised me!"). |

al., 2008). Figure 9.3 provides a summary of the recommended practices for ensuring a variety of instructional formats. Early childhood research and recommended practices literature acknowledge the importance of children's play, conversations, and storytelling experiences for the development of cognition, representational thought, social reasoning, and overall language competency. Through the use of play experiences, conversations, and storytelling, adults can learn what children know about their world. Specifically, play is deemed by early childhood experts as a right of young children and serves as an important vehicle for learning about the inner life of children as they engage with the physical world (Sheridan, Foley, & Radlinski, 1995). Partnering with children in conversations about their play and the events of their lives provides opportunities for children to exchange ideas, talk about the here and now as well as the past, demonstrate and formulate a sequence of events, and describe causally related events (Spencer & Slocum, 2010).

Effective ways to naturally incorporate play, conversation, and narrative development as well as other developmental skills through activity-based or routine-based approaches are well documented (McWilliam & Casey, 2008; Pretti-Frontczak & Bricker, 2004). Intentionally planning opportunities for children to talk to one another during opening circle or recalling their day at the closing circle ensures that functional oral narrative and conversational skills will be integrated into the classroom. The use of transition times to practice following directions with basic concepts ensures the purposeful use of transition times while building preschool concepts. Providing small group instruction opportunities reduces teacher–child ratios and supports teachers' abilities to provide highly differentiated speech, language, and listening instruction. Video clip 9.6 demonstrates use of the activity-based learning format for developing speech-language skills. Inviting children to explore a variety of ways to represent what they know and how they view their world by using different media supports children's development of representational thought (Edwards, Gandini, & Forman, 2012). This approach enables educators to acknowledge and respect children's internal conceptualizations, especially when linguistic abilities are limited. Documenting children's wonderings, explorations, and discoveries in daily communication notebooks and formal displays serves the purpose of making children's learning visible and accessible to all children, families, and educators. Video clip 9.7 demonstrates use of the Reggio Emilia project approach with peer supported communication. The presence of the following components ensures the use of a range of learning formats:

1.  The preschool program follows an identified curriculum framework.

2.  A range of activities is provided that supports sociodramatic play, reading, writing, math, science, social studies, art, and music development.

3.  Opportunities are provided for children to engage in conversations and storytelling.

4.  The daily schedule includes time for small differentiated instruction supporting speech, language, and listening skill development.

5. Social-emotional, cognitive, auditory, language, and speech instruction is embedded into functional activities, routines, and transitions.

6. Instruction is provided using a variety of visual, auditory, tactile, and kinesthetic strategies.

7. Opportunities are provided for the children to represent their ideas using a range of mediums.

8. Communication mechanisms are in place to inform families and children about daily activities and learning.

Table 9.5 provides intervention practices utilizing a variety of learning formats situated in the SCALES model.

## COMMUNICATION SUPPORT

Developing communication competence is essential in establishing interpersonal and learning connections. Preschool children who are D/HH often need specialized and intensive approaches to ensure that they develop effective communication. From the human development perspective, environments can support children's sense of agency and communication competence by providing them with opportunities to reveal who they are, express what they like or dislike, explain why they feel the way they feel, or demonstrate how they wish to learn. From an educational perspective, we know that home and early childhood environments supporting children's language abilities during the early years are creating an important foundation for later reading and academic achievement (Mashburn, Justice, Downer, & Pianta, 2009; Storch & Whitehurst, 2002).

All children in early childhood environments display an emerging sense of who they are as they develop linguistic competence. However, children who are D/HH may arrive in preschool settings with emergent or delayed social, emotional, and linguistic abilities. While it might be easy to assume that those children are delayed in language acquisition due to hearing loss alone, we know that multiple factors contribute to language competency, including degree of hearing loss, age of identification, enrollment in early intervention, age of access to audition through use of hearing technology, or age of access to visual language. We also know that all children's development of language and social skills is related in part to the cultural, socioeconomic, and linguistic environments in which they grow and learn (Hoff, 2006). Extensive research over the years has revealed that the quality and quantity of parental responsiveness, teacher linguistic input, and peer interactions can have an impact on language development and use (see Hoff, 2006, for a summary).

When children move from the home into early childhood environments, educators' use of particular strategies, specific levels of support, and small group instruction plays an important role in facilitating language development (Connor, Morrison, & Slominski, 2006; Girolametto & Weitzman, 2002; Justice, Mashburn, Pence, & Wiggins, 2008). For instance, educators' use of child-oriented strategies (e.g., wait and listen, follow the children's lead, engage face to face), interaction-promoting strategies (e.g., use a variety of questions,

**Table 9.5.** SCALES model: Instructional learning format practices

| Skills: Activity/routine instruction, transitions, plan- recall, daily oral language, conversation, and cooperative learning | | | | | |
|---|---|---|---|---|---|
| S = Social-emotional | C = Cognitive | A = Auditory | L = Language | E = Extra | S = Speech |
| Select specific social-emotional skills that need to be developed and utilize activity- and routine-based interventions to develop the skill. For example, if the children need to work on using appropriate greetings, build greetings into planned activities such as the opening circle or into routine-based activities at home such as every time someone enters the home. | Incorporate HighScope's Plan-Do-Recall format into play by asking the children where and or what they plan to do during playtime (Plan). During playtime, take pictures or draw pictures of what the children are doing (Do). After playtime is finished, use the pictures or photographs and ask children to share something about their play with the group (Recall). | Incorporate a variety of auditory development activities into all transitions (e.g., for transition to outdoor play, "If you want to play at the sand table, walk to the sand table," or, "If you want to play on the swings, tiptoe to the door."). | Incorporate enthusiasm for conversation into group activities by asking children to share their perspectives on identified topics (e.g., start a conversation with a lead such as "Let me tell you about when I had a problem with my car."). Encourage children to generate solutions to your problem. Model the use of sharing perspective language (e.g., "What's your idea?" or, "What do you think?"). | Support self-determination and self-regulation by working with the children to organize the order of activities. Using a planning board with three empty boxes, ask the children to plan the order of three activities and estimate how long work will be conducted on each activity. Place a picture or drawing of the activities in each of the empty boxes in the order designated and write the minutes for each activity. Set the timer for the work to begin. | Incorporate targeted speech sounds into a daily oral language format. For example, engage the children in picking out a sound for the week that they will use to help you create words or sentences. If the sound selected is /b/, work with the children to create meaningful word combinations with the targeted sound (e.g., "bye bobby," "big ball," "big baby," "bumble bee"). |

encourage turn taking, monitor the class to see who is engaged), and language-modeling strategies (e.g., use rich vocabulary, language expansion, idea extension) is significantly correlated with preschoolers' number of utterances, use of different words, and production of multiword utterances (Girolametto & Weitzman, 2002). In addition, language facilitation strategies used with appropriate emotional support are positively associated with children's receptive and expressive language achievement (Howes et al., 2008; Mashburn, 2008). Consideration must be given to child–teacher ratios, as lower ratios may have an association with higher expressive language skills (Mashburn et al., 2009).

Experts assert that exposure to abstract language is an important mech-anism for developing higher order linguistic skills (Massey, Pence, Justice, & Bowles, 2008). Accordingly, teachers have been encouraged to use comments and questions with increasing levels of abstraction while talking about experiences beyond the here and now. This practice supports children's ability to hypothesize, predict, and reason (van Kleeck, Vander Woude, & Hammett, 2006). Blank, Rose, and Berlin (1978) proposed a question abstraction model to support development of children's discourse abilities. The model uses the following four levels of question abstraction, which are ordered from basic to complex:

1.  Matching perception (e.g., "What do you see or hear?"; "What is this?")

2.  Selective analysis of perception (e.g., "Show me which one is big and round.")

3.  Reordering perception (e.g., "Tell me all the things I don't need."; "What will happen next?")

4.  Reasoning about perception (e.g., "What should we do to solve this problem?"; "Why do you think he decided to do that?")

The influence of peers' abilities on the language development of preschoolers has had far less research attention than that of parent or teacher influences on language development (Mashburn et al., 2009). What has become apparent is that care should be taken to ensure appropriate peer support is available for children who are D/HH, making sure that good peer language models are present. Research on children with normal hearing has shown that those who come from disadvantaged homes exhibit higher vocabulary growth when they are enrolled in economically diverse preschools as opposed to enrollment in programs that serve only children of lower economic status (Schechter & Bye, 2007).

While many curriculum frameworks focus on teacher-managed instruction for facilitating language competence, other experts have proposed that child-managed instruction during such activities as book reading or pretend play is crucial for social and communication development. Educators may need to examine their preference for use of particular types of strategies during specific types of activities. For example, some educators may engage in more teacher-directed communication (e.g., question asking) during book reading or may use more child-directed communication (e.g., extensions, expansions) during sensory activities (Connor et al., 2006; Girolametto & Weitzman, 2002). Knowing the various types of strategies and how to use the strategies to support peer interactions and conversations will assist educators to build peer communication competence. This is particularly important for children who are D/HH, as they may have difficulty sustaining peer interactions. A study of preschool peer interactions revealed that not only did children who are D/HH receive fewer invitations to interact or play from their hearing peers, but 83% of the initiations by children who are D/HH were ignored, compared to 52% for the children with typical hearing (DeLuzio & Girolametto, 2011).

Preschool programs that provide rich communication environments are necessary for children who are D/HH and at risk for language delays. In order for the children to develop communication competence, they need opportunities to practice talking in rich conversations, experiences with varying linguistic complexity, time to comprehend information, and multi-ple meaningful peer interactions. They need educators who ask a variety of questions, provide supports when they don't understand, use a variety of language strategies, implement peer interaction techniques, and integrate listening opportunities throughout the day. Attention to the following ques-tions can assist educators in creating communication environments that will support child–teacher and child–child interactions:

1. Is this a receptively based classroom where the teacher does the talking and the children do the listening, or is there a balance between teacher talk and child talk?

2. Is there a balance of spontaneous and imitated communication from the children?

3. Is there a balance of adult–child and child–child partnered conversations?

4. Are conversations and instructions provided using increasing complexity, with specific attention to presenting context-rich and context-limited information?

5. Is there frequent use of comprehension strategies to ensure understanding?

6. Does the teacher's speaking rate, volume, and intonation support the children's understanding of the language of instruction?

7. Does the teacher's sentence length and complexity match the children's comprehension level?

8. Does the teacher use a variety of question types incorporated throughout the daily routine?

9. Does the teacher use a variety of language facilitation strategies (e.g., expansions, elaborations, modeling, mirroring, self-talk, redirecting children to talk to children, repeating children's ideas)? See Video clip 9.8 for a demonstration of spoken and sign language communication support strategies.

10. Does the teacher use a variety of auditory strategies to develop listening skills (e.g., listening first, tell and then show, auditory highlight/lowlight, repetition, and rephrasing)? See Video clips 9.9 and 9.10 for demonstration of auditory and communication support strategies.

Refer to Cole and Flexer (2007), Esterbrooks (2012), and Chapter 7 for further details. Table 9.6 provides communication support practices situated in the SCALES model.

## Case Study: A Young Cochlear Implant Recipient

Emily is a 4-years-and-9-months-old child who was diagnosed at 35 months with progressive bilateral severe-profound sensorineural hearing loss. At 42 months of age, Emily received a cochlear implant. At that time, her speech, listening, and language skills were significantly below expectations for her age. Her family decided to use sign language prior to cochlear implantation to reduce Emily's communication frustrations. Emily was placed in a preschool classroom taught by an educator of the deaf who used simultaneous communication (i.e., spoken language and sign language) while focusing on the development of Emily's auditory, speech, and language skills. Emily's SCALES profile was presented earlier in Figure 9.1.

Over time, Emily settled into the preschool environment and began engaging with peers and adults with success. The family's use of sign language supported her social-emotional well-being, and Emily's communication frustrations reportedly decreased at home. However, Emily was not progressing in her listening and spoken language skills as expected. A meeting with the family was scheduled to discuss expectations. The discussion identified differences between what the parents thought and what the school staff observed was possible for Emily. The parents reported expectations for Emily to understand language in the "Va-V" zone (i.e., mostly understands using visual input with some auditory awareness; see Table 9.7 and DVD) and reported Emily's daily performance to be in the "Va-V" zone. The school staff reported expectations for Emily to understand language in the "A-Av" zone of support (i.e., mostly understands using auditory information with some visual support), and they reported Emily's daily performance to be in the "AV-Va" zone (i.e., currently understands using an equal emphasis on auditory and visual supports and sometimes needing more visual supports). Differences were also seen in the area of sign and spoken language use, with the parents noting Emily's practice of communicating using sign language without speech and the school staff noting potential for spoken language development. See Table 9.7 for Emily's expectations and performance inventory.

The exchange of perspectives resulted in raised expectations for Emily to develop her listening and spoken language skills. The New, Review, Routine approach (Carotta et al., 2014) was used to support Emily's auditory development. When Emily was introduced to new information, it was presented using spoken language and sign (AV). When the information was known (i.e., review), it was presented using spoken language with visual support, if n eeded (Av). When the information was routine, it was presented in the auditory condition alone (A). After 9 months in the program and upon transition to a kindergarten program, Emily was well on her way to using her listening and spoken language skills as well as continuing to develop her ability to communicate with her deaf friends using sign language, as her parents hoped. Emily's zone of use (i.e., solid arrows) incorporates the entire auditory-visual (A-V) and oral-visual (O-V) continuum. In other words, she is able to communicate with her deaf friends using sign language, and she communicates with her hearing friends using spoken language. Emily's zone of development is represented by dashed lines and

**Table 9.6.** SCALES model: Communication support practices

| | Skills: Choice giving, question variety, auditory strategies, memory, focus, attention, and natural imitation strategies | | | | | |
|---|---|---|---|---|---|---|
| S = Social-emotional | C = Cognitive | A = Auditory | L = Language | E = Extra | S = Speech |
| During closing circle, encourage self-determination and decision making by giving children the opportunity to choose from a variety of ways to say good-bye to their friends (e.g., handshake, wave, and bear hug). | Use Blank, Rose, & Berlin's (1978) question abstraction model during storytime to pose a variety of questions. For example, in level 1 (matching perception), ask, "What is this?" In level 2 (selective analysis), ask, "Can you find the animal that is big and white?" For level 3 (reordering perception), ask, "Which one of the animals does not belong in the zoo?" For level 4 (abstract reasoning), ask, "What should we do if the lion escapes from the zoo?" | In the "preparing to go home" routine, give a routine direction in auditory-only condition, then use the chaining strategy to support comprehension. Consider these examples: "Get your backpack" (auditory first). "Get your backpack" (visual look and point in direction of back pack; auditory-visual chain). "Right, get your backpack" (present direction again using an auditory-only presentation, sign it, or say it again; auditory sandwich). | Create a mechanism for children to assist each other in making sure everyone remembers or understands. During conversational or storytime activities, assign one child to be a "Rememberer" or "Repeater" of information that is missed or misunderstood. | Create opportunities to engage in intense focus and attention while performing specific tasks within a set period of time. For example, set a timer and ask children to focus on completing a task such as building a model, putting together a puzzle, dressing a doll, or picking up toys within the set time frame. | Use a self-talk language strategy to emphasize speech production and encourage natural imitation from children. For example, during a therapy session or small group instruction, comment on sounds you make: "I made the /s/ sound. Let me try that again: /s/"; "I can make the /b/ sound five times: /b-b-b-b-b/"; "I want to say the /ba/ sound slowly: / baaaaa/, /baaaaa baaaa/." |

**Table 9.7.** Expectation and performance inventory

| Receptive communication: Understanding language A = Auditory; V = Visual (print, speechreading, sign); D/HH = deaf or hard of hearing | | | | | |
|---|---|---|---|---|---|
| Expectations | A | Av | AV | Va | V Family |
| Family | | | • | | • |
| D/HH classroom teacher | • | • | | | |
| Speech-language pathologist | • | • | | | |
| Performance (spontaneous) | A | Av | AV | Va | V Home |
| Home | | | | • | • |
| Classroom | | • | | • | |
| Speech session | | • | | • | |

Adaptation of McConkey Robbins (2001); Nussbaum, Scott, Waddy-Smith, and Koch (2004).

| Expressive communication: Use of language O = Oral; V = Visual expression (print, sign, gestures) | | | | | |
|---|---|---|---|---|---|
| Expectations | O | Ov | OV | Vo | V |
| • Family | | | | • | • |
| • D/HH classroom teacher | • | • | | | |
| • Speech-language pathologist | • | • | | | |
| Performance (spontaneous) | O | Ov | OV | Vo | V |
| • Home | | | | • | • |
| • Classroom | | | • | | |
| • Speech session | | | • | | |

*Source:* Waddy-Smith (2004).

is located in the auditory-visual to auditory zone (i.e., Av-A zone). Emily's identified zone of development was highlighted in her kindergarten transition plan, which recommended continued enrollment in speech and listening sessions to enhance her spoken language and listening skills.

This case example demonstrates how knowledge of a child's needs and capacity for learning in new ways can emerge or change over time. Meeting this child's unique needs required an openness to a variety of options or strategies, periodic assessment to determine if these options or strategies were supporting development, and ongoing conversation to determine if the family's and school's expectations were in alignment with this child's development. See Video clip 9.11 for a sample of Emily's speech and language development.

## FUTURE DIRECTIONS

Whereas research-based advances in the establishment of recommended practices in early childhood intervention and early childhood special education are

**Table 9.8.** Communication performance summary

**Receptive communication: Understanding of language**

| Auditory | Av | AV | Va | Visual |
|---|---|---|---|---|
| Primarily uses auditory input | Mostly uses auditory input with some visual support | Equal use of auditory and visual input | Mostly uses visual input with some auditory awareness | Primarily uses visual input (print, speechreading, sign) |

Adapted from McConkey Robbins (2001); Nussbaum, Scott, Waddy-Smith, & Koch (2004).

**Expressive communication: Use of language**

| Oral | Ov | OV | Vo | Visual |
|---|---|---|---|---|
| Primarily uses oral communication | Mostly uses oral expression with some visual expression | Equal use of oral expression and visual expression | Mostly uses visual expression with some oral expression | Primarily uses visual expression (print, signs, gestures) |

Adapted from Waddy-Smith (2004).

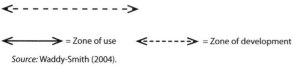

←——————→ = Zone of use   ←------→ = Zone of development

*Source:* Waddy-Smith (2004).

clearly present in and guiding educational programs, early childhood special education for children who are D/HH continues to be an area where there is limited research and agreed upon practices. To address this need, the following suggestions are provided:

1.  Numerous tools have been designed to examine early childhood environments. These scales serve their purpose for the general population of preschool children who are competent language users. However, they do not contain the specific practices needed to support the language and listening needs for children who are D/HH. More research is needed to identify the critical components and practices necessary for establishing quality educational environments for young children who are D/HH.

2.  Given the increase in the number of children in preschool programs who are speaking more than one language, it is especially important that early childhood special educators receive professional development that includes cultural sensitivity and responsiveness. Further, additional research is needed to identify the principles and practices for teaching children who are D/HH and who are dual-language learners and learning a third language, especially sign language and signing systems (see Chapter 6).

3.  Enhancement of teacher confidence and knowledge of social-emotional development is needed. Teacher preparation programs and ongoing professional development are needed in the areas of assessing and

supporting parenting interactions with children (Roggman et al., 2013), understanding child temperament and implementing practices that support a goodness of fit between the adult's and child's temperaments (Kristal, 2005), and implementation of activity-based intervention focused on social-emotional development in classrooms and routine-based interventions in the home (Squires & Bricker, 2007).

4.   Parents of children who are D/HH benefit from ongoing family support as they navigate the educational system with their child. Most early childhood programs spend the greatest number of hours educating the child and a lesser amount of time working with the family. Further emphasis in teacher preparation programs is needed in the areas of adult learning principles, interpersonal sensitivity, communication skills for difficult conversations, and coaching models for supporting adult learning.

## SUGGESTED READINGS

Barrera, I., & Kramer, L. (2009). *Using skilled dialogue to transform challenging interactions: Honoring identity, voice, and connection.* Baltimore, MD: Paul H. Brookes Publishing Co.

Participation in supportive conversations with families and teams of individuals serving young children is an essential competency for professionals. This conversational model is built on the following critical qualities: respect (honoring identity), reciprocity (honoring voice), and responsiveness (honoring connection). Case examples and guided questions assist professionals to develop an approach to addressing challenging situations.

Galinsky, E. (2010). *Mind in the making: The seven essential life skills every child needs.* New York, NY: Harper Studios.

Galinsky introduces seven critical competencies that children need most: 1) focus and control, 2) perspective taking, 3) communicating, 4) making connections, 5) critical thinking, 6) taking on challenges, and 7) self-directed engaged learning. Specific focus on the executive function of the brain and the social-emotional factors supporting cognitive connection provides future directions for developing optimal outcomes in young children.

Keogh, B. (2003). *Temperament in the classroom: Understanding individual differences.* Baltimore, MD: Paul H. Brookes Publishing Co.

This work assists educators in understanding how temperament impacts children's behavior and achievement. Methods for assessing temperament are introduced, and strategies for creating a "goodness of fit" between the child's temperament and the school environment are provided.

## LEARNING ACTIVITIES

1.   Observe an early childhood program for children who are D/HH. Using the developmentally appropriate practices model, write a report providing a summary of the practices observed and recommendations for consideration.

2.   Observe an early childhood program for typically developing children. Using the developmentally appropriate practices model, write a report providing a summary of the practices observed and recommendations for consideration.

3. After observing the two programs, write a report comparing and contrasting the manner in which the two programs are meeting the standards in the developmentally appropriate practices model.

## REFERENCES

American National Standards Institute (ANSI). (2010). *12.60-2010/part 1: Acoustical performance criteria, design requirements and guidelines for schools, part 1: Permanent schools.* New York, NY: Acoustical Society of America.

Bagnato, S.J., & Neisworth, J.T. (1991). *Assessment for early intervention: Best practices for professionals.* New York, NY: Guilford Press.

Bagnato, S.J., Neisworth, J.T., & Pretti-Frontczak, K. (2010). *LINKing authentic assessment and early childhood intervention: Best measures for best practices* (2nd ed.). Baltimore, MD: Paul H. Brookes Publishing Co.

Barrera, I., & Kramer, L. (2009). *Using skilled dialogue to transform challenging interactions: Honoring identity, voice, and connection.* Baltimore, MD: Paul H. Brookes Publishing Co.

Baumgartner, J.J., & Buchanan, T. (2010). Supporting each child's spirit. *Young Children, 65*(2), 90–95.

Bess, F., Dodd-Murphy, J., & Parker, R. (1998). Children with minimal sensorineural hearing loss: Prevalence, educational performance, and functional status. *Ear and Hearing, 19,* 339–354.

Blank, M., Rose, S.A., & Berlin, L.J. (1978). *The language of learning: The preschool years.* New York, NY: Grune & Stratton.

Bodrova, E., & Leong, D. (2007). *Tools of the mind: The Vygotskian approach to early childhood education.* Columbus, OH: Pearson.

Bricker, D., & Waddel, M. (2002). *Assessment, evaluation, and programming system for infants and children.* Baltimore, MD: Paul H. Brookes Publishing Co.

Bronfenbrenner, U. (1979). *The ecology of human development.* Cambridge, MA: Harvard University Press.

Carotta, C., Cline, K.M., & Brennan, K. (2014). *Auditory consultant resource network handbook.* Omaha, NE: Boys Town National Research Hospital.

Cole, E.B., & Flexer, C.A. (2007). *Children with hearing loss: Developing listening and talking, birth to six.* San Diego, CA: Plural.

Connor, C.M., Morrison, F.J., & Slominski, L. (2006). Preschool instruction and children's emergent literacy growth. *Journal of Educational Psychology, 98,* 665–689.

Copple, C., & Bredekamp, S. (2009). *Developmentally appropriate practice in early childhood programs.* Washington, DC: National Association for the Education of Young Children.

Crandell, C., & Smaldino, J. (2005). Acoustical modifications in classrooms. In C. Crandell, J. Smaldino, & C. Flexer (Eds.), *Sound field amplification: Applications to speech perception and classroom acoustics* (pp. 132–141). Clifton Park, NY: Tomson Delmar Learning.

DeLuzio, J., & Girolametto, L. (2011). Peer interactions of preschoolers with hearing loss. *ASHA Leader, 16*(11), 22–24.

Dewey, J. (1976). *Experience and education.* London, England: Colliers MacMillan.

Division of Early Childhood. (2007). *Promoting positive outcomes for children with disabilities: Recommendations for curriculum, assessment, and program evaluation.* Missoula, MT: Author.

Dodge, D.T., Colker, L.J., Heroman, C., & Bickart, T. (2010). *The creative curriculum for preschool* (5th ed.). Washington, DC: Teaching Strategies.

Edwards, C., & Carotta, C. (Eds.). (2015). *Listening to children, seeing possibilities: Stories from a Reggio-inspired inquiry circle at the Boys Town National Research Center, and beyond.* Omaha, NE: Boys Town National Research Hospital.

Edwards, C., Gandini, L., & Forman, G. (Eds.). (2012). *The hundred languages of children: The Reggio Emilia experience in transformation* (3rd ed.). Santa Barbara, CA: Praeger.

Eliot, L. (1999). *What's going on in there? How the brain and mind develop in the first five years of life.* New York, NY: Bantam Books.

Ensher, G.L., & Clark, D.A. (2011). *Relationship-centered practices in early childhood: Working with families, infants, and young children.* Baltimore, MD: Paul H. Brookes Publishing Co.

Esterbrooks, W. (2012). *101 FAQs about auditory-verbal practice.* Washington, DC: Alexander Graham Bell Association for the Deaf or Hard of Hearing.

Forman, G., & Fyfe, B. (2012). Negotiated learning through design, documentation, and discourse. In C. Edwards, L. Gandini, & G. Forman (Eds.), *The hundred languages of children: The Reggio Emilia experience of transformation* (3rd ed., pp. 247–271). Santa Barbara, CA: Praeger.

Galinsky, E. (2010). *Mind in the making: The seven essential life skills every child needs.* New York, NY: HarperCollins.

Gandini, L. (2012). Connecting through caring and learning spaces. In C. Edwards, L. Gandini, & G. Forman (Eds.), *The hundred languages of children: The Reggio Emilia experience of transformation* (3rd ed., pp. 317–341). Santa Barbara. CA: Praeger.

Girolametto, L., & Weitzman, E. (2002). Responsiveness of child care providers in interactions with toddlers and preschoolers. *Language, Speech, and Hearing Services in Schools, 33,* 268–281.

Gordon, A.M., & Browne, K.W. (Eds.). (2004). *Beginnings and beyond: Foundations in early childhood education* (6th ed.). Clifton Park, NY: Delmar Learning.

Grisham-Brown, J., Hemmeter, M.L., & Pretti-Frontczak, K. (2005). *Blended practices for teaching young children in inclusive settings.* Baltimore, MD: Paul H. Brookes Publishing Co.

Grisham-Brown, J., Hemmeter, M.L., & Pretti-Frontczak, K. (2011). *Assessing young children in inclusive settings: The blended practices approach.* Baltimore, MD: Paul H. Brookes Publishing Co.

Hoff, E. (2006). How social contexts support and shape language development. *Developmental Review, 26,* 55–88.

Hohmann, M., & Weikart, D.P. (1995). *Educating young children.* Ypsilanti, MI: High/Scope Press.

Holt, T., Gilles, J., Holt, A., & Davids, V. (2004). *HELP: The Hawaii early learning profile for preschoolers.* Palo Alto, CA: Vort.

Howes, C. (1999). Attachment relationships in the context of multiple caregivers. In J. Cassidy & P.R. Shaver (Eds.), *Handbook of attachment theory and research* (pp. 671–687). New York, NY: Guilford Press.

Howes, C., Burchinal, M., Pianta, R., Bryant, D., Early, D., Barbarin, C., & Clifford, R.M. (2008). Ready to learn? Children's pre-academic achievement in pre-kindergarten programs. *Early Childhood Research Quarterly, 23*(1), 27–50.

Howes, C., & Ritchie, S. (2002). *A matter of trust: Connecting teachers and learners in the early childhood classroom.* New York, NY: Teachers College Press.

Individuals with Disabilities Education Improvement Act (IDEA) of 2004, PL 108-446, 20 U.S.C. §§ 1400 *et seq.*

Johnson-Martin, N.M., Attermeier, S.M., & Hacker, B.J. (2004). *The Carolina curriculum for preschoolers with special needs* (2nd ed.). Baltimore, MD: Paul H. Brookes Publishing Co.

Justice, L.M., Mashburn, A., Pence, K., & Wiggins, A. (2008). Experimental evaluation of a preschool language curriculum: Influence on children's expressive language skills. *Journal of Speech, Language, and Hearing Research, 51*(4), 1–19.

Knecht, H., Nelson, P., Whitelaw, G., & Feth, L. (2002). Background noise levels and reverberation times in unoccupied classrooms: Predictions and measurements. *American Journal of Audiology, 11,* 65–71.

Kristal, J. (2005). *The temperament perspective: Working with children's behavior styles.* Baltimore, MD: Paul H. Brookes Publishing Co.

Losardo, A., & Notari Syverson, A. (2011). *Alternative approaches to assessing young children* (2nd ed.). Baltimore, MD: Paul H. Brookes Publishing Co.

Mashburn, A.J. (2008). Quality of social and physical environments in preschool and children's development of academic, language, and literacy skills. *Applied Developmental Science, 12*(3), 113–127.

Mashburn, A.J., Justice, L., Downer, J.T., & Pianta, R. (2009). Peer effects on children's language achievement during pre-kindergarten. *Child Development, 80*(3), 686–702.

Maslow, A.H. (1970). *Motivation and personality* (3rd ed.). New York, NY: Longman.

Massey, S., Pence, K.L., Justice, L.M., & Bowles, R.P. (2008). Abstract questioning in the preschool classroom. *Early Education and Development, 19,* 340–360.

McConkey Robbins, A. (2001). A sign of the times: Cochlear implants and total communication. *Advanced Bionics Loud and Clear, 4*(2), 1–7.

McWilliam, R.A., & Casey, A.M. (2008). *Engagement of every child in the preschool classroom.* Baltimore, MD: Paul H. Brookes Publishing Co.

Montessori, M. (1967). *The Montessori method* (Trans. A.E. George). Cambridge, MA: Transaction.

Moog, J.S., Bildenstein, J., & Davidson, L. (1995). *Speech perception instructional curriculum and evaluation (SPICE).* St. Louis, MO: Central Institute for the Deaf.

National Association for the Education of Young Children & National Association of Early Childhood Specialists in State Departments of Education. (2003). *Early childhood curriculum, assessment, and program evaluation: Building an effective accountable system in programs for children birth through age 8.* Retrieved January 27, 2004, from http:// www .naeyc .org/ about/ positions .asp

Nussbaum, D., Scott, S., Waddy-Smith, B., & Koch, M. (2004). *Spoken language and sign: Optimizing learning for children with cochlear implants.* Paper presented at Laurent Clerc National Deaf Education Center, Washington, DC.

Odom, S., & Wolery, M. (2003). A unified theory of practice in early intervention/early childhood special education: Evidenced-based practices. *Journal of Special Education, 37*(3), 164–173.

Palermo, F., Hanish, L., Martin, C., Fabes, R., & Reiser, M. (2007). Preschoolers' academic readiness: What role does the teacher-child relationship play? *Early Childhood Research Quarterly, 22*(4), 407–422.

Piaget, J. (1970). Piaget's theory. In P. Mussen (Ed.), *Carmichael's manual of child psychology* (Vol. 1, pp. 703–732). New York, NY: John Wiley & Sons.

Pinata, R.C., La Paro, K.M., & Hamre, B.K. (2008). *Classroom Assessment Scoring System™ (CLASS™).* Baltimore, MD: Paul H. Brookes Publishing Co.

Pretti-Frontczak, K., & Bricker, D. (2004). *An activity-based approach to early intervention* (4th ed.). Baltimore, MD: Paul H. Brookes Publishing Co.

Rinaldi, C. (2006). *In dialogue with Reggio Emilia: Listening, researching, and learning.* New York, NY: Routledge.

Rinaldi, C. (2012). The pedagogy of listening: The listening perspective from Reggio Emilia. In C. Edwards, L. Gandini, & G. Forman (Eds.), *The hundred languages of children: The Reggio Emilia experience in transformation* (3rd ed., pp. 233–246). Santa Barbara, CA: Praeger.

Roggman, L.A., Cook, G.A., Innocenti, M.S., Norman, V.J., Christiansen, K., & Anderson, S. (2013). *Parenting interactions with children: Checklist of observations linked to outcomes.* Baltimore, MD: Paul H. Brookes Publishing Co.

Rossi, K. (2003). *Learn to talk around the clock.* Washington, DC: Alexander Graham Bell Association for the Deaf and Hard of Hearing.

Rousseau, J.J. (1961). *Emile* (Trans. B. Foxley). London, England: J.M. Dent & Sons.

Rudasill, K.M., & Rimm-Kaufman, S.E. (2009). Teacher-child relationship quality: The roles of child temperament and teacher-child interactions. *Early Childhood Research Quarterly, 24,* 107–120.

Sandall, S.R., Hemmeter, M.L., Smith, B.J., & McLean, M.E. (Eds.). (2005). *DEC recommended practices: A comprehensive guide for practical application in early intervention/early childhood special education.* Longmont, CO: Sopris West.

Schechter, C., & Bye, B. (2007). Preliminary evidence for the impact of mixed-income preschools in low-income children's language growth. *Early Childhood Research Quarterly, 22,* 137–146.

Schein, D. (2014). Children's spiritual development and nature. In M.S. Rivkin & D. Schein, *The great outdoors: Advocating for natural space for young children* (pp. 57–72). Washington, DC: National Association for the Education of Young Children.

Sheridan, M., Foley, G., & Radlinski, S. (1995). *Using the supportive play model.* New York, NY: Teachers College Press.

Skinner, B.F. (1953). *Science and human behavior.* New York, NY: Simon and Schuster.

Spencer, T., & Slocum, T. (2010). The effect of a narrative intervention on story retelling and personal story generation skills of preschoolers with risk factors and narrative language delays. *Journal of Early Intervention, 32*(3), 178–199.

Squires, J., & Bricker, D. (2007). *An activity-based approach to developing young children's social emotional competence.* Baltimore, MD: Paul H. Brookes Publishing Co.

Storch, S.A., & Whitehurst, G.J. (2002). Oral language and code related precursors to reading: Evidence from a longitudinal structural model. *Developmental Psychology, 38,* 934–947.

Tyler Krings, A., & Robinson, S. (January 2011). *Designing speech-language and listening sessions.* Paper presented at the Boys Town National Research Hospital Conference on Cochlear Implants: Concept to Classroom, Omaha, Nebraska.

van Kleeck, A., Vander Woude, J., & Hammett, L. (2006). Fostering literal and inferential language skills in Head Start preschoolers with language impairment using scripted book-sharing discussions. *American Journal of Speech-Language Pathology, 15,* 85–95.

Vygotsky, L.S. (1987). *Thinking and speech* (Vol. 1). New York, NY: Plenum Press.

Waddy-Smith, B. (2004). *Spoken language and sign: Optimizing learning for children with cochlear implants.* Paper presented at Laurent Clerc National Deaf Education Center, Washington, DC.

Watkins, S., Taylor, D.J., & Pittman, P. (2004). *SKI-HI curriculum.* Logan, UT: Hope.

Wilkes, E. (1999). *Cottage Acquisition Scales for Listening, Language, and Speech (CASLLS).* San Antonio, TX: Sunshine Cottage School for Deaf Children.

# 10

# Internet Therapy

*Providing Listening and Spoken Language*
*Intervention to Children Who Are Deaf or Hard of Hearing*

Cheryl L. Broekelmann and David J. Ertmer

The use of the Internet to provide intervention services for children who are deaf or hard of hearing (D/HH) is in its infancy, and a consistent label for the practice has not yet been adopted across professions. The American Speech-Language-Hearing Association (ASHA) uses *telepractice* to describe the "application of telecommunications to the delivery of professional services at a distance by linking [a] clinician to [a] client or [a] clinician to [another] clinician, for assessment, intervention, and/or consultation" (ASHA, retrieved 2014). The U.S. Department of Health and Human Services (2012) defines *telehealth* as "the use of electronic information and telecommunications technologies to support long-distance clinical health care, patient and professional health-related education, [and] public health administration" (Health Resources and Services Administration, 2012). A related label is also offered by a special interest group of the American Telemedicine Association. They define *telerehabilitation* as "the delivery of rehabilitation services via information and communication technologies" (Houston, 2014, p. 346). The scope of *telerehabilitation* includes a variety of rehabilitative and habilitative services that are offered to children who are D/HH and their families, including intervention, education, and counseling (A.G. Bell, 2012; Houston, 2014).

For the purposes of this chapter, the term *Internet therapy* (IT) will be used to characterize the provision of assessment, intervention, and counseling services provided to children who are D/HH and their families through video conferencing via the Internet. This generic term was selected for three main reasons. First, it lacks the ambiguity of some of the previously discussed terms (e.g., *telerehabilitation*) and is easily understood by consumers. Second, *Internet therapy* clearly describes the most common approach to providing services at a distance to children who are D/HH from infancy through high school. Finally, because different names are used by various professional groups, this generic term is intended avoid the appearance of favoring one profession's label over another. By any name, however, IT greatly increases the availability of services for children who are D/HH. As noted in Chapters 3, 4, and 5, access to intervention services is especially important for the development of listening and language in infants and toddlers who are D/HH.

## A RATIONALE FOR INTERNET THERAPY

Approximately 2 or 3 of every 1,000 children born in the United States each year are D/HH (National Institute on Deafness and Other Communication Disorders [NIDCD], 2010). Unfortunately, almost one third of these children do not receive follow-up intervention services in a timely manner (Centers for Disease Control and Prevention, 2009).

Early intervention is a process of providing services, education, and support to young children who have a diagnosed physical or mental condition, have an existing delay, or are at risk of developing a delay that will affect development or impede education. Thus early intervention is intended to decrease the adverse effects of a child's disability or delay (Wright & Wright, 2002). Two common logistical problems can interfere with the provision of appropriate early intervention services to children who are D/HH: limited availability of services in given locations and the lack of trained service providers for this population.

Because hearing loss is a low incidence disability, the number of children who are D/HH in some locales can be quite small. As a result, early intervention programs (including programs for the 0- to 3-year age group mandated by the Individuals with Disabilities Education Act Amendments [IDEA] of 1997, part C, PL 105-17) and local school districts often lack service providers who are specially trained to work with children who are D/HH. A common approach to dealing with this problem is to form a cooperative special education agency with other school districts so that special services can be provided in children's homes or in a central location. However, recruiting well-trained service providers can be problematic, even when school systems cooperate.

A second, and related, logistical problem has to do with the limited availability of well-trained service providers. The American Speech-Language-Hearing Association (ASHA) reports that there are shortages of speech-language pathologists (SLPs) in urban and rural areas across the United States and around the world (ASHA, 2014). There are also shortages of teachers of children who are D/HH (ToD/HH) and other special educators according to the U.S. Department of Labor (2014). With the advent of newborn hearing screening and cochlear implants, there is also an urgent need for professionals who have specialty certification, such as Listening and Spoken Language Specialist Educators (LSLS Cert. AVEd) and Listening and Spoken Language Therapists (LSLS Cert. AVT). The A.G. Bell Association for the Deaf and Hard of

Hearing considers this shortage a "crisis in capacity" (Goldberg, Dickson, & Flexer, 2010, p. 134).

Data from the 2010 U.S. Census indicate that 76.6% of families of children ages 3 to 17 have Internet access in their homes (U.S. Department of Commerce, 2011). Such widespread Internet access has made IT a realistic option for most families of children who are D/HH and school districts that do not have qualified service providers. IT can overcome these logistical problems by enabling trained service providers to deliver intervention to most any location—including homes and schools in areas where specialized services for children who are D/HH are not available.

## OVERVIEW OF THE TECHNOLOGICAL REQUIREMENTS OF INTERNET THERAPY

IT places a technological filter between service providers (e.g., ToD/HH, SLPs, audiologists) and service receivers (e.g., children, their families, and local professionals). Although this filter becomes relatively transparent as voices and images are exchanged in real time, many sophisticated electronic components are needed to make the exchange seamless. A detailed description of these hardware and software components and various delivery options is beyond the scope of this chapter and has been addressed in other publications (see Houston, 2014). The purpose of the following section is to provide a brief overview of the technologies needed for satisfactory, reliable, and secure IT sessions.

High-speed access to the Internet is the most basic requirement for IT. Internet connection speed is measured in terms of signal bandwidth, with wider bandwidths resulting in better transmission of audio and video data. The National Center for Hearing Assessment and Management (NCHAM, 2012) has determined that at least 2.0 Mbps (**megabytes** per second) is the minimum speed for downloading adequate quality video and audio signals. Commercial Internet service providers typically offer higher download and upload speeds than this recommendation. Yet regardless of the advertised speed, various situations can reduce bandwidth between users. For example, the simultaneous use of other Internet devices (e.g., smartphones, video games, other computers), a high volume of Internet traffic in the system, and differences in bandwidth due to geographical locations (e.g., urban versus rural situations) can negatively affect signal transmission and the quality of an intervention session. It has been recommended that IT providers subscribe to the maximum bandwidth available through a digital subscriber line (DSL) or cable and use hardwire connections (as opposed to Wi-Fi) to ensure stable bandwidth and high quality video and audio (Crutchley, Alavares, & Campbell, 2014; Olsen, Fiechtl, & Rule, 2012).

Assuming adequate Internet access and bandwidth for both parties, two main types of systems are available for providing IT: dedicated and desktop systems (including laptops and tablets). A dedicated system can be thought of as a bundle of equipment and software that is available through a videoconferencing company or as a purchased product (e.g., Cisco, Tandburg, or Polycom systems). Dedicated systems require that both the provider site and the **remote site** have the same conferencing software, which typically includes wide-angle videocameras, omnidirectional microphones, and a **codec** for compressing and decompressing data. Although relatively expensive in terms of start-up costs ($1,000–$5,000), dedicated video conferencing equipment has very high quality video and audio capabilities (NCHAM, 2012).

Rather than purchasing a bundle of services and equipment, IT service providers might choose to subscribe to an online video conferencing service and use their own devices. In a "desktop" system, software is downloaded to computers at the professional hub and remote site, and microphones and cameras are purchased separately. If the video conferencing service is server-based, a virtual "room" is made accessible to both parties for intervention sessions. Universities, hospitals, schools, and clinics often purchase site licenses for video conference services to reduce costs. As Houston (2014) notes, group sites enable professionals to share materials and records with other professionals who have been cleared for access. Server-based systems also encrypt video and audio signals so that they cannot be accessed by unauthorized persons during transmission. These services further protect confidentiality by requiring unique passwords for access. Online sites often include useful tools such as cloud-based backup recordings of sessions, text chat, or whiteboards for illustrating concepts. Typically, the monthly costs of using the service are paid by the service provider; remote users are not charged ongoing service fees. These expenses must be considered when calculating the actual cost of providing services.

As with dedicated systems, the provider site must ensure that the remote site (e.g., home or school) has the necessary hardware and software for participating in IT. Newer computers typically have the needed hardware, software, and equipment, including built-in cameras, microphones, and speakers, although upgrades to microphones and videocameras might be needed to optimize video and audio signals at both the provider and remote locations. Users of desktop systems can access free video-conferencing tools such as Skype Premium, Adobe Connect, or Cisco WebEx to connect with their clients. Although the cost savings of connecting to an already purchased family or school computer (including laptops and tablets) and accessing free video-conferencing systems are substantial, this approach lacks important online capabilities (e.g., session recording and record keeping) and does not ensure confidentiality of sessions and client information as required by the Health Insurance Portability and Accountability Act of 1996 (HIPAA; PL 104-191). If intervention services are provided in educational settings, compliance with the Family Educational Rights and Privacy Act of 1974 (FERPA; PL 93-380) is also required. Thus, for users of desktop systems, subscription to secure server-based sys-tems is strongly recommended over free online systems.

Successful IT requires that families and professionals feel comfortable and confident in using technology. Selecting, setting up, and maintaining equipment and video conferencing systems are complex tasks. Organizations that offer IT will likely require consultation and collaboration with technology support personnel to make the process run smoothly. Finally, it should be noted that the costs of providing IT can be considerable and, in some cases, exceed the reimbursement limits of insurance (when IT is covered) and state and federal agencies. In fact, limited reimbursement for services may make IT unsustainable. Careful study is needed to determine whether savings in time and transportation costs outweigh the other expenses associated with IT.

## THE IHEAR MODEL AT THE ST. JOSEPH INSTITUTE

The ihear IT program was created by the staff and faculty at the St. Joseph Institute for the Deaf (SJI; St. Louis, MO) to provide effective, individualized, and interactive therapy via secure, HIPAA-and FERPA-compliant, high-speed Internet connections. Using ihear, children and adults participate in real-time therapy sessions with professionals who specialize in developing spoken language through listening. The sessions are interactive and based on digitized lesson plans that address specific objectives for each child. The ihear program was piloted in 2008–2009 and has been expanded and enhanced since that time.

Several core principles have guided the growth of the ihear program. First, the developers agreed that the privacy of information and sessions must be protected for every participating child and family. Second, it was recognized that a collaborative and adult-based learning approach was central to the success of the program—that is, the needs of adults who participate during IT sessions must be a primary focus of intervention. Third, it was recognized that IT must be conducted in a way that would keep children interested and engaged. This latter challenge has led to the development of a bank of digital lesson plans that require **active learning** and frequent responses on the part of the child. Lastly, it was required that the speed of the Internet connection be "as good as in person," so that interactions with parents, teachers, and children could flow naturally and without pause or interruption. The technologies needed to achieve this last principle are discussed next.

The ihear IT program is founded on the belief that listening and spoken language best prepare children who are D/HH for mainstream classrooms and social and vocational success. The program is available to infants, toddlers, and those already enrolled in schools. Just like in-person intervention, IT begins with a comprehensive evaluation of the children's communicative abilities.

### Internet Therapy for Families of Infants and Toddlers

Initial assessments for infants and toddlers who are D/HH examine auditory functioning, speech, spoken language development, adaptive behaviors, and play skills. These areas are assessed mainly through parent questionnaires such as the MacArthur-Bates Inventory of Communicative Development (Fenson, Dale, Resnick, & Bates, 1993) and the Hawaii Early Learning Profile (Parks, 2004), through information sharing and collaborations with the child's audiologist, and through direct observations of the child via the Internet. Following the initial assessment, a family-centered (F-C) approach is implemented.

A study of the effects of the child's age at entering the intervention (Moeller, 2000) provides evidence of the effectiveness of F-C intervention for D/HH infants and toddlers. Moeller found that children who were enrolled in communication intervention by 11 months of age achieved greater vocabulary and verbal reasoning scores than those enrolled after 11 months. A closer look at the data also revealed a strong correlation between parent involvement and language achievement levels—that is, the most successful children were those enrolled by 11 months *and* whose parents were highly involved in intervention. Parent involvement is the key component of F-C intervention. Detailed discussions of the methods used in F-C intervention can be found in Chapters 4 and 5.

The ihear program applies an adult-learning model in which parents are empowered to construct their own understanding of new knowledge and strat-e-gies through coaching. **Coaching** is a process that "builds a cooperative and col-laborative relationship" (Broekelmann, 2012, p. 419) between the ihear thera-pist and a participating parent or local professional. In coaching, ihear therapists share hearing-related information and therapeutic strategies (e.g., language stimulation techniques; see Chapters 4 and 5) while seeking out and valuing the knowledge and ideas of the participating adults. Effective coaching requires that IT providers have high-level counseling skills and integrity. As Hanft, Rush, and Sheldon (2004) note, a coach must be competent, objective, adaptive, caring, and honest. Effective coaching seeks to develop a good rapport with parents or professionals, treating the adult with respect so that the adult feels comfortable as a learner. This level of comfort requires that the ihear therapist values the experiences, knowledge, and skills that the adult already possesses. Ultimately, coaching seeks to help parents and local professionals become competent listen-ing and language coaches for the student.

Several studies of early intervention programming suggest that parent edu-cation through coaching is often neglected during face-to-face sessions (Mahoney et al., 1999; McBride & Peterson, 1997; Peterson, Luze, Eshbaugh, Jeon, & Kantz, 2007). In contrast, the consistent use of coaching in the ihear program has resulted in considerable learning and involvement. With few exceptions, ihear parents report being highly motivated to learn new strategies for stim-ulating listening and spoken language—possibly because the format promotes their realization that they must act as a therapist for their own child through-out the day. ihear therapists also note that coaching enables parents to take an active role in discussing intervention strategies, trying them out, evaluating their effectiveness, and making modifications as necessary. Parents routinely report using their new skills in a wide range of activities and environments—not just during IT sessions. It has also been noted that IT sessions are very rarely missed or cancelled. Some parents have even gone to great lengths to overcome Internet connectivity problems by arranging IT sessions in alternative settings (e.g., a relative's house). In addition to these anecdotal observations, data from the *ihear Parent/Coach Survey* (St. Joseph Institute, 2011; Figure 10.1) show that 31 survey respondents were highly satisfied with key elements of ihear services, including coaching. Thus highly focused interactions during IT sessions appear to promote successful coaching experiences, possibly because parents realize that they must be the actual "on-site" service provider both during and after each session.

### Internet Therapy for School-Age Children

In addition to infants and toddlers, school-age children who are D/HH are sometimes referred to the ihear program whenever appropriately trained pro-fessionals are not available. In these cases, ihear therapists provide comple-mentary support for local SLPs and teachers, as well as parents. Specific goals

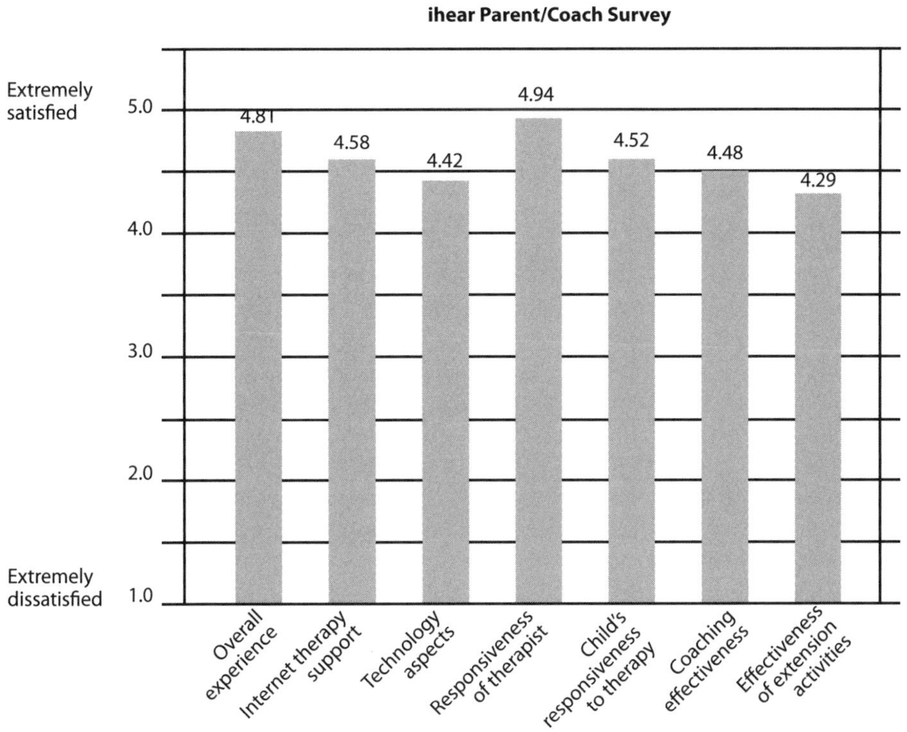

**ihear Parent/Coach Survey**

**Figure 10.1.** Parent satisfaction with the ihear program. (*Source:* Stredler-Brown, 2012).

for children are usually based on previous evaluation results and parent and professional input. The ihear therapist might also request that specific tests be given before goals are written.

Each ihear lesson plan includes individualized objectives in the areas of cognition, audition, receptive and expressive language, and speech (iCARES) and a coaching strategy. A progress record is kept in a digital file and shared with families and schools (Figure 10.2).

All lessons are based on a **constructivist educational philosophy** in which authentic activities are presented so that learners are drawn into meaningful communication (see Schunk, 2000, for discussion) and designed to create a learning environment in which children become curious about the world and have reasons to talk about their knowledge and experiences. For example, pictures that are related to weekend events could be used to help a child write/tell a personal experience story, or a child's interest in farming might be used to expand his or her ability to describe the pieces of equipment and explain their uses. School curriculum is also used to facilitate language growth and academic success in older children. Incorporating each child's interests and academic content into lessons ensures that new vocabulary and other language skills can be introduced, modeled, and practiced during personally meaningful activities. Through use of diagnostic teaching principles, the child's progress is assessed and future lesson plans are fine-tuned to improve or maintain skills. Formal and informal testing is also completed every 6 months to document

**ihear Lessons and Objectives**

Coaching strategy: _____

Objectives for student:

• Cognition: _____

• Audition: _____

• Receptive language: _____

• Expressive language: _____

• Speech: _____

**Figure 10.2.**   ihear lesson plan template.

progress and adjust objectives and instructional strategies as needed. Some of these tests are given via the Internet and others by local service providers. See the second case study for an illustration of how services were provided to a preschool child in a remote location.

As mentioned, the last component of the iCARES model involves coaching the school-based personnel. To do this, ihear therapists help the SLP/teacher to relate their prior knowledge and experiences to the kinds of interventions that the student needs. This approach encourages discussion, practice, application, and self-reflection (Bodner-Johnson, 2001). The *School Professional Questionnaire* (SPQ) was developed by the ihear staff to assess the experience, knowledge, and skills of school professionals who work with children who are D/HH. The topics covered on the SPQ include previous experience with children who are D/HH; cochlear implants, hearing aids, and assistive listening devices; interpreting audiograms; understanding children's aided hearing abilities; the impact of hearing on spoken language development; the use of communication repair strategies; and the transfer of learning to other environments. Responses to the SPQ are used to select and emphasize the areas in which the professional sees the greatest needs.

## Case Studies

### Case Study 1: Family-Centered Internet Therapy

Molly was born prematurely with complications in a rural area of the Midwestern United States. Following a 4-week stay in the neonatal intensive care unit, her parents were told that Molly had failed her newborn hearing screening. A severe-profound, bilateral, sensorineural hearing loss was confirmed through Auditory Brainstem Response (ABR) testing the following week. Molly was immediately referred for intervention services through the Individuals with Disabilities Educational Act (IDEA 1997, part C) and received hearing aids at 3 months. An early interventionist who had no formal training with children who are deaf or hard of hearing (D/HH) was assigned to provide intervention at the family's rural home. Following a suggestion from Molly's audiologist, the family contacted the St. Joseph Institute for the Deaf (SJI), and Molly was enrolled in the ihear program at 8 months of age.

Molly's initial evaluation revealed a total language score of 77, with an age equivalency of 4 months on the *Cottage Acquisition Scales for Listening, Language, and Speech—Preverbal* form (CASLLS-P). Observations from the ihear specialist and the parent revealed that Molly had begun to detect and localize some sounds with her hearing aids (HAs) and that she sometimes showed joint attention when playing with her mother. Molly and her mother participated in two 30-minute Internet therapy (IT) sessions per week. The local early interventionist was also present in some sessions.

The main focus of the sessions was to coach Molly's mother in specific strategies for creating a listening environment that would stimulate language. For example, when the phone rang during an ihear session, mom was taught to alert Molly to the presence of the ringing by point-ing at her ear while saying, "Molly, I hear something. Do you?" The value of using routine events as teachable moments was also highlighted. Molly's mother was encouraged to name objects during everyday routines such as eating, dressing, bathing, and playing (see Chapters 4 and 5 for more ideas). A coaching approach was used in which the ihear therapist would describe, demonstrate, and provide opportunities for the mother to practice new listening and language stimulation strategies. Molly's mother was encouraged to think of ways to implement strategies and evaluate their usefulness.

After approximately 8 months of HA use (chronological age [CA] = 11 months), it was deter-mined that Molly's progress could likely be enhanced through a cochlear implant (CI). The ihear therapist worked in partnership with the family and Molly's audiologist to determine candidacy for cochlear implantation. Molly was found to be a viable candidate and received a unilateral CI at 16 months of age. She continued wearing a HA in her nonimplanted ear.

After 1 year in the ihear program (CA = 20 months) and 4 months of robust hearing experience with her CI, Molly's total language score was 85, with an age equivalency of 17 months on the CASLLS. Testing also showed that she had acquired numerous foundational skills for spoken language, including participating in functional, relational, and self-directed play; understand-ing specific words and phrases without gestural cues; vocalizing at least two consonant sounds; producing two-syllable utterances; using a symbolic gesture (e.g., waving bye-bye); imitating some words; saying words (e.g., "more," "Elmo," "open," "up"); and producing a variety of consonant-vowel combinations.

Although Molly "graduated" from the ihear program when she entered a regular preschool, ihear assistance did not stop. Online mentoring was provided to Molly's local speech-language pathologist (SLP) because she had never worked with a child who had a CI. The SLP was shown a variety of techniques to improve listening, phonology, and language. She was also shown how to give the Ling Six-Sound Test (see Chapter 7 and its DVD demonstrations) and how to troubleshoot if the CI was not working properly. The SLP was appreciative of the support and indicated that she used the newly learned strategies with other students in her caseload in addition to Molly.

At age 4, Molly continues to increase her language abilities through the combination of CI-and HA-assisted hearing, preschool and home experiences, and local intervention services. She loves to sing and participate in "circle time," where she tells her classmates about her newest adventures with her dog, King. She is learning the alphabet and can count to 25. Her ihear therapist continues to provide services to Molly and her hospital-based CI team by sharing insights into how well Molly uses hearing at home and in preschool. The team uses this information to fine-tune her cochlear implant maps.

In addition to the ability to communicate with their daughter, Molly's family also gained less tangible—but equally important—benefits. According to Molly's mom, "ihear benefited our family by teaching us how to communicate with our daughter. We are learning so much from our sessions about meeting her needs, knowing what she wants, and giving her language to express those wants. Now we're more comfortable with the process of teaching her how to listen and talk. We no longer feel 'out there,' on our own without any support." These comments and Molly's progress confirm the value of IT when local expertise is in short supply.

### Case Study 2: Internet Therapy in a School Setting

Following a normal pregnancy and delivery, Robert failed his newborn hearing screening. Although he passed a second screening, his parents noticed that he did not become startled by loud sounds and that he did not babble or respond to his name during the first year of life. He was diagnosed with a bilateral, severe to profound sensorineural hearing loss and was fitted with hearing aids at 16 months. Robert received his first cochlear implant in his left ear at the age of 2 years, 3 months, and the second implant in his right ear at 3 years, 9 months. He began to attend a regular preschool in a rural school district when he turned 3. After a few months, his family did not feel that he was making sufficient progress at home or in the preschool. They heard about ihear from a special educator and made arrangements for an evaluation.

At the time of the evaluation, Robert was 4 years 6 months old. He was observed to have a few two-word utterances, some functional expressions, and spoken names for some common objects but very few verbs. Some examples of his language included "Mom look," "No blue," "My turn," "Help me," and "That scary." His receptive language age on the CASLLS was 18 to 21 months, and his expressive language age was 15 to 18 months. Robert's parents expressed the desire to have him learn to use his CIs better and to become an oral communicator. After enrollment, Robert and his mother participated in a 1-hour session each week. He also received speech-language therapy at his preschool four times a week for a half-hour each session.

At the end of the school year, Robert's parents requested that an ihear staff member be a part of his individualized education program (IEP) review meeting. At the meeting, it was decided that the school would incorporate ihear into his speech-language sessions once each week. His parents also agreed to continue IT at home, while reducing their sessions to a half-hour per week.

The relationship between the ihear therapist and the school SLP was not optimal at first. There was minimal participation by the SLP during sessions and little carryover of strategies into the classroom. Not surprisingly, Robert made little progress toward his spoken language objectives during the first year of service. The ihear therapist revisited the expectations of the IT program with the parents in hopes that they and school professionals would increase their efforts to address Robert's goals. A much improved collaboration began during the second year, when all parties began functioning as a team. Good working relationships with paraprofessionals, special education directors, and school district Internet technicians were also critical to the success of Robert's program.

The benefits of this teamwork were seen as Robert gradually began to increase his auditory skills (see Chapter 8 for examples of auditory training methods), began following directions containing up to five critical elements, and became more consistent in using complete sentences. His standardized test scores increased, and the gap between his chronological age and hearing age decreased as well. Robert is now near age level in receptive and expressive language according to his standardized assessments. According to the CASLLS, Robert scored between the 6-and 8-year level in all areas (CA = 8;8). Although he has moved to a different locale, his family has continued participation in the ihear program. This highlights another unique advantage to IT: Children can keep the same service provider even when their family moves.

Here are some examples of the complex sentences that Robert produced when discussing his family's move.

ihear therapist: "Have you already packed your things?"

Robert: "We're not putting our stuff in the truck now, because we're not leaving 'til after Christmas."

ihear therapist: How do you feel about moving?

Robert: "I'm feeling shy about going to a new school, since I won't know anybody there."

In sum, despite the delayed onset of services and less-than-optimal teamwork at first, Robert made substantial growth once Internet and local service providers began to work together. Further growth in spoken language appears likely, as Robert will continue to receive Internet therapy after his family settles into their new home.

## FUTURE DIRECTIONS FOR INTERNET THERAPY

Demand for IT has been growing steadily, and the need for these services is expected to increase in the United States and around the world. For that to happen, however, several barriers to service delivery will have to be overcome. Currently, service providers for children who are D/HH are required to hold licenses in the states where the consumer lives. IT will not expand efficiently if SLPs and teachers of the deaf or hard of hearing (ToD/HH) are required to have licenses in each state where their services could be implemented. A national license for IT providers would ensure IT availability for children in all parts of the country. Further, there is a need for formal recognition of Listening and Spoken Language Specialist Educators (LSLS Cert. AVEd) and Listening and Spoken Language Therapists (LSLS Cert. AVT) as highly qualified to provide IT to children learning spoken language who are D/HH. Relatedly, the critical shortage of LSLS specialists will limit access to specialized spoken language service providers. Increased numbers of qualified personnel are needed so that IT can overcome barriers in distance and availability.

Finally, research has shown that communication interventions such as cochlear implantation and follow-up services have resulted in increased mainstreaming opportunities and substantial reductions in special education costs (Niparko, Cheng, & Francis, 2000). IT has the potential to yield similar benefits for children who lack access to local specialized service providers. If such benefits are to be gained, however, consistent and adequate reimbursement from insurance companies and state and local agencies must become the norm, not the exception.

As mentioned at the beginning of this chapter, the field of IT for children who are D/HH is in its infancy. As the field grows, it is likely to change forms with advances in technology and new public policies. It is hoped that these changes will overcome the barriers discussed previously so that children who are D/HH can receive optimal services no matter where they live.

## SUGGESTED READINGS

A.G. Bell Association. (2012). Current knowledge and best practice in telepractice (Ed. A. Stredler-Brown). *The Volta Review, 112*(3), 1–255.

A wide-ranging discussion of Internet-based intervention practices for children who are deaf or hard of hearing.

American Speech-Language-Hearing Association. (2010). *Speech-language pathologists providing clinical services via telepractice.* Retrieved May 8, 2015, from http://www .asha.org/PRPSpecificTopic.aspx?folderid=8589934956&section=Overview

A review of the key issues and helpful resources for those interested in learning more about Internet therapy.

Houston, K.T. (2014). *Telepractice in speech-language pathology.* San Diego, CA: Plural. This edited textbook was written specifically for speech-language pathologists who want to know how Internet therapy can be used with families, preschoolers, school-age children, and adults who have communication disorders.

National Center for Hearing Assessment and Management. (2012). *A practical guide to the use of tele-intervention.* Retrieved May 8, 2015, from http://www.infanthearing .org/ti-guide/index.html

This comprehensive resource can be downloaded without charge.

## LEARNING ACTIVITIES

1.  Visit http://www.broadband.gov to find information on Internet bandwidth available in your area.

2.  Visit http://www.infanthearing.org/ti-guide to learn more about IT for young children who are D/HH.

3.  Visit the *PC World* magazine web site to learn more about video conferencing systems: http://www.pcworld.com/article/2017422/top-video-conferencing-services.html

4.  Make a list of the advantages of visiting with a friend via Skype. Make another list of the problems you have encountered with this service. In addition to privacy concerns, how might connectivity problems interfere with providing IT to children who are D/HH and their families?

5.  Starting an IT program requires considerable planning and evaluation. Read "The Business of Telepractice" (Brick, 2014) for a better idea of what is involved. Prepare a business plan to determine whether IT is a feasible option.

6. Contact a local speech-language pathologist (SLP) who provides private speech-language services to determine whether IT is available or being considered. Discuss the success of the program or the factors that have discouraged implementation.

## REFERENCES

A.G. Bell Association. (2012). Current knowledge and best practice in telepractice (Ed. A. Stredler-Brown). *The Volta Review, 112*(3), 1–255.

American Speech-Language-Hearing Association. (2014). *2014 school survey: SLP workforce/work conditions.* Retrieved May 8, 2015, from http://www.asha.org/uploadedFiles/2014-Schools-Survey-SLP-Workforce-Reportpdf#search=%222014%22&_ga=1.54517800.1488324507.1419623010

Bodner-Johnson, B. (2001). Parents as adult learners in family-centered early education. *American Annals of the Deaf, 146*(3), 263–269.

Brick, M. (2014). The business of telepractice. In K.T. Houston (Ed.), *Telepractice in speech-language pathology* (pp. 237–260). San Diego, CA: Plural.

Broekelmann, C. (2012). ihear Internet therapy program: A program by St. Joseph Institute for the Deaf. *The Volta Review, 112,* 417–422.

Centers for Disease Control and Prevention. (2009). *Early hearing detection and intervention (EDHI) hearing screening and follow-up survey* (revised November 2011). Retrieved May 8, 2015, from http://www.cdc.gov/ncbddd/hearingloss/ehdi-data2011.html

Crutchley, S., Alcares, R.L., & Campbell, M.F. (2014). Getting started: Building a successful telepractice program. In K.T. Houston (Ed.), *Telepractice in speech-language pathology* (pp. 51–82). San Diego, CA: Plural.

Family Educational Rights and Privacy Act (FERPA) of 1974, PL 93-380, 20 U.S.C., §§ 1232g *et seq.*

Fenson, L., Dale, P., Resnick, J., & Bates, E. (1993). *MacArthur communicative development inventories: User's guide and manual* (2nd ed.). San Diego, CA: Singular.

Goldberg, D.M., Dickson, C.L., & Flexer, C. (2010). A.G. Bell Academy Certification Program for Listening and Spoken Language Specialists: Meeting a world-wide need for qualified professionals. *The Volta Review, 110,* 129–144.

Hanft, B.E., Rush, D.D., & Shelden, M.L. (2004). *Coaching families and colleagues in early childhood.* Baltimore, MD: Paul H. Brookes Publishing Co.

Health Insurance Portability and Accountability Act (HIPAA) of 1996, PL 104-191, 42 U.S.C. §§ 201 *et seq.*

Health Resources and Services Administration. (2012). *The role of telehealth in an evolving healthcare environment.* Retrieved May 8, 2015, from http://www.hrsa.gov/ruralhealth/about/telehealth/telehealth.html

Houston, K.T. (2014). *Telepractice in speech-language pathology.* San Diego, CA: Plural.

Individuals with Disabilities Education Act Amendments (IDEA) of 1997, PL 105-17, 20 U.S.C. §§ 1400 *et seq.*

Mahoney, G., Kaiser, A., Girolametto, L., MacDonald, J., Robinson, C., Safford, P., & Spiker, D. (1999). Parent education in early intervention: A call for renewed focus. *Topics in Early Childhood Special Education, 19,* 131–140.

McBride, S.L., & Peterson, C.A. (1997). Home-based early intervention with families of children with disabilities: Who is doing what? *Topics in Early Childhood Special Education, 17*(2), 209–233.

Moeller, M.P. (2000). Early intervention and language development in children who are deaf and hard of hearing. *Pediatrics, 106*(3), E43. doi:10.1542/peds.106.3.e43

National Center for Hearing Assessment and Management (NCHAM). (2012). *A practical guide to the use of tele-intervention in providing listening and spoken language services to infants and toddlers who are deaf or hard of hearing.* Retrieved March 15, 2014, from http://www.infanthearing.org/ti-guide/index.html

National Institute on Deafness and Other Communication Disorders. (2010). *Quick statistics.* Retrieved May 8, 2015, from http://www.nidcd.nih.gov/health/statistics/Pages/quick.aspx

Niparko, J.K., Cheng, A.K., & Francis, H. (2000). Outcomes of cochlear implantation: Assessment of quality of life impact and economic evaluation of the benefits of the cochlear implant in relation to costs. In J. Niparko, K. Kirk, N.K. Mellon, A. McConkey Robbins, E.L. Tucci, & B.S. Wilson (Eds.), *Cochlear implants: Principles and practices* (pp. 269–288). Philadelphia, PA: Lippincott Williams & Wilkins.

Olsen, S., Fiechtl, M.S., & Rule, S. (2012). An evaluation of virtual home visits in early intervention: Feasibility of "virtual intervention." *The Volta Review, 112,* 267–281.

Parks, S.W. (2004). *The Hawaii early learning profile.* Menlo Park, CA: VORT.

Peterson, C.A., Luze, G.J., Eshbaugh, E.M., Jeon, H.J., & Kantz, K.R. (2007). Enhancing parent-child interactions through home visiting: Promising practice or unfulfilled promise? *Journal of Early Intervention, 29*(2), 119–140.

Schunk, D.H. (2000). *Learning theories: An educational perspective.* Upper Saddle River, NJ: Pearson Education.

St. Joseph Institute for the Deaf. (2011). *The ihear parent/coach survey.* Unpublished document.

Sunshine Cottage. (1999). *Cottage scales for acquisition of listening, language, and speech.* San Antonio, TX: Sunshine Cottage School.

U.S. Department of Commerce. (2011). *Computer and Internet use in the United States.* Retrieved May 9, 2015, from http://www.census.gov/prod/2013pubs/p20-569.pdf

U.S. Department of Health and Human Services, Institute of Medicine. (2012). *The role of telehealth in an evolving health care environment.* Retrieved May 8, 2015, from http://www.hrsa.gov/ruralhealth/about/telehealth/telehealth.html

U.S. Department of Labor. (2014). *Occupational outlook handbook.* Retrieved February 15, 2014, from http://www.bls.gov/ooh/education-training-and-library/special-education-teachers.htm

Wright, P.W.D., & Wright, P.D. (2002). *Wrightslaw: From emotions to advocacy—The special education survival guide.* Hartfield, VA: Harbor House Law Press.

# Language and
# Literacy in the School Years

# 11

# Reading the World

*Supporting Theory of Mind*
*Development in Deaf or Hard-of-Hearing Students*

Carol Westby and Deborah Wilson-Taber

Historically, individuals who are deaf or hard of hearing (D/HH) typically have exhibited low literacy (Lederberg, Schick, & Spencer, 2012; see Chapter 12). On average, median scores of 17-year-old students who are D/HH on the Stanford Achievement Test have been at the fourth-grade level and have not improved significantly in more than 40 years despite significant changes in deaf education (Qi & Mitchell, 2012). This low reading performance of students who are D/HH has been attributed to their difficulty accessing the oral speech code and reduced language skills. Early identification of young children with hearing loss and the provision of cochlear implants and hearing aids have given many D/HH individuals auditory access to spoken language models and a greater ability to develop oral language. Although some deaf children with cochlear implants reach levels of reading comprehension comparable to those of normal hearing children (Lyxell et al., 2011), there is considerable variability among children (Marschark, Rhoten, & Fabrich, 2007) and some indication that the gap between hearing children and children with implants increases by adolescence (Geers, Tobey, Moog, & Brenner, 2008). Reading abilities of students who are D/HH with and without cochlear implants cannot be explained by their hearing levels, phonological processing skills, and measured language skills alone. To understand and promote the reading abilities of students who are D/HH, researchers and service providers must consider other cognitive and social processes and abilities (Kronenberger, Colson, Henning, & Pisoni, 2014; Marschark, Sarchet, Rhoten, & Zupan, 2010).

A social cognitive process requiring more attention with students who are D/HH is theory of mind (ToM). Theory of mind (ToM) is defined as the ability to attribute mental states and emotions to oneself and others and to recognize that others have mental states and emotions that might be different from one's own (Premack & Woodruff, 1978). In this chapter, we describe 1) social-cognitive factors associated with reading development in students who are D/HH, 2) current neuroscience concepts regarding ToM, 3) how deficits in ToM can explain some of the reading comprehension problems exhibited by students who are D/HH, 4) how to evaluate potential ToM deficits, and 5) strategies to build the language and social/cognitive skills underlying ToM abilities to improve reading comprehension and social interactions.

## FACTORS ASSOCIATED WITH READING DEVELOPMENT IN CHILDREN WHO ARE DEAF OR HARD OF HEARING

A broad range of oral language skills has been identified as the foundation for long-term literacy success in children with normal hearing (Dickinson, McCabe, & Essex, 2006). Hearing loss affects the relationship between spoken language and literacy development in two ways. First, exposure to spoken language models is limited by hearing loss, and consequently, the lower literacy of these children is due in part to the discrepancy between their spoken language system and the demands of reading an orthographic system based on oral language. Second, deaf children whose first language is American Sign Language (ASL) or some other signed or non-English spoken language are challenged to develop literacy in a language they may not yet have acquired.

Limited language skills and difficulty in mastering the print code cannot, however, account for all the text comprehension difficulties exhibited by these students. Even students who are D/HH with adequate word recognition skills are likely to have difficulty analyzing the syntactic relations among the words in sentences. For example, consider the complexity of the relationships in this sentence from *Harry Potter and the Goblet of Fire* (Rowling, 2000, p. 46): "Indeed, from the tone of his voice when he next spoke, Harry was quite sure that Mr. Weasley thought Dudley was quite as mad as the Dursleys thought he was, except that Mr. Weasley felt sympathy rather than fear." The sentence processing of students who are D/HH better predicts their reading comprehension than their word recognition ability (Miller, 2010).

Narrative language abilities differ considerably between D/HH and hearing students (Crosson & Geers, 2001; Wellman et al., 2011), and these skills appear to be highly related to reading comprehension. Compared to hearing students, students who are D/HH produce narratives that are less complete (Boons et al., 2013), focus more on descriptions than causal relationships (Arfe & Boscolo, 2006), and have fewer mental state and evaluative words (Huttunen & Ryder, 2012). Students who are D/HH also exhibit deficits in metacognitive awareness, evidenced by the fact that college-age deaf readers profess a better understanding of what they read than they are able to demonstrate (Kelly, Albertini, & Shannon, 2001).

Marschark and colleagues suggest the reading comprehension difficulties of students who are D/HH are not really about reading because these students exhibit the same degree of comprehension difficulties regardless of whether the discourse stimuli is print, oral language, or sign (Marschark et al., 2009).

Clearly, comprehension of oral, written, and signed discourse requires inferences, and research has shown that many students who are D/HH exhibit marked difficulty making inferences. For example, both prelingually deafened adolescents who used spoken English to read short narratives and prelingually deafened adolescents who watched the same narratives signed to them responded at chance level to questions about the passages that required temporal or causal inferences (Doran & Anderson, 2003). The ability to make inferences when reading, listening to, or watching discourse and engaging in appropriate and effective social interactions requires a well-functioning ToM.

## THEORETICAL BASES FOR A THEORY OF MIND APPROACH TO DEVELOPING SOCIAL COGNITION AND READING COMPREHENSION

### Theory of Mind Dimensions

Social neuroscience in the last decade has provided new understanding of the nature of ToM and the role of ToM in social and academic development. Most of the research on ToM has viewed it as a unity cognitive construct and has focused on the ability to infer the thoughts, beliefs, and intentions of others. Recent advances in neuroscience, however, have shown that ToM is a multidimensional construct, with each dimension having different neurophysiological and neuroanatomical foundations. Basically, ToM can be differentiated into two main dimensions—cognitive and affective (Abu-Akel & Shamay-Tsoory, 2011; Keysers, 2011; Shamay-Tsoory et al., 2007)—and each of these dimensions includes both interpersonal (between individuals) and intrapersonal (within individuals) components. These are described and illustrated in Figure 11.1. Because each of these ToM dimensions has its own neuroanatomical substrates, individuals can have differing patterns of strengths and weaknesses in their ToM abilities (Shamay-Tsoory & Aharon-Peretz, 2007; Shamay-Tsoory, Aharon-Peretz, & Perry, 2009).

ToM research typically describes tasks that evaluate three levels of ToM, including first-order, **second-order**, and higher-order skills. Table 11.1 summarizes these levels and provides definitions, expected ages of development, and illustrative examples. Notably, research on children who are D/HH reveals they exhibit delays and deficits in all dimensions of ToM.

### Theory of Mind Deficits in Students Who Are Deaf or Hard of Hearing

*Cognitive Theory of Mind Deficits*   Most research on ToM in both children who are D/HH and their hearing, same-age peers has focused on first-order interpersonal **cognitive ToM**. The classic developmental milestone for first-order interpersonal cognitive ToM is the ability to attribute false cognitive belief—that is, to recognize that others can have beliefs about the world that are not true and that their actions are based on these false or mistaken beliefs (Wellman & Liu, 2004.) For example, mother keeps searching for her keys in her purse because she does not know they are hanging on the key hook in the kitchen. Numerous studies have documented first-order cognitive **interpersonal ToM** deficits in children who are D/HH (Peterson & Wellman, 2009),

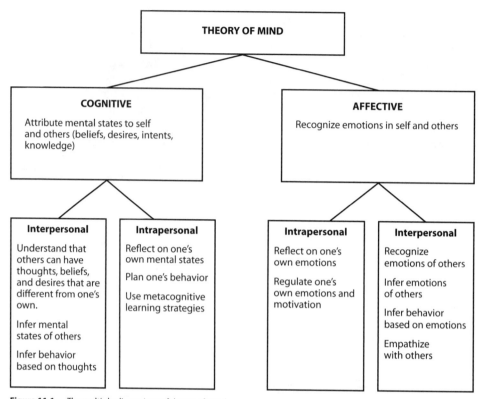

**Figure 11.1.** The multiple dimensions of theory of mind.

particularly those of hearing parents (Schick, de Villiers, de Villiers, & Hoffmeister, 2007). Deaf children of deaf parents perform markedly better than the latter group on ToM tasks (Courtin, 2000; Schick, de Villiers, de Villiers, & Hoffmeister, 2007). Deaf children's delays and deficits in cognitive interpersonal ToM have been attributed to their reduced interactive language experiences. The better performance of deaf children of deaf parents is explained by their higher quality communicative interactions with their parents. In contrast, the frequency and quality of communicative interactions between deaf children and their hearing parents are much more limited. Even hearing parents who sign with their deaf children use significantly fewer mental state words than hearing parents of hearing children. The frequency of exposure to mental state words has been correlated with children's ToM skills (Moeller & Schick, 2006). When discourses and texts involve information about the personalities and motivations of characters (e.g., "Winnie the Pooh" or "The Three Little Pigs and the Big Bad Wolf"), individuals must also possess interpersonal ToM to make inferences about goals and responses to situations.

Children who are D/HH also exhibit deficits in intrapersonal cognitive ToM. This dimension of ToM emerges around 18 months of age when children become aware of themselves as separate, unique individuals (Lewis, 2014). Beyond the preschool years, this self-awareness or intrapersonal cognitive ToM can be viewed as metacognitive development. Metacognitive knowledge involves

**Table 11.1.**   Three levels of theory of mind commonly evaluated in research

| Theory of mind level | Age of development | Example |
|---|---|---|
| *First order:* Ability to think about what someone else thinks or feels | 4 to 5 years | A child realizes that *her friend Jimmy* **thinks** *his dog is still in the garage* (and that's why Jimmy looks there even though the dog is really in the neighbor's yard). |
| *Second order:* Ability to think about what one person is thinking or feeling about what another person is thinking or feeling | 5 to 7 years | A child realizes that John *doesn't know* that Mary believes John **is angry** with her. |
| *Higher order:* Involves multiple embedding, comprehension of lies, sarcasm and figurative language (where what is said is not what is meant), and social faux pas (where what is said causes unintended hurt). | After 7 years | *She* **thinks** *that her mother* **knows** *that her brother* **hopes** *his girlfriend will* **want** *the gift.* |

awareness of what one knows and doesn't know about a topic, awareness of the strategies for doing tasks, knowledge of when to use the strategies, and how to plan, monitor, and evaluate one's learning (Baker & Brown, 1984). If students are to make inferences about spoken, signed, and written discourse, they must be aware of the need to make inferences—that is, they must have a metacognitive awareness that not all the information is in the discourse and that strategies are needed for making inferences, and they must have the ability to use this knowledge (termed executive functions) to implement and monitor the inference making. These behaviors require **intrapersonal ToM**: a conscious awareness of one's own thoughts and plans. Although few studies have examined the metacognitive skills of individuals who are D/HH, there is an indication of their deficits in **metacognition** (Borgna, Convertino, Marschark, Morrison, & Rizzolo, 2011; Strassman, 1997). Compared to hearing readers, D/HH readers are less aware of when they comprehend and do not comprehend a passage. They also have been shown to use fewer strategies to construct meaning, monitor, and evaluate their own comprehension (Schirmer, Bailey, & Lockman, 2004).

**Affective Theory of Mind Deficits**   Children who are D/HH also exhibit delays/deficits in affective interpersonal and intrapersonal ToM, including inferring the affective states of others and recognizing and regulating one's own affective states (Dyck, Farrugia, Shochet, & Holmes-Brown, 2004; Ludlow, Heaton, Rosset, Hills, & Deruelle, 2010; Wiefferink et al., 2012). **Affective ToM** deficits cannot as easily be attributed to insufficient language experiences as cognitive ToM deficits. For example, both oral and signing deaf children, ages 6 to 16 years, were less successful than hearing children in labeling photos and human and nonhuman cartoon faces as happy, sad, or angry. Ludlow and colleagues (2010) suggested two possible explanations for this difficulty in identifying emotions: First, in efforts to lipread and hear, oral deaf children may not give sufficient attention to other facial features, particularly the eyes, to interpret emotions correctly. Second, signing deaf individuals are used to observing the face for linguistic cues; this attention to linguistic cues may affect processing of emotional cues. Another possibility offered by Dye, Hauser, and Bavelier (2008) is that signing students who are D/HH may not be attending sufficiently to the face. They noted that students who are D/HH show greater attention to peripheral locations, whereas hearing individuals focus more on the center of the visual field.

Regarding children with cochlear implants (CIs), preschool CI recipients exhibited more difficulty on all aspects of emotional understanding than hearing preschoolers (Wiefferink et al., 2012), even when language was not involved. They were not as proficient at sorting faces that expressed emotion, in both positive versus negative expressions and sad versus angry expressions. (The hearing and deaf groups performed similarly when sorting cars and flowers or faces with and without hats.) They also exhibited greater difficulty in matching positive or negative emotional expressions to pictures of situations that might trigger that emotion (e.g., matching a happy face to a picture of a boy receiving an ice cream cone or a sad face with a boy falling off his bicycle). This difficulty with facial matching and linking facial expressions to situations would likely influence their interpersonal affective ToM (or their abilities to recognize and interpret the emotions of others).

Rieffe, Terwogt, and Smit (2003) reported that deaf children give different rationales for the occurrence of emotions than their hearing peers. In the case of negative outcome situations, children who are D/HH concentrated more on the loss of the desired state (which evokes sadness predictions), whereas their hearing peers focused more on the conditions that lead to the negative outcome (e.g., those that bring about anger predictions, especially when the situation does not seem totally hopeless yet). Also in contrast with hearing children, children who are D/HH ignored the controllability of the situation. This evaluation affects the way they attempt to regulate their emotions in situations, and they have more difficulty thinking of strategies to regulate their emotions in situations that trigger sadness or anger, which are aspects of intrapersonal affective ToM (Rieffe, 2012). Students who are D/HH also misinterpret the types and causes of emotions of characters in stories (Gray, Hosie, Russell, Scott, & Hunter, 2007). Such errors could significantly compromise their ability to adequately comprehend stories.

Affective ToM begins to emerge in infancy when infants and caregivers are in attunement. Attunement is being aware of and responsive to another. When there are high levels of attunement between caregivers and children, children develop an emotional resonance that influences their sensitivity to each other's minds (intersubjectivity). These early attuned interactions can be disrupted when infants are deaf, particularly if their parents are hearing. Deaf children are less likely to follow the line of regard of others (Scott, Russell, Gray, Hosie, & Hunter, 1999) and hence may be less likely to engage in activities requiring joint attention. Further research is needed to determine whether early identified children who receive family-centered intervention continue to be susceptible to disruptions of attunement.

## ASSESSMENT OF THEORY OF MIND

The research on ToM in children who are D/HH has focused on early emerging interpersonal cognitive ToM, generally evaluated by tasks that assess understanding of false belief. Very few studies have investigated higher order levels of ToM in children who are D/HH (Peterson, Wellman, & Slaughter, 2012), particularly higher level affective ToM. Studies of emotional understanding in children and adolescents who are D/HH have focused on simple, nonsocial emotions (happiness, anger, sadness, disgust, fear). If children who are D/HH have difficulty with these emotions, they are even more likely to have difficulty with more complex nonsocial emotions (disappointment, curiosity) and complex social emotions (jealousy, embarrassment, shame). If educators are to promote students' development of ToM as a means to improve their social and comprehension skills, they need to know the students' skills in each aspect of ToM.

### Assessing Cognitive and Affective Interpersonal Theory of Mind

Many research articles on ToM include the assessment protocols that can be used to assess the cognitive and affective ToM skills of students who are D/HH. Tables 11.2 and 11.3 show some of these tasks.

As of 2015, Hutchins and Prelock are refining and standardizing *The Theory of Mind Task Battery,* which includes tasks that assess some aspects of first and second-order cognitive and affective ToM, although the battery does not differentiate between the cognitive and affective tasks. The same researchers are also standardizing *The Theory of Mind Inventory* (Hutchins, Prelock, & Bonazing, 2012), a parent questionnaire that has parents rate their children on statements reflecting three levels of ToM understanding. Both of these assessments can be downloaded from http://www.theoryofmindinventory.com.

### Assessing Cognitive Intrapersonal Theory of Mind

Cognitive intrapersonal ToM is first observed when toddlers recognize themselves in a mirror. A task has been developed to assess this ability. Using rouge makeup, an experimenter surreptitiously places a dot on the nose or face of the child. The child is then placed in front of a mirror, and his or her reactions are monitored. If the child looks, adjusts to get a better view, touches the rouge, and perhaps acts embarrassed, it can be argued that the child recognizes the child in the mirror as an image of himself or herself (Lewis, 2014).

Another common assessment procedure is to ask students what they do in particular reading tasks. Students may be shown a text they are using in class and asked questions such as "What is the hardest part of answering questions like the ones in this book? Does that make you do anything differently?" (Wix-son, Bosky, Yochum, & Alvermann, 1984, p. 348). Or students may be given hypothetical situations that they are likely to have experienced and asked what they would do. For example, "You have to read a story silently. You need to understand the plot and characters, then retell the story. What do you do to understand the plot and characters? How can you remember and retell the story?" (Chamot & O'Malley, 1994, p. 77).

Individual interviews are time consuming and hence may not be practical when many students must be assessed. A variety of questionnaires for students from elementary school through college have been developed to evaluate metacognitive awareness and use of self-regulatory strategies (Israel, 2007; Schellings, 2011). Some have students rate statements in terms of how much

**Table 11.2.** Assessing cognitive interpersonal theory of mind

| First order | Second order | Higher order |
|---|---|---|
| *Knowledge access:* Child is shown a small box and asked what is in it. Evaluator opens the box and shows the child a small plastic toy dog. He or she then produces a toy figure of a girl and tells the child, "Polly has never seen what's inside this box. Here comes Polly. Does Polly know what's inside the box?" (Wellman & Liu, 2004). | *False belief:* Today is Peter's birthday and Mom is surprising him with a puppy. She has hidden the puppy in the basement. Peter says, "Mom, I really hope you get me a puppy for my birthday." Mom wants to surprise Peter with a puppy. So instead of telling Peter she got him a puppy, Mom says, "Sorry Peter, I did not get you a puppy for your birthday. I got you a really great toy instead." Now Peter says to Mom, "I'm going outside to play." On his way outside, Peter goes to the basement to get his roller skates. In the basement, Peter finds the birthday puppy! Peter says to himself, "Wow, Mom didn't get me a toy, she really got me a puppy." Mom does not see Peter go down to the basement and find the birthday puppy. Now the telephone rings. Peter's grandmother calls to find out what time the birthday party is. Grandma asks Mom on the phone, "Does Peter know what you really got him for his birthday?" | *Cognitive lie:* John hates going to the dentist because every time he goes to the dentist he needs a filling and that hurts a lot. But John knows that when he has a toothache, his mother always takes him to the dentist. Now John has a bad toothache at the moment, but when his mother notices he is looking sick and asks, "Do you have a toothache, John?" John says, "No, Mom." |
| *False belief contents:* Children are shown a crayon box and asked what they believe to be the contents of the box. After the children guess (usually) crayons, they are shown that the box contains ribbons. The adult recloses the box and asks the children what they think another person, who has not been shown the contents of the box, will think is inside (Gopnik & Astington, 1988). | | Higher order question: Was it true what John said? Why did he say that (Happe, 1994)? |
| | *Second-order ignorance question:* What does Mom say to Grandma? | *Figurative language:* Emma has a cough. All through lunch she coughs and coughs. Her father says, "Poor Emma, you must have a frog in your throat" (Happe, 1994). |
| | Then Grandma says to Mom, "What does Peter think you got him for his birthday?" | Higher order question: Is it true what father said? Why did he say that? |
| *False belief location:* Child is shown two dolls, Sally and Anne, who have a basket and a box, respectively. Sally also has a marble, which she places in her basket, and then leaves the room. While she is out of the room, Anne takes the marble from the basket and puts it in the box. Sally returns, and the child is then asked where Sally will look for the marble and why (Baron-Cohen, Leslie, & Frith, 1985). | Second-order false belief question: What does Mom say to Grandma? Why does Mom say that (Sullivan, Zaitchik, & Tager-Flusberg, 1994)? | *Cognitive sarcasm:* Joe went into the bank manager's office and couldn't find anywhere to sit down because there were papers on all the chairs and letters and documents were randomly set on the table. Joe said to the bank manager, "Your office is so tidy!" |
| | | Higher order question: Why did Joe say that? Did Joe think the office was tidy? Was the office tidy (Shamay-Tsoory, Tibi-Elhanany, & Aharon-Peretz, 2007)? |

**Table 11.3.** Assessing affective interpersonal theory of mind

| First order | Second order | Higher order |
|---|---|---|
| *Diverse desires:* Show the child a cartoon scenario with two boys, Mark and Jeff, on either side of a closed box with a movable flap. Tell the child, "Mark hates carrots. Jeff likes carrots very much." Check to make certain the child remembers this "story," and then ask the child to open the flap to see the contents of the box. There are carrots in the box. Ask, "How is Mark feeling? Is he happy, sad, just all right, or scared? How is Jeff feeling?" (Pons, Harris, & de Rosnay, 2004). | *False belief:* Joe and Anna are setting the table for dinner. Anna pours Joe a glass of water, but some water spills on his new shirt. Joe says, "It's nothing. I will change the shirt later." Anna puts the glass on the table and goes to look for a paper towel to dry Joe's shirt. When she leaves the dining room, Joe gets furious about the wet shirt and kicks the table. Anna peeks into the dining room, sees what Joe is doing, and feels guilty. Anna comes back to the dining room. What does Joe think that Anna feels about the wet shirt when she returns? What does Anna think Joe feels about the wet shirt? (Shamay-Tsoory, Tibi-Elhanany, & Aharon-Peretz, 2007). | *Affective lie:* One day Aunt Jane came to visit Peter. Now Peter loves his aunt very much, but today she is wearing a new hat—a new hat which Peter thinks is very ugly indeed. Peter thinks his aunt looks silly in it and much nicer in her old hat. But when Aunt Jane asks Peter, "How do you like my new hat?" Peter says, "Oh, it's very nice." Was it true what Peter said? Why did he say it? (O'Hare, Bremner, Nash, Happe, & Pettigrew, 2009). |
| *False belief affective:* The child judges how a person will feel, given a belief that is mistaken. The child is shown a book with a picture of a rabbit eating a carrot and told that the rabbit likes carrots very much. The child is then asked to lift a flap on the page, which reveals a hidden fox. Tell the child that the fox wants to eat the rabbit. Close the flap and ask the child if the rabbit knows the fox is there. If the child answers the false belief question correctly, say, "That's right—the rabbit doesn't know the fox is hiding behind the bushes. If the child answers incorrectly, say, "Well, actually the rabbit doesn't know the fox is hiding behind the bushes." Then ask, "How is the rabbit feeling? Is he happy, just all right, angry, or scared?" (Pons, Harris, & de Rosnay, 2004). | *Hiding emotions:* The child recognizes that there are situations where one should hide one's true emotions, such as showing pleasure rather than disappointment when receiving an undesirable birthday gift. The child is shown a picture of Chris and his grandmother and told, "This is Chris, and this is Chris's grandmother. Chris told his grandmother he wanted a really scary dinosaur costume for Halloween. His grandmother makes him a Barney costume. [Show a picture of the grandmother with the Barney costume.] What does Chris say to his grandmother? What would Chris's parents want him to say?" (Brinton, Spackman, Fujiki, & Ricks, 2007). | *Affective sarcasm:* Joe's dad was supposed to pick him up after chess club at 6 p.m. By the time he recalled that he had to pick up his son, it was 7 p.m. Dad found Joe standing tired and frightened out in the rain. When they got home, Joe was crying and told his mom what had happened. Mom said, "You are such a good father!" Why did Mom say that? Did Mom think Dad was a good father? Was Dad a good father on this occasion (Shamay-Tsoory, Tibi-Elhanany, & Aharon-Peretz, 2007)? |
| | | *Faux pas:* James bought Richard a toy airplane for his birthday. A few months later, they were playing with it and James accidentally dropped it. "Don't worry," said Richard, "I never liked it anyway. Someone gave it to me for my birthday." Did someone say something he should not have said? What did he say that should not have been said? Did Richard remember James had given him the toy airplane for his birthday (Baron-Cohen, O'Riordan, Stone, Jones, & Plaisted, 1999)? |

the statement is like them (from "very typical of me" to "not at all typical of me"; e.g., "I have difficulty identifying the important points in reading"; Weinstein & Palmer, 2002) or how often they employ an activity ("almost never," "sometimes," "often"; e.g., "I tried to draw conclusions from the text"; Schellings, 2011). Other questionnaires have students select a response from multi-ple choices. For example,

> When I'm reading, it's a good idea to 1) stop to retell the main points to see if I understand what happened so far, 2) read the story quickly to find out what happened, 3) read only the beginning and end of the story to find out what happens, and 4) skip the parts that are too difficult for me. (Schmitt, 1990)

### Assessing Affective Intrapersonal Theory of Mind

Assessments of affective intrapersonal ToM examine awareness of one's emotions and the ability to regulate one's emotions. The *Emotion Regulation Questionnaire for Children and Adolescents* (Gullone & Taffe, 2011) and the *Emotional Regulation Index* (MacDermott, Gullone, Allen, King, & Tonge, 2010) ask children 9 years and older to make judgments about their emotional awareness, self-control, and situational responsiveness. Children are asked to rate themselves on items such as "When things don't go my way I get upset easily"; "I am a happy person"; "I control my feelings by not showing them"; and "When I want to feel less bad, I think of something different." Adults can make judgments of children's and adolescents' affective intrapersonal ToM by observing how well they appear to understand and regulate their affect (Delaney, 2006). For example, does the child display awareness of his or her affect by labeling emotions, tying emotions to situations that generated them, displaying emotion appropriate to situations, or differentiating between two similar emotions (e.g., excitement and happiness)? Regulation of affect can also be revealing. Does the child regulate the intensity of affect (e.g., frustration does not escalate to intense anger); tolerate negative emotions such as sadness, disappointment, and frustration; discuss strong negative emotions; use self-soothing mechanisms when upset; and signal needs to adults when overwhelmed and accept their help?

### INTERVENTIONS TO PROMOTE THEORY OF MIND

Interpersonal and intrapersonal cognitive and affective ToM are essential for recognizing and interpreting emotions, making appropriate inferences in social interactions and academic contexts, regulating one's own learning and emotions, and evaluating one's knowledge; hence, ToM deficits can contribute to literacy, behavioral, and social difficulties exhibited by children who are D/HH. A number of the **Common Core State Standards** (National Governors Association Center for Best Practices and Council of Chief State School Officers, 2010) require perspective taking and ToM ability (e.g., students must acknowledge differences in the points of view of characters or describe how a narrator's or speaker's point of view influences how events are described). Because ToM deficits are commonly associated with deafness, and given the role of ToM in social and academic functioning, it is imperative that service providers for students who are D/HH have strategies for developing a range of ToM abilities. These strategies can be appropriate for children who are D/HH that are making steady progress in developing listening, spoken language, and literacy skills (i.e., a habilitative approach) and those who are not making expected progress in these areas (i.e., a rehabilitative approach).

Interventions to foster ToM development must take into account the various dimensions of ToM. This section will describe a variety of strategies to stimulate interpersonal and intrapersonal cognitive and affective ToM in children and adolescents who are D/HH. When seeking to develop the ToM skills of children and adolescents, adults must consider their own language and interactions as much or more than the language and interactions of their students. Although some aspects of cognitive ToM can be acquired through explicit teaching of vocabulary and syntax, affective ToM and effective use of both cognitive and affective ToM skills can only be learned through caring, empathic interactions with others who are skillful with their own understanding of ToM.

In the following section, we describe strategies to promote ToM development in children and adolescents who are D/HH as a way to foster social skills and reading comprehension. All the strategies have empirical bases—some in the developmental literature on ToM and some in intervention research on reading comprehension in neurotypical students and students with learning disabilities. Some strategies focus on one dimension of ToM, while others involve multiple dimensions.

### Developing Theory of Mind Foundations

***Developing Mental State and Emotion Words***   Development of ToM, particularly cognitive ToM, is highly dependent on children's language skills. If children are to develop ToM, they must converse with individuals who use words to refer to emotions and mental states and processes (see Video clips 11.1 and 11.2). Caregivers and service providers frequently use mental state and emotion words when remembering and reflecting on past experiences and thinking about and planning future experiences. Reflecting on past experiences promotes development of episodic **autobiographical memory** (or "time travel" to the past), and reflecting on possibilities of future experiences develops episodic autobiographical future time travel. This **mental time travel** requires development of a sense of self—an aspect of intrapersonal ToM. When one engages in mental time travel, one has a sense of oneself in the past or the future. These autobiographical memories or thoughts through time are different from semantic memory, which involves knowledge of an event or experience. For example, I have semantic knowledge that I have ridden most of the rides at Disneyland, but I have autobiographical memory of only a few. When I remember my first ride on the Space Mountain roller coaster, my autobiographical memory is activated—I remember the darkness, the irritating flashing lights, the sense of speed, and the dizziness I felt when I got off.

Children whose mothers engage in a highly elaborative reminiscing style, replete with description and evaluation, develop better autobiographical memories not only for those particular experiences but also for other experiences as they grow (Fivush, 2011). Adults are not only promoting children's understanding and use of mental state and emotion words in these interactions, but they are also promoting children's sense of self or intrapersonal ToM. Furthermore, these guided conversations highlight for children that different people can have different subjective perspectives on the same objective event, thus promoting development of interpersonal ToM. Children who have more opportunities to reminisce about emotional experiences show higher levels of emotional understanding and regulation (affective ToM; Laible, 2004a, 2004b). The better their autobiographical memories for the past, the better their future time travel skills. By being able to see themselves in the future, children are better able to self-regulate and plan their behaviors (intrapersonal ToM). In addition, children who have better autobiographical memories have their prior knowledge more accessible. This can facilitate their comprehension because discourse comprehension requires building mental models that are dependent on integrating information in the discourse or text with prior knowledge so that one can make necessary inferences. Providers of family-centered intervention (Chapter 4) can stimulate these affective and interpersonal abilities by modeling and encouraging parents to use elaborative reminiscing with their child who is D/HH.

In a classroom, educators can talk about earlier experiences or activities that have been completed. Class field trips provide excellent opportunities for using mental state and emotion words before and after the experience. For example, before a trip to the natural history museum, the teachers can ask children to *predict* what they might see and do. They might distinguish between what they *know* they will see (based on a brochure from the museum) and what they *hope* they might see (i.e., something they would *like* to see that they *think* might be in the museum, such as a stegosaurus). They can *decide* what they *want* to see first. While at the museum, teachers can comment on students' emotional responses to what they see. "You are *intrigued* with the sun dagger astronomical exhibit and *curious* about how the ancient ones could have made it." "You're *hypothesizing* about how they could have moved those huge boulders." After the trip, students can *reflect on* and *remember* what they saw and did. They can *evaluate* the predictions they made before the trip. "We didn't *expect* to walk through a volcano." "We were *disappointed* that the planetarium was not working." "We were *startled* by the visual effects of a meteor exploding in the dinosaur exhibit."

Many approaches to teaching reading involve teaching metacognitive strategies. If students are to engage in metacognitive strategies, it is critical that teachers engage in metacognitive talk such as suggesting a child use a particular strategy (e.g., "Remember how we figure out the meaning of a word"), asking metacognitive questions ("How can you tell that Jim's unhappy?"), or requesting information from memory and providing suggestions for strategies to facilitate remembering or retrieval of information (e.g., "How did you answer that last question about Jimmy?"). Children in classrooms where teachers engage in more metacognitive talk spend more time using strategies when asked to remember a variety of interesting objects than the children in the classrooms where teachers did not engage in frequent metacognitive talk—  and they remember significantly more items (Ornstein, Grammer, & Coffman, 2010; see Video clip 11.3).

***Recognizing and Interpreting Emotional Expressions***   A number of programs designed to build social/emotional and problem-solving skills in typically developing children and children with disruptive behavior disorders include activities to promote recognition, understanding, and regulation of emotions. Using a wait-list control design, Greenberg and Kusche (1998) implemented PATHS (Promoting Alternative Thinking Strategies) with children who are D/HH in first through sixth grades. The children who are D/HH in the program exhibited significant improvement in recognizing emotions, offered more positive, prosocial alternatives on problem-solving tasks, and exhibited greater self-regulation of their emotions and behaviors after participating in the program.

Several programs that have been developed to teach emotional recognition to children with autism spectrum disorders (ASD) have the potential to be useful with the D/HH population. *The Transporters* (http://www.thetransporters .com) DVD teaches children (4–7 years) how to recognize 15 emotions through the exploits of eight vehicles, including a train, a bus, a ferry, and a cable car. The vehicles have human faces grafted onto them, making focusing on human features unavoidable. *Mindreading* (Baron-Cohen, Golan, Wheelwright, & Hill, 2007) is an interactive computer program that guides players through a series of interactive game modules designed to teach basic face processing skills. *Mindreading* also has a library of 412 different emotions organized into 24 related groups. Six video clips are provided for each emotion, showing close-up performances by a wide range of people (old, young, men, women, boys, girls) in a variety of situations. *Let's Face It!* (Wolf et al., 2008), which can be downloaded free from http://web .uvic .ca/~letsface/letsfaceit/, is a set of computer games that teach following line of regard, facial discrimination, and emotion discrimination. Recognizing facial expressions is not the same as understanding an emotion or feeling empathy, but if you cannot recognize what someone is feeling, how are you going to respond emotionally to what they're feeling? These programs are not meant to stand alone or substitute for human interaction. Ideally, experiences with the programs should be linked with opportunities to use the skills in real-life situations.

Watching videos can also provide opportunities to study facial expressions in context. Short wordless narrative videos provide students with the opportunity to connect facial expressions with story events. The Max the Mouse videos (*Max in Motion* and *Adventuresome Max*, available for purchase from http://store .discoveryeducation.com), each only a few minutes long, show Max the Mouse in situations where he experiences a variety of emotions and intents to deal with the situations. Max exhibits specific and intense facial and gestural cues regarding his emotions. *Shawn the Sheep* and *Pingu* cartoons, two British claymation video series available for free on YouTube, can be useful for discussing emotions in contexts. The claymation nature of the videos does not provide as defined emotional cues as the Max videos. The emotional features in these videos are typically more stereotyped so students will need to use more contextual cues to interpret the characters' emotions and intents. Schick and Moeller (1998) produced a DVD version of the alphabet book, *C is for Curious: An ABC of Feelings* (Hubbard, 1995) as a way to discuss emotions with deaf children who use American Sign Language (ASL). For the DVD, the deaf poet, Peter Cook, created story vignettes in ASL to illustrate the meanings of each emotion word.

Although ToM is needed to understand stories, picture book stories can be used to develop interpersonal cognitive and affective ToM (see Video clip 11.4). Books by Jan Thomas are particularly useful for teaching mental state and emotion words and developing ToM. The books are geared toward preschool children, but they can be used with children through mid-elementary school. Each book typically has a single episode story told primarily through the voices of its animal characters. The amount of text is minimal. The characters' expressions are superb. In her drawings, Thomas conveys a variety of emotions—not only happy, sad, frightened, and angry, but additional emotions such as surprised, frustrated, concerned, puzzled, worried, enthusiastic, disappointed, confused, and relieved. The emotions are conveyed through the characters eyes/eyebrows, mouths, and body stances. The plots of the stories trigger the characters' emotions, and the emotions carry forward the stories.

An early stage in the development of ToM is awareness that people may have different desires and that they are happy when they get what they desire. The book *A Birthday for Cow!* (Thomas, 2008) provides a way to help young children understand this concept. Pig and Mouse are making Cow what they believe is the best birthday cake ever. They mix flour, sugar, and eggs into a big

**Figure 11.2.**    Pictures from *A BIRTHDAY FOR COW!* (Illustrations from A BIRTHDAY FOR COW! By Jan Thomas. Copyright © 2008 by Jan Thomas. Reprinted by permission of Houghton Mifflin Publishing Company. All rights reserved.)

bowl. Duck wants to mix in a turnip, which Pig and Mouse adamantly refuse to do. How can you mix a turnip into a birthday cake? As the cake is baked and about to be decorated, Duck keeps insisting that they add the turnip, but the other animals refuse to consider this suggestion, becoming progressively more irritated with Duck (moving from irritated, to angry, to furious). Duck is puzzled and confused by their refusal of the turnip. Mouse and Pig frost and decorate a beautiful cake, which they feel Cow is guaranteed to love. A surprised Cow is overjoyed when he arrives and, on seeing her friends, exclaims, "Is that what I think it is? Oh boy, this is the best birthday ever . . . a turnip!" Duck knew something about Cow that Mouse and Pig did not know. They acted on their false belief that Cow would want a cake for his birthday. Cow eats the turnip while Pig and Mouse eat the cake. The ending is surprising. Because most children would like cake, they are likely to expect that Cow will like cake. Children easily relate to this story. They understand about birthdays and recognize that they are happy if they get something they want for their birthday. The story helps them realize that not everyone likes or wants the same thing.

Using DVDs along with books that students are reading is another means to draw attention to interpreting emotions. Movies have been made of a number of stories that students read. Students can read an excerpt from the book and then watch the same excerpt on the video. Teachers can draw the students' attention to the characters' facial and body cues, as well as visual factors in the setting to assist them in interpreting the scene. They can then go back to the text and note the words the author used to convey this information. Reading comprehension requires the ability to make mental models (visual images) of the text one is reading. One cannot develop mental visual images when reading texts if one has not developed accurate interpretations of situations. Some books and videos are better matches than others. *Holes* (Sachar, 1998), a Newbery award book about an adolescent in a juvenile detention center in the desert of West Texas, and the accompanying movie screenplay were written by the same person and are a near perfect match. See Chapter 12 for more ideas on developing reading comprehension.

***Teaching Complex Syntax to Express Emotions and Intents***   Students must be able to do more than identify individuals' mental states and emotions; they must be able to recognize and express the reasons for and consequences of these mental states and emotions. This requires competency with some complex syntax. ToM skills are closely intertwined with syntactic skills. Students with language delays or disorders for any reason experience difficulty attempting to express an unfamiliar or abstract concept in complex syntax. This may be related to demands on working memory. Attempting to retrieve a syntactic pattern while manipulating multiple conceptual ideas may require more working memory than is available. Providing students with sentence frames to express their ideas can reduce working memory load, allowing students to more easily express the concepts. The use of sentence frames with students who are D/HH has been around for quite some time. *The Fitzgerald Color Coding Key* (Fitzgerald, 1976) has been used to teach students who are D/HH the parts of speech and the order of words in a sentence since 1929.

Table 11.4 presents a frame for expressing how characters feel when something happens and why they feel as they do. Examples in Table 11.4 are from the book *Holes* (Sachar, 1998). Typically, the adult enters the character names in the chart and describes the "when" situations. Students then complete the chart by putting in the appropriate feeling and explanation. The adult then models how this can be expressed: For example, "When Zero was looking over Stanley's shoulder as he was writing to his mother, Stanley felt annoyed because he didn't want Zero to see what he was writing," or, "Stanley felt annoyed when Zero was looking over his shoulder because he didn't want Zero to see what he was writing" (see Video clip 11.5).

The students are given a frame and shown that there can be more than one way of expressing this content. Adults can also write the clauses of these sentences on separate sheets of paper and have students put the pieces in an order that makes sense.

The essence of narratives lies in the intentions or goal-directed behaviors of their characters—all requiring that readers have interpersonal ToM. A character (a person or animal) wants something for some reason. The character tries to do something to accomplish a goal but frequently encounters one or more obstacles that must be overcome before the goal can be achieved. This content determines the story theme. According to the Common Core State Standards for Language Arts, fourth-grade students have to be able to determine narrative themes (National Governors Association Center for Best Practices and Council of Chief State School Officers, 2010). Table 11.5 presents a frame using the book *Percy Jackson and the Olympians: The Lightning Thief* (Riordan, 2005) for describing a character's goal, rationale for that goal, an obstacle to the goal, and what the character did in reaction to that obstacle.

## Developing Theory of Mind for Academics

*Think-Alouds*  The purpose of the think-aloud strategy is to model for students how skilled readers construct meaning from a text (Davey, 1983). The goal is for students to learn to monitor their thinking as they read. Students who are D/HH may be poor at monitoring their comprehension, often assuming that they have comprehended the text when they have not. Think-alouds

**Table 11.4.**  Syntactic frame for expressing emotions for different characters and situations from the novel *Holes*

| Characters | When | Feeling | Why (because) |
|---|---|---|---|
| Stanley | Zero was looking over Stanley's shoulder as he was writing to his mother. | Annoyed | He didn't want Zero to see what he was writing. |
| Stanley | X-ray takes the lipstick tube and turns it in. | Frustrated | Stanley found the tube, so he should get a day off. |
| Zero | He finds his mother. | Relieved, thrilled, happy | He thought she might have died or that she didn't want him. |
| The warden | Stanley's lawyer finds the boys in the hole. | Worried | The authorities will learn how she has been mistreating the boys, and she could go to jail. |

*Source:* Sachar, L. (1998).

**Table 11.5.** Syntactic frame for expressing rationales for intentions for *Percy Jackson and the Olympians: The Lightning Thief*

| Somebody | Wanted | But | So |
|---|---|---|---|
| Percy | Wanted to stop Medusa because she could stop him from finding the lightning thief | But if he looked at her when he swung his sword he would be turned to stone | So he looked at her reflection in a mirror and swung his sword behind him |
| Grover | Wanted to get permission to go in search of Pan, the god of the fields, because he has not been seen for many years | But he had failed on his previous tasks | So he had to prove himself by successfully protecting Percy |
| Annabeth | Wanted to leave Camp Halfblood because she had not seen much of the real world | But she could not live in the world with her stepfamily because she brought them into danger | So going on the quest with Percy was a way to get out of camp |

*Source:* Riordan, R. (2005).

require both intrapersonal and interpersonal ToM. Student must recognize if they are comprehending; if they are not, they must reflect on the strategies they could use (intrapersonal ToM). They must make inferences about the author's intent in writing the text or the characters' intents or reasons for their actions (interpersonal ToM). Recommended components of think-alouds include the following:

- *Making predictions:* "From the title, I think this will be about . . ."

- *Describing the pictures students form in their heads about the information:* "I have a picture of this scene in my head, and this is what it looks like . . ."

- *Developing analogies:* Showing how to link prior knowledge to new information in text. "This reminds me of . . ."

- *Making inferences from pictures and words:* "I think Stanley feels frustrated because . . ."

- *Demonstrating fix-up strategies:* Showing how to make sense of the passage. "I'd better reread," or "I'll read ahead and see if I can get some more information."

Think-alouds have been used with readers from the upper elementary grades through college. Traditionally, think-alouds are done with printed texts. For individuals with language deficits, however, thinking aloud while reading can be quite difficult and may actually disrupt and distort the reading process, particularly for students who are poor readers. The complexity of think-alouds places stress on working memory because the students must remember and reflect on what was read while simultaneously organizing a verbal response to explain what they are doing to comprehend the text. To teach the think-aloud process without compounding it with reading or listening to text, educators can model thinking aloud using pictures or wordless picture books. For upper elementary through high school students, we have found the books *The Invention of Hugo Cabret* (Selznick, 2007) and *Wonderstruck* (Selznick, 2011) particularly useful for teaching and using the think-aloud process. These books are between 530 and 630 pages long—but more than half of each book is pictures. The pictures do not represent the printed text; they are their own "text." *Wonderstruck* tells the story of two deaf individuals. The majority of the boy's story is told through printed text; the majority of the girl's story is  told through pictures. To follow the stories, the reader must carefully interpret the pictures (see Video clips 11.6, 11.7, and 11.8).

**Questioning the Author**    We integrate the think-aloud process with the "Question the Author" (QtA) process. Beck and McKeown (2006) proposed questions for students to use to QtA as a way of encouraging reflection on the text content. QtA encourages interpersonal ToM because students are asked to think like the author of the text. The Common Core State Standards for Language Arts (National Governors Association Center for Best Practices and Council of Chief State School Officers, 2010) require that by sixth grade, students should be able to interpret the author's intent and point of view.

A teacher may initiate a discussion by asking questions such as "What is the author trying to say here?"; "What is the author's message?"; or "What is the author talking about?" Follow-up queries assist students in integrating and connecting ideas to construct meaning. They are encouraged to consider the ideas behind the author's words—to consider what the text means rather than what it says: "What does the author mean here?" If the student rereads the words on the page, the teacher may say, "That's what she says, but what does she mean? What does she want us to understand? Does the author explain this clearly?" Other queries relate information from different parts of a text or make connections with something that may be missing from the text: "Does this make sense with what the author told us before? How does this connect to what the author told us here?" And finally, queries help students figure out an author's reason  for including particular information: "Does the author tell us why? Why do you think the author tells us this now?" (see Video clips 11.9 and 11.10).

When using QtA with pictures, teachers modify the questions slightly to refer to the artist's intent. Although the questions can foster development of metacognitive awareness, by themselves they will not lead students to self-regulation of the reading process. Educators need to employ strategies in which control of the process is gradually transferred from the educator to the student so that the students ask these questions themselves as they read. See Chapter 12 for additional related ideas.

**Question–Answer Relationships**    Students who are D/HH exhibit greater difficulty than hearing students in comprehending both literal and inferential questions, but their difficulty is more marked for inferential questions. Students may not always be aware of where to find the answers to questions; this would require metacognition or intrapersonal cognitive ToM. Students must monitor texts to determine the information that is explicitly provided and to recognize the situations in which they must infer information. Raphael and colleagues (Raphael, Highfield, & Au, 2006) engaged children in noting the types of relationships between questions that can be asked of texts and their answers. They proposed four types of question–answer relationships; examples of questions asked about the book *Passage to Freedom: The Sugihara Story* (Mochizuki, 1997) are provided in Table 11.6. This picture book tells about the experiences of the Sugihara family in Lithuania at the beginning of World War II. Mr. Sugihara was the Japanese ambassador to Lithuania. Jews, fleeing the German military, sought visas from Sugihara to leave the country. Sugihara's supervisors in Japan denied him the authority to issue visas, but he chose to do so anyway, putting himself and his family in danger.

Educators can ask students to identify the types of questions they are asked. In addition, they can ask students to develop questions of each type about a passage. In doing so, they can also use mental state terms when discussing the answers to the questions: "I know for sure the answers to 'right there' and 'think and search' questions"; "I'm inferring the answer to the 'you and the author' questions"; "For the 'on your own' question, I'm trying to remember; I think . . ."

***Teaching Text Structure*** Narrative comprehension requires more than understanding the individual words and sentences of the stories—the **discourse/ text microstructure**. One must also recognize the overall story organization— the **discourse/text macrostructure**—and to do this with narratives, the listener or reader must be able to view the action from the point of view of the story characters and to empathize with their motives and actions. Most stories in mainstream Euro-American culture have similar macrostructure organization. Stories have *characters* and a *setting*—the time and place where the events occur. They begin with some *initiating event* that is disequilibrating—a change of state or an action that creates a problem for the characters, which in turn motivates a character's *emotional reaction or response*. The reaction to the initiating event can be a behavior such as crying or yelling that is not goal directed or two

**Table 11.6.**   Question–answer relationship question types for *Passage to Freedom: The Sugihara Story*

| Type of question | Example | Rationale for type |
|---|---|---|
| *Right there:* The answer is explicitly stated in the text. | Why was the Sugihara family living in Lithuania? | The author says they were there because Mr. Sugihara was the Japanese ambassador to Lithuania. |
| *Think and search:* The answer is in the text, but the words in the question and the words in the text are not the same or the answer is not in just one location. | In what ways did Hiroki's life change after the Polish Jews came to his house? | As one reads, one learns that Hiroki, Mr. Sugihara's son, can no longer play outside; he keeps the curtains drawn, and the family is running low on food. |
| *You and the author:* This involves thinking about what you have learned from the text and using what you already know to answer the question. | Why didn't Mrs. Sugihara help write the visas? | The author tells us that Mr. Sugihara does not want his wife to get into trouble, but we are not told what this trouble might be. |
| *On your own:* The question is motivated by some information in the text, but the answer has to be generated from students' prior knowledge. | Can you think of someone else who has risked his or her own life to save other individuals? | The question requires text-to-self inference; the student must be able to identify a personal experience with the story. |

*Source:* Mochizuki, K. (1997).

types of internal responses such as an internal state (emotional feelings) or an internal plan that leads to overt reactions such as physical *attempts* to cope with the initiating event or problem. For a story to be perceived as a "good story," there must also be some *consequence or outcome* of the character's attempts—possibly a character's reaction to this consequence. In some stories, an obstacle blocks goal attainment, so the initial consequence of the character's attempts does not result in resolution of the problem. In these cases, the character must engage in further attempts to achieve the goal. There may be a reaction or *resolution* that relates to the characters' thoughts, feelings, or actions (behaviors) in relation to the consequence. There may also be an ending that may be as simple as "that's all" or "the end" or that in some way addresses the overall theme of the story or gives a summary or a moral. These components comprise a story episode, but not all are absolutely essential to a story. A minimally complete episode must contain at least some reference to the motivation or purpose of the character's behavior (an initiating event or an internal response), an overt goal-directed action (an attempt), and the attainment or nonattainment of the goal (a direct con-se-quence). (See Chapter 13.)

Explicitly teaching students the structure of narratives results in improved comprehension and production of stories but also improved syntax (Gillam, Gillam, & Reece, 2012). Narratives place a considerable load on working memory because students must engage in several activities simultaneously. When they listen, read, or tell a story, they must keep in mind the overall gist of the story, while simultaneously comprehending or organizing each utterance, linking the utterances together in a temporal/causal sequence, and making certain that all utterances link to the theme and overall organization of the story. Students who are D/HH have deficits in working memory that can contribute to their difficulties with discourse-level comprehension (Hall & Bavelier, 2010). Providing visual support can reduce the load on working memory. A variety of outlines, graphic organizers, and manipulatives are available for teaching narrative structure. For example, the *Story Grammar Marker®* (SGM; Moreau & Fidrych, 1994) is a manipulative that reminds students of the parts of stories and their sequence. The SGM is a braided yarn character with icons that repre-sent the components of stories. The furry ball with eyes at one end represents the character (or characters) in the story; the star represents the setting of the story; the shoe represents the "kickoff" (initiating event), which is the action or perception that gets the story going; and the heart represents the character's feeling about the initiating event. In most stories, characters decide to do something about the initiating event; they make a plan. The hand on the SGM represents the character's plan. Each bead represents an attempt. The yarn bow at the base of the beads represents the consequence of the attempts, and the small hearts at the end of braid represent the character's feelings about the consequence (see Figure 11.3).

Many studies teaching narrative structure have focused on having students identify and label the narrative components. Few have acknowledged that narrative structure arises from the narrative content. Something is an initiating event only when a character responds emotionally and behaviorally to it in some way. The attempts in the story arise because the characters intend or set goals to change something or accomplish something. Hence the

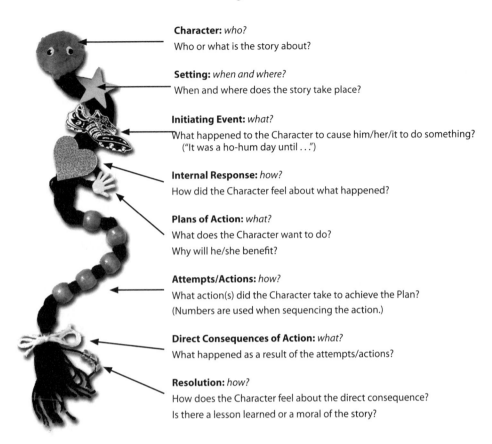

**Character:** *who?*
Who or what is the story about?

**Setting:** *when and where?*
When and where does the story take place?

**Initiating Event:** *what?*
What happened to the Character to cause him/her/it to do something?
("It was a ho-hum day until . . .")

**Internal Response:** *how?*
How did the Character feel about what happened?

**Plans of Action:** *what?*
What does the Character want to do?
Why will he/she benefit?

**Attempts/Actions:** *how?*
What action(s) did the Character take to achieve the Plan?
(Numbers are used when sequencing the action.)

**Direct Consequences of Action:** *what?*
What happened as a result of the attempts/actions?

**Resolution:** *how?*
How does the Character feel about the direct consequence?
Is there a lesson learned or a moral of the story?

**Figure 11.3.** Illustration of the Story Grammar Marker®, a manipulative that reminds students of the parts of stories and their sequence. (From Moreau, M.R., & Fidrych, H. [1994]. *The story grammar marker teacher's manual.* Story Grammar Marker®. Reprinted with permission from MindWing Concepts, Inc.)

essence of comprehending and producing narrative is dependent on ToM skills. Consequently, mapping narratives to text structure should not be taught as an isolated skill. Educators will need to use all the strategies discussed in this chapter for promoting ToM to build students' understanding of the narrative characters and how the characters' intentions, emotions, and beliefs drive the story structure.

***Reciprocal Teaching*** We have left discussion of reciprocal teaching (RT) until last in this chapter because it requires that students integrate skills in all ToM dimensions and all intervention activities described in this chapter. Although RT can promote development of intrapersonal and interpersonal ToM, students must have some foundation in ToM skills to engage in the RT process. Oczkus (2010) provides strategies for teaching the underlying concepts and strategies for students who require more support to engage in RT:

- *Predicting:* Using a think-aloud approach, model predicting by saying, "I think I will learn . . . because . . . ," or, "I think . . . will happen because . . ."

- *Questioning:* Model different types of questions. An adult might begin with "I wonder . . ." and then ask questions with who, what, how, where, when, and why. Explain that the answers to some questions are found in the text, whereas other answers have to be inferred. Use the question–answer relationship framework to have students think about where they can find the answer.

- *Clarifying:* Explain that readers use the clarifying strategy when they want to figure out tricky or hard words or ideas. Adults model their own thinking as they clarify. For example, they might model use of the phrase "I don't get . . . , so I . . ." Then give ideas for what they might do (e.g., read on, reread, ask a friend; see Video clip 11.11).

- *Summarizing:* Model summarizing, using language such as "So far . . ."; "This is mostly about . . ."; "First . . . next . . . then . . ."

## ONGOING ASSESSMENT TO GUIDE INTERVENTION

Initially, it is important to evaluate what ToM skills students have and do not have. The goal of intervention, however, is not to teach ToM skills so that students pass ToM assessment tasks but rather to use information from the assessment to know the types of language and thinking skills to teach to promote students' interpersonal and intrapersonal cognitive and affective ToM so they can comprehend texts and social discourse interactions. Based on the concepts discussed in this chapter, ongoing assessment can involve tracking the number and type of mental state and emotion words used in conversations, personal and fictional narratives, and narrative retells; the syntactic and discourse organization complexity of their personal (tapping autobiographical memory), historical, and fictional narratives; their responses to literal and inferential questions; and the number and types of strategies mentioned when students do think-alouds with pictures or texts.

Narrative comprehension and production is highly dependent on ToM skills. One must have good interpersonal cognitive and affective ToM to recognize how intents, beliefs, and emotions drive the heart of narratives, and one must have good intrapersonal ToM to monitor one's comprehension and production. Narrative assessment can be a time-consuming process. Peterson and Spencer (2012) have developed the *Narrative Language Measures* (NLM) as a quick way to evaluate children's personal narrative generation or retell of real-life short stories. The materials are meant for typically developing children from preschool through third grade, but the authors of this chapter have been able to use the materials with students with language impairments through middle school. The materials are available for free at http://languagedynamicsgroup .com/products.html. The NLM stories highlight events that children are likely to experience in their daily lives (e.g., getting hurt, losing something). Students either retell a short real-life story or generate a personal story. Scoring for narrative organization is based on story grammar elements, including description of a setting, a problem, attempts to solve the problem, and the consequence. Points are also awarded for referring to intention and emotions. A syntactic score is based on use of connecting words and subordinate clauses. The retell scoring rubric can be used across all ages.

The European Cooperation in Science and Technology (COST) sponsored development of narrative assessment materials for children ages 3 through 9. Four stories of six pictures each are on the COST web site (http://www.bi-sli .org/WG.htm). All stories include an instance of ToM false belief. Children's story retells or productions are scored for the elements of story structure that are included. For each story, children can also be asked a set of inferential comprehension questions. In addition, the number and types of mental state and emotion words in the students' stories are counted.

Getting beyond fourth-grade comprehension levels necessitates that students be able to read between the lines—to make inferences. The *Qualitative Reading Inventory* (QRI; Leslie & Caldwell, 2011) provides reading passages from preprimer through high school. Students listen to or read the passages, retell them, and answer four literal and four inferential questions. The answers to the inferential questions can be analyzed based on the type of inferencing they require. The QRI could be part of a yearly evaluation. Throughout the year, the educator should be certain to use both literal and inferential questions and have students generate these types of questions.

Engaging students who are D/HH in reciprocal teaching activities can improve their ability to make inferences and comprehend what they read, but speech-language pathologists (SLPs) and educators need to monitor the types of difficulties students have with the components of reciprocal teaching. Here are some examples:

- *Predicting:* Are students making imaginative predictions that are not based on textual cues and do not relate to the texts? After reading, are they failing to check the accuracy of their predictions?

- *Questioning:* Are they producing only literal or superficial questions?

- *Clarifying:* When they clarify, do they focus only on single words rather than ideas?

- *Summarizing:* Are they failing to recognize themes or main ideas? When they attempt to summarize, are they simply recounting anything they remember from the text?

## Case Study: Application to a Child

Thomas was a 4 lbs, 7 oz, 35-week preemie born by cesarean section. He was hospitalized for the first 11 weeks of his life and diagnosed with Mobius syndrome with involvement of the left sixth, bilateral seventh, and bilateral eighth cranial nerves. The sixth cranial nerve, the abducens, turns the eye laterally; the seventh cranial nerve, the facial, enables facial expression, some sense of touch on the face, and sense of the tongue in the mouth; the eighth cranial nerve, the vestibulocochlear, enables hearing and a sense of balance. Because of Mobius syndrome, Thomas is unable to move his eyes independent of moving his head, he can make no facial expression, he cannot eat by mouth or move his lips or tongue to produce any speech sound, and he is profoundly deaf.

Research on individuals with Mobius suggests that their inability to produce emotional expressions can compromise their ability to recognize emotional expressions in others (Bate, Cook, Mole, & Cole, 2013). Recognizing emotional expressions is an aspect of affective theory of mind (ToM). In neurotypical individuals, recognition of emotions in others is mediated by the mirror neurons. Mirror neurons fire both when individuals perform a motor act and when they witness another person perform the same act. Seeing emotional expressions in others triggers the neurons that one uses to produce the same emotional expressions, and this facilitates recognition of the emotion. If a person cannot perform the motor act, as is the case with Mobius, the neuron does not fire, and if the neuron does not fire to produce a motor movement, it will not fire when the motor movement of another is witnessed (Keysers, 2011). The mirror neuron system is the automatic or *low road* to emotion recognition and emotional empathy. Individuals who do not have access to this low road can still use a *high road*—a more cognitive or mentalizing approach—that uses language to reason about the situation and person to interpret emotional expressions (Krueger & Michael, 2012). As a profoundly deaf child of hearing parents, Thomas was likely to have delays in ToM development. Having Mobius syndrome could further compound his development of ToM. As a result of Mobius syndrome, Thomas lacked access to the automatic or low road to aspects of affective ToM. Consequently, he must rely on the high road, which in his case is also compromised because of his reduced access to language.

Thomas was fitted with hearing aids initially but did not gain any noticeable benefit. He received a Nucleus 24 cochlear implant (CI) at 2 years of age, but testing indicated no benefit from the implant. Thomas was enrolled in early intervention at 4 months of age and at 1 year began receiving support services through the state School for the Deaf early intervention program. At age 3, Thomas entered the School for the Deaf dual-language program.

Thomas's entire family attended sign language classes from the beginning of his life, and his mother entered the university sign language interpreting program when he was five to keep up with Thomas's rapid language acquisition. When he entered the School for the Deaf preschool program at age 3, his siblings were enrolled as peer models. Because Thomas could not convey any emotions through facial expressions, his mother searched for other cues of his emotions. She identified his "smile" and "happy state" with changes in respiration and belly movements. His laugh was a guttural sound and wiggling. Anger was a tensing of his body all over. Sometimes Thomas averted eye gaze to communicate discomfort or sadness and broadened his eyes to communicate fear or anxiety. By reading these subtle emotional cues,  Thomas's mother was able to engage in interactive, attuned interactions, which lay the foundation for ToM (see Video clip 11.12).

Staff of the preschool program gave considerable attention to ways to modify American Sign Language (ASL; see Chapter 6) so Thomas could communicate needs and emotions using strategies that were not dependent on the use of facial expressions and the facial grammatical markers of ASL. He would lean forward for questioning and back for laughter. He began to use the ASL sign for "question" to indicate when he was asking questions (because he was unable to show that with facial expressions). Games were played that required Thomas to watch and move in synchrony with his peers and respond to his peers' engagements. Thomas began to initiate and turn-take with meaningful discourse. All this was mediated and facilitated so that the other children learned along with Thomas how to respond to his unique ways of engaging.

When Thomas was five, the preschool staff began implementing further strategies to support the development of ToM. The preschool literacy team used the reciprocal teaching strategies, including think-alouds, cooperative learning, and mental state and emotional vocabulary words, when discussing stories and encouraged students to make predictions, ask questions, clarify confusions, and provide story summaries. Stories were selected that were rich in affective and mental states. To build autobiographical memory and the use of mental state and emotion words, children were scaffolded in producing personal narratives around activities and field trips at the preschool (see Video clip 11.13, showing Thomas's narrative about decorating for Halloween). Photographs and videos of the events supported retellings. Teachers encouraged the children to remember and evaluate the events, particularly discussing children's emotional responses and noting when children had different feelings about the experiences.

At age 7, Thomas's expressive and receptive ASL language scores were in the 55th and 75th percentiles, respectively, on the *One Word Expressive Vocabulary Test* (Brownell, 2000) and the *Carolina Picture Vocabulary Test* (Layton & Holmes, 1985). All instructions were given in ASL, and he responded in ASL. On the *Test of Early Reading Ability Deaf and Hard of Hearing* (Reid, Hresko, Hammill, & Wiltshire, 1991), Thomas scored in the average range with a percentile ranking of 66%. On a language sample, Thomas used language to think and reason (e.g., "Connie hold implant, why? I think broke . . . battery dead"); to make guesses and predictions (e.g., "The boy might play basketball or go home after he gets off his bike"); and to demonstrate metacognitive awareness (e.g., Thomas explained to his mother the five different ways one can sign the word "go" and how each has a slightly different meaning). He used "because" to answer "why" questions. In response to "Why do you think Isaiah is mad?" Thomas answered, "He mad . . . why . . . because John his cookie snatched!" Thomas showed empathy when other children were sad, hurt, scared, or angry and would comment "red face," a classifier phrase to describe a very upset boy and the sign for feeling sorry. He used dependent clauses but still had difficulty attending to multiple contextual cues. Thomas demonstrated all the foundations for **first-order ToM** and was on his way to becoming a reader.

## FUTURE DIRECTIONS

Actress Marlee Matlin, who is deaf, has said, "The handicap of deafness is not in the ear; it is in the mind." Early identification of infants with hearing loss and advances in hearing instrumentation have given many children who are D/HH access to spoken language and improved literacy. Hearing aids and implants, however, do not guarantee literacy skills comparable to hearing-age peers. Marschak and colleagues (2010) have emphasized that children who are D/HH cannot be compared to children who can hear with blocked ears. Research indicates that children who are D/HH, even those with CIs and well-fit hearing aids, process cognitive, social/emotional, and visual information differently from hearing children. Students who are D/HH, including CI users, exhibit greater delays and deficits in executive function and working memory than hearing children (Kronenberger, Colson, Henning, & Pisoni, 2014; Nittrouer, Caldwell-Tarr, & Lowenstein, 2013). Executive function and ToM are intertwined (Doherty, 2009). Developing ToM requires a certain level of executive functioning (one must inhibit behavior to reflect), but simultaneously, executive functioning requires ToM because one must consider one's knowledge, evaluate the situation or task, and determine the best course of action—which are aspects of intrapersonal and interpersonal ToM. Working memory is essential for ToM because one must be able to take more than one perspective on a situation and integrate multiple pieces of information to infer what a particular person might be thinking or feeling in a situation (interpersonal ToM) or to choose the best strategy to facilitate reading comprehension (intrapersonal ToM).

Improving oral and written discourse comprehension of students who are D/HH requires going beyond the ears; it requires understanding of the functioning of the mind and how to nourish that functioning. Additional research is needed into the multiple factors that influence comprehension in students who are D/HH, the ways these factors interact, and the strategies that are most effective in promoting development of ToM. Although ToM abilities are highly correlated with language, students must also employ executive function and working memory abilities to attend to, integrate, and interpret multiple sources of contextual information. Vermeulen (2012) maintains that some of the social difficulties and comprehension problems of individuals with autism arise because they do not know how to use all the available context cues to interpret people's behavior. The same may be true for individuals who are D/HH. Recently, a young woman with a severe hearing impairment from birth as a result of bilateral ear atresia (in her case, absence of both external and middle ears) told the authors of this chapter how as a child and adolescent, she realized she was missing a lot. She said that because of the severity of her hearing loss, in real-life situations she worked so hard on listening that she could not attend to other cues, and as a consequence, she did not really understand what was happening and how she should respond. (All of her working memory was being used to interpret sound, so she was unable to attend to the cues essential for employing interpersonal ToM.) To compensate, she watched television shows and movies over and over, looking for cues of what was happening and why people were acting as they were. With videos, she could focus on different elements of the individuals and contexts with each viewing. (She used executive function skills and intrapersonal ToM to compensate.) In the process, she taught herself the multiple cues she needed to attend to if she were to correctly interpret people's intents and emotions. Her story demonstrates how hearing loss can affect multiple factors that influence comprehension.

## SUGGESTED READINGS

Beck, I.L., & McKeown, M.G. (2006). *Improving comprehension with questioning the author.* New York, NY: Scholastic.

Krakower, C. (2013). *Practical theory of mind games.* Moline, IL: Linguisystems.

Moreau, M.R., & Fidrych, H. (1994). *The Story Grammar Marker® teacher's manual.* Springfield, MA: MindWing Concepts.

Oczkus, L.D. (2010). *Reciprocal teaching at work.* Newark, DE: International Reading Association.

Raphael, T.E., Highfield, K., & Au, K.H. (2006). *QAR now.* New York, NY: Scholastic.

Schick, B., de Villiers, J., de Villiers, P., & Hoffmeister, B. (2002). Theory of mind: Language and cognition in deaf children. *ASHA Leader, 7*(22), 6–7.

Wilhelm, J. (2001). *Improving comprehension with think-aloud strategies.* New York, NY: Scholastic.

## LEARNING ACTIVITIES

1. Using the activities and references listed in the sections for assessing cognitive and affective ToM, develop materials that you can use to assess the ToM abilities of students you work with.

2. Read *Wonderstruck* (Selznick, 2011) and develop lesson plans for how you will use it to develop the ToM skills necessary for comprehension of this text.

3. For what events in your life do you have semantic memories but not autobiographical memories? For what events do you have strong autobiographical memories? Investigate your students' autobiographical memories and ability to think about the future. Give them a word such as *friend, easy, naughty,* or *tired,* and ask them to describe a specific time in the past (a few weeks or a few months) they think of when they hear that word. Then ask them to imagine a time (a few weeks or months) in the future the word makes them think of.

## REFERENCES

Abu-Akel, A., & Shamay-Tsoory, A. (2011). Neuroanatomical and neurochemical bases of theory of mind. *Neuropsychologia, 49,* 2971–2984.

Arfe, B., & Boscolo, P. (2006). Causal coherence in deaf and hearing students' written narratives. *Discourse Processes, 42,* 271–300.

Baker, L., & Brown, A.L. (1984). Metacognitive skills and reading. In P.D. Pearson, R. Barr, M.L. Kamil, & P. Mosenthal (Eds.), *Handbook of reading research* (pp. 353–394). New York, NY: Longman.

Baron-Cohen, S. (2007). *Mind reading: The interactive guide to emotions.* Philadelphia, PA: Jessica Kingsley.

Baron-Cohen, S., Golan, O., & Ashwin, E. (2009). Can emotion recognition be taught to children with autism spectrum conditions? *Philosophical Transactions of the Royal Society B: Biological Sciences, 364,* 3567–3574.

Baron-Cohen, S., Golan, O., Wheelwright, S., & Hill, J.J. (2007). *Mind reading: The interactive guide to emotions.* London, England: Jessica Kingsley.

Baron-Cohen, S., Leslie, A.M., & Frith, U. (1985). Does the autistic child have a "theory of mind"? *Cognition 21,* 37–46.

Baron-Cohen, S., O'Riordan, M., Stone, V., Jones, R., & Plaisted, K. (1999). Recognition of faux pas by normally developing children and children with Asperger syndrome or high-functioning autism. *Journal of Autism and Developmental Disorders, 29,* 407–418.

Bate, S., Cook, S.J., Mole, J., & Cole, J. (2013). First report of generalized face processing difficulties in Mobius sequence. *PLOS ONE, 8,* 1–9.

Beck, I.L., & McKeown, M.G. (1996). Questioning the author: A yearlong classroom implementation to engage students with text. *Elementary School Journal, 96,* 385–414.

Beck, I.L., & McKeown, M.G. (2006). *Improving comprehension with questioning the author.* New York, NY: Scholastic.

Boons, T., de Raeve, L., Langereis, M., Peeraer, L., Wouters, J., & van Wieringen, A. (2013). Narrative spoken language skills in severely hearing impaired school-aged children with cochlear implants. *Research in Developmental Disabilities, 34,* 3833–3846.

Borgna, G., Convertino, C., Marschark, M., Morrison, C., & Rizzolo, K. (2011). Enhancing deaf students' learning from sign language and text: Metacognition, modality, and the effectiveness of content scaffolding. *Journal of Deaf Studies and Deaf Education, 16,* 79–100.

Brinton, B., Spackman, M., Fujiki, M., & Ricks, J. (2007). What should Chris say? The ability of children with specific language impairment to recognize the need to dissemble emotions in social situations. *Journal of Speech, Language, Hearing Research, 50,* 798–811.

Brownell, R. (2000). *Expressive one-word picture vocabulary test.* East Moline, IL: Linguisystems.

Cain, K., Oakhill, J., Barnes, M., & Bryant, P. (2001). Comprehension skill, inference-making, and their relation to knowledge. *Memory & Cognition, 29,* 850–859.

Chamot, A.U., & O'Malley, J.M. (1994). *The CALLA handbook: Implementing the cognitive academic language learning approach.* Reading, MA: Addison-Wesley.

Corina, D., & Singleton, J. (2009). Developmental social cognitive neuroscience: Insights from deafness. *Child Development, 80,* 952–967.

Cote, N., Goldman, S.R., & Saul, E.U. (1998). Students making sense of informational text: Relations between processing and representation. *Discourse Processes, 25,* 1–53.

Courtin, C. (2000). The impact of sign language on the cognitive development of deaf children: The case histories of mind. *Journal of Deaf Studies and Deaf Education, 5,* 266–276.

Crosson, J., & Geers, A. (2001). Analysis of narrative ability in children with cochlear implants. *Ear and Hearing, 22,* 381–393.

Dammeyer, J. (2010). Psychosocial development in a Danish population of children with cochlear implants and deaf and hard-of-hearing children. *Journal of Deaf Studies and Deaf Education, 15,* 50–58.

Davey, B. (1983). Think-aloud: Modeling the cognitive processes of reading comprehension. *Journal of Reading, 27,* 44–47.

Decety, J., & Jackson, P.L. (2004). The functional architecture of human empathy. *Behavioral and Cognitive Neuroscience Reviews, 3,* 71–100.

Delaney, K.R. (2006). Following the affect: Learning to observe emotional regulation. *Journal of Child and Adolescent Psychiatric Nursing, 19,* 175–181.

Dickinson, D.K., McCabe, A., & Essex, M.J. (2006). A window of opportunity we must open to all: The case for preschool with high-quality support for language and literacy. In D.K. Dickinson & S.B. Neuman (Eds.) *Handbook of early literacy research,* vol. 2 (pp. 11–28). New York: The Guilford Press.

Doherty, M.J. (2009). *Theory of mind: How children understand others' thoughts and feelings.* New York, NY: Psychology Press.

Doran, J., & Anderson, A. (2003). Inferencing skills of adolescent readers who are hearing impaired. *Journal of Research in Reading, 26,* 256–266.

Dyck, M.J., Farrugia, C., Shochet, I.M., & Holmes-Brown, M. (2004). Emotion recognition/understanding ability in hearing or vision-impaired children: Do sounds, sights, or words make the difference? *Journal of Child Psychology and Psychiatry, 45*(5), 789–800.

Dye, P., Hauser, P., & Bavelier, D. (2008). Visual attention in deaf children and adults: Implications for learning environments. In M. Marschark & P. Hauser (Eds.), *Deaf cognition* (pp. 250–263). New York, NY: Oxford University Press.

Fitzgerald, E. (1976). *Straight language for the deaf.* Washington, DC: Alexander Graham Bell Association for the Deaf.

Fivush, R. (2011). The development of autobiographical memory. *Annual Review of Psychology, 62,* 559–82.

Geers, A., Tobey, E., Moog, J., Brenner, C. (2008). Long-term outcomes of cochlear implantation in the preschool years: From elementary grades to high school. *International Journal of Audiology, 47,* 21–30.

Gillam, S.L., Gillam, R.B., & Reece, K. (2012). Language outcomes of contextualized and decontextualized language intervention: Results of an early efficacy study. *Language, Speech, and Hearing Services in Schools, 43,* 276–291.

Gopnik, A., & Astington, J.W. (1988). Children's understanding of representational change and its relation to the understanding of false belief and the appearance-reality distinction. *Child Development, 59,* 26–37.

Gray, C., Hosie, J., Russell, P., Scott, C., & Hunter, N. (2007). Attribution of emotions to story characters by severely and profoundly deaf children. *Journal of Developmental and Physical Disabilities, 19,* 145–159.

Greenberg, M.T., & Kusche, C.A. (1998). Preventative intervention for school-age deaf children: The PATHS curriculum. *Journal of Deaf Studies and Deaf Education, 3,* 49–63.

Gullone, E., & Taffe, J. (2012). The emotion regulation questionnaire for children and adolescents (ERG-CA): A psychometric evaluation. *Psychological Assessment, 24,* 409–417.

Hall, M.L., & Bavelier, D. (2010). Working memory, deafness, and sign language. In M. Marschark & P.E. Spencer (Eds.), *The Oxford handbook of deaf studies, language, and education* (Vol. 12, pp. 458–471). New York, NY: Oxford University Press.

Happe, F.G.E. (1994). An advanced test of theory of mind: Understanding of story characters' thoughts and feelings by able autistic, mentally handicapped, and normal children and adults. *Journal of Autism & Developmental Disorders, 24,* 129–154.

Hubbard, W. (1995). *C is for curious: An ABC of feelings.* San Francisco, CA: Chronicle Books.

Hutchins, T.L., Prelock, P.A., & Bonazing, L. (2012). Psychometric evaluation of the theory of mind inventory (ToMI): A study of typically developing children and children with autism spectrum disorder. *Autism and Developmental Disorders, 42,* 327–341.

Huttunen, K., & Ryder, N. (2012). How children with normal hearing and children with a cochlear implant use mentalizing vocabulary and other evaluative expression in their narratives. *Clinical Linguistics & Phonetics, 26,* 823–844.

Israel, S. (2007). *Using metacognitive assessments to create individualized reading instruction.* Newark, DE: International Reading Association.

Kelly, R.R., Albertini, J.A., & Shannon, N.B. (2001). Deaf college students' reading comprehension and strategy use. *American Annals of the Deaf, 146,* 385–400.

Keysers, C. (2011). *The empathic brain.* Kindle edition: Social Brain Press.

Kronenberger, W.G., Colson, B.G., Henning, S.C., & Pisoni, D.P. (2014). Executive functioning and speech-language skills following long-term use of cochlear implants. *Journal of Deaf Studies and Deaf Education, 19,* 456–470.

Krueger, J., & Michael, J. (2012). Gestural coupling and social cognition: Mobius syndrome as a case study. *Frontiers in Human Neuroscience, 6,* 1–14.

Laible, D. (2004a). Mother-child discourse surrounding a child's past behavior at 30 months: Links to emotional understanding and early conscious development at 36 months. *Merrill Palmer Quarterly, 50,* 159–80.

Laible, D. (2004b). Mother-child discourse in two contexts: Links with child temperament, attachment security, and socioemotional competence. *Developmental Psychology, 40,* 979–992.

Layton, T.L., & Holmes, D.W. (1985). *Carolina picture vocabulary test for deaf and hearing-impaired students.* Austin, TX: Pro-Ed.

Lederberg, A.R., Schick, B., & Spencer, P.E. (2012). Language and literacy development of deaf and hard-of-hearing children: Successes and challenges. *Developmental Psychology, 49*(1), 15–30.

Leslie, L., & Caldwell, J.S. (2011). *Qualitative reading inventory.* Boston, MA: Pearson.

Lewis, M. (2014). *The rise of consciousness and the development of emotional life.* New York, NY: Guilford Press.

Lucariello, J. (2004). New insights into the functions, development, and origins of theory of mind: The functional multilinear socialization model. In L. Lucariello et al. (Eds.), *The development of the mediated mind* (pp. 33–58). Mahwah, NJ: Erlbaum.

Ludlow, A., Heaton, P., Rosset, D., Hills, P., & Deruelle, C. (2010). Emotion recognition in children with profound and severe deafness: Do they have a deficit in perceptual processing? *Journal of Clinical Experimental Neuropsychology, 32,* 923–928.

Lyxell, B., Wass, M., Sahlén, B., Uhlén, I., Samuelsson, C., Asker-Árnason, L., . . . Hällgren, M. (2011). Development of cognitive and reading skills in deaf children with CIs. *Cochlear Implants International: An Interdisciplinary Journal, 12,* 98–100.

MacDermott, S.T., Gullone, E., Allen, J.S., King, N.J., & Tonge, B. (2010). The emotional regulation index for children and adolescents (ERICA): A psychometric investigation. *Journal of Psychological Behavior Assessment, 32,* 301–314.

Marschark, M., Lang, H.G., & Albertini, J.A. (2002). *Educating deaf students: From research to practice.* New York, NY: Oxford University Press.

Marschark, M., Rhoten, C., & Fabrich, M. (2007). Effects of cochlear implants on children's reading and academic achievement. *Journal of Deaf Studies and Deaf Education, 12,* 269–282.

Marschark, M., Sapere, P., Convertino, C.M., Mayer, C., Wauters, L., & Sarchet, T. (2009). Are deaf students' reading challenges really about reading? *American Annals of the Deaf, 154,* 357–370.

Marschark, M., Sarchet, T., Rhoten, C., & Zupan, M. (2010). Will cochlear implants close the reading achievement gap for deaf students? In M. Marschark & P.E. Spencer (Eds.), *The Oxford handbook of deaf studies, language, and education* (pp. 127–143). New York, NY: Oxford University Press.

Michalson, L., & Lewis, M. (1985). What do children know about emotions and when do they know it? In M. Lewis & C. Saarni (Eds.), *The socialization of emotions* (pp. 1–17). New York, NY: Plenum.

Miller, P. (2010). Phonological, orthographic, and syntactic awareness and their relation to reading comprehension in prelingually deaf individuals: What can we learn from skilled readers? *Journal of Developmental and Physical Disability, 22,* 549–580.

Miller, P., Kargin, T., & Guldenoglu, B. (2013). The reading comprehension failure of Turkish prelingually deaf readers: Evidence from semantic and syntactic processing. *Journal of Developmental and Physical Disabilities, 25,* 221–239.

Mochizuki, K. (1997). *Passage to freedom: The Sugihara story.* New York, NY: Lee & Low Books.

Moeller, M.P., & Schick, B. (2006). Relations between maternal input and theory of mind understanding in deaf children. *Child Development, 77,* 751–766.

Moreau, M.R., & Fidrych, H. (1994). *The Story Grammar Marker® teacher's manual.* Springfield, MA: MindWing Concepts.

Murdock, T.B., & Lybarger, R.L. (1997). An attributional analysis of aggression among children who are deaf. *Journal of the American Deafness and Rehabilitation Association, 31,* 10–22.

National Governors Association Center for Best Practices and Council of Chief State School Officers. (2010). *Common Core State Standards for English language arts and literacy in history/social studies, science, and technical subjects.* Washington, DC: Authors.

Nittrouer, S., Caldwell-Tarr, A., & Lowenstein, J.H. (2013). Working memory in children with cochlear implants: Problems are in storage, not processing. *International Journal of Pediatric Otorhinolaryngology, 77,* 1886–1898.

Northoff, G., Heinzel, A., de Greck, M., Felix, B., Dobrowolny, H., & Panksepp, J. (2006). Self-referential processing in our brain—A meta-analysis of imaging studies on the self. *NeuroImage, 31,* 440–457.

Oczkus, L.D. (2010). *Reciprocal teaching at work.* Newark, DE: International Reading Association.

O'Hare, A.E., Bremner, L., Nash, M., Happe, F., & Pettigrew, L. (2009). A clinical assessment tool for advanced theory of mind performance in 5 to 12 year olds. *Journal of Autism & Developmental Disorders, 39,* 916–928.

Ornstein, P.A., Grammer, J.K., & Coffman, J.L. (2010). Teachers' "mnemonic style" and the development of skilled memory. In H.S. Walters & W. Schneider (Eds.), *Metacognition, strategy use, and instruction* (pp. 23–53). New York, NY: Guilford Press.

Petersen, D.B., & Spencer, T.D. (2012). The narrative language measures: Tools for language screening, progress monitoring, and intervention planning. *Perspectives on Language Learning and Education, 19*(4), 119–129.

Peterson, C.C., & Slaughter, V.P. (2006). Telling the story of theory of mind: Deaf and hearing children's narratives and mental state understanding. *British Journal of Developmental Psychology, 24,* 151–179.

Peterson, C.C., & Wellman, H.M. (2009). From infancy to reason: Scaling deaf and hearing children's understanding of theory of mind and presence. *British Journal of Developmental Psychology, 27,* 297–310.

Peterson, C.C., Wellman, H.M., & Slaughter, V. (2012). The mind behind the message: Advancing theory-of-mind scales for typically developing children, and those with deafness, autism, or Asperger syndrome. *Child Development, 83,* 469–485.

Pons, R., Harris, P., & de Rosnay, M. (2004). Emotion comprehension between 3–11 years: Developmental periods and hierarchical organization. *European Journal of Developmental Psychology, 1,* 127–152.

Premack, D., & Woodruff, G. (1978). Does the chimpanzee have a theory of mind? *Behavioral and Brain Sciences, 1,* 515–526.

Qi, S., & Mitchell, R.E. (2012). Large-scale academic achievement testing for deaf and hard-of-hearing students: Past, present, and future. *Journal of Deaf Studies and Deaf Education, 17,* 1–18.

Rachford, D., & Furth, H.G. (1986). Understanding of friendship and social rules in deaf and hearing adolescents. *Journal of Applied Developmental Psychology, 7,* 391–402.

Raphael, T.E., Highfield, K., & Au, K.H. (2006). *QAR now.* New York, NY: Scholastic.

Reid, D.K., Hresko, W.P., Hammill, D.D., & Wiltshire, S. (1991). *Test of early reading ability: Deaf or hard of hearing.* Austin, TX: Pro-Ed.

Reutzel, R.D., Smith, J.A., & Fawson, P.C. (2004). An evaluation of two approaches for teaching reading comprehension strategies in the primary years using science information texts. *Early Childhood Research Quarterly, 20,* 276–305.

Rieffe, C. (2012). Awareness and regulation of emotions in deaf children. *British Journal of Developmental Psychology, 30,* 477–492.

Rieffe, C., Terwogt, M.M., & Smit, C. (2003). Deaf children on the causes of emotions. *Educational Psychology, 23,* 159–168.

Riordan, R. (2005). *Percy Jackson and the Olympians: The lightning thief.* New York, NY: Puffin.

Rowling, J.K. (2000). *Harry Potter and the goblet of fire.* New York, NY: Scholastic.

Sachar, L. (1998). *Holes.* New York, NY: Farrar, Straus and Giroux.

Schellings, G. (2011). Applying learning strategy questionnaires: Problems and possibilities. *Metacognition and Learning, 6,* 91–109.

Schick, B., de Villiers, P., de Villiers, J., & Hoffmeister, R. (2007). Language and theory of mind: A study of deaf children. *Child Development, 78,* 376–396.

Schick, B., & Moeller, M.P. (1998). *Exploring feelings with your child.* Omaha, NE: Boys Town National Research Hospital.

Schirmer, B.R., Bailey, J., & Lockman, A.S. (2004). What verbal protocols reveal about the reading strategies of deaf students: A replication study. *American Annals of the Deaf, 149,* 5–16.

Schmitt, M.S. (1990). A questionnaire to measure children's awareness of strategic reading processes. *The Reading Teacher, 43,* 454–461.

Schneider, P., Hayward, D., & Dubé, R.V. (2006). Storytelling from pictures using the Edmonton Narrative Norms Instrument. *Journal of Speech-Language Pathology and Audiology, 30,* 224–238.

Scott, C., Russel, P.A., Gray, C.D., Hosie, J.A., & Hunter, N. (1999). The interpretation of line of regard by prelingually deaf children. *Social Development, 8,* 412–426.

Selznick, B. (2007). *The invention of Hugo Cabret.* New York, NY: Scholastic.

Selznick, B. (2011). *Wonderstruck.* New York, NY: Scholastic.

Shamay-Tsoory, S., & Aharon-Peretz, J. (2007). Dissociable prefrontal networks for cognitive and affective theory of mind: A lesion study. *Neuropsychologia, 45,* 3054–3067.

Shamay-Tsoory, S., Aharon-Peretz, J., & Perry, D. (2009). Two systems for empathy: A double dissociation between emotional and cognitive empathy in inferior frontal gyrus verson ventromedial prefrontal lesions. *Brain, 132,* 617–627.

Shamay-Tsoory, S., Tibi-Elhanany, Y., & Aharon-Peretz, J. (2007). The ventromedial prefrontal cortex is involved in understanding affective but not cognitive theory of mind stories. *Social Neuroscience, 1,* 149–166.

Snow, C. (2002). *Reading for understanding: Toward an R&D program in reading comprehension.* Santa Monica, CA: Rand Corporation.

Southam-Gerow, M.A. (2013). *Emotion regulation in children and adolescents.* New York, NY: Guilford Press.

Stevenson, J., McCann, D., Law, C.M., Mullee, M., Petrou, S., Worsfold, S., . . . Kennedy, C.R. (2011). The effect of early confirmation of hearing loss on the behaviour in middle childhood of children with bilateral hearing impairment. *Developmental Medicine & Child Neurology, 53,* 269–274.

Stevenson, J., McCann, D., Watkin, P., Worsfold, S., & Kennedy, C. (2010). The relationship between language development and behaviour problems in children with hearing loss. *Journal of Child Psychology and Psychiatry, 51,* 77–83.

Strassman, B.K. (1997). Metacognition and reading in children who are deaf: A review of the research. *Journal of Deaf Studies and Deaf Education, 2*(3), 140–149.

Sullivan, K., Zaitchik, D., & Tager-Flusberg, H. (1994). Preschoolers can attribute second-order beliefs. *Developmental Psychology, 30,* 395–402.

Tanaka, J.W., Wolf, J.M., Klaiman, C., Koenig, K., Cockburn, J., Herlihy, L., . . . Schultz, R.T. (2010). Using computerized games to teach face recognition skills to children with autism spectrum disorder: The Let's Face It! program. *Journal of Child Psychology & Psychiatry, 51,* 944–952.

Terwogt, M.M., & Rieffe, C. (2004). Behavioural problems in deaf children: Theory of mind delay or communication failure. *European Journal of Developmental Psychology, 1,* 231–240.

Thomas, J. (2008). *A birthday for cow!* Orlando, FL: Harcourt.

Vermeulen, P. (2012). *Autism as context blindness.* Shawnee Mission, KS: Aperger Autism Publishing Company (AAPC).

Weismer, S.E. (1985). Constructive comprehension abilities exhibited by language-disordered children. *Journal of Speech and Hearing Research, 28,* 175–184.

Wellman, H.M., & Liu, D. (2004). Scaling of theory-of-mind tasks. *Child Development, 75,* 523–541.

Wellman, R.L., Lewis, B.A., Freebairn, L.A., Avrich, A.A., Hansen, A.J., & Stein, C.M. (2011). Narrative ability of children with speech sound disorders and the prediction of later literacy skills. *Language, Speech, & Hearing Services in Schools, 42,* 561–579.

Wiefferink, C.H., Rieffe, C., Ketelaar, L., De Raeve, L., & Frijns, J.H.M. (2012). Emotion understanding in deaf children with a cochlear implant. *Journal of Deaf Studies and Deaf Education, 18,* 175–186.

Weinstein, C.E. & Palmer, D.R. (2002). LASSI: *User's manual for those administering the learning and study strategies inventory* (2nd Ed.). Clearwater, FL: H&H Publishing Company, Inc.

Wixson, K.K., Bosky, A.B., Yochum, N., & Alvermann, D.E. (1984). An interview for assessing students' perceptions of classroom reading tasks. *The Reading Teacher, 37,* 346–352.

Wolf, J.M., Tanaka, J.W., Klaiman, C., Cockburn, J., Herlihy, L., Brown, C., . . . Schultz, R.T. (2008). Specific impairment of face processing abilities in children with autism spectrum disorder using the Let's Face It! skills battery. *Autism Research, 1*(6): 329–340.

# 12

# Models for Facilitating
# Literacy Development

John L. Luckner

Many definitions of **literacy** exist. The United Nations Educational, Scientific, and Cultural Organization (2004) wrote one that captures the complexity and importance of becoming literate:

> Literacy is the ability to identify, understand, interpret, create, communicate and compute, using printed and written materials associated with varying contexts. Literacy involves a continuum of learning in enabling individuals to achieve their goals, to develop their knowledge and potential, and to participate fully in their community and wider society. (p. 13)

Becoming literate is a complex task. Yet, once mastered, these skills open opportunities for a lifetime of learning and enjoyment. Moreover, in our current rapidly changing, global, technological world where social and political participation takes place both physically and virtually, the acquisition of literacy skills and the advancement and application of such skills throughout life is crucial. And unfortunately, many individuals who do not become literate struggle to take part in the world around them and to reach their full potential as individuals, employees, parents, and citizens.

One interesting lens through which to examine the importance of literacy is through the concept of quality of life (QOL). As explained by Schalock, Gardner, and Bradley (2007),

> Quality of life involves the degree to which people have life experiences that they value; reflects the domains that contribute to a full and interconnected life; considers the contexts of physical, social, and cultural environments that are important to people; and includes measures of experience both common to all humans and those unique to individuals. (p. 169)

Table 12.1 provides a list of frequently researched QOL domains, common indicators of each domain, and examples of how literacy benefits an individual's functioning in that domain.

## THEORETICAL BASIS

### Models and Stages of Reading Development

Skilled readers scan print effortlessly, extracting meaning and making connections between ideas in the text and their existing knowledge (Pearson, 1985). They figure out new words and names quickly, consciously employing a sounding out strategy or using **context clues**. If they happen to misread a word or phrase or do not comprehend something, they adapt by rereading to clarify what was unclear. Simultaneously, they form mental models for the meanings just constructed that are encoded into a logical framework that allows them to remember what they read (Moats, 2005).

While multiple models of literacy development currently exist, most support a systems perspective in which language skills play a prominent early role in organizing cognitive and other affective-behavioral systems that support literacy-related activities (Dickinson, McCabe, & Essex, 2006). Interrelationships among language, print-related skills, social development, self-regulation, **motivation**, home environment, and teacher knowledge exist and interact so that interconnections among systems can be shaped into mutually reinforcing systems (e.g., Joshi & Aaron, 2102; Vellutino, Tunmer, Jaccard, & Chen, 2007).

The systems perspective and the interaction of nature and nurture in the development of literacy skills is demonstrated in the model of reading development proposed by Chall (1996) and revised by Minskoff (2005). Examination of Figure 12.1 indicates that the stages of reading development are aligned with

**Table 12.1.**   Quality of life domains and examples of how literacy benefits functioning in each domain

| Domain | Indicators | Benefits of literacy |
|---|---|---|
| Physical well-being | Health, health care | Increasing understanding of nutrition, hygiene, exercise, and medication use |
| Interpersonal relations | Relationships | Texting, e-mailing, or writing family, friends, or acquaintances |
| Emotional well-being | Coping ability, productivity | Accessing resources to successfully adapt to life's demands |
| Personal development | Education, competence | Improving oneself by participating in activities that develop talents and potential |
| Material well-being | Employment, finances, housing | Career attainment and maintenance that provides economic resources that can be used for daily living |
| Self-determination | Autonomy, goals, choices | Being able to gather sufficient information to make choices and establish and achieve goals |
| Social inclusion | Community participation | Being able to find out about and participate in community events |
| Rights | Legal status, citizenship | Being able to vote and understand laws, disability rights, and patient rights |

language and cognitive development and that the acquisition of skills at each stage is essential to progress to the successive stages. And, as noted previously, how well individuals progress through the stages depends on genetic, environmental, educational, and experiential factors. In addition, it shows how the challenges of learning and teaching reading change over time.

### How Do Students Who Are Deaf or Hard of Hearing Learn to Read?

Do children and youth who are deaf or hard of hearing (D/HH) learn to read in the same way as their typical hearing peers? This is a question that has been asked for quite some time (e.g., Hanson, 1989). Some researchers say yes. They contend that reading development is qualitatively similar: Individuals who are D/HH proceed through the same developmental stages and use similar reading strategies as typical hearing individuals do, although the development may be quantitatively slower or delayed (e.g., Paul & Lee, 2010; Trezek, Wang, & Paul, 2010).

Written English alphabets, like other alphabets, were developed to match symbols to the sounds they represent. Consequently, print encodes spoken language. Letters represent the component sounds or phonemes of the language

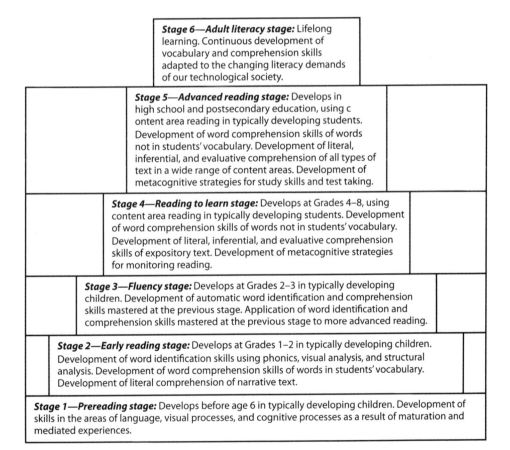

**Figure 12.1.**   Stages of learning to read. (*Source:* Minskoff, 2005.)

(Adams, 1990; McGuinness, 2004, 2005). The awareness that words are composed of letters and that these letters are a representation of spoken language in writing is referred to as the knowledge of the **alphabetic principle** (i.e., knowledge that speech sounds, phonemes, correspond to print, graphemes).

The beginnings of reading emerge from birth onward as children acquire language, including **phonological awareness**, and develop skills in the areas of visual processing and cognitive processing, along with exposure to educationally supportive experiences (Minskoff, 2005; National Early Literacy Panel, 2008; National Reading Panel, 2000). The importance of providing language and literacy experiences from birth onward, including reading to children, playing with language through rhyming and games, and encouraging writing activities, is well documented (e.g., Hart & Risley, 1995, 2003; Weizman & Snow, 2001; Wells, 1986). These activities encourage **vocabulary** development and enhance verbal reasoning, as well as semantic and syntactic abilities (Birsh, 2005).

In addition, in order to understand the alphabetic principle and apply this knowledge to beginning reading, many young children require direct, **explicit instruction** in letter–sound relationships (i.e., **phonics**; Chall, 1996; National Reading Panel, 2000). For children who are D/HH to obtain an awareness of the sound structures of words, supplementary systems such as speechreading (Kyle & Harris, 2010, 2011; Spencer & Oleson, 2008), cued speech (Leybaert, Aparicio, & Alegria, 2011), or visual phonics (Trezek & Malmgren, 2005; Trezek, Wang, Woods, Gampp, & Paul, 2007; Wang, Spychala, Harris, & Oetting, 2013) may need to be used, depending on the child's level of auditory access.

In contrast, many researchers assert that the reading acquisition process is significantly different for individuals who are D/HH and that they use alternative routes to become proficient readers (e.g., Allen et al., 2009; Miller & Clark, 2011; Morere, 2011). They contend that a permanent, profound hearing loss from birth or during early childhood limits access to the auditory signal and is likely to interfere with an individual's ability to acquire knowledge of the alphabetic principle and that the most accessible pathway for full access to linguistic information for many children who are D/HH is through vision. Simultaneously, research (e.g., Mayberry, 1993, 2010; Newport, 1990) has demonstrated the negative effects of delayed first language acquisition on the language performance and processing skills of children who are D/HH. The brain is most receptive to language acquisition during "sensitive periods" early in the child's development, from birth to age 6 (Mayberry & Lock, 2003). Consequently, in order to avoid delaying language, acquisition time should not be spent developing phonemic awareness and phonics skills, but instead students who are D/HH should develop their first language (i.e., American Sign Language [ASL]) and then the teaching of English literacy should be based on complex linguistic knowledge accessed through the first language, ASL (e.g., Chamberlain & Mayberry, 2008; Mayberry, del Guidice, & Lieberman, 2011).

Natural sign languages, such as ASL, demonstrate similar linguistic properties as spoken languages, and children exposed to sign languages from birth demonstrate that they acquire these languages on a similar maturational time line as hearing children acquiring spoken language (Schick, 2011). Bilingualism, the acquisition of both a natural sign language, ASL, and the spoken and/or written form of the majority language, English, is based on the premise that children who acquire language early can more easily acquire a second or third language, whether that language is visually or auditorily based (Cummins, 2000; Grosjean, 2010). Early exposure to a visual language that is fully accessible, such as ASL, encourages language development and provides opportunities to develop critical thinking and reasoning skills that can be applied to literacy development in the second language, written English (Fish & Morford, 2012).

**Bilingual** methods are characterized by instruction in ASL, with the expectation that the students will use ASL for communication and will learn English through the written form (Lange, Lane-Outlaw, Lange, & Sherwood, 2013). Most bilingual programs for students who are D/HH are based on English-as-a-second-language models. ASL is introduced as the child's first language, and English is taught as a second language. ASL is used for the full range of social interactions (e.g., conversations, discussions, questions, and answers); to teach curriculum subjects such as science, humanities, social studies, and mathematics; as well as to teach reading and writing skills in English. In addition, children are surrounded with books, storytelling, and reading, as well as the use of English for real-life situations such as using the Internet, texting, and report writing (Snodden, 2012).

### Dual Perspectives: Auditory Learners and Visual Learners

Given the diversity of the population of students who are D/HH, it is practical to consider assessments and interventions that are effective for two separate groups of individuals: 1) students who are D/HH with functional hearing and 2) students who are D/HH with limited functional hearing (Easterbrooks, 2010; Easterbrooks & Beal-Alvarez, 2013; Lederberg, Schick, & Spencer, 2013). In addition, the dual-route cascaded (DRC) model of word recognition and reading (Coltheart, Rastle, Perry, Langdon, & Ziegler, 2001) posits two distinct routes to reading—the phonological route and the lexical orthographic route. Similarly, the dual-coding theory (Paivio, 1986, 2008; Sadoski & Paivio, 2004) also contends that there are two separate and distinct systems that individuals use to represent and process information—the verbal system and the visual system. As a result, assessments and instructional practices appropriate for students who are D/HH who use different approaches to access print are provided in the following sections.

### THE USE OF ASSESSMENTS TO IDENTIFY INTERVENTION PRIORITIES

Assessment is the process of collecting and reviewing data for the purpose of making decisions about students (Salvia, Ysseldyke, & Bolt, 2013). Assessment is an essential component of any literacy program for students who are D/HH. Ongoing use of assessments maximizes student progress by providing educators with information that can be used to structure successful learning experiences for students.

Although assessments vary across a wide variety of factors, for the purpose of this chapter, four types of literacy assessment (screening, progress monitoring, diagnostic, and outcomes) are discussed. In the following section, each type of assessment is briefly described, an explanation of how it benefits professionals and students is provided, and examples of tools that are frequently used with students who are D/HH are included.

## Screening Assessments

These are brief, easy to administer tests, rating scales, and checklists that determine general levels of performance. They are often used early in the school year so that students who might be at risk for experiencing difficulties with literacy can be identified and additional instruction or further assessment can be provided. Educators use screening assessments to answer questions such as the following: Which students are likely to experience reading difficulties now and in the future? Which students will need additional instruction to meet their reading goals? Examples of commonly used screening assessments include *Stages of Literacy Development Checklist* (French, 1999); *Early Reading Checklists* (French, 1999); *Dynamic Indicators of Basic Early Literacy Skills, Sixth Edition (DIBELS)—Benchmark Screening* (Good & Kaminski, 2007); *The Texas Primary Reading Inventory (TPRI)—Benchmarking Kit* (Texas Education Agency and University of Texas System, 2010); and AIMSweb (Pearson, 2012).

## Progress Monitoring Assessments

These are brief assessments given throughout the school year to determine if students are making adequate progress toward meeting their grade-level reading ability. If students are not making sufficient progress, educators can use the data to make adjustments to the instruction that students receive in an effort to get them back on track. Educators use progress monitoring assessments to answer questions the following: Are individual students on track for meeting end-of-year goals? Is instruction working? Is the instruction being provided enabling students to make sufficient progress? Examples of commonly used progress monitoring assessments include *Qualitative Reading Inventory 5* (Leslie & Caldwell, 2011); *Edcheckup* (2013); *The Basic Reading Inventory: Pre-Primer Through Grade 12 and Early Literacy Assessments, 11th edition* (Johns & Elish-Piper, 2012); *Dynamic Indicators of Basic Early Literacy Skills, Sixth Edition (DIBELS)—Progress Monitoring Materials* (Good & Kaminski, 2007); *The Texas Primary Reading Inventory (TPRI)—Progress Monitoring for Emergent and Beginning Readers* (Texas Education Agency and University of Texas System, 2010); and AIMSweb (Pearson, 2012).

## Diagnostic Assessments

These measures are used to gather in-depth information about students' strengths and areas of concern. Diagnostic assessments are longer and more in depth than screening and progress monitoring measures. The results of diagnostic assessments can help explain why a student is not performing at an expected level and help educators adjust or intensify instruction to meet the individual needs of students. Most diagnostic tests are norm referenced, which allows educators to compare a student's score against the scores of other students. Also, most diagnostic tests include standardized procedures, which include prescribed methods for the administration, scoring, and interpretation that must be strictly followed. Educators use diagnostic assessments to answer questions such as the following: Which specific literacy skills have students mastered or not mastered? Which instructional programs are most likely to be effective based on the specific needs of this student? Examples of commonly used diagnostic assessments include *Woodcock Reading Mastery Tests* (Woodcock, 2011); *Qualitative Reading Inventory 5* (Leslie & Caldwell, 2011); *Group Reading Assessment and Diagnostic Evaluation* (Williams, 2001); *Woodcock-Johnson III Diagnostic Reading Battery* (Woodcock, Mather, & Schrank, 2004); and *Stanford Diagnostic Reading Test 4* (Karlsen & Gardner, 1996).

## Outcome Assessments

These measures are used to evaluate students' performance and the effectiveness of the overall academic program. Educators administer outcome assessments at the end of the school year to document students' achievement. Students' performance on outcome assessments can be compared to grade-level standards, to students' performance from previous years, or to national normative samples. Educators use outcome assessments to answer questions such as the following: Did students improve from last year? How do specific students compare with similar-age students? Is our academic program meeting the needs of students? How can we make our educational programs better? How does our school compare with other schools? Examples of commonly used outcomes assessments include state assessments, *Stanford Achievement Test Series, 10th edition* (Pearson, 2007); *Woodcock-Johnson III—NU Tests of Achievement* (Woodcock, McGrew, & Mather, 2007); the ACT; and the SAT.

## INTERVENTIONS TO PROMOTE LITERACY

Cambourne and Turbill (1987) proposed optimal conditions for literacy learning (Table 12.2). Although their work focused on typical hearing children, the

**Table 12.2.**  Optimal conditions for literacy learning

| | |
|---|---|
| Immersion | • Written text is everywhere—on signs, charts, labels, and bulletin boards; in books, magazines, and newspapers; and on the computer.<br>• The day is filled with story-reading time, sharing time, and many other language-rich activities. |
| Demonstration | • Model reading and writing for students.<br>• Have active, meaningful conversations.<br>• Use questions to activate background knowledge and encourage predictions—before, during, and after reading. |
| Engagement | • Language is used for real-life purposes, providing opportunities for students to use language and literacy for personal, social, and school needs.<br>• Cooperative planning of events takes place and plans are recorded and displayed along with other useful documents and charts. |
| Expectation | • All students will learn—everyone will succeed.<br>• Adults have an understanding of the developmental stages of becoming literate and support students via assessment, scaffolding, and instruction. |
| Responsibility | • The environment is set up to promote self-direction.<br>• Students have many opportunities to work cooperatively in creating, planning, and carrying out both large and small projects. |
| Approximation | • Mistakes are accepted.<br>• Approximations are not wrong; they are a step toward being right.<br>• Language learners of all ages need positive reinforcement as they acquire more sophisticated language forms and acquire literacy skills. |
| Feedback | • Language and literacy learners need lots of feedback in order to evaluate their progress, draw new or revised conclusions, and move forward.<br>• Celebrate successes. |

conditions are applicable to students who are D/HH, at home and school. Educators and parents/caregivers should be aware of these principles as they work to promote literacy development in students who are D/HH.

### Components of a Comprehensive Literacy Program for Auditory Learners

For students with functional hearing, interventions should be guided by the recommendations of the National Reading Panel (2000) and the National Early Literacy Panel (2008) for a balanced reading program (Luckner, Sebald, Cooney, Young, & Goodwin Muir, 2005/2006; Schirmer & McGough, 2005; Trezek, Wang, & Paul, 2010). The five components of reading and a brief definition of each are provided in Table 12.3.

The majority of core basal reading programs (e.g., Success for All, Read Well, Literacy Express) provide systematic instruction in each area. Although basal reading programs differ, they usually have four similar features: 1) student texts adjusted to approximate grade levels containing narrative (a story or account of events) and expository (intended to explain or describe some-thing) selections; 2) a teacher's guide that provides lesson plans and suggestions for teaching the reading selections; 3) a student workbook to support the skills taught and provide opportunities for practice and reinforcement; and 4) end of unit tests to assess skills taught.

In contrast to using a core basal reading program, some teachers and educational programs prefer to use a literature-based approach. Literature-based programs tend to use sets of literature books and rely on teacher initiative and teacher decisions on skills selection, sequencing, and development. Teachers who use a literature-based approach tend to 1) have small groups of students read and respond to the same book; 2) facilitate discussions related to students' **background knowledge**, ideas derived from the text, and students' reaction to the text; 3) structure end of book summary and synthesis activities; and 4) use informal observation to assess student progress (Ruddell, 2009). Some teachers and educational programs enhance their literature-based programs by using supplemental reading programs (e.g., Read Naturally, Sound Partners) to help address each of the five components discussed previously.

**Table 12.3.**  Components of a balanced reading program for students who are auditory learners

| | |
|---|---|
| Phonological awareness | "The ability to manipulate the sound system of spoken language, including words, rhymes, syllables, onset-rimes, and phonemes. Phonological awareness is a broad term encompassing phonemic awareness" (Vaughn & Linan-Thompson, 2004, p. 138). |
| Alphabetic principle | "The basic idea that written language is a code in which letters represent the sounds of spoken words" (Hougen & Smartt, 2012, p. 286). |
| Vocabulary | "The words we must know to comprehend and communicate effectively" (Trezek, Wang, & Paul, 2010, p. 213). |
| Fluency | "The ability to perform reading skills such as naming letters, reading words, and reading connected text quickly, smoothly, and automatically" (Vaughn & Linan-Thompson, 2004, p. 136). |
| Comprehension | "The active process of constructing meaning from text; it involves accessing previous knowledge, understanding vocabulary and concepts, making inferences, and linking key ideas" (Vaughn & Linan-Thompson, 2004, pp. 98–99). |

To help students who are D/HH gain access to phonological-related information, quasi-experimental research (e.g., Beal-Alvarez, Lederberg, & Easterbrooks, 2011; Smith & Wang, 2010; Trezek & Hancock, 2013; Trezek & Malmgren, 2005; Trezek, Wang, Woods, Gampp, & Paul, 2007) indicates the benefits of visual phonics (International Communication Learning Institute, 1996)—a multisensory instructional tool that consists of 46 hand cues and written symbols that are used in conjunction with speech and/or speechread-ing to represent the individual phonemes of a language. These hand cues were developed to mimic the articulatory features of phonemes, and simple line-drawn symbols mirror the gestures used to produce the cues.

## Components of a Comprehensive Literacy Program for Visual Learners

Children's language and literacy skills develop simultaneously rather than sequentially (Whitehurst & Lonigan, 2001). They reinforce each other and should be introduced into children's lives as soon as possible (Lonigan, Farver, Phillips, & Clancy-Menchetti, 2011). Because some children who are deaf do not have access to auditory stimulus, use of the visual modality and exposure to natural sign languages such as ASL provides an alternative pathway to developing language and literacy skills. Early and consistent access to language is vital to its acquisition and continued development, and this access provides the foundation for later literacy development (Gárate, 2012). In contrast, lack of access to language during the optimum period for language development negatively affects literacy as well as behavior and academic development (e.g., Chamberlain & Mayberry, 2008; Mayberry, 2007, 2010; Newport, 1990; Quittner et al., 2010).

Research with children who are deaf and exposed to sign language from birth indicates that they acquire language on a similar maturational timeline as hearing children acquire spoken language (e.g., Morford & Mayberry, 2000; Petitto, 2000). Research also has demonstrated a positive correlation between high levels of ASL proficiency and English literacy skills (e.g., Chamberlain & Mayberry, 2000, 2008; Mayberry, 2007; Mayberry, del Guidice, & Lieberman, 2011).

Table 12.4 contains examples and brief descriptions of strategies that have been found to be effective for creating a bridge from the first language, ASL, to the second language, written English.

## Supplementary Literacy Instruction

Many students who are D/HH need additional instruction beyond what is provided to their typical hearing peers. In the following sections, suggestions for supplementary literacy instruction that may be beneficial for any student who has not attained age-appropriate literacy skills are provided.

***Functions of Communication***    Despite the tendency of educators to support one communication approach (e.g., oral, sign language, sign systems) over the others, there is a paucity of research indicating that one approach is more effective than the others (Spencer & Marschark, 2010). Instead, an abundance of research exists documenting the language and literacy delays and difficulties that many children and youth who are D/HH experience (e.g., Kyle & Harris, 2010; Luckner & Cooke, 2010; Mayberry, 2007).

**Table 12.4.**   Strategies for creating a bridge from American Sign Language to written English

| | |
|---|---|
| Storybook reading | Shared storybook reading has been defined as the "joint use of picture books to talk about the pictures, read the text, and discuss the story ideas" (Kerr & Mason, 1993, p. 133). Storybook reading contributes to language development and provides learning opportunities associated with later reading ability (Dickinson & Tabors, 2001). Children learn how to connect the text to their daily life experiences and become exposed to textual features associated with written English. Interactions using language facilitative techniques (e.g., open-ended questions, expansions, and recasts) while sharing books can increase vocabulary development (e.g., Fung, Chow, & McBride-Chang, 2005). Storybook reading also promotes an awareness of story grammar and provides opportunities for adults to use more complex language in explanations, descriptions, and definitions. In addition, storybook reading allows adults to introduce concepts of print such as the direction one reads, identification of letters and words, punctuation, capitalization, and clarification of story meaning (Snow, 1983). |
| Child-directed signing | Establishing and maintaining eye-to-eye joint attention with infants and toddlers is essential for language and cognitive development when using a visual-gestural language (Waxman & Spencer, 1997). Adult responsiveness to a child's eye gaze provides opportunities to name people and objects in the child's immediate environment. In addition, adults tend to sign at a slightly slower rate, increase the size and the duration of their signs, maintain a high rate of redundancy, and modify the placement of signs so they are within the child's field of vision (Bailes, Erting, Erting, & Thumann-Prezioso, 2009). |
| Fingerspelling | Fingerspelling has been defined as "the use of handshapes to represent letters of the alphabet" (Baker, 2010, p. 2). Deaf parents of deaf children fingerspell to their children early and often (Padden, 2006). Consequently, deaf children of deaf parents sometimes begin to fingerspell as early as 8 months of age (Pettito, 1983) but more frequently around 13 months of age (Anderson & Reilly, 2002; Padden & LeMaster, 1985). Several studies (e.g., Emmorey & Petrich, 2012; Haptonstall-Nykaza & Schick, 2007; Puente, Alvarado, & Herrera, 2006; Roos, 2013) have documented the important role that fingerspelling plays in American Sign Language (ASL) acquisition and contend that adults should expose children to fingerspelling when conversing as well as when teaching in order to establish a manually based linguistic bridge between ASL and written English (Crume, 2013; Erting, Thumann-Prezioso, & Sonnenstrahl-Benedict, 2000). |
| Chaining | Chaining is an interaction and teaching strategy for introducing vocabulary or concepts. Chaining creates associations by using multiple communicative techniques to help individuals learn the word or concept (Humphries & MacDougall, 2000). Two frequently used sequences include 1) point to the word written on the board (e.g., *flood*), fingerspell *F-L-O-O-D*, and sign *flood*, or 2) fingerspell *F-L-O-O-D*, sign *flood*, and write *flood* on the board. Use of pictures or objects may be helpful as well. |
| Sandwiching | Sandwiching is similar to chaining; however, the written step is eliminated. The three-step process that is often used is 1) fingerspell *F-L-O-O-D*, 2) sign *flood*, and 3) fingerspell *F-L-O-O-D* again, or 1) sign *flood*, 2) fingerspell *F-L-O-O-D*, and 3) sign *flood* again. |
| Preview-view-review (PVR) | The initial phase of PVR, "Preview," is undertaken to access background knowledge, provide an overview, and prepare students for the story or content of the lesson. This phase is conducted in ASL. The second phase, "View," occurs in written English using books, a document camera, or a SMART board. The third phase, "Review," is the discussion of the story or the wrap-up of the lesson, and this occurs in ASL (Andrews, Winograd, & DeVille, 1994; Gárate, 2012; Miller & Rosenthal, 1995). |
| American Sign Language educational media | Educational materials, such as signed educational television shows, multimedia ASL storytelling, and specially developed educational videos in ASL may be beneficial for several reasons, including 1) they are motivating for students; 2) they build on students' first language, ASL; 3) they employ multiple modes of communication (e.g., pictures, ASL, print); and 4) they integrate aspects of Deaf culture. A variety of small intervention studies have demonstrated positive outcomes (e.g., Andrews & Jordan, 1998; Cannon, Frederick, & Easterbrooks, 2010; Gentry, Chinn, & Moulton, 2004/2005; Golos & Moses, 2011, 2013; Guardino, Cannon, & Eberst, 2013; Mueller & Hurtig, 2010; Snodden, 2012). |

With an awareness that mode of communication is not as important as the quantity and quality of interaction that takes place between language learners and skilled users of that language (e.g., Hart & Risley, 1995; Wells, 1986), increasing attention has been given to helping children and youth acquire a wide range of language functions to serve different purposes in various environments (Halliday, 1978; Kretschmer & Kretschmer, 1995). Individuals' need to interact with others and to express different information (pragmatics) is currently viewed as the driving force for the words that they choose to use (semantics) and the form that is used to send the message (syntax).

From this perspective, it is understood that adults need to establish learning opportunities that require communication for real purposes, whereby the natural use of language emerges. With sufficient exposure to language and meaningful interactions with skilled language users, students who are D/HH can develop appropriate communication skills. Thus instead of teaching language in isolation, educators now emphasize content material while simultaneously infusing language objectives (e.g., Bullard & Luckner, 2013; Luckner, 2002).

People communicate for a variety of purposes. The functions, along with a brief explanation, include the following (Clarke School for the Deaf, 1995; North Dakota School for the Deaf, n.d.):

1. *Conversation*—An informal interaction between two or more people that generally involves an opening, an exchange of information, and a closing

2. *Description*—To convey an image or impression

3. *Narration*—To give an account of a real event or to tell a fictional story

4. *Explanation*—To make factual information clear and understandable

5. *Direction*—To give instructions for completing a task

6. *Negotiation/persuasion*—To reach an agreement with others or to influence the actions of others

7. *Questioning*—An expression of inquiry that invites or calls for a reply

8. *Writing*—The process of developing, selecting, combining, and arranging ideas into effective sentences, paragraphs, or longer units of information on paper or on other material or mediums (e.g., computers)

Obviously, the functions overlap. For example, a colleague could describe a friend that visited for the weekend while telling you what they did as part of a conversation you were having. Yet skilled communicators are able to use each of the functions when appropriate.

The functions of communication can be applied to stories as well as content. By aligning the language objectives with the story or the content, vocabulary and concepts can be reinforced and exposure and practice using the functions can occur. See Chapters 5, 6, and 7 for additional information about promoting language development.

**Motivation**    Humans are inherently curious and self-directed (e.g., Deci & Ryan, 2003). Motivation, which has been defined as "an internal state that arouses us to action, pushes us in particular directions, and keeps us engaged in certain activities" (Ormrod, 2008, p. 452), is critical for learning language and forming positive attitudes about reading. Motivated readers read more and become increasingly skilled (Parault & Williams, 2010). In contrast, unmotivated readers read infrequently and are likely to fall behind (Stanovich, 1986). Actions teachers can take to promote reading motivation include the following:

1. Be enthusiastic about reading.

2. Model reading, discuss books and stories, and promote interaction among students about literature.

3. Be knowledgeable of students' current level of functioning and help students choose materials they can read.

4. Provide opportunities for choices about what to read.

5. Understand and respect students' interests and provide appropriate selections.

***Vocabulary***   Research has consistently demonstrated a strong correlation between vocabulary and reading **comprehension** for hearing students (e.g., Cunningham & Stanovich, 1997; Snow, Griffin, & Burns, 2005) and for students who are D/HH (e.g., Fagan, Pisoni, Horn, & Dillon, 2007; LaSasso & Davey, 1987). Children learn vocabulary indirectly as well as directly (Armbruster, Lehr, & Osborn, 2003). During the preschool years, the majority of vocabulary knowledge is acquired indirectly through daily interactions with adults, siblings, and peers that occur through conversations around routines, games, nursery rhymes, songs, and reading activities (Landry & Smith, 2006). More specifically, young children learn words indirectly through conversational exchanges with sophisticated language users who pay close attention to the young child's communication attempts and who respond to the child about the object or activity of interest to the child (Luckner & Cooke, 2010). Simultaneously, the skilled language user models new vocabulary, expands on the child's utterances, prompts to keep the conversation going, and/or repairs conversation breakdowns (DesJardin & Eisenberg, 2007).

For hearing students, vocabulary knowledge develops rapidly from preschool through adulthood. It is estimated that hearing students expand their vocabulary at the rate of 2,700 to 3,000 words per year (Ruddell, 2009). In contrast, research indicates that the vocabulary knowledge of students who are D/HH is quantitatively reduced when compared with typical hearing peers. Qualitatively, it has been reported that students who are D/HH are delayed in vocabulary acquisition, have smaller lexicons, acquire new words at slower rates, and have a narrower range of contexts that result in word learning (e.g., Lederberg & Spencer, 2009; Marschark & Wauters, 2008; Trezek, Wang, & Paul, 2010).

For many students who are D/HH, insufficient vocabulary begins to negatively affect learning in the late primary and intermediate grades (Easterbrooks & Beal-Alvarez, 2013). This occurs because content area texts, such as science and social studies, tend to have different organizational patterns than narrative texts and include more sophisticated vocabulary (e.g., amphibian, vertebrates) as well as text organization patterns that include description and information, cause and effect, problem and solution, and comparison and contrast (Ruddell, 2009). Students are expected to extract, integrate, and retain main ideas, details, and specialized vocabulary.

Actions teachers can take to increase the depth and breadth of vocabulary knowledge of students who are D/HH include the following:

- *Teach high frequency words:* Many students who are D/HH do not have common words in their vocabulary (Paul & Gustafson, 1991). An important aspect of teaching high frequency words is providing sufficient repetition and practice for students to be able to apply word meanings to what they read. Research with hearing students (e.g., Roberts, Torgeson, Boradman, & Scammacca, 2009) suggests that up to 12 exposures may be necessary to develop a deep understanding of a new word.

- *Explicitly teach key words that are critical to understanding the text or the content:* The National Reading Panel (2000) as well as researchers in deaf education (e.g., Cannon et al., 2010; deVilliers & Pomerantz, 1992) reported the benefits of teaching specific words before reading to foster vocabulary learning as well as reading comprehension.

- *Explicitly teach compound words and affixes:* Being able to infer the meaning of words by using morphological clues becomes significantly more important as students move into the reading-to-learn stage (Nagy & Anderson, 1984). Many students who are D/HH have a difficult time figuring out what an unknown word means (Gaustad, Kelly, Payne, & Lylak, 2002). When introducing prefixes and suffixes, educators will want to begin with examples that are frequently used. White, Sowell, and Yanighara (1989) identified 111 prefixes (*un, re, in, dis, en/em, non, in/im, over, mis, sub, pre*) and six suffixes (*s/es, ed, ing, ly, er/or, ion/tion*) that account for 80% of all prefixed and suffixed words.

- *Explicitly teach students how to use context clues:* Learning to use context clues to figure out the meaning of words is an important independent vocabulary strategy students need to know (Bursuck & Damer, 2011). Context clues provide hints about the meanings of unknown words through the words, phrases, and sentences that surround the words. An instructional strategy for teaching how to use context clues suggested by Blachowicz and Fisher (2010) is 1) look (before, at, and after the word); 2) reason (connect what you know with what the author has written); 3) predict a possible meaning; and 4) resolve or redo (decide if you know enough, should try again, or consult an expert or a reference like a dictionary or thesaurus).

**Fluency**   Researchers (e.g., Fuchs, Fuchs, Hosp, & Jenkins, 2001; Theirren, 2004) have found high correlations between reading **fluency** and reading comprehension with hearing readers. The positive effect of fluency on reading comprehension appears to occur because fluent readers are able to process text effortlessly, which frees up working memory resources to focus on higher level reading processes such as word and phrase recognition, accessing prior knowledge, analyzing syntax, and checking for comprehension. In contrast, individuals with fluency problems tend to read text laboriously and spend large quantities of their cognitive resources focused on lower level skills such as decoding and word recognition, which limits the processing resources required to focus on meaning (Kelly, 2003; Swanson & O'Connor, 2009).

A synthesis of the research on reading fluency and students who are D/HH by Luckner and Urbach (2012) suggests that the primary action teachers can take to improve the fluency of students who are D/HH is the use of repeated reading. Through practice, students can increase their accuracy and rapid recognition of letters, words, phrases/sentences, and passages (e.g., Enns & Lafond, 2007; Schirmer, Therrien, Schaffer, & Schirmer, 2009). The guidelines for developing fluency skills adapted from Minskoff (2005) suggest providing explicit modeling of fluent reading; focusing on mastery of accuracy before working on speed; charting student progress; providing frequent, short periods of practice; and making practice varied and fun.

**Comprehension** The central purpose of reading is comprehension—constructing meaning from text. Luckner and Handley (2008) conducted a comprehensive review of the reading comprehension research. They identified five reading comprehension teaching interventions that have some evidence of effectiveness. Since 2008, additional studies (e.g., Banner & Wang, 2011) have been conducted that have provided additional support for the following interventions:

1.  *Explicit comprehension strategy instruction:* Explicit instruction means that teachers clearly explain to students (in language they understand) what it is they are going to do and why they are going to do it. Learning strategies are the techniques that successful students use to learn, behave, and do well in academic and social situations (Salend, 2008). Unfortunately, many students who are D/HH are strategy inefficient (Strassman, 1997)—that is, they do not know the procedures that successful learners use. Consequently, many students who are D/HH need **strategy instruction** that includes having specific strategies broken down into small steps, viewing multiple demonstrations of each strategy, and practicing each strategy several times in order to learn to apply it (Friend & Bursuck, 2009). The most frequently taught strategies are prediction, questioning, imagery, connecting (i.e., activating prior knowledge before, during, and after reading), and summarizing. A typical teaching sequence for explicit comprehension instruction includes the following steps: 1) direct explanation (the teacher explains to students why the strategy helps comprehension and when to apply the strategy); 2) modeling (the teacher models or demonstrates how to apply the strategy while reading the text that the students are using); 3) guided practice (the teacher guides and assists the students as they learn how and when to apply the strategy); and

4) application (the teacher helps students practice the strateg y until they can apply it independently).

2. *Text structure:* Texts are generally organized in two patterns—narrative (fiction) and expository (nonfiction). When students have an awareness of these patterns, they have an easier time understanding what they read. Narrative story structure or story grammar involves an understanding of the setting, the main characters, the problem, the attempts to solve the problem, and the resolution. The same steps for explicitly teaching comprehension strategies discussed previously can be used to teach students narrative story structure. Also, story maps, which are a form of graphic organizer, can be used as a visual guide to understand and retell narrative stories.

3. *Modified directed reading thinking activity:* The modified directed reading thinking activity (DRTA) is designed for group comprehension instruction. The goals of the DRTA are to help students set a purpose for reading, make predictions using personal background information and text-based knowledge, gather information as they read, verify and revise predications, and reach a conclusion about the story (Ruddell, 2009). In general, there are two distinct phases of the DRTA. The first involves getting the students ready for the story and guiding their thinking and interaction with the story. The second is the extension phase, which focuses on skill development and follow-up activities.

4. *Background knowledge:* A person's knowledge of the world that is stored in long-term memory is often referred to as prior knowledge, schemata, or background knowledge. This type of knowledge serves as the foundation for reading comprehension. Skilled readers connect their background knowledge to the new knowledge they read in a text (Fountas & Pinnell, 2006a). Educators can activate students' background knowledge by 1) bringing in objects for hands-on exploration, 2) showing pictures or videos pertaining to the topic (e.g., picture sources, YouTube videos, described and captioned media programs), 3) providing conceptually related books that span a wide range of reading levels, and 4) previewing the reading material (for narrative text, examine the title, headings, and pictures, and for expository text, examine the side headings, pictures, graphics, bold-faced words, and study questions).

5. *Well-written, high-interest materials:* Teachers can expose students to good writing and motivate them to build their interest in and love for good books and diverse forms of literature by providing a variety of high-interest books in an environment that promotes individual and small-group reading and responding (Edmunds & Bauserman, 2006). Strategies for using literature include 1) storybook reading, 2) storytelling, 3) literature-response journals, 4) literature-response groups, and 5) reader's theater.

***Writing***   Reading and writing skills are intimately connected processes. Reading helps individuals learn **text structure**s and language they can use when they write, and writing helps individuals build their reading skills by developing critical thinking skills such as questioning, recalling, analyzing, and synthesizing (Langer & Applebee, 1987). The development of writing skills requires opportunities to write as well as properly designed and sequenced instruction (Albertini & Schley, 2011). See Chapter 13 for information about promoting written language development.

## Use of Ongoing Assessments to Guide Intervention

Progress monitoring has been defined as the "frequent and ongoing measurement of student knowledge and skills and the examination of student data to evaluate instruction" (Vaughn, Bos, & Schumm, 2007, p. 74). As noted, progress monitoring is one of the four types of literacy assessment that educators typically undertake. Progress monitoring differs from traditional assessment in that it tends to focus on students' performance on a few critical skills (e.g., concepts of print, letter naming, **sight words**, passage reading fluency), using repeatable (e.g., weekly, monthly, quarterly) and brief probes (e.g., 1–3 minutes). Advantages of progress monitoring over traditional assessments include the following: 1) it can be hand scored, 2) it allows teachers to conduct error analyses to identify specific targets for intervention, and 3) the graphing of students' progress allows teachers, students, and parents to see how students are performing (Quenemoen, Thurlow, Moen, Thompson, & Morse, 2003). The National Center on Student Progress Monitoring (n.d.) reports that the benefits of progress monitoring include 1) accelerated learning because students receive more appropriate instruction, 2) more informed instructional decisions, 3) more efficient communication with families and other service providers about students' progress; 4) documentation of student progress for accountability purposes, and 5) higher expectations for students by teachers.

Specific progress monitoring instruments that are frequently used with students who are D/HH are noted. In addition, the National Center on Intensive Intervention provides a resource professionals can use to identify academic progress monitoring tools for reading, writing, and math. Included on the web site are three tabs (Psychometric Standards, Progress Monitoring Standards, and Data-Based Individualization Standards), as well as ratings on the tech-nical rigor of the tools (http://www.intensiveintervention.org/chart/progress -monitoring). Another valuable resource is Intervention Central, which has a link for the Curriculum-Based Measurement Warehouse for free progress monitoring resources (http://www.interventioncentral.org/curriculum-based -measurement-reading-math-assesment-tests).

## Addressing Unique Needs in Intervention

The population of students who are D/HH is very heterogeneous. In the following section, additional strategies for working with students who have unique needs, in addition to being D/HH, are provided. Also, general suggestions for working with parents/caregivers are included.

***Delayed Adolescent Readers***   Students are expected to read to learn beginning in the upper elementary grades. As students progress through middle and high school, reading to learn becomes increasingly important in subject areas such as science and social studies, with information derived from text becoming the primary way that students access course content. However, some adolescents who are D/HH have not developed the fundamental skills of learning to read by this time, such as word recognition, fluency, and comprehension, and as a result, they develop a negative attitude about reading and actively avoid texts, neglect reading homework, and rarely read for pleasure. Unfortunately, like most skills, reading requires practice. Limited reading results in a lack of vocabulary development, less background knowledge acquired, and less familiarity with narrative and expository text structure, which all lead to lowered text comprehension. To help delayed readers, teachers will want to collect assessment data to identify students' strengths, areas of concern, and interests as well as their approximate reading level. Analysis of the assessment data can help educators plan systematic instruction in the areas that students demonstrate skill deficits. By identifying students' interests and approximate reading level, teachers can provide students with texts that they can read, thereby increasing their opportunities to practice the skills they are learning in the context of real reading material that contains stories or information.

One way teachers can encourage delayed readers to read more is by matching texts to students' reading level. This can be done using a leveled book approach. For example, Fountas and Pinnell (2006b) provide an online list of more than 46,000 books that have been reviewed and leveled (http://www .fountasandpinnellleveledbooks.com). Another option is to use high-interest, low-vocabulary books. Many book publishers produce books that are interesting to adolescents but written at lower reading levels so they can understand what they are reading and feel successful. In addition, many publishers produce nonfiction trade books that can be used to provide students access to content that is too complex for them to read in traditional textbooks.

Professionals can also help students increase their comprehension of content in textbooks using a variety of methods. First, they can explicitly teach students how to use expository text structures (e.g., key vocabulary, headings, graphs, charts, guide questions). Second, prior to reading the textbook, they can conduct "chapter tours" with students to look at and discuss the title, headings, bold-faced words, and visuals. Third, they can activate background knowledge by showing videos (e.g., YouTube, TeacherTube, described and captioned media programs) or pictures from the Internet aligned with the content in the textbook. Fourth, they can develop graphic organizers that provide a visual representation that depicts the relationships of the critical content that students are expected to learn.

One final essential point to take into consideration with delayed readers is their motivation—or, more accurately, their lack of motivation. When students fail to develop automatic word recognition, struggle to understand words, and don't comprehend a passage, they avoid reading because it makes them feel inadequate, frustrated, and sometimes embarrassed (Ruddell, 2009). In addition to the aforementioned information as well as the suggestions on ways to promote motivation presented earlier, teachers can 1) help students create mastery goals for themselves related to improving specific reading skills, 2) provide students choices about what they read, and 3) establish opportunities for social interaction with peers about what they are reading (Guthrie, 2008).

**Students Who Have Additional Disabilities**    It has been consistently reported that between 25% and 50% of students who are D/HH also have an additional disability (e.g., Blackorby & Knokey, 2006; Gallaudet Research Institute, 2011; Knoors & Vervloed, 2003). The presence of an additional disability does not merely add to the challenges of acquiring literacy skills; it compounds them exponentially. Consequently, some students may be delayed readers and bene-fit from the suggestions provided, while others will require a more functional reading program that focuses on life skills (e.g., self-care, budgeting, planning meals, travel, community safety, using medications, employment, recreation and leisure; Luckner, 2010).

Professionals need to take into consideration the current and future needs of all the students they serve. When students who are D/HH complete their pre-K–12 educations, they can continue on to postsecondary training, enter the world of work, or collect Social Security Disability Insurance. They also are required to perform adult tasks (e.g., have meals, use money, travel from place to place, deal with illness, use the Internet). Most of these tasks require reading in order to access information. For some students with additional disabilities, explicit instruction in reading materials that they will encounter in their daily lives once they leave school will need to be provided while they continue to receive educational services. Some examples include menus, road signs, directions for food preparation, forms, directions on medications, bills, classified ads, and job applications. Fortunately, multiple publishers produce instructional materials that can be used to help students achieve the reading skills they will need in real-life situations (Cronin, Patton, & Wood, 2007).

**Students Who Are Culturally and/or Linguistically Diverse**    The Gallaudet Research Institute (2011) suggests that approximately 53% of students who are D/HH are culturally and/or linguistically diverse. The same report indicates that for approximately 22% of the students, Spanish is the language regularly used in the home and that for approximately 25%, a language other than English, Spanish, or ASL is regularly used in the home.

A review of the literature on interventions for students who are D/HH and culturally and/or linguistically diverse conducted by Cannon and Guardino (2012) indicates that a paucity of research has been conducted. One intervention that has demonstrated positive results is the use of preteaching vocabulary and viewing math expository books read in ASL on a DVD (Cannon, Frederick, & Easterbrooks, 2010; Guardino, Cannon, & Eberst, 2013). Gersten et al. (2007) reviewed the literature for typical hearing students who are English language learners and identified five evidence-based practices: 1) screen for reading problems and monitor progress, 2) provide intensive small-group reading interventions, 3) provide extensive and varied vocabulary instruction, 4) develop academic English, and 5) schedule regular peer-assisted learning opportunities.

In addition to using many of the previously discussed interventions, Drucker (2003) suggests that teachers preview material before reading and use paired reading, multicultural literature, and the language experience approach when teaching students who are English language learners. Similarly, Gerner de Garcia (1995) advises that educators use the thematic teaching of units that includes the use of trade books with pictures to help students who are D/HH and culturally and/or linguistically diverse learn vocabulary and increase their understanding of the content.

**Working with Parents/Caregivers**    Children are not born with an interest in reading. Most often, parents/caregivers read with children, and as a result of these shared experiences, children come to think of reading as enjoyable and valued. Joint parent and child book reading has demonstrated positive language development, school readiness, literacy development, and a desire to read for typical hearing children (e.g., Bus, van IJzendoorn, & Pellegrini, 1995; Weizman & Snow, 2001). Although not as rigorously studied, similar positive results have been found for children who are D/HH (e.g., Delk & Weidekamp, 2001; DesJardin, Ambrose, & Eisenberg, 2009, 2011; Kaderavek & Pakulski, 2007).

Zupan and Dempsey (2013) discuss the importance of collaboration between teachers and parents/caregivers. They suggest that it is critical for teachers to work with families of children who are D/HH to help them create language and literacy rich environments and to demonstrate how specific literacy-based activities can be integrated into existing daily routines. Examples of specific language and literacy activities that educators can share with parents/caregivers, drawn from Armbruster, Lehr, and Osborn (2003) and DesJardin and Ambrose (2010), include the following: 1) talk with the child while you do things together; 2) read to the child each day; 3) use and repeat important words such as names of buildings, food, events, and places you visit; 4) point out and name familiar signs and logos to the child (e.g., McDonald's, shopping stores, street signs); 5) have conversations about recent family photographs; and 6) talk about what is going on when watching television programs or videos/DVDs together.

## Case Study: Application to a Child

Diego is 9 years old and attends third grade at Roosevelt Elementary School in Blue Sky, Colorado. He has a bilateral, profound, sensorineural hearing loss, which was identified through newborn hearing screening. He is the only member of his family who is deaf and the cause of his deafness is unknown. He lives with his parents; his two older brothers, both in high school; and a younger brother who is in first grade. His parents speak Spanish in the home. He has been wearing hearing aids since he was 1 year old and received a cochlear implant in his right ear a month before his fourth birthday. His primary mode of communication is spoken English, but he also uses sign and speechreading.

Diego's family received early intervention services from the Colorado Home Intervention Program. After that, he attended the district's preschool program for students who are deaf or hard of hearing (D/HH) for half a day, 4 days a week. Since kindergarten, he has attended his home school, which is also the center-based elementary program for students who are D/HH in the district.

He spends the majority of the day in the general education classroom and receives speech and language services from a speech-language pathologist (SLP) twice a week for 30 minutes each time. The educational audiologist provides auditory training once a week for 30 minutes, and the resource room teacher of students who are D/HH also provides reading and math tutoring 4 times a week for 30 minutes a day. Each of these services has been in place since kindergarten.

Diego has friends at school and at home. He is active in sports (e.g., soccer, basketball, and base-ball). At the last individualized education program (IEP) meeting, his parents indicated through an interpreter that Diego has a good relationship with family members and likes to spend time with his younger brother and his cousins. They also indicated that he is active in their church.

As part of his triennial evaluation, Ms. Bowen, the resource room teacher for students who are D/HH, interviewed the general education teacher and observed Diego in the general educa-tion classroom. The general education teacher, Mrs. Rudolph, reported that Diego is a hard worker, gets along with his classmates, and demonstrates difficulty in the areas of vocabulary, reading, and writing. The district uses the Success for All reading program, and Diego is in the lowest group in the class. During the classroom observation of his reading period, Diego was off task 30% of the time, which was approximately twice as much as two of his peers in the same classroom. Diego was administered a variety of assessments that focused on literacy. The results are presented in Table 12.5.

*Sample Literacy Objectives Developed by Diego's Multidisciplinary Team*

By the end of the school year, Diego will be able to do the following:

- Describe characters, settings, and major events in a story, using key details with 80% accuracy.
- Retell stories, including key details, and demonstrate understanding of their central mes-sage with 80% accuracy.
- Ask and answer 90% of questions about key details in a text read independently.
- Increase the number of sight words he knows by 20%.
- Decode words with common prefixes and suffixes with 80% accuracy.
- Read grade-appropriate irregularly spelled words with 80% accuracy.
- Demonstrate understanding of figurative language, word relationships, and nuances in word meanings with 80% accuracy.
- Use sentence-level context as a clue to the meaning of a word or phrase with 80% accuracy.
- Read a second-grade-level text with 80% accuracy, appropriate rate, and expression.
- Use the illustrations and details in an expository text to describe the key ideas with 90% accuracy.

## FUTURE DIRECTIONS

As described in Chapter 1 and noted multiple times throughout this text, stu-dents who are D/HH are a heterogeneous population. Professionals need a

**Table 12.5.**   Diego's assessment data

| Woodcock Reading Mastery Test (3rd ed.) | | |
| --- | --- | --- |
| Subtest | Grade equivalent score | Standard score (90% Confidence Intervals) |
| Readiness | | |
| Word identification | 1.8 | 68 (59–77) |
| Word attack | 1.4 | 73 (66–80) |
| Basic skills cluster | | |
| Word comprehension | 1.5 | 71 (63–79) |
| Passage comprehension | 1.2 | 68 (59–77) |
| Reading comprehension cluster | | |
| Oral reading fluency | 1.6 | 62 (57–67) |
| Total reading cluster | 1.9 | 73 (69–77) |
| Qualitative Reading Inventory 5 | | |
| Subtest | Score | |
| Word list | First-grade-level narrative: 70% accuracy | |
| Passage reading | Miscues: 46 reading miscues out of 250 words | |
| | Fluency: 250 words read minus 46 miscues = 204 words read correct in 4.2 minutes = 46 correct words per minute | |
| | Retelling: 15 out of 44 items listed on the checklist for the retell = 34% | |
| | Number correct explicit questions: 2/3 | |
| | Number correct implicit questions: 0/3 | |
| | Total: 2/6 | |
| Reading interest inventory results | | |

Reads on his own "once in a while."

He likes magazines such as *Sports Illustrated for Kids*.

He likes the *Magic Tree House* books, *Cloudy with a Chance of Meatballs*, and *Bunnicula*.

He likes to watch *SpongeBob SquarePants* and *Gravity Falls*.

He has a library card but never uses it.

variety of practices, materials, strategies, and interventions to use in order to have positive outcomes with students. Although improving, to date a paucity of research has been undertaken that can guide educators about the most effective practices to use with students who are D/HH. Many studies are correlational and not experimental. Simultaneously, most intervention studies have not been replicated. As a result, there is a need for replication studies in all aspects of literacy for students who are D/HH. Specific research that has been demonstrated to be effective by one set of researchers in one setting with one group of students needs to be repeated by different researchers with another set of students in order to increase the body of evidence. Similarly, interventions that have a strong evidence base with typical hearing students or students who receive special education services need to be examined with students who are D/HH. The What Works Clearinghouse (WWC; http://ies.ed.gov/ncee/wwc) provides intervention reports that summarize the research conducted on educational programs, practices, or policies aimed at improving student outcomes.

## SUGGESTED READING AND RESOURCES

Easterbrooks, S.R., & Beal-Alvarez, J. (2013). *Literacy instruction for students who are deaf or hard of hearing.* New York, NY: Oxford University Press.
Florida Center for Reading Research. (2010). *Florida Assessments for Instruction in Reading (FAIR) Search Tool for Links to Instructional Materials.* Retrieved from http://www.fcrr.org/FAIR_Search_Tool/FAIR_Search _Tool .aspx
The IRIS Center has nine modules focused on reading, literacy, and language arts at http://iris.peabody.vanderbilt.edu

## LEARNING ACTIVITIES

1.  Choose one of the objectives identified for Diego. Identify three activities you would use to attain the objective with him.

2.  Nolan is 14 years old. He is 3 years behind his classmates in reading and becoming less motivated to read daily. Prioritize the actions you could take to help him become more motivated about improving his reading skills.

3.  Identify a comprehension reading strategy (e.g., summarizing, creating mental images) you want to teach a small group of middle school students who are hard of hearing. Make a list of the steps you would include to effectively teach them the strategy.

## REFERENCES

Adams, M.J. (1990). *Beginning to read: Thinking and learning about print.* Cambridge, MA: MIT Press.
Albertini, J.A., & Schley, S. (2011). Writing: Characteristics, instruction and assessment. In M. Marschark & P. Spencer (Eds.), *Handbook of deaf studies, language, and education* (2nd ed., Vol. 1, pp. 130–143). New York, NY: Oxford University Press.
Allen, T.E., Clark, M.D., del Giudice, A., Koo, D., Lieberman, A., Mayberry, R., & Miller, P. (2009). Phonology and reading: A response to Wang, Trezek, Luckner, and Paul. *American Annals of the Deaf, 154*(4), 338–345.
Anderson, D., & Reilly, J. (2002). The MacArthur Communicative Development Inventory: Normative data for American Sign Language. *Journal of Deaf Studies and Deaf Education, 7,* 83–106.
Andrews, J. F., & Jordan, D. L., (1998). Multimedia stories for deaf children. *Teaching Exceptional Children, 30*(5), 28-33.
Andrews, J.F., Winograd, P., & DeVille, G. (1994). Deaf children reading fables: Using ASL summaries to improve reading comprehension. *American Annals of the Deaf, 139,* 378–386.
Armbruster, B.B., Lehr, F., & Osborn, J. (2003). *Put reading first: The research building blocks of reading instruction, kindergarten through Grade 3* (2nd ed.). Washington, DC: Partnership for Reading.

Bailes, C.N., Erting, C.J., Erting, L.C., & Thumann-Prezioso, C. (2009). Language and literacy acquisition through parental mediation in American Sign Language. *Sign Language Studies, 9*(4), 417–456.

Baker, S. (2010, July). *The importance of fingerspelling for reading* (research brief no. 1). Visual Language and Visual Learning Science of Learning Center. Retrieved from http://vl2 .gallaudet .edu/assets/section7/document100 .pdf

Banner, A., & Wang, Y. (2011). An analysis of the reading strategies used by adults and student deaf readers. *Journal of Deaf Studies and Deaf Education, 16*(1), 2–23.

Beal-Alvarez, J., Lederberg, A.R., & Easterbrooks, S.R. (2011). Grapheme-phoneme acquisition of deaf preschoolers. *Journal of Deaf Studies and Deaf Education, 17,* 39–60. doi:10.1093/deafed/enr030

Beck, I.L., & Beck, M.E. (2013). *Making sense of phonics: The hows and whys.* New York, NY: Guilford Press.

Beck, I., McKeown, M., & Kucan, L. (2013). *Bringing words to life: Robust vocabulary instruction* (2nd ed.). New York, NY: Guilford Press.

Birsh, J. (2005). *Multisensory teaching of basic language skills* (2nd ed.). Baltimore, MD: Paul H. Brookes Publishing Co.

Blachowicz, C., & Fisher, P.J. (2010). *Teaching vocabulary in all classrooms.* Boston, MA: Allyn & Bacon.

Blackorby, J., & Knokey, A. (2006). *A national profile of students with hearing impairments in elementary and middle school: A special topic report from the Special Education Elementary Longitudinal Study.* Menlo Park, CA: SRI International.

Bullard, C., & Luckner, J.L. (2013). *The itinerant teacher handbook* (2nd ed.). Hillsboro, OR: Butte.

Bursuck, W.D., & Damer, M. (2011). *Teaching reading to students who are at risk or have disabilities* (2nd ed.). Upper Saddle River, NJ: Pearson Education.

Bus, A.G., van IJzendoorn, M.H., & Pellegrini, A.D. (1995). Joint book reading makes success in learning to read: A meta-analysis of intergenerational transmission of literacy. *Review of Educational Research, 65,* 684–698.

Cambourne, B., & Turbill, J. (1987). *Coping with chaos.* Portsmouth, NH: Heinemann.

Cannon, J.E., Frederick, L.D., & Easterbrooks, S.R. (2010). Vocabulary instruction through books read in American Sign Language for English-language learners with hearing loss. *Communication Disorders Quarterly, 31,* 98–112.

Cannon, J.E., & Guardino, C. (2012). Literacy strategies for deaf/hard of hearing ELLs: Where do we begin? *Deafness & Education International, 14*(2), 78–99.

Chall, J.S. (1996). *Stages of reading development.* (2nd ed.). New York, NY: McGraw-Hill.

Chamberlain, C., & Mayberry, R.I. (2000). Theorizing about the relationship between American Sign Language and reading. In C. Chamberlain, J. Morford, & R. Mayberry (Eds.), *Language acquisition by eye* (pp. 221–260). Mahwah, NJ: Lawrence Erlbaum Associates.

Chamberlain, C., & Mayberry, R.I. (2008). American Sign Language syntactic and narrative comprehension in skilled and less skilled readers: Bilingual and bimodal evidence for the linguistic basis of reading. *Applied Psycholinguistics, 29,* 367–388.

Clarke School for the Deaf. (1995). *Language arts curriculum.* Northampton, MA: Author.

Coltheart, M., Rastle, K., Perry, C., Langdon, R., & Ziegler, J. (2001). DRC: A dual-route cascaded model of visual word recognition and reading aloud. *Psychological Review, 108,* 204–256.

Cronin, M.E., Patton, J.R., & Wood, S.J. (2007). *Life skills instruction: A practical guide for integrating real-life content into the curriculum at the elementary and secondary levels for students with special needs or who are placed at risk* (2nd ed.). Austin, TX: Pro-Ed.

Crume, P.K. (2013). Teachers' perceptions of promoting sign language phonological awareness in an ASL/English bilingual program. *Journal of Deaf Studies and Deaf Education, 18*(4), 464–488.

Cummins, J. (2000). *Language, power, and pedagogy: Bilingual children in the crossfire.* Clevedon, England: Multilingual Matters.

Cunningham, A.E., & Stanovich, K.E. (1997). Early reading acquisition and its relation to reading experience and ability 10 years later. *Developmental Psychology, 33,* 934–945.

Deci, E.L., & Ryan, R. (2003). *The handbook of self-determination research.* Rochester, NY: University of Rochester Press.

Delk, L., & Weidekamp, L. (2001). *Shared reading project: Evaluating implementation processes and family outcomes.* Washington, DC: Gallaudet University.

DesJardin, J.L., & Ambrose, S. (2010). The importance of the home literacy environment for developing literacy skills in young children who are deaf or hard of hearing. *Young Exceptional Children, 13,* 28–44.

DesJardin, J.L., Ambrose, S.E., & Eisenberg, L.S. (2009). Literacy skills in children with cochlear implants: The importance of early oral language and joint storybook reading. *Journal of Deaf Studies and Deaf Education, 14*(1), 22–43. doi:10.1093/deafed/enn011

DesJardin, J. L., Ambrose, S. E., & Eisenberg, L.S (2011). Maternal involvement in the home literacy environment: Supporting literacy skills in children with cochlear implants. *Communication Disorders Quarterly, 32*(3), 135-150.

DesJardin, J.L., & Eisenberg, L.S. (2007). Maternal contributions: Supporting language development in young children with cochlear implants. *Ear and Hearing, 28*(4), 456–469.

deVilliers, P.A., & Pomerantz, S.B. (1992). Hearing impaired students learning new words from written context. *Applied Psycholinguistics, 13,* 409–431.

Dickinson, D.K., McCabe, A., & Essex, M.J. (2006). A window of opportunity we must open to all: The case for preschool with high-quality support for language and literacy. In D.K. Dickinson & S.B. Neuman (Eds.), *Handbook of early literacy research* (Vol. 2, pp. 11–28). New York, NY: Guilford Press.

Dickinson, D. K., & Tabors, P. O., (2001). *Beginning literacy with language.* Baltimore, MD: Paul H. Brookes Publishing Co.

Drucker, M.J. (2003). What reading teachers should know about ESL learners. *The Reading Teacher, 57*(1), 22–29.

Easterbrooks, S.R. (2010). Evidence-based curricula and practices that support development of reading skills. In M. Marschark & P. Spencer (Eds.), *Oxford handbook of deaf studies, language, and education* (Vol. 2, pp. 111–126). New York, NY: Oxford University Press.

Easterbrooks, S.R., & Beal-Alvarez, J. (2013). *Literacy instruction for students who are deaf or hard of hearing.* New York, NY: Oxford University Press.

Edcheckup. (2013). *Welcome to Edcheckup!* Retrieved January 11, 2014, from http://www.edcheckup.com.

Edmunds, K., & Bauserman, K. (2006). What teachers can learn about reading motivation through conversations with children. *The Reading Teacher, 59*(5), 414–424.

Emmory, K., & Petrich, J.A. (2012). Processing orthographic structure: Associations between print and fingerspelling. *Journal of Deaf Studies and Deaf Education, 17,* 194–204.

Enns, C., & Lafond, L.D. (2007). Reading against all odds: A pilot study of two deaf students with dyslexia. *American Annals of the Deaf, 152*(1), 63–72.

Erting, C., Thumann-Prezioso, C., & Sonnenstrahl-Benedict, B. (2000). Bilingualism in a Deaf family: Fingerspelling in early childhood. In P. Spencer, C. Erting, & M. Marschark (Eds.), *The deaf child in the family and at school* (pp. 41–54). Hillsdale, NJ: Lawrence Erlbaum Associates.

Fagan, M.K., Pisoni, D.B., Horn, D.L., & Dillon, C.M. (2007). Neuropsychological correlates of vocabulary, reading, and working memory in deaf children with cochlear implants. *Journal of Deaf Studies and Deaf Education, 12*(4), 461–471.

Fish, S., & Morford, J.P. (2012, June). *The benefits of bilingualism: Impacts on language and cognitive development* (research brief no. 7). Visual Language and Visual Learning Science of Learning Center. Retrieved January 20, 2014, from http://vl2.gallaudet.edu/research/research-briefs/

Fountas, I.C., & Pinnell, G.S. (2006a). *Teaching for comprehension and fluency: Thinking, talking, and writing about reading, K–8.* Portsmouth, NH: Heinemann.

Fountas, I.C., & Pinnell, G.S. (2006b). *Leveled books K–8: Matching texts to readers for effective teaching.* Portsmouth, NH: Heinemann.

French, M.M. (1999). *The toolkit appendices for starting with assessment: A developmental approach to deaf children's literacy.* Washington, DC: Gallaudet University.

Friend, M., & Bursuck, W.D. (2009). *Including students with special needs: A practical guide for classroom teachers* (4th ed.). Boston, MA: Pearson/Allyn & Bacon.

Fuchs, L.S., Fuchs, D., Hosp, M.K., & Jenkins, J.R. (2001). Oral reading fluency as an indicator of reading competence: A theoretical, empirical, and historical analysis. *Scientific Studies of Reading, 5*(3), 239–256.

Fung, P.C., Chow, W.Y., & McBride-Chang, C. (2005). The impact of a dialogic reading program on deaf and hard-of-hearing kindergarten and early primary school-aged students in Hong Kong. *Journal of Deaf Studies and Deaf Education, 10,* 82–95.

Gallaudet Research Institute. (2011, April). *Regional and national summary report of data from the 2009–10 annual survey of deaf and hard of hearing children and youth.* Washington, DC: Gallaudet University.

Gárate, M. (2011). Educating children with cochlear implants in an ASL/English bilingual classroom. In R. Paludneviciene & I. Leigh (Eds.), *Cochlear implants: Evolving perspectives* (pp. 206–228). Washington, DC: Gallaudet University Press.

Gárate, M. (2012, June). *ASL/English bilingual education: Models, methodologies, and strategies* (research brief no. 8). Visual Language and Visual Learning Science of Learning Center. Retrieved January 22, 2014, from http://vl2.gallaudet.edu/research/research-briefs/

Gaustad, M.G., Kelly, R.R., Payne, J.A., & Lylak, E. (2002). Deaf and hearing students' morphological knowledge applied to printed English. *American Annals of the Deaf, 147*(5), 5–21.

Gentry, M.M., Chinn, K.C., & Moulton, R.D. (2004/2005). Effectiveness of multimedia reading materials used with children who are deaf. *American Annals of the Deaf, 149*(5), 394–403.

Gerner de Garcia, B.A. (1995). ESL applications for Hispanic deaf students. *The Bilingual Research Journal, 19*(3), 453–467.

Gersten, R., Baker, S.K., Shanahan, T., Linan-Thompson, S., Collins, P., & Scarcella, R. (2007). *Effective literacy and English language instruction for English learners in the elementary grades: A practice guide* (NCEE 2007-4011). Washington, DC: National Center for Education Evaluation and Regional Assistance, Institute of Education Sciences, U.S. Department of Education. Retrieved from http://ies.ed.gov/ncee/wwc/publications/practiceguides

Golos, D.B., & Moses, A.M. (2011). How teacher mediation during video viewing facilitates literacy behaviors. *Sign Language Studies, 12*(1), 98–118.

Golos, D.B., & Moses, A.M. (2013). Developing preschool deaf children's language and literacy learning from an educational media series. *American Annals of the Deaf, 158*(4), 411–425.

Good, R.H., & Kaminski, R.A. (Eds.). (2007). *Dynamic indicators of basic early literacy skills* (6th ed.). Eugene, OR: Institute for the Development of Education Achievement.

Grosjean, F. (2010). Bilingualism, biculturalism, and deafness. *International Journal of Bilingual Education and Bilingualism, 13*(2), 133–145.

Guardino, C., Cannon, J.E., & Eberst, K. (2013). Building the evidence-base of effective reading strategies to use with deaf English-language learners. *Communication Disorders Quarterly, 35*(2), 59–73.

Guthrie, J.T. (2008). Growing motivation: How students develop. In J.T. Guthrie (Ed.), *Engaging adolescents in reading* (pp. 99–113). Thousand Oaks, CA: Corwin Press.

Halliday, M.A.K. (1978). *Language as social semiotic.* London, England: Edward Arnold.

Hanson, V. (1989). Phonology and reading: Evidence from profoundly deaf readers. In D. Shankweiler & I. Lieberman (Eds.), *Phonology and reading disability: Solving the reading puzzle* (pp. 69–89). Ann Arbor: University of Michigan Press.

Haptonstall-Nykaza, T.S., & Schick, B. (2007). The transition from fingerspelling to English print: Facilitating English decoding. *Journal of Deaf Studies and Deaf Education, 12*(2), 172–183.

Hart, B., & Risley, T.R. (1995). *Meaningful differences in the everyday experiences of young American children.* Baltimore, MD: Paul H. Brookes Publishing Co.

Hart, B., & Risley, T.R. (2003). The early catastrophe: The 30 million word gap by age 3. *American Educator, 27*(1), 4–9.

Hougen, M.C., & Smartt, S.M. (Eds.). (2012). *Fundamentals of literacy instruction and assessment: Pre-K–6.* Baltimore, MD: Paul H. Brookes Publishing Co.

Humphries, T., & MacDougal, F. (2000). "Chaining" and other links: Making connections between American Sign Language and English in two types of school settings. *Visual Anthropology, 15,* 84–94.

International Communication Learning Institute. (1996). *See the sound visual phonics.* Edina, MN: Author.

Johns, J., & Elish-Piper, L. (2012). *The basic reading inventory: Pre-primer through Grade 12 and early literacy assessments* (11th ed.). Dubuque, IA: Kendall/Hunt.

Joshi, R.M., & Aaron, P.G. (2012). Componential model of reading (CMR): Validation studies. *Journal of Learning Disabilities, 45*(5), 387–390.

Kaderavek, J.N., & Pakulski, L.A. (2007). Mother-child story book interaction: Literacy orientation of pre-schoolers with hearing impairment. *Journal of Early Childhood Literacy, 7*(1), 49–72.

Karlsen, B., & Gardner, E.F. (1996). *Stanford Diagnostic Reading Test* (4th ed.). San Antonio, TX: Harcourt Educational Measurement.

Kelly, L. (2003). Considerations for designing practice for deaf readers. *Journal of Deaf Studies and Deaf Education, 8*(2), 171–186.

Kerr, B.M., & Mason, J.M. (1993). Awakening literacy through interactive story reading. In F. Lehr & L. Osborn (Eds.), *Reading, language and literacy* (pp. 133–148). Mahwah, NJ: Lawrence Erlbaum Associates.

Knoors, H., & Vervloed, M.P.J. (2003). Educational programming for deaf children with multiple disabilities: Accommodating special needs. In M. Marschark & P. Spencer (Eds.), *Oxford handbook of deaf studies, language, and education* (pp. 82–94). New York, NY: Oxford University Press.

Kretschmer, R.R., & Kretschmer, L.W. (1995). Communication-based classrooms. *The Volta Review, 97*(5), 1–18.

Kyle, F.E., & Harris, M. (2010). Predictors of reading development in deaf children: A 3-year longitudinal study. *Journal of Experimental Child Psychology, 107*(3), 229–243. doi:10.1016/j.jecp.2010.04.011

Kyle, F.E., & Harris, M. (2011). Longitudinal patterns of emerging literacy in beginning deaf and hearing readers. *Journal of Deaf Studies and Deaf Education, 16*(3), 289–304.

Landry, S.H., & Smith, K.E. (2006). The influence of parenting on emerging literacy skills. In D. Dickinson & S. Neuman (Eds.), *Handbook of early literacy research* (Vol. 2, pp. 135–148). New York, NY: Guilford Press.

Lange, C.M., Lane-Outlaw, S., Lange, W.F., & Sherwood, D.L. (2013). American Sign Language/English bilingual model: A longitudinal study of academic growth. *Journal of Deaf Studies and Deaf Education, 18*(4), 532–544. doi:10.1093/deafed

Langer, J.A., & Applebee, A.N. (1987). *How writing shapes thinking: A study of teaching and learning.* Urbana, IL: National Council of Teachers of English.

LaSasso, C., & Davey, B. (1987). The relationship between lexical knowledge and reading comprehension for prelingually, profoundly hearing-impaired students. *The Volta Review, 89,* 211–220.

Lederberg, A.R., Schick, B., & Spencer, P.R. (2013). Language and literacy development of deaf and hard-of-hearing children: Successes and challenges. *Developmental Psychology, 49*(1), 15–30.

Lederberg, A.R., & Spencer, P.E. (2009). Word-learning abilities in deaf and hard-of-hearing preschoolers: Effect of lexicon size and language modality. *Journal of Deaf Studies and Deaf Education, 14*(1), 44–62.

Leslie, L., & Caldwell, J.S. (2011). *Qualitative Reading Inventory 5.* Upper Saddle River, NJ: Pearson.

Leybaert, J., Aparicio, M., & Algeria, J. (2011). The role of cued speech in language development of deaf children. In M. Marschark & P. Spencer (Eds.), *Handbook of deaf studies, language, and education* (2nd ed., Vol. 1, pp. 276–289). New York, NY: Oxford University Press.

Lonigan, C.J., Farver, J.M., Philips, B., & Clancy-Menchetti, J. (2011). Promoting the development of preschool children's emergent literacy skills: A randomized evaluation of a literacy-focused curriculum and two professional development models. *Reading and Writing Quarterly: An Interdisciplinary Journal, 24,* 305–337.

Luckner, J.L. (2002). *Facilitating the transition of students who are deaf or hard of hearing.* Austin, TX: Pro-Ed.

Luckner, J.L. (2010). Preparing teachers of students who are deaf or hard of hearing. In M. Marschark and P.E. Spencer (Eds.), *Oxford handbook of deaf studies, language, and education* (Vol. 2, pp. 41–56). New York, NY: Oxford University Press.

Luckner, J.L., & Cooke, C. (2010). A summary of the vocabulary research with students who are deaf or hard of hearing. *American Annals of the Deaf, 155*(1), 38–67.

Luckner, J.L., & Handley, C.M. (2008). A summary of the reading comprehension research undertaken with students who are deaf or hard of hearing. *American Annals of the Deaf, 153*(1), 6–36.

Luckner, J., Sebald, A.N., Cooney, J., Young, J., & Goodwin Muir, S. (2005/2006). An examination of the evidence-based literacy research in deaf education. *American Annals of the Deaf, 150*(5), 443–456.

Luckner, J.L., & Urbach, J.E. (2012). Reading fluency and students who are deaf or hard of hearing: Synthesis of the research. *Communication Disorders Quarterly, 33*(4), 230–241.

Marschark, M., & Wauters, L. (2008). Language comprehension and learning by deaf students. In M. Marschark and P.C. Hauser (Eds.), *Deaf cognition: Foundations and outcomes* (pp. 309–350). New York, NY: Oxford University Press.

Mayberry, R.I. (1993). First-language acquisition after childhood differs from second-language acquisition: The case of American Sign Language. *Journal of Speech and Hearing Research, 36,* 1258–1270.

Mayberry, R.I. (2007). When timing is everything: Age of first-language acquisition effects on second-language learning. *Applied Psycholinguistics, 28*(3), 537–549.

Mayberry, R.I. (2010). Early language acquisition and adult language ability: What sign language reveals about the critical period for language. In M. Marschark & P. Spencer (Eds.), *The Oxford handbook of deaf studies, language, and education* (Vol. 2, pp. 281–291). New York, NY: Oxford University Press.

Mayberry, R., del Guidice, A., & Lieberman, A. (2011). Reading achievement in relation to phonological coding and awareness in deaf readers: A meta-analysis. *Journal of Deaf Studies and Deaf Education, 16,* 164–188.

Mayberry, R., & Lock, E. (2003). Age constraints on first versus second language acquisition: Evidence for linguistic plasticity and epigenesis. *Brain and Language, 87*(3), 369–384.

McGuinness, D. (2004). *Early reading instruction: What science really tells us about how to teach reading.* Cambridge, MA: MIT Press.

McGuinness, D. (2005). *Language development and learning to read: The scientific study of how language development affects reading skill.* Cambridge, MA: MIT Press.

Miller, K. J. & Rosenthal, L. L. (1995). Seeing the big picture: Deaf adults' development of summarization through book discussion in American Sign Language. *Journal of Adolescent and Adult Literacy, 39,* 200–206.

Miller, P., & Clark, M.D. (2011). Phonemic awareness is not necessary to become a skilled deaf reader. *Journal of Developmental Physical Disabilities, 23,* 459–476. doi:10.1007/s10882-011-9246-0

Minskoff, E. (2005). *Teaching reading to struggling readers.* Baltimore, MD: Paul H. Brookes Publishing Co.

Moats, L.C. (2005). *Language essentials for teachers of reading and spelling: Module 1—The challenge of learning to read.* Boston, MA: Sopris West Educational Services.

Morere, D.A. (2011, June). *Reading research and deaf children* (research brief no. 4). Visual Language and Visual Learning Science of Learning Center. Retrieved January 24, 2014, from http://vl2.gallaudet.edu/research/research-briefs/

Morford, J.P., & Mayberry, R. (2000). A reexamination of "early exposure" and its implications for language acquisition by eye. In C. Chamberlain, J. Morford, & R. Mayberry (Eds.), *Language acquisition by eye* (pp. 111–127). Mahwah, NJ: Lawrence Erlbaum Associates.

Mueller, V., & Hurtig, R. (2010). Technology-enhanced shared reading with deaf and hard of hearing children: The role of a fluent signing narrator. *Journal of Deaf Studies and Deaf Education* 5 (1): 72–101.

Nagy, W.E., & Anderson, R.C. (1984). How many words are there in printed school English? *Reading Research Quarterly, 19,* 304–330.

National Center on Student Progress Monitoring. (n.d.). *What are the benefits of progress monitoring?* Retrieved from http://www.studentprogress.org

National Early Literacy Panel. (2008). *Developing early literacy: Report of the National Early Literacy Panel.* Washington, DC: National Institute for Literacy. Retrieved June 4, 2009, from http://lincs.ed.gov/publications/pdf/NELPReport09.pdf

National Reading Panel. (2000). *Teaching children to read: An evidence-based assessment of the scientific research literature on reading and its implications for reading instruction. Reports of the subgroups.* Bethesda, MD: National Institute of Child Health and Human Development.

Newport, E. (1990). Maturational constraints on language learning. *Cognitive Science, 14,* 11–28.

North Dakota School for the Deaf. (n.d.). *Language: The bridge to the future.* Devils Lake, ND: Author.

Ormrod, J.E. (2008). *Human learning* (5th ed.). Upper Saddle River, NJ: Pearson Education.

Padden, C. (2006). Learning to fingerspell twice. Young signing children's acquisition of fingerspelling. In B. Schick, M. Marschark, & P. Spencer (Eds.), *Advances in the sign language development of deaf children* (pp. 189–201). New York, NY: Oxford University Press.

Padden, C., & LeMaster, B. (1985). An alphabet on hand: The acquisition of fingerspelling in deaf children. *Sign Language Studies, 47,* 161–172.

Paivio, A. (1986). *Mental representation.* New York, NY: Oxford University Press.

Paivio, A. (2008). How children learn and retain information: The dual coding theory. In S.B. Neuman (Ed.), *Educating the other America* (pp. 227–242). Baltimore, MD: Paul H. Brookes Publishing Co.

Parault, S.J., & Williams, H.M. (2010). Reading motivation, reading amount, and text comprehension in deaf and hearing adults. *Journal of Deaf Studies and Deaf Education* 15(2), 120–135.

Paul, P.V., & Gustafson, G. (1991). Comprehension of high-frequency multimeaning words by students with hearing impairment. *Remedial and Special Education, 12*(4), 52–62.

Paul, P.V., & Lee, C. (2010). The qualitative similarity hypothesis. *American Annals of the Deaf, 154*(5), 456–462.

Pearson. (2007). *Stanford Achievement Test series* (10th ed.). San Antonio, TX: Author.

Pearson. (2012). *AIMSweb.* Retrieved February 2, 2014, from http://www.aimsweb.com

Pearson, P.D. (1985). Changing the face of reading comprehension instruction. *The Reading Teacher,* 724–738.

Petitto, L.A. (1983). From gesture to symbol: The relationship between form and meaning in the acquisition of personal pronouns in American Sign Language. *Papers and Reports on Child Development, 22,* 100–107.

Petitto, L.A. (2000). On the biological foundations of human language. In K. Emmorey & H. Lane (Eds.), *The signs of language revisited: An anthology in honor of Ursala Bellugi and Edward Klima* (pp. 449–473). Mahwah, NJ: Lawrence Erlbaum Associates.

Puente, A., Alvarado, J., & Herrera, V. (2006). Fingerspelling and sign language as alternative codes for reading and writing words for Chilean deaf signers. *American Annals of the Deaf, 151*(3), 299-310.

Quenemoen, R., Thurlow, M., Moen, R., Thompson, S., & Morse, A.B. (2003). *Progress monitoring in an inclusive standards-based assessment and accountability system* (synthesis report 53). Minneapolis, MN: University of Minnesota, National Center on Educational Outcomes. Retrieved from http://education.umn.edu/NCEO/OnlinePubs/Synthesis53.html

Quittner, A.L., Barker, D.H., Cruz, I., Snell, C., Grimley, M.E., Botteri, M., & CDaCI Investigative Team. (2010). Parenting stress among parents of deaf and hearing children: Associations with language delays and behavior problems. *Parenting: Science and Practice, 10*(2), 136–155.

Roberts, G., Torgeson, J.K., Boradman, A., & Scammacca, N. (2009). Evidence-based strategies for reading instruction of older students with learning disabilities. *Learning Disabilities Research & Practice, 23*(2), 63–69.

Roos, C. (2013). Young deaf children's fingerspelling in learning to read and write: An ethnographic study in a signing setting. *Deafness & Education International, 15*(3), 149–178.

Ruddell, R.B. (2009). *How to teach reading to elementary and middle school students: Practical ideas from highly effective teachers.* Boston, MA: Pearson Education.

Sadoski, M., & Paivio, A. (2004). A dual coding theoretical model of reading. In R.B. Ruddell & N.J. Unrau (Eds.), *Theoretical models of processes of reading* (5th ed., pp. 1329–1362). Newark, DE: International Reading Association.

Salend, S.J. (2008). *Creating inclusive classrooms: Effective and reflective practices* (6th ed.). Upper Saddle River, NJ: Pearson Education.

Salvia, J., Ysseldyke, J.E., & Bolt, S. (2013). *Assessment in special and inclusive education* (12th ed.). Belmont, CA: Wadsworth.

Schalock, R.L., Gardner, J.F., & Bradley, V.J. (2007). *Quality of life for people with intellectual disabilities and other developmental disabilities: Application across individuals, organizations, communities, and systems.* Washington, DC: American Association on Intellectual and Developmental Disabilities.

Schick, B. (2011). The development of American Sign Language and manually coded English systems. In M. Marschark & P. Spencer (Eds.), *Handbook of deaf studies, language, and education* (2nd ed., Vol. 1, pp. 229–240). New York, NY: Oxford University Press.

Schirmer, B.R., & McGough, S.M. (2005). Teaching reading to children who are deaf: Do the conclusions of the National Reading Panel apply? *Review of Educational Research, 75*(1), 83–117. doi:10.3102/00346543075001083

Schirmer, B.R., Therrien, W.J., Schaffer, L., & Schirmer, T.N. (2009). Repeated reading as an instructional intervention with deaf readers: Effect on fluency and reading achievement. *Reading Improvement, 46*(3), 168–177.

Smith, A., & Wang, Y. (2010). The impact of visual phonics on the phonological awareness and speech production of a student who is deaf: A case study. *American Annals of the Deaf, 155*(2), 124–130.

Snodden, K. (2012). *American Sign Language and early literacy: A model parent-child program.* Washington, DC: Gallaudet University Press.

Snow, C.E. (1983). Literacy and language: Relationships during the preschool years. *Harvard Educational Review, 53,* 165–189.

Snow, C.E., Griffin, P., & Burns, M.S. (Eds.). (2005). *Knowledge to support the teaching of reading: Preparing teachers for a changing world.* San Francisco, CA: Jossey-Bass.

Society for Neuroscience. (2012). *Neuroscience core concepts: The essential principles of neuroscience.* Retrieved February 7, 2014, from http://www.sfn.org/coreconcepts

Spencer, L.J., & Oleson, J.J. (2008). Early listening and speaking skills predict later reading proficiency in pediatric cochlear implant users. *Ear and Hearing, 29,* 270–280.

Spencer, P.E., & Marschark, M. (2010). *Evidence-based practice in educating deaf and hard-of-hearing students.* New York, NY: Oxford University Press.

Stanovich, K.E. (1986). Matthew effects in reading: Some consequences of individual differences in the acquisition of literacy. *Reading Research Quarterly, 21*(4), 360–407.

Strassman, B.K. (1997). Metacognition and reading in children who are deaf: A review of the research. *Journal of Deaf Studies and Deaf Education, 2*(3), 140–149.

Swanson, H.L., & O'Connor, R. (2009). The role of working memory and fluency practice on the reading comprehension of students who are dysfluent readers. *Journal of Learning Disabilities, 42*(6), 548–575.

Texas Education Agency and University of Texas System. (2010). *The Texas Primary Reading Inventory (TPRI)*. Baltimore, MD: Paul H. Brookes Publishing Co.

Therrien, W.J. (2004). Fluency and comprehension gains as a result of repeated reading: A meta-analysis. *Remedial and Special Education, 25*(4), 252–261.

Trezek, B.J., & Hancock, G.R. (2013). Implementing instruction in the alphabetic principle within a sign bilingual setting. *Journal of Deaf Studies and Deaf Education, 18*(3), 391–408.

Trezek, B.J., & Malmgren, K.W. (2005). The efficacy of utilizing a phonics treatment package with middle school deaf and hard-of-hearing students. *Journal of Deaf Studies and Deaf Education, 10*, 257–271.

Trezek, B., Wang, Y., & Paul, P. (2010). *Reading and deafness: Theory, research and practice*. Clifton Park, NY: Cengage Learning.

Trezek, B.J., Wang, Y., Woods, D.G., Gampp, T.L., & Paul, P. (2007). Using visual phonics to supplement beginning reading instruction for students who are deaf or hard of hearing. *Journal of Deaf Studies and Deaf Education, 12*(3), 373–384.

United Nations Educational, Scientific and Cultural Organization (UNESCO). (2004). *The plurality of literacy and it implications for policies and programmes: UNESCO education sector position paper*. Paris, France: Author.

Vaughn, S., Bos, C.S., & Schumm, J.S. (2007). *Teaching students who are exceptional, diverse, and at risk in the general education classroom* (4th ed.). Boston, MA: Pearson Education.

Vaughn, S., & Linan-Thompson, S. (2004). *Research-based methods of reading instruction: Grades K–3*. Alexandria, VA: Association for Supervision and Curriculum Development.

Vellutino, F.R., Tunmer, W.E., Jaccard, J.J., & Chen, R. (2007). Components of reading ability: Multivariate evidence for a convergent skills model of reading development. *Scientific Studies of Reading, 11*, 3–32.

Wang, Y., Spychala, H., Harris, R.S., & Oetting, T.L. (2013). The effectiveness of a phonics-based early intervention for deaf and hard of hearing preschool children and its possible impact on reading skills in elementary school: A case study. *American Annals of the Deaf, 158*(2), 107–120.

Waxman, R., & Spencer, P.E. (1997). What mothers do to support infant visual attention: Sensitivities to age and hearing status. *Journal of Deaf Studies and Deaf Education, 2*(2), 104–114.

Weizman, Z.O., & Snow, C.E. (2001). Lexical input as related to children's vocabulary acquisition: Effects of sophisticated exposure and support for meaning. *Developmental Psychology, 37*(2), 265–279.

Wells, G. (1986). *The meaning makers: Children learning language and using language to learn*. Portsmouth, NH: Heinemann.

White, T.G., Sowell, J., & Yanighara, A. (1989). Teaching elementary students to use word-part clues. *The Reading Teacher, 42*, 302–308.

Whitehurst, G.J., & Lonigan, C.J. (2001). Emergent literacy: Development from pre-readers to readers. In S. Neuman & D.K. Dickinson (Eds.), *Handbook of early literacy research* (Vol. 1, pp. 11–29). New York, NY: Guilford Press.

Williams, K.T. (2001). *Group reading assessment and diagnostic evaluation*. Circle Pines, MN: American Guidance Service.

Woodcock, R.W. (2011). *Woodcock Reading Mastery Tests* (3rd ed.). Circle Pines, MN: American Guidance Service.

Woodcock, R.W., Mather, N., & Schrank, F.A. (2004). *Woodcock-Johnson III Diagnostic Reading Battery*. Itasca, IL: Riverside.

Woodcock, R.W., McGrew, K.S., & Mather, N. (2007). *Woodcock-Johnson III Normative Update (NU) Tests of Achievement*. Itasca, IL: Riverside.

Zupan, B., & Dempsey, L. (2013). Facilitating emergent literacy skills in children with hearing loss. *Deafness & Education International, 15*(3), 130–148.

# 13

# Teaching Writing

*Principles into Practice*

Connie Mayer

With respect to literacy development, far less attention has been paid to writing than reading in research and practice for both children who are typically developing and those who are deaf or hard of hearing (D/HH; Kress, 1994; Marschark, Lang, & Albertini, 2002; Mayer, 2010; Moores, 1987). Troia (2007) contends that "instructional research in writing is not as mature as that in reading and does not enjoy the same level of distinction," going on to suggest that there is a critical need to elevate the status of writing instruction and its associated research (p. 130). This lack of attention seems incongruous, given that the majority of students would describe writing as more challenging than reading, with writing often being regarded as the most demanding, complex cognitive activity that learners typically undertake (Singer & Bashir, 2004).

Based on the available research evidence, it would certainly be reasonable to characterize many learners who are D/HH as being among the group who find writing and learning to write particularly demanding, and it has been well documented that historically they have demonstrated poor performance in this area. A review of studies from the early 20th century onward reveals a consistent finding—that writers who are D/HH struggle with the process of text generation and do not achieve at a level commensurate with their hearing, same-age peers (see Mayer, 2010, for a discussion and overview) or even relative to their own signed productions (Marschark, 1993). Difficulties have been identified in the areas of morphology, lexicon, syntax, grammar, conceptual coherence, and text and discourse structures (e.g., Conte, Rampelli, & Volterra, 1996; Musselman & Szanto, 1998; Taeschner, 1988; Yoshinaga-Itano,

Snyder, & Mayberry, 1996) and in the strategies employed in the composing process (e.g., Albertini, Meath-Lang & Harris, 1994; Kelly, 1988; Mayer, 1999).

In this chapter, a framework for understanding written language development in learners who are D/HH will be presented, and this framework will be the basis for describing what constitutes recommended practice in teaching writing, planning an appropriate program, differentiating instruction, and identifying interventions. (Although English will be the language referenced most often in this chapter, the discussion is applicable to other alphabetic languages and with some adaptation to syllabic and logographic languages as well.) Effective pedagogical strategies will be described, taking into account the changing context in the field (e.g., universal newborn hearing screening [UNHS], cochlear implants, evidence-based practice, increasing numbers of learners in general education settings) and the changing needs of the learner from the primary years through high school.

## THEORETICAL BASIS

The starting point for this discussion will be the assertion that with respect to writing development, children who are D/HH must follow the same developmental process from language to literacy as their hearing counterparts if they are ultimately to become proficient writers (Mayer,2007; Mayer & Trezek, 2011; Paul & Lee, 2010; Trezek, Wang, & Paul, 2010). Specifically, if the measure of success is taken as the development of grade-level, age-appropriate writing, there is no convincing theoretical argument or body of research evidence from learners who are D/HH to make a case that the process of learning to write should be different from that of their hearing, same-age peers. This view is consistent with the evidence from other groups such as language-minority learners, those from low socioeconomic status (SES), and those with learning disabilities. For example, it has been demonstrated that language-minority children develop literacy in ways that are similar to their native-English-speaking peers, and instructional approaches effective with the majority are equally efficacious with these learners (see Ehri, 2009, for discussion).

An underlying premise of this chapter is that writers who are D/HH must master the same set of knowledge and skills as their hearing counterparts if they are to become proficient writers. The differences between hearing and D/HH writers in the activity of learning to write do not rest in the nature of the process or foundational requisites but in the nature of what these learners bring to the activity. The most fundamental requisite that underpins learning to write for any child is a threshold level of competence in the primary form of the language to be written. Language provides the foundation not only for the morphosyntactic and semantic understandings needed for learning to write but also for the development of phonological awareness and other code-related abilities (Whitehurst & Lonigan, 1998; see also Dickinson, McCabe, Anastasopoulos, Peisner-Feinberg, & Poe, 2003, for a review). For all learners who struggle with literacy development, there is a broad consensus that a core difficulty in literacy learning manifests itself as a deficiency within the language system, including phonological awareness skills—particularly as to how these affect development in the early years (Pugh, Sandak, Frost, Moore, & Mencl, 2006).

Given the central role language proficiency plays in this process, there are significant implications for learners who are D/HH, as they have often faced challenges in acquiring communicative competence in an auditory-oral language such as English. In the absence of this language foundation, writers who are D/HH are put in the untenable position of learning to write when they have minimal control of the language that has to be committed to paper. As Geers (2006) argues, "The frequently reported low literacy levels among students with severe to profound hearing impairment are, in part, due to the discrepancy between their incomplete spoken language system and the demands of reading [and writing] a speech-based system" (p. 244).

There is a view that learners who are D/HH in a bilingual situation can bypass proficiency in the language to be written (e.g., English as the second language, or L2) and rely on their knowledge of the signed first language (L1; e.g., American Sign Language [ASL]) to become proficient writers. However, this claim is counter to the evidence available from the context of hearing bilingual learners, where it is well documented that in the absence of L2 proficiency, limitations are imposed on a writer's ability to conceptualize and organize meanings in text in the L2 (Berman, 1994; Bialystok, 2011; Cummins, 2000; Freedman, Pringle & Yalden, 1983; Yau, 1991). While it is the case that L1 proficiency can be supportive of learning the L2, as there is some cross-linguistic transfer or interdependence between languages (especially between the written forms of L1 and L2), this is a complex relationship in which there are "sometimes benefits for bilingual children, sometimes deficits, and sometimes no consequences at all" (Bialystok, 2011, p. 121).

Given that the effects of transfer can be positive, negative, or neutral, and in the absence of any robust research evidence to support the view, it seems an oversimplification to suggest that proficiency in a face-to-face form of L1 ensures development of proficient writing in L2, particularly in the singular context of a signed L1 (e.g., ASL) and a spoken L2 (e.g., English) in which the L1 has no written form (see Mayer, 1999; Mayer & Akamatsu, 2011; Mayer & Leigh, 2010; Mayer & Trezek, 2015; Mayer & Wells, 1996, for discussions). In other words, L1 proficiency alone is not sufficient for learning to write in the L2; developing proficiency in the face-to-face form of the L2 is also necessary and cannot be bypassed.

Therefore, it is essential to emphasize that the first consideration in teaching writing to any learner who is D/HH is to ensure that they have the requisite, age-appropriate foundation in place *in the same language that is to be read and written*—as is the case for their hearing peers. All following claims made in this chapter with respect to teaching writing are grounded in this premise.

It is also important at this juncture to point out that even when this language competence is in place, writing presents a singular and unique set of challenges for all learners irrespective of audiogram. As Kress (1994) remarks with respect to the early years, "Considering how painlessly children learn to talk, the difficulties they face in learning to write are quite pronounced. Indeed some children never learn to write at all, and many fall far short of proficiency in the task" (p. ix). These challenges can be accounted for by the fact that communication through the written mode takes place in the absence of physically present interlocutors and of the auditory and visual-gestural features of face-to-face discourse (Olson, 1977, 1993, 1994), thus demanding a greater precision of expression, expansion, and elaboration of thought and a clearer sense of audience than spoken or signed language (Halliday, 1989). Gaining control of this kind of language is challenging for all children, as they must "learn to construe their experience in two complementary modes: the dynamic mode of everyday commonsense grammar and the synoptic mode of the elaborated written grammar" (Halliday, 1993, p. 112).

Many hearing children and those children who are D/HH (e.g., with cochlear implants) who face challenges in writing development beyond the early stages often do so as a consequence of not having this "synoptic mode" in place, even though in most cases they have established basic communicative competence in the language. In other words, although proficiency in the language is the necessary starting place, writing requires the learner to use this language in ways that become increasingly differentiated from the structures that characterize face-to-face communication (e.g., use of lower frequency vocabulary, greater morphosyntactic complexity, textual coherence), accounting for the challenges that face developing writers and the teachers who are trying to support them.

## Pedagogical Frameworks

The dominant pedagogical framework underpinning the instructional approaches that will be described in this chapter is a ***process writing*** model (Graves, 1978) that integrates reading and writing instruction (Clay, 1982, 1983). Adopting this perspective is consistent with a broader view in the field of literacy education that writing is best learned when it is used purposefully and communicatively, used as an authentic means for expression with accuracy and correctness subordinate to meaning making, and aligned with the understanding that writing is a messy process that involves managing the tensions between meaning and form (Collins & Gentner, 1980).

A process writing approach is informed by models of the composing process (both cognitive and sociocultural) in which writing is a complex, recursive activity that involves planning, generating, and revising (Bereiter & Scardamalia, 1987; Flower & Hayes, 1980). In their model, Bereiter and Scardamalia propose a dialectic between two problem spaces in the process of writing—one defined by the writer's content knowledge (i.e., what the writer wants to say) and the other by the rhetorical problem of how to say what is meant. The content space is tied up with issues of meaning and understandings that can be expressed in the language of everyday discourse; however, in moving these ideas to the rhetorical space, the writer must reformulate these meanings in the language of the text and under the constraints of text production.

Beginning writers address the challenge of capturing their meaning in written language by using a think-say pattern of composing, essentially talking their way into text. In these early stages, children must sort out how to represent in print the meanings they have made in spoken and/or signed language as they simultaneously grapple with managing the mechanics of the writing process (e.g., encoding and forming letters). Experienced writers face the same fundamental challenge of realizing what is meant in a written form, but they have the advantage of having developed automaticity in terms of certain aspects of the composing process (e.g., spelling, handwriting). This allows them to focus more cognitive attention on considering whether what they have written has captured what is meant (i.e., reading like a writer, developing a sense of audience). In this way, writing becomes a recursive process between meaning and form, as writers revise what is written to better reflect what is meant.

It is this model of composition that informs the process writing approach—an approach that mirrors the process in which proficient writers engage, that of planning, independently composing, writing multiple drafts, and reviewing and revising numerous times based on feedback from editors and peers along the way (Wong & Berninger, 2004). Other features of this model include using written language for genuine purposes, making strong relationships between reading and writing, and authentic assessment via a consideration of written language samples.

A process writing approach is the predominant pedagogical model employed with hearing learners. Although it has been argued that even though there has been widespread implementation, the evidence base for the efficacy of the approach remains variable. At least in part, this can be explained by the fact that the basic understanding of what the process model entails has evolved over time (to include a greater emphasis on aspects such as explicit instruction) and that the implementation of a process writing approach has been uneven, with teachers having different perspectives of what the model looks like in practice. Even researchers have differing views on what the process approach involves, with this difference resting primarily on the extent to which direct instruction plays a role (see Pritchard and Honeycutt, 2006, for a detailed discussion). That said, it remains the preferred option for writing instruction in general education across the age and grade range, and the widespread consensus is that there is no strong evidence to desert the model:

> The writing process has its weaknesses; it is poorly implemented in many instances; it is not a panacea. But it is a better candidate for improving writing performance than the traditional approach . . . we must listen to the critics; we must be willing to rethink and adjust our theories, procedures and practices. But there is not sufficient evidence to cause us to abandon the writing process. (Cramer, 2001, as cited in Pritchard and Honeycutt, 2006, p. 282)

This applies equally to the situation of learners who are D/HH. It is well documented that traditional, structured approaches to teaching writing did not engender strong outcomes, and while there are relatively few intervention studies in the field to demonstrate the efficacy of any writing instruction or approach (e.g., only three in 20 years for emergent writers; Williams & Mayer, 2012; see Strassman & Schirmer, 2013, for a review), there is some evidence to indicate that moves to process-oriented approaches have realized a positive shift in some aspects of writing and learning to write (e.g., Conway, 1985; Ewoldt, 1985; Mayer, 1994; Williams, 1993, 2011). Overall, the findings of these studies indicate that students developed a more positive attitude to writing, saw the process as meaningful and purposeful, and learned that writing was a powerful tool for communication and making meaning. However, the same improvements were not evidenced in the area of linguistic structure and form (e.g., grammar, syntax, textual coherence; see Mayer, 2010, for a discussion). In this respect, many writers who are D/HH have much in common with other struggling writers whose texts tend to be poorly organized and contain more irrelevant information and mechanical and grammatical errors, rendering them weaker in overall quality and less readable. Troia (2007) argues that these problems are attributable to some extent to the difficulties these struggling writers have "in executing and regulating the processes underlying proficient composing, especially planning and revising" (p. 131)—weaknesses that a process approach has the potential to address.

In the following sections, the process writing model will be described in more detail, particularly as to how it can be realized in practice. However, before going on to this description, it is important to address the issue of assessment—a necessary aspect informing the implementation of any pedagogical approach.

## ASSESSMENT INFORMING PRACTICE

Assessment and evaluation are critical for designing writing programs and planning appropriate interventions, yet assessing writing has not provoked the same level of concern and attention as assessing reading (Troia, 2007) and has been identified as a major area of concern for all populations of learners (National Commission on Writing, 2003), including writers who are deaf (Mayer, 2010). In some sense, this seems ironic, in that writing, in contrast to reading, produces a tangible product that can be reviewed and analyzed. It has nevertheless proven to be challenging to assess this product, especially if the goal is to use this information to drive instruction and set goals. One aspect that is arguably less problematic in assessing writing in learners who are D/HH is that issues of test bias and questions of compromising validity and reliability as a consequence of test administration (e.g., how to sign test items) are not significant concerns, as these are not integral to what is being evaluated (i.e., the quality of the written product). Therefore the following measures to assess written language in hearing learners would be appropriate for learners who are D/HH as well.

Standardized tests of writing (e.g., Test of Written Language, Slosson Written Expression Test, Written Expression Scale) or subtests of other standardized measures (e.g., Woodcock-Johnson; see Pierangelo & Giuliani, 2006, for descriptions) can provide summative information that can be useful in reporting outcomes (e.g., for a research study), but they do little to inform teaching. They also do not capture the complexity of the writing that students do over the course of a school year and across the curriculum, because in these sorts of assessments, students are often writing to a prompt or responding to questions.

The richest pedagogical information comes from evaluating authentic pieces of writing and the strategies that writers employ in creating these texts. In a process-writing classroom there are many opportunities to assess these areas, as the students are regularly writing and producing texts, allowing the teacher to observe the writer at work and to collect many writing samples. These samples are then housed in a portfolio, described as the purposeful collection of students' authentic writing over time, representing the range of what a learner can do. In other words, the portfolio paints a picture of the writer and is an excellent way to illustrate and capture growth. The portfolio can take many forms, depending on the age of the student. It can be as simple as a folder for younger writers in which it is important to capture the broad range of ways children are making meaning with text (e.g., a painting with a sentence written underneath, a sign posted in the house center). For older writers, it might be a virtual folder on the computer where it is possible to store multiple versions of the same text (i.e., from first draft to final product). This record of one piece of writing over time is important, as one of the criticisms of portfolio assessment is that it can be difficult to sort out how much of a final version is legitimately attributable to the student author and how much is a consequence of assistance. In any case, whatever format is chosen for housing the samples, the portfolio provides the evidence for making judgments as to current performance and setting goals.

While collecting the samples is relatively straightforward, assessing and evaluating them is much more complex, particularly in the case of writers who are D/HH, as their texts may exhibit idiosyncratic, nonstandard uses of language. The tools used to assess these written language samples generally fall into two major categories: **rubrics/exemplars** or checklists (Harp, 2006). Exemplars can be useful because they provide a benchmark for comparing writers who are D/HH to their hearing, same-age peers (e.g., Nova Scotia Writing Exemplars: Grades One to Eight, 2005). Many school authorities have developed assessments of this type, and they are often included as part of the curriculum package. There are some versions of these assessments that have been developed expressly for use with learners who are D/HH (e.g., Burman, Evans, Nunes, & Bell, 2008; Mayer, 2006; Schirmer, Bailey, & Fitzgerald, 1999), and to varying degrees, they put more emphasis on considerations of form (e.g., English grammar), as this can be an area of concern for many writers who are D/HH.

There are also measures available that provide insights into the composing processes and strategies writers are using to create a text and the extent to which they are engaging with the process writing approach. These often take the form of surveys or observation checklists (see Rhodes, 1993, for examples). One version that aligns particularly well with a process writing approach is the Portrait of Writers/Writing Continuum Checklist (see Harp, 2006, appendix A), which outlines nine levels of writing development from preconventional to independent, providing descriptors and indicators of performance at each level.

## WRITER'S WORKSHOP: PROCESS WRITING IN PRACTICE

A process writing approach (which considers writing a process that involves the planning, generating, and revising of text) is most often realized pedagogically in the context of a **writer's workshop** (Calkins, 1994)—an approach that can be actualized in a range of ways depending on the nature and needs of the learner. Although there is not a single way to implement a writer's workshop, it typically follows a format that begins with writing time. During this period, while the students are working individually at some stage in the development of a piece of writing (e.g., writing a first draft, planning the outline for a new piece), the teacher works with individual students (or small groups) to support the writers in generating or revising their text.

This individual **conferencing** is at the core of the writer's workshop approach, as it is through these conferences that the teacher provides the feedback and scaffolding that will aid the student in improving their text and identifies the strategies that a student might use to accomplish this. These conferences are not lengthy and can be as brief as a few minutes, with the length being dictated by the age of the writer and the number of children in the class. No matter the length, the conference begins with a reading of the text so that the teacher can get a sense of what the writing is about in order to ask questions and provide feedback. In other words, the initial focus is always on meaning—on what the student wants to say in their text. The teacher can then work with the student to identify areas for revision, modeling strategies and practicing them with the student, with the goal that the student can make revisions not only to the current piece but also to future work. Record keeping is central to the process, and the teacher keeps track of the date and the focus of each conference, helping the teacher (and students themselves) monitor progress. There can also be value in peer conferences, when children read their texts to a classmate, as this also aids in developing a sense of audience.

The workshop concludes with some broader sharing of the written work. For example, the session can end with an "author's chair." This is when the student author reads a piece of writing aloud to the class not only to share their work but also to get feedback from the group. In some sense, this mirrors what is happening during the teacher conferencing but with a wider audience. The classmates ask questions and make comments and observations to which the student author responds. This gives the writer insights into how an audience perceives the text and where revisions need to be made in order clarify the meaning.

Minilessons are another feature of the writer's workshop. These are typically 10 to 15 minutes in length and often occur at the beginning of the session, before the students actively begin writing. But this is not immutable, and they can happen at the end of the session instead. The key point is that the focus of these minilessons is on discrete aspects of the writing process that warrant explicit attention and can be modeled or taught (e.g., adding more descriptive vocabulary, writing a strong opening sentence, using direct narration, combining sentences with conjunctions). The teacher identifies these targets, choosing them on the basis of what may have arisen in the conferencing process, what would be of general concern to the class, or what is mandated by the curriculum.

Although the writer's workshop is most often talked about in terms of elementary-age students, there is no reason that (with adaptations) it cannot be implemented with older learners, even at the end of high school. One of the key differences in the way the program works for beginning and more advanced writers is in the length of the texts produced and the time that is spent on one piece of writing. For example, high school students may work on a text such as an essay for an extended period and conference this same piece of writing multiple times.

It is also possible to use an adapted version of this approach when working with individual students (e.g., teachers of the deaf working in itinerant settings). The primary difference would be that the teacher would have the opportunity to conference more regularly and extensively with one student, arguably the reason a student is working with an itinerant teacher in the first place. One challenge is that there is always an audience of one (i.e., no opportunity for a version of the author's chair), so it would be important to create opportunities for the student to share their writing with a wider group.

## Considerations for Implementation

The following guidelines should inform the implementation of any process writing approach.

1. *Adequate time must be devoted to writing instruction in the school day:* It is typically the case that not enough time is devoted specifically to the teaching of writing. To effectively implement a process approach such as writer's workshop, 90 minutes per week would be seen as a bare minimum, and the research indicates that most teachers do not meet this threshold (Troia, 2007). If this is the baseline for hearing writers, it would seem reasonable to suggest that writers who are D/HH would need at least the same amount of time—and arguably more, given that they are a group that has traditionally struggled to develop proficiency in this area.

2. *Establish routines for how the writing class is managed so that students know what is expected of them:* This includes strategies such as 1) a system for checking in at the beginning of the class to indicate where students are in the process (e.g., revising a text, writing a first draft), 2) records of ideas and topics for future writing, 3) sign-up sheets for conferencing or taking a turn in the author's chair, 4) folders for housing completed work and work in progress, and 5) editing sheets listing the writing and revising strategies that have been discussed during conferencing or minilessons.

3. *Address all aspects of the writing curriculum within the process writing approach:* Teachers must be mindful of the knowledge and skills that are to be developed at each grade level so that they can be appropriately addressed. This becomes especially relevant for teachers working with children who are deaf in general education settings where the expectation is that they will be working on the same content as their hearing, same-age peers.

4. *Use written language for authentic purposes:* Students must learn how to use text for a broad range of purposes. An excellent framework for thinking about this is the functions of language (Halliday, 1975). Although Halliday's focus was on the use of language for face-to-face communication, this hierarchical framework applies equally well to communicating in written language (see Table 13.1). The earliest developing functions are the instrumental ("What do I want") and regulatory ("Do as I say"), with the more complex uses of language—the heuristic ("Tell me why") and informative ("I've got something to tell you")— developing later.

**Table 13.1.**   Functions of language

| | |
|---|---|
| Instrumental ("I want") | Request, cajole, persuade |
| Regulatory ("Do as I say") | Direct behavior |
| Interactional ("Me and you") | Disagree, promise, criticize, compliment |
| Personal ("I feel") | Complain, justify, express emotions |
| Imaginative ("Let's pretend") | Tell stories, role play |
| Heuristic ("Tell me why") | Clarify, predict, probe |
| Informative ("I've got something to tell you") | Describe, compare, discuss, suggest |

Based on Halliday (1975).

For each of these functions, it is possible to identify written language forms (genres) that are used to accomplish the task—to use writing for a real purpose and in a meaningful way. For example, a note in the classroom mailbox can accomplish the instrumental function for a 7-year-old writer (see Figure 13.1). As a writer develops and written language becomes more sophisticated, there are a range of ways in which this same function can be communicated. Consider how we might use text to request compensation from an airline for lost luggage as we attempt to persuade and make a case to get what we want. Thinking about written language use in this way ensures that students learn to use a broad range of genres for a variety of purposes with varying levels of complexity, avoiding one of the pitfalls of many writing programs— that teachers focus inordinately on one text type (e.g., the daily journal).

**Figure 13.1.**   Instrumental function, 7-year-old writer. (Transcription: Could I use your eraser please? But I need it only sometimes.)

5. *Ensure a balance between the writing of narrative and expository texts:*
This is an important balance to achieve, as the bulk of the writing that
students need to do in schooling (and ultimately in life) is expository (e.g.,
report writing, essays). Yet it is often the case that the focus is predominantly on the **narrative** form in the early grades, and when students
encounter **expository text** in the middle school years, they are ill-pre-
pared. It is also the case that expository texts are typically more complex
and challenging to write, but students have had much less experience
with them. By the time children are asked to write their first narrative,
they have already had many stories read to them (or have read them
themselves), and they have a good idea as to what constitutes a well-written story. Yet children are often asked to write a book report or an essay
before they have ever read one or had one read to them.

For older students, it can be valuable to use the writer's workshop
Therefore it is important to develop the writing of expository,
nonfiction text from the earliest grades. This can be as simple as having
children record observations at a center in the primary classroom. See the
example in Figure 13.2, illustrating how a 7-year-old child documented
her findings about a cough drop ("cothe jroup").

For older students, it can be valuable to use the writer's workshop
as an opportunity to work on the expository texts that are required in
other subject areas (e.g., summaries, essays, reports). For all students,

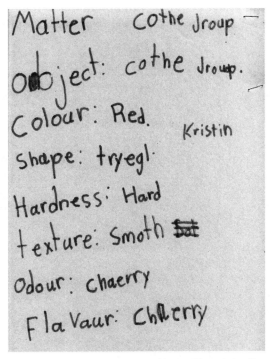

**Figure 13.2.** Expository text, 7-year-old writer. (Transcription: Matter: Cough drop; Object: Cough drop; Colour: Red; Shape: Triangle;
Hardness: Hard; Texture: Smooth; Odour: Cherry; Flavour: Cherry)

it is useful to have expository texts read to them to develop the sense of the language and structure that characterize these forms.

6.  *Be thoughtful about the choice of topic:* To motivate interest in writing, students should be given opportunities to write about the topics that are most meaningful to them. However, this does not preclude the teacher also assigning some topics or a genre for a particular purpose. This ensures that all aspects of the writing curriculum are addressed (see point 5 above), provides a means for introducing genres that might not otherwise emerge, and helps maintain a balance between narrative and expository text.

7.  *Integrate writing done in other subject areas into the writing classroom:* A writer's workshop can be the perfect forum for the class to work on developing the writing skills needed in other subject areas (e.g., a compare and contrast essay in social studies, a summary of a chapter, a science report). This can be especially true at the middle and secondary school level, where writing is central to completing the assignments that provide a basis for evaluation in a given subject area.

8.  *Create opportunities for sharing and publishing work and reading aloud:* With younger children, the author's chair provides an excellent opportu-nity to share writing with the class, get feedback, and develop a sense of audience. But even with older students, reading a text aloud to the class or having students share work in small groups or pairs is useful. Learn-ing to read like a writer—to understand how and whether a text can be  understood by others—is central to becoming a proficient writer.

9.  *Provide explicit modeling:* It is has been demonstrated that simply being exposed to the writing process is not enough. It is critical that teachers explicitly model both the steps of the writing process and the strategies that are employed in developing a text. One of the best ways to do this is to use a "think aloud" strategy (i.e., overt mental dialogue; see also Chapter 11) that allows the developing writer to gain insights into how a more skilled writer gets the job done. In time, the novice writer takes these on board to use as self-regulation strategies—self-statements and questions that aid a writer in being more systematic and reflective as they compose a text (Zimmerman, 2002). This explicit modeling has been shown to be a critical pedagogical element for all writers, but especially those who struggle (see Troia, 2007, for a discussion).

10. *Use minilessons for explicit teaching:* Minilessons provide an excellent forum for the explicit teaching of those aspects of the writing process that can be directly taught (e.g., using capital letters, joining two independent clause with a conjunction) and for the explicit modeling of composing strategies as described previously.

## SPECIFIC STRATEGIES AND INTERVENTIONS

At each stage of the writing process, there are strategies that can be taught to support students in creating a text. This is an area that warrants attention, as research indicates that although many teachers implement a writer's workshop approach, there is great variability in the extent to which composing strategies are explicitly taught (Troia, 2007) and adaptations are made for struggling writers (Graham, Harris, Fink, & MacArthur, 2003). In the following paragraphs, specific strategies will be described that target the challenges writers typically encounter at each step of the writing process—planning, generating, and revising.

## Planning

Struggling writers will often begin writing a text in the absence of any prior planning or broader sense of how the text will be organized, composing in a linear, think-say pattern resulting in texts that lack coherence and a recognizable structure, often rendering them difficult to read. This can be the result of weaknesses in the areas of form (e.g., poor knowledge of the genre) and/or meaning (e.g., content knowledge). Although a knowledge-telling, think-say strategy is an approach used by all beginning writers, including those who are deaf (Mayer, 2007), it is not characteristic of proficient writers beyond the early years. That said, there are strategies that can be explicitly taught to students to aid them in the planning process and assist them in moving beyond a knowledge-telling approach.

In terms of focusing on content, it can be helpful to brainstorm, discuss, or explore potential topics in advance (with individual students or as a group) and then make a list of key ideas, points, reflections, and vocabulary. These can be documented in some way (e.g., a writer's notebook, a word wall, a semantic web) as the starting place for planning a text. If the topic has involved researching a subject, the content information from other sources can be included here as well.

Once the students have the key content defined, they need to sort out a plan as to how this content will be organized in their text. One of the best strategies for doing this is graphic organizers, as they provide a visual scheme for managing the written content (for examples, see http://www.educationoasis.com/curriculum/graphic_organizers.htm). These are incredibly flexible tools, as they can be used across the age and grade range to plan both narrative and expository texts and to analyze various written genres (e.g., a compare and contrast essay). While they can be used to plan a text that will be written, they can also be used "in reverse" to analyze a text that has been read, allowing a budding writer to see how a more mature author has used a particular genre to make meaning.

## Generating

While planning is an important aspect of the process, it is only the first step. From this plan, the student must generate a written text. This requires writers to tap into their implicit knowledge of the language (phonologic, morphosyntactic, and semantic) to formulate meaning (i.e., what I want to say) in text (i.e., how I say it). In other words, writers must realize their thoughts in words and sentences and in linguistic units that capture the intent of what is meant (Olson, 1977; Singer & Bashir, 2004). In addition to this challenge, the writer must also manage the issue of **transcription**—the **encoding** of language that includes spelling, writing conventions, and mechanics (i.e., handwriting, typing). An inordinate amount of the attention of beginning writers is taken up with these skills, and in the early going, this constrains their ability to write. As automaticity and fluency develop, the transcription load lightens and students write increasingly longer texts, with research indicating that in more mature writers, longer texts are linked to higher quality writing.

Many struggling writers who are D/HH face profound challenges at this generation stage. In the absence of proficiency in a face-to-face form of the language, they lack the implicit (automatic) knowledge required for text creation—for composing orally in spoken and/or signed language. This harkens back to a point made earlier—that it is not possible to learn to write without a foundation in a face-to-face form of the language of the text (e.g., communicative competence in spoken English if the goal is to write in English). It would not be overstating the issue to say that the intervention for these students would be to develop the language base that is the necessary prerequisite for learning to write. This is consistent with the research indicating that struggling hearing writers with deficits in oral language generation also experience marked difficulties in text generation (see Singer & Bashir, 2004, for a discussion). These struggling hearing writers can face a further challenges in simultaneously formulating and transcribing the text (i.e., committing to print what they orally compose).

Writers who are D/HH who first compose a text in a natural signed language (e.g., ASL; see Chapter 6) have an even more daunting task, as they are not transcribing but translating from one language to another in the writing process. In this sense, it becomes a two-step process—translating ASL into English and then capturing the English on the page. Thought about in this way, it is not surprising that these writers who are D/HH have had difficulties learning to write, even if they have relatively strong signed language (ASL) abilities (Singleton et al., 2004).

Assuming a threshold level of competence in the language to be written, there are strategies that can be used to support writers at this stage. One of the most robust is dictation. While this is a strategy that is often used with younger learners, it can be equally efficacious with older writers. Dictation allows for the separation of text formulation and transcription so that the writer can focus on only one aspect at a time, thus lightening the cognitive load. For example, if the student dictates a story to the teacher, the focus for the student is on the generation of the language to capture the intended meaning. The teacher transcribes the student's oral composition, and this can be read together, allowing the student to see how the meaning has been captured in the text so that it can become an object for reflection and analysis. If the roles are reversed and the teacher dictates, the student can concentrate on text transcription. But in reading the completed text together, both the teacher and student can focus on how the language has been used to convey meaning. In both cases, the teacher can identify ways in which the student can improve the text, and these become goals for revising and editing.

Spelling is an aspect of text generation that affords a unique window into how younger children are coming to terms with making the connection between language and text—at least at the sublexical (i.e., phoneme to grapheme correspondence) and lexical level, providing insights into the process of encoding words that are already in the young writer's spoken or signed vocabulary. In some sense, in the early stages of learning to write, spelling *is* writing, as the bulk of the child's attention is taken up by figuring out how to represent spoken and/or signed language in print (i.e., transcription).

**Invented spellings**, characteristic of hearing children's work at this stage, demonstrate how beginning writers are making sense of the transcription process as they make use of what they know about phoneme–grapheme correspondences to commit spoken language to paper (Kress, 1997). Figure 13.3 provides an example of how a 7-year-old deaf writer (implanted at 1.3 years) used invented spelling in writing about a picture prompt in the Test of Written Language (TOWL). This use of invented spelling should be encouraged, as it has been shown to be associated with the development of stronger reading and writing abilities and is a predictor of progress in understanding the alphabetic principle (i.e., decoding and encoding; see Chapter 12; Pressley, 2006; Whitehurst & Lonigan, 2001).

**Abot the Wor**

I'm thinking wher did they kam from. I see peple.
Tha are killing the elifins kas thay don't wont the elifins.
The stiks are sorp. Thy end.

**Transcription: About the War**

I'm thinking where did they come from. I see people.
They are killing the elephants because they don't want the
elephants. The sticks are sharp. The end.

**Figure 13.3.** Use of invented spelling, 7-year-old deaf writer with a cochlear implant.

## Revising

Of all the aspects of the writing process, it is revising that can be the most problematic:

> The notion of implicit (automatic) versus explicit (reflective) encoding of the language distinguishes the generating process from the revising process . . . they encode ideas implicitly, then reflect on the degree to which they have accurately represented their intentions, and when necessary, explicitly use their knowledge of language to reformulate, clarify or elaborate. (Singer & Bashir, 2004, p. 565)

In this sense, the initial generation of text is more instinctive or natural, while the revising process necessitates identifying where the writing has gone wrong in achieving its intended goal with respect to meaning and/or form. Improving the writing may involve making changes in sentence, paragraph, or text structure; word choice; spelling; grammar; and punctuation.

It can be useful to think about this revising challenge on two levels: The first involves identifying the more obvious errors in form (e.g., spelling), and the second involves reading the text as if the content was unknown (i.e., reading like a writer). The latter instance is the more demanding of the two, as the writer must take the perspective of the intended audience to determine whether the way in which the text has been organized and presented accurately captures the intended meaning. This is particularly difficult, given the meaning is already known to the writer (i.e., it makes sense to you if you have written it). The challenge is in sorting out whether the text makes sense to others.

It is often the case that in the revising process, teachers focus on the first challenge—on the surface features of writing that can be relatively easily addressed (e.g., adding periods at the end of sentences, indenting paragraphs, plural "s"). However, the real work of the revising process is in addressing the more substantive issues of content and text structure, figuring out where and how to add information when the meaning is unclear or how to reorganize the text to make an argument more coherent. It is characteristic of all struggling writers to focus on the more superficial aspects of writing in the revision process, and even when they are able to identify mismatches between intended meaning and text, they usually do not know how to resolve the problem (Troia, 2007).

One of the ways in which writers can be supported in the revising process is by reading their texts aloud and getting feedback. Through the comments and questions of the audience, they gain insights into how a reader perceives their text and the places in which it falls short of making the intended meaning. As this audience does not see the printed page, surface issues of form such as spelling are not a focus. With younger writers, the author's chair can serve this function. For example, in a second-grade classroom, a young writer who was deaf read aloud her story of "My Bad Baby." Her classmates asked her the name of the baby, how old he was, and whether he always did bad things. She was able to incorporate these details into her story when she revised it (Mayer, 1994). Older writers can benefit from a similar approach, sharing their work with a classmate or teacher.

It can also be useful to read the text aloud to the writer, as in hearing it read aloud, the writer has the opportunity to identify errors in wording and sentences structure and gaps in meaning. Even experienced writers will read texts aloud to themselves to aid in the revision process. It is at this point in the writing process that weaknesses in reading comprehension can have a profound impact on learning to write, as students can struggle not only to decode and comprehend their own writing but to evaluate its effect on a potential reader (Singer & Bashir, 2004).

## Adaptations for Writers Who Are Deaf or Hard of Hearing

Consistent with the view that students who are D/HH must master the same set of knowledge and skills as hearing children if they are to become proficient writers, approaches and strategies that have been proven to be efficacious for hearing learners would apply equally to students who are D/HH. However, there are two aspects of writing instruction that necessitate differentiation beyond what might be typically necessary with hearing students, even those who are struggling writers.

The first of these areas relates to the challenge beginning writers who are D/HH face in the transcription process—in encoding an auditory-oral language in print. For hearing children, this relies heavily on phonological abilities (i.e., making phoneme–grapheme relationships), and for some children who are D/HH, this presents a challenge. For these learners, access to phonological information can be provided via the implementation of visual strategies such as the use of visual phonics (Trezek & Wang, 2006; Trezek, Wang, Woods, Gampp, & Paul, 2007), cued speech (see Chapter 6; Cupples, Ching, Crowe, Day, & Seeto, 2014; Leybaert, Colin, & LaSasso, 2010), and speechreading (see Chapter 12; Harris and Moreno, 2006; Kyle & Harris, 2011). Although the use of these alternate strategies is usually discussed in relation to decoding and reading, there is no reason to think that they would not be equally effective in the encoding process. These strategies would allow all writers who are D/HH to invent spellings (that rely on making sound–symbol correspondences in the process of learning to write)—a strategy that has been positively linked to improved development in both reading and writing (Pressley, 2006).

Fingerspelling can also play a role in writing development, although it does not provide the same kind of phonological information as visual phonics or cued speech in the process of learning to write (i.e., an understanding that graphemes have a relationship to phonemes). Rather, fingerspelling represents the grapheme directly (e.g., the hand shape for the letter "a" stands for the written letter) and can be used to highlight some aspects of language as writers who are D/HH attempt to capture their language on paper (e.g., using the manual alphabet to mark word endings such as "s" that can be difficult to hear, almost as a form of manual highlighting). This is a tool that can also be exploited in the dictation process to highlight morphology and function words (e.g., *of, the, as*). Writers who are D/HH have also reported using fingerspelling in the composing process to aid in spelling a word—even if they cannot fingerspell it with complete accuracy (Mayer, 1999).

The second area relates to the issue of language and the challenge that some writers who are D/HH can face in generating, reading, and revising their texts. For those writers who cannot use spoken language alone to mediate the creation of a text, it is important to provide additional visual modalities to aid in the process (e.g., sign supported spoken language, cued speech). This becomes particularly evident in the revising process when the writer must read over what has been written to determine whether the text conveys the intended meaning and whether the correct language and grammar have been used. This "reading over" must be done in the language of the text. This is the stage when writers must read every word on the page to see if it "sounds right." This understanding of what is correct can come from visual as well as auditory information or from whatever combination of modalities allows the writer to represent the text "through the air" in the language in which it is encoded. Undoubtedly this can be the most challenging aspect of learning to write for some learners who are D/HH, but there are ways in which the ear and eye can work in concert to mediate this aspect of the writing process.

## FUTURE DIRECTIONS

Of all aspects of literacy education for learners who are D/HH, writing development and instruction represent an area that has been sorely neglected. To address this gap in both research and practice, the following suggestions are noted:

- As a necessary start, there is simply a need for more research in this area, particularly for intervention studies that 1) are longitudinal and track writers over time, 2) include learners from a range of educational settings (e.g., general education, schools for the deaf), 3) include out-come measures, 4) implement interventions with fidelity, and 5) include comparison groups when possible. Research of this type will be particularly important at this juncture in the field as greater numbers of learners who are D/HH are developing age-appropriate competence in the language of the text as a consequence of earlier intervention and improvements in hearing technologies. It will be important to determine the extent to which these writers meet age-appropriate literacy outcomes and to consider any implications for instruction.

- Writing instruction needs to be accorded greater attention in educational programming. The first step in making this change would be as straightforward as designating time in the school day for the teaching of writing. All students should be given daily opportunities to experiment with writing, linking the use of text with real-life experiences and the active use of language.

- Writing programs, instruction, and interventions for learners who are D/HH should be designed to reflect what is known to be recommended practice for other literacy learners (including those who struggle with writing), affording opportunities for the development of the linguistic, phonologic, and orthographic understandings and skills that are necessary to engage meaningfully in the writing process. Programs that have been designed specifically for learners who are D/HH are not needed, nor have they historically evidenced improvements in outcomes. Rather, the focus should be on differentiating instruction based on robust assessment in ways that address the unique individual needs of writers who are D/HH (e.g., using visual phonics to support encoding), taking advantage of those strategies that have been reported to be efficacious in supporting all writers.

- Well-designed programs should reflect a balance between a focus on meaning (i.e., writing in use) and skills instruction, taking advantage of the strengths of both (Pressley, 2006; Stanovich, 2000). For at-risk learners, including those who are deaf, the balance in an integrated literacy program may need to be adjusted to provide extra support in areas of weakness (Xue & Meisels, 2004), but this should not be taken as an endorsement for reducing writing programs to the teaching of a discrete set of skills. Rather, areas of need should be identified via assessment and interventions designed to address any gaps (e.g., direct teaching of vocabulary).

- Given the central role language plays in learning to write, it is critical to ensure that children who are D/HH have the requisite foundation in place (in the face-to-face form of the language of the text) and that there is a continued emphasis on the development of this language. To achieve this, all writers who are D/HH must have access to this language through auditory input via hearing technologies, visual modalities, or both (e.g., speechreading, sign support, cued speech) so that the language can be acquired and continue to develop. This focus needs to be taken into account in planning any writing program.

- A focus on teaching writing needs to be given greater prominence in teacher education programs and in ongoing professional development for practitioners.

## SUGGESTED READINGS

Calkins, L. (1994). *The art of teaching writing* (2nd ed.). Portsmouth, NH: Heinemann.

This is the updated version of the classic text in which Calkins first launched the idea of a writer's workshop. Since that time, this pedagogical approach has become a staple in language arts education, and in this second edition, she updates the work in light of what has been learned after years of implementation, expanding the volume to include sections on assessment, writing across the curriculum, reading–writing connections, publishing, and nonfiction writing. Although there are now descriptions of writer's workshop approaches in many curricula and language arts textbooks, Calkins's book remains the "go-to" resource for understanding what is critical in implementing this pedagogical approach.

Graves, D.H. (1978). *Writing: Teachers and children at work.* Portsmouth, NH: Heinemann.

Graves's book provided the theoretical and philosophical framework for Calkins's work. Graves was one of the first to recognize that teaching writing needed to go beyond a focus on teaching grammar and spelling. He argues that children should be encouraged to see writing as an active process of making meaning and communicating via text and that this could be best accomplished if children were taught to engage in a writing process that mirrored what proficient writers did—planning, revising, editing, and publishing.

Mayer, C. (2010). The demands of writing and the deaf writer. In M. Marschark & P. Spencer (Eds.), *Oxford handbook of deaf studies, language, and education* (Vol. 2, pp. 144–155). New York, NY: Oxford University Press.

In this chapter, Mayer provides a summary and analysis of the studies examining written language development and achievement in the D/HH population in terms of the challenges that writing and learning to write present for all learners, whether the process is viewed from a cognitive or a sociocultural perspective. Discussion includes an overview of shifts in pedagogical approach and the challenges related to assessing written language for the purposes of both research and practice.

Strassman, B.K., & Schirmer, B. (2013). Teaching writing to deaf students: Does research offer evidence for practice? *Remedial and Special Education, 34*(3), 166–179.

In this article Strassman and Schirmer review the research on writing instruction with deaf students to identify those pedagogical practices that are supported by evidence. They found that the research base in this area is small and fragmented, identifying only 16 studies in the past 25 years. They concluded that while some approaches showed promise, outcomes were equivocal, indicating the critical need for further research.

## LEARNING ACTIVITIES

1. Using Halliday's (1975; Table 13.1) functions of language as a framework, identify types of writing (genres) that can be used to accomplish each function (e.g., posters, instructions, recipes, advertisements, and warning signs can be used for the regulatory function). Consider how each of these could be taught and how this might change, given the writing level of the student. Think about how communication technologies such as e-mail, texting, and Facebook can play a role in executing some of these language functions and can be a motivating factor for student writers.

2. Develop a plan (schedule) for how you would implement a writer's workshop for students who are D/HH in the educational setting where you teach (e.g., on an itinerant caseload, in a school for the deaf, in a self-contained classroom in a mainstream school). Include the amount of time that would be devoted to teaching writing and describe the strategies you would use to track and monitor progress (e.g., topic/idea sheets, revised checklists).

3. Look at a first draft of a student's writing. Develop five questions that you would ask this student in an individual writing conference. Remember that the focus should first be on the meaning (the content) and second on the form (the surface features). Identify one strategy that the student might add to their revising checklist.

4. Visit the following web site, which provides examples of graphic organizers: http://www.edhelper.com/teachers/graphic_organizers.htm. Identify the graphic organizers that could be used to support students in planning and writing various text types. Look at some examples of student writing and analyze them in terms of these organizers. Outline the ways in which you could use a graphic organizer to plan a piece of writing with a student.

5. Look at a writing curriculum from your local school district and make note of the writing goals for the age/grade level of students you are teaching. Identify which of these could be explicitly taught in a minilesson.

6. Write a script for a "think-aloud," showing how you would model an aspect of the composing strategy or the steps in the writing process. For example, how would you describe the thinking process (step by step) that goes into writing an appropriate title, deciding where to include paragraph breaks, or making a particular word choice?

## REFERENCES

Albertini, J., Meath-Lang, B., & Harris, D.P. (1994). Voice as muse, message, and medium: The views of deaf college students. In K.B. Yancey (Ed.), *Voices on voice* (pp. 172–190). Urbana, IL: National Council of Teachers of English.

Ambrose, S.E., Fey, M.E., & Eisenberg, L.S. (2012). Phonological awareness and print knowledge of preschool children with cochlear implants. *Journal of Speech, Language, and Hearing Research, 55*(3), 811–823. doi:10.1044/1092-4388(2011/11-0086)

Bereiter, C., & Scardamalia, M. (1987). *The psychology of written composition.* Hillsdale, NJ: Lawrence Erlbaum Associates.

Berman, R. (1994). Learners' transfer of writing skills between languages. *TESL Canada Journal, 12,* 29–41.

Bialystok, E. (2011). Language proficiency and its implications for monolingual and bilingual children. In A.Y. Durgunnoğlu & C. Goldenberg (Eds.), *Language and literacy development in bilingual settings* (pp. 121–138). New York, NY: Guilford Press.

Burman, D., Evans, D., Nunes, T., & Bell, D. (2008). Assessing deaf children's writing in primary school: Grammar and story development. *Deafness and Education International, 10*(2), 93–110. doi:10.1002/dei.238

Calkins, L. (1994). *The art of teaching writing.* Portsmouth, NH: Heineman.

Clay, M. (1982). Research update: Learning and teaching writing: A developmental perspective. *Language Arts, 59,* 65–70.

Clay, M. (1983). Getting a theory of writing. In B. Kroll & G. Wells (Eds.), *Explorations in the development of writing* (pp. 259–284). London, England: John Wiley and Sons.

Collins, A.M., & Gentner, D. (1980). A framework for a cognitive theory of writing. In L.W. Gregg & E. Steinberg (Eds.), *Cognitive processes in writing* (pp. 51–72). Mahwah, NJ: Lawrence Erlbaum Associates.

Conte, M.P., Rampelli, L.P., & Volterra, V. (1996). Deaf children and the construction of written texts. In C. Pontecorvo & M. Orsolini (Eds.), *Children's early text construction* (pp. 303–319). Hillsdale, NJ: Lawrence Erlbaum Associates.

Conway, D. (1985). Children (re)creating writing: A preliminary look at the purpose of free choice writing of hearing impaired kindergarteners. *The Volta Review, 87,* 91–107.

Cummins, J. (2000). *Language, power and pedagogy: Bilingual children in the crossfire.* Clevedon, England: Multilingual Matters.

Cupples, L., Ching, T., Crowe, K., Day, J., & Seeto, M. (2014). Predictors of early reading skill in 5-year-old children with hearing loss who use spoken language. *Reading Research Quarterly, 49*(1), 85–104. doi:10.1002/rrq.60

Dickinson, D.K., McCabe, A., Anastasopoulos, L., Peisner-Feinberg, E., & Poe, M.D. (2003). The comprehensive language approach to early literacy: The interrelationships among vocabulary, phonological sensitivity, and print knowledge among preschool-aged children. *Journal of Educational Psychology, 95*(3), 465–481.

Dickinson, D., McCabe, A., & Essex, M. (2006). A window of opportunity we must open to all: The case for pre-school with high-quality support for language and literacy. In D. Dickinson & S. Neuman (Eds.), *Handbook of early literacy research* (Vol. 2, pp. 11–28). New York, NY: Guilford Press.

Ehri, L. (2009). Learning to read in English: Teaching phonics to beginning readers from diverse backgrounds. In L.M. Morrow, R. Rueda, & D. Lapp (Eds.), *Handbook of research on literacy and diversity* (pp. 292–319). New York, NY: Guilford Press.

Ewoldt, C. (1985). A descriptive study of the developing literacy of young hearing-impaired children. *The Volta Review, 87,* 109–126.

Flower, L.S., & Hayes, J.R. (1980). The dynamics of composing: Making plans and jug-gling constraints. In L.W. Gregg & E. Steinberg (Eds.), *Cognitive processes in writing* (pp. 31–50). Mahwah, NJ: Erlbaum.

Freedman, A., Pringle, I., & Yalden, J. (1983). The writing process: Three orientations. In A. Freedman, I. Pringle, & J. Yalden (Eds.), *Learning to write: First language/second language*. London, England: Longman.

Geers, A. (2006). Spoken language in children with cochlear implants. In P. Spencer & M. Marschark (Eds.), *Advances in spoken language development of deaf and hard of hearing children* (pp. 244–270). New York, NY: Oxford University Press.

Graham, S., Harris, K.R., Fink, B., & MacArthur, C.A. (2003). Primary grade teachers' instructional adaptations for struggling writers: A national survey. *Journal of Educational Psychology, 95,* 279–292.

Graves, D.H. (1978). *Writing: Teachers and children at work.* Portsmouth, NH: Heinemann.

Halliday, M.A.K. (1975). *Learning how to mean.* London, England: Edward Arnold.

Halliday, M.A.K. (1989). *Spoken and written language.* Oxford, England: Oxford University Press.

Halliday, M.A.K. (1993). Towards a language-based theory of learning. *Linguistics and Education, 5,* 93–116.

Harp, B. (2006). *The handbook of literacy assessment and evaluation* (3rd ed.). Norwood, MA: Christopher-Gordon.

Harris, M., & Moreno, C. (2006). Speech reading and learning to read: A comparison of 8-year-old profoundly deaf children with good and poor reading ability. *Journal of Deaf Studies and Deaf Education, 11,* 189–201.

Kelly, L.P. (1988). Relative automaticity without mastery: The grammatical decision making of deaf students. *Written Communication, 5*(3), 325–351.

Kress, G. (1994). *Learning to write* (2nd ed.). New York, NY: Routledge.

Kress, G. (1997). *Before writing: Rethinking the paths to literacy.* New York, NY: Routledge.

Kyle, F.E., & Harris, M. (2011). Longitudinal patterns of emergent literacy in beginning deaf and hearing readers. *Journal of Deaf Studies and Deaf Education, 16*(3), 289–304.

Leybaert, J., Colin, S., & LaSasso, C. (2010). Cued speech for the deaf students' mastery of the alphabetic principle. In C. LaSasso, K.L. Crain, & J. Leybaert (Eds.), *Cued speech and cued language for deaf and hard of hearing children* (pp. 245–283). San Diego, CA: Plural.

Marschark, M. (1993). *Psychological development of deaf children.* New York, NY: Oxford University Press.

Marschark, M., Lang, H., & Albertini, J. (2002). *Educating deaf students: From research to practice.* New York, NY: Oxford University Press.

Mayer, C. (1994). Action research: The story of a partnership. In G. Wells (Ed.), *Changing schools from within: Creating communities of inquiry* (pp. 151–170). Portsmouth, NH: Heinemann.

Mayer, C. (1999). Shaping at the point of utterance: An investigation of the composing processes of the deaf student writer. *Journal of Deaf Studies and Deaf Education, 4,* 37–49.

Mayer, C. (2006). *Beyond rubrics: Assessing the written language of deaf students.* Presented at the Annual Conference, American College Educators of the Deaf and Hard of Hearing, Denver, Colorado.

Mayer, C. (2007). What matters in the early literacy development of deaf children. *Journal of Deaf Studies and Deaf Education, 12,* 411–431.

Mayer, C. (2010). The demands of writing and the deaf writer. In M. Marschark & P. Spencer (Eds.), *Oxford handbook of deaf studies, language, and education* (Vol. 2, pp. 144–155). New York, NY: Oxford University Press.

Mayer, C., & Akamatsu, C.T. (2011). Bilingualism and literacy. In M. Marschark & P. Spencer (Eds.), *Oxford handbook of deaf studies, language and education* (2nd ed., Vol. 1, pp. 144–155). New York, NY: Oxford University Press.

Mayer, C., & Leigh, G. (2010). The changing context for sign bilingual education programs: Issues in language and the development of literacy. *International Journal of Bilingualism and Bilingual Education, 13*(2), 175–186.

Mayer, C., & Trezek, B.J. (2011). New (?) answers to old questions: Literacy development in D/HH learners. In D.F. Moores (Ed.), *Partners in education: Issues and trends from the 21st international congress on the education of the deaf* (pp. 62–74). Washington, DC: Gallaudet University Press.

Mayer, C., & Trezek, B.J. (2015). *Early literacy development in deaf children.* New York, NY: Oxford University Press.

Mayer, C., & Wells, G. (1996). Can the linguistic interdependence theory support a bilingual model of literacy education for deaf students? *Journal of Deaf Studies and Deaf Education, 1*(2), 93–107.

Moores, D. (1987). *Educating the deaf: Psychology, principles and practices.* Boston, MA: Houghton Mifflin.

Musselman, C., & Szanto, G. (1998). The written language of deaf adolescents: Patterns of performance. *Journal of Deaf Studies and Deaf Education, 3,* 245–257.

National Commission on Writing in America's Schools and Colleges. (2003). *National assessment of educational progress (NAEP).* Washington, DC: U.S. Department of Education.

Nova Scotia Writing Exemplars: Grades One to Eight. (2005). Retrieved from http://nswritingexemplars.ednet.ns.ca/overview.htm

Olson, D. (1977). From utterance to text: The bias of language in speech and writing. *Harvard Educational Review, 47,* 257–281.

Olson, D. (1993). Thinking about thinking: Learning how to take statements and hold beliefs. *Educational Psychologist, 28,* 7–23.

Olson, D. (1994). *The world on paper.* Cambridge, England: Cambridge University Press.

Paul, P.V., & Lee, C. (2010). The qualitative similarity hypothesis. *American Annals of the Deaf, 154*(5), 456–462.

Pierangelo, R., & Giuliani, G. (2006). *The special educator's comprehensive guide to 301 diagnostic tests.* San Francisco, CA: Jossey-Bass.

Pressley, M. (2006). *Reading instruction that works: The case for balanced teaching* (3rd ed.). New York, NY: Guilford Press.

Pritchard, R.J., & Honeycutt, R.L. (2006). The process approach to writing instruction: Examining its effectiveness. In C.A. MacArthur, S. Graham, & J. Fitzgerald (Eds.), *Handbook of writing research* (pp. 275–290). New York, NY: Guilford Press.

Pugh, K.R., Sandak, R., Frost, S.J., Moore, D.L., & Mencl, W.E. (2006). Neurobiological investigations of skilled and impaired reading. In D. Dickinson & S. Neuman (Eds.), *Handbook of early literacy research* (Vol. 2, pp. 64–74). New York, NY: Guilford Press.

Rhodes, L. (1993). *Literacy assessment: A handbook of instruments.* Portsmouth, NH: Heinemann.

Schirmer, B., Bailey, J., & Fitzgerald, S.M. (1999). Using a writing assessment rubric for writing development of children who are deaf. *Exceptional Children, 65,* 383–397.

Singer, B.D., & Bashir, A.S. (2004). Developmental variation in writing composition skills. In C. Stone, E. Silliman, B.J. Ehren, & K. Apel (Eds.), *Handbook of language and literacy: Development and disorders* (pp. 559–582). New York, NY: Guilford Press.

Singleton, J.L., Morgan, D., DiGello, E., Wiles, J., & Rivers, R. (2004). Vocabulary use by low, moderate and high ASL-proficient writers compared to hearing ESL and monolingual speakers. *Journal of Deaf Studies and Deaf Education, 9*(1), 86–103.

Stanovich, K. (2000). *Progress in understanding reading: Scientific foundations and new frontiers.* New York, NY: Guilford Press.

Strassman, B.K., & Schirmer, B. (2013). Teaching writing to deaf students: Does research offer evidence for practice? *Remedial and Special Education, 34*(3), 166–179.

Taeschner, T. (1988). Affixes and function words in the written language of deaf children. *Applied Psycholinguistics, 9,* 385–401.

Trezek, B.J., & Wang, Y. (2006). Implications of utilizing a phonics-based reading curriculum with children who are deaf or hard of hearing. *Journal of Deaf Studies and Deaf Education, 10*(2), 202–213.

Trezek, B.J., Wang, Y., & Paul, P.V. (2010). *Reading and deafness: Theory, research and practice.* Clifton Park, NY: Cengage Learning.

Trezek, B.J., Wang, Y., Woods, D.G., Gampp, T.L., & Paul, P. (2007). Using visual phonics to supplement beginning reading instruction for students who are deaf or hard of hearing. *Journal of Deaf Studies and Deaf Education, 12*(3), 373–384.

Troia, G. (2007). Research in writing instruction: What we know and what we need to know. In M. Pressley, A.K. Billman, K.H. Perry, K.E. Reffitt, & J. Moorehead-Reynolds (Eds.), *Shaping literacy achievement: Research we have, research we need* (pp. 129–156). New York, NY: Guilford Press.

Whitehurst, G., & Lonigan, C. (1998). Child development and emergent literacy. *Child Development, 68,* 848–872.

Whitehurst, G., & Lonigan, C. (2001). Emergent literacy: Development from prereaders to readers. In S. Neuman & D. Dickinson (Eds.), *Handbook of early literacy research* (Vol. 1, pp. 11–29). New York, NY: Guilford Press.

Williams, C. (1993). Learning to write: Social interaction among preschool auditory/oral and total communication children. *Sign Language Studies, 80,* 267–284.

Williams, C. (2011). Adapted interactive writing instruction with kindergarten children who are deaf or hard of hearing. *American Annals of the Deaf, 156,* 23–34.

Williams, C., & Mayer, C. (2012). *Writing in young deaf and hard of hearing children: A review of the literature.* Presentation at the American Educational Research Association (AERA) Annual Meeting, Vancouver, B.C.

Wong, B.Y.L., & Berninger, V.W. (2004). Cognitive processes of teachers in implementing composition research in elementary, middle and high school classrooms. In C. Addison-Stone, E.R. Silliman, B.J. Ehren, & K. Apel (Eds.), *Handbook of language and literacy: Development and disorders* (pp. 600–624). New York, NY: Guilford Press.

Xue, Y., & Meisels, S. J. (2004). Early literacy instruction and learning in kindergarten: Evidence from the early childhood longitudinal study—kindergarten class of 1998–1999. *American Educational.*

Yau, M. (1991). The role of language factors in second language writing. In L. Malave & G. Duquette (Eds.), *Language, culture and cognition.* Clevedon, England: Multilingual Matters.

Yoshinaga-Itano, C., Snyder, L.S., & Mayberry, R. (1996). How deaf and normally hearing students convey meaning within and between sentences. *The Volta Review, 98,* 9–38.

Zimmerman, B.J. (2002). Becoming a self-regulated learner: An overview. *Theory into Practice, 41*(2), 64–70.

# 14

# Educational Advocacy Across the Curriculum

Cheryl DeConde Johnson

The auditory and communication abilities of students who are deaf or hard of hearing (D/HH) have changed dramatically in recent years, indicating a new era in educational practice for this population. Due to the success of early hearing detection and intervention (EHDI) programs, improved technologies, and inclusive education philosophies, the majority of today's students receive special education services in mainstream, general education classrooms, and many more are no longer eligible for special education services because of effective communication skills and near age-level academic functioning. As a result, the role of teachers of the deaf or hard of hearing (ToD/HH) has become increasingly consultative and collaborative, and the traditional model of providing instruction in self-contained classrooms is most often reserved for students with language learning difficulties or multiple disabilities. Due to these changing demographics, expectations for teachers of children who are D/HH now include greater emphasis on the following:

- Comprehensive knowledge of effective educational supports that extend beyond classroom instruction

- "Coaching" general education teachers to implement the specialized classroom practices previously provided by teachers of the D/HH

- Identification of needs that are unique to students who are D/HH, such as expanded core curricula for understanding the communication implications of partial hearing or deafness, social and pragmatic language skills, and specialized and assistive technology

- Collaboration with members of multidisciplinary teams, children's primary audiology facilities, parents, and other relevant professionals

- Continuous collection and management of student data across a variety of academic settings to track performance and, when indicated, modify services

This new era brings many opportunities and challenges for professionals who work with children who are D/HH. Opportunities for thoughtful discussion of service options with other stakeholders (e.g., parents, regular teachers, administrators) exist well beyond individualized education program (IEP) meetings. In fact, teachers of children who are D/HH may find that their most important role has changed from classroom instruction to providing daily support for instructional accommodations and **communication access**. Yet the education of children who are D/HH remains a complex and challenging process. Each child must be considered as an individual in all areas of their development and education. This calls for detailed evaluations of language, academics, and social abilities and specialized plans to meet each child's needs. In addition, the pedagogical practices and beliefs of regular classroom teachers might not be easily influenced by consultation with specialists. True collaboration results from mutual respect and a well-balanced "give and take" of information. The purpose of this chapter is to explore these issues and various approaches to optimizing learning for students who are D/HH.

## THEORETICAL BASIS

Changing student demographics and evolving educational practices call for a new model for serving students who are D/HH. This new model must address not only students who qualify for special education services and their curricular supports but also students who are making reasonable academic progress without an IEP yet could benefit from *prevention* and *sustainability* supports.

### Federal Laws that Support Services for Children Who Are Deaf or Hard of Hearing

Before discussing a contemporary model of education for children who are D/HH, a brief review of the Individuals with Disabilities Education Improvement Act of 2004 (IDEA; PL 108-446) and Section 504 of the Rehabilitation Act of 1973 (PL 93-112) is needed to establish an understanding of their main distinguishing components. Although IDEA and Section 504 provide similar protections, some important differences exist:

- IDEA requires the existence of a condition (as identified in the IDEA-B regulations, 34 CFR Part 300, Section 300.5) that adversely affects educational performance, thus necessitating special education and related services. Section 504's broader definition of individuals with disabilities does not require "adverse effect." This means that a wider group of individuals are eligible for services under 504 plans than under IDEA. Thus according to Section 504, the obligation to provide an appropriate education extends beyond students served in special education programs.

• The term *eligibility* provides another opportunity to differentiate IDEA and Section 504. Special education means *specially designed instruction* provided *at no cost to the parents* and designed *to meet the unique needs of a child with a disability* (300.39[a][1]). According to IDEA, once a disability is diagnosed, eligibility for special education is based on whether the disability adversely affects educational performance (i.e., the child's ability to obtain reasonable benefit from regular education alone). In contrast, according to Section 504, children can be eligible for services even if they do not exhibit a disability that negatively affects their educational performance.

• Section 504 is a civil rights law and complaints are filed with the Office of Civil Rights. Noncompliance with a 504 plan may result in corrective actions, fines, or other sanctions. In contrast, due process for IDEA is managed through each state department of education and includes mediation and impartial hearings for disagreements regarding the evaluations, records, or placements of students with disabilities.

## A Contemporary, Tiered Model of Supports and Services for Learners Who Are Deaf or Hard of Hearing

The model illustrated in Figure 14.1 is based on the response to intervention model (RTI; also referred to as the multitiered systems of support paradigm proposed by the National Association of State Directors of Special Education [NASDSE, 2005]). For the purposes of this chapter, it has been modified to represent a continuum of services for educating learners who are D/HH. All students who have atypical hearing levels are included in this model. Thus the model is unique in that it does not identify D/HH students' needs and levels of service solely on the basis of eligibility for IDEA.

According to the model in Figure 14.1, students in Tier 1 would have minor or no documented adverse effects of their hearing status. Their educational performance would be at or above grade level. These students might receive monitoring support and/or special accommodations via either an IEP or a 504 plan. For example, such students might have an IEP goal to continue monitoring progress in academic areas or to remain eligible for use of assistive listening devices or interpreting services. Unfortunately, some students who are D/HH who could benefit from special education or support services do not receive them because their academic performance is comparable to peers who have normal hearing. Section 504 plans can provide important learning accommodations for such students, but as the following data show, they are underused.

Data from the Departments of Education in Colorado, Washington, and Iowa (personal communication with Colorado on June 1, 2005; with Washington on August 5, 2012; and with Iowa on October 4, 2012) reveal several patterns of service provision for students who are D/HH. Table 14.1 shows that about half of the students in these states received services based on special education IEPs. In contrast, relatively few children received services under a 504 plan. As the last column shows, the percentage of students who are D/HH and being educated without any formal services is significant in each state.

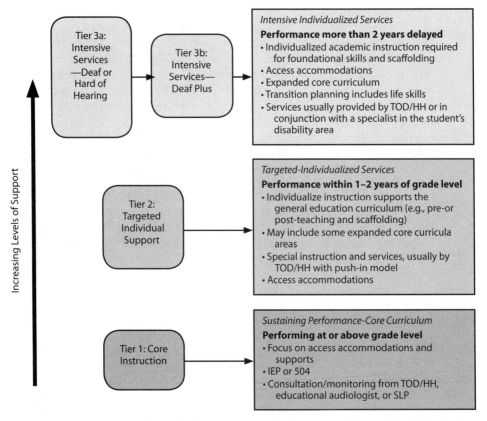

**Figure 14.1.**    Increasing levels of support.

Key: *TOD/HH*, teacher of the deaf or hard of hearing; *SLP*, speech-language pathologist; *IEP*, individualized education program

This is a serious concern because, at a minimum, children who are D/HH typically require close monitoring to ensure that their educational needs are being met and that their hearing status is stable.

It is essential, then, that designated professionals be responsible for monitoring the progress of students who are D/HH and determining the need for further assessments and accommodations. In most cases, this professional is an educational audiologist, a teacher of the D/HH, or a speech-language pathologist. These service providers are responsible for understanding and gathering the following information:

- The names, hearing levels, and classroom placements of all students with atypical hearing status

- The performance levels for each student based on the three-tiered model (Figure 14.1)

- The referral procedures and qualification criteria for IDEA and 504 plans

- The assessments that are required by the school district to determine eligibility for IDEA

- The procedures for developing 504 plans

- The professionals who are assigned to monitor each student's performance levels, especially those on 504 plans

The data in Table 14.1, if representative of other states, clearly suggest that there is a sizable population of children who require monitoring (at a minimum) and who could benefit from 504 plans even though relatively successful in the classroom. Changing the tendency to underserve these children will require sustained advocacy on the part of the parents and professionals who serve children who are D/HH.

In light of the substantial proportions of children who are not receiving services, *advocacy* may be the most important role of service providers for children who are D/HH in schools. Broadly, advocacy encompasses the customary instruction and support duties of teachers of the D/HH, audiologists, speech-language pathologists, and other providers. The main difference between an advocate and a service provider involves the way in which supports are provided. An advocate is a person who pleads, supports, or promotes the cause of another. To be effective, teachers of students who are D/HH must advocate for educational opportunities that allow children to reach their full potentials as well as the accommodations that allow them to fully participate in their education. As an empowering practice, advocacy may be viewed as opening the door to opportunities by building awareness in others and creating supportive environments that can sustain learning. Ideally, advocacy by parents and teachers leads to self-advocacy by students themselves.

Statistics from the U.S. Department of Education's Annual Report to Congress on the implementation of IDEA illustrate the increase in regular classroom placements for children who are D/HH. In 1992–1993, 49.2% were placed in regular classrooms at least 40% of the school day (U.S. Department of Education, 1995). By the 2007–2008 school year, this percentage had grown to 70.8% (U.S. Department of Education, 2010). Clearly, sustained advocacy will also be needed to ensure that general classroom educators and school administrators understand the special needs and learning potential of children who are D/HH.

**Table 14.1.**   Service profile of students who are deaf or hard of hearing

| State | Percentage of students with an IEP | Percentage of students with a 504 plan | Percentage of students without services |
|---|---|---|---|
| Colorado (2005) | 43 | 2 | 55 |
| Washington (2012) | 57 | 17 | 26 |
| Iowa (2012) | 54 | No data available | 46 |

*Source:* Personal communication (with Colorado on June 1, 2005; with Washington on August 5, 2012; and with Iowa on October 4, 2012).

**New Expectations for Students Who Are Deaf or Hard of Hearing**

Just as the demographics of students who are D/HH have changed, so too have expectations for academic success. The often-cited third-grade reading level for high school graduates who are deaf (Traxler, 2000) is no longer relevant for today's students who are D/HH. Results of a longitudinal study of main-streamed D/HH elementary and high school students in Colorado and Arizona reported that their average academic performance was within one standard deviation of their hearing peers (Antia, Jones, Reed, & Kreimeyer, 2009). Anal-ysis of scores for all 3rd to 10th graders who are D/HH on the Colorado Student As-sessment Program (CSAP) found that within 1 school year, 82% of students made >1 year of growth in reading and 92% made >1 year of growth in writing and in math (Johnson, 2006). These data strongly suggest that it is reasonable to expect at least one grade-level growth per school year in all academic areas. For students who are behind in academic areas by more than 1 year, even greater gains must be realized if they are to catch up with peers. If adequate gains are not made, then service providers and teachers are accountable for examining the effectiveness of their instruction, educational placements, and accommodations, as well as further evaluating children's language and learn-ing abilities.

The diversity of students who are D/HH must also be acknowledged. Instructional approaches and accommodations that work for one student do not necessarily work for another, especially for students who are repre-sented at Tiers 2 and 3 in Figure 14.1. Service providers address individual differences by completing comprehensive assessments (of language, communi-cation, social, and academic skills), consulting with classroom teachers, devel-oping and implementing evidence-based intervention programs (i.e., IEPs or 504 plans) based on assessment results, monitoring learning, and modifying approaches as needed. Carefully following these steps allows service providers to determine whether children's intervention plans are producing the intended results. Without careful assessment and analysis, this process is guided sub-jectively and will lack the specificity needed to produce desirable results.

## USE OF ASSESSMENT TO IDENTIFY INTERVENTION PRIORITIES

The assessment and intervention approaches discussed in the remainder of this chapter are focused on five areas: 1) the Iowa Expanded Cored Curriculum for Students Who Are Deaf or Hard of Hearing (Iowa Department of Educa-tion, 2010), 2) classroom listening abilities, 3) communication access for stu-dents, 4) learning environments, and 5) **classroom acoustics**. Assessments of students' language and academic abilities are presented in Chapters 7, 8, 12, and 13.

### Expanded Core Curriculum Areas

Some states have identified content beyond the basic core academic areas to address skills that are pertinent for academic success for students who are D/HH. For example, the Iowa Department of Education (2010), a national leader in developing services for children who are deaf or hard of hearing, identified the following content areas of unique importance for students who are D/HH in the Iowa Expanded Core Curriculum: audiology, career education, communication, Deaf culture, family education, functional educational skills, listening and speaking, self-determination and self-advocacy, social-emotional skills, and technology. Each area of the Iowa Expanded Core Curriculum includes a rubric for placing children's abilities and knowledge into early, emerging, intermediate, and advanced levels. These supplemental instructional areas are frequently overlooked in educational assessments, yet they represent knowledge and skills that are foundational to the development and education of students who are D/HH. Instruction in these areas requires the expertise of teachers of the deaf, speech-language pathologists, educational audiologists, and other related service professionals. Functional measures such as teacher and parent observation reports and student self-assessments are often the basis for evaluating areas of the **expanded core curriculum**. Although not standardized, such functional measures add authentic information that helps complete a profile of each student's strengths and needs. D/HH educational teams (composed of teachers of the deaf, educational audiologists, speech-language pathologists [SLPs], and others as pertinent) should review all expanded core content areas to consider their impact on special education eligibility; appropriate assessment, data collection, and measurement tools; and team members who have primary instructional responsibilities. Areas of the expanded core curriculum are included in the curricular modification section of the IEP/504 plan checklist found in Appendix 14.1.

## Assessment of Children's Classroom Listening Abilities

As more children who are D/HH receive the majority of their education in general education classrooms (National Association of State Directors of Special Education, 2005; U.S. Department of Education, 2010), increased attention has been devoted to assessing children's ability to listen and learn in this challenging environment. The importance of audition for early reading development (National Institute of Child Health and Human Development, 2000) further highlights the importance of consistent and adequate auditory access to spoken language in the classroom setting. For children who are D/HH, this access comes through the filters of hearing aid technology, cochlear implants, and/or the use of hearing assistance devices (Lauer, 2004; Stelmachowicz, 2005; Zwolan, 2009). Advocacy for the accommodations that allow students to fully participate in their educational programs is paramount. To be most effective, advocacy must be based on evidence from assessment measures that examine listening abilities within the classroom setting (Johnson, 2010a).

Objective protocols are now available to assess listening in the classroom. For example, the **Functional Listening** Evaluation (FLE; Johnson, 2013) is designed to examine the effects of the noise and reverberation found in the classroom as well as other communication issues encountered by students (e.g., distance from the teacher and other speakers, audibility and intelligibility of the teacher's and student's voices, availability of visual cues). The FLE was developed to assess students using their typical hearing mode (e.g., unaided hearing, hearing aids, cochlear implants, or other hearing technology) and can also be used to examine the benefits of hearing assistance technology (see Chapter 2).

The FLE uses the student as his or her own control to compare listening abilities across eight conditions (quiet, noise, auditory only, auditory-visual, each in close and distant arrangements). A variety of stimulus material (e.g., words, phrases, sentences) can be chosen to match the developmental needs of each student, but the "Common Children's Phrases" lists available from http://www.adevantage.com/resources.html are recommended to provide a stimulus that is long enough to account for classroom reverberation characteristics. When using the FLE, classroom noise is simulated by presenting recordings of classroom or multitalker noise as background to the stimuli. Presentation variables must be carefully controlled in this "live" presentation so that there is consistency across conditions. For children who use hearing assistance technology, noise and distance conditions can be repeated to validate the device. Table 14.2 illustrates a sample FLE "score box" and the accompanying "interpretation matrix" for a child using a cochlear implant. The effects of noise, distance, and visual input across conditions as well as the benefits of frequency-modulated (FM) technology are evident. The goal of hearing assistance technology is to mitigate the detrimental conditions by providing a consistent auditory input to the student. It is apparent that, for this child, FM technology made an important difference in listening ability.

## Communication Access Assessment

Communication access considers the combined skills and conditions that result in shared meaning between communication partners (Johnson & Seaton, 2012, p. 470). Whether through auditory, visual, tactile, or combined modalities, access is also dependent on the individual's attention and processing skills as well as the language level of the message conveyed. External factors such as room acoustics, talker diction, and signer accuracy also affect communication access. As a result of these variables, assessment of communication access is vital for identifying students who have access problems, defining the nature of the problems, making accommodations to address the problems, and often, providing counseling and support for students to learn to manage their own communication access.

A recent study by Antia et al. (2011) reported that classroom participation was a powerful predictor of social outcomes as measured by the domains of social skills and problem behaviors in the Social Skills Rating System (SSRS; Gresham & Elliott, 1990). The Classroom Participation Questionnaire (CPQ; Antia, Sabers, & Stinson, 2007) was used in this study. It examines the quality and frequency of classroom participation by students who are D/HH. The CPQ consists of 16 statements (Table 14.3) that a student rates on a four-point scale (1 = almost never; 2 = seldom; 3 = often; 4 = almost always). Self-assessment questions focus on how well the student understands his or her teacher and classmates and the student's feelings about those communication interactions.

Through self-assessments like the CPQ, students reveal information about themselves that opens the door for discussion and counseling, an opportunity that should not be missed. A follow-up discussion can reinforce what is working well and highlight problem situations that should be addressed.

**Table 14.2.** Sample functional listening evaluation score box and interpretation matrix: Cochlear implant only versus cochlear implant with personal frequency-modulated (FM) technology

Score box (*asterisks mean percent correct with FM)

| | Close/Quiet | Close/Noise | Distant/Quiet | Distant/Noise |
|---|---|---|---|---|
| Auditory-visual | 95% | 75% 100%* | 80% 95%* | 40% |
| Auditory | 80% | 65% | 65% 95%* | 25% 95%* |

Interpretation matrix

| | Noise | | Distance | |
|---|---|---|---|---|
| | Quiet | Noise | Close | Distant |
| Close/Auditory | 80% | 65/95%* | 80% | 65/95%* |
| Close/Auditory-visual | 95% | 75/100%* | 95% | 80/95%* |
| Distant/Auditory | 65/95%* | 25/90%* | 65/95%* | 25/90%* |
| Distant/Auditory-visual | 80/95%* | 40/95%* | 75/100%* | 40/95%* |
| Average of above scores | | | | |
| Cochlear implant only | 80% | 51.25% | 77.75% | 52.5% |
| Cochlear implant with FM | 91.25%* | 95%* | 92.5%* | 93.75%* |

| | Quiet/Auditory | Quiet/Auditory-visual | Noise/Auditory | Noise/Auditory-visual |
|---|---|---|---|---|
| Close | 80% | 95% | 65/95%* | 75/100%* |
| Distant | 65/95%* | 80/95%* | 25/90%* | 40/95%* |

| | Visual input | |
|---|---|---|
| | Auditory-visual | Auditory |
| Close/Quiet | 95% | 80% |
| Close/Noise | 75/100%* | 65/95%* |
| Distant/Noise | 40/95%* | 25/90%* |
| Distant/Quiet | 80/95%* | 65/95%* |
| Cochlear implant only | 72.5% | 58.75% |
| Cochlear implant with FM | 96.25%* | 90%* |

Scores represent the percentage of short phrases recognized in each condition.
Reprinted with permission from Johnson, C.D., and Seaton, J. (2012). Educational audiology handbook, second edition, Delmar Cengage Learning.

**Table 14.3.**   Questions from the Classroom Participation Questionnaire

| Understanding teacher | I understand my teacher. |
| --- | --- |
| | I understand my teacher when she gives me homework assignments. |
| | I understand my teacher when she answers other students' questions. |
| | I understand my teacher when she tells me what to study for a test. |
| Understanding student | I understand the other students in class. |
| | I join in class discussions. |
| | I understand other students during group discussions. |
| | I understand other students when they answer my teacher's questions. |
| Positive affect | I feel good about how I communicate in class. |
| | I feel relaxed when I talk to my teacher. |
| | I feel happy in group discussions in class. |
| | I feel good in group discussions in class. |
| Negative affect | I feel frustrated because it is difficult for me to communicate with other students. |
| | I get upset because other students cannot understand me. |
| | I get upset because my teacher cannot understand me. |
| | I feel unhappy in group discussions in class. |

*Source:* From Stinson, M., Long, G., Reed, S., Kreimeyer, K., Sabers, D., and Antia, S. (2006). Classroom Participation Questionnaire.

Students can then be coached in strategies to improve communication access/participation as well how to self-advocate for better communication access.

## Learning Environment Assessment

In order to support student success, it is also necessary to evaluate the student's proposed or existing learning environment. Doing so helps determine whether there is a good fit between the needs of the student and the various aspects of classroom instruction and routines. The Placement and Readiness Checklists (PARC; Johnson, 2010b) provide very functional information for making placement and programming decisions. Most students are considered for placement in the general education classroom for at least part of their school day. Ultimately, inclusion in the general education classroom should mean that when provided the necessary accommodations, modifications, and supports, students can actively and meaningfully participate in communication, instruction, and social activities by using their selected communication mode(s). The increasing use of educational technology in classrooms may complicate access for some students. Web-based resources, YouTube videos, and computer-based instruction require captioning, audio connections, and other accommodations to ensure full access to learning materials. There are two main criteria that should be considered when evaluating placement and service delivery. First, the student should demonstrate the prerequisite skills needed for the placement, and second, the learning environment should provide the supports needed for success.

Assessment tools such as the "Readiness" checklists of the PARC can assist the IEP team in examining the many factors that influence how well a student will be able to function in various classroom settings. In some cases, students may be "ready" for some classes or situations while not ready for others. The four readiness checklists can be used in combination or independently, depending on the student and the purpose of the review. The General Education Inclusion Readiness checklist is used to evaluate overall readiness for entry into regular education classrooms and is appropriate for most students.

The Interpreted/Transliterated Education and the Captioning/Transcribing Readiness checklists identify skills that students need to fully benefit from these services within a general education classroom. The Instructional Communication Access checklist analyzes how well a student accesses instruction using listening and spoken language, sign or cues, or both. This checklist may help determine what communication approach and supports are needed in the general education classroom, a resource room, or a special classroom. When deficiencies are identified, IEP goals should specify the requisite student skills and instructional modifications necessary to ensure success in the desired learning environment. The checklists can also be used to address supports and accommodations for 504 plans as well as monitor the acquisition of the targeted skills. Other protocols that may be useful to evaluate readiness include the Screening Instrument for Targeting Educational Risk (SIFTER; Anderson, 1989), which compares teachers' perceptions of classroom function for children with and without hearing loss, and the Assessment of Mainstream Progress (AMP; Chute & Nevins, 2006), which was developed specifically for children with cochlear implants to determine their readiness for and progress in mainstream classroom placements.

The learning environment itself must also be examined. The placement checklist of the PARC examines the physical environment, the general learning environment, the instructional style of the teacher, the school culture, and how well the learning environment is matched to the student's communication, language, and social needs through observation and interview with the classroom teacher. Available in three versions (preschool/kindergarten, elementary, and secondary), the placement checklists provide a basis for a guided discussion with teachers and administrators regarding appropriate classroom instruction and management that is conducive to learners who are D/HH. To specifically address the classroom listening environment, consider the Listening Inventory for Education (LIFE-R; Anderson, Smaldino, & Spangler, 2011), which assesses 10 typical classroom listening situations and five additional nonclassroom or social situations. Students in third grade and above can self-rate their ability to hear and understand in each situation. "Before LIFE" questions delve into student awareness of the classroom listening setting, and "After LIFE" questions provide a baseline of self-advocacy strategies. These checklists can be used whenever the student's classroom environment changes.

## Assessing Classroom Acoustics

An important part of the classroom assessment is consideration of classroom acoustics. The detrimental effects of excessive noise and reverberation times are well-documented and particularly affect children who are D/HH or otherwise have compromised auditory systems (e.g., auditory processing difficulties), children with limited English language proficiency, and children with attention deficits (American Academy of Audiology, 2011; American Speech-Language-Hearing Association, 2005; Bistafa & Bradley, 2000; Boothroyd, 2004; Crandell & Smaldino, 2000; Houtgast, 1981; Nelson & Soli, 2000; Nelson, Soli, & Seltz, 2002; Neuman & Hochberg, 1983). The American National Standards Institute (ANSI) and Acoustical Society of America (ASA) *Acoustical Performance Criteria, Design Requirements, and Guidelines for Schools* (ANSI/ASA, 2010) proposes guidelines with set recommended limits of 35 dBA for classroom ambient noise and a maximum of 0.6 seconds for reverberation time for permanent classrooms ≤10,000 cu ft. A reduced reverberation time of 0.4 seconds is also recommended for children with special listening needs (ANSI/ASA). Measuring classroom acoustics is a critical first step to designing appropriate accommodations for students who are D/HH. It is also important to identify and control excessive noise and reverberation in the classroom. Table 14.4 provides a checklist of common culprits in these areas. Noise and reverberation times can also be easily estimated with apps such as "Audio Tools" by Studio Six Digital (available from the iTunes store). These tools can be used by teachers, audiologists, SLPs, and parents. Many audiologists have access to sound level meters and reverberation time analysis equipment to verify acoustic conditions prior to requesting modifications or other treatments. Recommendations for hearing assistance technology should only be made after speech-in-noise assessments and classroom acoustic measurements are conducted.

**Table 14.4.**   Observation checklist for classroom noise and reverberation problems

A classroom observation is a preparatory step for making classroom acoustics measurements. The observation provides information about acoustic parameters of the classroom as well as the style of instruction, seating arrangement, and status of communication access.

Background noise

Listen in the classroom and check for the following; a "yes" is an indicator of potentially excessive levels of noise.

| Classroom features | Yes | No |
|---|---|---|
| Heating and ventilation system is audible. | | |
| Mechanical equipment must be turned off during important lessons. | | |
| Noise from playground is audible. | | |
| Noise from automobile traffic is audible. | | |
| Noise from air traffic is audible. | | |
| With heating and ventilation system turned off, sounds from other classrooms, learning spaces, or hallway are audible. | | |

Reverberation

Overall reverberation is determined by the volume of the room and the absorptive characteristics of the materials making up the classroom walls, floors, and ceilings. Check the classroom for the following surfaces; a "yes" is an indicator of potentially high reverberation times.

| Classroom features | Yes | No |
|---|---|---|
| A hard surface, flat ceiling without acoustic ceiling tiles | | |
| Ceiling height is over 11 feet/3.35 meters | | |
| Acoustic ceiling tiles have been painted | | |
| Walls are constructed of sound reflective materials (e.g., plasterboard, concrete, wood paneling) | | |
| Floors are constructed of sound reflective materials (e.g., concrete, tiles, wood) | | |

*Source:* From American Academy of Audiology. (2008, 2011). Clinical practice guidelines: Remote microphone hearing assistance technologies for children and youth from birth to 21 years.

Measuring *critical distance* is another important component of a classroom acoustics assessment. This term refers to the location where near (e.g., the area where the auditory signal is received directly by the listener without being contaminated by room surface reflections) and far (e.g., the area in which the auditory signal contains reflections from wall, floor, ceiling, and other room surfaces) sound fields meet. It is at this location that the effects of late reflections of speech begin to interfere with speech perception ability. Critical distance is calculated based on the room size and reverberation time of the classroom. Classroom teachers should be aware of the critical distance in their classrooms in order to optimize communication access for students. A protocol for conducting a classroom acoustics survey is contained in the American Academy of Audiology *Clinical Practice Guidelines: Remote Microphone Hearing Assistance Technologies for Children and Youth from Birth to 21 Years* (American Academy of Audiology, 2008, 2011).

## INTERVENTIONS TO PROMOTE ACADEMIC AND SOCIAL/COMMUNICATION SUCCESS

A primary purpose of the previously described assessments is to identify student and environmental deficiencies that require intervention plans. Typically, assessment outcomes and multidisciplinary discussions guide the development of intervention plans. These plans are then documented through the IEP process or through 504 plans for students who are not eligible for special education. The principles of RTI described by NASDSE (2005) highlight the ongoing cycle of intervention: assessment, instruction, monitoring, and adjustment. The core beliefs of this approach include the following:

- All children can be effectively taught using research-based, scientifically validated methods.

- Assessment is used for screening, diagnostic, and progress monitoring purposes.

- Intervention should be provided early and strategically.

- A multitier model of service delivery ensures optimal placements.

- Decisions are made through a data-driven, problem-solving approach.

- Student progress is monitored and used to inform instruction.

Earlier in this chapter, a variety of assessments from the Iowa Expanded Core Curriculum were discussed. These areas related to the student (e.g., audiology, self-advocacy, listening, communication access) and the learning environment (e.g., classroom acoustics, instructional and classroom management). These same categories can also be potential areas for intervention (see Table 14.5). For student-related goals, intervention often involves explaining new concepts (e.g., the audiogram, self-advocacy), discussing them, and checking for comprehension. Other areas might require a constructive approach in which a specific problem is identified and the student is encouraged to develop potential solutions and try them out. For example, if a teacher's voice is difficult to hear, the student could think of and practice ways to ask for a change in seating. In this way, both listening access and self-advocacy are addressed. Finally, it is important that students be involved in the development and implementation of their intervention plans whenever possible. Interventions and accommodations are often most effective when developed with student input. Examples of student-centered intervention resources are listed in Table 14.5.

Goals that are related to the learning environment are more often the concern of the adults in the situation. For example, reducing classroom noise levels, ensuring adequate participation, and encouraging self-advocacy can be addressed through the collaboration of classroom teachers and service providers. Teachers of the D/HH, educational audiologists, and other specialists often serve as consultants to teachers to ensure that recommendations are understood and implemented appropriately. Issues that involve facility management (e.g., excessively noisy heaters, installation of sound-field assistive devices; see Chapter 2) typically require the involvement of school principals or other administrators. The IEP/504 checklist in Appendix 14.1 is an effective guide for identifying accommodations and services. Service providers must become "pleasantly persistent" advocates for children who are D/HH so that agreed-upon goals and accommodations are implemented in a timely fashion.

**Table 14.5.** Student intervention options

| Area | Content | Resources |
|------|---------|-----------|
| Audiology | Understanding hearing and hearing deficiencies' impact on language development and communication access, and hearing assistance technologies | • *Knowledge Is Power,* Mississippi Bend Area Education Agency (2002), available from http://www.edaud.org <br> • *Demystifying Hearing Assistance Technology: A Guide for Service Providers and Consumers,* C.D. Davis, S.R. Atcherson, and M.L. Johnson (Northridge, CA: PEPNet West, National Center on Deafness, California State University, Northridge, 2007), available from http://www.wou.edu/~davisc <br> • Hearing aid manufacturer web sites |
| Self-determination and advocacy | Understanding self, disability rights, and personal responsibility | • Books on Deaf culture by Gallaudet University Press, http://gupress.gallaudet.edu/catalog.html <br> • *101 Ways to Encourage Self-Advocacy,* Clarke Mainstream Services (2010) <br> • *Self-Advocacy for Students Who Are Deaf or Hard of Hearing,* K. English (1997), available from http://www .phonakpro.com/us/b2b/en/pediatric/GAP.html <br> • *Guide to Access Planning,* available from http://www.phonakpro.com/us/b2b/en/pediatric/GAP.html <br> • *A Nuts and Bolts Guide to College Success for Deaf and Hard of Hearing Students,* J. Bourgeois and K. Treubig (Knoxville: University of Tennessee, 2002) |
| Communication access and listening | Listening skill development, and strategies and accommodations to mitigate adverse listening conditions | • There are numerous auditory skill curricula and programs available that are discussed in other chapters of this text; skill areas should be determined according to assessment data. <br> • See resources listed previously for self-determination, advocacy, strategies, and accommodations. <br> • *Guide to Access Planning,* available from http://www.phonakpro.com/us/b2b/en/pediatric/GAP.html |

It is often expected that the interventions and supports provided to children who are D/HH will be aligned with school district curriculum and, if adopted by the state, with the Common Core State Standards (National Governors Association and Council of Chief State School Officers, 2010). Thus IEP and 504 plan objectives are often embedded in the reading, writing, speaking, listening, and language standards of the English language arts and literacy areas. For example, an intervention that targets syntactic and morphological comprehension (e.g., understanding passive sentences such as "The boy was chased by the girl") can support the content standard of reading fluency for comprehension. Similarly, an auditory discrimination goal (e.g., identifying final consonants in spoken words) can be tied to the content standard for phonological awareness. These linkages help interventions become directly related to the general education curriculum and increase joint responsibility between classroom teachers and specialists. Additional examples of linking intervention to the content areas of reading and writing can be found in Chapters 12 and 13, respectively.

## EVIDENCE-BASED PRACTICE

The aforementioned intervention approaches are a mix of prior recommended practices and responses to the recent changes in the demographics of children who are D/HH. Empirical investigations of these approaches are currently in short supply. Although a review of the treatment efficacy literature is beyond the scope of this chapter, interested readers are referred to Spencer and Marschark (2010) for a thorough consideration of intervention practices for children who are D/HH.

The interventions described here have been developed through clinical expertise and collaboration among educators of children who are D/HH, educational audiologists, and speech pathologists. They are also based on well-accepted educational philosophies, and they include children and caregiver perspectives in the formation and implementation of goals and activities. For example, the Iowa Expanded Core Curriculum areas identify new and authentic ways to support student success based on adult and student input. Finally, the Contemporary Tiered Model of Supports and Services for D/HH Learners was developed in response to rapidly changing educational placements and performance. This model is evidence-based in that it is flexible enough to accommodate students with a wide variety of needs and abilities whether they receive special education services or not.

Finally, it must be acknowledged that the evidence generated by monitoring individual progress is child-specific rather that population-specific. As such, it is useful and essential for developing effective intervention plans but not for verifying efficacy across groups of students who are D/HH. However, substantial increases in the percentage of mainstream placements and high percentages of students who are making appropriate annual gains in academic areas clearly indicate that the combination of early hearing detection and intervention programs, improved hearing technologies, and inclusive educational and intervention practices is having very positive effects in this new era of service provision for children who are D/HH.

## Case Study: Luke

This case study illustrates how a classroom listening assessment can provide evidence of the potential benefits of a frequency-modulated (FM) system and how counseling can be used to address goals in the Iowa Expanded Core Curriculum areas of audiology, self-advocacy, and communication access accommodations.

### Background

Luke is 8 years old and in a third-grade general education classroom. He has a bilateral sensorineural hearing loss that slopes from mild at 250–1000 Hz to moderate-severe above 1000 Hz. Audibility index scores are .62 for the right ear and .65 for the left ear, estimating that Luke understands on average 64% of speech at typical conversational loudness levels. Unaided word recognition scores are 80% for the right ear and 78% for the left ear. He uses behind-the-ear hearing aids bilaterally but no FM at this time. His teacher reports that he is a good student and is performing within the average range for his grade level. However, she notes that he often misses spoken information and is not aware of what he misses. He receives services from the itinerant teacher of the deaf or hard of hearing (D/HH) for 1 hour each week. These services provide indi-vidual instruction on academic concepts that his teacher identifies as needing extra support.

### Assessment

The following list identifies the assessment tools used with Luke and the results of each one. His assessment was intended to answer the following questions: What are Luke's listening challenges? What are his strengths? What conclusions can be drawn? What other information is needed to understand Luke's learning environment? What recommendations would help Luke be more successful in his classroom?

1.  *Classroom observation summary:*

    Overall, the classroom environment is sufficient to support Luke. The areas that could ben-efit from some improvement include, first, reducing the teacher's movement around the room, as this is making it difficult for Luke to follow her voice when she is at a distance from him (e.g., the teacher was observed making an announcement while Luke was look-ing in a different direction and he had to be told by another student what she said), and second, helping Luke improve attention and listening in background noise (which was also made evident in other assessments as well as reports by the teacher).

2.  *Classroom participation questionnaire (CPQ):*

    Luke reported no difficulty listening to his teacher and some difficulty understanding peers. He primarily uses listening and spoken language, including some lip cues, when communicating. Luke reported some difficulty with how he feels when he is communicat-ing in class; however, he also reported a positive affect when working with others.

    Scores:

    Understanding teacher: 4.0 (desirable scores = 3.0–4.0)

    Understanding students: 3.3 (desirable scores = 3.0–4.0)

Positive affect: 4.0 (desirable scores = 3.0–4.0)

Negative affect: 2.0 (desirable scores = 1.0–2.0)

3.  *Children's auditory performance scale (CHAPS):*

    The CHAPS (Smoski, Brunt, & Tannahill, 1998) is a teacher-rated scale that compares the listening abilities of learners who are D/HH to their hearing peers in the areas of listening in noise, quiet, and ideal conditions; listening when additional inputs are present (e.g., visual, tactile); auditory memory sequencing; and auditory attention span. Luke's teacher reports that he has difficulty with most listening situations. Ratings revealed that he is in the "at risk" category for most listening situations, especially in noise and those that require auditory memory sequencing. His best listening condition is when he has multiple inputs such as watching the teacher's face while she is talking.

    Scores:

    Noise: 2.5

    Quiet: 0.5

    Ideal: +1.0

    Multiple: +1.0

    Memory: 3.5

    Attention: 1.5

    Total: 1.2

4.  *Functional listening evaluation (FLE) interpretation matrix (identification of spoken phrases):*

    Noise: 93% (quiet), 78% (noise)

    Distance: 96% (close), 76% (distance)

    Visual input: 91% (auditory-visual), 81% (auditory only)

    Most difficult condition: Distance/noise/auditory only = 45%

5.  *Classroom acoustics measurements:*

    Noise average: Unoccupied classroom with heating, ventilation, air conditioning (HVAC) off = 43 dBA; unoccupied classroom with HVAC on = 50 dBA; occupied classroom with HVAC off = 55 dBA; occupied classroom with HVAC on = 51 dBA

    Teacher voice average (with HVAC on): 57 dBA, speech-to-noise ratio (SNR) +6 dBA; at Luke's desk, SNR +9 dBA

    Reverberation time: 0.4 seconds

    Critical distance: 5 feet

## Analysis Considerations

*Summary of Listening Challenges*

- *Observation:* Luke is missing spoken information from his teacher when there is no visual access, when he is not aware that the teacher is speaking, and when his classroom is noisy.

- *CPQ:* Luke has some difficulty understanding other students and some frustration with communication access.

- *CHAPS:* Luke's poorest scores were for the noise and auditory memory sequencing areas.

- *FLE:* Luke has poorer scores for noise, distance, and situations without visual cues than other situations.

- *Classroom acoustics measurements:* Luke's classroom exceeds the maximum noise standard of 35 dBA established by the American National Standards Institute (ANSI) and the Acoustical Society of America (ASA). The SNR is poorer than the +15 dB recommended level. It was also noted that the recommended critical distance (5 feet) limits the teacher's movement around the classroom.

## Luke's Strengths

- His teacher reports that he is performing in the average range as compared to his peers and is not behind in any academic area.

- Luke feels pretty good about his communication in the classroom.

## Conclusions

- Classroom SNR needs to be improved.

- Luke would benefit from instruction regarding communication access and self-advocacy to gain responsibility for managing his accommodations.

- Academic test scores are needed.

- A self-advocacy assessment should be completed.

## Recommendations

1. The assessment evidence supports the need for improving auditory access for Luke in his classroom. As such, he is a candidate for an FM system to deliver the talker's voice (e.g., teacher and other students) directly through his hearing aids (see Chapter 2 for more information). This will help him overcome the problems associated with classroom noise, distance from the talker, and lack of visual access to the talker. The educational audiologist should discuss the FLE results with Luke to illustrate how these factors affect his ability to understand the person speaking. An FM system should be discussed and demonstrated to engage Luke's support for a trial with the technology. The trial will include fitting and verification. The FLE distance conditions for noise and no visual access should be repeated with the FM system to validate the improvement in understanding and ease of listening. If there are no contraindications (e.g., lack of support, problems with self-esteem or motivation), the use of the FM system should be added to his individualized education program (IEP) as assistive technology needed to access instruction and content standards. The educational audiologist will provide orientation and training in the use of the FM system for Luke, his teachers, and others who may also use the FM system.

2. Counseling should be provided to address three areas: 1) Luke's difficulty understanding peers, 2) his feelings about communicating with peers, and 3) the need to develop solutions to problem situations. Luke does not always recognize that he has misunderstood

until he responds to a question or makes a statement that is slightly off topic or one that has already been made. Lessons should be provided to help Luke better understand his hearing situation and the resulting communication challenges.

3.  Assessment of self-advocacy skills using the *Audiology Self-Advocacy Checklist* (elementary level; Johnson & Spangler, 2014) should be followed by lessons from the *Self-Advocacy for Students Who Are Deaf and Hard of Hearing* curriculum (English, 1997).

4.  The results and recommendations should be reviewed with Luke's classroom teacher and other pertinent school staff, as well as his parents. These discussions will help them understand his communication challenges, allow them to support his attempts to address them, and provide basic communication accommodations at school and home.

5.  Luke's auditory and communication access should be reviewed at monthly intervals by discussing how well his strategies are affecting his classroom communication.

## FUTURE DIRECTIONS

Educational services for children who are D/HH will continue to evolve as the improved capabilities of these students become evident in classroom performance and standardized testing. Four suggestions are highlighted to further enhance this process.

Foremost, there is an urgent need for more research to identify effective, evidenced-based practices. These explicit instructional practices (see Chapters 12 and 13) must be directly applicable to the variety of communication modalities used by students who are D/HH, specific to educational settings (e.g., general education classrooms, itinerant services), and appropriate for students from kindergarten through high school.

There is also a need for broader recognition of the much-improved academic potential of learners who are D/HH by school administrators and classroom teachers. This recognition is essential for ensuring that students receive the accommodations and adjustments needed to optimize both classroom learning and social development.

Unique complications must be anticipated when children use hearing instruments. As educational technology expands in classrooms, it may actually become disruptive—rather than helpful—for students who are D/HH if not managed properly. For example, computer-based instruction will require special connections to accommodate personal hearing instruments and/or hearing assistive technology and provide a clear signal (e.g., without interference, background noise, others talking). Captioning, whether live or remote, for speech, music, video, and other auditory inputs is also necessary for many students. Whereas modern hearing technologies can "level the playing field" in many situations, it is important that the benefits of educational technologies be fully available to all students who are D/HH.

Finally, general and special educators will require substantial support as they integrate children who are D/HH into their classrooms. In particular, in-service education and continuous "just-in-time" support for general education classroom teachers must be built into schedules so that teachers can implement recommendations, accommodations, and instructional strategies appropriately and effectively.

## SUGGESTED READINGS

Spencer, P., & Marschark, M. (2010). *Evidenced-based practices in educating deaf and hard of hearing students.* New York, NY: Oxford University Press.

This informative textbook should be required reading for every professional in deaf education. It carefully describes and documents practices that have research support and dispels myths for those practices for which there is inadequate evidence of effectiveness.

Wehmeyer, M., Palmer, S., Agran, M., Mithaug, D., & Martin, J. (2000). Promoting causal agency: The self-determined learning model of instruction. *Exceptional Children, 66*(4), 439–453.

The development of self-advocacy skills is identified as one of the expanded core curriculum areas by Iowa and other states. Wehmeyer and colleagues provide an instructional model to support student self-advocacy skills as part of self-determination. Through this model, students develop relevant goals, make decisions and choices, solve problems, self-advocate, and evaluate their progress.

## LEARNING ACTIVITIES

1. Meet with a local teacher for children who are D/HH. Ask her to consider where children on her caseload fit into the Tiered Model of Supports and Services in Figure 14.1. Also ask whether there are students who are not receiving support and students who are on 504 plans. Who is monitoring those students?

2. Conduct a classroom acoustics survey using the form from the *Remote Microphone Hearing Assistance Technologies for Children and Youth from Birth to 21 Years* (American Academy of Audiology, 2011). How does the classroom measure up to the ANSI/ASA standard? What recommendations would you make?

3. Contact a local school that has children who are D/HH and ask to interview a parent about their personal journey with their son or daughter. Be sure to discuss experiences as they navigated the early hearing detection and intervention system, early intervention services, and current educational services. How might this parent's journey influence your future practice?

4. Visit the Hands and Voices web site (http://www.handsandvoices.org). This web site contains descriptions of personal experiences being a parent of or living as a person who is deaf or hard of hearing. These journeys can affect our perceptions of family priorities and opportunities. The web site also contains other useful articles, tools, and resources that support educational advocacy.

5. Visit pepnet 2 (http://www.pepnet.org), which is a U.S. Department of Education funded project that supports transition activities and resources for students who are D/HH to prepare them for postsecondary education and employment. The web site contains e-learning opportunities as well as relevant resources for teachers and parents.

## REFERENCES

American Academy of Audiology. (2008, 2011). *Clinical practice guidelines: Remote microphone hearing assistance technologies for children and youth from birth to*

*21 years.* Retrieved November 5, 2014, from http://www.audiology.org/publications -resources/document-library/hearing-assistance-technologies

American National Standards Institute (ANSI) and Acoustical Society of America (ASA). (2010). *American national standard: Acoustical performance criteria, design requirements, and guidelines for schools, part 1, permanent schools, and part 2, relocatable classroom factors.* ANSI/ASA S12.60-2010. Melville, NY: Acoustical Society of America.

American Speech-Language-Hearing Association (2005). Acoustics in educational settings: Position statement. Retrieved July 11, 2015 from http://www.asha.org/policy/ PS2005-00028.htm

Anderson, K. (1989). *Screening instrument for targeting educational risk (SIFTER).* Retrieved October 14, 2014, from http://successforkidswithhearingloss.com/tests

Anderson, K., Smaldino, J., & Spangler, C. (2011). *Listening Inventory for Education (LIFE)—Revised.* Retrieved October 14, 2014, from http://successforkidswithhearing loss.com/tests

Antia, S., Jones, P., Luckner, J., Kreimeyer, K., & Reed, S. (2011). Social outcomes of students who are deaf and hard of hearing in general education classrooms. *Exceptional Children, 77*(4), 489–504.

Antia, S., Jones, P., Reed, S., & Kreimeyer, K. (2009). Academic status and progress of deaf and hard-of-hearing students in general education classrooms. *Journal of Deaf Studies and Deaf Education, 14*(3), 293–311.

Antia, S., Sabers, D., & Stinson, M. (2007). Validity and reliability of the classroom participation questionnaire with deaf and hard of hearing students in public schools. *Journal of Deaf Studies and Deaf Education, 12,* 158–171.

Bistafa, S., & Bradley, J. (2000). Reverberation time and maximum background-noise level for classrooms from a comparative study of speech intelligibility metrics. *Journal of the Acoustical Society of America, 107,* 861–875.

Boothroyd, A. (2004). Room acoustics and speech reception: A model and some implications. In D. Fabry & C. DeConde Johnson (Eds.), *ACCESS: Achieving clear communication employing sound solutions—2003* (pp. 207–216). Stafa, Switzerland: Phonak.

Chute, P.M., & Nevins, M.E. (2006). *Assessment of Mainstream Progress (AMP): School professionals working with children with cochlear implants.* San Diego, CA: Plural.

Crandell, C.C., & Smaldino, J.J. (2000). Classroom acoustics for children with normal hearing and with hearing impairment. *Language, Speech, and Hearing Services in Schools, 31,* 362–370.

English, K. (1997). *Self-advocacy for students who are deaf and hard of hearing.* Austin, TX: Pro Ed.

Gresham, F.M., & Elliott, S.N. (1990). *Social skills rating system.* Circle Pines, MN: American Guidance Service.

Houtgast, T. (1981). The effect of ambient noise on speech intelligibility in classrooms. *Applied Acoustics, 14,* 15–25.

Individuals with Disabilities Education Improvement Act (IDEA) of 2004, PL 108-446, 20 U.S.C. §§ 1400 *et seq.*

Iowa Department of Education, Bureau of Student Family Support Services. (2010, August). *The expanded core curriculum for students who are deaf and hard of hearing.* Des Moines, IA: Author.

Johnson, C.D. (2006). *Performance levels vs. growth: A comparison of Colorado assessment data for students who are deaf and hard of hearing.* Alexandria, VA: National Association of State Directors of Special Education (NASDSE).

Johnson, C.D. (2010a). Making a case for classroom listening assessment. *Seminars in Hearing, 31,* 177–187.

Johnson, C.D. (2010b). *Placement and readiness checklists (PARC).* Retrieved November-ber 5, 2014, from http://www .ADEvantage .com/resources .html

Johnson, C.D. (2011). *Common children's phrases.* Retrieved May 12, 2015, from http:// www.ADEvantage.com/resources.html

Johnson, C.D. (2013). *Functional listening evaluation.* Retrieved May 12, 2015, from http://www.ADEvantage.com/resources.html

Johnson, C. DeConde, & Seaton, J.B. (2012). Educational considerations for students who are deaf and hard of hearing. In *Educational audiology handbook* (2nd ed.). Clifton Park, NY: Cengage Learning.

Johnson, C.D., & Spangler, C. (2014). *Audiology self-advocacy checklist.* Retrieved May 12, 2015, from http://www.ADEvantage.com

Lauer, S. (2004). Wireless solutions—The state of the art and future of FM technology for the hearing impaired consumer. In D. Fabry and C.D. Johnson (Eds.), *ACCESS—Achieving clear communication employing sound solutions, 2003: Proceedings of the first international conference* (pp. 31–37). Stafa, Switzerland: Phonak.

National Association of State Directors of Special Education. (2005). *Response to intervention.* Alexandria, VA: Author.

National Governors Association Center for Best Practices and the Council of Chief State School Officers. (2010). *Common Core State Standards Initiative.* Retrieved October 5, 2014, from http://www.corestandards.org

National Institute of Child Health and Human Development. (2000). *Report of the National Reading Panel. Teaching children to read: An evidenced-based assessment of the scientific research literature on reading and its implications for reading instruction, NIH publication no. 00-4769.* Washington, DC: U.S. Government Printing Office.

Nelson, P., & Soli, S. (2000). Acoustical barriers to learning: Children at risk in every classroom. *Language, Speech, and Hearing Services in Schools, 31,* 356–361.

Nelson, P., Soli, S., & Seltz, A. (2002). *Classroom acoustics II: Acoustical barriers to learning.* Melville, NY: Acoustical Society of America.

Neuman, A., & Hochberg, I. (1983). Children's perception of speech in reverberation. *Journal of the Acoustical Society of America, 73,* 2145–2149.

No Child Left Behind Act of 2001, PL 107-110, 115 Stat. 1425, 20 U.S.C. §§ 6301 *et seq.*

Rehabilitation Act of 1973, PL 93-112, 29 U.S.C. §§ 701 *et seq.*

Smoski, W., Brunt, M., & Tannahill, J.C. (1998). *Children's auditory performance scale.* Educational Audiology Association. Retrieved October 5, 2014, from http://www.edaud.org

Spencer, P., & Marschark, M. (2010). *Evidenced-based practices in educating deaf and hard of hearing students.* New York, NY: Oxford University Press.

Stelmachowicz, P. (2005). Pediatric amplification: Past, present, and future. In R. Seewald & J. Bamford (Eds.), *A sound foundation through early amplification, 2004: Proceedings of the third international conference* (pp. 27–40). Stafa, Switzerland: Phonak.

Traxler, C.B. (2000). Measuring up to performance standards in reading and mathematics: Achievement of selected deaf and hard of hearing students in the national norming of the ninth edition Stanford Achievement Test. *Journal of Deaf Studies and Deaf Education, 5,* 337–348.

U.S. Department of Education. (1995). *Seventeenth annual report to U.S. Congress on the implementation of the Individuals with Disabilties Education Act (Table AB2).* Retrieved October 5, 2014, from http://www2.ed.gov/pubs/OSEP95AnlRpt/ch1c .html

U.S. Department of Education. (2010). *Thirty-second annual report to U.S. Congress on the implementation of the Individuals with Disabilities Education Act (p. 46).* Retrieved May 12, 2015, from http://www2.ed.gov/about/reports/annual/osep/2010/parts-b-c/32nd-idea-arc.pdf

Wehmeyer, M., Palmer, S., Agran, M., Mithaug, D., & Martin, J. (2000). Promoting causal agency: The self-determined learning model of instruction. *Exceptional Children, 66*(4), 439–453.

Zwolan, T. (2009). Cochlear implants. In J. Katz, L. Medwetsky, R. Burkhard, & L. Hood (Eds.), *Handbook of clinical audiology* (pp. 912–933). Baltimore, MD: Lippincott Williams & Wilkins.

**APPENDIX 14.1**

# IEP/504 Checklist: Accommodations and Modifications for Students Who Are Deaf or Hard of Hearing

Name: _____ Date: _____

Note: Accommodations provide access to communication and instruction and are appropriate for 504 or individualized education program (IEP) services; modifications alter the content, the expectations, and the evaluation of academic performance and usually require an IEP amplification.

## ACCOMMODATIONS

- Personal hearing instrument (hearing aid, cochlear implant, bone anchored, tactile device)
- Personal hearing assistance technology (HAT; includes hearing aid and HAT)
- HAT only (without personal hearing instrument)
- Classroom sound distribution system (CADS)

## ASSISTIVE DEVICES ACCOMMODATIONS

- Videophone or text phone
- Alerting devices
- Other _____

## COMMUNICATION ACCOMMODATIONS

- Priority seating arrangement: _____
- Ensure student's attention prior to speaking
- Reduce auditory distractions (background noise)
- Reduce visual distractions
- Allow student time/assistance to locate speaker in small or large group setting

- Enhance speechreading conditions (avoid hands in front of face, mustaches well-trimmed, no gum chewing)
- Present information in simple, structured, sequential manner
- Enunciate speech clearly
- Allow extra time for processing information
- Repeat or rephrase information when necessary
- Frequently check for understanding
- Use speech to text software (speech recognition)
- Provide interpreting (e.g., American Sign Language [ASL], signed English, cued speech, oral)

## INSTRUCTIONAL ACCOMMODATIONS AND MODIFICATIONS

- Visual supplements (overheads, charts, vocabulary lists, lecture outlines)
- Interactive whiteboard (e.g., Smart Board, Mimio)
- Classroom captioning (CART, CPrint, TypeWell)
- Captioning and/or scripts for television, videos, movies
- Buddy system for notes, extra explanations, and directions
- Check for understanding of information
- Downtime or break from listening/watching
- Extra time to complete assignments
- Step-by-step directions
- Interpreting (ASL, signed English, cued speech, oral)
- Speech to text software (speech recognition)
- Tutoring
- Notetaker
- Direct instruction (indicate classes): _____

## PHYSICAL ENVIRONMENT ACCOMMODATIONS

- Noise/reverberation reduction (carpet and other sound absorption materials) reASA/ANSI S 12.60 2010
- Special lighting
- Room design modifications: _____
- Flashing fire alarms/smoke detectors

## CURRICULAR MODIFICATIONS

- Modified reading assignments (shorten length, adapt phonics-based instruction)
- Modified written assignments (shorten length, adjust evaluation criteria)
- Extra practice
- Preteach, teach, postteach vocabulary, concepts
- Strategies to adapt oral/aural curriculum/instruction to accommodate reduced auditory access
- Supplemental materials to reinforce concepts of curriculum
- Alternative curriculum
- Expanded core curriculum:
    - Advocacy/self-determination
    - Audiology (understanding hearing loss and resulting communication accommodations, technology options [hearing assistive technology, connectivity])
    - Assistive technology
    - Communication/pragmatic language
    - Deaf studies
    - Disability rights
    - Functional skills
    - Family education
    - Listening skill development
    - Sign language
    - Social-emotional skills
    - Transition planning

## EVALUATION ACCOMMODATIONS AND MODIFICATIONS

- Reduce quantity of tests
- Alternate tests or methods
- Reading assistance with tests for clarification of directions, language of test questions (nonreading items)
- Extra time
- Special setting
- Other

## OTHER NEEDS/CONSIDERATIONS

- Counseling
- Family supports and training
- Sign language instruction for family members
- Peers who are deaf or hard of hearing (D/HH)
- Role models who are D/HH
- Recreational/social opportunities
- Transition services:
  - Disability rights
  - Financial assistance
  - Linkages to higher education, job training
  - Vocational rehabilitation services
- Other _____

_____

_____

*Source:* From Johnson, C.D., and Seaton, J. (2012). *Educational Audiology Handbook* (2nd ed., p. 528–529). Cengage Delmar Learning; reprinted by permission.

# Afterword

Mary Pat Moeller, David J. Ertmer, and Carol Stoel-Gammon

After hundreds of years of educating children who are deaf or hard of hearing (D/HH) and engaging in simmering controversies about the ways in which children should communicate, we have reached the dawn of a new era in helping children achieve their potential. This era has emerged mainly because of new technologies; increased knowledge about spoken and sign language development; new insights into children's needs in the areas of theory of mind, literacy, and social development; and opportunities to introduce language within an age range when the brain is naturally organizing itself to receive and express meaning. It is indeed an era of optimism, in which we can work together to ensure that all children and families reap the benefits of these advancements and their own hard work. These exciting times give us much hope, yet pressing challenges keep us searching for ever-better solutions.

As we close this volume, we want to reflect on some "big picture considerations" that should guide our clinical/educational practice with this current generation of children.

First, it is important to recognize that technologies (e.g., newborn hearing screening, digital hearing instruments, and cochlear implants) have advanced rapidly over the past 15 years and, in many ways, outpaced research into the effectiveness of interventions. This means that frontline clinical and educational efforts often led the way in discovering and testing new intervention approaches, while research in treatment efficacy lagged behind. Each of the chapter authors has pointed to the gaps and limitations in evidence supporting specific approaches. Limitations in evidence are not surprising, given that early identification and other technological advancements have only recently become standard practices. Fortunately, there has been a resurgence of interest within the scientific community in documenting factors that influence communicative, academic, and psychosocial outcomes in children who are D/HH. Early identification, in fact, has enabled researchers to examine linguistic development at earlier stages than ever before, giving us a better grasp on factors that really matter within intervention programs.

This brings us to the second consideration: Service providers must keep abreast of the emergent body of research. A number of large-scale, longitudinal research collaborations are underway both in the United States and internationally. These studies circumvent some of the historical problems in our literature of small and/or restricted samples of children who are D/HH. Collectively, they suggest that average outcomes are improving, yet many children continue to lag markedly behind typically developing peers in linguistic and academic development. These disparate outcomes suggest the value of individualized approaches to intervention, which is our third consideration. Service providers must be skilled at identifying and applying intervention approaches that make the most sense for each individual child and family on a case-by-case basis. The optimal intervention approach for one family may be quite different from another. In other words, "one size does not fit all." Disparate outcomes also point to the pressing need to continue to gather treatment efficacy data so that many more children experience social and academic success.

The fourth consideration focuses on the importance of incorporating interdisciplinary research as a guide to our practices. Many of the intervention strategies used with children who are D/HH and their families have empirical support from studies in allied fields (e.g., typical development, infant mental health, special education, speech-language pathology, pediatric audiology). This suggests that service providers need to recognize the inherently interdisciplinary nature of our practice and engage in transdisciplinary reading and discussion to enrich our interventions by applying the current best evidence available.

A fifth consideration is the value of recognizing that evidence-based practice involves both a science and an art. The "science" involves the process of continually evaluating and integrating research evidence with practitioner expertise. The "art" entails working in partnership with families and supporting them with sensitivity and openness as they navigate the complexities of the various interventions to find individualized solutions that promote the child's potential in communication, language, and literacy. This means that service providers must become skilled consumers of evidence from clinical and translational research, carefully evaluating the quality of studies so that appropriate conclusions are drawn. In addition, a commitment to evidence-based practice requires that providers recognize when their own skills represent an appropriate match to the individual needs of the family and when there is a need to recruit additional expertise to meet family goals. Service providers also need to become skilled at supporting families in clarifying their own goals and support needs. This is an iterative process that accommodates and shifts as family goals alter in response to the child's changing needs. Finally, service providers must learn to effectively support the informed decision-making process with families, recognizing that ultimately the decision-making authority rests with the family. Multiple authors in this text have highlighted the value of family-centered intervention, developmentally appropriate educational environments for preschoolers, visual-gestural language and signing systems, as well as new approaches for stimulating listening, spoken language, literacy, and social-cognitive skills. They have illustrated ways in which children's abilities can be optimized within educational settings and through innovative routes (e.g., Internet therapy).

A final consideration is the fact that a number of broad, societal challenges remain when considering the needs of special populations of children who are D/HH. As unified professionals, we need to work toward reducing the number of newborns who are lost to follow-up after newborn hearing screening, increasing and diversifying services for children who come from economically disadvantaged environments, and ensuring that bilingual children receive services that enable the acquisition of the linguistic skills they need for success at home and in school. Above all, the clinical and educational efforts of this new era must be based on research that explores the efficacy and efficiency of various intervention practices while expanding knowledge to support the development of new and innovative approaches aimed at enhancing the capabilities of today's children who are D/HH.

We have many reasons for optimism, but further progress will only come from untiring efforts to optimize the abilities of every child who is deaf or hard of hearing. As Anne Frank said, "How wonderful it is that nobody need wait a single moment before starting to improve the world." Her statement fits our contemporary era in intervention and education for children who are D/HH. As long as we are responsive to the "changing tides," we join a movement that is indeed improving the world for children who are D/HH and their families.

# Key Words and Definitions

**Acoustic highlighting**  Techniques used to enhance the auditory salience of spoken language features, including suprasegmental, segmental, and linguistic.

**Active learning**  A method of instruction in which the learner is expected to be engaged in acquiring new knowledge and problem solving.

**Activity-based intervention**  An approach focused on using authentic learning opportunities that are embedded in daily activities.

**Affective theory of mind**  Ability to recognize emotions in oneself and others, to reflect on one's own emotions, to regulate one's emotions, and to empathize with others.

**Alphabetic principle**  The basic idea that written language is a code in which letters represent the sounds of spoken words.

**American Sign Language (ASL)**  A visual-gestural language that uses hand shapes, varied body positions, facial expressions, and hand/body movements to convey meaning and express thoughts and ideas. ASL is an independent language that has its own grammar and syntax. It has no written or spoken form.

**Analytic auditory development**  A type of listening practice in which children learn to distinguish between speech sounds and speech features, often using minimal pair words (e.g., "cat" versus "cap"; "meat" versus "mat").

**Appraisal**  Personal judgment made about an individual, group, issue, or situation that involves a degree of evaluation based on knowledge, values, and experience.

**Audibility**  Extent of child's access to the speech spectrum, including through technology.

**Authentic assessments**  Flexible processes of systematically recording observations of behaviors over time in natural settings.

**Autobiographical memory**  A form of memory that moves beyond recall of experienced events to integrate perspective, interpretation, and evaluation across self, other, and time to create a personal history.

**Background knowledge**  What an individual already knows about a topic.

**Barrier games**  Games where two players who are separated by a barrier must arrange materials in exactly the same configuration, using only spoken language exchanges. These games address use of specific, not vague, language and taking another's perspective.

**Bilingual (ASL and English)**  A language acquisition and communication approach that utilizes American Sign Language and English in the spoken, written, signed, or cued form.

**Bimodal**  A combination of acoustic (hearing aid) and electric (cochlear implant) stimulation of the auditory system.

**Blended framework**  The integration of practices from the fields of early childhood, early childhood special education, and deaf education.

**Boss Your Brain techniques**  A set of working memory and executive function strategies that enhance retention and retrieval of information.

**Canonical babbling**  Nonmeaningful productions formed of consonant-vowel syllables (e.g., "baba" or "mido"); these usually appear around 7 to 9 months in children who are developing typically.

**Capacity building**  A primary goal of early intervention where providers seek to recognize and build on family strengths, working in partnership to increase the capability of the family to adjust to the child's diagnosis and promote developmental growth.

**Chronic**  Continual rather than episodic or time bounded.

**Classroom acoustics**  Noise and reverberation characteristics that affect listening in the classroom.

**Coaching**  A form of instruction in which the learner is supported by someone with greater expertise as they develop competencies.

**Codec**  A computer device or software that encodes and decodes digital data streams.

**Cognitive theory of mind**  Ability to attribute mental states—beliefs, intents, desires, pretending, knowledge, and so forth—to oneself and others and to understand that others have mental states that are different from one's own.

**Common Core State Standards**  Knowledge and skills for K–12 education developed and adopted by the National Governors Association and Council of Chief State School Officers, 2010.

**Communication access**  Considers visual, auditory, and other parameters of classrooms and educational environments that may facilitate or deter learning.

**Communication approaches**   The typical ways in which people who have limited hearing communicate (e.g., listening or speaking, watching and signing, cueing).

**Communication continuum**   A method for describing how children use auditory and visual means to understand and use language.

**Communication temptation**   An enticing situation set up by the clinician whose purpose is to prompt (elicit) communication from the child.

**Complementarity**   A term used to describe the beneficial interaction of hearing aid and cochlear implant inputs to a listener.

**Comprehension**   The active process of constructing meaning from text; it involves accessing previous knowledge, understanding vocabulary and concepts, making inferences, and linking key ideas.

**Conferencing**   A one-to-one strategy integral to a writer's workshop approach in which the teacher confers with the student writer to work on the processes and skills necessary to create a written text.

**Constructivist educational philosophy**   A philosophy of instruction that seeks to involve the learner in constructing meaning and personal understanding; intended to encourage critical thinking and independent learning.

**Context clues**   The words and sentences occurring before and after an unknown word or phrase that provide hints about its meaning.

**Contingent responses**   Caregiver social responses that are closely linked to the child's utterance or behavior.

**Criterion-referenced measures**   Child's behaviors are compared to specific learning objectives or performance expectations rather than test norms.

**Cross-cultural competence**   Knowledge and skills needed by providers to appropriately partner with families from culturally and linguistically diverse (CLD) backgrounds.

**Cued speech**   A sound-based visual communication system that incorporates a number of hand shapes placed in a variety of different positions on or around the face that, when combined with speech, give individuals who are deaf or hard of hearing visual access to all of the sounds of speech. Cue systems have currently been created to represent 38 different languages. North American English Cued Speech incorporates eight hand shapes placed in four possible positions to represent all of the phonemes of spoken English.

**Cultural reciprocity**   A process of dialogue where professionals discuss with families cultural values and practices so as to appreciate their perspectives and address them in early intervention.

**Cumulative practice**   The additive benefit of repeatedly performing a skill over time.

**Curriculum framework**   A set of concepts or a structure of organizing the many elements and processes used to create learning environments.

**Deaf community**   Deaf and hard-of-hearing individuals who share common goals, similar life experiences, common values, and perhaps most importantly, a common language to convey thoughts, ideas, and information.

**Deaf culture**   Incorporates the behaviors, social boundaries, beliefs, shared history, art, literature, and valued institutions that are shared by communities of individuals who are deaf and hard of hearing.

**Deaf mentor**   A trained deaf or hard-of-hearing adult who acts as a guide to hearing families who are raising deaf or hard-of-hearing children to help them in learning American Sign Language, learning about Deaf culture, and experiencing the Deaf community in a safe and comfortable way.

**Developmental dyssynchrony**   Uneven rates of development across various capacities of the child (as often seen in the presence of sensory disability such as deafness or blindness).

**Developmentally appropriate practice**   The outcome of a process of teacher decision making that is based on knowledge and application of principles for how children learn and grow.

**Discourse/text macrostructure**   The global meaning or gist of the discourse and the overall organization of the discourse.

**Discourse/text microstructure**   The vocabulary, syntactic structures, and cohesive linguistics elements (pronouns, connective words) used in discourse.

**Early intervention**   Providing hearing instruments and intervention services to infants and toddlers to minimize or prevent communication delays.

**Effect size**   A quantitative measure of the strength of an effect, such as how much more effective one intervention approach is compared to another.

**Electroacoustic measurement**   The process of measuring the sound output of an amplifier such as a hearing aid.

**Embellishments**   Strategies parents incorporate throughout the day to maximize communication and auditory opportunities and make them accessible.

**Encoding**   The ability to translate spoken language into print by employing knowledge of sound–symbol (phoneme–grapheme) correspondences.

**Evidence-based practice**   An intervention approach in which research evidence is integrated with service provider expertise and client preferences and values.

**Exemplars**  Representative examples of writing performance at a particular grade or stage of development against which other texts are evaluated.

**Expanded core curriculum**  Content areas that are unique to the education of students who are deaf and hard of hearing (i.e., listening and speech, audiology, sign language, self-advocacy, self-determination, Deaf culture).

**Expansions**  Responses that repeat part or all of the child's previous utterance and add to it with semantic content, grammatical cues, or both.

**Explicit instruction**  Overtly teaching the steps required to complete a task.

**Expository text**  A form of written discourse that functions to describe, explain, or inform.

**Family-centered early intervention**  Approaches that seek to build on family strengths and support families' efforts to gain confidence and competence in parenting their children who are deaf or hard of hearing.

**First-order theory of mind**  Predicting what someone is thinking/feeling.

**Fluency**  The ability to perform reading skills such as naming letters, reading words, and reading connected text quickly, smoothly, and automatically.

**Functional**  Able to achieve a specified purpose and continue to do so (opposite = dysfunctional).

**Functional listening**  Considers the impact of typical classroom variables such as noise, reverberation, distance from the talker, and lack of visual access on a learner's ability to access verbal information.

**Habilitative intervention**  Efforts to facilitate further growth in listening, language, and speech development in children who are D/HH and acquiring some spoken language in the context of everyday activities.

**HAT (hearing assistance technology)**  Any device that enhances sound detection or provides a substitute for sound through visual or tactile input.

**Health literacy**  The degree to which individuals have the capacity to obtain, process, and understand basic health information and services needed to make appropriate health decisions.

**Hearing status**  Refers to whether a person has full hearing, has limited hearing such as a hard-of-hearing person, or is deaf.

**Hundred languages**  Refers to children using a variety of media, such as cloth, textiles, paint, wire, clay, wood, or dance, to express themselves and represent their ideas.

**Incidental learning**   Learning that is acquired spontaneously through natural exposure (as opposed to didactic learning, which is adult directed and occurs in teaching situations).

**Inconsistent access**   Intermittent problems in hearing and understanding spoken language due to distance from speaker, background noise, or other factors.

**Individualized approach to intervention**   Meeting the diverse communication, cultural, and learning needs of the child and family.

**Interpersonal theory of mind**   Cognitive and affective theory of mind for others.

**Intrapersonal theory of mind**   Cognitive and affective theory of mind for oneself.

**Invented spelling**   An attempt to encode a word based on a young writer's knowledge of sound–symbol correspondences that typically results in a nonstandard representation.

**Language Environment Analysis (LENA)**   A wearable digital language processor and associated software that can be used to analyze features of a child's own speech and language environment.

**Literacy**   The ability to read and write for a variety of purposes.

**Manually Coded English (MCE) systems**   Visual communication methods created to present English visually on the hands. Unlike "natural" Deaf sign languages, MCE systems typically follow the grammar and syntax of spoken English and are typically expressed using simultaneous communication (signing and speaking at the same time). Examples of MCE systems include Signed Exact English (SEE) and Conceptually Accurate Signed English.

**Megabyte**   One million bytes of information. Megabytes per second (MB/s) is the measure of the speed of an Internet connection.

**Mental time travel**   The ability to think about one's past and future.

**Metacognition**   Awareness of what one knows and doesn't know about a topic, about strategies for doing tasks, and about when to use the strategies; one's control or regulation of learning—planning, monitoring/evaluating, and revising; an aspect of intrapersonal theory of mind.

**Modality**   The sensory system that is used while learning or while teaching. Modalities are typically described as visual, auditory, or tactile.

**Model**   A means of conceptualizing an issue that has a theoretical basis and privileges some processes, actions, and explanations over others.

**Motivation**   An internal state that arouses us to action, pushes us in particular directions, and keeps us engaged in certain activities.

**Multiple means of expression**   A principle supporting children's ability to express themselves using multiple formats to demonstrate what they know or to inform others of their preferences.

**Multiple means of representation**   A principle supporting children's ability to participate and understand classroom content by attending to individual ability levels and learning styles.

**Narrative text**   A form of written discourse that relates an event or a series of events that can be fiction or nonfiction.

**Neuroplasticity**   The brain's ability to reorganize itself by forming new neural connections.

**Ontology**   A branch of philosophy and research that focuses on "being" rather than "knowing."

**Osseointegrated**   Anything that is implanted into bone and becomes fused into it; for audiology applications, it refers specifically to a fixture implanted in the skull that can be attached to a bone conduction hearing aid.

**Participatory practices**   Those that actively engage the family in activities that strengthen existing competencies while responding to their self-identified needs.

**Phonics**   The systematic process of teaching sound–symbol relationships to decode words.

**Phonological awareness**   The ability to manipulate the sound system of spoken language, including words, rhymes, syllables, onset-rimes, and phonemes.

**Phonological system**   The organization of the sound system of a language, including phonemes (consonants, vowels), suprasegmental features (stress, intonation, rhythm), and phonotactic properties (permissible sequences of phonemes).

**Piggyback technique**   A method for creating songs where invented lyrics are sung to the tune of a familiar melody.

**Pragmatic auditory development**   Practice in applying strategies to avoid communication breakdowns (e.g., "Let's move to a quieter area.") or to repair breakdowns after they occur (e.g., "I thought I heard you say Wednesday. What happened on Wednesday?").

**Prelinguistic vocal development**   Stages of early speech development that precede and overlap with early word production.

**Prelinguistic vocalizations**   Nonmeaningful vocalizations produced prior to the appearance of first words, usually following a predictable sequence of stages between birth and 12 months of age.

**Process writing**   The overlapping phases of text production that include planning, generating, drafting, and revising.

**Reauditorization**   Verbal rehearsal by talking to oneself, either aloud or silently.

**Rehabilitative intervention**   Efforts to facilitate listening, language, and speech development in children who make slow or limited progress in these areas after receiving their hearing instruments.

**Relational practices**   Provider behaviors such as compassion, active listening, empathy, and partnership-building skills, as well as sensitivity toward families and cross-cultural competence.

**Relationship-focused**   A term that reinforces the need to focus in early intervention on the interactions between family members and children, which should be accomplished by forming parent–professional partnerships.

**Remote site**   The location of the receiver of Internet therapy.

**Robust hearing experience**   The amount of time that a child has had auditory access to speech at conversational intensity levels.

**Rubric**   A scoring tool for assessing writing that is based on a set of criteria or standards.

**Second-order theory of mind**   Predicting what someone is thinking or feeling about what someone else is thinking or feeling.

**Self-efficacy**   The strength of parents' *beliefs* about their own ability to parent, learn, or complete certain tasks.

**Self-reflection**   A strategy of using guided questions and introspection to evaluate one's own behaviors, values, and effectiveness.

**Sight words**   Words that are read fluently and automatically at first sight.

**SII (Speech Intelligibility Index)**   A number from 0 to 1 that quantifies the amount of speech that is loud enough to be heard.

**Simultaneous communication**   Signing and talking at the same time.

**Social constructionism**   Reality/realities defined and understood as resulting from subjective experiences through interactions in context and how these are portrayed.

**Soundscape**  The sense and understanding of the full variety of sounds that surround each individual listener. This can include speech, noise, and environmental sounds.

**Speech intelligibility**  The degree to which a person's speech is understood by a listener.

**Sphere of relevance**  Those topics and activities with which people are familiar and which are of personal import.

**SPLogram**  A graphical illustration of the output of a hearing aid in relation to hearing sensitivity.

**Stimulability**  The degree to which nonoccurring or misarticulated phonemes can be produced correctly via imitation.

**Strategy instruction**  An evidence-based teaching approach that teaches students ways to acquire, store, and express information and skills as well as to plan, execute, and evaluate their performance on a task and its outcomes.

**Stress**  A natural human response to pressure that involves physiological and psychological aspects.

**Synthetic auditory development**  A type of listening practice with the goal of understanding the meaning of an utterance or utterances rather than to identify phonemes and speech features.

**System**  Made up of constituent parts that interact and are codependent; the whole works together to achieve an aim or maintain a state.

**Temperament**  A constellation of inborn traits that influence the ways in which the child is likely to experience and react to the world.

**Template in therapy**  An established practice or routine used by a clinician that provides scaffolding, organization, or predictability to a child.

**Text structure**  The organization of the content in written material.

**Therapeutic alliance**  The bond formed between clinicians and families over time that is based on collaborative problem solving, accountability, and alignment of purpose.

**Tiered model of supports and services for learners who are D/HH**  Derived from the response to intervention/multitiered systems of support model to illustrate a continuum of supports based on levels of performance rather than eligibility for special education.

**Transcription**  The encoding of language in print that includes spelling, writing conventions, and mechanics such as handwriting and typing.

**Verification**   Confirmation of a hearing device's settings and function.

**Visual language and visual communication**   Communication or language that is expressed using a visual modality.

**Vocabulary**   The words we must know to comprehend and communicate effectively.

**Writer's workshop**   A model of writing instruction that develops competency through a process approach.

**Zone of proximal development (ZPD)**   In Vygotskian theory, the area between a child's independent and assisted performance levels where the most powerful instruction should be aimed.

# Index

Tables and figures are indicated by *t* and *f*, respectively.